Sharing the Book

Religion and Human Rights Series

Series Editors
John Witte Jr.
Abdullahi Ahmed An-Na'im
Emory University

Board of Advisors
Azizah al-Hibri, University of Richmond
Donna Arzt, Syracuse University
Irwin Cotler, McGill University
Frances Deng, The Brookings Institution
Jean Bethke Elshtain, University of Chicago
David Little, United States Institute of Peace
Ann Elizabeth Mayer, University of Pennsylvania
José Míguez Bonino, Facultad Evangélica, ISEDET, Buenos Aires
Chandra Muzzafar, University of Malaysia
John T. Noonan Jr., U.S. Court of Appeals
Kusumita P. Pedersen, St. Francis College
Lamin Sanneh, Yale University
Max Stackhouse, Princeton Theological Seminary
M. Thomas Thangaraj, Emory University

Other Books Published in the Series

Proselytization and Self-Determination in Africa
Abdullahi Ahmed An-Na'im, Editor

Religious Freedom and Evangelization in Latin America: The Challenge of Religious Pluralism
Paul E. Sigmund, Editor

Proselytism and Orthodoxy in Russia: The New War for Souls
John Witte Jr. and Michael Bourdeaux, Editors

RELIGION AND HUMAN RIGHTS SERIES

Sharing the Book

Religious Perspectives on the Rights and Wrongs of Proselytism

John Witte Jr.
Richard C. Martin
Editors

ORBIS BOOKS

Maryknoll, New York 10545

Copyright © 1999 by the Law and Religion Program at Emory University, Atlanta, Georgia.
Published by Orbis Books, Maryknoll, New York, U.S.A.

Manufactured in the United States of America.

Copy editing and typesetting by Joan Weber Laflamme.

Library of Congress Cataloging-in-Publication Data

Sharing the book   :   religious perspectives on the rights and wrongs of proselytism /
   John Witte, Jr., Richard C. Martin, editors.
      p.   cm.   —   (Religion & human rights series)
   Includes bibliographical references and index.
   ISBN 1-57075-276-1 (paper)
      1. Proselytizing.   I. Series. II. Witte, John 1959– III. Martin, Richard C.

BL637.S53 1999
291.7 21—dc21

                                                                99-04487

CONTENTS

PART THREE
MAINLINE CHRISTIANITY

PART FOUR
MODERN MISSION MOVEMENTS

THE RELIGION AND HUMAN RIGHTS
SERIES PREFACE

The relationship between religion and human rights is both problematic and unavoidable in all parts of the world. Religion, broadly defined to include various traditional, cultural, and customary institutions and practices, is unquestionably a formidable force for violence, repression, and chauvinism of untold dimensions. But religion is also a natural and necessary ally in the global struggle for human rights. For human rights norms are inherently abstract ideals—universal statements of the good life and the good society. They depend upon the visions and values of human communities to give them content, coherence, and concrete manifestation. Religion is an inherent condition of human lives and human communities. Religion invariably provides the sources and scales of dignity and responsibility, shame and respect, restitution and reconciliation that a human rights regime needs to survive and to flourish.

This book series explores the interaction of religious ideas and institutions with human rights principles and practices. It seeks to discover the religious sources of human rights—both their cultivation and their corruption in the discourse of sacred texts, the activism of religious organizations, and the practices of religious polities. It seeks to uncover the legal sources of human rights—both their protection and their abridgment in international human rights instruments and in domestic constitutions, statutes, and cases. It seeks to address some of the cutting edge issues of religion and human rights in theory and practice.

This series is made possible, in part, by the generous funding of The Pew Charitable Trusts, Inc. and the Ford Foundation. Pew's support came through its funding of a three-year project on "Soul Wars: The Problem and Promise of Proselytism in the New World Order." Ford's support came through its funding of a three-year project on "Cultural Transformation in Africa: Legal, Religious, and Human Rights Perspectives." Several of the early volumes in this series are parts and products of these two projects. They provide pilots and prototypes for the type of rigorous interdisciplinary and interreligious analysis that the subject of religion and human rights requires.

We wish to express our gratitude to our friends at the two foundations for their generous support of this effort. We also wish to thank the Maryknoll Fathers and Brothers and Bill Burrows and Bernadette Price of Orbis for their sage stewardship of this series.

— JOHN WITTE JR.
ABDULLAHI AHMED AN-NA'IM
EMORY UNIVERSITY, ATLANTA

PREFACE

The world has entered something of a "Dickensian era" in the past two decades.[1] We have seen the best of human rights protections inscribed on the books but some of the worst of human rights violations inflicted on the ground. We have celebrated the creation of more than thirty new constitutional democracies since 1980 but lamented the eruption of more than thirty new civil wars. We have witnessed the wisest of democratic statecraft and the most foolish of autocratic belligerence. For every South African spring of hope, there has been a Yugoslavian winter of despair.

These Dickensian paradoxes of the modern human rights revolution are particularly striking when viewed in their religious dimensions.

On the one hand, the modern human rights revolution has helped to catalyze a great awakening of religion around the globe. In regions newly committed to democracy and human rights, ancient faiths once driven underground by autocratic oppressors have sprung forth with new vigor. In the former Soviet bloc, for example, numerous Buddhist, Christian, Hindu, Jewish, Muslim, and other faiths have been awakened, alongside a host of exotic goddess, naturalist, and personality cults.[2] In postcolonial and post-revolutionary Africa, these same mainline religious groups have come to flourish in numerous conventional and inculturated forms, alongside an array of Traditional groups.[3] In Latin America, the democratic revolution has not only transformed long-standing Catholic and mainline Protestant communities but also triggered the explosion of numerous new evangelical and pentecostal movements.[4] Many parts of the world have seen the prodigious rise of a host of new or newly minted faiths—Adventists, Bahí'ás, Jehovah's Witnesses, Latter-day Saints, among others.

One cause and consequence of this great awakening of religion around the globe is that the ambit of religious rights has been substantially expanded. In the past two decades, more than 150 major new statutes and constitutional provisions on religious rights have been promulgated—guaranteeing liberty of conscience, religious pluralism and equality, free exercise of religion, nondiscrimination on religious grounds, autonomy for religious groups, among other norms. These national guarantees have been matched with a growing body of regional and international norms, notably the 1981 U.N. Declaration on Religious Intolerance and Discrimination Based upon Religion and Belief and the long catalogue of religious group rights set out in the 1989 Vienna Concluding Document and its progeny.[5]

On the other hand, this very same human rights revolution of the world has helped to catalyze new forms of religious and ethnic conflict, oppression, and belligerence, of tragic proportions. In the former Yugoslavia, local religious and ethnic rivals, previously kept at bay by a common oppressor, have converted their new liberties into licenses to renew ancient hostilities, with catastrophic results. In Sudan and Rwanda, ethnic nationalism and religious extremism have conspired to bring violent dislocation and death to hundreds of rival religious believers each year, and persecution, false imprisonment, forced starvation, coerced conversions, and savage abuses to thousands of others. In America and Western Europe, political secularism and nationalism have combined to threaten a sort of civil denial and death to a number of believers, particularly "sects" and "cults" of high religious temperature or of low cultural conformity. In a host of nations around the globe, Jews, Christians, and Muslims, when in minority status, have faced sharply increased restrictions, repression, and, at times, martyrdom.

In Russia and other parts of Eastern Europe, in various nations of subSaharan Africa, and in a number of nations in Latin America, the modern human rights revolution has also brought on something of a new war for souls between indigenous and foreign religious groups. This is the most recent, and the most ironic, chapter in the Dickensian drama. With the political transformations of these regions in the past decade, foreign religious groups were granted rights to enter these regions for the first time in years. In the early 1990s, they came in increasing numbers to preach their gospels, to offer their services, to convert new souls. Initially, local religious groups welcomed these foreigners. Today, they have come to resent these foreign religions, particularly those from North America who assume a democratic human rights ethic. Local religious groups resent the participation in the marketplace of religious ideas that democracy assumes. They resent the toxic waves of materialism and individualism that democracy inflicts. They resent the massive expansion of religious pluralism that democracy encourages. They resent the extravagant forms of religious speech, press, and assembly that democracy protects.

An increasingly acute war has thus broken out over the cultural and moral souls of these newly transformed societies and over adherents and adherence to competing forms of faith and ethnic identity. In part, this is a theological war— as rival religious communities have begun actively to defame and demonize each other and to gather themselves into ever more dogmatic and fundamentalist stands. The ecumenical spirit of the previous decades is giving way to sharp new forms of religious balkanization. In part, this is a legal war—as religious groups have begun to persuade local political leaders to adopt regulations restricting the constitutional rights of their religious rivals. Beneath a shiny constitutional veneer of religious rights and freedom for all, many East European, African, and Latin American countries have recently developed a legal culture of overt religious favoritism of some and oppression of others. A whole brace of antiproselytism laws and policies has recently appeared on the books.

Such Dickensian paradoxes have exposed the limitations of a secular human rights paradigm standing alone. And they have inspired the earnest search for additional resources to deter violence, resolve disputes, cultivate peace, ensure security—in dialogue, liturgical healing, ceremonies of reconciliation, and more.[6]

Human rights are as much the problem as they are the solution in a number of current religious and cultural conflicts. In the current war for souls in Eastern Europe and Latin America, for example, two absolute principles of human rights have come into direct conflict: the foreign religion's free exercise right to share and expand its faith versus the indigenous religion's liberty of conscience right to be left alone on its own territory. Further rights talk alone cannot resolve this dispute. At the heart of a number of the conflicts between Christian and Muslim groups in Africa is a fundamental controversy over the right to change one's religion, to convert. Most Western Christians believe in relatively easy conversion into and out of the faith. Most Muslims believe in easy conversion into the faith but allow for no conversion out of it. Whose rites get rights? At the root of current waves of Christian and Muslim antisemitism are ancient theological resentments toward Jewish notions of being an elect nation under Yahweh's blessing and now a select nation under America's patronage. Here, too, further rights talk alone avails us little.

The purpose of this volume is to summon some of the religious traditions that have an authoritative written scripture at the core of their identity, and to analyze and compare their insights respecting human rights in general, and the rights to proselytism among members of other faith communities in particular. Gathered herein are authoritative presentations of these insights in both the classic traditions of Judaism, Christianity, and Islam as well as the modern traditions of Latter-day Saints, Jehovah's Witnesses, Seventh-day Adventists, and Bahá'í's.

The religious traditions analyzed in this volume do not, of course, exhaust the range of available religious interpretations of the right to proselytize. No single volume could pretend to such comprehension. In the United States alone, there are more than a thousand recognized and registered religious groups, many of which are religions of revelation that reach out to others. The numbers increase exponentially as one crosses the religious landscapes of Asia, Africa, and Europe. Selection, truncation, and distillation have thus been necessary to keep the volume to manageable size. Invariably, specific denominations have been slighted in this process, others ignored altogether. The point of this collection is to provide a representative range of theological expressions and experiences of the rights and wrongs of proselytism—with an eye to fostering greater mutual understanding across the religions of the Book and to prompting many other comparative studies of this sort.

Likewise, the contributors chosen to present each tradition do not exhaust the range of opinions in and of that tradition. Particularly the classic traditions of Judaism, Islam, and Christianity have whole millennia of insights that can only be lightly illustrated and interpreted by an individual author. Contributors have been chosen because of their command of the subject matter, not because of the nature of their profession or confession. Not only theologians, but also jurists, historians, ethicists, linguists, and comparativists are all gathered herein. Some are insiders, with high positions within the religious tradition on which they are writing. Some are outsiders, with deep insights into a particular aspect of another religious tradition. Every effort was made to secure authors who could speak with authority and sensitivity to their assignments—in terms and with terminology designed to be accessible to English-speaking insiders and outsiders alike. Invariably, something is lost in the translation of Arabic, Hebrew, and Latin sources into modern English parlance, and in the translation of Islamic, Judaic, and Christian mysteries into Western analytical categories. But what is lost in translation is more than amply offset by the gain in mutual understanding afforded by these chapters.

Each contributor has been asked to speak candidly about the theology and practice of proselytism in the texts and traditions of a particular faith. What is the faith's understanding of the nature and purpose of proselytism and mission, religious pluralism and toleration, religious rights and liberties for coreligionists and for all others? What are regarded as legitimate and illegitimate forms and methods of demonstrating or sharing the faith with insiders and outsiders? What are the respective responsibilities and rights of religious officials and political officials to define and monitor the rights and duties of preaching, educating, writing, and other methods of transmitting and sharing the faith? What is the attitude of the tradition to being the object of proselytism, or evangelism, by members of other faiths?

The candor and cogency of the chapters gathered herein illustrate the complexity of the modern problem of proselytism. Each tradition stands firmly on its natural and constitutional rights and duties to proselytize, but each casts these rights and duties in a rather distinctive manner.

Many Jews regard proselytism primarily as a form of *inreach,* a method of gathering into the community those born of a Jewish mother who have strayed from *halakha.* Jews resent being the object of proselytism by other faiths. They do little to encourage or attract non-Jews to convert into Judaism, and they place ample substantive and procedural requirements before those who nonetheless choose to convert. Their most urgent plea is to be left alone to their own faith, to their own tradition, and, since 1948, to their own nation.

Many Muslims regard proselytism primarily as a form of *outreach,* a *jihad* designed to invite all to see the wisdom of the revelation of Allah in the Qur'an and the Sunna. Once confronted with the wisdom of the Prophet's words and actions, a person—and, historically, whole communities whom that person represents—will see the virtue and value of conversion to Islam. The message of Islam should be particularly cogent for Jews and Christians (the *dhimmi*), who have had access to partial revelation in their Torah and Bible, and in their great prophets Moses and Jesus. But it should also be cogent for all people, regardless of their faith, particularly if the message of Islam is demonstrated forcefully—which today often means presenting the message in its full spiritual, moral, cultural, rational, and aesthetic splendor. According to more conservative schools of Islamic law today, Muslims neither accept being the object of proselytism by other faiths, nor do they accept conversions out of the faith from those who have properly converted into it.

The Catholic, Orthodox, and Protestant traditions of Christianity array themselves all along the spectrum between these two hard positions. On one end of this spectrum are a number of evangelical Protestants who emphasize that, in order to be saved, every person must make a personal, conscious commitment to Christ—to be born again, to convert. Any person who has not been born again, or who once reborn now leads a nominal Christian life, is a legitimate object of evangelism—regardless of whether and where the person has been baptized. The principal means of reaching that person is through proclamation of the gospel, rational demonstration of its truth, and personal exemplification of its efficacy. Any region of the world that has not been open to the gospel is a legitimate "mission field"—regardless of whether the region might have another Christian church in place. On the other end of the spectrum are Orthodox Christians. They, too, believe that each person must come into a personal relationship with Christ in order to be saved. But such a relationship comes more through birth than rebirth, and more through regular sacramental living than through a one-time conversion. A person who is born into the church has by definition started *theosis*—the process of becoming acceptable to God and ultimately coming into eternal communion with God. Through infant baptism, and later through the mass, the Eucharist, the icons, and other services of the church, a person slowly comes into fuller realization of this divine communion. Proclamation of the gospel is certainly an important means of aiding the process of *theosis*. But, for the Orthodox, mission work is designed not to transmit rational truths, but to incorporate persons into communion with Christ and fellow believers. Each territory is united under the spiritual protectorate of the local Orthodox church. Any person who has been baptized into that local Orthodox church is no longer a legitimate object of evangelism—regardless of whether that person leads only a nominal Christian life.

Between and beyond these two juxtaposed positions the chapters herein reveal a wide range of alternative views of the rights, duties, and restrictions on proselytism. Several contributors emphasize that proselytism must be a form of gentle and genial invitation to "come and see" the riches of a particular religious tradition. Others emphasize that proselytism is a process, an ongoing dialogue among the proselytizer, proselytizee, and the religious communities they represent. Others emphasize that proselytism must involve not only religious proclamation but also cultural transformation—an effort to transform local communities to grant greater respect not only to civil and political rights, but also to social, cultural, and economic rights. At the same time, several contributors emphasize that conversion is not a one-time event, but a process by which a person slowly develops in relationship with God even if he or she makes no change in adherence to a particular religious community. Indeed, a number of writers today, most notably represented herein by the Bahá'ís, commend both intensely inculturated forms of communal faith as well as a person's adherence to multiple religious communities at once.

Mining these juxtaposed theologies of proseltyizing traditions does not resolve the Dickensian paradoxes of the modern human rights revolution. But it does open pathways to a fuller, and perhaps more pacific, understanding of modern formulations and applications of religious rights. Particularly, a long historical view of the positions of some of the antagonists in some of the current wars for souls sometimes provides considerable enlightenment.

Permit me just one example of the benefits of such theological discourse for modern formulations of religious rights—namely, the conflict between Christian and Muslim groups over the right to change one's religion, to convert. As we saw, most Western Christians believe in relatively easy conversion into and out of the faith. Most Muslims believe in easy conversion into the faith but allow for no conversion out of it. How can these juxtaposed rights claims be balanced?

International human rights instruments initially masked these conflicts, despite the objections of some Muslim delegations. Article 18 of the 1948 Universal Declaration included an unequivocal guarantee: "Everyone has the right to freedom of thought, conscience, and religion; this right includes the right to change his religion or belief. . . . " Article 18 of the 1966 International Covenant on Civil and Political Rights, whose preparation was more highly contested, became more tentative: "This right shall include to have or adopt a religion or belief of his choice. . . . " The 1981 Declaration on Religious Intolerance and Discrimination Based Upon Religion and Belief repeated this same tentative language, but the dispute over the right to conversion contributed greatly to the long delay in the production of this instrument. Today, the issue has become more divisive than ever.

"A page of history is worth a volume of logic," the great American jurist Oliver Wendell Holmes Jr. once said.[7] And, on an intractable legal issue such as this, recollection might be more illuminating than ratiocination.

It is discomfiting, but enlightening, for Western Christians to remember that the right to enter and exit the religion of one's choice was born in the West only after centuries of cruel experience. To be sure, a number of the early church fathers considered the right to change religion as essential to the notion of liberty of conscience, and such sentiments have been repeated and glossed continuously until today. But in practice the Christian church largely ignored these sentiments for centuries. As the medieval church refined its rights structures in the twelfth and thirteenth centuries, it also routinized its religious discrimination, reserving its harshest sanctions for heretics. The communicant faithful enjoyed full rights. Jews and Muslims enjoyed fewer rights, but full rights if they converted to Christianity. Heretics—those who voluntarily chose to leave the faith—enjoyed still fewer rights, and had little opportunity to recover them even after full and voluntary confession. Indeed, in the heyday of the Inquisition, heretics faced not only severe restrictions on their persons, properties, and professions, but sometimes unspeakably cruel forms of torture and punishment. Similarly, as the Lutheran, Calvinist, and Anglican churches routinized their establishments in the sixteenth and seventeenth centuries, they inflicted all manner of repressive civil and ecclesiastical censures on those who chose to deviate from established doctrine—savage torture and execution in a number of instances.

It was, in part, the recovery and elaboration of earlier patristic concepts of liberty of conscience as well as the slow expansion of new theologies of religious voluntarism that helped to end this practice. But, it was also the new possibilities created by the frontier and by the colony that helped to forge the Western understanding of the right to change religion. Rather than stay at home and fight for one's faith, it became easier for the dissenter to move away quietly to the frontier, or later to the colony, to be alone with his conscience and his co-religionists. Rather than tie the heretic to the rack or the stake, it became easier for the establishment to banish him quickly from the community with a strict order not to return.

Such pragmatic tempering of the treatment of heretics and dissenters eventually found theological and legal rationales. By the later sixteenth century, it became common in the West to read of the right, and the duty, of the religious dissenter to emigrate physically from the community whose faith he or she no longer shared. In the course of the next century, this right of physical emigration from a religious community was slowly transformed into a general right of voluntary exit from a religious faith, without encumbrance. Particularly American writers, many of whom had voluntarily left their European faiths and territories to gain their freedom, embraced the right to leave—to change their faith, to abandon their blood, soil and confession, to reestablish their lives, beliefs, and identities afresh—as a veritable sine qua non of religious freedom. This understanding of the right to choose and change religion has now become an almost universal feature of Western understandings of religious rights.

To tell this peculiar Western tale is not to resolve current legal conflicts over proselytism and conversion that divide Muslims and Christians, especially in Africa and Eastern Europe. But it is to suggest that even hard and hardened religious traditions can and do change over time, in part out of pragmatism, in part out of fresh appeals to ancient principles long forgotten. Even certain Shi'ite and Sunni communities today, that have been the sternest in their opposition to a right to conversion from the faith, do have resources in the Qur'an, in the early development of *shari'a,* and in the more benign policies of other contemporary Muslim communities, to rethink their theological positions.

Moreover, the Western story suggests that there are halfway measures, at least in banishment and emigration, that help to blunt the worst tensions between a religious group's right to maintain its standards of entrance and exit and an individual's liberty of conscience to come and go. Not every heretic needs to be either executed or indulged. It is one thing for a religious tradition to insist on executing its charges of heresy, when a mature adult, fully aware of the consequences of his or her choice, voluntarily enters a faith, and then later seeks to leave. In that case group rights must trump individual rights—with the limitation that the religious group has no right to violate, or to solicit violation of, the life and limb of the wayward member. It is quite another thing for a religious tradition to press the same charges of heresy against someone who was born into, married into, or was coerced into the faith and now, upon opportunity for mature reflection, voluntarily chooses to leave. In that case, individual rights trump group rights—with the limitation that the individual has no right to remain within the former religious community to foment reform or nonconformity therein.

Where a religious group exercises its trump by banishment or shunning and the apostate voluntarily chooses to return, he does so at his peril. He should find little protection in state law when subject to harsh religious sanctions—again, unless the religious group threatens or violates his life or limb. Where a religious individual exercises her trump by emigration, and the group chooses to pursue her, it does so at its peril. It should find little protection from state law when charged with tortious or criminal violations of the wayward former member.

Current categorical formulations of both religious group rights and religious individual rights simply restate the problems rather than resolve them. It will take new arguments from history and experience and new appeals to internal religious principles and practices, along the lines just illustrated, to blunt, if not resolve, these tensions. The chapters in this volume hold out many such possibilities for the discerning reader.

It was a privilege for me to collaborate with my friend and colleague Richard C. Martin on the editing and production of this volume. A distinguished scholar of Islamic theology, law, and history, Professor Martin not only took the lead in soliciting and editing the chapters herein on Islam, but contributed his own highly valuable chapter on the Islamic understanding on the concept of conversion by invitation.

I would like to thank Ms. Eliza Ellison, associate director of the Law and Religion Program at Emory University, for her invaluable criticisms of several of the chapters herein, and Mr. Joel A. Nichols and Ms. Louise Jackson for their work in preparing the final manuscript.

This volume and other early titles in this series on religion and human rights are parts and products of a three-year project made possible by a generous grant from The Pew Charitable Trusts, Inc., in Philadelphia, Pennsylvania, to the Law and Religion Program at Emory University. On behalf of my colleagues in the Law and Religion Program, I wish to offer my warmest thanks to the Trusts, particularly President Rebecca M. Rimel, and Dr. Luis Lugo and his predecessor, Dr. Joel Carpenter, of the Religion Division, for their continued solicitude for this vital work.

—JOHN WITTE JR.

Introduction

Proselytizers and Proselytizees on the Sharp Arête of Modernity

———————◆———————

Martin E. Marty

The dictionary offers rich variations on the word that signals efforts by one to convert another, to *proselytize*: *proselyte* as noun; *proselyte* as verb; *proselytess; proselytism; proselytist; proselytization; proselytize; proselytizer.*

The *proselytess* curiously makes no appearance on these pages. But Michael Broyde makes up for that by using another word in his chapter herein that belongs penultimately on the dictionary's list and provides a dramatic match for the ultimate one. In his chapter Broyde pairs *proselytizer* with a logically named counterpart: *proselytizee.*

If the *proselytizer* is someone who induces someone to convert, then the *proselytizee* is someone who is induced or toward whom someone makes an effort at inducement. In this chapter we will speak both of those with whom the inducing proselytizer was successful and of those with whom he or she was not as the proselytizee.

At the root of all these words is the Greek *proseelutos,* "one who has come to a place." Behind that is the Ur-root, *proserch-esthai,* "to come to, to approach." In the dramas that follow, the proselytizer is in one place, specifically, in a religious community or situation. This person approaches another with the intent to convert, to help or make this proselytizee come to the same place. In negative imagery that usually colors such incidents, one is to picture the proselytizer assessing the scene, spotting a potential proselytizee, stalking her, watching for a weak moment, getting poised, and then pouncing.

Meanwhile the proselytizee, on the point of being approached, has been occupying a different place than does the one who would convert her. She has her scene, becomes wary of being overtaken, does her own measuring of the distance between her and the proselytizer, tries to stay strong but may grow vulnerable, and then gets confronted.

All that imagery suggests that a shadow of violence shrouds the two. Notice, as you read: not all the authors in this book, who represent a scholarly approach to a variety of religions, themselves think there is something very wrong with proselytizing. But they at least write with an awareness that in the present-day cultures in which most readers of this book reside, the sound of the word has pejorative overtones and undertones. In these cultures it is ordinarily not considered good to proselytize. Those who speak positively about doing so on any scale have to know that they are inviting complex criticism or even simple dismissal.

Why should this be so? In many cultures, past and present, proselytizing was and is considered in many circumstances to be a good. It is a favor done the other, the cause, and the truth. The proselyte is simply "one who has come over from one opinion, belief, creed, or party to another; a convert." Several authors herein cite the central and widely appreciated figures of specific religions—Jesus and Mohammed among them, down to Joseph Smith and Charles Taze Russell among the Mormons and Jehovah's Witnesses—as having authorized, legitimated, and even commanded followers to make converts. How, one asks, can one show respect to some such figures—no one respects them all!—and then grow wary about proselytizing?

The shortest answers, elaborated upon in the following pages, would include these, by reference to what we might call the late modern period: This is an age, first, that celebrates freedom and autonomy, including the freedom to be alone and to choose one's own opinion, belief, creed, or party without intrusion on the part of a would-be converter.

This is, next, an age of pluralism, when free polities assure that differing peoples with differing opinions, beliefs, creeds, or parties can coexist creatively, or at least neutrally. Efforts to convert others across the boundaries of sub-communities violate at least the implicit rules of the pluralist game. The proselytizer seeks homogeneity and resents the persisting presence of the other. He must make all the same.

This is, third, an age in which identities are insecure. People have great difficulty knowing who they are, to whom they belong, whom they can trust, and to what they should show loyalty and commit themselves. The fabric of social relations is gossamer, easily pulled at and torn. Bombarded from all sides by advertisers, public relations experts, strangers, and seducers, people have few psychic defenses that will help them keep to boundaries and uphold traditions. The proselytizer violates boundaries and disrupts traditions. He is more concerned with enlarging his own community than caring for the integrity of others. Now, especially, one must be wary of anyone who would see another as a prospective proselytizee. Be caught off guard, and, whether or not one succumbs, there is a challenge to personal and social identity. The message: proselytizer, stay home.

This is, finally, an age of relativism, or at least an age that poses absolutisms against relativism. So long as the potential proselytizee is unaware of alternatives, he can blissfully and productively think and act his way through the mazes of life. The opinions, beliefs, creeds, and parties inherited from ancestors will sustain such a one who is "pluralistically ignorant" and naive. The English social philosopher Ernest Gellner quotes the medieval Muslim thinker al-Ghazali to this point: "There is no hope of returning to a traditional faith after it has once been abandoned, since the essential condition in the holder of a traditional faith is that he should not know he is a traditionalist."[1] He has become a chooser, whether he decides to stay or depart from the tradition. He chooses what elements from the tradition to accent.

Thereupon the proselytizer awakens doubt: Are you sure that your elders and peers have taught you the truth? Are you sure that you might not better yourself by converting? Here, says this proselytizer, is my alternative. Here, says a competitor, is another option. There are many more. Uncertain, bewildered, the prospect is overwhelmed by relativism and loses the sense of integrity that opinions, beliefs, creeds, and parties must command. Or he must be confirmed in his own absolutism so that he can ward off challenges and seductions. To prevent all this from happening, the word becomes: proselytizer, stay home.

So the fateful encounter between proselytizer and proselytizee goes on. But, as the authors in this book uniformly show, the stakes are higher than before. The engagements between the two are ever more noteworthy and noticed.

When we spoke a moment ago of this being "an age of . . . " something or other, we were pointing to the contemporary world, call it late modern or postmodern, and investing that "age of" designation with as many meanings as are relevant here. Not all the authors are convinced that modernity represented a qualitatively different situation from circumstances in the past. Certainly when Gentiles converted to Judaism, when the early Jewish and Gentile Christians sought proselytizees in Greco-Roman and pagan cultures, or when Mohammed and his successors spread their prophecy and formed communities, they were also in ages bearing many marks in common with our own.

In these earlier ages, freedoms might have been restricted to only some elite individuals, but the freedoms could be dizzying. Those, too, were ages of pluralism and relativism. The apostle Paul confirmed an impression: "Indeed, even though there be many so-called gods in heaven or on earth—as in fact there are many gods and many lords—yet for us there is one God, the Father, from whom are all things and for whom we exist, and one Lord, Jesus Christ, through whom are all things and through whom we exist" (1 Cor 8:5, NRSV). Then, as now, it was difficult to know who one was, and to what he or she belonged.

So it would be unproductive to make too big a case for a qualitative difference between proselytism now as opposed to then, as if the present age had to be the climax of all others, and had to outstrip them in drama. Still, the age as described is our own, and contemporaries must deal with it, however informed and marked they are by previous controversies and experiences. And many inventions and circumstances, among them mass media of communication, rapid means of travel, mass higher education in many cultures, free or forced migrations on huge scales, and the development of competitive business cultures, conspire to heighten the drama.

As I read the following accounts, trying to be sympathetic toward but not uncritical of the proselytizers and proselytizees, some lines from poet W. H. Auden kept coming to mind. They capture well the tensions, paradoxes, and persistently problematic character of life on this front. It may well be that others will share the uneasiness and awareness of the irresolvability when it comes to the issues of proselytism.

In the years before mid-century, poet Auden was much given to metaphors and images from landscapes: valleys, islands, and, most of all, mountains and ridges. In a very long "New Year Letter" to friend Elizabeth Mayer in 1940, after the start of the Second World War in Europe, he wrote:

> So, perched upon the sharp arête,
> Where if we do not move we fall,
> Yet movement is heretical,
> Since over its ironic rocks
> No route is truly orthodox.[2]

The arête is a very narrow, almost razorlike mountain ridge. Contrast the gingerly dances of both proselytizer and proselytizee with those that went on or could go on elsewhere on the landscape.

Picture proselytizers and proselytizees of old or in violent present places, pacing in aggression and defense in the dark forest, where few would be aware of their movements. This is figuratively the situation of what we and others have called "pluralistic ignorance." There may be some readers of this book who picture religion as authentic or authentically grasped only if those who hold it firmly have a passion to persecute others, and for whom aggressive proselytizing is an ideal. But the majority have come to terms with nonaggression and no doubt put a premium on other approaches.

Keeping the precarious mountain hikers in mind, picture next two in a valley. Interestingly, in extending his landscape metaphors, Auden in his "Paysage Moralise" saw valleys as "wretched places where the harvests are rotting, inhabited by moping villagers, who, for all their wretchedness, will not leave their valley homes." In another poem, valleys are "silent" and in them we cannot "guess in what direction lies the overhanging precipice." It is the place of "spiritual emptiness and the desperation of the modern world."[3]

From the figurative to the real world: in such places prospective proselytees enjoy some forms of moderate protection and stability. They seem thus to be able to contribute to the serenity of the world. Among them is little adventure, risk, or spiritual innovation. In that place, if they do make a move, it can be cautious and safe. This is what we might call gradual, subtle, almost unnoticeable shifts in opinion, creed, belief, or party—elisions so gentle that they do not threaten the rest of the community in the valley of each. The temptation to proselytize or to be induced to convert hardly reaches such places for the listless.

Picture the proselytizer and proselytizee on islands, spaced apart, as they would not be in the city or wherever cultures clash. To many critics of proselytism, figurative island life is the ideal solution. The stranger, the other, is not near enough or easily capable of getting to be near enough to present alternatives and induce change. Once again, we can draw on Auden, this time for the way he poses island versus city. Again in "Paysage Moralise" he speaks of the resolve to "rebuild our cities, not dream of islands." In his "The Dog beneath the Skin," the poet contrasts islands to mountains, for the way one can there "escape from reality, from fear." In "Letters from Iceland," he says: "This is an island and therefore Unreal." Beach comments: "The island, then, is a place where the disturbing realities of the world are not present." Choosing to be insulated and isolated is one way to avoid the issues of proselytism and dealing with the other. But it is a fantasy world, and means stagnation.[4]

Inevitably, then, in a world where communities and cultures come into contact and conflict, proselytism is an element in encounters, stimulant to exertion—however full of risk and discomfort they may be. Picture proselytizer and proselytizee there, perched and dangerously poised, as Auden's figures find themselves. They must move, both of them. If they do not, they fall. The proselytizer will fall into disfavor in her community for not having followed the founders' orders or for not having been attentive to the community that has sent her out, the community that would grow.

The proselytizee, meanwhile, must move in either of two directions. The first is into the already described isolation and insulation, there to be protected from the proselytizer's beguilements or aggressions. The second is into her host community, but a community that will henceforth look different because she has visibly entertained an alternative to it. She has taken fate and turned it into choice, and that is dangerous.

The two figures at first do not move; they must move lest they fall. Yet "movement" is heretical. Peter Berger, in a book title dealing with the necessary choice, speaks of The Heretical Imperative. On the ironic rocks that make up the late modern landscape, no move is truly orthodox. We pause to make more of the word *heretical*. The root of that term is *haireesis*, which simply meant a "choosing," a "choice." For the proselytizee, the circumstances are particularly precarious. Choosing to resist conversion inspires one set of criticisms and even ostracism. Choosing to convert means disruption from community and its ways, and risking a place in the new space.

For the proselytizer, too, the choice is risky. Venturing forth from the protective community to approach others means going into the unknown. There is always a chance that in open encounter the now heretical, which means the "choosing" proselytizer, might become the proselytizee. Each partner may work on the other. They are roped together, as it were. From the mountain vista he may find greener grass, more lush growth, more entanglements that at least rouse doubts about the opinions, beliefs, creeds, or parties to which he had held. This kind of thing occurs frequently in religiously mixed marriages. One partner may be lured to the community of the other and abandon attempts either to convert her or to be faithful to her own.

For all the tension that attends the scene of these proselytizer-proselytizee circumstances, we have only looked at one approach to all this approaching. So far there has been only brief mention that the proselytizer claims to have been called, sent, commanded to seek converts. It is time now to look at the engagement from the opposite angle, leaders in many religions and cultures will say.

Precisely because this is an age of freedom and autonomy for millions, it will be said that this is a good time to exercise the option and seek to make proselytes. For too long potential converts have been enslaved by tradition, community, habit, and forced conformity. Along comes someone who liberates them, takes them to high and high-risk places. From that precarious perch the converter is able to point to new places for the spirit. Further, we hear the argument from the pro-conversion faction that doing such pointing and then cajoling is doing the proselytee-to-be a favor. The world community should not scorn; rather, it should applaud those who care enough to try to rectify old errors and accidents of misplacement and help locate people where they belong.

Precisely because this is an age of pluralism, it will be said, the proselytizer must be set loose to do his work as never before. This time the argument goes: One can be benumbed when there are too many choices. People turn unproductive when confronted with so many arrays of options that they get paralyzed. Because they are surrounded by so many neighbors and their influences, they lose the values that come with singularity and commitment in isolation.

Look around. Neighbors, by being good neighbors with other ultimate commitments, without trying, lead them to call into question the opinions they were told to have, but do not help replace them. Different people function with different sets of beliefs, and to see others functioning reasonably through being different calls into question the hold a person has on her old beliefs. The presence and invitation of the other from another creed call into question the creeds already being held. And the multiple-party situation is paralyzing.

It is on that scene that the proselytizer comes. He is charismatic, well-equipped, ambitious to be successful, profoundly committed, and, most of all, he gives the impression that he knows he is right. He represents the truth among the half-truths and lies. In a culture of freedom that produces protean personalities, people who make ephemeral and trivial commitments, here comes someone who can guide them so that they become integral human beings in integral communities. The proselytizer, meanwhile, if successful, helps reduce the number of choices within pluralism and thus helps the basic and decisive ones come into bold relief and bald outline.

Similarly, precisely in an age characterized by insecure identities, the proselytizer does a favor. He would not even begin to get a hearing were the possible proselytizee satisfied and properly located in community. The door would never open at all; it would be slammed in his face. But the proselytizer does not rely upon artificial constructs and props, arbitrarily gained. Among these would be identities based upon race, ethnicity, gender, taste, class, region, and all the rest. These have to be assaulted and tend to be eroded in such a time as ours, says the typical proselytizer.

Onto such a scene comes that proselytizer. He may be the ancient Jew who welcomed the Gentile who was ready to move out of chaos to become part of the people of God. He may be the Christian who can assert that in Jesus Christ there is no Jew or Greek, no male or female, no bond or free, for all are "one in Christ." The Muslims built *umma*, a more profound and secure community. They point out, in nation after nation, that semi-secular, corrupt, military regimes corrupt the true faith and true community and thus contribute to the erosion of identity. Identity comes when one joins an international, trans-tribal, multi-class, increasingly universal community of opinion, belief, creed, and practice.

In these cases, this means that the proselytizee gains for once and at last an identity that can help her withstand other assaults and beguilements by lesser convert-seekers. Who can gainsay the proselytizer with credentials and staying power, and decry the good she can do to the other, the proselytizee?

Precisely in an age called relativist, the defenders of the proselytizer will say, strenuous efforts to make converts demand applause, not condescension or dismissal. Why? Because relativism does not have to be the first and last word about life circumstances that God or philosophy ordained. Many great philosophers have guided their disciples into simple and hence more sure essences of thought and foundations for action. True religion does not leave one half-convinced between whole repertories of opinion options.

One will hear: let the proselytizers have free competitive range, and let the best man win. Or, exclude all proselytizers but one and let him make converts, and the polity will be stronger. Note what advantages the Iranian Shi'ite Muslims had because they could mobilize mass sentiment during the revolution of 1979. Note what a disadvantage a much larger and more powerful United States had because it had to incorporate and hear the voice of dissent and multiple busying and dizzying opinions. The proselytizer may not solve all philosophical and religious issues—who claims to?—but he could help one come to choose the firm stand, to be accepted into the community that has and knows the truth.

Picture, then, the struggle of proselytizer and proselytizee on that sharp arête, visible to those below, whether observers and analysts or potential wrestlers themselves. Know that many in the gathering below not only see nothing wrong with proselytism, but see much wrong among those who do not undertake or support it. Their indictment is strong, and to entertain it carefully is to call into question the solitary advocacy of other systems of opinion, belief, creed, or party. Now we must pose a third figure on the sharp arête of late modernity. This is the one who is neither proselytizer nor proselytizee, but someone who has trouble holding footing while the other two climb and wrestle. He is put off by the crowding, the jangle of opinions, the risk to his own footing. But he is mainly there on other business and would be just as happy if the contenders would simply leave the scene, to be replaced by no others.

The judgment of the proselytizing community falls on such. He is apathetic, indifferent to truth and commitment, which also means he may hold his beliefs so lightly that he does not trust himself to ask others thus to be committed. Or he has only a tenuous attachment to his own belief, creed, and cult, so tenuous that it allows him to be indifferent to the good he could bring others.

The judgment of the proselytizing community directs itself against those who are so uncertain of their values, or so ready to give higher respect to opinions of others that they become uncertain. Meanwhile, absolutists, even across boundaries of faith communities, prefer the celebration of absolutes of others to mere relativism by any. Let the pope take a controversial stand, or let there be eavesdropping on a Nation of Islam community, and one is likely to hear, "Well, at least, by God, they believe in something." And, by God, they can help the uncertain make a best and final choice.

The only time proselytizers honor one who does not proselytize is when the spiritual stay-at-homes who do not convert many make clear that they do not or need not seek converts at all. Judaism is in that situation, as it holds the identification of only about fourteen million people around the world—a world where the largest Protestant denomination in the United States has more than fifteen million. The accusation comes, one that is well supported by the authors on Judaism in this book, that Judaism, by conceiving itself as the elect of God, is so exclusivistic that it makes little effort to draw converts, so it turns arrogant. Worst of all, where Jews concentrate, as in Jerusalem, they forbid proselytizing by others. There may be flaws in the Jewish system, say these critics, but these are the downside of an otherwise enviable position: they are established in the Holy Land and can use it as a base where they can begin to live out their prophecy of being "a light to the nations."

Not to proselytize, in sum, turns out to be an insult to the tired religious bodies and their leadership, just when such bodies need new energies and imagination. It is an insult, further, because it shows too little interest in the integrity of true portrayals. It is an insult because it suggests that there is so little life in the particular community that one would not dream of moving out of the sanctuary to do some of the ministry in the public forum, there to be unsequestered and no longer silenced.

While numerous authors in this book speak about ways to address proselytism, none of them pictures it disappearing from the world. If some religions choose not to seek converts, others do and will. In fact, the relative passivity of many religious communities relaxes boundaries and makes their nominal adherents and their rare hungry zealots vulnerable to proselytism. If the community to which they belong does not offer sufficiently strong opinion, belief, creed, and parties, they can be won to some that do. And in a world of religious "supply-side economics," there will always be plenty at hand who will supply options.

If proselytism is to remain on the scene, people who bring various valuations to it are learning that they have to understand it better than most of them have before, and all of them have to understand it in the new landscape of late modernity, where they or those they observe are perched upon the sharp arête where step and misstep are part of the drama of their choice. All the essays in this book are efforts to contribute to such understanding. Different participants in the colloquia that produced it, different readers during these years of preparation, and different readers now may take differing insights from it.

For me, if not a new revelation, then at least a reinforcement of a previously half-finished view, came now to appear to be fundamental. I will note and propose it for the sake of other readers who will be drawing on the mass of information and insight in the book as they seek what they would grasp. Mine is this:

The essays do not deal with proselytism but with proselytisms. Of course, there can be coordinating and comprehending categories. As William James reminded himself and us, it is impossible to understand phenomena without typifying and classifying them. But doing so can mean the loss of particularity. In *Varieties of Religious Experiences*, James used the vivid picture of the crab, who, given a choice and a voice, "would be filled with a sense of personal outrage if it could hear us class it without ado or apology as a crustacean, and thus dispose of it. 'I am no such thing,' it would say; 'I am MYSELF, MYSELF alone.'"

In this book, written at the distance from most proselytizees that this format and the current intention dictates, the authors cannot get very close to many of the "MYSELF, MYSELF" people. Now and then we will meet a Maimonides or a named convert, but they tend to be leaders, not typical of the ordinary folk who make up most of the recruited pool for proselytizers through history. But if we cannot deal with those perched on arêtes one by one, it is possible to find them, as this book does, on particular mountains and ridges, in this case, communities of faith.

We will, in short, understand proselytizing better if we discern ever more of the impulses, resources, and intentions of particular religions. No one can walk away from this book and credibly say that "all proselytizers do so and so" or "all proselytizees have this particular psychological disposition or sociological setting." Certainly not all proselytizers and proselytizees will avoid heresy and, during their climbs on precarious arêtes, make only orthodox moves. But there will be certain families of approach, and learning them by learning the context of faith and its development in each case will be helpful.

A word of philosopher George Santayana is here in place as a reminder and pointer: "Any attempt to speak without speaking any particular language is not more hopeless than the attempt to have a religion that shall be no religion in particular. . . . Thus every living and healthy religion has a marked idiosyncrasy. Its power consists in its special and surprising message and in the bias which that revelation gives to life. The vistas it opens and the mysteries it propounds are another world to live in; and another world to live in—whether we expect ever to pass wholly over into it or no—is what we mean by having a religion."[5]

It is impossible here to follow these particularities through all the chapters. The best way to begin is at the beginning, since David Novak's essay on proselytism in classic Judaism is a rather pure form and exemplary case study. To condense it to almost brutally curt terms: while Jews did some proselytizing two thousand years ago, producing many Gentile converts, it does not characteristically do so now. There are several reasons for this, all of them integral to Judaism and not or at least not precisely similar to those of other faiths.

First, Judaism is transmitted through the genes, but not the territory. That is, while Jerusalem and Israel have always been a territorial focus and a dream, most Jews for nineteen centuries and even after 1948 live in diaspora and are not unfaithful for that. So Jewish proselytizees today do not have to make *aliyah*, to immigrate and live in Israel.

Second, the reference to the genes has to do with the fact that if you have a Jewish mother, you are a Jew. No proselytizer interferes with that transaction. This is not the case in most faith communities.

Third, and most to the point: Jews classically have believed they are an elect people, a point underscored by Jocelyn Hellig. However arrogant and offensive this sounds to others, including to all others who see themselves as elect—as American civil religionists do—Jews have this realization and make the claim that they are God's chosen people. Let others be offended; Jews do not mean to offend. They are stating a fact about their existence, and they often claim that being chosen, being elect, carries so much responsibility and makes one so visible that it is a burden. But it is simply there.

What, then, is the point of proselytizing? To be sure, one can become a Jew, through some tests and delays and even painful—especially to adult males!—experiences. Does the Jew believe the world will be saved when all are converted to Judaism? Not at all. Jews do believe, however, that the world will not be saved if Jews are not faithful to the covenant. Michael Broyde shows some of the ways with which Jewish law reinforces these understandings, creating obligations for Jews and minimizing the appeal of and reasons for proselytizing.

So it is that, where proselytism is viewed negatively, as it so often is, Jews can relax and escape condemnation on this one front, at least. Let others break the bounds of civility; we do not proselytize. At the same time, Jews realize that not to proselytize keeps this diaspora small. Having lost millions in Europe during the Holocaust, and more to persecutions in the Soviet Union; producing small families; experiencing a great deal of exogamy and emigration on the part of the Jewish partner in many marriages; and not proselytizing, makes their very future precarious. Novak and Broyde know that, but they would say that classic Judaism turns over the answers about outcomes to this question to the God of Israel. And Jews are particularly vulnerable therefore, and lose some to aggressive proselytizers, especially Messianic Christians and Jews for Jesus, but also to the New Religious Movements, the "NRMs" that used to be called cults.

In sum, to use Santayana's words, you know at once when you are in the contexts of Judaism. The vistas it opens and the mysteries it reveals show that it is "another room to live in." Living there, one certainly sees the logic of the non-proselytism presented here.

A different world, another room, presents itself when Luke Timothy Johnson and James Muldoon open the door to earliest Christianity and the later canon law traditions. That this "another room" is always capable of change in the form of windows opened for the breezes to blow through (which was one of Pope John XXIII's images for the Second Vatican Council, 1962-65) is apparent. But it is a Catholic room, not a Muslim room or a Mormon room.

Generalizing about 1,800,000 people worldwide called is harder than doing so about 15 million Jews. There are about 25,000 separate Christian denominations worldwide, and they present astonishing variety. Among them are heirs of European establishments and highly acculturated American mainstream Protestants, not to mention millions of similarly accommodated and acquiescent Catholics who never make an effort to convert others and are embarrassed by aggressive fellow Christians who do. They are moderates, tolerant, ecumenically experienced, friendly to interfaith ventures, not uncomfortable being in intimate contexts with other believers and nonbelievers. The wags say that sociologists, having asked Episcopalians when they last invited someone to church, conclude that on the average an Episcopalian invites someone to church every twenty-nine years. In such mainstream Protestant company it is hard to suffer criticism for belonging to proselytizing communities. Most members have never seen their kind in action trying to convert anybody. They tend to be on the side of the anti-proselytizers and are subject to the criticism of Protestant evangelizers.

At the same time, Max L. Stackhouse and Deirdre King Hainsworth present a more mixed and complex picture of Protestant approaches to the subject. It is not likely that one will be able to generalize about Protestantism so readily in the era when the center of its gravity and impulses has shifted beyond Europe and to some extent beyond North America. While mainstream Protestant missionaries in Africa, Asia, and elsewhere do not concentrate on proselytizing—conversion is almost a byproduct of other features of ministry—Protestants in the "poor world," as in subSaharan Africa, tend to engage in vigorous efforts to convert, sometimes in competition, as with Muslims in Nigeria. Stackhouse and Hainsworth do not take us on a world tour, but they help explain the diversities around the world.

Orthodoxy, as described by Vigen Guroian, follows a different tack. It has engaged in proselytizing efforts and dominates in the Greek, Russian, and Middle Eastern worlds because there were historic proselytizers who won over the rulers and the populations, as at Kiev a millennium ago. But today the Orthodox are less concerned with expansion through their own proselytizing efforts and more concerned about proselytizers from the West invading their communities and, they say, by winning proselytizees to extravagant Protestant sectarian life, thus hindering efforts to gather energies for Orthodox renewal.

As for the Evangelicals, in whose every fiber is an instinct to convert, some of them tend to be aggressive in proselytizing. While most of them follow the implied rules of the game within pluralist republics, they may well target particular communities. While some eschatology-minded Evangelicals turn the question of the conversion of Jews over to God, who, in their belief, will act when Jesus Christ returns, others do precisely the opposite. They set up strategies and summon energies to convert Jews as part of their reading of premillennial visions of Christ's second coming.

Evangelical and evangelistic Protestants and Catholics will be more ready than others to send missionaries into any and all cultures and seek converts there. They will still often do so without showing sensitivity to the ways of those cultures or entertaining the possibility of seeing positive values in the religions that are on the scene when they arrive. As Jozef Tomko reports, with evident mixed feelings, this impulse has been changing since the bishops at Vatican II in the declaration *Nostra Aetate* made more positive mention than before of the values and integrities of non-Catholic Christianity and of non-Christianity.

Even so, the convert-seekers have many New Testament texts and examples on their side and thus call upon textual reasons for chiding fellow Christians who do not proselytize, just as they have little patience for those of other and no religions who do not live in the "another room" that happens to have been or was providentially provided to be theirs. They agree with Johnson and Muldoon, in those two scholars' very different ways, that Christianity perches its adherents on a sharp arête of its own. It poises them between universalism and particularism. It aspires to be the new light to the nations, complementing or replacing Israel's role, and to win as many proselytizees as possible. As the historians in this book show, and rivers of ink in libraries elaborate, after the flow of rivers of blood by militant convert-seekers and imperialists, proselytizing was often done by force of arms. It was done.

In the case of the third "People of the Book"—a concept with which some of the scholars of Islam here are uneasy—Muslims, like Christians, can be aggressive proselytizers, by sword and persuasion alike. The concept Richard C. Martin hears them using is "invitation," but Donna Arzt shows how the command to proselytize is integral, thanks to interpretations of the Qur'an and reinforced in many rules against apostasy.

There is no question but that Jehovah's Witnesses, Latter-day Saints, and Seventh-day Adventists engage in vigorous proselytization. The door-to-door visitations engaged in by some of these groups and the overt repudiation of all other Christian churches as false, in this case by Jehovah's Witnesses, show that they live with ease with the idea and reality of proselytization. Dallin Oaks and Lance Wickman do make the case for the discernment of civility and some live-and-let-live spirit in emergent Mormonism. On the other hand, while Bahá'ís welcome new members, their rather syncretic approach leads them from overt proselytization. In all these cases, each religion represents its own "another room." Know the room and you will have a good idea about the attitudes toward proselytization.

As for the future, it is not the purpose of the chapters in this book to do much projecting. The authors were assigned the sufficiently difficult task of accounting for the attitudes and practices of each. In many ways, they have put together a kind of data bank for those who do want to project a variety of futures. We can deduce some.

First, no one foresees a serene future in which everyone agrees with everyone else to be sensitive to other cultures and peoples with other commitments than those of the proselytizers. Jews, mainstream Protestants, and others who welcome converts in various ways are not likely to become organized around the conversionist agenda and will be sensitive about those who do. Jews in particular resent efforts to convert them, but mainstream Protestants can also be heard grumbling when aggressive pentecostal, charismatic, or fundamentalist Christians woo away their active members or intrude upon their cultures.

These irritations are minor and selective when compared with what can go on on the world scene. We have already mentioned Muslim-Christian racing to convert in Nigeria as a sample of tension where two large and aggressive cultures meet. Another instance was the former Soviet Union, now approached and, some Orthodox say, overrun by exploitative evangelistic and sectarian groups, to use their terminology for those they see to be intruders.

Whether or not these culture clashes over proselytism will lead to open physical warfare, as tribalisms and fundamentalisms on occasion do, is another question. In tribalisms and fundamentalisms of the most militant sort, the goal is to subjugate or eliminate the other as enemy, not to win him or her to your camp and community. But there are other kinds of wars than shooting ones, so anticipate disturbances of the peace.

On the other hand, we can expect to hear legitimations of proselytizing strategies from many who justify them. One frequently hears their assessment that proselytizing goes on all the time, in secular and religious worlds alike. It is difficult to have enthusiasm for a product, a way of life, or an object of ultimate concern, and then not to bid others to entertain sharing it with others. A person or community certifies its own authenticity and depth of commitment by instinctively wanting to share it. Even Judaism's strenuous efforts at non-proselytizing, in the eyes of some, look like a form of advertising designed to make membership alluring. And most mainstream Protestant congregations, in a variety of activities from "Everybody Welcome" signs to evangelism committees, are delighted when new members come from whatever source, and put the highest premium on those who are converted as if from scratch.

One of the contending approaches to explaining religious adherency these years is the Rational Choice Theory option. Its proponents argue that those groups not firm or dedicated and ambitious enough to proselytize will continue progressively to wane and may well disappear. Those that are most aggressive, make most demands, and are most sure of their product, will prosper. There is no perching on sharp arêtes in such supply-side marketing approaches. It is all very clear: proselytize or die. Be as civil as possible, if that does not distract from the efforts to convert, but those efforts must predominate over everything else. If that looks invasive and uncivil, let those who would celebrate ecumenism and interfaith relations enjoy the luxury as they decline.

The authors in this book spend little time breaking the bounds of their assignments to ask whether it is possible to combine commitment and civility, passionate attachment to one's own "another room" and seek to bid others to it with regard for the others as they now are. There are individual exemplars of this kind of approach. Some of the modern popes set out to exemplify this approach, as did the Vatican Council document *Nostra Aetate*. Yet critics within Catholicism argue that this affirmation of the commitment of others sapped the energies of missionaries and undercut the enterprise.

Taunted by those who use "macho" approaches to faith and proselytism, if they do not turn aggressive, and chastised by those for whom respect for diverse cultures and peace among them is the highest premium, civil-minded people who undertake to proselytize will no doubt remain in conflicted and ambiguous situations. So will those who are subjects of their efforts. We picture them, not settled or secure, but perched upon the sharp arête, uncertain about moving and unwilling to fall, aware of the heretical character of their moves and yet sure that the orthodox addresses of old will not give them balance.

The chapters in this book accurately trace those orthodoxies and suggest why heretical moves and orthodox stances are in conflict now as never before. They are proselytizers for the cause of accuracy and the stimulation of understanding and empathy. I hope others will join me in being henceforth better informed proselytizees.

Part One

JUDAISM

1.

PROSELYTISM IN JUDAISM

———————◆———————

David Novak

INTRODUCTION

In order to understand the role of proselytism in Judaism, one must first understand the role of conversion from Gentile to Jewish status. Though proselytism presupposes the possibility of conversion, conversion does not necessarily entail proselytism. A Gentile may very well join the Jewish people without any overt action by Jews to attract him or her to join them. We shall discover that the possibility of Gentiles becoming Jews has always been recognized in Judaism, in one way or another. But the active Jewish encouragement of Gentiles to convert to Judaism has been much more limited in scope. Indeed, the concept of the convert (*ger*) could be seen as a "border concept" in Judaism; that is, a concept whose constitution at various points in Jewish history tells us a good deal about how Jews viewed their identity in distinction from that of the Gentiles who surround them.[1] As such, the conversion of Gentiles into Jews tells us something essential about Judaism itself, whereas the intermittent advocacy of active proselytizing tells us the views of more selected groups of Jews in regard to the whole issue of distinctive Jewish identity. So, in order even to entertain the notion of Jewish proselytizing, we need to know a good deal about the institution of conversion to Judaism (*gerut*) throughout the ages. Nevertheless, the fact that one could never rule proselytism out of Judaism altogether tells us of a potential within the Jewish tradition that might well have important ramifications for the whole question of proselytism and human rights, which is of much current political interest internationally.

THE BIBLICAL PERIOD

Because Judaism, Christianity, and Islam have definite rites of conversion, one assumes that becoming a Jew or a Christian or a Muslim is essentially an event

17

in which the convert chooses to participate. In current parlance and conceptuality, religious "conversion" seems to denote a distinct act whereby one changes his or her fundamental religious affiliation; that is, one *becomes* a member of one religious communion, and thereby *ceases to be* a member of a previous one, at a definite point in time. One moves from being a religious *outsider* by simultaneously becoming an *insider*. Though free choice is a necessary condition for valid conversion, it is not a sufficient condition for it. One's personal choice to become a member of another religious communion does not automatically make one a member of that communion: one must also be accepted by those in authority within that communion. Joining a religious communion and gaining full acceptance into it are two sides of the very same event.

During much of the biblical period, one can make a better case for conversion being a process rather than a single event, and even the free choice of the convert as a necessary condition for it is something that is not altogether clear.[2] During the pre-exilic period, namely, before the destruction of the First Temple in 586 B.C.E. and the exile of the Judean community into Babylonia, the term *ger*, which later came to denote *convert* in the sense it has come to be known since the rise of Christianity and Islam, meant a *resident-alien,* someone having more or less status in common with native-born Israelites. The term is used in a number of different contexts.[3] At times it seems to denote religious parity as, for example:

> And when a *ger* dwells with you and makes Passover for the Lord, you shall circumcise him, every male, and then he shall draw near to do it, and he shall be like a person native-born on the land (*k'ezrah ha'arets*).
> . . . There shall be one Torah for the native-born and for the *ger* who dwells among you (Exodus 12:48-49).[4]

Other times, the term *ger* seems to denote a political outsider living among the people of Israel on a permanent enough basis to qualify for his or her own status in the polity, where one has a certain number of civil rights. Thus we read elsewhere: "You shall not abuse a needy and destitute laborer, whether a countryman (*me'amekha*) or your *ger* who is in your land in your cities (*bi'sha'arekha*)" (Deuteronomy 24:14).[5]

Other than the requirement of circumcision to be able to partake of the Paschal sacrifice, the biblical texts do not tell us exactly how one *became* a *ger* in the first place. But considering the fact that in pre-exilic Israel one's political-religious status was determined by his or her connection to a landed family, it would seem that intermarriage was the only way a Gentile could become part of the people of Israel on a truly permanent basis. Accordingly, a male Gentile would be at a disadvantage, at least during his own lifetime, because of his inability to own land in Israel on a permanent basis, even if he had married an Israelite woman and had children with her.[6] This comes out in the following:

And the Lord spoke to Moses in the steppes of Moab at the Jordan near Jericho saying: Speak to the sons of Israel and say to them that when you cross the Jordan into the land of Canaan, you shall disinherit all the inhabitants of the land from before you. . . . And you shall cause the land to be inherited by lot for your families: with many increase their share (*nahalato*), and with few decrease their share . . . according to ancestral tribes (*le-mattot avoteihem*) they shall be apportioned (*titnehalu*) (Numbers 33:50-51, 54).[7]

Full status in pre-exilic Israelite society required one to be landed, or to have official and permanent attachment to cultic shrines, as in the case of the Aaronide priests (*kohanim*).[8] Both the status of the tribes and that of the priests were determined by patrimony. In such a society, a person without patrimony would be in essence landless, for even if he or she purchased real estate, it would revert to its original tribal owner by ancestral right during the Jubilee year, that is, once in a fifty-year cycle. Any purchase of real estate by a tribal outsider would, in effect, be a lease, the longest term possible being forty-nine years.[9] Hence, when Moses implored his Midianite father-in-law, Jethro, to join the Israelites in their journey to the Promised Land and settle there with them, Jethro replied, "I shall not go [with you], but only back to my land and my birthplace shall I go" (Numbers 10:29). The good reason for this refusal is given in one of the oldest rabbinic texts: "because *gerim* have no portion therein."[10] From all of this, it seems rather clear that the rights and privileges of a *ger* were limited; that is, he was a second-class citizen living under Israelite rule, although not subject to Israelite caprice. Being landless, he was more often than not reduced to hiring out his services as some sort of laborer to those who were themselves landed.

This situation was not unique to ancient Israel. Throughout the ancient world, where full citizenship was determined by patrimony, provision had to be made for resident aliens living in the society, for it was neither possible nor practical to enslave them all. Following a term originally used in Athens, such persons are generally known as *metics*, namely, *sojourners*.[11] In order to distinguish *metics* in Israel, whose actual legal status the Rabbis themselves regarded as part of ancient, per-exilic history, the Rabbis drew a clear distinction between a *ger toshav*, a "sojourner in residence," and a full convert a *ger tsedeq*, a "righteous proselyte."[12] According to a number of biblical scholars, the *gerim* in the original sense consisted primarily of those original non-Israelite residents of Canaan who were not exterminated but, rather, were subjugated by the Israelite conquerors of the land.[13] In the Pentateuch there are various numbers of generations stipulated for residence in Israel before members of these various nations might actually "come into the congregation of the Lord," that is, marry full Israelites.[14] And even actual members of the seven Canaanite nations, about whom it was commanded "you shall not let one of them live" (Deuteronomy 20:16), are mentioned in the early prophetic books as living among the people of Israel with impunity.[15] It would seem that this obvious fact lies behind a later rabbinic attempt to exempt from punishment any "Canaanite" who was willing to live in Israel under the minimal rules required of any Gentile, especially the rule to refrain from practicing idolatry.[16]

In the case of women, it seems that they could become members of the people of Israel directly by marrying an Israelite man.[17] At least as far as biblical sources go, there was only an explicit prohibition of intermarriage with men and women from the seven Canaanite nations.[18] The most vivid presentation of this situation is found in the book of Ruth, which even though written in the post-exilic period, is set in the pre-exilic period, indeed in the early period of the Judges.

Ruth was a Moabite woman (a nation distinguished from the seven Canaanite nations) married to a Judean man, who, because of famine in his ancestral land, had taken up residence in Moab with his parents and brother. But Ruth's husband had died childless, leaving her a widow, in limbo, so to speak. If she had been married to him in the land of Israel, the levirate would have automatically taken place: it would be the obligation of one of her late husband's male relatives to "redeem" her by marrying her.[19] Had children resulted from this new union, they would have continued the patrimony of the family, thereby including their formerly Gentile mother therein. However, since Ruth had not become a member of the people of Israel, inasmuch as that status would have required residence in the ancestral land itself, her status became questionable. Indeed, because her late husband and his family had moved out of Israel into Moab, their status seems to have become questionable too. Because of the doubtful circumstances of the entire family, Naomi, Ruth's mother-in-law, strongly urged Ruth (and Orpah, the Moabite widow of her other deceased son) to "go, return, each woman to her mother's house" (Ruth 1:8). As the Rabbis were later to say, "when confronted with the certain and the doubtful, the certain takes precedence."[20] Ruth's Moabite status was certain, especially since she had not yet left her ancestral homeland; whereas her status in Israel would be doubtful as a single, non-Israelite woman. Accordingly, Orpah took what was no doubt the more certain course of action and returned to (that is, remained at home in) Moab, but Ruth took a considerable chance and emigrated to Israel with Naomi.

Ruth expressed her intentions by saying, "your people are my people and your God my God" (Ruth 1:16). Later rabbinic texts, written during a time when "conversion" had become a precise event with stipulated steps therein, saw in these words of Ruth a description of a definite conversion ceremony. But the biblical text itself seems to record nothing but a statement of intention on Ruth's part to gradually *become* a member of the people of Israel.[21] And, indeed, her becoming a member of the people of Israel did not really become a fait accompli until Boaz, a wealthy kinsman of her late husband, himself, chose to exercise his levirate right and responsibility by marrying Ruth. Before that happened, Ruth referred to herself as a "stranger" (*nokhriyah*) (Ruth 2:10). But Boaz, emphasizing what would come to be, said to Ruth, "the Lord will recompense your labor, and let your reward be complete from the Lord God of Israel, to whom you have come to take shelter under his wings" (Ruth 2:12). Hence, in this earlier time, Ruth did not become "like Rachel and Leah" (Ruth 4:11), who were the ancestresses of the entire house of Israel, until she is taken in marriage by Boaz. (In a later time, Ruth's becoming a Jew would have had to precede her marriage to Boaz or any other Jewish man.) No particular rite other than the event of the marriage itself seems to have been involved in Ruth's final change from Gentile to Israelite status. Her now unquestionable Israelite status is emphasized by the author, who at the end of the book points out that she is the ancestress of no one less than King David.[22] But things would become different later on in biblical times.

The exile of the Judean community to Babylonia in 586 B.C.E. had profound ramifications for Jewish life in many ways. As had been the case with the earlier exile of the northern kingdom of Israel by the Assyrians, the Babylonians exiled the Judeans in order to force them to assimilate into a larger Gentile society and thus lose their identity as a people. This strategy had worked in the case of all the other peoples who were exiled by the Assyrians and the Babylonians. They did assimilate and so no longer posed a threat to their conquerors. The Judeans were the notable exception. "Judaism," as we know it, begins with them.

The factor that enabled the Judeans (or by now the "Jews" as the remnant of the full people of Israel) to maintain their identity was their adherence to their God, whose reign they assumed to be universal. Indeed, because the Lord God of Israel was to be served anywhere his people happened to be, they were able to maintain their identity in exile and to return to their ancestral land of Israel. But after the exile, no one could assert again that to leave the land of Israel was the real equivalent of leaving the covenant between God and the people of Israel.[23] Remaining part of the people of Israel and its covenant with God now became much more a matter of personal conviction and less a matter of simple patrimony. For patrimony involves a more or less uninterrupted social and political life, a fact that the exile had permanently ruptured.

This new sense of more voluntary Jewish identity meant that becoming part of the people of Israel was no longer tied to a particular connection to the land. Living in the land of Israel remained an important part of Judaism, but it could no longer be taken as its sine qua non. Furthermore, after the return from the Babylonian exile, no one was really living on his old ancestral portion anymore. Thus the main difference between native-born Israelites and sojourners before the exile no longer obtained. Gentiles now had to become full converts in order to secure for themselves any permanent status among the Jewish people.[24] Thus in post-exilic texts we read of "Gentiles (*bnei nekhar*) becoming attached (*ha-nilvim*) to the Lord to serve him and to love the name of the Lord by becoming his servants" (Isaiah 56:6). Although the texts do not outline exactly how Gentiles became "attached," clearly this was more a matter of their volition than their assimilation into the people of Israel as was the case in the pre-exilic period with the old "sojourners in residence." What we have in post-exilic writings is the beginning of the current meaning of *conversion*.

POST-BIBLICAL JUDAISM

Josephus recounted the instance early in the first century C.E. of the conversion to Judaism of the pagan king, Izates, by a Palestinian Jew, Ananias. The king was ready to be circumcised in order to be "a genuine Jew," but his mother dissuaded him from doing so because this would not have been acceptable to his subjects.[25] His Jewish teacher assured him that he could be a genuine Jew "if indeed he had fully decided to be a devoted adherent of Judaism."[26] However, another Palestinian Jew urged him to become circumcised, and Izates followed his suggestion. Nevertheless, it is important to note here that even Eleazar did not declare the earlier conversion with Ananias to be invalid, but only indicated that Izates *as a Jew* was not upholding the law of the Torah that every male Jew be circumcised.[27] Thus there is no doubt that Josephus regarded circumcision to be an essential part of the conversion process, but he seemed to regard it as something that could, under certain circumstances, come later in the process.[28]

With one notable exception, conversion to Judaism after the return from Babylonian exile seems to have been an individual matter, and a matter that was the result of personal volition on the part of the convert. The exception to this general trend was also recorded by Josephus. It concerns the forced conversion of the Itreans and the Idumeans (the descendants of ancient Edom) by the Maccabean king John Hyrkanus in the second century B.C.E.[29] Undoubtedly, this was a political move designed to integrate these conquered peoples into the Judean polity. However, this political strategy did not really work out well. Instead of leading to the integration of these peoples into the Jewish people, it created a lingering resentment among them toward their conquerors. Indeed, the Idumeans got their revenge when the Romans made one of them, Herod, the king of the Jews. Herod's cruelty to "his" people became legendary in his own time and afterward.[30] This whole experience seems to have taught the Jews that conversions could only be real when the converts came to Judaism out of their own free choice, to answer what had to be regarded as the personal summons of the God of Israel.[31] It also seems to have resulted in the rabbinic insistence that a conversion without the explicit consent of the convert himself or herself is invalid.[32] This was a definite step in the development of the whole institution of conversion in Judaism.

Even in the second century C.E., when conversion was much more officially circumscribed as a definite event, there was still a major dispute as to the exact moment one converted from being a Gentile to being a bona-fide Jew.

> Our Rabbis taught: If a convert was circumcised but not immersed, Rabbi Eliezer says he is a convert . . . if immersed but not circumcised, Rabbi

Joshua says he is a convert. . . . And the Sages say that one who was either immersed but not circumcised, circumcised but not immersed, he is not a convert until he is both circumcised and immersed.[33]

The point here is not whether circumcision can be waived for entrance into God's people.[34] The point of dispute is, rather, exactly *when* in the process of conversion one can be considered fully Jewish. The view of the Sages, which became the normative one, is that in the narrowest sense the process of conversion begins with circumcision and ends with immersion.

None of this indicates in a conclusive way just how much effort was being made by the Jewish community to attract Gentiles to Judaism by what we now call *proselytization*. Nevertheless, there arose among the Hellenistic Jews a group that was designated as the "fearers of the Lord" or the *sebomenoi*. Both Jewish and non-Jewish sources acknowledge a group of Gentiles who observed Jewish religious practices in varying degrees, short of full conversion to Judaism.[35] They were, for all intents and purposes, quasi-Jews. Whether the Jews actually went out and sought such people is debatable.[36] But we certainly do have enough evidence to conclude that they often encouraged such people to move closer and closer to Judaism, eventually resulting in circumcision and immersion. What is also clear is that in the first and second centuries C.E., and perhaps beyond, Jews and Christians were in competition for which community would attract more of these former pagans, who had become dissatisfied with their ancestral polytheism. These people were seen as being on their way to some sort of monotheism, which was either Jewish or Christian—and later Muslim as well.

The attempt to make Judaism attractive to Gentiles searching for a new and more humanly satisfying way of life, even if not the type of overt proselytizing we know today, was usually done by presenting the superiority of the laws of the Torah over any other competing way of life. In what must be seen as having a proselytizing intent, the first century C.E. Hellenistic Jewish thinker Philo of Alexandria makes the following claim for Judaism's universal appeal:

Thus all the laws are shown to be desirable (*zelotai*) and precious in the eyes of all, ordinary citizens and rulers alike, though our nation has not prospered for many a year. . . . But if a fresh start should be made to brighter prospects, how great a change for the better might we expect to see! I believe that each nation would abandon its peculiar ways and throwing overboard their ancestral customs, turn to our laws alone.[37]

Since the services in the Alexandrian synagogues were held in Greek, including the central feature of the service, the reading of the Torah and its exposition, it was not uncommon to find a considerable number of Gentiles in regular attendance. There is also little doubt that they were made to feel welcome, probably being regarded in one way or another as potential Jews. And, since the synagogue service was the first religious service in the ancient world not involving sacrificial worship, none of the purity distinctions between Jews and Gentiles that pertained in the Jerusalem Temple would have applied there.[38] Aside from the actual leading of these services, which would have had to be done by bona-fide Jews, there seems to have been no distinction made between Jewish and Gentile worshipers. Even Gentile spectators seem to have been made to feel welcome.

Even in earlier rabbinic sources from Palestine, where the religious primacy of the Hebrew language was certainly maintained, we see an emphasis on what seems to be a form of proselytizing. Thus when Scripture states that Abraham and Sarah "had made (*asu*) souls in Haran" (Genesis 12:5), one source assumes that this does not refer to increasing their slave population, which is what the plain meaning of the text would indicate, but, rather, to the converts they had made.[39] Another source emphasizes how Abraham would use his constant hospitality to strangers as an occasion to get them to thank God and not himself for the kindness extended to them.[40] And Jethro, the father-in-law of Moses, is considered to be a paradigmatic convert because of his exclamation upon his arrival in the Israelite camp at Sinai: "And now I know that the Lord is greater than all the other gods" (Exodus 18:11).[41] Moreover, he refused to accompany the Israelites to the Promised Land because he wanted to return to his homeland of Midian to convert all his countrymen by "drawing them near to the wings of the divine presence (*Shekhinah*)."[42] From these sources it is clear that some sort of active proselytizing is being endorsed. How much of it was actually put into practice is debated by historians of the period in which these texts were written, however.

What seems to have been a program of proselytizing is also seen in the career of Hillel the Elder, who lived in Palestine in the first century B.C.E., after having immigrated there from Babylonia in his youth in order to study under the Pharisaic teachers Shemaiah and Abtalyon, themselves reputed to have been the descendants of converts to Judaism.[43] Hillel became renowned for his open personality, which attracted many to the Pharisee way of life. In one of the most famous stories in the Talmud, Hillel is approached by a Gentile who wants to be taught the whole Torah "while standing on one foot."[44] Although this seemingly outrageous request was rejected by Hillel's sterner colleague Shammai, Hillel accepts it by responding, "what is hateful to you, do not do to your fellow human. This is the whole Torah; the rest is commentary. Go and learn." The answer, though, is hardly distinctly Jewish. Positive reciprocity as a moral norm is found in numerous other traditions, including those contemporary with Hillel and his Gentile interlocutor.[45] However, this was not a reduction of Judaism to some kind of universally evident morality, which could well be a means to assimilation out of Judaism rather than an attraction to it. Instead, it was an admission that in universally accepted morality there is already the potential for Judaism.[46] Once the would-be convert sees that, he is on the way to rising from the lower and more general to the higher and more singular, which is within uniquely Jewish revelation.[47] But without that initial potential, it is hard to see how Hillel could have made intelligible contact with this Gentile, or any intelligent Gentile seeker of higher truth. Indeed, one of Hillel's favorite sayings was: "Love humankind (*ha-beriyot*) and draw them near to the Torah."[48] Although later rabbinic sources, perhaps reflecting a time when proselytizing was already out of favor, seem to confine the application of this norm to Hillel's fellow Jews, the original meaning seems to have a wider application. Indeed, the New Testament may have had Hillel or someone like him in mind when it spoke of the zeal of the Pharisees in attracting converts.[49]

A number of historians have noted that after the rise of Christianity and its rapid success in what might be termed the "war for the converts," rabbinic references to the "fearers of the Lord" virtually disappeared.[50] For it was from this group that Paul and his successors made many converts to the new religion. In his discourses in diaspora synagogues he repeatedly refers to "God-fearers" as well as to his fellow Jews.[51] Perhaps as a response to this, the Rabbis began to emphasize a strict demarcation between Jews and non-Jews. Eventually, Gentiles who followed what the Rabbis regarded as the basic laws applying to all humankind, especially the renunciation of idolatry, were regarded as law-abiding humans who were acceptable to God as they were.[52] One could no longer assume all Gentiles idolaters simply because they are not Jews and, as such, conclude that none of them could have a valid relationship with God.[53] To make the distinction between Jews and Gentiles as clear as possible, becoming a Jew now required what amounted to an almost instant acceptance of Judaism and all its practices.[54] In fact, the earlier rabbinic acceptance of partial observance of Judaism by quasi-Jews became discouraged in the third century C.E.[55] This, of course, made proselytization much harder because no compromise with the Gentile's original culture was now allowed in order to make Judaism more congruous with it, even for the sake of easing a Gentile into Judaism. Moreover, since more and more Jewish thinkers were accepting the view of first-century Rabbi Joshua ben Hananiah that "the righteous of the nations of the world have a portion in the world-to-come," one could no longer present Judaism as the only alternative to idolatry, which, by the time of the Rabbis, was considered to be universally prohibited.[56] This, of course, made the type of proselytizing that offers heaven for its own community and hell for everyone else impossible. (In the Middle Ages it made Jewish respect for the Gentile communities of Christianity and Islam possible, although arguable.)

Maimonides, although writing much later, captured the spirit of the sharp distinctions between Jews and Gentiles—even monotheistic Gentiles—as follows:

> The essence of the matter is that we do not allow them [Gentiles] to innovate a religious practice and to make commandments for themselves according to their own opinion, but a Gentile should either become a full convert (*ger tsedeq*), or remain with his own law and neither add to it nor subtract from it.[57]

THE TALMUDIC INSTITUTION OF CONVERSION

At the time when Paul's view prevailed in the early Christian community—namely, that full conversion to Judaism was not required for a Gentile to become part of God's covenant with Israel—the requirements for conversion to Judaism were codified during the administration of Rabban Yohanan ben Zakkai, just before the destruction of the Second Temple in 70 C.E. The necessary requirements for conversion became: (1) circumcision; (2) immersion (what the New Testament calls *baptism,* that is, full immersion of the whole body in a natural pool of water); and (3) bringing a sacrifice to the Temple. The event of conversion was compared to the event of covenantal commitment made by the people of Israel when they accepted the Torah at Mount Sinai. Thus the presupposition for the performance of these rites of conversion is the unconditional acceptance of the authority of Scripture (*torah she-bi-khtav*) and Jewish tradition (*torah she-b'al peh*). Conversion became one, multifaceted, cultic event, involving acceptance of the kingship of the Lord God of Israel and all his commandments and public acts unmistakably marking this ontological transition.

> Rabbi [Judah the Prince] says that "like you" (*kakhem*—Numbers 15:15) means like your ancestors. Just as your ancestors did not enter the covenant except through circumcision, immersion, and being sprinkled with sacrificial blood, so they may not enter the covenant except through circumcision, immersion, and being sprinkled with sacrificial blood.[58]

The requirements of circumcision and being sprinkled with sacrificial blood are explicitly scriptural; as for the requirement of immersion, it is seen as being the prerequisite for being sprinkled with sacrificial blood.[59] Indeed, immersion was seen as the necessary transition for the assumption of any new sacred state. However, inasmuch as the sacrificial system was already endangered just before the destruction of the last Temple in 70 C.E., could the requirement of sacrificial blood as a sine qua non of conversion spell the end of the institution of conversion to Judaism?[60] The answer of Jewish tradition was an unambiguous *no*. The decision not to allow the involuntary loss of the Temple and its sacrificial rites to end conversion indicates how central this whole institution was considered to be to Judaism itself. But how was the legal problem to be solved?

One solution proposed was that the minimal price for a sacrifice be put in escrow by the convert. Here it was assumed that the Temple would be rebuilt shortly, and then the convert could take the money and purchase his conversion sacrifice after the fact, as it were. But Rabban Yohanan ben Zakkai eliminated even this conditional act as entailing more problems than it would solve. In effect, he did not allow the involuntary loss of a formerly necessary aspect of the conversion event to eliminate the whole institution itself. Quoting the verse, "when a *ger* dwells among you throughout your generations" (Numbers 15:14), it is assumed in the Talmud that there must be converts in every generation and that the law must now find a modus operandi for legitimizing this ubiquitous historical reality.[61]

A similar problem arose in connection with the possibility of disqualifying all rabbinical judges, who after the demise of the Sanhedrin no longer had the full ordination (*semikhah*) instituted by Moses and passed on to Joshua and his successors.[62] According to the earlier law, there could be no conversion without the supervision and approval of these fully ordained rabbinical judges.[63] A medieval authority solved this problem by citing another talmudic source which rules that even Rabbis who do not have this full ordination are still allowed "to function as the agents" of the earlier Rabbis who did have this full ordination.[64] What is important in the use of this obvious legal fiction is that its use is to be limited to those areas of the law whose application is regularly required by the Jewish community.[65] Conversion is considered to be such a regular requirement. In addition to this highly formal legal reasoning, conversion is also justified by the historical fact that the Babylonian Rabbis, who themselves did not have full ordination, nevertheless conducted conversions, and these conversions could not be invalidated because of the different juridical status of these Rabbis. Even though their authority as the "agents" of the earlier Rabbis was not actually given to them by these earlier Rabbis, except in certain areas of law, they exercised it anyway in other places at their own initiative.[66] Here we have a clear recognition of how the law must respect popular consensus. The fact is that the Jewish people themselves regarded the acceptance of converts to be a necessary part of their overall covenantal life. Thus the book of Ruth came to be read on the festival of *Shavuot*, which celebrates the Sinaitic covenant and the giving of the law for it there.[67] For Ruth was seen as a paradigmatic convert, who had accepted the Torah willingly just as the people of Israel was seen as having accepted the Torah willingly.

The very essence of the conversion event, and the process leading up to it, are seen as being the acceptance of the commandments of the Torah as binding upon oneself without exception.[68] This is preceded by the commitment of the conversion candidate to cast his or her lot with the Jewish people for better or for worse. In other words, conversion is to both the Jewish people and Judaism in tandem. It is an irrevocable commitment to the reality of the covenant in the living Jewish people and to the idea of the covenant in the Torah. Without the reality of the covenant in the people, the idea of it is empty; without the idea of the covenant in the Torah, the reality of it is blind. This comes out in the *locus classicus* of the procedure for conversion in the Talmud:

Our Rabbis taught: When one comes to convert in this time, they are to say to him, "What benefit do you see in coming to convert? Do you not know that Israel at this time is beset, downtrodden, lowly, distraught, and persecuted?" If he says, "I know and I am not worthy to be part of them," they are to accept him immediately. They are to inform him of some of the less consequential commandments and some of the more consequential commandments . . . but this is not to be overdone. When he accepts them, they are to circumcise him at once.[69]

Here is a clear statement that the convert's acceptance of both the Jewish people and Judaism, and the Jewish community's acceptance of him or her (which is not necessitated by the would-be convert's desire to become a Jew), are to be conscious, deliberate, public acts. Later authorities insist that whereas in certain cases of circumcision and conversion the acts need not be done publicly to be valid—at least ex post facto—acceptance of the binding character of all the commandments must be done in public.[70] This once again affirms the rabbinic emphasis of the point that it is the Torah that makes Jews what they are, and that even native-born Jews who do not accept the authority of the Torah and its commandments are still "Jews" only because the Torah teaches that no one, native born or convert, can ever remove himself or herself from God's everlasting covenant with the people of Israel.[71]

Even though there probably was no overt proselytizing in the talmudic period, there seems to have been a considerable number of Gentile converts to Judaism. In fact, one of the problems dealt with in the talmudic discussion of conversion is whether everyone claiming to be a convert should be accepted as one. Apparently, being a convert to Judaism was a desirable status for a considerable number of people. That should belie the notion that after the destruction of the Temple, Jews were constantly despised by all Gentiles.

> Our Rabbis taught: Someone who came and said, "I am a convert," are we to accept him as such? Scripture states "with you" (Leviticus 19:23)— namely, one who has been so ascertained (be-muhazaq) with you. If he came with evidence, how do we know he is to be believed? Scripture teaches, "when a stranger dwells with you in your land" (Leviticus 19:33) . . . the Sages say whether in the land of Israel or outside it, he must bring proof (ra'yah).[72]

Nevertheless, in the Middle Ages there were considerable debates as to how far the investigation of converts need go. For some authorities, proof was only required if the convert had been previously known as a Gentile in the very community in which he wanted to now be accepted as a Jew.[73] For others, proof was always required of anyone who even appeared to be a convert rather than a native-born Jew.[74]

The concern of the Talmud about someone announcing "I am a convert" is whether that person had been converted in a properly supervised rabbinical context. "Rabbi Judah said that one who had been converted under the auspices of a rabbinical court (be-vet din) is a convert, but if he converted by himself, he is not a convert."[75] Because of this concern, the practice gradually arose to issue to a convert a certificate (te'udat gerut), signed by the three judges who officiated at the conversion, indicating that everything required had been properly done.

Another way that Gentiles have become Jews is through the conversion of children to Judaism. This is most often the case when Jews, usually childless Jewish couples, take children born to non-Jewish parents and raise them as their own children. The *locus classicus* of this whole question is seen in the following talmudic text:

> Rav Huna said that a convert who is a minor may be immersed under the supervision of a rabbinical court. What does this imply? One may benefit someone without his consent. . . . What are we dealing with here specifically? It is with a convert whose children converted with him. Indeed, what their father did was for their benefit. Rav Joseph said, nevertheless, when they become adults, they may repudiate (*li-mhot*) the conversion. . . . Once she [or he] has reached the age of majority for even one hour and did not repudiate it, she [or he] may never repudiate it again.[76]

At first glance, it would seem that a child may be converted only when his or her biological parents are bringing him or her along with themselves for the conversion of the whole family. This might well be regarded as a special privilege inasmuch as conversion legally severs previous biological ties, even parenthood.[77] Thus only a biological parent could bestow such a "benefit" on his or her child, because the benefit totally changes their relationship. Some are of the opinion that this is the automatic right of the father, whereas a mother's request for the conversion of her child would require a formal legal ruling by a court.[78]

However, Gentile parents do have the right to transfer full control of their children to Jews, irrespective of whether they themselves convert.[79] In other words, they have the right to put their children up for adoption. Accordingly, Maimonides writes: "A Jew who took a Gentile child or found a Gentile infant and had him immersed, if this is for the sake of conversion, then he is a convert."[80] Other medieval authorities rule similarly.[81] But what is meant by the right of repudiation by the child so converted when he or she becomes an adult?

One can understand the right of repudiation as meaning only a possibility de jure, but not something applicable de facto. Thus the fourteenth-century authority Nissim Gerondi wonders how the right of repudiation can be compressed into the very first hour of one's adulthood. If the converted child is living a Jewish life, then that fact alone indicates the person accepts what was done for him or her in childhood retroactively.[82] Accordingly, neither Nissim Gerondi nor Maimonides before him regards this possibility of repudiation as an actual procedure that must be presented to the convert who has just now become an adult. It would seem that, for them and others, becoming a Jew is in effect a privilege that one cannot really renounce, even if it was a privilege bestowed before he or she could possibly give literal consent.[83] Indeed, following this line of thinking, there hardly seems to be any reason to have to even inform this convert of his or her biological origins.

Of course, the earlier talmudic ruling about the right of repudiation could not very well be ignored by any traditional authority, but it could be played down to a considerable extent. Thus the conversion of the child to Judaism is an event that happens to the child with or without his or her consent just by virtue of being taken into a Jewish family to be raised in its midst. This is much the same situation as birth itself, a matter in which a native-born child also has no consent. For both, Jewish identity is determined by either the literal event of birth or an event of "rebirth" shortly thereafter. Indeed, to play down conversion as an essentially voluntary matter, the Talmud says that "a convert who is converted is like a newborn child (ke-qatan she-nolad)."[84] As such, the only significant difference between native-born Jewish children and those adopted from Gentile parents is that the adopted child has the possibility, but need not be given the opportunity, to repudiate subsequently what was done on his or her behalf by others earlier in his or her life. However, there are some authorities who insist that the adopted child be informed of his or her right of consent, which can be exercised at whatever point in one's adult life he or she has been so informed. For without the opportunity for the exercise of this right, the Jewish status of one converted as a child might remain doubtful.[85]

Nevertheless, there are medieval authorities who require at least some consent to the conversion on the part of the Gentile parents, even if they themselves do not convert to Judaism.[86] Following this view, it would seem to be prohibited to convert children whose biological parents put them up for adoption not knowing that Jews would eventually adopt them, let alone not specifically approving the conversion of their children to Judaism. Still others emphasize that even if the biological parents do not initiate the conversion, the child himself or herself must be capable of intelligently requesting the court, in loco parentis, to fulfill his or her choice to convert to Judaism.[87] Following this view, it would seem to be prohibited to convert any infant. The court would have to be assured by the child that this was indeed what he or she truly wanted. The age of conversion, then, would no doubt vary from child to child. However, eventually the conversion of infants to Judaism became an almost universally accepted Jewish practice.

CIRCUMCISION

Circumcision has always been seen as the chief way Jewish males have been distinguished from other peoples.[88] Yet, it was known in both Jewish and non-Jewish sources that there are circumcised Gentiles too.[89] The question arose, therefore, in early rabbinic sources whether the circumcision of a Gentile, when he was still a Gentile, is sufficient ex post facto for his conversion to Judaism.

Rabbi Simon ben Eleazar said that the School of Shammai and the School of Hillel . . . disputed about a convert who converted when he was already circumcised (*mahul*): the School of Shammai say that the covenantal blood needs to be drawn from him; and the School of Hillel say that the covenantal blood does not need to be drawn from him.[90]

Though the law generally follows the Hillelites, in this case it does not.[91] That is because in a later text this version of the dispute is rejected in favor of a reading that assumes that the Hillelites agree with the Shammaites on the necessity of drawing "the covenantal blood" (*hatafat dam berit*), which is a symbolic gesture whereby a drop of blood is drawn from the place on the penis where the foreskin had formerly been connected to it.[92]

By the time of later rabbinic sources, no authority dispensed with the requirement of a symbolic recircumcision of a convert whose foreskin had already been removed.[93] But there was a dispute in the Middle Ages concerning the exact procedure and its meaning. Some were of the opinion that this recircumcision is required because of the possibility that some minute residue of the foreskin remained.[94] The assumption here seems to be that when Gentiles do circumcise their own, they are not as precise as Jews, who, after all, place great religious significance on all the details of the circumcision procedure. But others opined that the act of drawing the covenantal blood is an act *de novo* and is thus not at all a correction of something done incompletely in the Gentile past of the convert. The thirteenth-century authority Nahmanides emphasized that the drawing of the covenantal blood is for circumcised men what circumcision itself is for uncircumcised men. The earlier circumcision is totally irrelevant one way or another in cases of conversion. The circumcision of the convert is thus part of the process whereby he is "born again." Not being a case of doubt, Nahmanides insists that the benediction recited at a real circumcision also be recited in this case too.[95]

IMMERSION

The last component of the conversion procedure is immersion in a natural body of water (*miqveh*) sufficient for other purification rites, especially postmenstrual immersion.[96] *Ab initio*, this act of immersion (*tevilah*) is to be in the presence of a court of three. It is required of both women and men. The question arose, however, to what extent an earlier immersion in a *miqveh* for purposes other than that of conversion is acceptable ex post facto for purposes of conversion. What if the immersion had been for a specifically sacred matter but not for the purpose of conversion per se? In other words, there is proper sacred intent here, as signified by the recitation of a benediction (*berakhah*), but it is not specifically an intention of conversion per se.[97] On this question there is a medieval dispute. It revolves around the following passage in the Talmud:

The slave of Rav Hiyya bar Ammi had a certain Gentile woman immersed for purposes of marriage. Rav Joseph said, "I am able to legitimize her and her daughter based on the view of Rav Assi who said, 'who has not immersed herself after menstruation?' . . . Rabbi Joshua ben Levi said, 'who has not immersed himself after a seminal emission?'"[98]

The point being made in this text is that anyone living in a normative Jewish community could be assumed to be observant of immersion as a regularly mandated purification rite. The important thing to note here is that there was no formal acceptance of the commandments on the part of the Gentile woman. Her acceptance of the commandments was not part of any discernible event. Instead, it was a process that is presumed by virtue of her observance of the Jewish laws of female purity. The later dispute is concerned with the extent to which we are to follow the above text.

Maimonides qualified it in this way:

When we have seen a female convert continually behaving in a Jewish manner, for example, immersing herself following menstruation . . . and similarly so with a male convert: these persons are presumed to be full converts (gerei tsedeq), even though there are no witnesses to testify before whom they were actually converted. Nevertheless, if they came to marry with other Jews, we are not to permit them to do so until they bring witnesses, or until they immerse themselves in our presence. That is because they are presumed to have been Gentiles.[99]

Maimonides is making two points here: First, marriage requires greater proof of pedigree than other religious acts. Second, the most that would be required in such cases is another immersion for purposes of completing the conversion procedure. That is sufficient because their observant Jewish life is enough of a presumption that they have already accepted the commandments of the Torah.

Nahmanides, however, questioned why Maimonides chose regular immersion as evidence of leading a normative Jewish life, but not being sufficient to validate fully the Jewish status of the former Gentile. Wouldn't Sabbath observance be a more public act if that is what we are looking for? Therefore, he considered the regular practice of immersion as efficacious for both the presumption of the acceptance of the commandments and the legal fact of full conversion.[100] He explicitly based himself on the Palestinian Talmud, which states:

A convert who was circumcised but not immersed is acceptable (kasher) because there is no convert who has not immersed himself after a seminal emission. But this is difficult, for it suffices for purification of a lesser impurity, yet does it suffice for purification of a more serious impurity?

Rabbi Yose ben Bun said that because both of these acts were for the sake of the sanctity of Israel, one suffices for the sake of the other.[101]

Nahmanides indicated that this text is the support for his point of view, namely, ordinary immersion for any religious purpose can be accepted ex post facto as being sufficient for both the acceptance of the commandments, which initiates the conversion procedure, and the immersion itself, which terminates it.

THE CHILDREN OF CONVERTS

There is a tendency in the Talmud to be more lenient in matters of doubt regarding the children of converts than with converts themselves.

> There is the case of someone who came before Rabbi Judah and said to him, "I converted by myself." Rabbi Judah said to him, "Do you have proof?" He responded, "no." [Rabbi Judah said to him] "Do you have children?" He responded, "yes." He said to him, "you are believed to disqualify yourself, but you are not believed to disqualify your children."[102]

A number of suggestions are made in the text as to what Rabbi Judah's reasoning actually is in this case. The most likely suggestion is that since the man declares himself to be, on legal grounds, a Gentile, his subsequent testimony about his children's status (even though coming on the heels of his testimony about himself) is invalid because Gentiles cannot be witnesses about matters of Jewish status.

In such cases, we see a dialectic at work between conversion as an event and conversion as a process, which is an issue we have already seen in biblical times between pre-exilic and post-exilic times. For the convert himself or herself, conversion is meant to be an event, one clearly discernible in all its components. However, the convert sets in motion a process of Jewish identification for his or her descendants, in the same way that the ancestors of the Jewish people set in motion a process of Jewish identification for all subsequent generations of their descendants. A number of legal factors concerning doubtful identity impinges on this question of those who are taken to be Jews as the result of a process begun by their ancestors.

First, there is the talmudic principle, "a family that has become intermingled is considered intermingled."[103] In other words, presumption of Jewish familial identity over a number of generations is taken to be sufficient for accepting such a family as fully Jewish. Now this principle is stated concerning families in which there is a suspected strain of bastardy (*mamzerut*), something the Rabbis considered to be essentially not rectifiable, at least when it is ascertained.[104] However, if a process of eventual absorption into the marriageable

Jewish community is accepted in a situation essentially not rectifiable when ascertained, how much more so should a process of absorption be accepted in a situation whose initial event can be rectified by the subsequent recognition of a recognizably Jewish religious life on the part of the first Jewish ancestor? In other words, the principle of not asking questions about pedigree, when nothing on the part of the life of the family here and now seems to warrant it, would seem to have very wide application.

Second, there is also the question of violating the commandment against casting aspersions on those already presumed to be fellow Jews. The Mishnah states:

> Just as there is oppression in buying and selling, so is there oppression (*ona'ah*) in words. . . . If one is the child of converts, do not say to him, "remember the deeds of your fathers," as Scripture says, "and the sojourner (*ger*) you shall not oppress or persecute" (Exodus 22:20).[105]

The special status of the children of converts, in distinction from converts themselves, is seen in the following talmudic text:

> Our Rabbis taught: If he was the son of converts, one should not say to him, "remember the deeds of your fathers." If he was a convert coming to study Torah, one should not say to him, "the mouth that ate nonkosher meat, detestable and creeping things, is coming to study Torah that was uttered by the mouth of God!"[106]

From all this it seems clear that the forbidden taunt to the children of converts is not about their ultimately non-Jewish origins. That would be a taunt to the converts themselves.[107] The taunt to the children of the converts regarding "the deeds of your fathers" (*ma'aseh avoteikhem*) seems to be about the validity of the conversion of their ancestors.[108] Moreover, the Palestinian Talmud notes that even those who rule that converts may not recite the liturgical formula "God of our fathers" do not hold that this applies to the children of converts.[109] In other words, the process initiated by even a forgotten conversion in the past can now be taken to be irreversible.

PROSELYTIZATION IN THE THEOLOGY OF RABBI JUDAH HALEVI

With the rise of Christianity and Islam and their eventual political domination of the areas of the world where virtually all Jews lived, the question of Jews proselytizing Gentiles became a moot point de facto. It was usually forbidden by the respective Christian and Muslim authorities under whom Jews were now living. In fact, in many localities, even the acceptance of Gentile converts to Judaism who came of their own accord, without any overt Jewish efforts to attract them to Judaism, was forbidden; hence it was quite dangerous for Jewish communities to accept them at all.[110] Nevertheless, even under these difficult circumstances, Jews were not willing simply to abandon the institution of conversion altogether. Accordingly, various subterfuges were devised in order to enable Gentiles to convert to Judaism without danger to themselves and the Jewish communities that accepted them as members.

Despite the virtual end of any overt Jewish proselytizing, and even the serious curtailment of the more passive acceptance of converts altogether, the issue of proselytizing in principle took on a new life on the intellectual level in the Middle Ages. Here the question was not so much the reality of proselytizing as the possibility of it. This possibility emerged as a Jewish reaction to the supersessionist claims of both Christianity and Islam against what for both of them is the older religion of Judaism. Each in its own way, both Christianity and Islam had to acknowledge the greater antiquity of Judaism. But antiquity was not the issue per se—if it were, Hinduism might have a prior claim over even Judaism. Instead, Christianity and Islam had to claim, mutatis mutandis, that each had taken up into itself everything true that Judaism had already taught, and then each had gone beyond Judaism, teaching a greater truth than that of the parent religion. Indeed, each asserted that the truth it now teaches is unsurpassable by any other faith community in this world. The task of each of these new communities (in relation to Judaism, that is) was now defined as proselytizing the entire world, that is, bringing the world to its truth, which it believes to be universal. In principle, that message was to be first carried to the Jews, for, after all, they were deemed better prepared to accept it than the pagans. But the fact that the vast majority of the Jews resisted the proselytizing efforts of both Christianity and Islam caused a great deal of animosity against them from both Christians and Muslims.

Intelligent Jews confronted with these supersessionist claims could not very well remain indifferent to them. For a major part of both Christian and Muslim supersessionism is that Jews have no further raison d'être as a faith community and, therefore, they should become what has superseded them historically. That is, the inner logic of the initial Jewish truth claims should carry the Jews over to the community in which these claims take their final form. And, of course, that new community itself could not be superseded by another as it superseded Judaism. In addition, there was a powerful political argument; namely, Jews had lost their own sovereignty and were living under the rule of either Christian or Muslim authorities. This was supposed to be proof that God had already favorably judged those who had superseded the Jews, and thus had already judged the Jewish persistence in remaining an intact community unfavorably.

What Jews had to do, if for no other reason than to still be convinced why they had to remain Jews, was to counter these new truth claims with a renewed version of their own. Just as in the Hellenistic age Jews like Philo had to devise cogent arguments as to why pagan philosophy could not supersede Judaism, so in the Middle Ages Jews like Judah Halevi had to devise cogent arguments as to why Christianity or Islam had not superseded Judaism. And the basic logical strategy had to be similar; namely, any so-called supersession of Judaism was in effect a falling beneath it, not a going beyond it. Thus whatever truth Christianity or Islam taught was really a diluted version of what Judaism had always taught with purer cogency. And whatever Christianity or Islam taught that is inconsistent with Judaism is false ipso facto. And whereas Hellenistic Judaism had to invent legends about great Greek thinkers supposedly having learned their deepest insights into the truth from Jewish prophets, the derivation of Christianity and Islam from Judaism is a historical point that no one could deny, not even Christians or Muslims.[111] Christians derive their claims from the Hebrew Bible as their "Old Testament." Muslims venerate the prophets of Israel as necessary predecessors of Mohammed.

If Jews were to counter these claims with anything more than ethnic obstinacy, they were going to have to argue that the optimal community for any human being created in the image of God is Israel. The truth of God and the world, which all humans by their nature seek to know, is to be found in Judaism more than anywhere else. If this is the case, then Jews have all the potential they need for actively proselytizing Gentiles for Judaism. It would seem that the only factor preventing Jews from actualizing this potential in the real world was political; namely, Christians and Muslims had such power over the Jews in this pre-messianic world and simply would not let the Jews proselytize—under threat of death or expulsion. And no Jewish authority taught that a Jew need die as a martyr or even suffer as a result of proselytizing (which would be the case if a Jew were offered the choice of conversion to any other religion—including, of course, Christianity or Islam).[112]

Actual proselytizing, therefore, would have to wait for an improved political climate for Jews. Nevertheless, the persuasive arguments for it were already in place, certainly after Judah Halevi, who lived in eleventh-century Spain, wrote his great theological dialogue *Kuzari*, which he subtitled "an argument for the despised religion," that is, the religion despised by both Christianity and Islam for both theological and political reasons.

Halevi's dialogue, like those of Plato, begins in a historical context, which is the conversion to Judaism of the king of the Khazars and his people in Crimea earlier in history. Halevi imagined what led the king to convert to Judaism and to bring his whole people along with him. As the narrative begins, the king has had a disturbing dream in which an angel tells him that "your intention is acceptable to the Creator but not your action."[113] Since the king had been punctilious in his observance of the ancestral religion of his nation, it is first obvious to him that some change in his way of life is called for. But the fact that the message of the dream makes an immediate claim upon him indicates that the desire to live in accordance with God's will is universal, something that even pagans have. So, he begins a series of consultations with the representatives of various points of view on the God-human relationship.

The first person the king consults is a philosopher, who tells him that as long as he lives according to some moral code, even if he has to devise one for himself, that is sufficient because the true relationship with God is on the theoretical not the practical level.[114] This position is very much that of Aristotle, who saw the true philosophical life being devoted to theoretical matters, practical matters being something to be transcended as much as is humanly possible.[115] However, this is unsatisfactory even for a philosopher, which the king seems to be and which is indicated by a philosopher being the first person he consults in his quest for an answer to the claim of the dream.[116] So far, he seems to be closer to the position of Plato, for whom metaphysics and politics are to be fully integrated in a truly fulfilled rational life.[117]

Next, he turns to representatives of Christianity and Islam, initially not wanting even to bother with a representative of Judaism because of the lowly political status of the Jews in the world. The Christian representative presents his theology as beginning in Judaism, which has been superseded by Christianity with the coming of Jesus as the Messiah or Christ.[118] Next, the king consults a representative of Islam, who, like the Christian, ultimately bases his claims on the history of the Jews that preceded the coming of Mohammed as the final prophet.[119] Only then does the king feel that he has to turn to a representative of Judaism, since the claims of both the Christians and the Muslims go back to Judaism.

Finally, the king turns to a Jewish theologian, who bases all his claims on history. There is an unbroken tradition of what God did for Israel and what God taught them in the Torah.[120] It is that continuity, which goes back to creation itself, that enables the Jewish claims to have an original cogency that cannot pertain to the other two faiths. In the end, Christianity and Islam are not only derivative of Judaism but are deviants from it. Religions of revelation are superior to philosophy because they provide a coherent system of practice in their respective laws. Ultimately, practice must be based on what we know God has done in the world, that is, in history where all worldly action takes place. Therefore, Christianity and Islam are not improvements on Judaism but regressions from it, and it stands to reason that the king must turn to Judaism as the best way to fulfill the claims of his dream. Of course, the Judaism to which he turns is already a Judaism that is able to pass philosophical muster; that is, it goes beyond what is known by human reason and not beneath it.[121]

By the end of the first of the five books of the *Kuzari*, the king and the general of his army, whom he has convinced to join him in his quest, leave their country and are clandestinely converted to Judaism according to the standards of Jewish law for proper conversion. They then return to their land, at first keeping their conversion secret. Once they proselytize the other members of their nation, they import Jewish scholars and Jewish books to continue the process of education in Judaism that began with the conversion of the Khazar nation.[122]

Whether this actually happened as Halevi presumed is beside the point. The point is that he made a case for the universal superiority of religions of revelation over philosophy by using arguments that, if not totally persuasive to philosophers, could not, nonetheless, be refuted by them. And, on the heels of this argument, he made a case for the superiority of Judaism over the other two religions of revelation: Christianity and Islam. To be sure, there might be reasons why the Jews would choose not to proselytize Gentiles. In the Middle Ages, these reasons seem to be largely based on political prudence. In the modern period, there might be other reasons for such reluctance, as we shall see later. Nevertheless, the potential for proselytizing was now established, and it could easily be actualized by anyone who saw a good reason for doing so in his or her own time. The presence of this potential, even if not actualized, is an important indication of the fact that Jews can, and perhaps should, see the truth claims of Judaism as being in principle universal, which under the right circumstances can, and perhaps should, be universally proclaimed.

PROSELYTIZING IN MAIMONIDES' JURISPRUDENCE

The philosophical theology of Maimonides, who lived in the twelfth century in Egypt, is in many significant ways quite different from that of Halevi. In fact, at this level of discourse they are often contrasted one with the other. However, in his legal writings Maimonides comes very close to the endorsement of proselytizing we have just seen in Halevi. In fact, he is even more explicit about it and, in addition, shows how it can be put into practice within the context of Jewish law. We can best begin to see Maimonides' position on this whole question by looking at how he treats the legal question of teaching the Torah to the Gentiles, which is the main component of any proselytizing program.

In his complete code of Jewish law, which he wrote in the middle of his career, Maimonides stated that a Gentile should only be instructed in the seven Noahide laws.[123] These laws, which for him especially are all based on the prohibition of idolatry, were considered by the Rabbis in the Talmud to be universally binding.[124] This is in contrast with the six hundred thirteen commandments of the written Torah (the Pentateuch—and the tradition that explicates it and supplements it), which are binding only on the Jewish people. However, in his enumeration of the six hundred thirteen commandments, which formed the introduction to his code of Jewish law, Maimonides goes much farther, stating: "He has commanded us to sanctify the name of God . . . to proclaim (le-farsem) this true faith to the world."[125] Clearly, the proclamation of the "true faith to the world" involves more than just teaching the very general, and incomplete, Noahide laws. Furthermore, in a *responsum* he wrote later in his career, Maimonides states:

It is permitted (*muttar*) to teach the commandments to Christians and draw them to our law. But it is not permitted to teach anything from it to Muslims because it is known to you about their belief that this Torah [of ours] is not from God . . . and if one can convince the Christians of the correct interpretation [of Scripture], it is possible that they might return to what is good.[126]

Here Maimonides seems to be advocating a kind of Jewish proselytizing of Gentiles, especially those Gentiles who already have something significant in common with Judaism. (And, of course, that is exactly the reason Christians have regarded proselytizing Jews to be so special; namely, Jews are seen to have more potential than any other people for becoming Christians because their scriptures are seen to be the indispensable preparation for Christ.) In talmudic teaching, on the other hand, Gentiles are only to be taught the Torah after they have explicitly and voluntarily presented themselves as candidates for conversion.[127] In his emphasis of the obligation (*mitsvah*) to proclaim Judaism as the true faith to and for the world, Maimonides advocates teaching the Torah even before any Gentile who hears it decides to become a candidate for conversion. And in his *responsum*, Maimonides permits teaching the Torah to Christians based only on the possibility that they *might* subsequently decide to become candidates for conversion. In both cases, then, we have a considerable innovation on Maimonides' part.

The key to more fully understanding what Maimonides is up to on this whole question lies in discerning just what he means by Gentiles, especially Christians, "*returning* to what is good." How can they "return" to where they have never been? But Maimonides talks about such a return elsewhere, too. In writing about the Messianic Age, which all Jews are to affirm and hope for, Maimonides states:

> It should not enter one's mind that in the days of the Messiah any aspect of the normal world order will be abrogated or that there will be any innovation in the created order, for the world will run as usual . . . [but] all of them [Jews and Gentiles] will return to the true law (*la-dat ha'emet*). . . . The sages and prophets did not desire the days of the Messiah in order to rule over the whole world nor to exercise authority over the Gentiles nor that the nations might lift them up over them.[128]

But what is this "*return* to the true law"? Is it to take place in preparation for the coming of the Messiah, or is it a necessary result of the Messiah's realm when it is already in place? In the former case, the connection of non-Jews to Judaism is something that can be persuasively effected by Jews in the present. In the latter case, it is something that must wait for a seismic change in the political order of the world, even though nature will remain the same.

The answer to this question comes from another statement of Maimonides' messianic theology. After dismissing the messianic claims of Jesus of Nazareth, Maimonides nevertheless writes:

> However, the thoughts of the Creator of the world are beyond the ability of humans to apprehend . . . and all the deeds of Jesus of Nazareth and this Arab [Mohammed] who arose after him, they are only to prepare the way for the Messiah-King and to order (*le-taqqen*) the whole world to serve the Lord together, as it is said in Scripture, "For then I will turn

to the united peoples with clear speech to call all of them in the name of the Lord and to serve him with one accord" (Zephaniah 3:9).[129]

From this text (one that was removed from the printed additions of Maimonides' code by Christian censors) we see that the role of Christianity and Islam is to prepare the world for the reign of the Messiah-King. His reign promises to be the best form of polity possible in this world, combining the highest theoretical ability with the most extensive practical ability.[130] That is, he will teach the truth about God and the relation of the world to him, and he will teach the good that God wants his human creatures to practice in the world. Since the Torah already contains the content of these two excellences superlatively, the chief distinction of this polity is that the complete law of the Torah will be fully authoritative and wholly effective politically. In other words, the Messiah-King will actualize the full potential of the Torah of Moses, not introduce changes into it that have come from Christian and Muslim misunderstandings. "Returning to what is good" in the *responsum* suggests that Christians especially should return to the Jewish roots of their faith, roots from which Christian doctrine has partially, but not wholly, deviated.[131] If conversion from Christianity to Judaism is a return, not to the historical roots of the individual convert's own life, but to the true roots of Christianity itself, then the conversion is in essence the actualization of an authentic religious potential, which Christianity began but could not finish. For Christians, conversion would mean a return to the true meaning of biblical faith and practice. For Muslims, as Maimonides points out in another *responsum*, conversion would be a return to the primeval monotheism of Abraham, whom Muslims and Jews alike venerate as their monotheistic founder.[132]

Maimonides emphasizes in the *responsum* about teaching the Torah to Gentiles that the main advantage Christians have over Muslims, and what should make them the prime objects of Jewish proselytizing, is that, unlike the Muslims, "the uncircumcised ones [Christians] believe that the text of the Torah has not changed."[133] Having a common revealed text is more important than certain abstract theological commonalities: for instance, at the level of philosophical theology, Islamic monotheism seems to be much less problematic for Jews than Christian trinitarianism.[134] Not only is Scripture the source of the most complete knowledge of God possible in this world, but it is also the most perfect law possible for the governance of the body politic. At the level of practice, Christianity's merit is its full acceptance of Mosaic revelation as it pertains to inter-human relations and God's universal relationship with the world. Indeed, Christianity only regarded as historically limited those practices of the Torah linked to the particular historical experience of the Jewish people and designed to preserve their particular identity until the coming of Christ.[135] The Christian acceptance of Jewish morality, then, became what some medieval Christian theologians would eventually designate as "natural law."[136]

Although earlier in his career Maimonides designated Christianity as idolatry pure and simple, in his later works he clearly changed his mind.[137] Whether this change of mind was due to further study of the literature of the Christians, or due to deeper reflection on the Christian theology he already knew, or due to new contacts with Christians themselves, it is hard to say. But what is so amazing about Maimonides' more mature view of Christianity is that it developed as part of an overall project that at last wished to restore the Jewish proselytization of Gentiles. Of course, Maimonides was aware of how hypothetical his views were in the political climate of his day. Thus he concludes the *responsum* we have been examining with the thought that even if Jewish efforts to convince Christian biblicists of the superiority of Judaism are unsuccessful and "they do not return as they [their Jewish teachers] would like them to return, there is no harm that will come to us from this."[138] It would seem that by "no harm," he means no harm to either the theory or practice of any Jew who engaged in this proselytizing activity. But, of course, in many of his contemporary societies, it very well could have led to grave political dangers.

PROSELYTIZING IN MODERN JUDAISM

Modern Judaism began with the emancipation of European Jewries in the eighteenth and nineteenth centuries, as a consequence of the rise of the modern, secular nation-states. The main feature of these new states, which profoundly changed the political situation of the Jews, was the elimination of membership in a particular religious community as a prerequisite for citizenship. Jews as individuals could now acquire political equality with non-Jews. This meant that Christianity could no longer claim that its political hegemony was proof that it had superseded the Jewish people in the divine governance of the universe. After the emancipation, Christian supersessionist arguments against Judaism would have to remain on the purely theological level. Indeed, although the majority of the citizens of the new nation-states remained affiliated with Christianity, Christians were now faced with a task somewhat similar to that which had always faced the Jews: having to justify one's own place in a society and culture grounded in a different source of authority than one's own religion. In many cases, Christian survival depended upon proving that it was an integral part of the culture within which it now had to live.[139] In other words, whereas in the Middle Ages Christianity was taken to be the foundation of society and culture, it now had to appeal to other political and cultural realities for its own social validation. This had a profound effect on Christian attempts to proselytize Jews and Jewish attempts actively to resist it.

In the medieval past, active Jewish resistance to Christian proselytizing attempts had taken the form of showing the superiority of Judaism over Christianity. This was done, as we have seen, on the level of philosophically influenced theology for the most part. But in the modern world, this formerly face-to-face theological confrontation (whether personally, as in the famous medieval disputations between Christian and Jewish theologians, or intellectually, through books) now had to go through a formidable *tertium quid*:

fundamentally secular culture. Both Christian and Jewish thinkers had to justify their respective beliefs and practices, to their own communities and to
others, in terms of their cultural relevance. As such, more often than not Christian efforts to proselytize Jews began to be made on nationalistic lines. Thus to
be a good German or Englishman, for example, meant including Christianity
of one type or another.

Because of this, Jewish resistance to Christian proselytizing depended less
on countering real theological claims than had been the case in earlier centuries. Instead, what Jews had to argue was that being a Jew is just as conducive
to good citizenship in a secular polity as is being a Christian.[140] A few more
daring European Jewish thinkers actually argued that Judaism was more suited
to the new secular political and cultural reality, precisely because its theology
is more rational and more respectful of religious differences within one polity
than is Christian theology.[141] In a political and cultural climate where tolerance was one of the highest values, Jews seemed to have more resources for it
than did Christianity. Here, at least at the intellectual level, the long experience of being a vulnerable minority, who sought simply to be left alone, seemed
to give Judaism a polemical edge. Thus Jews no longer had to demonstrate the
theological superiority of Judaism in order to make a place for themselves,
even religiously. What they had to do was show that in the new secular environment each religious tradition had to redefine itself in order to be relevant.
Proselytizing efforts seemed to violate the new atmosphere where religion in
general could no longer claim to be the foundation of anything of public significance. That is why, to this very day, Jewish resistance to Christian proselytizing efforts usually takes the form of protesting that such efforts violate the
spirit of democratic cultural diversity. It is thus exceptionally rare that Jewish
efforts take on the theological urgency they once had.

Nevertheless, this avoidance of the theological directness of medieval Jewish responses to Christian (and Muslim) attempts to proselytize Jews has served
to obfuscate the question that Jews have always had to answer for themselves:
why should we remain Jews? The medieval answer was that Jews are to remain Jews *because* God has elected them for a special, covenantal relationship
with himself, and has given them a law (*torah*) by which to live this relationship in the world. And that law was considered to be theoretically and practically superior to any other law available to human beings. Aside from the
kabbalists, who saw the Jews as a separate species from the rest of humankind, virtually all of the other medieval Jewish thinkers argued for the universal superiority of Judaism for any human being.[142] In essence, that meant that
Judaism was the best way for any human being here and now. That is, Judaism
is the highest truth available to human beings in this world, and *to either
remain or become a Jew* is the highest good for all humans. As we have seen,
this belief is the necessary condition for any proselytizing effort, even if circumstances, political or otherwise, make actual proselytizing impractical in
one way or another. Derived from creation theory, that all humans share one
universal nature, designated in Scripture as the "image of God" (*tselem elohim*),

this belief assumes that the messianic culmination of history will obtain universally among all humankind.

Most modern Jews have been too busy justifying their presence in a secular world to be much concerned with these truth claims. But without them, the question "why should we remain Jews?" goes unanswered. In fact, it usually goes unasked. Jewish survival is talked about as if it were self-evident. Yet the undeniable fact of the voluntary defection from Judaism by many Jews in modern times clearly belies any such "natural" explanation of Jewish survival. And those Jews, liberal and even traditional, who in the nineteenth and early twentieth centuries did talk about "the mission of Israel," usually did so by showing Judaism to be in the vanguard of liberal or even socialist notions of human moral progress.[143] Surely, the Holocaust, of which the Jews were the chief victims, not only shows unmistakably how little influence Judaism has had on human morality, but how utterly dispensable the Jews themselves really are. With very few exceptions, one hardly hears anymore about the mission of Israel after 1945.[144]

Just as in the Middle Ages, when there were very good political reasons for the Jews not to engage in proselytizing Gentiles, so in the modern world there are some very good moral reasons for a reluctance to proselytize Gentiles. Indeed, one can be derived from the aversion most Jews have to Christian efforts to proselytize them. Those of us who have been exposed to these efforts, and that includes most Jews who interact with non-Jews at all, have been deeply resentful of the arrogance of those who proselytize. They inevitably come across as men and women who are so self-righteous that they feel no moral compunction in denigrating other faiths and their cultures for the sake of cajoling their adherents to cease being what they have been and change their identity by becoming what the missionaries are. It is little wonder, then, that missionary efforts have often proved quite useful for various forms of political imperialism. Thus proselytizing can well be seen as a pride that is opaque to the transcendence of God rather than a humility that is transparent to it.

One could make a good argument, on moral grounds and on theological grounds, that it is for God, not for humans, to bring the rest of the world into the covenant with Israel. In other words, proselytization will be the result of the messianic event, not a forerunner of it. Israel's task in the present world is intensely to live the life of the covenant prescribed in the Torah. Those individual Gentiles who somehow or other believe themselves to be part of that covenant are certainly to be welcomed into the covenantal community, once they have demonstrated their sincerity to that community—as best the human eyes of the authorities of the community can discern it. The conversion of the Gentile masses, however, will have to wait for the time when "the nations will go towards your light" (Isaiah 60:3).[145] At present, Jews can argue with moral and theological cogency: "Let every nation, each one, go in the name of its god, but we will go in the name of the Lord our God forever and ever" (Micah 4:5). They can cogently argue that short of the kingdom of God on earth, which is to be an apocalyptic event brought about by God, not humans, political, religious, and cultural diversity is more open to the true authority of God than any pseudo-messianic urgency that insists that the world must join my community or be made subordinate to it here and now. But to affirm that, without the inner conviction that Judaism is the highest truth and the greatest good, is to argue for a tribalism that cannot answer the question posed to its separateness: Why? Accordingly, Jews are to remain more separate from the world than being in common with it, until the time God ends the separateness of the Gentiles from his chosen people and brings a final commonality truly worthy of human nature as the image of God.

2.

Proselytism and Jewish Law

Inreach, Outreach, and the Jewish Tradition

———————◆———————

Michael J. Broyde

> Who is happy? One who is content with his place in the
> world. *Ethics of the Sages 4:1.*

The Jewish legal[1] tradition desires not to participate in proselytizing and conversion, either as proselytizer or proselytizee.[2] It desires to be left alone, and to focus on inreach, the process by which Jews make Jews into better Jews. It recognizes some limited ability to accept proselytes and, thus, does have a mechanism, albeit complex and limiting, for joining the Jewish faith. There is no right of exit in the Jewish tradition.

It is important to understand how different the issues of inreach and outreach are to normative Jewish law, and how deep the contrast is with other faiths. On the one hand, the Jewish tradition directs a categorical imperative that Jews must observe Jewish law and that Jews who observe Jewish law are obligated to persuade or compel those Jews who do not observe Jewish law to start doing so. Absent observance of Jewish law, Jews are viewed as sinners by the tradition. On the other hand, however, Jewish law obligates its adherents not to solicit converts and indeed affirmatively to reject converts as an initial matter, and denies any duty to observe Jewish law by Gentiles. In many circumstances, Jewish law forbids the observance of Jewish law by Gentiles.[3]

In light of this theological and legal construct, this chapter will proceed along three different, but interrelated, tracks. The first section will review the theological background for how Judaism and Jewish law view Jews and Gentiles in relationship to proselytizing. The second section will address the basis for the Jewish legal and theological view that directs inreach. The third section will address the conversion conundrums—the outreach problems.

"WE ALL HAVE BUT ONE CREATOR"[4]: THE STATUS OF JEWS AND GENTILES REGARDING CONVERSION

The Limits of Jewish Law

The Jewish tradition is neither universalistic nor particularistic. It does not maintain that only Jews can enter heaven; both Jews and Gentiles can. It does not maintain that Jewish law is binding on all; Jewish law binds Jews, Noahide law binds Gentiles. It does not maintain that all must acknowledge the "Jewish" God; it recognizes that monotheism need not be accompanied by recognition of the special role of the Jewish people.[5] Maimonides' opening formulation of the Jewish view of messianic times is revealing:

> One should not think that in messianic times that the normal practices of the world will change or that the laws of nature will change. Rather the world will be as it always is. The words of the prophet Isaiah "and the wolf will dwell with the lamb, and the leopard shall lie down with the goat" are metaphors meaning that the Jews will live peacefully among the heathen nations of the world.[6]

Even in messianic times, the Jewish tradition avers that there will *and should be* Gentiles—people who are not members of the Jewish faith. The existence of those who are not Jewish is part of the Jewish ideal, which requires that all worship the single God, although not exclusively through the Jewish prism of worship. Indeed, the Talmud insists that in messianic times conversion into Judaism will not be allowed; Jews and Gentiles will peacefully coexist.[7]

The universalistic law code governing those who are not Jewish (called the Noahide code) requires the observance of many commandments that are basic to the moral existence of people. The Talmud[8] recounts seven categories of prohibition: idol worship, taking God's name in vain, murder, prohibited sexual activity, theft, eating flesh from a living animal, and the obligation to have a justice system or enforce laws. As is obvious from this list, these seven commandments are generalities with many particular specifications. Thus, for example, the single categorical prohibition of sexual impropriety includes both adultery and the various forms of incest.[9] These Noahide laws appear to encompass nearly sixty of the six hundred and thirteen biblical commandments traditionally enumerated as incumbent on Jews from the Bible itself, which is nearly one-fourth of those biblical commandments generally applicable in post-Temple times.[10] The majority of the commandments found in Jewish law that are unrelated to ritual activity are also found in the Noahide code.[11] The Noahide code was intended to be a practical legal code and to form a system that satisfied the social, legal, and religious needs of peoples outside the framework of Judaism.[12] Jewish law is not the ideal legal code for all—only for

Jews. For example, consider the remarks of Rabbi Juda Loewe of Prague concerning the Jewish law prohibition of cross-breeding in animals:

> The creativity of people is greater than nature. When God created in the six days of creation the laws of nature, the simple and complex, and finished creating the world, there remained additional power to create anew, just like people can create new animal species through inter-species breeding. . . . People bring to fruition things that are not found in nature; nonetheless, since these are activities that occur through nature, it is as if it entered the world to be created. . . . *There are those who are aghast of the interbreeding of two species. Certainly, this is contrary to Jewish law which God gave the Jews, which prohibits inter-species mixing. Nonetheless, Adam (the First Person) did this.* Indeed, the world was created with many species that are prohibited to be eaten. Inter-species breeding was not prohibited because of prohibited sexuality or immorality. . . . Rather it is because Jews should not combine the various species together, as this is the way of Jewish law. As we already noted, the ways of the Jewish law, and the [permissible] ways of the world are distinct. . . . Just like the donkey has within it to be created [but was not created by God]. . . but was left to people to create it. *Even those forms of creativity which Jewish law prohibits for Jews are not definitionally bad.* Some are simply prohibited to Jews.[13]

What flows most clearly from this is that there is nothing intrinsically wrong with cross-breeding, even if it violates Jewish law; indeed, Rabbi Loewe nearly states that such conduct by Gentiles is good. It was prohibited by Jewish law because it was not part of the divine mission for the Jewish people. What flows from this type of argument is that Jewish law is not a general ethical category governing the conduct of all. Its scope and application are limited to Jews, not merely jurisdictionally, but even theologically.

THE PARTICULARISM OF JEWISH LAW

This recognition of diversity within God's kingdom is just one side of the Jewish-Gentile relations coin, however. The Jewish tradition also does have a clear concept of the Jews being the chosen people, to whom God revealed the Jewish tradition on Mount Sinai. This revelation imposed on the Jewish tradition special obligations and rights that create special legal duties that bind Jews. Jews have duties one to another,[14] to God, and to society, which Gentiles bear no duty to keep.[15] The Jewish tradition makes it clear that a Gentile observant of Noahide law is a more righteous person than a Jew whose observance of Jewish law is incomplete, even if that Jew observes all of Noahide law.[16] But the Jewish tradition is equally clear in its insistence that proper observance of the Jewish tradition by Jews brings Jews closer to God. Jewish theology sees the Jews as designated for holiness, a nation of priests[17] on a mission of holiness. There is little doubt that the Jewish tradition views the Jewish ideal as "closer to God" than the monotheistic Noahide ideal. Indeed, the same Jewish sources that recognize the right (and perhaps even the duty) of people who are not Jewish to remain such, recognize that the complete Jewish ideal is closer to the Divine.[18]

SUMMARY

What flows from these two sides of the same coin is that the Jewish tradition does not seek to convert individuals to the Jewish faith; Jewish law imposes at least a minimal affirmative duty to push potential converts away a number of times.[19]

One of the classical colloquia Jewish law requires that one have with converts before they undergo the final, irrevocable, part of the conversion ritual is designed to deter the conversions. It requires the court performing the conversion to state to the convert: "Before you convert to Judaism, if you eat this unkosher foodstuff, there is no violation; if you violate the Sabbath, there is no death penalty violation. . . ." So, too, Jewish law requires that one ask the potential convert: "Why did you decide to convert? Do you not know that the Jewish people nowadays are marginalized, oppressed and troubles come to them?"[20] Soliciting converts is not a *mitzvah* (a good deed or a positive act), and accepting converts is not a required or encouraged act.[21]

In sum, the Jewish tradition is relatively balanced on the question of proselytism and conversion, and has so been since recorded history. The Jewish tradition does not seek to proselytize and has created significant internal barriers to it. Hand in hand with that approach, it desires not to be the object of another tradition's proselytism. It does not recognize the right of a Jew to change his or her faith, whether such conversion to another faith is motivated by love, threat, financial need, or deeply-held religious motivations. It is extremely difficult to convert into Judaism, and according to the overwhelming majority of decisors, absolutely impossible to convert out of Judaism.[22]

THE THEORY OF INREACH

The Jewish tradition focuses not on *outreach* (bringing converts into the Jewish tradition) but on *inreach* (strengthening the Jewish tradition in those who are Jewish). Indeed, even activities that seem apparently motivated solely by the desire to reach a Gentile audience sometimes have inreach motives and desires. Consider the famous story, often recounted, that Rabbi Israel Salanter, a Jewish scholar of the nineteenth century, favored the translation of the Talmud into German and its introduction into the curriculum of German universities. People were surprised that he would advocate such a project, given the apparent proscriptions in Jewish law against such outreach efforts directed toward Gentiles. In response to such questions, he replied that if the Gentiles think Talmud study is important, maybe the Jews will study it also![23] Outreach can be a form of inreach.

Inreach—proselytizing Jews to increase their Jewishness—creates a host of dilemmas within the Jewish tradition. These issues inevitably focus on the religious and ethical problems caused by seeking to persuade (or in rare circumstances, compel) the observance of Jewish law. In the theoretical realm, they focus on three different concepts: (1) When is one obligated to coerce compliance with the dictates of Jewish law? (2) When is a Jew obligated to inform another Jew that his or her conduct violates Jewish law and ethics? (3) May one ever encourage a violation of Jewish law?

Jewish law, in essence, bases its duty to engage in inreach on the answers provided to these questions. When dealing with Jews—who are bound to observe Jewish law—one is obligated to compel observance of much of Jewish law, seek to persuade full observance of Jewish law, and never to facilitate a violation of Jewish law (unless it leads to increased observance of Jewish law later[24]). Bundled together, these three duties compel inreach, when it will be effective.

COMPELLING OBSERVANCE OF JEWISH LAW

Within the Jewish legal tradition, there has always been a clear recognition of the multifaceted nature of the duty to compel observance, and the problems—both theological and practical—that result from such compulsion. There are a variety of distinctly different categories of obligations found in Jewish law, each with its own status in terms of compelling observance.

The first category is those commandments that affect and effect significant social norms. Thus, the Jewish legal tradition recognizes that society can prevent murder, theft, and other social crimes as they are disruptive of the social order of life. Sometimes these laws are enforced through the pursuer (*rodef*) principle, sometimes through the seven-elders-of-the-city rule, sometimes through the social compact precept, and sometimes through exigent jurisdiction of the Jewish law courts.[25] Whatever the precise rationale, it is clear that Jewish law permits—indeed mandates—enforcement of these norms, either through the Jewish law courts, communal regulation, or even through the secular legal system.[26]

The second category is enforcement of the communitarian aspects of religious law. Consider, for example, the building of a ritual bath used for conversions and ritual purity by community members. Jewish law allows the whole community to be taxed, or compelled to do physical labor on the bath, based on the principle that religious benefits for all are to be paid for by all.[27] Indeed, even those who are under no religious duty to use a ritual bath, and never will, are compelled to participate in its building. The ability to compel participation in the community through the building of communal institutions—through both the power to tax and the power to compel actual participation—is present in the Jewish tradition. Shunning and excommunication are among the modern tools used to enforce these communal religious norms.[28]

Yet other aspects of Jewish law are recognized as un-compellable. Consider problems that would ensue if society sought to enforce the duty to love God, the first precept found in Maimonides' *Book of Commandments*.[29] Two different views are adduced within Jewish law as to what exactly are the parameters of this exemption. Some limit the exemption from compulsion strictly to "duties of the heart" but argue that positive ritual law commandments, such as daily prayer, worship in booths during the feast of Tabernacles, grace before and after meals, as well as other examples, actually can be compelled.[30] Yet other authorities seem to limit the duty to compel to cases where there is something more at stake than one's relationship with the Creator; they argue that compulsion is limited to such *mitzvot* as the duty to repay one's creditors. However, ritual matters alone, this view insists, are beyond the reach of the law to compel.[31]

Finally, a variety of negative prohibitions are enforced, whether "religious" or "secular" in nature. For example, Jewish law directs that one refrain from eating foods prohibited by the dietary (kosher) laws, avoid desecration of the Sabbath, prohibit even consensual adultery, as well as a host of ritual, financial, and other laws. The Jew so compelled to avoid actively violating the law is better off, in that the Jew is not, in fact, violating Jewish law, and will not be punished, whether by God or man.[32] The argument is that Jewish law requires that one—as an act of love to a fellow Jew—force a Jew to avoid sinning.

All this is true in theory. In practice, however, Jewish law for more than two centuries has not had the ability to compel observance of these rules. Yet the values contained in these views are of considerable theological importance. The Jewish tradition views the obligation to obey Jewish law as real—no different, in many ways, from the way that others view secular law and the duty to obey it. This very much affects how one views those who do not observe Jewish law.

REBUKING VIOLATORS OF JEWISH LAW

Jewish law obligates its adherents to admonish another Jew[33] seen violating Jewish law, but one cannot (or should not) compel this person to cease the violation. So, too, when one sees a person unintentionally violating Jewish law, one must tell the person what Jewish law requires so that the person can correct his or her ways. This obligation is known as collective responsibility. These two obligations compel, at least in theory, each Jew to engage in inreach with the goal of encouraging the observance of Jewish law.

While it is true that, as a matter of theory, one is not obligated to admonish a person who has completely left the path of observance and has no ideological fidelity to Jewish law at all,[34] such a status is rarely thought applicable to a person whom one can contemplate returning to the community of observance through theological discussion or religious motivation. Indeed, even in circumstances where the technical obligation to assist another might be inapplicable, in situations where one can assist a person in his or her religious return, one must do so.[35] However, admonition is to be performed with care lest it not accomplish its goal,[36] or even worse, distance people from Judaism.[37]

ASSISTING IN A VIOLATION OF JEWISH LAW

Hand in hand with the Jewish law obligation to return people to the fold, Jewish law prohibits one from facilitating, or sometimes merely assisting, one in a violation of Jewish law. This prohibition is derived from Leviticus 19:14, which reads, "You shall not curse a deaf person and before a blind person you shall not put a stumbling block; you shall fear your God, I am the Lord."

The Talmud advances an expansive definition of the prohibition of placing a stumbling block in front of a blind person by defining "blindness" broadly. The Talmud quotes the following statement:

> Rabbi Nathan said: "From where do we know that one may not extend a cup of wine to one who swore not to drink wine [a *nazir*] nor a limb of a live animal to a Noahide [who, like all others, may not eat such flesh]?" The source is from the verse "before a blind person thou shall not put a stumbling block."[38]

Since the Talmud does not distinguish between an intentional and an unintentional violation in this regard, it may be inferred that this conduct is prohibited even when the one who may not drink wine or eat flesh from a living animal is aware that these actions are prohibited. Support for this inference can also be found in the Talmud's assertion[39] that a father may not strike his grown child, because the child may retaliate physically—an act which is a capital offense.[40] The Talmud bases its opinion on the verse in Leviticus 19:14 concerning tripping a blind person (*lifnei ivver*), even though the child is fully aware of the consequences of the action.

Another talmudic discussion in *Bava Metzia* provides a further application of this prohibition. Biblical law proscribes both charging and paying interest. In addition to the standard prohibitions,[41] the Talmud states that all people who participate in or facilitate a transaction involving interest—including the guarantor, witnesses, and even the scribe of the document—violate the prohibition of assisting in a violation (*lifnei ivver*).[42] The notion that even the ancillary and supportive participants in the transaction are in violation of this prohibition broadens our understanding of the scope of the prohibition even further. The participation, as a scribe or witness, in such a transaction violates the prohibition only because, by enabling the transaction to occur, one is deliberately helping *blind* people to sin. A *blind* person thus includes one who voluntarily sins as a result of an intentional *stumbling block*.

Blindness is thus not limited to the case where the sinner is blinded by ignorance or naivete, but also encompasses the case where the person is blinded by a desire. Thus the biblical verses concerning tripping a blind person (*lifnei ivver*) prohibit aiding in any violation of the law. They not only prohibit one from maliciously misguiding another but also prohibit cooperating with one who is misguided by his or her own material needs or improper understanding of law.

SUMMARY

The Jewish tradition views Jewish law as a binding legal system whose yoke of observance compels—at least as a matter of theory—observance of Jewish law. The Jewish tradition recognizes little theoretical right for a Jew to decline to observe, although it has grown very untroubled, on a practical level, living in a society where Jewish law cannot be enforced except in limited communitarian areas. However, even within that normative society, the Jewish tradition sees a clear religious and legal compulsion to try to convince those people bound by the yoke of Jewish law to obey it.

THE THEORY OF OUTREACH:
THE CONVERSION PROCEDURE

As noted, the Jewish tradition does not seek out individuals for conversion. Instead, it imposes an affirmative duty to rebuff initially potential converts and denies that conversion to Judaism is a good deed. To be sure, the rabbinic literature contains aphorisms indicating that conversion to Judaism is meritorious—"whoever brings a heathen near to God and converts him, is as if he had created him"[43] or "beloved are the converts to Judaism."[44] But for each commendatory aphorism, there is a less flattering one—"trouble after trouble comes to one who receives converts"[45]; "Converts . . . delay the arrival of the messiah."[46] Jewish law and the resulting legal tradition certainly accept that conversion is never mandatory—and is to be discouraged, whether any given conversion is bad.

The process of conversion to Judaism, in its technical procedure, is relatively simple; in times of old it involved six different steps for men and five for women; currently, only five steps for men, and four for women, are possible. A short elaboration on five of these will help explain the details of the conversion process. The sixth—acceptance of the commandments—will be the subject of a lengthy analysis in the next section.

THE CONVERSION PROCEDURE

The minimal requirements for conversion are:

1. *A commitment to join the Jewish people by the potential convert.* The desire to join the Jewish people is a political and social commitment. Jews form not only a faith community of common beliefs, laws, and ideals, but a common social and political community. One must desire to join that community to be considered a Jew. As has been noted by others,[47] this commitment is not related to the acceptance of the commandments or immersion in a *mikva*. Rather, it is the recognition that one is linking one's fate with the Jewish people, such that one is united with them.[48] One who refuses to identify as a Jew has not converted to Judaism, as that person has refused to join the Jewish people.

2. *The acceptance of this person as a member of the Jewish faith by a Jewish court.* The reasons for such a formal process of acceptance are obvious. Only a properly constructed Jewish court may formally accept the convert into the community, for it represents the interest of the community in the conversion.[49] This Jewish court determines whether the person is fit to join, has no ulterior motives, and otherwise is eligible to join the community and to marry within it. Just as one cannot become an American citizen without a formal swearing-in ceremony, one cannot become Jewish without appearance in front of a Jewish court. A Jewish court need not accept every convert and has discretionary authority to reject otherwise qualified converts.[50]

3. *Circumcision of a male convert.* Circumcision for men is part of the biblical conversion of Abraham, a unique indication of a man's Jewishness, and the classical first step in conversion. Jewish legal theory is unclear why circumcision is a prerequisite for a man joining the Jewish people. Indeed, contrary to popular Jewish folk belief, a Jew who declines to be circumcised remains Jewish, and while such conduct is a sin, it is no greater a sin than declining to bring the mandatory Passover sacrifice in the times of the Temple, or a variety of other serious transgressions of Jewish law. Such a sinner remains Jewish. This is not the case for a male Gentile who wishes to convert to Judaism. In order for a male Gentile to join the Jewish people, the man must be circumcised.[51]

4. *Immersion in a mikva or ma'ayan.* Immersion is the process used throughout Jewish law and tradition to denote changes in spiritual status, both for people and inanimate objects.[52] Indeed, medieval codifiers of Jewish law note that apostates who desire to return to Judaism should be immersed in a mikva[53] or ma'ayan[54] as part of their "return to tradition," even though their status as Jews was never genuinely in question.[55] A convert undergoes such a change, and thus must immerse.

5. *Sacrifice of an animal in the Temple.* Sacrifice of an animal in the Temple in Jerusalem was one of the ways that converts signified their membership in the Jewish people. Since the destruction of the Temple in the first century C.E., conversions have continued without the sacrifice being offered. The exact theoretical reason why sacrifice is not needed in post-Temple times remains in dispute,[56] but a wide consensus has developed in Jewish law that sacrifice is not a requirement for conversion in cases where a sacrifice cannot be brought

for reasons independent of this particular conversion; in this case, because the Temple has been destroyed.[57]

6. *Acceptance of the commandments by the convert in front of a Jewish court.* This final, and perhaps most significant requirement is, in fact, the most difficult. Unlike each of the other five steps in the conversion process, this one is substantive and involves a change in one's daily life and existence, in that one submits to the daily obligations of Jewish law. Indeed, as this next section of the chapter will explore, the validity of the whole conversion process can be questioned when that change does not occur.

ACCEPTANCE OF THE COMMANDMENTS

Four of the above five requirements of conversion are primarily procedural, not substantive. While some might be painful (such as circumcision)[58] or technically difficult (such as full immersion in a prescribed body of water), none of them involves a fundamental reorientation of one's permanent existence. The desire to join the Jewish people, while a significant and substantive requirement for conversion, is a political belief and an orientation. It does not require a fundamental change in how one conducts one's daily life, particularly when one lives in an open society with only hints of antisemitism, or in Israel, where Judaism is the cultural norm for most of the population.

The essence of classical Judaism is life through Jewish law, a legal system that undertakes to regulate every aspect of one's conduct in this world. Judaism is, more than most faiths, a system of deed and not creed. Thus, the most significant issue present in the modern discussion of conversion addresses what level of commitment to Jewish law as the touchstone of one's personal ethics and morality must be required of converts in order for conversion to be proper.

UNDERSTANDING THE COMMANDMENTS

The question of commitment by a potential convert to Jewish law as a standard of personal observance must first be understood in terms of the obligation upon the Jewish court dealing with the potential convert. While one might expect the Jewish court to require that the convert be informed of the whole substance of Jewish law before he or she converts—for how can one commit to observe that which one does not understand?—in fact, the exact opposite is true. While Jewish law requires that the convert be informed of "some of the hard commandments, and some of the easy commandments,"[59] there is absolutely no obligation to inform the potential convert of all of the duties directed by Jewish law. The rationale for this is easy to understand and has its ready counterparts in the requirements for citizenship in most countries. Fidelity to Jewish law is a mindset, which requires converts to accept that Jewish law— whatever it might say—is binding on them.

The paradigm parallels the covenant between the Jewish people and God, as it is portrayed implicitly in the Bible and explicitly in the rabbinic homiletic discourses. The Jewish people accepted the oral and written Torah at Sinai, without a full or complete understanding of its detailed rules. Rather, they did so in the belief that whatever the Bible said, it was the word of the Lawgiver. This is the process the convert must go through as well. Obviously, one cannot accept Jewish law without a sampling of its requirements and without a rudimentary understanding of its rules. However, even basic, elementary duties could be left out of the explanation. Indeed, the Talmud explicitly states that a convert who fully accepts Jewish law without being informed that there is a concept called the Sabbath day of rest, and who thus does not observe the Sabbath in any way, has validly converted to Judaism if his mindset was that he desires to accept Jewish law, whatever it might be, and whatever it might direct—even if ignorance of fundamental precepts is present.[60] Ignorance of the commandments is not a failure in the duty to obey or the commitment to observe.

ACCEPTANCE OF COMMANDMENTS AS THE BASIC REQUIREMENT

The Talmud recounts the following rule:

> A Gentile who accepts all the laws of the Torah except for one, one should not accept him. Rabbi Yossie the son of Rabbi Judah states, "even if he rejects one detail of rabbinic law, one should not accept him."[61]

Theologically, this rule is simple enough. The Jewish tradition views Jewish law and theology as an integrated whole, grounded in the divine commandment to the Jewish people and the Jewish people's voluntary acceptance of the commandments. Absent a full acceptance of the "yoke of heaven," there is no acceptance. Indeed, this is true even when there is full observance, without any acceptance of obligation.[62]

The above talmudic statement would seem complete, but it is not. Elsewhere, the Talmud recounts:

> Our Rabbis recount: There was a case involving a Gentile who came to Shamai and stated to him, "How many Torahs do the Jews have?" Shamai responded: "Two. A written Torah and an oral Torah." The Gentile responded, "I believe in the written Torah, and not the oral Torah; convert me to Judaism so that I may learn the written Torah." Shamai shouted at him, and left in anger. The same Gentile came to Hillel, who converted him. The next day, Hillel taught him four concepts and the day after he taught him the same four concepts differently. The Gentile asked, "Yesterday you taught me differently." Hillel responded, "Do you not trust me? Do you not rely on my oral traditions as well?"[63]

The question is obvious. What right did Hillel have to convert this Gentile, who was obviously deficient in one area of his acceptance of Jewish law? Indeed, this incident provides the background to the general discussion of the flexibility of Jewish law to varied levels of observance by potential converts.

So, too, the acknowledgment of a duty to obey Jewish law is not the same as the commitment actually to obey it. One can categorize intentional violators of Jewish law into three broad categories.

1. There are those individuals who are genuinely committed to a full and complete observance of Jewish law, but who occasionally violate Jewish law due to temptation. Such individuals genuinely seek to observe Jewish law.

2. There are those individuals who recognize the binding nature of Jewish law and yet recognize that they cannot adhere to the requirements of Jewish law because of their own human frailties; they recognize that such conduct is a violation of Jewish law, and yet continue to violate—acknowledging their violation. The modern Jewish law *responsa* literature refers to these individuals as ones who have accepted the commandments but are not observing them.

3. There are those individuals who either do not think that Jewish law is binding or who do not think that all of Jewish law is binding, and thus violate Jewish law, aware of what it states, but yet uncaring and not desirous to repent, as they do not feel that any "sin" has occurred.[64]

The question addressed at great length by modern Jewish law decisors is, What is the status of the acceptance of commandments of individuals in any of these three categories? Since Jewish law mandates that acceptance of the commandments is a requirement for conversion, a determination that a person has not validly accepted the commandments is synonymous with a determination that a person is, in fact, not properly converted to Judaism and remains a Gentile according to Jewish law.[65] This is no small matter in Jewish law and remains the heart of a very significant controversy within Jewish law as well as the Jewish community both in Israel and in America.[66]

COMMITMENT TO OBSERVE AND ACTUAL OBSERVANCE

The status of those converts in category 1—those who fully commit to fidelity to Jewish law and occasionally sin as tempted to do so—seems clear. Such individuals have validly converted to Judaism. Consider the most problematic example of this, the case of the convert who at the time of the conversion has both fully committed to observing Jewish law and yet has—at the same time as his or her immersion—planned a violation of Jewish law out of financial need, which the convert deeply regrets but feels a need to do for economic reasons. Even in such a case the conversion is valid, and the individual's planned sin is not considered a failure to accept Jewish law. Rather, it is a sin by a Jew motivated by economic (or other) need, and such never voids a conversion.[67]

What, however, is the status of those converts in categories 2 and 3? The answer to that question depends on how one understands the talmudic story of Hillel and the convert. In the case of the convert of Hillel who appeared to be denying the validity of the oral tradition, three basic approaches are taken.[68]

Rashi, the premier commentator on the Talmud, explains that this potential convert did not deny the obligation to obey the oral law but simply did not feel that it came from God. Hillel, Rashi claims, was sure that he could convince him of this fact, and thus converted him.[69] Rashi seems to aver that one can convert a person who will immediately be a heretic, so long as that person is not also a sinner! This explanation is difficult. As noted by others, Rashi must mean that this Gentile accepted all that he knew was from God. That which he did not know was from God, he would not observe. However, he had accepted the "yoke of heaven" and merely questioned the validity of the current generation of interpreters.[70]

A second possibility is that Hillel worked with this person to elaborate on the Jewish tradition and its beliefs but did not actually convert this person until he had fully complied with all relevant provisions of Jewish law that he knew to be true; he only did not observe that which he did not believe that Jewish law mandated. "But when one says to the convert that such is a *mitzvah*, or he knows for himself that such is a *mitzvah* and he sees that such is how the Jewish people conduct themselves in a particular *mitzvah*, and the convert states that this *mitzvah* they do not wish to accept—in these circumstances one does not accept such a convert."[71] "It is obvious that when a convert does not accept even one biblical commandment, he is not a convert."[72]

A final approach is much more expansive. This approach notes that the obligation to accept all of Jewish law is itself only the *ab initio* ideal. One may accept a convert with a less than full acceptance of the commandments, if the rabbinical court that is supervising this conversion deems that approach to be wise in any given case. Rabbi Isaac Schmlekes states simply: "It appears to me post-fact that one is a proper convert even if one did not accept all the commandments, as the incident in Shabbat 31 [quoted above] indicates that Hillel accepted a convert who accepted only the written law" and whose observance must have been thus incomplete.[73] Rabbi Schmelkes is prepared to accept the conversion of a person who announces a lack of complete loyalty to portions of Jewish law. Of course, even he notes that when a person's lack of observance goes to fundamental issues, such as Sabbath observance, illicit sexual relations, or the like, such a person cannot successfully convert; such a person is not seeking to convert but to be exempt from many fundamental duties.[74] Other decisors, particularly those residing in modern-day Israel, have advanced similar arguments, focusing on the acceptance of Jewish traditions generally, even if there is a resistance to acceptance of the details of Jewish law.[75]

Even within the school of thought that categorically disagrees with Rabbi Schmelkes and requires full fidelity to Jewish law, there remains a significant dispute as to the second category of potential convert—those who without reservation accept the binding nature of Jewish law and, simultaneously, without reservation accept that they will live a life which is in an ongoing manner inconsistent with their obligations. Such a case revolves around the basic definition of what a convert must accept. One view accepts that a convert could be obligated to accept as binding Jewish law a set of duties that, until this point, Jewish law did not rule this particular person must accept, or even is better for the person to accept.[76]

The exact formulations of Rabbi Haim Ozer Grodzinski, the leader of prewar European Jewry, are worth citing:

> Thus, it appears that the rule which states that a Gentile who comes to convert, and accepts all the commandments except for one small rabbinic commandment, may not be accepted as a convert, is limited to a case where the convert has a precondition that his acceptance is predicated on his being permitted to do this otherwise prohibited act; in this circumstance, conversion cannot be done, as there is not partial conversion. But, one who accepts all the commandments, and rather intends to violate them out of a non-ideological sense of need, this is no deficiency in the acceptance of the commandments.[77]

However, Rabbi Grodzinski continues:

> However, when it is obvious that this convert will continue to wantonly violate Jewish law, such as the Sabbath laws or Kosher laws, and we know for certain his intent is not truly to convert and his heart is not committed to this, it is an apparent presumption that his acceptance of the commandments is nothing, and this failure to accept *mitzvot* voids the conversion.[78]

In essence, Rabbi Grodzinski concedes that when one converts without any intent to accept Jewish law (that is, a person in category 3 above), that conversion is absolutely void, as the acceptance of commandments is lacking. Such is true, even of the convert who pledges to observe but does not (category 3 above). However, if a person genuinely desires to convert but sins out of desire and knows that at the time of conversion he or she will sin, that conversion is valid. For that person genuinely accepts the *yoke* of commandments, even while recognizing his or her propensity to sin.

This view—treating incomplete observance with full acceptance as a complete acceptance of the yoke of commandments—is rejected by others who insist that a convert must voluntarily accept to obey Jewish law as a fundamental duty, and not merely accept a theoretical concept that the commandments are binding. The argument defining this position must be that acceptance of the yoke of commandments with the equally clear self-understanding that one will routinely, and intentionally, violate them deliberately is not called the acceptance of the commandments. To invoke the classical formulation used by these authorities, "acceptance of the commandments without observance of the commandments is void." One recent writer summarized the view of Rabbi Feinstein in its pristine form:

> Rabbi Feinstein opines many times that it is not sufficient for the convert to undergo the formal requirements of conversion—circumcision, immersion, and verbal acceptance of the commandments in front of a bet din. When one is certain that this acceptance is not genuine, "it is obvious and apparent that this conversion is void."[79]

Under this view, incomplete observance is tantamount to incomplete acceptance, which voids the conversion *ab initio*, so claims this school of thought.[80]

SUMMARY

In my opinion, there is little theoretical difference between the two views of acceptance of the yoke of commandments articulated by Feinstein and Grodzinski. Both acknowledge that in order successfully to convert into the Jewish faith, one must at the time of conversion genuinely desire to accept the yoke of the commandments. They differ only in two very small details, albeit very practical ones. First, how does one classify persons who pledge to observe and commit to observe, but do not? Should one consider their verbal commitment as dispositive of their state of mind, or argue that their actions reveal the truth about the value of their commitment? Second, what is the significance of a full-fledged acceptance of commandments, when not accompanied by a full-fledged observance? Should one assume that it is the observance which evaluates the acceptance, or does one recognize that acceptance and observance are separate?[81] A categorically different view is advanced by Schmelkes and others, who think that there is a place for the convert who will not commit to observance of all of Jewish law.

CONCLUSIONS

The Jewish tradition's view on proselytizing—both inward and outward—is unique among the Peoples of the Book. It absolutely prohibits proselytizing among Gentiles, in the sense of soliciting converts. It creates barriers—whose exact height are in some dispute—to conversion generally. And it views insincere conversions to Judaism as problematic. Proselytizing to the nations of the world is not a priority. Calling Jews to heightened observance of Jewish law is a priority; indeed, this is not viewed as a form of proselytizing at all. Jews are obligated to obey Jewish law, and anything one can do to facilitate such observance is a good thing.

This stark dichotomy of values between inreach and outreach has its origins in the theological view of the Jewish tradition that there are many proper paths to the top of the mountain, and Jews were chosen by God for one particular path—the one directed by Jewish law—which is not (necessarily) the right path for others to take.

"Who is happy? One who is content with his place in the world." This is the talmudic aphorism with which this paper opened. Such is the Jewish view on those who seek to change the religious identity of others. Those who are obligated to obey Jewish law should be content with their place in the world and should not seek to abandon the yoke of commandments. Those who are free from the obligation to obey Jewish law should be content with their place in the world, and should not generally seek the yoke of commandments. That is how one is content and lives in peace with oneself and with one's neighbors.

3.

Antisemitism and Proselytism

Judaism, Christianity, and Islam

———————◆———————

Jocelyn Hellig

The relevance of a chapter on antisemitism in a volume dealing with proselytization lies in the fact that antisemitism would be inexplicable without reference to the part that interreligious dynamics, particularly with regard to Jewish-Christian relations, have played in its formation. Antisemitism can be seen as the flip side of Christian mission. However, as this chapter will make clear, it was not only in Christianity but also in Islam that negative images of the Jew developed. Judaism, Christianity, and Islam each make absolute claims based on one core tradition, the Abrahamic tradition. Ironically, although the anti-Jewish stereotype of the Jew developed by Christian tradition was ultimately far more damaging and deep-rooted than that developed in Islam, today Muslim antisemitism (which is generally expressed in anti-Zionist terms) appears to be the more threatening of the two. This chapter will examine the dynamics inherent in this development, first with reference to Christianity and then to Islam.

PROBLEMS OF DEFINITION

Antisemitism, an imprecise word that is notoriously difficult to define, has as its irreducible meaning a dislike of Jews.[1] What makes definition so difficult is the fact that the term *antisemitism* can be applied to everything from vague

This chapter is an excerpt and partial revision of Jocelyn Hellig, "Antisemitism in Sub-Saharan Africa with a Focus on South Africa," in *Proselytism in Southern Africa,* ed. Johan D. van der Vyver (forthcoming), and is used with the kind permission of the editor and author.

feelings of dislike of or discomfort about Jews, at one end of the spectrum, to outright murder of them at the other. Between the two extremes one observes various forms of limitation on Jews' lives. These range from legislation that denies immigration of Jews to various countries or limits their social, economic, or educational aspirations, to active, often violent, persecution of Jews. Since a level of antisemitism exists in all societies, particularly the type limited to negative feelings about Jews, or what may be termed "genteel" antisemitism, one of the ways of assessing the seriousness of antisemitism is to examine the way in which it serves to hinder the lives of Jews. A variety of factors—political, social, economic, and religious—determine the development, nature, and extent of antisemitism. Thus, antisemitism fluctuates from period to period and from region to region.

Added to the difficulty of definition is the fact that words like *anti-Israeli, anti-Judaic,* and *anti-Zionist* are constantly confused with the word *antisemitism.* These essentially different concepts are used interchangeably, sometimes as a result of simple linguistic imprecision, but sometimes by design, as a tactic for achieving specific political and ideological ends. Although anti-Zionism is not necessarily antisemitism—in that criticism of the government of Israel, or even opposition to the establishment of the secular State of Israel, finds adequate representation among Jews themselves—anti-Zionism may also be seen to be a transmuted antisemitism. Robert Wistrich has suggested that because, after the Holocaust, it became unacceptable to mouth antisemitic sentiments, antisemitism was expressed through anti-Zionism.[2]

Difficulty with regard to definition of the term *antisemitism* notwithstanding, there is an underlying quality to antisemitism that seems to separate it from all other forms of ethnic and racial prejudice and that goes beyond mere denigration or even persecution. Although all forms of racism are dehumanizing in that they treat racial groups as monoliths and endow all members of a racial group with permanent—usually negative—characteristics, it is the demonization of Jews and the attribution to them of a quality of cosmic and eternal evil that mark antisemitism. Antisemitism has, as its most influential roots, the mythic structure of Christianity in its relation to Judaism. A particular role is assigned to the Jews in the Christian drama of salvation. This designated role, according to Richard L. Rubenstein, reveals a logic in Christian theology that, when pushed to the extreme, ends with justification of, if not incitement to, the murder of Jews. The Holocaust of the Second World War was thus "the terminal expression of Christian anti-Semitism."[3] At this level dehumanization becomes so complete that it denies to Jews all human rights—the rights to possession, dignity, citizenship, and ultimately the right to life itself.

The Holocaust was enacted under cover of war and was made possible by the fact that Jews were stripped, through legislation, of all power. Power, as Yehuda Bauer has defined it, is the "capability to influence decisions of others either through the implied or explicit threat of sanctions or through promise of political advantages deriving from military, economic, electoral, or other assets."[4] By this criterion the Jews of the Third Reich were absolutely power-less, and it was this experience and its disastrous entailments that made the Jewish return to Israel as an independent homeland so essential. Jews were returned to political sovereignty for the first time in almost two thousand years. Some scholars, notably Emil Fackenheim, regard this as a return of the Jewish people to history itself.[5] No longer the objects of history, Jews, by being in a position to make their own power decisions, are now participants in history. The Holocaust and the reestablishment of the State of Israel, the two *kairoi* of modern Jewish history, have influenced all aspects of modern Jewish thought. No Jewish community can be examined in isolation from them.

CHRISTIAN ANTISEMITISM

Dislike of Jews seems as old as Judaism itself. There was a significant amount of Jew-hatred in ancient times, but it was vastly exacerbated by the Christian "teaching of contempt" against the Jews. Long before the inception of Chris-tianity, in classical times, expression of antisemitism could take on quite vi-cious forms, as is evidenced in the diatribes of Apion of Alexandria. The source of Jew-hatred appears to be resentment of Jewish monotheism, the Jewish claim to chosenness, and the religious laws that maintained Jewish separate-ness. As David Berger points out, however, "if ancient paganism had been replaced by a religion or ideology without an internal anti-Jewish dynamic, it is likely that the anti-Semitism of the classical world would have gradually faded. Instead, it was reinforced. The old pedestrian causes of anti-Jewish ani-mus were replaced by a new, powerful myth of extraordinary force and vital-ity."[6]

Christianity's anti-Jewish teaching became explicit in three areas: (1) the Jewish rejection of Jesus as the Messiah; (2) the doctrine of Jewish chosenness; and (3) the deicide accusation against the Jews. Each of these will now receive brief consideration.

REJECTION OF JESUS AS THE MESSIAH

Christian antisemitism, as Rosemary Ruether argues, is not peripheral but central to Christianity. Relating to Christianity's core doctrine of Christology, antisemitism is found in the New Testament itself. The New Testament be-comes an "anti-Jewish midrash" of the Old Testament (itself a term of deni-gration of the Jewish scriptures), which sets out to prove that the church was the rightful heir to the promises of God, while the Jews were punished and rejected, and Judaism discredited.

Within the Hebrew Bible, there is an implicit promise of a Messianic Age; for Christians, the promise was fulfilled with the life, death, and resurrection of Jesus. However, since the Jews rejected the validity of that claim, they were seen to be blind to the true purport of their own scriptures, and the church developed a polemic against them in the form of an exegetical tradition that attempted to prove that Jesus was the messiah predicted in the Old Testament. Jewish blindness was to assume great significance, not only with regard to discrediting Judaism's religious law, leadership, and worship, but with regard to its history as a whole, dating back to the time of Moses. "The dialectic of judgment and promise is rendered schizophrenic, applied not to one elect people, but to two peoples; the reprobate people, the Jews, and the future elect people of the promise, the Church."[7] In divine intentionality, it now appeared, there had always been two peoples: the people of faith, who are the rightful heirs of the promise to Abraham; and the fallen, disobedient people, who never obeyed God or heard the prophets. The church becomes the true heir of the promises to Abraham, while the Jews are the heirs of an evil history of perfidy, apostasy, and murder. The result is that the Jews are cut off from their divine election. As a punishment, they were destined to be kept alive as witnesses to Christian verities, but they were to live a reprobate existence, outside of their Promised Land and scattered throughout the world. This interpretation often complicates Christian attitudes to the State of Israel.[8]

THE DOCTRINE OF CHOSENNESS

The doctrine of Jewish chosenness is another potent cause of antisemitism. Never regarded by Jews as a doctrine of racial superiority, but rather as one of special responsibility, it has resulted in several difficulties. First, it has been consistently misunderstood and distorted by outsiders. Second, it has been emulated throughout the world in order to legitimate a host of racist theories. The most notable of these is Nazism, an ideology which, according to George Steiner, boomeranged catastrophically against the Jews themselves in a "hideous relationship of parody."[9] Third, in a dynamic not unlike sibling rivalry, it serves to alienate Jews and Christians in that both claim chosenness. Fourth, it plays an important role in the dehumanization of Jews.

With the lack of logic inherent in two peoples being chosen by the same God, the church saw itself as the "New" or "True" Israel, while the promises to the Jews were seen as abrogated. This resulted in a myth of "displacement" of, or of "superseding," the "old Israel" with the "new Israel." The idea that the mission of the Jewish people was finished with the coming of Jesus Christ is, for Franklin H. Littell, the cornerstone of Christian antisemitism. This writing off of the old Israel, he claims, rings a genocidal note. "To teach that a people's mission in God's providence is finished, that they have been relegated to the limbo of history, has murderous implications which murderers will in time spell out." The murder of six million Jews by baptized Christians, from whom membership in good standing was not (and has not been) withdrawn, raises, for Littell, the most insistent question about the credibility of Christianity.[10]

One of the most destructive entailments of the doctrine of chosenness with regard to antisemitism is that it has thrust the Jews into an unwanted supernatural vocation as central actors in the salvation of the world. According to Richard Rubenstein, it may be impossible for Christians to remain Christians without regarding the Jews in mythic, magic, and theological categories. "Jews alone of all the people in the world are regarded as actors and participants in the drama of sin and innocence, guilt and salvation, perdition and redemption."[11] Unable to conceive of Jews as ordinary people, capable of the same virtues and vices as others, people dehumanize them. By condemning the Jews to the realm of the sacred, chosenness places them in a special category of expectation. Either praised as Jesus-like or condemned and murdered as Judas-like, Jews become the objects of decisive hatred.

So potentially damaging is the doctrine of chosenness that Rubenstein has called for its demythologization. Yet, this would not be an easy matter, as Judaism and Christianity are equally dependent on its retention. For Arthur Hertzberg, the doctrine is so central that he has claimed that "the essence of Judaism is the affirmation that the Jews are the chosen people; all else is commentary."[12] But the chosenness of the Jews is equally central to Christianity. "Unless Jews have a supernatural vocation," avers Rubenstein, "the Christ makes absolutely no theological difference."[13]

THE DEICIDE ACCUSATION

The dehumanization engendered by the doctrine of chosenness has been vastly exacerbated by the deicide accusation, which not only dehumanizes Jews but demonizes them. Although responsible theologians attempt to spread the blame for killing Christ to all humanity, Matthew 27:25 confirms Jewish guilt for all generations. One who can kill God is not beyond the most heinous of crimes. This slander against the Jewish people acts as a justification for the persecution and murder of Jews and was a powerful motivating factor during the Holocaust.[14] Alice L. Eckhardt points out that the German churches, during the 1930s, generally emphasized the curse upon Israel. She cites the words of a Protestant bishop in 1936, the year after the issuing of the Nuremberg racial laws:

> When the Jews crucified Jesus, they crucified themselves, their revelation and their history. Thus the curse came upon them. Since then that curse works itself out from one generation to another. This people has . . . become a fearful and divinely ordained scourge for all nations, leading to hatred and persecution.[15]

While the deicide accusation was not the cause of the Holocaust, Emil Fackenheim suggests that "had there been no two-thousand-year-old slander of Jews as a deicide people, the Holocaust could not have happened."[16]

The negative potential of the deicide accusation must be assessed against the power of the myth that encapsulates it. Hyam Maccoby regards the myth of the crucifixion of Jesus as the most powerful the world has ever known. In a breathtaking drama designed to lift the burden of guilt from those who believe, the Jews do *not* play the role of the scapegoats. Jesus himself is the scapegoat who takes upon himself the sins of the world. The function of the Jews was to bring about the necessary death of the scapegoat in order to save humankind from crisis. For Christianity, the cruel, sacrificial death of Jesus was a necessity, and the Jews were the evil instruments by which it was brought about. The Jews are thus the earthly agents of the cosmic powers of evil. They are the deicides who, by their wickedness, unwittingly save the world, but who are thus doubly damned in that the death of Christ is not efficacious for *them*, and because, with the deicide, they crown a long career of sin with the greatest of all sins, the murder of God. They become the embodiment of evil and excite a combination of awe and hate that, as the hallmark of antisemitism, separates it from all other forms of xenophobia.

Because the Jews were cast as cosmic villains in the Christian doctrine of atonement, their role demanded that any sign of happiness or prosperity among them should arouse anxiety for Christians, for if the Jews did not suffer, who would bear the guilt for the sacrifice of Jesus? As antisemitism is so ingrained in the central myth of Christianity, the only solution, according to Maccoby, is the return of the repressed, namely, a real understanding of Christendom's irrational prejudice against the Jews and its determination always to think of them in negative terms.[17] It is the idea that Jews are cosmic villains that makes views about world conspiracy, such as *The Protocols of the Elders of Zion*, so plausible. Without the decisive religious significance of Jews in Christianity's central drama, such theories would surely be dismissed by rational people as absurd.

When Christianity became the official religion of the Roman Empire in the fourth century, Christendom's negative perception of the Jews was translated into concrete legislation. The triumph of the church was interpreted as proof of divine favor, and Jews were seen as an anachronism, sustained merely by stubbornness. Jewish practice was circumscribed by law. In the medieval world Jews were an easily identifiable minority of nonconformists in a conformist world. This resulted in them being perceived and treated as alien to European society. Over the centuries a formidable anti-Jewish stereotype was developed, originally based on religiously inspired antipathy but later adapting itself around various foci. During the nineteenth century the focus was racial, and antisemitism was transmuted into a pseudo-scientific form. With emancipation Jews had become equals before the law in European society. In order to confirm their status as fundamentally and irrevocably alien to the rest of society, however, it became necessary to focus attention on allegedly permanent, unchanging characteristics such as race. Their equality could thus be delegitimated. This, in effect, meant that whereas escape from violent antisemitism had previously been allowed through conversion, no escape was now possible. Antisemitism was later to develop political ramifications and become fused with anti-Zionism.

Christian teaching had formed the basis for these developments and has had an ineradicable influence. As Claire Huchet-Bishop has suggested, the negative image of the Jew fostered by Christian teaching has "permeated our Western culture so thoroughly that even people wholly detached from the church, including atheists, are no longer unbiased in their reactions toward Jews, though they may think they are."[18] "What Christian teaching has done," she avers, "it has to undo; and it will take a long time."[19]

ISLAMIC ANTISEMITISM

Traditional Views

Antisemitism, in the forms manifest in the Christian tradition, is not apparent in Islamic tradition. Yet, as Bernard Lewis points out, since 1945 certain Arab countries have been the only places in the world where hardcore Nazi-style antisemitism is publicly and officially endorsed and propagated.[20] When Islam arose in the seventh century of the common era, Jews were a homeless and powerless people. In accordance with its claims of superiority over Judaism and Christianity, Islam regarded the Jews and Christians as *dhimmi* (protected peoples). Judaism was a tolerated religion in the Muslim world, and Jews were to adopt a low profile and self-effacing attitude.

The Qur'an distinguishes between warfare against pagans, which is to be total and unrelenting, and toleration of Jews and Christians. Jews and Christians should be tolerated, provided that they pay a special tax and are humiliated. These Qur'anic teachings, Jane S. Gerber suggests, created a formula for religious pluralism in which Jews could survive and even prosper, but if they became too ostentatious in their success, there was no guarantee that the original relationship of contractual protection would be honored.[21] While the notion of "toleration-protection *cum* humiliation"[22] took varied and sometimes outrageous forms, the radical isolation of the Jew as an outsider in Christian Europe was never approximated in the Muslim world. "Jews were objects of officially legislated contempt, but they were not intended to be objects of officially instituted hatred."[23]

Traditional Islam, although it did display hostility against Jews, did not demonize them. Mohammed had a complex and ambivalent attitude to Jews. His conflict with the Jewish tribes of Medina, along with the bitterness that it engendered, is reflected in the Qur'an and in the Hadith. Jews were labeled corrupters of scripture (Q. 3:63), were accused of falsehood (Q. 3:71), and were seen as enemies of Islam. "Thou wilt surely find that the strongest in enmity against those who believe are the Jews and the idolaters" (Q. 5:85). Yet, Mohammed did not outlaw the Jews or remove them entirely from Arabia. His conflict with them ended in the destruction of the Jewish tribes, *not* in Mohammed's. Because there was no equivalent of the deicide myth in traditional Islam, the Jews were not demonized.[24] This made it possible for Muslims to adopt a more relaxed and less embittered attitude toward their Jewish subjects. In the Islamic world, Jews were one minority among several and, although the Qur'an favors Christians over Jews, they received equal treatment under Islamic law. Jews were never free of discrimination under Islamic rule but were only occasionally subject to persecution. Their situation, according to Lewis, was never as bad as in Christendom at its worst, nor ever as good as in Christendom at its best. While prejudice was always present, it was usually muted, rarely violent, and mostly inspired by disdain and contempt rather than by the explosive mixture of hate, fear, and envy that fueled the antisemitism of Christendom.[25]

MODERN VIEWS

"European-style" antisemitism among Muslims arose out of various political developments, most particularly out of the Jewish resettlement in Palestine, the establishment of the State of Israel in 1948, and the series of Arab-Israeli wars that followed. From a political perspective the first development was the rise to world domination of the European empires during the nineteenth and early twentieth centuries. Along with European ideas, such as liberalism, constitutionalism, and socialism that were conveyed to the Arab world came antisemitism.[26] At the same time, Muslim and other minorities were weakened by the breakdown and collapse of the old political structures and the loyalties and traditions associated with them. New patriotic and nationalist loyalties made it more difficult to tolerate any kind of diversity. Because it is easier to be tolerant from a position of strength than it is from a position of weakness, Muslims began to mete out far harsher treatment to religious, ethnic, and even ideological minorities.[27]

From a Muslim religious perspective the return of Jews to sovereignty in Israel, in the midst of the Islamic world, runs against the grain of the understanding of Jews as *dhimmi*. The most potent reason for the development of European-style antisemitism in the Muslim world, therefore, was the Jewish return to Israel. Starting out as marginal to the main Arab struggle, antisemitism started to become dominant after the 1956 Sinai War and was accelerated by the Six Day War of 1967—both of which were swift and overwhelming Israeli victories.[28] While the war of 1948-49 was a hard-fought struggle that lasted many months and in which Israel won the prize of survival at high cost, these later defeats presented a terrible problem of explanation for the vanquished Arabs, particularly in that they had been thwarted by a people traditionally perceived as cowardly and lacking in all the military virtues. As the local media put it: "The Jew in his very soul and character has not the qualities of a man who bears arms. He is not naturally prepared to sacrifice for anything, not even for his son or wife. . . . "[29] Imposed by "cowards," these more recent humiliating defeats demanded recourse to an explanation that was beyond the normal processes of rational thought and that invoked demonic, conspiratorial powers. Such an explanation had already been offered in Christendom and had gained wide currency, even in the Arab world. Islamic antisemitism thus departed from its traditional historic manifestation and demonized the Jew, taking as its model Christian-inspired documents, such as the *Protocols of the Elders of Zion.*

Antisemitism was now generally disguised as anti-Zionism, which postulated a dangerous, shadowy, international conspiracy with its Jewish center in the Middle East. While the geographic focus has changed, the content of the mythology remains familiar. In the view of Robert Wistrich, there is a continuity between Nazi antisemitism and current militant anti-Zionism. Hitler unleashed an attack on the Jews that has not yet been fully spent, in that it has been resuscitated by Arab nationalism.[30] The problem today lies not so much in the resurfacing of antisemitism, but in the reintroduction of antisemitism as a legitimate ideological tool, and its acceptance as part of "respectable" public discourse.[31]

ANTI-ZIONISM AND ANTISEMITISM

It is a vexing question whether anti-Zionism is a new form of antisemitism, indeed, whether it is antisemitism at all. One has to distinguish between opposition to Israeli policy as a legitimate political criticism, and ideological anti-Zionism which persistently denies any legitimacy to a Jewish homeland in the Middle East. There is so much malevolence and sheer malice in the attack on Zionism that it is hard to see it as part of legitimate political opposition to a political movement. The word *Zionist,* as Dan Segre points out, has acquired an autonomous derogatory meaning of its own that transcends both time and space and is applied as an epithet to denote total evil. The term has, in the process, lost all rational connotation in relation to history or geography, and Zionists have ceased to be seen as human beings. Zionism is thus perceived not merely as a bad political phenomenon but as a cancerous growth. Thus, "the ongoing state of war with the Arabs does not imply—as it does for other states—a situation of military occupation so much as one of automatic colonial racism."[32] Unremitting hostility against the State of Israel in much of the Arab world and the Jewish involvement in the Middle East crisis serve merely to propel anti-Zionism but not to explain totally its nature.

So virulent is the denunciation of Zionism that some scholars believe that it is not merely an extension of antisemitism but that the roots lie, in part, elsewhere. They assert that there are other complex causative factors. Although antisemitism and anti-Zionism have common roots, anti-Zionism possesses a logic of its own. It can, according to Segre, be attributed in large part to deep-seated psychological fears that derive their logic from a need to exorcise threatening developments with which rationality cannot cope. One of these is the strength of separate Jewish identity, not only in the past but now also in the context of a nation-state. The dispersion of Jews was historically seen as divinely sanctioned. The growth of rationalism, historical criticism, and secularism, however, overturned this shielding interpretation. The Gentile world has always seen Jewish survival as an enigma. With the establishment of the Jewish State in Israel, this enigma has now been transferred from the individual to the political plane and is exacerbated by the peculiar nature of Israeli nationalism. There is a widespread inability to come to terms with Israel as a transnational state—one whose affiliates or centers of identification lie outside of it.[33] This results in deep fears about a kind of "pan-Judaism" with its focus in Israel, and is one of the dynamics underlying the accusation that Zionism is racism, an accusation that continues to mitigate against the ultimate normalization of the State of Israel.

The charge that Zionism is racism, though an outrageous canard, contains, according to Nathan Glazer, a modicum of meaning. This meaning is based on the special relationship of Israel to the Jewish people. Because it was established under the ideology of Zionism as a home for the Jewish people, Israel must be a home for *all* the Jewish people. However, because of its internal politics—and possibly other considerations—Israel must accept the orthodox Jewish religious definition of who is a Jew. This results in a questioning of the Jewish status, for example, of the Falashas who were airlifted to Israel. The issue is, therefore, not one of racism, but results from this chain of religious, historical, and political circumstances. Zionism, an overwhelmingly *secular* movement for the *national* liberation of Jews, who are defined by *religious* criteria, opens itself to attack as racist.[34] Factors such as these arouse widespread hostility, which finds support in antisemitism. But these factors may now, themselves, serve to support antisemitism. The identification of Zionism with racism opened the way for another cruel twist. Jews, previously victims of racism, were now themselves seen as racists. This exonerated the world from any sense of guilt toward the Jews for the Holocaust and from any sense of commitment to a Jewish state. It allowed the Israeli Jews to be perceived as "Nazis," while the Palestinians were now perceived as the victims or "Jews."[35]

The fact that Israel has not managed to achieve normality is another factor that underlies the development of anti-Zionism. Although the State of Israel was established in order to normalize the life of the Jewish people, it has not managed to achieve this. The reasons underlying the world's inability to perceive Israel as a state like any other are the ongoing hostility to Israel of some of its neighbors; the continuing unwillingness of these neighbors to accord Israel legitimacy, in spite of early international legal recognition of the state; and the special relationship of the state to the Jewish people.

An important conduit of anti-Zionist sentiment in Africa is third-world ideology, the dynamics of whose development has been illuminatingly traced by Rivlin and Fomerand.[36] Though disparate, they point out, third-world countries are united by certain psychological and social predispositions that have a critical bearing on their perception both of Israel and the Arabs. Having been passive subjects of the politics of others rather than active participants themselves, third-world countries have in common their recent emergence on the international scene as independent actors. Generally lacking in industrialization and crippled by social and economic underdevelopment, their common experience of political subordination and economic poverty has implanted within them and their elites bitter memories of victimization by foreign exploiters. These provide the foundation for the emergence of anti-colonialism and anti-imperialism as the dominant motifs underlying their struggle for self-determination. Characteristic of this ideology is a concern for all the oppressed peoples of the world.

Israel originally shared many major attributes of the third-world states, and, with the heterogeneity apparent in the Third World, could have been—and in fact originally desired to be—part of it. It should be noted at the outset that Israel had originally hoped to pursue a policy of nonalignment with either the United States or the Soviet Union. Long victimized and oppressed, like third-world countries, Jews had fought a war of national liberation in Palestine against a colonial regime. Like countries of the Third World, Israel had to confront problems of economic development, social mobilization, political integration, and modernization. Its inhabitants, with the exception of its Ashkenazi leadership, had come largely from the Third World. These oriental Jews, like members of the Third World, had suffered the cutting of their traditional cultural moorings under the impact of modernism.

Despite all these similarities, Israel was not accorded third-world status. Its inhabitants were not viewed as natives but as foreigners, who, as exponents of Western culture, were agents of Western imperialism. Far from Israel's struggle against Great Britain being accepted as part of the struggle of dependent peoples in Asia, it was seen as thwarting a colonial people, the Arabs of Palestine, in their own fight for independence.[37] The ideological lens of anti-colonialism and anti-imperialism directed the Third World toward a pro-Palestinian Arab and anti-Israeli position. This was reinforced by the bourgeois style of life that developed in Israel, by Israel's treatment of the Arab minority, and by Israel's collusion with Great Britain and France (the arch-imperialists) in the 1956 Suez operation. Israel's heavy dependence on the United States for military and economic aid after the Six Day War of 1967 further honed this negative image of Israel.[38]

Much of this negative perception of Israel was engendered by Arab propaganda, which was aimed at alienating Africa from Israel and was aided by the dominant presence of Islam in the Third World. As African and Asian colonies attained independence, Islam experienced increased solidarity, which was reinforced by meetings of the Islamic elite at world Islamic meetings. Exchange of diplomatic representation, meeting at the United Nations, and general contact with the Islamic world, brought about through the *hajj* and the media, determined the preeminent place of Islam in the world view of much of the Third World and influenced it toward an anti-Israeli and pro-Arab stance.

The development of anti-Zionist attitudes in the Third World was facilitated by lack of contact with Jews and an unfamiliarity with their historical travail. This helped to impede sympathy for the return of Jews to Palestine and the establishment of the State of Israel. People of the Third World, who do not have large Jewish communities in their midst, do not share any guilt that the Western world may have for the Holocaust. They cannot, therefore, be expected to react as Westerners did. Major antisemitic events, including the Holocaust, were not part of their close experience. Given all these factors, it took a surprisingly long time for the Third World to become totally alienated from Israel.

In fact, there were, originally, and for over a decade, positive attitudes to Israel. Sharing with Israel the challenges of nation-building and changing the face of the land, and confident that they would not be dominated by a more powerful partner, African states turned initially to Israel for technical assistance. They had developed their own negative images of the Arabs, were grossly unfamiliar with the details of the Palestine problem, and were almost totally ignorant of the existence of a human tragedy involving the Arabs of Palestine. All these factors had provided a climate favorable to Israel in Africa.[39]

The shift in black Africa's attitude to Israel did not take place abruptly. Wanting to cultivate black support without risking the loss of continental unity, the Arabs' goal was to loosen the African states' ties with Israel and persuade them to accept the Palestine issue as a legitimate concern of black Africa. This strategy only gained its initial breakthrough in 1961 at the Casablanca Conference, where Israel, in addition to being viewed as siding with apartheid because of an influential Jewish population in South Africa, was condemned as "an instrument in the service of imperialism and neo-colonialism not only in the Middle East but also in Africa and Asia." Deep concern was expressed over "depriving the Arabs of Palestine of their legitimate rights."[40] Even so, the Arab-Israeli dispute was not a matter of direct concern to black African states, and only became so in 1967. With Israel's spectacular victory in the Six Day War, black Africa could no longer avoid getting involved. Nor could it resist Egyptian pressure for support at Organization for African Unity meetings. The Six Day War saw the beginning of a change in the perceptual maps of third-world leaders. No longer perceived as a biblical David fighting against impossible odds, the Jewish state was now seen as a militarily invincible power. This view emerged just as the Third World was being transformed into a cohesive coalition of the underdog and underprivileged peoples of the world, and was fueled by the growing frustration at the third-world coalition's inability to bridge the gap with the rich, industrialized world. This led to an anti-imperialism and anti-colonialism directed primarily against the United States and its allies, most important, Israel.[41]

Israel's friendly relations with white Southern Africa at a time when the African community was mobilizing world opinion against the fascist and colonialist regimes of South Africa, Rhodesia, and Portugal simply added to its dereliction.[42] There was also heightened suspicion of Israel because of its closeness to the United States, for whom disillusionment had set in among African leaders. With the 1973 occupation by Israel of a portion of Egyptian territory on the West Bank of the Suez Canal, the Arab-Israeli conflict was propelled from a purely regional problem to an African one. Because it was a "threat to African soil," it became an issue affecting the entire African continent.[43] By 1973, the estrangement reached its nadir with seventeen African countries breaking relations with Israel. Israel was now seen to exhibit close parallels with the hated South Africa. Both were viewed as nations of alien settlers, oppressing indigenous populations and serving as outposts of imperialist ventures against the Africans.[44] These perceptions were exacerbated by economic realities, as could be discerned in the 1974 statement of President Senghor of Senegal: "The Arabs have the numbers, space and oil. In the Third World, they outweigh Israel."[45]

An essential part of all these developments is the Middle East conflict, which is just one part of the anti-Zionist picture. Its outcome will have an effect on the development of antisemitism. Future prospects with regard to Muslim-Jewish relations are inextricably tied with peace in the Middle East. Bernard Lewis maintains that "for Christian antisemites, the Palestine problem is a pretext and an outlet for their hatred; for Muslim antisemites, it is the cause. Perhaps if that cause is removed or significantly diminished, the hostility too may wane, not disappear, but at least return to the previous level of prejudice."[46] There is an awesome choice that confronts Jews, Arabs, and the world at the present day. This is the willingness for Israel and the Palestinians to enter into genuine dialogue and the preparedness by Israel to respond appropriately. If there is no solution or alleviation, Lewis avers, and the conflict drags on, there is no escape from an unending downward spiral of mutual hate, which will embitter the lives of Arabs and Jews alike. Any optimism concerning Arab-Jewish relations, however, has to be tempered by the possibility that the virus of a demonizing antisemitism may already have "entered into the bloodstream of Islam to poison it for generations to come as Christendom was poisoned for generations past. If so, Arab and Jewish hopes will be lost in the miasma of bigotry."[47]

CONCLUSION

This chapter has examined the ways in which two proselytizing religions—Christianity and Islam—negatively view Jews. The relationship among Judaism, Christianity, and Islam is hostile precisely because the three religions share a common tradition. The antisemitic stereotype, which demonizes Jews and attributes to them cosmic powers for evil, finds its most potent origin in the mythic structure of Christianity as it relates to Jews. Though present in the ancient world, anti-Judaism was given a powerful new impetus by Christianity's central myth, the drama of the crucifixion, and the role that was assigned to the Jews therein. The Jews became the embodiment of evil, the alien "other," in Christian Europe. Although modern antisemitism has centered on other foci, such as race, the fact that its roots are religious and, hence, are located within an area of ultimate concern, accounts for its irrationality, depth, and pervasiveness.

The relationship between Judaism and traditional Islam is intrinsically far less problematic. Yet Muslim countries are today the only countries in the world in which Nazi-style antisemitism is officially endorsed and propagated. Traditionally, Judaism was a tolerated religion and Jews a minority among several others in Muslim lands. The notion of the *dhimmi*—a minority alternatively protected and humiliated—laid the basis for religious pluralism in Muslim society. While there was prejudice against Jews, it was inspired by disdain and contempt rather than by the explosive mixture of hate, fear, and envy that characterized the antisemitism of Christendom. Demonization of the Jews was not automatic in that traditional Islam lacks a deicide myth. This was, however, to undergo changes.

The active propagation of antisemitism does not occur in a vacuum. While continually present in its "genteel" form, the practical expression of antisemitism requires a disruption of political, economic, and social conditions. Accordingly, European-style antisemitism among Muslims arose primarily out of political developments, the most decisive of which was the return of the Jews to their homeland in Israel in 1948 and the Arab-Israeli wars that followed. This was especially true of those—such as the Six Day War of 1967—in which a humiliating defeat was imposed on the Arabs by a people hitherto perceived as powerless and "cowardly." Not only did a Jewish homeland in the Middle East fly in the face of the Muslim idea of the Jews as *dhimmi*,[48] but the humiliating defeats required an explanation inaccessible to ordinary logic. This was supplied by a recourse to the antisemitic stereotype that had developed in Christendom. With the rise to world domination of the European empires of the nineteenth century, and the attendant spread of European ideas into the Muslim world, came antisemitism. Christendom's antisemitic stereotype was ready for the taking. Presenting the Jews as global conspirators, it supplied an answer to such inexplicable occurrences.

Anti-Zionism has become a primary vehicle through which antisemitism is expressed in the Muslim world. It is sometimes indistinguishable from antisemitism. This chapter suggests that while anti-Zionism is sometimes identified as antisemitism or seen as an extension of it, it has its own complex causative dynamics. Employed in response to irrational, deep-seated fears, it could, of course, only find an object after 1948. A prominent factor in the spread of anti-Zionism is third-world ideology. This has had the effect of extending the antipathy against Jews and Zionism beyond the confines of interreligious rivalry. But, in the case of Africa, it is also associated with the spread of Islam and an attempt to alienate African countries from Israel.

It is paradoxical that while antisemitism derives its pervasiveness and depth from interreligious rivalry, the religions themselves exercise some control through the moral restraints that inhere in them. Religions hold safeguards against wholesale slaughter of others. It is when the antisemitic stereotype is adopted into ideologies such as Nazism and the distorted religious ideas of Islamism (as contrasted with Islam), that all restraint is abandoned. Hitler, while mocking Christianity, took it seriously in the one aspect that demonized the Jews. In the absence of Christian moral restraints he enacted a program of mass destruction in which Jews were treated as subhuman and were therefore stripped of the most basic of human rights. In the new terrorist warfare promoted by fundamentalist Islam, the perceived enemy is not only America but Jews. They are also a stated target.[49] The random activity of terrorists infringes human rights on another level.

The aim of proselytization is positive, but there are always negative implications. One is the denigration of the target individual's previous religion. This is particularly so with regard to indigenous religions. The other, at least in the case of Christianity and Islam, is the spreading of an anti-Jewish stereotype. Antisemitism, even if only at the level of ill-feeling, will never disappear. In the modern world Jews have their greatest opportunity and freedom in democratic societies, which place controls on human rights abuses. In the face of anti-American (and hence anti-Jewish) terrorism, these may, however, prove to be ineffectual.

Part Two

ISLAM

4.

JIHAD FOR HEARTS AND MINDS

Proselytizing in the Qur'an and First Three Centuries of Islam

Donna E. Arzt

INTRODUCTION

*J*ihad. "Holy War." A *fatwa* "decree" of death for apostasy (*ridda*). These are words that evoke for many Americans images of Middle Eastern holy wars led by sword-yielding horsemen (or, their modern-day equivalent, anthrax-tipped missiles) and assassins' bullets targeted at authors and their publishers and translators.[1] While these allusions are in one sense far removed from the kinds of questions raised by problems of proselytism in the new democracies of Africa, Latin America, and Eastern Europe, in another sense they raise the specter of social conflict above a national and regional level to the global arena, for they are suggestive of a pivotal conflict between East and West.

But what if these images are based on fundamental misunderstandings—or worse, outright ignorance shaped by hostile propagandists—about Islam's basic principles and obligations? The only way to be certain is to go to the source. It is therefore the purpose of this chapter to explore the classical origins of the concepts of *jihad* and apostasy in Islam. I leave to other authors in this volume the task of determining whether contemporary Muslim spokespersons and issuers of *fatwas* are speaking in terms consistent with the classical traditions of Islam.

Ultimately, the question of proselytism is about freedom of choice or, given the reality that all human choices are to some extent determined by social and cultural factors, at least the degree of independence accorded to the individual will. In order to evaluate what role coercion may have played in conversions during any historical era, it is useful to examine what the process of conversion, as well as its consequences, looked like at that time. Regarding the classical period of Islam, this will not be an easy task, as few records remain—or, indeed, were ever kept—of the process, and few efforts have been made to study it formally.[2] For purposes of this essay, the term *classical era* of Islam refers to the period from 622 C.E., when the Prophet Mohammed and his followers left Mecca to establish the first Islamic community in Medina, until the middle of the tenth century, with what Muslims refer to as the closing of the door of *ijtihad*, the post-Qur'anic reasoning and creative interpretation of Islamic law that epitomized Muslim thought after the death of Mohammed in 632 C.E. through the religion's first three centuries.

Although I shall attempt to present the concept of proselytizing within Islam as a coherent doctrine, in this chapter I divide the subject into two parts: conversion *to* Islam and conversion *from* Islam. I am inherently suspicious of actions that involve coercion or other interference with individual freedom of belief. Because of the controversial nature of *jihad*, the Islamic prohibition on apostasy, and other aspects of conversion to and from Islam, full disclosure of my own bias on these issues is appropriate: As a specialist in contemporary international human rights, my perspective is reflected in the U.N. Human Rights Committee's 1993 General Comment on Freedom of Religion or Belief (interpreting Article 18 of the International Covenant on Civil and Political Rights):

> [F]reedom to "have or to adopt" a religion or belief necessarily entails the freedom to choose a religion or belief, including, inter alia, the right to replace one's current religion or belief. [International law] bars coercion that would impair the right to have or adopt a religion or belief, including the use or threat of physical force or penal sanctions to compel believers or non-believers to adhere to their religious beliefs and congregations, to recant their religion or belief or to convert.[3]

While such a point of view may, on first impression, appear hostile to Islam as it is popularly perceived in the West, closer examination will reveal that *jihad* as a militaristic method of proselytizing is but one version, for there are multiple interpretations of the Qur'an's injunctions to struggle in God's cause.[4] Similarly, the nature of the classical Islamic punishment for apostasy is open to interpretation. As seen below, a multiplicity of viewpoints applies both to the case of conversion *to* Islam and conversion *from* Islam.

CONCEPTUAL FRAMEWORK

Before addressing the texts and early history of Islamic proselytizing movements, this preliminary section provides a short primer in *shari'a* for readers who are unfamiliar with the structure and purpose of Islamic law. It then introduces the major Arabic terms and concepts which are necessary to understand the issue of proselytism in the Islamic context.

Sources and Tenets of Shari'a

Islamic law, like Jewish law, is a comprehensive and organic body of religious duties governing political, economic, and social life as well as the spiritual realm of worship and ritual—that is, behavior as well as belief. Law and theology are inseparable in Islam, as are the spiritual and the temporal realms of human life. The term for Islamic law, *shari'a*, literally means "the path" or "road to follow" (not unlike the Jewish term *halakha*). *Shari'a* is comprised of two categories of sources: the primary sources, which consist of the Qur'an and the Sunna; and the secondary sources, *ijma* and *qiyas*, which are not per se sources but rather methods of discovering *shari'a*.[5]

The Qur'an is the collection of recitations that Allah (Arabic for the universal concept of God) revealed to Mohammed the Prophet through the angel Gabriel between 610 and 632 C.E. Muslims believe that Mohammed was human, not divine, though he was Allah's Messenger and the last and greatest of prophets (lesser ones of whom include Moses and Jesus). The Qur'an's one hundred and fourteen chapters (suras) were written down by scribes after Mohammed's death, during the reigns of the first three caliphs. The early revelations, transcribed in Mecca, deal primarily with questions of morality and belief, while the later principles, revealed after Mohammed migrated to Medina, often concern legal topics such as contracts, crime, inheritance, and constitutional and commercial law. Considered supremely authoritative and infallible, as it is the word of God, the Qur'an cannot be altered. "There is no changing the words of Allah" (Q. 10:65).[6]

When the Qur'an is silent or unclear, one turns to the Sunna, a compilation of commands, prohibitions, and rules deduced from the sayings or the conduct (*hadith*, meaning "tradition" or story) of Mohammed during his lifetime. The Sunna was compiled by thousands of scholars beginning about one century after the death of the Prophet, as a means of resolving interpretive disputes. Together the Qur'an and Sunna are said to constitute an integrated whole, though in cases of conflict, the former prevails, according to traditionalist jurists. Although there is only one authoritative Qur'an, the original in Arabic, collections of Sunna (also in Arabic) can differ depending on who compiled them.

In addition to the two primary sources, a third source, *ijma*, meaning "consensus," provides a body of fixed rules reflecting the unanimous agreement of Islamic scholars, so long as their collective view does not conflict with the Qur'an and Sunna. According to a leading contemporary scholar, "The authority of *ijma* is based upon distrust of individual opinion. There is assurance of freedom from error in the communal mind."[7] Finally, when none of these three revealed or communal sources provides a relevant rule, individual Islamic scholars can derive one through logical inference from the primary sources and reasoning by analogy (*qiyas*), much as common law jurists do. The mental exertion involved in this independent interpretive process, which requires special training, is called *ijtihad* (related to the term *jihad*, discussed more extensively below).

The eighth and ninth centuries were a fruitful time for Islam. Through the process of *ijtihad*, Islamic jurists were able to interpret unclear passages of the Qur'an and Sunna in dynamic ways and to discern new rules or apply old ones where the two primary sources of law were silent. When the fresh interpretations achieved a scholarly consensus (*ijma*), they attained a legal status of their own. Moreover, through exposure to cultures as diverse as the Hellenic, Christian, Syrian, Persian, Judaic, Byzantine-Roman, and Zoroastrian in the regions that had been conquered, both Islamic culture and Islamic law were creatively enriched.[8] Thus, through *ijma* and *ijtihad* the classical community of Islam was able to develop the law to meet evolving needs, despite the formal notion that *shari'a* is rigid and immutable.

By the tenth century, however, it was generally felt among the more traditionalist jurists that independent efforts to ascertain God's law were no longer valid and that the door of *ijtihad* should close. Thereafter, with the door shut, or at least presumed shut as a hermeneutical principle, Islamic law became much more formalistic and confined to technicalities. It is probably no coincidence that this conceptual retrenchment corresponded to political retrenchments, for it was in the early eleventh century that Christian powers began to force back Muslim expansion, from Sicily and Spain, for instance.

During the second century after Mohammed's death, a variety of schools of jurisprudence developed, which began to diverge in their interpretations of Qur'an and Sunna. But these divisions are not of major significance regarding the question of proselytizing. Even between orthodox Sunni and heretical Shi'i jurists, interpretations over the obligation of *jihad* primarily differed only over whether the head of the Muslim community, who would lead the *jihad*, must be a divinely appointed religious leader, known as the imam.[9] The obligation to undertake the struggle was held in common.

In fact, universality is a predominant theme within the religion, given its fundamental teaching that Islam is the primordial faith that began with Adam and Eve, the first humans, developed through Abraham and his son Ishmael (Isma'il in the Qur'an), modified by Jesus, and finally coming to revealed fruition with Mohammed.[10] Thus, anyone, of any race, can become Muslim, simply by consciously submitting to God by reciting the *shahada*, the profession of faith, which is the first of Five Pillars of Islam that every Muslim, regardless of location or school of jurisprudence, shares: "There is no God but Allah, and Mohammed is his Messenger."[11] Conversion requires no other initiation ritual, such as baptism in Christianity. As Thomas Arnold and others have emphasized: "Assent to these two simple doctrines is all that is demanded of the convert. . . . Unencumbered with theological subtleties, it may be expounded by any, even the most unversed in theological expression."[12]

Shari'a is, in Islamic doctrine, the "Whole Duty of Mankind," not merely of the Muslims. "But it is nothing less than a Message to all the world" (Q. 68:52).[13] "We have sent thee not, except to mankind entire, good tidings to bear, and warning" (Q. 34:27). Its ethical, moral, and spiritual norms are intended for all. Concomitantly, Islam is a worldwide religious, cultural, and spiritual community that disregards race, nationalism, and territory.[14] Many passages of the Qur'an are accordingly addressed to "humankind" and the "Children of Adam," or refer to Mohammed's message to "all creatures" or "the peoples."[15] Muslims, therefore, have a duty to propagate the Qur'an's message to the rest of humanity, in order to establish a universal civilization. The key questions, then, are, when is that duty to be performed, and how?

ISLAMIC VOCABULARY OF PROSELYTIZING

Although Islam accepts both the Jewish and Christian Testaments as books of revelation, albeit inferior to the Qur'an, it does not adopt their use of the term *proselyte* as either "a resident alien in the land" or one who has left a religious community and converted to another religion.[16] The more positively connoted term *evangelical* is, similarly, of Christian origin, while *missionary* is associated by Muslims with Western colonialism and Orientalist thinking. *Conversion*, too, evokes images of the Crusades.[17]

In modern Arabic, the term *tabligh* roughly translates as "proselytization," while the more classical *al-da'wa* connotes "the call to preaching." But these terms are used much less often than *jihad*, which itself is frequently misunderstood by non-Muslims when translated into English as "holy war." According to contemporary scholar Abdulaziz Sachedina, this misconception is due in part to the writings of individual eighth- to tenth-century Islamic scholars who sought to provide a "religious legitimation for the territorial expansion of the Muslim rulers," overlooking the Qur'an's uses of an entirely different term, *qital*, for military action, and *harb* for military war.[18]

Jihad is perhaps best translated into English as the duty to "struggle" or "sacrifice" in the path of God, based on the Qur'anic use of the term as a means to "make Allah's cause succeed."[19] The struggle can be personal and internal, as against cravings and temptations that prevent one from behaving virtuously, or it can be communal and external, which requires combating evil, establishing a just political order, and spreading the cause of Allah among the unbelievers. "Ye should believe in Allah and His messenger, and should strive for the cause of Allah with your wealth and your lives" (Q. 61:11). In this verse, the phrase containing *jihad* literally means "striving in the path of Allah." But in other passages, the Muslims are directly authorized to fight—in defense against those who aggress against them, or who breach an armistice. "Fight in the way of Allah against those who fight against you, but begin not hostilities. Lo! Allah loveth not aggression" (Q. 2:190). "Sanction is given unto those who fight because they have been wronged" (Q. 22:39). It is unclear in these passages whether being "wronged" and "aggressed against" are generic provocations or refer specifically to being attacked militarily; other verses indicate that provocations include, for instance, "persecution."[20]

Even in the most militant versions of the term *jihad* in the Qur'an, unbelievers were not to be attacked outright without first receiving a summons (*da'wa*) either to convert or to submit to the *jizya* tax that shari'a imposed on non-Muslims.[21] Two passages in the Qur'an support this doctrine:

> Call unto the way of thy Lord with wisdom and fair exhortation, and reason with them in the better way. Lo! thy Lord is best aware of him who strayeth from His way, and He is best aware of those who go aright (Q. 16:125).

> We never punish until we have sent a messenger (Q. 17:15).[22]

These are further supported by a *hadith:* "the invitation to Islam is essential before declaring war."[23] According to Rudolph Peters, "The function of the summons is to inform the enemy that the Moslems do not fight them for worldly reasons, like subjecting them and taking their property, but that their motive is a religious one, the strengthening of Islam."[24]

Like any great book, the Qur'an's one hundred fourteen suras contain verses that support a variety of (even contradictory) perspectives—more militant versions of *jihad* as well as more passive and defensive ones. Contrast harsh passages such as, "But those who did wrong changed the word which had been told them for another saying, and We sent down upon the evil-doers wrath from heaven for their evil-doing" (Q. 2:59), with one that recommends tolerance: "If ye punish, then punish with the like of that wherewith ye were afflicted. But if ye endure patiently, verily it is better for the patient. Endure thou patiently (O Mohammed)" (Q. 16:126-27).[25] Other passages indicate that it is Allah, not the Muslim armies, who is to inflict punishment: "Whoso disbelieveth the revelations of Allah (will find that) lo! Allah is swift at reckoning" (Q. 3:19). "The duty of the messenger is only to convey (the message). Allah knoweth what ye proclaim and what ye hide" (Q. 5:99). Even the most harsh verse from sura 3 indicates that wrath comes later, from heaven, not from Muslims in the here-and-now: "And whoso seeketh as religion other than the Surrender (to Allah) it will not be accepted from him, and he will be a loser in the Hereafter" (Q. 3:85).

Yet classical Islam saw the world as a battleground where Muslim believers and unbelieving infidels waged war. The jurists accordingly divided it into two parts: the territory under Islamic rule, called *dar al-Islam*, and the rest of the world ruled by non-Muslim powers, called *dar al-Harb*, the territory of war, or *dar al-Kufr*, the sphere of unbelief. There was no such state as that of neutrality. A *harbi*, or member of the *dar al-Harb*, was an unsubjugated unbeliever and, by definition, an enemy of Islam. According to Majid Khadduri: "The territory of war was the object, not the subject, of Islam, and it was the duty of the *Imam*, head of the Islamic state, to extend the validity of its Law and Justice to the unbelievers at the earliest possible moment."[26]

But only overtly hostile infidels had to be vanquished; thus, *jihad*, according to some schools of jurisprudence, was only to be invoked defensively. Early scholars such as Abu Hanifa and Shaybani, who stressed tolerance toward nonbelievers, did not say that *jihad* was a war to be waged against non-Muslims on the grounds of disbelief. However, another early scholar, Shafi'i, formulated the doctrine that *jihad* was to be waged on unbelievers for reason of their disbelief, not only when they openly fought Muslims.[27] These varying interpretations are further complicated by the linguistic confusion between the words *surrender* and *convert*, as the Arabic for surrender or submit, *aslama*, is related to the word *Muslim*, literally, "one who submits."[28] Clearly, *some* of the people who submitted, the *dhimmi* People of the Book (discussed below), did *not* also convert.

Intended to protect the welfare of the Muslim community against enemies, *jihad* might be analogized to the modern concept of national security as a justification for state action and all it entails.[29] Like national security, which realistically may be needed to protect the state, the concept of strengthening Islam could also be abused in the form of imperialism abroad and human rights violations at home, particularly given that dying in battle has always been considered the highest form of witness to Allah, for which one will attain paradise in the hereafter.[30] Once force is justified in the name of a greater good, it is a short step to using force arbitrarily and disproportionately. Moreover, it is easy to bootstrap a legitimate justification, used in an appropriate context, into another altogether illegitimate setting.

Jihad, along with its corollary *hijra*, meaning "migration,"[31] has historically served as a rallying cry for territorial expansion of Islamic rule. "[M]igration has been a persistent and recurring feature in the Islamic faith, and its successful evolution and propagation. Migration was intended to protect the faithful from further persecution, weaken the society of 'non-believers,' and enable them to take part in the creation of a new Islamic community."[32] Some Islamic jurists have argued that the only legitimate reason for Muslims to remain outside the *dar al-Islam* (sphere of believers), that is, outside their own states, is for purposes of proselytization (*da'wa*).[33] Indeed, the first *hijra* was that of Mohammed and his followers, who left Mecca for Medina in 622 C.E. It was then that Mohammed engaged in armed battles with the Quraysh tribe, thereby launching the expansion of his power, territory, and claim to a universal message, directed not only to the Arabian peninsula but to the whole world.[34]

CONVERSION TO ISLAM

This section reviews the actual historical record of treatment of non-Muslims during Muslim conquests through the tenth century C.E., followed by an approximation, as best can be reconstructed, of what converting to Islam at that time entailed, both for the individuals involved and the societies as a whole.

HISTORICAL EXPANSION OF ISLAM

By the time of Mohammed's death in 632 C.E., his message had been more or less spread throughout the Arabian peninsula. His immediate successor, Abu Bakr, lived only two more years, which were devoted to crushing a revolt among Arabian tribes who claimed they had only accepted Mohammed's political rule, not his religion. It was the next caliph (*khalifa*), 'Umar ibn al-Khattab (r. 634-44), who began the vast expansion of the empire. One of the first targets was the city of Jerusalem, holy to Jews and Christians, an indication that 'Umar's intentions were religious and not simply military. His forces defeated enemy armies in Palestine, Syria, Iraq, Egypt, and Persia during his ten-year rule. By the end of the first century after Mohammed, the Umayyad dynasty had conquered Spain and North Africa to the West, Byzantium to the North, and India and present-day Afghanistan and Pakistan to the East. The only empires that would later surpass it in contiguous geographical magnitude would be Genghis Khan's Mongol empire and that of the Soviet Union.[35]

Because *jihad* was a permanent duty, truces were only entered into by the Muslim armies on a temporary basis, and only if the vanquished tribe agreed to accept the Islamic order, usually meaning the obligation of prayer and regular giving of financial donations. Following Mohammed's initial agreement with the Meccans to postpone war for a ten-year period, later *khalifahs* entered into treaties that were no longer than ten years in duration. The Hanafi and Maliki schools of jurisprudence, arguing that Mohammed's Meccan treaty actually lasted only three years, limited their treaties accordingly. In typical peace treaties of these kinds, non-Muslim hostages were taken as collateral, in case of breach by the non-Muslims. If the Muslims breached the treaty, they would return the hostages.[36]

Most of what can be said to constitute Islamic international law (*siyar*, literally, "to move"), that is, the law concerning Muslim relations with other nations, is derived not from the Qur'an or Sunna but from juridical scholars writing at the height of the expansionary period, the second century after Mohammed's death. The most prominent of these was al-Shaybani, of the Hanafi school of jurisprudence. Shaybani's conception was not a law of nations but a law of one nation, Islam. All Muslims should form a single state, whose purpose is to conquer non-Muslim nations, to subordinate them to Islam and *shari'a*.[37] But *siyar* must be comprehended in the setting in which it was first developed. In the Middle East of the seventh and eighth centuries, military force was the normal method of conducting foreign relations, so it was therefore natural that Islam should also endorse the use of force in that context. "In doing so, however, shari'a introduced new norms to control the reasons for going to war as well as its actual practice," which was an actual advance over existing customary practices.[38] Indeed, it was not until the end of World War II, over eleven centuries after Shaybani, that international law began to make serious progress in putting limits on justifications for the use of force.

As noted, the Qur'an does not authorize *first strike* attacks on the uncon-verted. In historical practice, territorial expansion did not necessarily correlate to conversion—forcible or otherwise. In the classical era, it probably corre-lated to forcible coercion in only two situations, involving pagans, and Arabi-ans who had become Christian before the birth of Islam. The latter were given the choice of accepting Islam or leaving the Arabian peninsula. "[T]he early Muslims felt that all Arabs . . . should be Muslim. On the other hand, this meant that there was no need to try and cajole non-Arabs into accepting the faith of Islam."[39] Thus, it is not correct to say—as popular Western caricatures of Islam would have it—that Islam the religion was spread by the sword. Only the Muslim political empire was spread that way, imperialism being a conse-quence of, if not an outright motive for, *jihad*.

According to Sachedina, "[U]ndoubtedly there were many instances of *jihad* in Islamic history in which the actual motivation was an interest in territorial expansion."[40] The *dar al-Islam* was not only to be defended but to be spread. As Poston notes in this regard, "[I]n short, the entire program of Muslim ex-pansion may be interpreted as a measure by means of which the world may be made safe for islamicity."[41] Rapid migrations and remigrations within the empire bolstered the military campaigns. In Spain, for instance, a first wave of Arabi-ans and newly converted North African Berbers landed in 710 and were there-after followed by a second wave of Muslim soldiers who had previously been in Syria. It took until about the end of the tenth century for the majority of the indigenous Spaniards to be converted to Islam.[42] "What was required to make the society of the Middle East and North Africa as a whole a single Islamic society was, first, the completion of the conversion process at least to the point at which internal threats to the dominance of the Islamic religion became in-conceivable and, second, the elaboration and spread of a more or less uniform set of social and religious institutions."[43]

WHAT CONVERSION MEANT

In provinces throughout the early Islamic empire, Muslim military governors were appointed and taxes were imposed on non-Muslim subjects who did not convert to Islam.[44] Although different territories would develop distinctive cultural forms, a common Arabic language and urban architecture, not to mention a single coinage (proclaiming in Arabic the oneness of God and the truth of Mohammed's message) and trading system, began to link the wide-spread parts of the Muslim world, in which the non-converted also partici-pated. Indigenous craftsmen were attracted to the urban centers where, over time, they eventually became converts.[45]

But Muslim soldiers, governing administrators, and religious personnel did not engage in any deliberate process of proselytizing. They were usually segre-gated in garrisoned cities (*amsar*) or portions of cities, probably in order to prevent their assimilation into the local cultures; after all, they themselves were usually rather fresh converts to Islam.[46] Instead, conversion of the newly conquered seems to have come about by osmosis, through exposure to an Islamic ambiance, the purpose of which was to allow Islam gradually to pervade the culture at all levels and thus make conversion more socially acceptable than it would have been had Islam remained a completely alien faith. In short, Muslims entered a society at the uppermost levels and extended their influence downward to the masses.[47]

In other words, the military and political conquests of the non-Muslim world were intended, as Poston has remarked, to "create a milieu, an environment in which the Muslim faith could be planted, tended and harvested," an indirect rather than a direct form of proselytization.[48] This followed the Qur'anic injunction: "And if anyone of the idolaters seeketh thy protection (O Mohammed), then protect him so that he may hear the Word of Allah, and afterward convey him to his place of safety. That is because they are a folk who know not" (Q. 9:6).[49]

Of course, for many converts the motive may have been the avoidance of the special taxes and other burdens imposed on non-Muslims rather than a pure attraction to the faith. According to Bulliet, "[T]he initial decision to join the religious community of the rulers had more to do with attainment or maintenance of status than it did with religious belief."[50] Economics played a part in another way as well. In the absence of professional missionaries (which do not exist in Islam),[51] it was primarily itinerant Muslim traders who spread the faith outside of the cities, as well as in lands that were not under Muslim military control, though more by example than by actual preaching. Because the credit system was controlled by Muslims, it was advantageous for a trader to convert, to adopt the Islamic lifestyle that would admit him into the system.[52] The absence of an elaborate ritual or even a course of Qur'anic study made the actual process of conversion quite simple. In fact, as there was no system of registration of new converts, the only way to determine who was a Muslim was to observe who prayed five times a day, who adopted an Arabic name and who adopted proper Muslim dress. In the early period, few of the converts probably had much intellectual knowledge of Islam and may have had actual misinformation.[53]

H. A. R. Gibb believed that the earliest conversions within Arabia occurred on three different levels: (1) a small group of total converts who inwardly accepted Islam's laws and principles; (2) a group of formal adherents, mainly merchants, who accepted Islam's easy outward prescriptions and duties because of the economic advantage of conversion, but who did not assimilate the new faith on a spiritual level; and (3) the pagan tribes whose adherence was enforced by threat of military sanctions.[54] By contrast, outside of Arabia, non-Arab polytheists converted to Islam with such alacrity that they far outnumbered the ruling Arab class and often caused fiscal crises by becoming exempt from the poll taxes.[55]

Nevertheless, despite Mohammed's proclamation that "all Muslims are brothers," non-Arab converts were not always received wholeheartedly. Although often well educated, they were rarely accepted socially and had to attach themselves to an Arab family or tribe as clients (*mawali*). In Spain, the *mawali* eventually became Arabicized, causing this meaning of the term *mawali* itself to disappear by the eighth century. But in the eastern part of the empire the Arabs were ultimately absorbed by their subjects, and while Islam remained the dominant religion, Iranian, Turkish, Berber, and Indian culture prevailed.[56]

CONVERSION FROM ISLAM

This section of the chapter focuses on the early restrictions placed on non-Muslims' practice of their own religion, which were both explicitly and implicitly intended to discourage conversion of Muslims, followed by an exploration of classical Islam's attitude toward its own adherents who did leave the faith, the apostates.

RELIGIOUS LIMITATIONS ON NON-MUSLIMS

While Muslims have a duty to propagate Islam among non-Muslim infidels, *shari'a* prohibits non-Muslims living under Muslim rule from propagating their faith among Muslims and from preventing one of their own from converting to Islam.[57] However, "recognition of the right of non-Muslims to live according to their convictions and at the same time in peaceful harmony and close cooperation with Muslims was one of the Prophet's prominent achievements," according to a contemporary commentator.[58]

Non-Muslims in the *dar al-Islam* were treated differently, depending on whether or not they were People of the Book—those whose faith was based, like that of Muslims, on revealed scripture (*ahl al-kitab*). Islamic law granted the protected status of *dhimma* (meaning "contract" or "guarantee") to communities of the other scriptural monotheisms, Christianity, Judaism, and Zoroastrianism. Freedom to practice their religion, including freedom from pressure to convert, was one of the traditional privileges of *dhimmis* (also known as *kitabis*).[59] This freedom also included protection from desecration of their holy sites and autonomy in appointment of religious leaders, as well as juridical autonomy in civil matters and equality with Muslims of punishment and restitution in criminal matters.[60] Mohammed had decreed that the People of the Book be treated with tolerance. "Lo! those who believe, and those who are Jews, and Sabaeans, and Christians—whosoever believeth in [God] and the Last Day and doeth right—there shall be no fear come upon them, neither shall they grieve" (Q. 5:69).[61] The justification was that monotheistic, revelatory religions that originated before Islam were embryonic, incomplete, and flawed, if not distorted, versions of Islam itself, but deserving of at least a limited tolerance.

The Sunna reports the Prophet as stating: "Whoever wrongs a *dhimmi* or lays on him a burden beyond his strength, I shall be his accuser on the Day of

Judgment."[62] Mohammed guaranteed to the Christians of Najran and the neighboring territories that

> the security of God and the pledge of his Prophet are extended for their lives, their religion and their property—to the present as well as the absent and others besides; there shall be no interference with [the practice of] their faith or their observances; nor any change in their rights or privileges; no bishop shall be removed from his bishopric; nor any monk from his monastery; nor any priest from his priesthood, and they shall continue to enjoy everything great and small as heretofore; no image or cross shall be destroyed; they shall not oppress or be oppressed; they shall not practice the rights of blood vengeance as in the Days of Ignorance; no tithes shall be levied from them nor shall they be required to furnish provisions for the troops.[63]

Nevertheless, *dhimmis* were conquered peoples who had agreed to submit to Muslim rule. The benefits of the *dhimma* contract carried concomitant burdens, the badges of *dhimmis'* second-class status. *Dhimmis* could not hold political or judicial office outside their local community structure and could not testify in litigation involving Muslims. They could not marry Muslim women and were forbidden to carry arms, to ride horses or mules, to walk in the middle of the street, to sell their books or religious articles in marketplaces, to raise their voices during worship, or to build churches or synagogues, tombs or houses, higher than those of Muslims. *Dhimmis* were also required to wear distinctive clothing and hairstyles, which set them apart from Muslims, and to stand in the presence of Muslims.[64] They were not to convert Muslims to their religion or prevent one of their own from converting to Islam. Moreover, if the People of the Book refused the *dhimma* compact, in theory they had only the choice of death or conversion to Islam—either before or after their defeat in war.

The other class of non-Muslims who were not *dhimmis* were slaves, the fate of polytheists and idolaters who had been captured as prisoners of war rather than slain in or after battle. They had the choice only of slavery, conversion to Islam, or death; no special communal contract allowed them to practice their religion quietly or even humbly. "Then, when the sacred months have passed [when a treaty with idolaters has expired], slay the idolaters wherever ye find them, and take them (captive), and besiege them, and prepare for them each ambush. But if they repent and establish worship and pay the poordue [that is, convert to Islam], then leave their way free. Lo! Allah is Forgiving, Merciful" (Q. 9:5).

The Islamic toleration of slavery offered various advantages to Muslims— "economically, through the profitable slave trade, socially through the institution of concubinage and the harem, and politically as individual slaves gained power as favorites, bodyguards, and rulers."[65] But like the *dhimma* compact that established a legal segregation of Muslims and non-Muslims, with clearly inferior status for the latter, slavery could also be justified on theological grounds:

> Since the Islamic state is basically an ideological state, only those persons are to be primarily entrusted with its administration who believe in its ideology, are conversant with its spirit, and have dedicated themselves to the promotion of the objectives of the state. . . . This does not mean that the Islamic state taboos the utilization of non-Muslims in the service of the state. This only means that, while availing of the services of non-Muslims, due care should be taken that the Islamic character of the state is not compromised and the ideological demands are not sacrificed on the altar of so called "tolerance."[66]

A further explanation for slavery, which also accounts for the second-class status accorded *dhimma* religions, may expose Islam's defensive attitude about its own potential apostates, a subject to be explored below. The Qur'an warns: "O ye who believe! If ye obey a party of those who have received the Scripture, they will make you disbelievers after your belief" (Q. 3:100). "O Ye who believe! Choose not for guardians such of those who received the Scripture before you, and of the disbelievers, as make a jest and sport of your religion. But keep your duty to Allah if ye are true believers" (Q. 5:57). Bat Ye'or believes these passages may reflect a concern that the Bedouin Arab tribes who staffed the Muslim foreign legions, "many of whom had recently converted from paganism to Islam, could have been attracted by the civilizations of the conquered peoples among whom they were a minority," particularly given that the indigenous religions were more established. "Thus the abasement of the other religions, no less than the privileges of the conquerors, served to reinforce the Muslim Arabs' feelings of superiority."[67] Or perhaps, is it also related to their feelings of insecurity in relation to older monotheisms?

PROHIBITION ON APOSTASY

Because orthodox Muslims consider Islamic law to constitute, comprehensively, the Whole Duty of Mankind, and to be divine, eternal, correct, and immutable, any allegation that all or any aspect of it is less than ideal would inevitably be seen not only as an affront but as a disloyal act of treason against Allah and against the unity and eternal values of the believing community. Such allegations must, therefore, be resisted and punished, in order to protect believers not only from injury but also from the possibility of change, which challenges to immutability represent. Accordingly, in classical Islam, those Muslims who renounced their belief in Islam—who "disbeliev[ed] after having believed"[68]—were considered apostates. On the basis of the Qur'anic verse, "Whoso judgeth not by that which Allah hath revealed: such are disbelievers" (Q. 5:44), some Islamic scholars placed any Muslim who refused to judge or be judged by *shari'a* into that category.[69] One contemporary scholar comments that "apostasy in Islamic law is a much worse offense than the Christian notion of heresy because Islam perceives itself as a political community, not just a religious community. It follows that apostasy is a form of treason against a very basic and all-encompassing group identity and loyalty. . . . "[70]

Apostasy (*ridda*) was one of the seven *hudud* offenses against God, the mandatory punishment for which involved physical pain. (The six others were theft, armed robbery, drinking alcohol, adultery, slanderous claims of unchastity, and armed rebellion against the leadership). Apostasy could be committed by word (blasphemy),[71] by deed, or by omission of a duty, so long as the offender intended the word, act, or omission with awareness of the penalty of death.[72] The *hudud* crimes were those acts that infringed not only on religion but also threatened community interests in public order, thereby requiring state control. For instance, the Qur'an calls for the death, mutilation, or expulsion of those who take up arms against Allah, "create discord on earth and strive after corruption" (Q. 5:33).

No passage of the Qur'an, however, actually specifies any penalty per se for apostasy. The closest approximations state: "And for those who disbelieve in their Lord there is the doom of hell, a hapless journey's end" (Q. 67:6). "And whoso seeketh as religion other than the Surrender to Allah (*Islam*), it will not be accepted from him, and he will be a loser in the Hereafter" (Q. 3:85). Numerous other verses cajole the Muslim into adhering to the faith, to avoid the temptation, ostensibly posed in particular by the People of the Book, to convert, but the exhortation is moral, not penal. Moreover, during his lifetime, Mohammed is said never actually to have executed persons who, once having adopted Islam, later renounced it.

Nevertheless, conversion to another religion was considered apostasy and sometimes in practice carried the death penalty. The Qur'an orders those who "turn back" to enmity to be slain, "wherever you find them" (Q. 4:89). This verse may have justified Mohammed's victory over pagan tribes when he returned to conquer Mecca between the years 624 and 630 C.E. More directly, Mohammed is reported to have said that "he who changes his religion must be killed," unless he repents.[73] This *hadith* is attributed to the period during the wars of apostasy after Mohammed's death, when some of the previously converted Arab tribes in Medina renounced Islam by refusing to pay the alms tax. The first *khalifah*, Abu Bakr, who was keen to legitimize his authority as successor, violently subdued the tribes after reminding them of their agreement with God's Prophet. He may have relied as precedent on Mohammed's order to dismember and slowly kill a band of apostates who murdered Muslim herdsmen and stole their cattle.[74] But Mohammed's original order may have been imposed for murder and theft, not for apostasy. Alternatively, it is possible that the early Muslim leaders and jurists were confused over the Qur'anic tension between religion and politics, thereby improperly treating disobedience, communal betrayal, murder, theft, and perhaps mere breach of contract as apostasy.[75] As the apostates in the original situation had taken up arms against the Muslims, the death penalty could also be considered an act of self-defense in wartime, rather than a criminal punishment during peacetime.[76]

The Qur'anic statement, "There is no compulsion in religion" (Q. 2:256), is often cited to support the view that death was not an authorized punishment for conversion. However, the remainder of that same verse implies that the non-coercion rule applied only to those who convert *to* Islam, not those who leave it: "There is no compulsion in religion. The right direction is henceforth distinct from error. And he who rejecteth false deities and believeth in Allah hath grasped a firm handhold which will never break. Allah is Hearer, Knower" (Q. 2:256). This would constitute a double standard. Although conversion to Islam must be freely chosen, without fear and without coercion, "it is practically impossible," it is often acknowledged, "once inside Islam, to get out of it."[77]

Regardless of the actual punishment rendered, about which there may have been no consensus, it is fair to conclude that conversion to a religion other than Islam was treated as apostasy, a definite crime. And if the apostasy was deemed to constitute an outright act of rebellion or sedition, it could, with Qur'anic sanction, be punished by death. Short of physical death, apostates who did not repent suffered various elements of "civil death," including suspension of the right to dispose of property and to inherit property. Marriage contracts were dissolved upon the apostasy of either spouse, and their children were declared illegitimate.[78]

CONCLUSION: CHOICE OR COERCION?

It is difficult to summarize a body of legal principles that is as open to interpretation as those of *jihad* and *ridda*. Did the Qur'anic principle, "no compulsion in religion," apply to all non-Muslims or only to *dhimmis*?[79] Did it apply only to persons seeking to convert from another religion to Islam, but not vice versa? Assuming that non-scriptural peoples of the *dar al-Harb* were not formally compelled to convert to Islam, if their only choices were to die in battle, serve as slaves for their rest of their lives, or convert, would not the third choice necessarily have been coerced? And if death was, at least under some interpretations, the punishment imposed on Muslims who renounced Islam, is it any surprise that conversion to other religions was generally a rare occurrence? More broadly, if to become—and to remain—a Muslim meant, quite literally, to "submit," how would one know if a case of new or continued "submission" were a voluntary act?[80]

To understand how these questions would have been answered in the first three centuries of the Islamic era, one needs to avoid thinking in twentieth-century individualistic terms, which tends to interpret religious creed as an entirely personal matter. For what if, as Bulliet suggests, "conversion to Islam in the early Islamic period was more a matter of social behavior than of religious belief"?[81] Or if, to most of the peoples who came under Muslim rule, "it did not much matter whether they were ruled by Iranians, Greeks or Arabs," and in fact, they had good reasons for *not* being ruled by Iranians or Greeks?[82]

The Qur'an required but three things of converts: to repent, to pray, and to pay alms (Q. 9:5).[83] To become, or remain, a Muslim in the classical era of Islam was more a matter of outward appearance than a question of either spiritual faith or existential identity. If we can understand this, we should also be able to understand how a sacred book recorded in the seventh century could be reinterpreted in a myriad of ways one, two, or even thirteen centuries later.

5.

CONVERSION TO ISLAM BY INVITATION

*Proselytism and the Negotiation
of Identity in Islam*

———————◆———————

Richard C. Martin

That proselytism has both textual and historical foundations in early Islam
has been set forth in the preceding chapter by Donna Arzt. Arzt has done an
exegesis of the terms often translated as *proselytism*: *da'wa* and *tabligh* (the
latter being a more recent, especially South Asian, usage). Arzt argues that
da'wa must be understood in the context of related concepts, such as the theological and physical arm of Islamic expansion, *jihad fi sabil Allah* (striving in
the Path of God). An important point made by Arzt is that "holy war" is a
much too narrow understanding of *jihad*. Moreover, the Islamic understanding of proselytism and of dealing with the issue of converting into and out of
Islam has significant differences with the phenomena of proselytism and conversion in early and medieval Christianity.

This chapter attempts to bridge what Arzt has established about proselytism
and *jihad* in the early centuries of Islam with the contemporary Muslim theological rethinking of the problem of proselytism in a pluralistic, interconnected,
and often conflicted world, by Farid Esack in the next chapter. The following
pages adduce additional theological implications of *da'wa* in early and medieval Islamic civilization. They explore further the social phenomenon of conversion to Islam and inquire into some of the possible theoretical explanations
for the growth and spread of Islam after the initial waves of Arab conquest.
The question is then raised: What happened when the conquests of the first
decades after the Prophet Mohammed's death reached a period of military
stalemate on the borders with Byzantium, Europe, and Asia; when the caliphate began to weaken in the tenth century; and when a new discourse of *jihad*
emerged to focus on psychological and theological enemies within *dar al-Islam?* The latter part of this chapter will focus on what might be called the

95

"poetics" of religious conflict, the verbal and performative confrontations between Muslims and other faith communities living within and contiguous to lands under Islamic rule. An implicit question in the following pages is whether proselytism, as distinct from missiology or conversion, is a valid category in the comparative study of religions to which a study of Islam can make a contribution.

DA'WA AND EXPANSION: HISTORICAL PERSPECTIVES

The Arabic term most commonly translated as proselytism, *da'wa*, comes from the root *d-'-w,* which means "to summon, call, invite; pray." It appears in various noun and verb forms over two hundred times in the Qur'an. In addition to the frequent meaning of inviting or summoning non-Muslims to Islam, the verb *da'a* and its substantive form *du'a'* mean prayer or supplication to God. As compared to *salat*, the canonical prayer required five times each day of all Muslims, *du'a'* is informal and personal and can be more urgent. Toshihiko Izutzu comments that *du'a'* is structurally the counterpart of revelation, God's sending down his Word to humankind: "Corresponding to the verbal type of communication from God to man, which is nothing but revelation, there is *du'a'* '(personal) prayer,' conversation of the human heart with God, calling on God for His favor and aid, as the verbal type of communication in the ascending direction."[1] Thus God says to Mohammed in Qur'an 2:186: "And when my servants question you about Me, truly I am near; I answer the supplication of the petitioner who cries out to me" (*da'wat al-da'i idha da'ani*). There are many passages like this last one, which indicate that humans often "cry out" to God in times of great need. Another connotation is the Qur'anic taunt to unbelievers: "The gods other than Allah whom they invoked availed them not when your Lord's command came; they gained nothing save ruin" (Q. 11:101). Indeed, God himself calls his creatures to the Straight Path, largely through prophets, the last of whom was Mohammed.

The Qur'an is replete with verses that speak of the successful supplications (*du'at*) of the prophets versus the vain petitions of idolaters and unbelievers. So, too, the latter are blind, deaf, and indifferent to the invitation to the Path of Allah (*da'wa ila sabil allah*). A cultural calk on the notion of calling, inviting outsiders into Islam is to be found, perhaps, in the phenomenon of adepts being called to submit to the discipline of a Sufi master (*pir*) through a dream, still known, for example, in South Asia.[2] The vehicle of dreams as bearers of the call or invitation to become Muslim, or to become *more truly* Muslim, has other expressions in literature, going back to early centuries. According to legend, the patronymic founder of the orthodox (Ash'arite) school of theology, Abu l-Hasan al-Ash'ari (d. 935), was called in a dream to leave the rationalist Mu'tazilite school of theology to found a more orthodox school of thought.[3]

If the historical context of *da'wa* we are trying to understand is the pagan culture of seventh-century Arabia, soon to be infused with the developed religious forms of Judaism and Christianity in Iraq and beyond, the symbolism that forms the subtext of that history is the *Heilsgeschichte* of the Qur'anic worldview. It is not surprising, therefore, that the eschatological significance of *da'wa* is the dreaded "call" from the Summoner, the angel who sounds the trumpet on the Last Day (Q. 20:102-8; see 54:1-8 where the call that goes out on the Last Day is compared to the summoning in the days of Noah).

Arzt has proposed that *da'wa*, when understood in the light of *jihad*, has more to do with politics and expansion of the body politic, such as during periods of military expansion, than with missionary activity as such. For the latter, another phrase that occurs several times in the Qur'an was more fundamental to early theological discourse and connoted a potentially less political notion of *da'wa*, namely, *al-amr bil-ma'ruf wal-nahy 'an al-munkar*, "commanding the good and prohibiting evil." Like *jihad*—striving in every way possible to live in the path of God—commanding the good and prohibiting evil expresses a duty that applies to all Muslims. In the case of "commanding the good," the meaning is to encounter what is contrary to Islamic teaching actively, to witness to the Qur'anic commands and prohibitions in the world of human affairs.

PROSELYTISM AND CONVERSION

That Mohammed and his followers sought to enlarge the nascent Muslim community (*umma*) by asking others to accept Islam is indicated in Muslim scripture (Qur'an) and in the recorded sayings (Hadith) of the Prophet Mohammed. In one signal Qur'an passage we read: "Invite [non-Muslims] in the Way of your Lord in good judgment and with elegant exhortation, and dispute with them concerning that which is the better [Way], for truly your Lord knows best who strays from His Way and He knows best who is guided [in the right Path]" (Q.16:125). Seeking to bring converts to Islam (a connotation of the Arabic term *islam*, which literally means "to submit"[4]) became a significant religious activity in early Islamic history, as the Muslim faith spread with Arab militias throughout Arabia and the Middle East in the seventh century. In the nature of things, proselytism was, therefore, also a political activity. As new convert members from outside the Arab tribal communities in Arabia altered the texture of the Muslim *umma*, theological and legal debates arose about the legitimate composition of the society that was forming under Islamic rule. That society took its rudimentary form in the last ten years of the life of the Prophet Mohammed (d. 632) in Medina. During the next thirty years Arab generals marched into North Africa, pushed back the armies of the Christian Byzantine Empire from Syria north into Anatolia, and soundly defeated the Mazdaean (Zoroastrian) Sasanian Empire of Iran to the east of the Fertile Crescent. This vast new territory was ruled for the next ninety years by the Umayyad Arab Kingdom, based in Syria.

By the middle of the eighth century C.E., after a series of civil wars, Damascus was defeated and replaced by a much more cosmopolitan empire, led at first by the Abbasid caliphs. Unlike the ruling elite of the Umayyad Arab Kingdom, Abbasid politics and society comprised many ethnic groups, languages, and religious communities. Much that came under Islamic rule was not in fact Islamic at all in the religious sense. Christian, Jewish, and other communities continued to live in large numbers under Islamic rule. Yet, Islamic imperial rule, the development of Arabic and later Persian as lingua francas, and the growing influence of Islamic cultural forms on the rest of society produced what Hodgson has called an "Islamicate" society.[5] It was in the early Abbasid period, with its rich social and theological diversity, that Islam—a new universal missionary religion on the world stage—gained enough adherents to become the majority religion within the lands ruled by the caliphs.

Conversion to Islam, then, is part of the broader context in which the study of proselytism must be understood. The purpose of "inviting" non-Muslims to submit to Islam meant renouncing one religion (and religious community) and accepting another, Islam. Michael Morony has made the obvious point, still worth recalling, that virtually the entire first generation of Muslims in the seventh century were adult members of non-Muslim religious communities. Most of those who accepted the call to submit to Allah from 622 to 660 were pagans who worshiped tribal deities ensconced in polytheistic cosmologies.[6] Converts also included Christians, Jews, Mazdaeans (Zoroastrians), and others. In most lands under Islamic rule, however, it was not until the ninth century that Jews and Christians in particular, who had traditional scriptural cosmologies similar to the Qur'anic cosmology, began to convert to Islam in large numbers. And it would be another century before massive conversions would reach a majority Muslim population density and begin to taper off. In the generation of the Prophet Mohammed and the followers and companions who survived him, responding to the call or invitation to become Muslim was a relatively simple and straightforward affair. Sometimes whole tribal communities followed their sheikhs in accepting Islam and Mohammed as their prophet.

Typical of the many accounts of early conversions to Islam is a passage on how the kings of Himyar sent a letter to the Prophet Mohammed, indicating their intention to submit to Islam and reject polytheism (*shirk*). According to Mohammed's chief early biographer, Ibn Ishaq, the Prophet sent these kings the following message in return, thus stipulating what answering the call to Islam entailed. Although the authenticity of this correspondence is subject to question, the text may be taken as indicative of what conversion entailed in nascent Islam:

> In the name of God the Compassionate, the Merciful, from Mohammed the apostle of God, the prophet. . . . I praise God the only God unto you. Your messenger reached me on my return from the land of the Byzantines and he met us in Medina and conveyed your message and your news and informed us of your Islam [lit., submission] and of your killing the polytheists. God has guided you with His guidance. If you do well and obey God and His apostle and perform prayer, and pay alms, and God's fifth

of booty and the apostle's share . . . and the poor tax which is incumbent on believers from [land and property] . . . [t]his is what God has laid upon the believers. Anyone who does more it is to his merit. He who fulfills this and bears witness to his Islam and helps the believers against the polytheists . . . is a believer with a believer's rights and obligations and he has the guarantee of God and His apostle. If a Jew or a Christian becomes a Muslim, he is a believer with a [Muslim's] rights and obligations. He who holds fast to his religion, Jew or Christian, is not to be turned from it. He must pay the poll tax. . . . He who pays that to God's apostle has the guarantee of God and His apostle, and he who withholds it is the enemy of God and His apostle.[7]

The subtext of this passage seems to be that Mohammed's new teaching, which he attributed to the revelations he was receiving from God through the Angel Jibril (Gabriel), was severely challenged by the predominantly polytheist Arab tribes throughout Arabia during his own lifetime. The message of Islam sought its first articulation and raison d'être in a conflicted, agonistic Arabian context.

Unlike the Christians and Jews, who were allowed to remain adherents of their own religions within their own communities, the polytheists posed a serious threat, which had to be dealt with more harshly. Typical of the stories recorded by Ibn Ishaq and his editor of the next generation, Ibn Hisham, is the following, in which Mohammed sent his redoubtable general, Khalid ibn al-Walid, to the tribe of al-Harith ibn Ka'b in Najran, Arabia, ordering him to

> invite them to Islam three days before he attacked them. If they accepted then he was to accept it from them; and if they declined he was to fight them. So Khalid set out and came to them, and sent out riders in all directions inviting the people to Islam, saying, "If you accept Islam you will be safe," so the men accepted Islam as they were invited. Khalid stayed with them teaching them Islam and the book of God and the *Sunna* of His prophet, for that was what the apostle of God had ordered him to do if they accepted Islam and did not fight.[8]

Later in the same passage and in several similar passages, Ibn Ishaq adds that in addition to teaching the Qur'an (at that time, presumably the passage of choice) and the Sunna of the Prophet, he taught them the *ma'alim al-islam*, meaning the characteristic teachings of Islam.[9] In an earlier passage Ibn Ishaq makes the point that commanders like Khalid ibn al-Walid were sent by the Prophet Mohammed to Arab tribes that resisted and opposed him with the instruction to function "as a missionary"; that is to say, "[the Prophet] did not send [Khalid] to fight." When Khalid put to the sword anyway a number of those who had submitted, and news of that reached the Prophet, the latter is said to have "raised his hands to heaven and said, 'O God, I am innocent before Thee of what Khalid has done.'" Mohammed subsequently sent his son-in-law and cousin, 'Ali ibn Abi Talib, to pay the requisite bloodwit, the reparations for the loss of life and property.[10] From this and other reports about the earliest missionary activities by Mohammed's generals and closest companions, we sense the strong but troubled link between spreading the faith and the use of physical force to do so. Qur'anic and prophetic warnings against the use of force in conversion were often subverted by tribal enmity and resistance to the growing success of Mohammed's troops and those of his followers in the next generations.

Curiously, in early and medieval Islam (as well as modern times) there was no technical term in Arabic theological language (like *da'wa* for proselytism) that denoted the general concept of religious conversion. In pre-Islamic culture the Arabs of Mohammed's tribe of Mecca used the term *sabi'* (verb *saba'a*) to mean "one who departs from one religion and adopts another." For example, the Arabs called the Prophet Mohammed a *sabi'* because he left the religion of the Meccan Quraysh to adopt Islam. A *sabi'* could also refer more specifically to a Sabean, an adherent of a pagan religious community that, in the Qur'anic worldview was recognized as being among the People of the Book (*ahl al-kitab*).[11] Only one kind of conversion, *aslama*, "he submitted" (i.e., "became Muslim") is prevalent in the historical literature about such forms of religious change. To become Muslim in the time of the Prophet and the first generations, then, was known by the Arabic verb *aslama*, "he submitted" or "he became Muslim." *Aslama* was the cultural, if not also the linguistic, antonym of *ashraka*, "he associated [other deities with Allah]" or "he committed *shirk*, became a polytheist." No other general theological term for conversion as such was used. Conversion was accepting, and being accepted into, particular religious communities. Conversion to Christianity was known in the early sources as *tamassah* from the substantive form *masihi*, "Christian" (from *masih*, "messiah"). Conversion to Judaism was expressed by *tahawwada* from the noun *hud*, meaning Jew.

Accepting the call to submit to Islam entailed a formulaic response, as the following story about the conversion of Abu l-'As in the second year after the first *hijra* (624 C.E.) indicates. Abu l-'As had married Zaynab, the Prophet's daughter, prior to the moment the divine injunction had been revealed that Muslim women should not marry non-Muslim males. Abu l-'As was a well-to-do trader from Mecca. On his way to Medina with a caravan of goods to visit his wife he was waylaid by troops loyal to the Prophet. Although they captured his goods, he managed to escape and clandestinely found his way to Zaynab's apartment in Mohammed's family compound in Medina, creating something of a problem for his father-in-law, the Prophet. Mohammed said to his men who had captured Abu l-'As's merchandise: "'You know this man's relationship to us, and you have seized his property. If you would do him a kindness and return his property to him, we would like that, but if you do not wish to, then it is God's booty which he has bestowed upon you, and you have a better right to it.' They replied, 'O Messenger of God, we will return it to him.' When it was all returned to him, the grateful and astonished Abu l-'As said: 'I testify that there is no deity but God and that Mohammed is his servant and his Messenger.'" In this case, there seems to have been more carrot than stick; *da'wa* or proselytism is not mentioned at all.

Similarly, when 'Umayr ibn Wahb went from Mecca to Medina in revenge to kill the Prophet, whose forces had captured his son, 'Umayr was spotted and brought to the Prophet. Mohammed revealed that he knew of 'Umayr's plot earlier in Mecca to kill him. When 'Umayr surmised that the Prophet had divine knowledge of what he could not have known through natural means, according to the tenth-century historian al-Tabari,

> he pronounced the *Shahadah* ["I bear witness that there is no deity but God; I bear witness that Mohammed is the Messenger of God"], and the Messenger of God said to the Muslims present, "Instruct your brother in his faith, teach him to recite and understand the Qur'an, and release his captive [i.e., his son] for him."[12]

Again, the story of how 'Umayr came to convert is constructed around motives and causes other than proselytism, although the latter might still have been a factor and simply not mentioned in the story.

POSTSCRIPT ON *DA'WA* IN EARLY ISLAM

Important conclusions may be drawn from these narratives quoted above, which are typical of the biographical and historical literature of early Islam. First, it was polytheists and pagans who became the chief target of proselytism in the time of the Prophet and the next few generations of conquest and territorial expansion. Christians and Jews, though they were permitted to convert to Islam, apparently did not do so in large numbers in the seventh and eighth centuries. In Islamic law and in actual political life they were considered *dhimmis*, scriptuary religious communities that came under the protection of the Islamic imperium. The Mazdaeans of Iran were the only scriptuaries to convert in large numbers during the first two centuries after the Prophet, and the sincerity of their conversion was often under suspicion by Arab Muslims. The other established confessional communities (primarily Christians and Jews) began to convert in larger numbers only in the ninth and tenth centuries, when Islamic populations spread beyond the military encampments into urban centers, such as Baghdad and Nishapur, and the old military encampments themselves, such as the ones at Basra and Kufa, developed into powerful Islamic political and intellectual centers.

Second, the nascent Islamic drive to proselytize and convert pagans and to destroy their religion had a larger context that was contemporary with Mohammed's strong antagonism toward Arabian paganism. During Mohammed's lifetime, in the late sixth and early seventh centuries, Christians were active in Iraq, especially, seeking converts from among the pagans who lived there in large numbers. Michael Morony writes that "toward the end of the Sasanian period [ca. 600] . . . [t]he sites of pagan temples or shrines were appropriated for churches and monasteries. The breaking of idols, destruction of temples, and the building of churches and monasteries in their place is a recurring theme in contemporary Christian hagiography."[13] Indeed, when we realize the extent of Christian (and to a lesser extent Jewish) efforts to destroy various forms of paganism and cults of magic, Mohammed's angry destruction of the idols in the Ka'ba in Mecca during his Farewell Pilgrimage in 632 makes broader historical and Middle Eastern cultural sense, as do the many Qur'anic warnings against associating other deities with Allah, the Arabic term for God. So, too, the loathing Mohammed's closest followers had toward Musaylima and other Arabs who arose as false (rival) prophets toward the end of Mohammed's life and mission is more understandable. According to the ninth-century Arab litterateur, al-Jahiz, Musaylima used to learn the tricks of magicians, snake charmers, and soothsayers in the marketplaces between Iran and Iraq, and he employed them in acts of subterfuge in order to dupe Arabs into converting to his religion rather than Mohammed's Islam.[14] Paganism became the victim of ethical monotheism at first with the rise of imperial Christianity in the fourth century. It may not be wrong to see the active proselytism of pagans by Muslims and Christians in the sixth and seventh centuries as a continuing consequence of imperial monotheism, established first under the emperor Constantine in fourth-century Byzantium.[15] The world from the Nile to Oxus rivers,[16] within which Islamic civilization had spread successfully during the seventh and eighth centuries, was to become more cosmopolitan. Idiosyncratic pagan communities could no longer remain isolated from the larger world. One theory, which we shall examine more closely in the next section, is that the universal cosmologies that Christians (and now Muslims) were retailing held more explanatory power than local deities, with their more parochial cosmologies.

DA'WA AND CONVERSION: THEORETICAL PERSPECTIVES

CONVERSION BY THE SWORD?

Why did Islam attract large numbers of converts from paganism and polytheism in Arabia and elsewhere in the Middle East during the first Islamic (seventh C.E.) century? Why did Mazdaeans and, eventually, Jews and Christians convert to Islam, reaching a peak in most parts of the Islamic world in the tenth century? Social scientists and social historians in recent decades have addressed these questions with new methods and theories.

It has been a longstanding myth from the time of the conquest of Egypt, Arabia, Palestine, Syria, Iraq, and Iran in the seventh century that Islam is a religion of the sword. The earliest critiques of Islam by Christian polemicists held that Islam became a powerful world religion by military expansion and conquest, not by rational or spiritual appeal. In later centuries Islam was accused, accurately in some cases, of forcing conversions, especially of Christians and Jews. These long-held views of Islam induced Sir Thomas Arnold in his famous history of proselytism and conversion (1896) to warn his readers that they

> should clearly understand that this work is not intended to be a history of Mohammedan persecutions but of Mohammedan missions—it does not aim at chronicling the instances of forced conversions which may be found scattered up and down the pages of Muhammadan histories. European writers have taken such care to accentuate these, that there is no fear of their being forgotten. . . . In a history of Christian missions we should naturally expect to hear more of the labours of St. Liudiger and St. Willehad among the pagan Saxons than of the baptisms that Charlemagne forced them to undergo at the point of the sword.[17]

Arnold's prevenient political correctness led him to dismiss the exaggerated claims made against Islam as a religion of the sword and of forced conversions; he regarded such as inappropriate to a discussion of the history of the Islamic mission enterprise. Yet he was in possession of demographic data that would have allowed him to challenge such claims (although his data were inaccurate at points). He stated accurately, it now seems, that "[t]hese stupendous conquests which laid the foundations of the Arab empire, were certainly not the outcome of a holy war, waged for the propagation of Islam." Nonetheless, Arnold believed that the conquests were, in his words, "followed by such a vast defection from the Christian faith that this result has often been supposed to have been their aim."[18] That defection, we now know, was insignificant, or at least not sustained, in the first century of Islam and did not reach a climax until at least the third to fifth (ninth to eleventh C.E.) centuries, depending on the region of Islamic rule, as we shall show in more detail below. Arnold himself, following the views of the Italian Orientalist Leone Caetani, held that "religious interests appear to have entered but little into the consciousness of the protagonists of the Arab armies."[19] We may set aside the claim that the Muslim conquerors were actually passé about Islam and that religion did not figure as a motivating factor in their march on Africa and Asia. However, if forced conversion to Islam had been the impetus behind the conquests, they were a miserable failure. It is more likely that massive and forced conversions were not the motive or the objective or the actual outcome of the Arab militias that quickly and efficiently defeated Byzantine and Sasanian troops in Syria, Iraq, and Iran in the mid-seventh century.

In his history of the early Muslim conquests, Fred Donner has reviewed some of the major theories of why the conquests, carried out by tribal militias from Arabia, were so successful. Writing in the nineteenth century and reflecting much more the hostile view toward Islam mentioned by T. W. Arnold above, Sir William Muir advanced what we would now regard as a racist view; namely, that the Arabs were possessed by an innate drive to plunder and destroy, thus making them victorious over their more civilized neighbors to the north and east. In the early part of the twentieth century Leone Caetani speculated on an ecological explanation, contending that the Arabian peninsula was undergoing an environmental change toward greater desiccation and shrinking of water resources for the pastoral Arab lifestyle. The Arabs were forced into Syria and Iraq and Egypt to survive, according to Caetani. A political theory was advanced by C. H. Becker, who argued that the weakness of the Byzantine and Sasanian empires in the seventh century produced the conditions for successful Arab assaults on larger armies and civilizations. The religious intensity of early Arab Muslims as the chief reason for their military success was emphasized in a theory advanced by G. H. Bousquet. Donner and other contemporary scholars are disinclined to accept single causes of events as extraordinary as the early Muslim conquests. The causes were many and complex. Donner does agree with Bousquet that religion was a factor, but the falling back of Christian and Zoroastrian political boundaries was not due to Islamic religious fervor alone. Donner makes the case that Islam provided a moral force and an organizing set of ideals for social and political formation that transformed the raids into Byzantine and Sasanian territory into a new religious civilization.[20] The historical significance of Islam for Mediterranean and Middle Eastern political economy would take several generations to realize.

Conversion and Cosmology

The historical phenomenon that still lacks adequate explanation is why and how Islamic monotheism displaced tribal varieties of paganism and polytheism so dramatically in the Arabian peninsula itself. The traditional religious view has generally explained conversion through the agency of the outsider, the proselytizer or preacher or bearer of a new revelation. Contemporary historians tend to argue that the changing social, political, and cultural circumstances of those who are converted are necessary, if not sufficient, explanations of conversion. Richard M. Eaton, a specialist in South Asian social history, has studied the conversion in the subcontinent from a comparative perspective. His studies include Christian and Muslim conversion in India, both in medieval and modern times. In order to explain the massive movement from ethnic and local religions to world religions at various times and places in South Asian history, Eaton has applied Robin Horton's "intellectualist theory." Horton himself has worked on conversion in Africa, which has provided ethnographers and historians with ample case studies of conversion from tribal to universal religions, and the competition among the latter for souls.[21]

Horton has noticed in African traditional religions a pattern of cosmological shifts, not unlike those that took place in Arabia during the seventh century when Islam appeared. Many traditional African religions have an impersonal high god who is ritually and spiritually remote from everyday concerns. A second tier of lesser beings consists in gods and spirits and other superhuman beings that are more particular to daily ritual needs, and thus are more personal and familiar. Horton's hypothesis is that as local tribal communities in Africa have been drawn into more cosmopolitan political economies, the more local gods have receded in importance while the high god becomes more powerful and representative of the larger world of the expanding new social and political experience. According to this hypothesis, the cosmological shift or evolution toward a more universal and powerful god within the traditional African worldview has made the intellectual acceptance of Christianity and Islam more feasible. So, too, in Arabia in the sixth and seventh centuries, the Quraysh tribe of Mecca into which Mohammed was born, like Bedouin society more generally, was polytheistic. Local gods, spirits, and jinns inhabited objects and places where Arabs lived their everyday lives. Less formally represented was the high god known as Allah. As Arab tribes were drawn more and more into the wider Near Eastern world of Byzantium and Sasanian Persia (as well as northeast Africa), through trade and the overspilling war between the principal powers, the more the universal Allah grew in importance. Speaking about the more recent African context, Horton concluded: "There is now a very general agreement that the phenomenon of 'conversion' can only be understood if we put the initial emphasis, not on the incoming religious messages, but rather on the indigenous religious frameworks and on the challenges they face from massive flows of novel experience."[22]

Eaton tested Horton's theory on instances of conversion both to Islam and to Christianity.[23] In an article on conversion to Christianity in South Asia, he studied data on three communities in the Naga Hills in South Asia, all of which had been subject to proselytizing by Christian missionaries since the nineteenth century. Separated by rugged mountains from the religious influences of Hinduism, Islam, Jainism, and other more universal religions, the Naga communities had religions described in missionary and census reports as having a high god and many local spirits and deities, some benevolent and other malevolent. With British imperialism came Christian missionary activity, which lasted well into the twentieth century. Missionary proselytism varied in approach and success within the three communities Eaton analyzed. One of his findings was that rates of conversion varied according to various factors, such as how rapidly each community was confronted with larger social and political realities than just the political economy of kin within their local villages. Another factor was that the village which converted more readily was one where the missionaries had identified the Christian god with the high god, because that particular group already had a fairly developed conception of the high god, which was a product of its greater encounter with the world beyond the village. In the case of early Islam, where increased trade and the relevance of the high God "Allah" seemed to go hand in hand, Horton's theory may help us understand how and why Arabs living in the Hijaz in the seventh century converted in remarkable numbers to the new expression of universal religion, Islam. How and why Christians, Jews, Zoroastrians, and members of other universal religions converted to Islam requires more theories as well as methods for adducing and testing them.

MEASURING CONVERSION

How quickly and pervasively did polytheists, Mandaeans, Jews, Christians, and others convert to Islam during the first few centuries? Richard W. Bulliet has studied the problem of how to assess the rates of conversion in six different parts of the Islamic world through the medieval period.[24] Bulliet assumed that the territories conquered by Arab militias during the seventh (first Islamic) century C.E. must have converted to Islam at different rates, given the varying linguistic, religious, and social identities of the inhabitants of lands as disparate as Spain, North Africa, Egypt, Syria, Iraq, and Iran. Islamic institutional development depended largely on the successful process of conversion to Islam, and hence on the rate of conversion. In order to test his theory, Bulliet needed a method for estimating rates of conversion. The method he chose was to measure the changing rate of Arabic/Muslim name-giving, which could be reconstructed from such sources as contemporary biographical dictionaries and historical annals, with their long genealogical chains of authorities for each report. Arabic biographical dictionaries are particularly useful because the long names given for each entry indicate the given names at birth, father or mother of so and so, lineage (son of so and so, son of so and so, etc.), honorifics, and both place and trade affiliation.[25] This method is highly speculative and has drawn some criticism. For example, it assumes the ratio of Muslim to non-Muslim names in Muslim biographical dictionaries represents the ratio of Muslims to non-Muslims in the total population. Nonetheless, Bulliet's method provides the only means of assessing conversion to Islam in those centuries and parts of Africa and West Asia when and where Islamic rule was transformed into Islamic society. Therefore, it is worth reviewing Bulliet's conclusions before returning to the problem of proselytism and conversion.

Bulliet has done most of his work on Iran and the biographical dictionaries of early to medieval Islamic history in Iran. Given the importance of Iran as a large non-Arab land that came under Islamic rule early (by ca. 650) and which retained a strong measure of its linguistic and cultural identity while at the same time converting to Islam at about the same rate as other central lands under Muslim rule, his work on Iran may be taken as indicative of his methods and conclusions as a whole. Bulliet has translated his findings on the rate of conversion in Iran in a graph with an S curve. The curve shows the rate of conversion to be gradual until the eighth (second Islamic) century, the end of the Umayyad Arab Kingdom and the rise of the more diverse Abbasid empire. The curve then rises sharply to represent about 50 percent of the total population of Iran in the middle of the ninth century—the early Abbasid period—and only begins to taper off again at the beginning of the tenth century, at about 75 percent of the population. Bulliet submits that many of the important political developments during the first four centuries can be plotted along this logistic curve, which indicates, in his words, "the degree to which Islam had made converts among the Iranian population." He continues:

An aspiring political leader at one period would have to choose policies and symbols appropriate to a largely unconverted population dominated by an Arab Muslim elite, whereas a similar leader at a later period would have an overwhelmingly Muslim population to deal with. During the period of most rapid increase according to the logistic curve of conversion, the political and religious possibilities could change markedly in twenty or thirty years' time.[26]

An example of the kind of intellectual change that took place at the steepest part of the conversion-rate curves, both in Iraq and Iran, was the transition among intellectuals from Mu'tazili to Ash'ari theology, from Hanafi to Shafi'i legal interpretation.[27] What this meant in the simplest terms was a shift from rationalist theology directed toward disputation with non-Muslims to a neo-Orthodoxy in theology and law that increasingly presumed a strong Sunni Muslim identity within Islamicate society.

Conversion to Islam during the first four centuries was not necessarily the product of *da'wa*, proselytizing non-Muslims. Other factors were probably also at play to produce an increasing conversion rate in the ninth century. Bulliet explains: "Conversion was a one-way street. . . . Islam did not tolerate backsliding. Therefore, the rate of growth was logarithmic. Children of Muslims were Muslims, and each generation's contribution of new converts was a permanent increment. With more Muslims came greater probability of the unconverted population coming into meaningful contact with members of the new faith."[28] *Da'wa* was not an insignificant theological or missionary enterprise, however. As conversion to Islam peaked and began to level off with about 80 percent of the population becoming Muslim, *da'wa* found new focus within Islam in an interesting form, among Muslims themselves. Indeed, the *da'wa* activities of Isma'ili Shi'i Muslims became something of a problem for the ruling elites of Abbasid society in the eleventh and twelfth centuries.

DA'WA AFTER EXPANSION:
CONVERTING THE OTHER IN MEDIEVAL ISLAM

In later generations after the mission of the Prophet (610-32) and the Rightly Guided Caliphs (632-61), the Islamic faith was carried to the newly conquered territories of Arabia, North Africa, Syria, Iraq, and Iran by Muslim missionaries (*du'ah*, singular *da'i*). Sufi mystics, who were often found in the entourages of traders and the armies of local warlords, found their way into Africa and Asia. Many stayed on to preach the message of Islam after the enterprises of commerce and conflict had played themselves out. A more serious form of *da'wa*, politically and theologically, developed among the Shi'a. This might be called "the *da'wa* within," that is, soul wars that erupted in the context of Islamic sectarianism and political dissidence.

THE ISMA'ILI *DA'WA*

Most of the Shi'a, known as the Itha 'Ashari Shi'a or Twelvers, believe eleven imams (charismatic religious leaders and authorities on the Qur'an and Sunna) descended from 'Ali, Mohammed's cousin and son-in-law. Since the Prophet had no sons who survived infancy, descent from the House of the Prophet has been traced through 'Ali. A group of dissident Shi'a in the eighth century believed that the seventh Imam in this line had not been Musa al-Kazim, as the majority believed, but his older brother Isma'il, whom Sunnis say predeceased his father, the sixth Imam. These became known as the Seveners and also as the Isma'ili. They claimed that Isma'il had not died but had gone into occultation (*ghayba*) and that he would appear again as the *mahdi*, the messianic-like figure in Islamic apocalypticism who is expected to return to this world to restore social justice. (The Twelvers in the next century were to claim that the twelfth Imam, a descendant of Musa al-Kazim, was the one who went into *ghayba* and would return as the *mahdi*.)

Whereas for Twelver Shi'a (the majority) the appearance of the Hidden Imam is an eschatological belief and still anticipated, for Isma'ili Shi'a the Imam appeared in history to lead revolts and other subversions against oppressive regimes. The Isma'ili Shi'a generated a virulent form of messianism in medieval Islam. Like the Shi'a generally in the early centuries of Islam, the Isma'ili formed a minority that was often persecuted by the Abbasid rulers and their Sunni judges and theologians. The Abbasid discourse against the Shi'a is recorded in Sunni historiographical and theological literature. Sunni intellectuals disputed the Shi'i claim that Mohammed had designated 'Ali, his cousin and son-in-law, to be leader (*imam*) of the Muslim community (*umma*). While the Twelvers and another group known as the Fivers made certain accommodations to Sunni theological and juridical practices, settling for social space as a minority within or on the fringes of Abbasid society, the Isma'ili went underground to pursue a sometimes violent posture against medieval Islamicate society, as in the case of the Assassins of Alamut. They also possessed the ability to construct a rival Shi'i Isma'ili government and society, as in the case of the Fatimids of North Africa and Egypt (909-1171). At the heart of their conflict with orthodox Islamic polities and religious authority was their own *da'wa*.

Shi'ite Muslims trained as religious propagandists (*du'ah*) in Isma'ili states and enclaves in North Africa and Egypt, and subsequently in the mountainous region south of the Caspian Sea known as Daylam. This form of proselytism was directed toward (some would say against) the Sunni Abbasid Empire in Iraq and Iran. The absolute teaching or *ta'lim* of the various Isma'ili movements,[29] such as the Fatimids, Qarmatians, and Assassins, was not directed outward toward pagans, Christians, and Jews, but rather within Islam toward Sunni Muslims, and, more specifically, against the Abbasid state. Elsewhere in this volume we learn of reformist forms of proselytism in the modern world: proselytism to bring secular Jews and Christians back to the true faith. Although the Isma'ili *da'wa* was directed toward other Muslims, the intent was not reform. Rather, it can be understood as a form of minority subversion. The Abbasid Empire was beginning to crumble, first at the hands of the Buyid warlords, themselves mostly Shi'i (945-1055), and then the Seljuq Turks, who were rigidly Sunni (1055-1258). The most daring and chilling effect of the Isma'ili *da'wa* for Abbasid rulers and Sunni intellectuals came in 1092, when the erudite Sunni vizier (prime minister) and patron of learning, Nizam al-Mulk, was assassinated in Baghdad by an agent of the Isma'ili sect known as the Assassins.

The more extreme expressions of the medieval Isma'ili *da'wa* generated a religious and political counterculture not unlike the militias and Christian Identity in the United States in the latter part of the twentieth century. In the Isma'ili case, Gnostic cosmological doctrines evolved out of the Qur'an and the sayings of the Prophet Mohammed, as well as the teachings of earlier Shi'i imams. The Shi'i concept of *da'wa* generally held that Muslims could not decide matters of religious doctrine and practice on their own authority. Yet the public understandings of Islamic doctrine and practice, by which the majority of Muslims lived, informed by the scholarly disputes and interpretations of the *'ulama*, the learned scholars of Qur'an and Sunna, were radically transformed by the Isma'ili theologians and *da'is* (agents). Propounding a Gnostic understanding of sacred and religious textuality, the Isma'ili agents appealed to Sunni Muslims to see that sacred texts had both an outer (*zahir*) and an inner (*batin*) meaning. Sunni Islam, with its religious duties, *'ulama*, schools of law, social codes of conduct, and so forth, practiced the *zahiri* meaning of Qur'an and Sunna. The *batini* or secret, interior meaning of revelation and Mohammed's interpretation of revelation (the Qur'an) were known only to Mohammed, who passed it on to 'Ali, who passed it on through the imams to Isma'il, and on to the Isma'ili leaders and agents who brought these secret teachings to ordinary Muslims living under Abbasid rule. The Shi'i theology of transcendence was such that the meaning of revelation had to be mediated through the imams—those chosen by God to receive those meanings from Mohammed through 'Ali; to assume that ordinary Muslims could grasp and teach the *ta'lim*, the interior doctrine, was a form of blasphemy. That the Isma'ili *da'wa* was successful to a degree is given evidence by the bloody response of Abbasid troops sent against various Isma'ili communities and agents. The actual appeal of the *da'wa* was characterized by Hodgson thus:

> The summons to allegiance to the imams descended from Ja'far's son Isma'il was called the Isma'ili da'wa. Representing this da'wa, travelling *da'is*, summoners, aroused and directed from a concealed central headquarters a general attack against the Baghdad Caliphate and against other rulers who theoretically recognized its authority. The appeal to the nomads would have been a combination of plunder, Shi'ite loyalism, and tribal independence; to the settled populations it was the usual Shi'a promise of justice as against the apostate and usurping dynasties of the world.[30]

PROSELYTISM AND CONVERSION IN MEDIEVAL LITERATURE

We turn now to ask whether *da'wa* became an object of theological specula-
tion and legal determination in the Abbasid Age after the main expansion of
Islam—when Christians, Jews, and other protected religious communities
constituted the largest category of non-Muslim others within Islamicate society. On a simple level, the answer is that the term *da'wa* receives no heading or subheading in the theology *(kalam)* manuals composed in the ninth to
eleventh centuries. Nor does it form a category or subcategory of discussion
in law manuals, the more modern summaries of which can be found in such
works as *Kitab al-fiqh 'ala l-madhahib al-arba'a (Book of Fiqh According to
the Four [Sunni] Schools)* by 'Abd al-Rahman al-Jaziri, or *al-Fiqh 'ala l-
madhahib al-khamas* by Muhmammad Jawid al-Mughniyya. By the time
Islam had established itself as the predominant religion in the tenth century,
da'wa became less effective as a way of dealing with non-Muslims, especially
those who lived as *dhimmis* (people with scriptures under the protection of
Islamic law).

The textual record of theological disputes with non-Muslims is rich, and to
this we will turn below. No *mutakallim* (theologian), however, posed his arguments with Christians and Jews about God, prophets, and scriptures as *da'wa
ila sabil allah*, an invitation to submit to Allah and the Islamic way of life, the
way the Qur'anic and early historical narratives, discussed above, had done.
That more urgent function of *da'wa* was more characteristic, as was shown
above and in the preceding chapter, of nascent Islam in Arabia and during the
first decades of conquest and expansion, especially in regard to pagan Arabs
and nonscriptured peoples.

Already during the ninth and early tenth century it was primarily *dhimmi*
faith communities, such as Christians and Jews, not the pagans, polytheists,
and prophetic pretenders of Mohammed's time and that of his immediate successors, that constituted the other with which Muslims had to deal. The missionary impetus to invite non-Muslims to submit *(islam)* and actively to command the good and prohibit evil was transformed into a poetics of religious
disputation, a warring with words, among Muslim sects and between Muslims and other scriptuaries. Inviting non-Muslims to accept Islam, as a religious duty, is not referred to by the noted early jurist of Medina, Malik ibn
Anas (d. 795), in his well-known extant text, *Kitab al-muwatta'*. Nor is *da'wa*
a main or subheading in the major Hadith collections, which, having been
compiled in the ninth and tenth centuries, reflected the taxonomies of major
social and legal interest in the early Abbasid Age. Where reference to *da'wa* is
found in these manuals and collections is primarily under the heading of *jihad*,
and even there the mention of it is surprisingly slight. Confronting the other,
the non-Muslim, evolved into verbal rituals that were at once more structured
and, the historical record seems to show, more entertaining among Muslims
and other faith communities with which they were willing to negotiate. Proselytizing did continue in various locales, but a strenuous, somewhat universal

discourse about the need for *da'wa* directed at non-Muslims does not reappear until the postcolonial age in the twentieth century.

When we put the question differently, asking as we did above, whether, when, and how non-Muslims converted to Islam during this period, the answer has to be that Christians and others did convert to Islam in the ninth and especially the tenth (fourth Islamic) century. Often, it seems, they did so voluntarily, for reasons other than force. Social historians like Eaton and Bulliet have gone beyond the strictly theological and legal texts of this and later periods to adduce the social, political, and economic factors that would explain why, in specific contexts, people convert to a universal missionizing religion. Another factor, studied by Maya Shatzmiller, is gender. Voicing a critique of Bulliet's quantitative methods, Shatzmiller says of the first three centuries: "Any attempt to discuss the size of the convert community in definitive terms, as some historians have done, without taking women into account, is hazardous at best, if not entirely misleading."[31]

Conversion (as opposed to proselytism) was discussed in the law manuals and Hadith collections under the heading of marriage (*nikah*). Thus, the medieval Islamic discourse about conversion was largely a gendered and often an economic matter. Shatzmiller also discovered a rich source of information about conversion, especially of women to Islam, in recorded conversion certificates. These consisted in a credal declaration of several parts, followed by a discussion of the legal issues that pertained to property and other rights. The latter often stipulated what property a woman could or could not bring as a Christian, Jew, or pagan to the new or reconstituted marriage under Islamic law. She examined in particular a set of documents from tenth-century Spain pertaining to Christian, Jewish, and pagan males and females, all of whom converted to Islam. The documents were prepared by notaries and thus were formal and detailed. Shatzmiller concluded that a wife's conversion to Islam was not a necessary legal consequence of her husband's conversion. "Conversion," she concluded, "was an individual undertaking, and the law regarded it as such."[32] Not surprisingly, the superior rights and powers of males in Muslim marriages applied to converts as well. Nonetheless, Islamic law was generous in granting property rights and in allowing women, including convert women, to manage and dispose of their property. A woman who converted on her own and then married under Islamic law could keep her own property separate from her husband's. Muslim women, including converted women, could earn and keep wages, as well as income from property they rented. More study of marriage law and conversion certificates is warranted in order to establish more clearly the reasons why non-Muslims converted, or not, during the Islamic Middle Ages.

Though a full review of such literature on conversion to Islam lies beyond the task of this chapter, the general conclusion of social historians and others writing on this topic has been that social (including marital), economic, and political reasons, and not changed theological convictions, often explained why non-Muslims chose, usually more or less freely, to convert to Islam. We next move toward a conclusion of this chapter by considering the theological expression of *da'wa* in an age when elective conversion was on the increase, the eighth to tenth (second to fourth Islamic) centuries.

THE POETICS OF *DA'WA* AS THEOLOGICAL CONFRONTATION

The earliest theologians (*mutakallimun*) had sought to rationalize the call to Islam in the face of increasing civil strife and sectarian factionalism in the eighth century. It was necessary to sort out scriptural and rational answers to such questions as Who is a Muslim?, Does sin require punishment?, and Who should decide that—God or the Muslim *umma*? The theologians also undertook disputations with Christian, Jewish, Manichaean, and other missionaries and agents working within the lands increasingly coming under Islamic rule. Known as the *Mu'tazila*, the theologians in the late eighth and early ninth centuries established as one of the five pillars of their theological system, in addition to God's unity (*tawhid*) and justice (*'adl*), the active stance discussed previously of commanding the good and prohibiting evil (*al-amr bi l-ma'ruf wa l-nahy 'an al-munkar*). Commanding the good and prohibiting evil was in fact a Qur'anic injunction. Qur'an 22:41 refers approvingly to "[t]hose who, if We empower them in the land, establish the Canonical Prayer (*salat*) and pay the Tithe for the poor (*zakat*) and command the good and forbid evil." In Qur'an 9:112, this phrase is added: "and those who keep the absolute commandments (*hudud*) of God and give glad tidings to believers," thus adding moral force to the duty to bear witness among non-Muslims. Commanding the good and prohibiting evil became the scriptural and theological basis for the earliest Muslim theologians to carry their construal of Mohammed's mission to the world.[33]

The *mutakallimun* were scholarly practitioners of oral and written *kalam*, the term for the formal discourse about such matters as God, God's attributes, God's messengers to humankind, other religions, and the valid leadership of the Muslim *umma* (the Imamate). The art of disputation (*mujadala*) lent itself to *kalam*. So did the multi-faith cultural environment of the Middle East in which Islam emerged and which it soon came to dominate politically. Recall the Qur'anic passage (16:125): "Invite [non-Muslims] in the Way of your Lord in good judgment and with elegant exhortation, and dispute with them concerning that which is the better [Way], for truly your Lord knows best who strays from His Way and He knows best who is guided [in the right Path]." The Qur'an presumes and anticipates a dialogical, disputational context for the propagation of its teachings. It is also important to note that the Arabic term *mutakallimun* applied to Christian and Jewish theologians as well as to Muslims. The *mutakallimun* were, among other things, spokespersons for their religious communities in public debates. The rules of engagement by which they operated when they debated with one another were known as *adab al-jadal*, the art of disputation. The verbal noun for this highly developed public debating skill was *mujadala*, and its synonym *munazara*.

The verb *jadalahu* in the third form means "he contended in an altercation, or disputed, or litigated with him." In the Qur'an, *mujadala* often meant disputing with the Arabs of Mecca, who followed the religious form of polytheistic paganism, referred to above, known as *shirk*. The *da'wa* or calling them to the Guidance was often met not with acceptance and conversion but rather with disputes and vain arguments of resistance. Indeed, in the Qur'anic cosmology it is Satans who inspire unbelievers to dispute with Mohammed and believers (Q. 6:121). There was, in fact, an eschatological urgency for believers to take on nonbelievers. Yet it is a theme of both the Meccan and the Medinan suras of the Qur'an that those who disbelieve, the *kuffar*, dispute using falsehoods and lies (Q. 18:56; see 22:3,8; 31:20).

Among the jurists and theologians after the early conquests and expansion, *mujadala* had the technical meaning of "he compared evidences [in a discussion with another person, or persons] in order that it might appear which of those evidences was preponderant." *Mujadala* additionally had the connotation of "disputing respecting a question of science [i.e., religious and legal sciences] for the purpose of convincing an opponent, whether what he says be wrong in itself or not."[34] By the eighth and ninth centuries C.E., religious disputation became an art form practiced by scholars and theologians among the various religious communities comprised by Islamicate culture; students of law, theology, and other religious disciplines trained in the rhetorical and dialectical art of *mujadala* (or *munazara*). Educated Muslims, Christians, Jews, philosophers, atheists, poets, politicians, and others would gather for an evening of entertainment while two famous jurists or theologians disputed points of doctrine, law, or Arabic grammar.[35]

Not all Muslims saw the dialectics of religious disputation, following rules of debate, among religious intellectuals in Abbasid society as a good thing for Islam. For these followers of Ahmad ibn Hanbal, the Islamic *da'wa* could not be negotiated with non-Muslims, indeed, not even with non-Sunni Muslims. A traditionalist scholar, Abu 'Umar Mohammed ibn Sa'di al-Faqih, during a visit to Baghdad, was asked by his host one day if he had attended the sessions of the *mutakallimun*. He replied that he had done so twice before leaving, never to return. "Why?" he was asked. Abu 'Umar described a hall that was crammed with members of all the sects, including Sunni Muslims, the innovators (referring to Shi'a and Mu'tazili theologians), Zoroastrians, Materialists, Manichaeans, Jews, Christians, and other unbelievers. Each sect had its own head who spoke (i.e., a *mutakallim*) on behalf of his religious school or doctrine (*madhhab*) and debated about it. If the head of any sect whatsoever, Muslim or non-Muslim, came forward, the entire assembly stood and remained standing until he sat, a show of respect that

Hanbali Muslims were loathe to confer on any but their own *'ulama* in Abbasid society and, even then, sparingly. One session Abu 'Umar attended was convened by a *mutakallim* from among the unbelievers who said to those assembled:

> You are gathered for the purpose of disputation. The Muslims shall not argue against us, using their Book (Qur'an) or the sayings (Hadith) of their prophet, for we do not recognize these as truth. . . . We will conduct the disputation only with rational argument and with what *nazar* [speculative reasoning] and *qiyas* [analogical reasoning] will permit.

When asked by his interlocutor if the other Muslims present were willing to dispute with non-Muslims and were satisfied with the ground rules that limited the disputation, Abu 'Umar conceded (disapprovingly, we may assume) that they seemed to be.[36]

What seemed to matter most, when the Islamic *da'wa* was transformed by the ending of conquest and the beginning of rule over a diverse commonwealth of cultures and confessional communities, was the expression of the "invitation" in rational and intellectual, rather than confrontational and absolute, terms. The need to make a case for Islam among scriptuary communities in particular, even those under Islamic rule, called for theological finesse, not physical force, though the latter was never entirely absent. The difficulty yet promise of the situation already in early Abbasid times can be seen from the following quote from a Nestorian polemicist, author of *Kitab al-masa'il wa-l-ajwiba (Book of Questions and Answers)*, which was written to prepare Christians to be able to negotiate their theological identity among Muslims and other People of the Book:

> How are we to distinguish between a religion having an order and consistency, which depends on signs and proof (*burhan*), and a religion that is due to human contrivance, having no signs or proof? We see many different peoples professing contrasting religions. In their possession are scriptures that differ about commands and prohibitions, laws and statutes, as well as raising [of the dead] and resurrection. Each sect of them claims that their book is God's covenant for his creation, which his messengers have brought, and that in its behalf he has made manifest his signs and his proof at their hands.[37]

If the reference to the raising of the dead and resurrection were dropped from 'Ammar al-Basri's words, the text could just as easily be Muslim or Jewish, right down to the technical terms of this kind of discourse. Only the atheists and philosophers, who also took part in disputes with Muslims and other confessional theologians, would have demurred at the claim that scripture was backed by divine assurance.

In disputing their differences with Christians, Jews, Zoroastrians, and others over which community is truly in possession of the Truth—which prophet or envoy had most completely delivered his community from the errors and ignorance of other religious communities—the Muslims and their theological opponents had found ways to ritualize communal conflict. Through their theological debates, they were able both to define and to manage the conflicts that naturally arose among confessional communities sharing a public language (Arabic in most cases) and culture (Islamicate, in Hodgson's sense). The traditionalists and other fundamentalist (*usuli*) reformers looked back into their Qur'anic and cultural heritage and saw the religious other as far too serious a threat to be engaged on equal ground. Similar to Abu 'Umar in the quotation above, traditionalists like Ibn Hanbal (d. 855), Ibn Taymiya (d. 1328), Mohammed ibn 'Abd al-Wahhab (d. 1787), and the Muslim Brothers in Egypt in the twentieth century have preferred sharper boundaries between Muslims and non-Muslims. The concept of *shari'a*—divinely revealed ritual, ethical, social legislation—and recollection of a putative moment when the Muslim umma was governed entirely by the *shari'a*, have been the inspiration of traditionalist reform movements throughout Islamic history. The Mu'tazilites and other Muslims who engaged in these verbal forms of combat with their spiritual enemies were presumably no less willing to witness to their faith than the Hanbali traditionalists who refused to grant Christians, Jews, and other non-Muslims a public hearing.

FINAL THOUGHTS

The argument of this chapter has been that once the conquests had more or less reached stasis, and the pagan Arabs had either been converted or isolated from political participation in the developing Islamicate society, the original, rather pointed *invitation* to convert to Islam became largely sublimated or otherwise transformed into controlled rituals of theological disputation. It was a form of conflict management that worked reasonably well for about three centuries.

Learning to dispute, yet accommodate, ritual and doctrinal differences was an important achievement of Islamicate society in the early centuries of the Abbasid Age (750-1055). Although Christians, Jews, and other non-Muslim scripturaries were severely restricted by Islamic law in their ability to proselytize Muslims, the Mu'tazili rationalist influence in Islam permitted and encouraged non-coercive disputes in which all interested parties could participate. These verbal, performative skirmishes were rather widespread in medieval Islamicate culture, producing both a literature about such debates, as well as separate treatises by Muslims, Jews, or Christians for their own communities on how to engage the other (the latter often in the vernacular languages of the given faith community).

Those discursive patterns and public performances did not last much longer, however. By the ninth century the Mu'tazilites were under severe attack by newer theologians, who undertook to defend the more puritanical, traditionalist expression of Islam represented by Ahmad ibn Hanbal and his followers. By the eleventh century the Mu'tazili influence was all but gone, save for a few places of retreat, in the Yemen and Central Asia. The new theologians, the Ash'arites, though often at odds with the Hanbalites themselves, attacked and destroyed the more porous boundaries between Islam and other religions, replacing them with more clearly defined walls between Sunni Muslims and others. The new orthodoxy was rooted less in rational argument and more in the authority of revelation. It should not be overlooked in this regard that the authority of the Abbasid caliphate began to crumble in 945, the first European Christian crusade began in 1095, followed by the Mongol invasions, destroying Baghdad in 1258. The need for stronger walls that clearly defined Islamic identity—and all else as forms of otherness that should be avoided, even in controlled disputes—is not difficult to imagine.

The twentieth century has seen a return of interest among Muslim intellectuals in Mu'tazili theology and the rationalist critique of Hanbali and other forms of traditionalism. The label often applied to this movement in general is Islamic modernism.[38] While very few modernists or neo-Mu'tazilites practice medieval dialectics with their opponents, the spirit of open, rational inquiry and discursive encounter with theological and religious opponents of Islam is to be found among a growing number of Muslim intellectuals and in their books and treatises. They generally argue two things: First, that Islam continues to be a valid way of life for humankind; indeed, some like Hassan Hanafi, professor of philosophy in Egypt, believe that Islam is more able, because of its historical embracing of religious pluralism, to replace Christianity as the intellectual background for the comparative study of religion in the next century. Second, the modernists also believe that Islam must adapt to the post–World War, indeed, post–Gulf War intellectual, political, and cultural conditions. The views defended by Farid Esack in the following chapter are indicative of the new wave of Islamic modernism among younger Muslim theologians. Yet, as Esack warns us, the tendency to develop and maintain sharp boundaries between orthodox Sunni Islam and non-Muslims is still quite strong and deeply engrained within the traditionalist Muslim faith community.

These two ways of "calling" or "inviting" humankind to Islam—the rationalist and the traditionalist—are really quite old and, I would argue, equally rooted in Islamic worldviews. As in the Abbasid Age, renewal and reform seems to be the impetus of the traditionalist expression of Islam, sometimes called Islamist and sometimes fundamentalist. Their work, throughout Islamic history, has been to restore an imagined pristine Islamic past. The more ardent traditionalists imagine a future in which all of humankind will answer the call and submit to Allah or, as in the early days of Islam, accept dhimmi status. The movement with stronger intellectual links to the non-Muslim world, known as

Mu'tazilism in the past and *modernism* at the moment, has usually been on the defensive against traditionalist Islam. Nonetheless, this view of Islam persists. It imagines a future in which Muslims and non-Muslims will use their religious traditions as separate resources for solving the problems of humankind. The more ardent among them believe that in the future such solutions will become Islamo-centric, replacing European modernism in the next century.

6.

MUSLIMS ENGAGING THE OTHER AND THE *HUMANUM*

———————◆———————

Farid Esack

Call unto the path of your Lord with wisdom, and good counsel, and engage them by those means which are the finest.

—Qur'an 16:125

INTRODUCTION

How do Muslims engage the religious other in a world that increasingly defies geographical, political, religious, and ideological boundaries? This is a world where the "enemy" is often the internal self (the Saudi, Iranian, or Sudanese regime, or the Shi'a, Qadiani, or modernists), and the asylum provider is the external other (Christian relief organizations, Amnesty International, or the non-Muslim neighbor). How do Muslims respond when we come face to face with the *humanum*, the essentially human, and its manifestation in lives of a tireless quest for compassion and commitment to justice that the other may lead? How do the various forms of engagement with the other facilitate or militate against efforts to challenge unjust socioeconomic systems and create possibilities for more humane alternatives?

The first part of this chapter is a broad overview of the various ways in which different tendencies among Muslims relate to the other, along with a brief comment on the ideological function of each. This relationship is discussed within a broader context of liberalism and globalization. A liberal

---

Another version of this chapter appears in Abdullahi Ahmed An-Na'im, ed., *Proselytization and Self-Determination in Africa* (Maryknoll, N.Y., 1999) and is used herein with the permission of the publisher.

critique of overt religious or ideological proselytism often occurs when the object to which one is invited is nonmaterial (faith, God, or salvation) but accepts more obviously similar covert *selling* when the objects are clearly material in the form of market commodities.

The second part of this chapter advocates an alternative to the form of proselytization that regards the other as being in various states of damnation. Despite the risk of essentializing Muslims, after locating myself within the debate about Muslims and the other, I nevertheless state the three main generalized assumptions that underpin my own understanding of Muslim responses to the question of engaging the other and the *humanum*.

The conclusion calls for intra-religious and extra-religious "proselytization" based on liberating praxis aimed at creating a world of socioeconomic and gender justice where all human beings are free to explore and attain their unique fullness, intended with their creation.

I am a South African Muslim, belonging to a small minority community that has survived, lived, and thrived among the "other" for three hundred and forty years. My years in Pakistan as a student of Islamic theology alerted me to the oppression of Christians in a Muslim country, and my involvement in the South African struggle for liberation alerted me to the need to value religiousness and spirituality in the other.[1] The challenges of poverty and AIDS that face Africa particularly, and those of consumerism and the ongoing ravaging of our planet and its peoples by the forces of a faceless God, the Market, in general, lead me to believe that my South African Muslim appreciation of the other serves two purposes: First, it enables others to see how some Muslims are dealing with the challenges of pluralism in a world of injustice. Second, it offers my Muslim co-religionists elsewhere a possible theological path whereby one can be true to one's faith and to the voice of one's conscience in a world where virtue is clearly not the monopoly of one's co-religionists, nor vice a monopoly of the other. Other than my own sociohistorical context, the following assumptions about Muslims underpin my appreciation of how we relate to the other.

First, the overwhelming majority of Muslims, regardless of the nature and extent or even complete absence of their religiosity, have an indomitable belief that the world would be a better place if people followed the religion of Islam. Comments such as "He's such an intelligent guy; how come he's not a Muslim?" or "Desmond Tutu is such a decent person, if only he were a Muslim" are common among Muslims. The notion of Islam as a given and all else as aberration is both based on and supported by a hadith (tradition) of the Prophet Mohammed that "every person is born in a natural state, it is the parent which makes the child a Christian or a Jew." The fact that Christianity and Judaism are portrayed as nonnatural religions leads to the refrain that Islam is *al-din al-fitrah* ("the natural," also understood as "the obvious") religion.

Second, the notion that the "world is hungry for Islam; if only we were better examples" is widespread among Muslims. Many Muslims are, therefore, genuinely surprised when encountering someone who has studied Islam and has not embraced it. When, for example, they first encounter a non-Muslim person interested in Islam, they are generally patient and happy to assist. After an extended period, when they realize that such interest is not transforming the researcher into a searcher ready to discover Islam, then, for most Muslims, there is only one conceivable motive for that person's interest in Islam: "He or she is learning about us in order to undermine us." This contributes to the widespread suspicion and antagonism that lurk underneath the polite surface of interreligious and even academic forums toward the professional non-Muslim Islamicist.

Third, much of conscious religiously motivated interaction with the other is based on the assumption that there is a stable "self" or "own community" with a package of essential and unchanging values, principles, and beliefs that stand in contrast with the other equally stable, even if invariably "lesser," other. The presentation of this package is intended to destabilize the other and, upon this instability, open the other to embrace this new package. Muslims, of course, engage non-Muslims all the time and at different levels. In this chapter I am concerned with consciously religiously based forms of engagement, where the responses to the other are made on the basis of that putative or actual otherness.

MUSLIM ENGAGEMENT WITH THE OTHER

THE OTHER AS ENEMY

At this level of engagement all manifestations of non-Islam—the definition of *Islam* being the sole prerogative of that particular Muslim group and/or its leader—is viewed as a perversion of the natural order. This order, in turn, is regarded as synonymous with the divine order. For many, such as the al-Takfir wa-l-Hijra group in Egypt,[2] or the Spain-based Murabitun, this evaluation of the other may include merely *nominal* or *cultural* Muslims or those whose appreciation of Islam differs from theirs. While invoking the hadith "rejection or disbelief is a single community" (*al-kufr millatun wahidah*), the latter group is usually the object of greater vilification, given its betrayal of the "real" Islam.

This level of engagement is usually the terrain of those described as Islamic fundamentalists, who often come from a professional background and have a more pronounced ideological thrust. These groups, which include the Jordanian Hizb al-Tahrir, the Egyptian al-Jama'at al-Islamiyya, and the Algerian Armed Islamic Group (GIA), follow a program aimed at destroying the political structures of *kufr* (literally "rejection," that is, rejection of Islam) and replacing them with an Islamic state. While always welcoming converts to the true Islam, their proselytization work is in large measure aimed at other Muslims in preparation for the eventual showdown with *kufr*. A small segment of this persuasion regards the other in general—and more particularly, the ideological leadership of the other—as beyond redemption. They would, therefore, either resort to withdrawing from "kafir society" along the lines of al-Takfir wa-l-Hijra or those, such as the GIA, who engage in active, often armed combat, against the agents of *kufr*. In these circles, hostage-taking would be justified, as would the death of civilians in the active *jihad* against *kufr*.

Much has been written on the subject of religious fundamentalism as a response to modernity.[3] Whatever the varying sociological circumstances in different contexts, many of these Muslims feel moved and/or sustained by their religious sensitivities to seek refuge in what they believe is the ultimate certainty: an ahistorical and reified Islam. The following are some of the factors responsible for this: (1) the unfettered global hegemony of the United States of America and the many agencies such as the World Bank and International Monetary Fund, which are viewed as mere adjuncts of neocolonialism; (2) the virtual powerlessness of Muslim states and their seeming collaboration in their own subjugation; (3) the moral, particularly sexual, flexibility of modernity; and (4) the intellectual and philosophical tentativeness of postmodernity.

While many of the activists at this level are familiar with the discourse of modernity and utilize its instruments, such as the Internet, they lack an appreciation of how inextricably interwoven the fate of humankind has really become. Thus they still believe that one can carve out pieces of liberated territories and make them into *dar al-Islam*—the abode of Islam[4]—freed from foreign videos, CNN, and mini-skirts. More pertinently, they are indifferent to the attempts of numerous other entities throughout the world who share their concern and disdain for the way globalization is becoming synonymous with "McDonaldization," with the hypocritical and self-centered nature of American foreign policy and the lack of political freedom and abundance of repression in their own societies.

In this lack of recognition of shared concerns lies both the greatest weakness and strength of many Islamist groups. As isolated entities, they are destined to remain on the margins of humankind, occasionally bursting to the fore in acts of raw terror, such as the massacre of tourists at Luxor, Egypt, or of covert terror, such as the closing of medical-care facilities for women in Afghanistan under the *Taliban*. Equally, as isolated entities, they can march forth undisturbed by questions of the humanness of the other, which will confront them as soon as they discover a commonness in objectives to create a more just world.

THE OTHER AS POTENTIAL SELF

The second level of conscious engagement with the other is that of active proselytism with the stated intention of saving souls and increasing the numbers of "the believers." This level is usually the domain of those who espouse a traditionalist and putatively apolitical view of Islam. They focus on personal sin, reformation, and salvation in the hereafter. Occasionally some form of charitable work serves as an adjunct to their proselytism. This view, conversely, lacks an awareness of socioeconomic justice and an appreciation of its structural causes. Faith is narrowly defined as verbal testimony to a set of creeds and morality to the personal sphere with the focus on matters pertaining to sex. This group confines its activity to relatively mild forms of engaging the other. While the Tablighi Jama'a may concentrate on knocking on the doors of the non-praying or "unrighteous" internal other, those who opt for increasing the numbers of the nominally faithful adopt a wide range of strategies. These include the following: (1) coercion, such as withholding of food ration cards or complicating access to them in Pakistani villages; (2) the incessant anti-Christian haranguing over mosque loudspeakers in Bangladesh and Indonesia; (3) the exploitation of social problems such as lack of health and educational facilities by combining *da'wa* (literally "invitation") with concrete assistance in these fields by the Africa Muslim Agency in Southern Africa; and (4) the regular public debates with Christian evangelists by the world-renowned South African Muslim polemicist Ahmed Deedat, an exception in a world where *da'wa* is rarely individualized.

The latter form of engagement is particularly meaningful to Muslims who feel disempowered through colonialism and the seeming religio-cultural hegemony of the West. It is thus not unusual to find up to fifty video tapes of Deedat in a single Muslim home in Britain or Abu Dhabi. The compulsion appears to be: What we are losing daily in the world of economic and cultural power can be compensated for by our victories in religious slanging matches.

THE OTHER AS UNAVOIDABLE NEIGHBOR

There are numerous Muslims who are engaged in interfaith or interreligious dialogue in various parts of the world. With the exception of the Ahl al-Bayt Institute in Jordan, such activity rarely enjoys the support of mainstream Muslim institutions in the Arab world. Significant pockets of such initiatives, however, are found in countries such as Nigeria, Indonesia, and Malaysia, and, more particularly, in those countries where Muslims are in a minority. Other than the occasional high-powered and largely symbolic gatherings of an organization such as the World Conference of Religion and Peace, much of interreligious dialogue at a local level comprises one or more of the following: (1) clarifying some basic guidelines for proselytization; (2) promoting good neighborliness; and (3) learning the basics of the other's religion. In the case of the latter, presentations usually border on apologetics, with each side keen to show the finest side of the religion's heritage and careful to avoid reference to the actual historical or contemporary conduct of its adherents.

The number of Muslims, usually individuals rather than groups, engaged in such dialogue with the other are few and far between, and where they are organized in forums these have generally been organized by Christians. At this level there is some appreciation of the other, recognition of some worth attached to them and of the need to nurture this worth. ("These are good people; they would be even better if they were Muslim.") While there is an explicit acknowledgment of the duty of proclaiming *good news* or *da'wa*, the participants acknowledge the need to learn about the other for effective religious tolerance or proselytization. A number of Muslims initially enter such dialogues under the misunderstanding that their (usually) Christian counterparts are engaged in conversation because of the wavering nature of their own faith and, therefore, present to Muslims fertile opportunities for Islamic *da'wa*.

While many participants in interreligious dialogue start at this level, for some at least, the perception of the other changes and, along with it, their objectives in the dialogue. This is due to the inherent lack of closure for most such dialogue, as well as the unpredictability of the outcome of any true listening experience. As for those who are incapable of listening, they normally just disappear after a few meetings, dismissing the exercise as a waste of time. At a more scholarly level there are a number of Muslim intellectuals who form an intrinsic part of the dialogue scene. Some of them, such as Jamal Badawi, the Toronto-based scholar, and Mahmoud Ayoub, the Lebanese scholar based in Philadelphia, believe that exposing the other to the intellectual face of Islam, represented by them, is itself an invitation to Islam. There is little awareness among them that this very intellectualizing of the face of Islam means a transformation of the product and is, in effect, a denial of an essentialist Islam.

Despite the apparent objective nature of this approach, it is still essentially characterized by an assumption of superiority. First, it is not atypical to find suggestions in these circles that the Christian or Jewish partner—the *noble savage*, as it were—is actually a Muslim, even if he or she is unaware of it. This notion of the anonymous Muslim assumes that goodness is synonymous with, even exclusive to, Islam. Many Muslims, when coming face to face with goodness, cannot relate this with integrity to the person as a person or as a Christian. Instead, they feel compelled to go through the initial act of making him or her "one of us."

While the activities of this tendency are usually characterized by political noninvolvement, it does often tolerate moderate political action in support of what are considered to be righteous causes. At other times, those involved at this level may also cooperate with each other in seemingly benign activities such as tree planting or literacy campaigns. Seldom, if ever, in the forefront of challenging unjust sociopolitical systems or practices, they often play a significant role in the agenda of national states struggling to fuse diverse cultural religious identities into a broader national one.

THE OTHER AS SELF AND INTELLECTUAL/THEOLOGICAL SPARRING PARTNER

"In our age," says Ghrab, "the purpose of dialogue must be solely knowledge . . . of the other as the other wishes to be and not as it pleases us to imagine him, and on the basis of his texts, and his heritage and not merely on the basis of our texts."[5] This scholarly and objective approach to the other is the position of a growing number of individual Muslim intellectuals, such as Mohammed Arkoun and Ebrahim Moosa, who eschew any hint of an agenda of *da'wa*, however subtle, in interactions with non-Muslims. These individuals, often working on the margins of Muslim society, nonetheless embrace a calling that Arkoun refers to as "the creation of a new space of intelligibility and freedom."[6] Utilizing this space, they may embrace ideals of finding areas of commonality. In many ways this approach is a classic liberal one, which values individual freedom, space, and the intellectual quest for their own sake.

What is often ignored at this level is that liberal ideology is not without its hegemonic interests. Leonard Binder has raised the pertinent question whether the critique of Muslim liberals has not been a "form of false consciousness, an abject submission to the hegemonic discourse of the dominant secular Western capitalist and imperialist societies, an oriental Orientalism, or whether it was and is practical, rational and emancipatory."[7] Mohammed Arkoun's call for knowledge as a sphere of authority independent of ideologies does little more than further the ideological interest within which such knowledge is located and formulated. Knowledge, like any other social tool, while it can be critical, is never neutral. As Segundo has argued, "Every hermeneutic entails conscious or unconscious partisanship. It is partisan in its viewpoint even when it believes itself to be neutral and tries to act that way."[8] While this group of scholars make for the most interesting partners on the dialogue circuit, I do not share the enthusiasm of those who insist on letting a million thoughts bloom for the fun of diversity and pluralism, a kind of social venture that often claims to not take sides because, as theologian David Tracy reminds us, "this is the perfect ideology for the modern bourgeois mind. Such a pluralism makes a genial confusion in which one tries to enjoy the pleasures of difference without ever committing oneself to any particular vision of resistance, liberation and hope."[9]

A second area of concern with dialogue at this level is that it is essentially confined to those whom Muslims regard as People of the Book, that is, Jews and Christians. In some ways, this reflects the relative Qur'anic gentleness toward the People of the Book as well as the social location of these thinkers. However, I believe that this preference also betrays a more serious prejudice, a subject to which I will later revert: that people of the Fourth World, often adherents of pagan traditions, are of little or no consequence.

THE OTHER AS SELF AND SPIRITUAL PARTNER

For a number of Muslim scholars, such as David Chittick, Fritchoff Schuon, Martin Lings, and Seyyed Hossein Nasr, as well as a few Muslim groups, such as the Deutsche Muslim Liga, and a host of loosely organized Sufi groups in different parts of the world, dialogue is also considered to be an act of mutual spiritual enrichment. They view dialogue against what they see as the march of modernity and postmodernity toward a world wherein God as the sacred is dethroned or confined to the margins of human life. Dealing with the negative impact of Western education, Martin Lings, for example, argues that one needs to teach "as far as possible, the whole truth, which would mean teaching many truths that were not taught in better times, for the needs of the eleventh hour are not the same as those of the sixth and seventh hour."[10] The extent of the acceptance of otherness is also reflected in Lings when he argues that a sense of the glory of God is one of the main objectives of religion.[11] "For those who are not prepared to sacrifice that glory to human prejudices it has become abundantly clear that none of the so-called world religions can have been intended by Providence to establish itself over the whole globe."[12]

The Other as Self and Comrade

All of the forms of engagement cited above avoid any conscious political discourse. Some Muslims would preach and work against those who seek some political expression of their Islam, even though they themselves are often players within political situations. In conditions of socioeconomic or gender injustice, where abstinence from overt political activity is invoked, this abstinence, willingly or unwillingly, acquires a political character. It serves a political purpose because it usually results in the accruing or maintenance of politico-economic advantages to the abstaining party and ruling class. These religious groups thus lose their spiritual disinterestedness and become an intrinsic part of the dominant political and ideological discourse.

BEYOND A DISEMBOWELED PLURALISM

I now turn to the problem of disengaged pluralism before proposing a path of engagement with the other that not only nurtures the intellectual potential of the participants but also seeks to discover the humanity of all within the context of a broader struggle to create a more humane world.

First, we live in a world where individuals are less and less formed by the wealth of their traditions and their own cultures. Rather, the world is one where the Market is so all-pervasive that all of our so-called freedom of choice is steered into particular directions—all of them ultimately serving the Market and impoverishing the human spirit. While one must guard against essentializing any community and culture, even more so against glossing over the multifarious injustices ranging from xenophobia to homophobia often intrinsic to these, the truth is that globalization and the celebration of individual liberty are not ideologically neutral. For me, as a Muslim theologian, this represents the single most significant ideological and spiritual difficulty. I can only truly be who I am in my unceasing transforming self within the context of personal freedom. In today's world this freedom is intrinsically connected to all the ideological baggage of the modern industrial state along with the "Cocacolonization" of global consciousness through a process of relentless "McDonaldization." In other words, my freedom has been acquired within the bosom of capitalism along with all of its hegemonic designs over my equally valued cultural and religious traditions.

While many "enlightened" Muslims are embarrassed by Ahmed Deedat's video-cassette peddling, or irritated by the Tablighi Jama'a's door-knocking, there is little awareness of the proselytization of the global *Taliban*-like nature of the Market—every bit as ruthless, tenacious, and dogged as its Afghani counterparts. Thus I am afraid of the other which, for me, is not another community or other individuals but one which has entered my consciousness, the intangible and faceless Market forces, my eternal companion in my back pocket in the form of my credit cards.

The dominant public Muslim discourse, of course, rather simplistically reduces this problem to Islam versus the West or Muslims versus Christians and Jews. The underlying assumption in this defensive posturing is that the other is "the enemy." In *Qur'an, Liberation and Pluralism* I argued that for those who struggle to survive on the margins of society, living under the yoke of oppression and struggling in the hope of liberation with those from other religions who are equally oppressed, a pluralism of splendid intellectual neutrality or gentle coexistence within unjust socioeconomic or personal relationships is not a dignified option. We need to ask what causes are being advanced by our commitment to pluralism and shared existence.

When "objective" scholars fail or refuse to recognize that all human responses and refusals to respond are located within a sociopolitical context, then "understanding" and "living together," de facto, become an extension of the dominant ideological status quo. When such a status quo is characterized by injustice and exploitation, the reduction of people to commodities and death by starvation and over-consumption, then the pursuit of understanding is itself reduced to cooption to strengthen the overall ideological framework of the powerful. I am thus arguing for a theological and concrete engagement with the other that recognizes the intrinsic human worth of each person and that takes place within the context of a struggle to transform our world into a more just one.

The nature of the world wherein we live today and the potency of our weapons of destruction mean that the fate of all of humankind is irretrievably interwoven. There is no selective existence for any particular community. The cake of humankind is beyond unbaking; we cannot now separate the sugar from the flour or the water. We sink or swim together. For people committed to the noblest in their religious heritage, though, the question is not merely one of the survival of our own. Today the survival of the self depends on the survival of the other as much as the survival of the human race depends on the survival of the ecosystem. We have gone beyond "no man is an island unto himself" to "no entity is an island unto itself." A vague and sentimental sense of attachment to the clan is not going to see us through the turbulent future of a world threatened by the gradual reemergence of Nazism, environmental devastation, a triumphalist New World Order based on the economic exploitation of the so-called Third World (that is two-thirds of the world), a world where women continue to just survive on the margins of dignity. There are many ways of dying. There is, however, only one way to live: through discovering what the self and other and their ever-changing nature are really about; to understand how much of the other is really reflected in us; and to find out what it is that we have in common in the struggle, to strive together in a world of justice and dignity for all the inhabitants of the earth. To do so requires transcending theological categories of self and other that were shaped in and intended for another era and context.

BEYOND THE PEOPLE OF THE BOOK

Early in this chapter I referred to the preference that Muslims have for either converting or conversing with the People of the Book. The tension in the religious-ideological relationship between the Muslims and the People of the Book was inevitable from the dawn of Islam. The Qur'an claimed an affinity with scriptural tradition and, furthermore, claimed to be its guardian. An unwelcome response was inevitable on the part of those who claimed their own scriptures to be legitimate and final, in and by themselves. Much of the Qur'an's attention to the other is, therefore, devoted to this tension.

There are several reasons for the preoccupation with this category of the People of the Book. First, since most of the *mushrikun* (literally, associationists, that is, the pagans who associated other deities with God) converted to Islam after the liberation of Mecca (630 C.E.), at the earliest stages of its history, Jews and Christians were essentially the communities with which Muslims and their jurisprudence had to deal. Second, the historical encounter over territory (both ideological and geographical) was largely between Muslims and Christians. Third, in the modern period, as Muslims are struggling to overcome the divisions of the past and to find avenues of coexisting and cooperating with those of other faiths, they find it theologically easier to focus on a category with which the Qur'an seems to have some sympathy. Fourth, the present preeminence of the Western world—itself a product of a predominantly Christian and, to a lesser extent, Jewish heritage—in the fields of technology, science, and politics requires some Muslim focus on relations with the People of the Book, if only as one way of coming to terms with the fact of this preeminence or domination.

There are a number of problems in focusing on the People of the Book as a distinct contemporary religious group in the belief that this is the same referent as that in the Qur'an. The Qur'anic position toward the People of the Book and even its understanding as to who constitutes the People of the Book went through several phases. There is, however, agreement that the term has always applied to the Jews and Christians whom Mohammed encountered during his mission. The Qur'an naturally dealt only with the behavior and beliefs of those of the People of the Book with whom the early Muslim community was in actual social contact.

To employ the Qur'anic category of People of the Book in a generalized manner of simplistic identification of all Jews and Christians in contemporary society is to avoid the historical realities of the society of Medina to which Mohammed and his early followers emigrated, as well as the theological diversity among both earlier and contemporary Christians and Jews. To avoid this unjust generalization, therefore, requires a clear idea of the sources of beliefs as well as the many nuances that characterized the various communities encountered by the early Muslims. Given the paucity of such extra-Qur'anic knowledge, one would either have to abandon the search for a group with corresponding dogma today or shift one's focus to an area of practice and attitudes rather than dogma.

In practice, the latter option has always been exercised. In none of the disciplines of exegesis, Islamic history, or legal scholarship have Muslims known anything approximating consensus about the identity of the People of the Book. There was even disagreement as to which specific groups of Christians and Jews made up the People of the Book. At various times, Hindus, Buddhists, Zoroastrians, Magians, and Sabeans were included among or excluded from the People of the Book depending on the theological predilections of the Muslim scholars and, perhaps more important, the geopolitical context in which they lived. In all of these attempts to extend the boundaries of the Qur'anic People of the Book, Muslim scholars implicitly acknowledged the situation-boundedness of the Qur'anic categories.

A recognition of the need of solidarity of all oppressed people in an unjust and exploitative society requires going beyond the situation-bound categories of the Qur'an. I do not wish to suggest that there are no Christians who, for example, believe in the concept of a triune deity. Justice, however, requires that no one be held captive to categories that applied to a community or to individuals fourteen centuries ago merely because they share a common descriptive term, a term which may even have been imposed on them by Muslims and rejected by them. "These are a people who have passed on. They have what they earned and you shall have what you have earned" (Q. 2:141).

There is another significant reason why the category of People of the Book should be regarded as of dubious relevance in our world today. In the context of the political and technological power exercised by the Judeo-Christian world, on the one hand, and Arab monetary wealth, on the other, Muslim rapprochement with that world, based on the simplistic analogy that Jews and Christians are the contemporary People of the Book, could easily, and probably correctly, be construed as an alliance of the powerful. A Qur'anic hermeneutic concerned with interreligious solidarity against injustice would seek to avoid such alliances and would rather opt for more inclusive categories that would, for example, embrace the dispossessed of the Fourth World.

This rethinking also has to extend to another category the Qur'an particularly singles out for demonization, the *mushrikun*. Initially referring to the Meccans who revered physical objects such as sculptures or heavenly bodies as religiously sacred entities worthy of obeisance, the term *mushrikun* was also employed to refer to the People of the Book by some Muslim jurists. Two factors led to an early recognition that all *mushrikun* are not the same and were not to be treated equally: (1) the Qur'anic accusation of *shirk* against the People of the Book (e.g., Q. 9:31), while simultaneously regarding them as distinct from the *mushrikun*; and (2) the subsequent wider Muslim contact with the world of non-Islam. Later, as the *Shorter Encyclopaedia of Islam* observes, "in the course of the dogmatic development of Islam, the conception of *shirk* received a considerable extension . . . [because] the adherents of many sects had no compunction about reproaching their Muslim opponents with *shirk*, as soon as they saw in them any obscuring of monotheism, although only in some particular respect emphasized by themselves." *Shirk* has thus become no longer simply a term for unbelief prevailing outside of Islam but a reproach hurled by one Muslim against another inside of Islam.[13] As with the category of the People of the Book, here too one finds that the actual application of the neat divisions has been far more problematic than most traditional scholars are wont to admit. There is evidently a need to rethink these categories and their contemporary applicability or otherwise. It is now more apparent than ever that the religious situation of humankind and the sociopolitical ramifications thereof are far more complex than previously understood.

The following are but a few indications of this complexity: (1) the emergence of the new religious movements where, in some cases, people claim to be both Christians and pagans, or Buddhist and Hindu Catholics, in Japan and India respectively; (2) the situation in large parts of Asia, Australia, Latin America, and Africa, where people combine a commitment to Islam, Christianity, and even Judaism with other traditional "pagan" practices, such as the veneration of graves and sacred relics and the invoking of deceased ancestors for spiritual blessings or material gain; and (3) in the aforementioned areas, formal and institutional religion has been systematically used to oppress, exploit, and even eliminate entire nations among the indigenous people. In these situations the marginalized and oppressed have often resorted to their ancient religions as a means of asserting their human dignity.

Like *tawhid*, "divine unity," *shirk* had its socioeconomic implications in Meccan society, and one needs to retain a sense of this in a contemporary consideration of the believers in *tawhid* and *shirk*. Referring to the early Qur'anic texts, Fazlur Rahman has argued that they can only be understood against their Meccan background, "as a reaction against Meccan pagan idolworship and the great socioeconomic disparity between mercantile aristocracy of Mecca and a large body of its distressed and disenfranchised population."[14] "Both of these aspects," he says, "are so heavily emphasized in the Qur'an that they must have been organically connected with each other."[15]

QUR'ANIC UNIVERSALISM
AND INCLUSION OF THE OTHER

The Qur'an presents a universal and inclusivist perspective of a divine being who responds to the sincerity and commitment of all His servants. From this, two questions arise: First, how does traditional Qur'anic interpretation present a parochial image of a deity that does not differ from that postulated by the Medinan Jews and Christians and denounced in the Qur'an, an image of a deity who belongs to a small group of people and who, having chosen His favorites, turns a blind eye to the sincere spiritual and social commitments of all others outside this circle? Second, how does the universality of the Qur'an's message relate to the exclusivism and virulent denunciation of the other, indeed, even its exhortation to wage an armed struggle against the other?

While the context of individual verses dealing with the other is often carefully recorded by the earlier interpreters, they do not show any understanding of the overall historical context of a particular revelation. The task of shedding historical light on various texts has, until recently, been primarily the domain of non-Muslim scholars. Muslim reluctance to deal with the question of contextualization beyond the search for an isolated occasion of revelation has led to a generalized denunciation of the other, irrespective of the sociohistorical context of the texts used in support of such rejection and damnation. The Qur'anic position toward the other unfolded gradually in terms of their varied responses to the message of Islam and to the prophetic presence. Any view to the contrary would invariably lead to the conclusion that the Qur'an presents a confused and contradictory view of the other. The idea of the gradual and contextual development of the Qur'anic position toward the other has significant implications. First, one cannot speak of a "final Qur'anic position" toward the other, and second, it is wrong to apply texts of opprobrium in a universal manner to all those whom one chooses to define in an ahistorical fashion as "People of the Book" or as "nonbelievers."

Beliefs and behavior are not genetically determined as are, for example, the color of one's eyes. It is to guard against the injustices of such generalizations that texts of opprobrium referring to other religious communities or the associationists are usually followed or preceded by exceptions (e.g., Q. 3:75). Furthermore, qualifying or exceptive expressions such as "from among them" (Q. 3:75), "many among them" (Q. 2:109; 5:66; 22:17; 57:26), "most of them" (Q. 2:105; 7:102; 10:36;), "some of them" (Q. 2:145), and "a group among them" (Q. 3:78), are routinely used throughout the Qur'anic discourse on the other. The Qur'an provides only the basis for the attitude of Muslims at any given time toward the other. The Qur'anic position, in turn, was largely shaped by the varying responses of the different components that comprised the other to the struggle for the establishment of an order based on divine unity (tawhid), justice ('adl), and islam. More often than not, these responses assumed concrete political form in decisions to side with the Muslim community or against it. Much of the Qur'anic opprobrium is directed at the way doctrine was used to justify exploitative practices and tribal chauvinism. It was not as if the Qur'an avoided the discourse on power or denounced the exercise of political power; it was concerned about whom political power served and who suffered as a consequence of it.

The Qur'an, in general religious terms, refers to various groups or types of people by various expressions, of which the following are the most frequent: believers (*mu'minun*), righteous, "those who submit to Allah" (*muslimun*), People of the Book, Jews, Christians, associationists, "ingrates or unbelievers" (*kafirun/kuffar*), and "backsliders or hypocrites" (*munafiqun*). I want to make some brief observations about the Qur'anic use of these terms before I examine the context of its attitude toward the other.

First, the terms usually used in translation are often, at best, approximations of the Arabic meanings. The Qur'an, for example, does not use the equivalent of the words "non-Muslim" or "unbeliever"; yet these are the most common English renderings of "*kafirun/kuffar*" in both the process of translation as well as internal usage within the Arabic language.

Second, some of these terms are frequently used interchangeably in the Qur'an, such as *mu'minun* (literally, "the convinced ones") and *muslimun* (literally, "submitters"), or People of the Book and Christians or Jews. It is essential to maintain the Qur'anic distinctions in their various uses in order to avoid a generalized and unjust rubbishing of the other.

Third, in addition to these nouns, the Qur'an also employs descriptive phrases such as *alladhina amanu* (literally "those who are convinced") instead of *mu'minun*, and *alladhina kaffaru* (literally, "those who deny/reject/are ungrateful") instead of *kafirun* (literally, "deniers, rejecters or ingrates"). These descriptive phrases express specific nuances in the text and indicate a particular level of faith conviction or of denial/rejection/ingratitude in much the same way as "one who writes poetry" has a different nuance than "poet."

Fourth, references to these groups are occasionally to a specific community within a historical setting and, at other times, to a community in a wider sense, transcending one specific situation.

Fifth, besides the terms of opprobrium such as *kafir*, *munafiq*, and *mushrik*, the other terms are rarely used in a negative or positive manner without exceptions. While praise or reproach is usually inherent in some of these terms, this is not without exception. Indeed, the Qur'an, at times, describes the reprehensible acts committed by some of those from among the Muslim or believing community as *kufr* or *shirk* (Q. 39:7).

Sixth, these terms are often used in the sense of a historic, religious, or social group, but not always. The hypocrites and righteous were invariably referred to as individuals, and the term *muslim* and its various forms, for example, are also frequently invoked to refer to the characteristic of submission in an individual, group, or even an inanimate object.

QUR'ANIC RECOGNITION OF RELIGIOUS PLURALISM

The Qur'an's general attitude toward the other, which underpins the more specific injunctions and doctrinal issues that it raises from time to time, is based on a number of fundamental principles. First, the Qur'an relates dogma to socioeconomic exploitation and insists on connecting orthodoxy with orthopraxis. This is equally applicable to the communities and individuals, in Mecca as well as Medina, who rejected the Prophet's message of *tawhid* and social justice. The Qur'an makes it clear that it was both the rejection and ignorance of *tawhid* that had led to social and economic oppression in Meccan society (e.g., Q. 83:1-11, 102:1-4, 104). Chapter 90 asserts that a denial of the presence of an all-powerful God causes people to squander their wealth: "Does he think that no one has power over him? He will say: I have spent abundant wealth" (Q. 90:5-6). Furthermore, this chapter links faith to an active social conscience: "to free a slave," "to feed on a day of hunger," and "to exhort one another to perseverance and to mercy" (Q. 90:13-15). By implication, it also links *kufr* to the refusal to display mercy toward others. In this text those who reject "the signs of Allah" are those whose actions do not correspond with the ones who have chosen to "ascend the steep path." The rejecters of "the signs of Allah," therefore, are those who deny mercy and compassion. This linking of the rejection of Allah and *din* (religion) to the denial of mercy and compassion is even more explicit in Chapter 107: "Have you observed the one who belies *al-din*? That is the one who is unkind to the orphan, and urges not the feeding of the needy. So, woe to the praying ones, who are unmindful of their prayer. They do good to be seen, and refrain from acts of kindnesses" (Q. 107:1-7).

The texts of opprobrium revealed in Medina, which relate to the various Jewish and Christian communities and individuals encountered there by the Prophet and the early Muslims, reveal a similar relationship between erroneous beliefs and the socioeconomic exploitation of others. Equally significant is the fact that, although the Jews were closer to Muslims in creed, the Qur'an often reserves the severest denunciation for some of them. Similarly, the Sabeans were widely believed to have worshiped stars, even angels, yet they were included among the People of the Book.[16] According to the Qur'an, the Jews and Christians justified their exploitation of their own people by claiming that their scriptures permitted such practices.

The Qur'an denounced this exploitation of the ignorance of ordinary illiterate people who had no "real knowledge of the Scriptures" (Q. 2:78) by the priests of the People of the Book. The contempt for and exploitation of the marginalized by some of the People of the Book are further seen in their justification that they had no moral obligation to be just toward the illiterate (Q. 3:75). This text is followed by a denunciation of those who "barter away their bond with Allah and their pledges for a trifling gain" (Q. 3:77) and of "a section among them who distort their Scripture with their tongues, so as to make you think that it is from the Scripture while it is not" (Q. 3:79). Thus, we see that while their bond and their pledges were with a transcendent God, their crimes were very much about the exploitation of the people of God.

Second, the Qur'an explicitly and unequivocally denounces the narrow religious exclusivism that appears to have characterized the Jewish and Christian communities encountered by Mohammed in Hijaz. The Qur'an is relentless in its denunciation of the arrogance of Jewish religious figures and scathing about the tribal exclusivism that enabled them to treat people outside their community, especially the weak and vulnerable, with contempt. This contempt for other people, the Qur'an suggests, was very much rooted in notions of being the chosen of God. According to the Qur'an, many among the Jews and the Christians believed that they were not like any other people whom Allah had created, that their covenant with Allah had elevated their status with Allah, and that they were now the "friends of Allah to the exclusion of other people" (Q. 62:6). The Qur'an alleges that they claimed a privileged position with Allah merely by calling themselves Jewish or Christian. In other words, it was a claim based on history, birth, and tribe rather than on praxis and morality. Thus, they claimed to be "the children of Allah and His beloved" (Q. 5:18) and "considered themselves pure" (Q. 4:48). In response to these notions of inherent purity, the Qur'an argues, "Nay, but it is Allah who causes whomsoever He wills to grow in purity; and none shall be wronged by even a hair's breadth" (Q. 5:49). The same text links these notions of being Allah's favorites to their socioeconomic implications and suggests that this sense of having an exclusive share in Allah's dominion leads to greater unwillingness to share wealth with others: "Have they perchance, a share in Allah's dominion?" the Qur'an asks, and then asserts: "But (if they had) lo, they would not give to other people as much as (would fill) the groove of a date stone!"(Q. 4:53).

The Qur'an denounces the claims of some of the People of the Book that the afterlife was only for them and "not for any other people" (Q. 2:94, 111), that the fire (of hell) will only touch them "for a limited numbered days" (Q. 3:24), and that "clutching at the fleeting good of this world will be forgiven for us" (Q. 7:169). The Qur'an, furthermore, takes a rather dim view of the boasts of the Jews and the Christians that their creeds are the only ones of consequence. While the Qur'an does not accuse Christians of claiming to be free of any moral accountability in their behavior toward non-Christians, they, too, according to the Qur'an, held that they were the beloved of Allah:

> And they say: "None shall enter paradise unless he be a Jew or a Christian." Those are their vain desires. Say: "Produce your proof if you are truthful." Nay, whoever submits his whole self to Allah and is a doer of good, will get his reward with his Lord; On such shall be no fear nor shall they grieve. . . .
>
> And the Jews say the Christians have nothing [credible] to stand on and the Christians say the Jews have nothing to stand on while both recite the Book. Even thus say those who have no knowledge. So Allah will judge between them on the Day of Resurrection in that wherein they differ (Q. 2:111-13).

Attempts to appropriate the heritage of Abraham and to make it the property of a particular socioreligious group is also denounced (Q. 3:69). "It is not belonging to the community of Jews or Christians which leads to guidance, but the straight path of Abraham" (Q. 2:135) who "was neither a Jew nor a Christian, but an upright person who submitted to Allah" (Q. 3:67).

Third, the Qur'an is explicit in its acceptance of religious pluralism. Having derided the petty attempts to appropriate Allah, it is inconceivable that the Qur'an should itself engage in this. The notion that Abraham was not a Jew or a Christian but "one of us" (that is, a Muslim) is at variance with the rejection of all exclusivist claims in these texts. For the Qur'anic message to be an alternative one, it had to offer the vision of a God who responds to all of humankind and who acknowledges and responds to the sincerity and righteousness of all believers. The Qur'an thus makes it a condition of faith to believe in the genuineness of all revealed religion (Q. 2:136; 2:285; 3:84). The Qur'an acknowledges the de jure legitimacy of all revealed religion in two respects: (1) it takes into account the religious life of separate communities coexisting with Muslims, respecting their laws, social norms, and religious practices; and (2) it accepts that the faithful adherents of these religions shall also attain salvation and that "no fear shall come upon them neither will they grieve" (Q. 2:62). These two aspects of the Qur'an's attitude toward the other may be described as the cornerstones of its acceptance of religious pluralism. Given the widespread acceptance, among the most conservative Muslims, of respect for the laws of the other, even if only in theory, and the equally widespread rejection of their salvation, I want to focus on the latter.

The Qur'an specifically recognizes the People of the Book as legitimate socioreligious communities. This recognition was later extended by Muslim scholars to various other religious communities living within the borders of the expanding Islamic domain. The explicit details, restrictions, and application of this recognition throughout the various stages of the prophetic era, and subsequently in Islamic history, point to a significant issue at stake in dealing with the other. The socioreligious requirements of the Muslim community, such as community building and security, rather than the faith convictions, or lack thereof, in these other communities shaped the Qur'an's attitude toward them.

There are a number of indications in the Qur'an of the essential legitimacy of the other. First, the People of the Book, as recipients of divine revelation, were recognized as part of the community. Addressing all the prophets, the Qur'an says: "And surely this, your community [umma], is a single community" (Q. 23:52). Furthermore, the establishment of a single community with diverse religious expressions was explicit in the Charter of Medina, which was established as the basis of the Prophet's settling there. Second, in two of the most significant social areas, food and marriage, the generosity of the Qur'anic spirit is evident: the food of "those who were given the Book" was declared lawful for the Muslims and the food of the Muslims lawful for them (Q. 5:5). Likewise, Muslim males were permitted to marry "the chaste women of the People of the Book" (Q. 5:5). If Muslims were to be allowed to coexist with others in a relationship as intimate as that of marriage, then this seems to indicate quite explicitly that enmity is not to be regarded as the norm in relations between Muslims and others. Interestingly, this text mentions the believing women in the same manner as the women of the People of the Book: "[Permissible in marriage] are the virtuous women of the believers and the virtuous women of those who received the Scripture before you" (Q. 5:5). The restriction of permission for marriage to the women of the People of the Book indicates that this ruling related to the social dynamics of early Muslim society and the need for community cohesion. The fact which also reflects this point is that most jurists, while agreeing on the permissibility of marriage to women of the People of the Book, who are also the people of *dhimma* (protected under Islamic law), differ as to whether it is permissible if they are from states hostile to Islam.[17] Third, in the area of religious law, the norms and regulations of the Jews and of the Christians were upheld (Q. 5:47) and even enforced by the Prophet when he was called upon to settle disputes among them (Q. 5:42-43). Fourth, the sanctity of the religious life of the adherents of other revealed religions is underlined by the fact that the first time that permission for armed struggle was given was to ensure the preservation of this sanctity: "But for the fact that God continues to repel some people by means of others, cloisters, churches, synagogues and mosques, [all places] wherein the name of God is mentioned, would be razed to the ground" (Q. 22:40).

The Qur'anic recognition of religious pluralism is not only evident from the acceptance of the other as legitimate socioreligious communities but also from an acceptance of the spirituality of the other and salvation through that otherness. The preservation of the sanctity of the places of worship alluded to above was thus not merely in order to preserve the integrity of a multi-religious society in the manner in which contemporary states may want to protect places of worship because of the role that they play in the culture of a particular people. Rather, it was because it was Allah, a God who represented the ultimate for many of these religions, and who is acknowledged to be above the diverse outward expressions of that service, who was being worshiped therein. That there were people in other faiths who sincerely recognized and served Allah is made even more explicit in the following text:

> Not all of them are alike; among them is a group who stand for the right and keep nights reciting the words of Allah and prostrate themselves in adoration before Him. They have faith in Allah and in the Last Day; they enjoin what is good and forbid what is wrong, and vie one with another in good deeds. And those are among the righteous (Q. 4:113).

If the Qur'an is to be the word of a just God, as Muslims sincerely believe, then there is no alternative to the recognition of the sincerity and righteous deeds of others, and their recompense on the Day of Requital. Thus, the Qur'an says:

And of the People of the Book there are those who have faith in Allah and in that which has been revealed to you and in that which has been revealed to them, humbling themselves before Allah, they take not a small price for the messages of Allah. They have their reward with their Lord. Surely Allah is swift to take account (Q. 3:198).

And whatever good they do, they will not be denied it. And Allah knows those who keep their duty (Q. 3:112-14).

THE QUR'ANIC RESPONSE TO RELIGIOUS DIVERSITY

The Qur'an regards Mohammed as one of a galaxy of Prophets, some of whom are mentioned specifically in the Qur'an while "others you do not know" (Q. 40:78). The same faith, the Qur'an declares, "was enjoined on Noah, Abraham, Moses and Jesus" (Q. 42:13). "You are but a warner," the Qur'an tells Mohammed, "and every people has had its guide" (Q. 13:08, see also Q. 16:36 and Q. 35:24). The fact that the Qur'an incorporates some of the accounts of the lives of these predecessors of Mohammed and makes it part of its own history is perhaps the most significant reflection of its emphasis on the unity of faith. These prophets came with identical messages that they preached within the context of the various and differing situations of their people. Basically, they came to reawaken the commitment of people to *tawhid*, to remind them about the ultimate accountability to Allah, and to establish justice. "And for every *umma* there is a messenger. So when their messenger comes the matter is decided between them with justice, and they will not be wronged" (Q. 10:47).

We have revealed to you the Book with the truth, verifying that which is before it of the Book and a guardian over it. So judge between them by what Allah has revealed and follow not their desires, [turning away] from the truth that has come unto you. For every one of you we have appointed a *shir'ah* and a *minhaj*. And if Allah had pleased, He would have made you a single *umma*. However, He desires to try you in what He gave you. So vie with one another in righteous deeds. To Allah you will all return, so that He will inform you of that wherein you differed (Q. 5:48).

In a similar vein, it says: "To every community, We appointed acts of devotion, which they observe; so let them not dispute with you in the matter, and call to your Lord. Surely you are on a right guidance" (Q. 22:67).

Viewing the deceased adherents of supposedly abrogated *shari'as* as the addressees of this text, as many orthodox exegetes have done, dispensed with the need for any detailed discussion on the text itself or its implications for religious pluralism. The traditional interpretations of the text present several difficulties and are evidently inconsistent with both its context and apparent meaning. These difficulties compel me to choose an alternative inclusivist interpretation. First, the entire Qur'anic discussion, including the preceding sentences of the same verse and the subsequent verse, refer to the relationship between the Prophet as arbitrator in an actual community. The context of this text makes it plain that other religious communities coexisting with the Muslims in Medina are addressed and not a historical community existing in a nonphysical world or in a different historical context. Second, the text under discussion says that, upon returning to Allah, "He will inform you of that wherein you differed." If one supposes that this text referred to the pre-Mohammedan communities whose paths are acknowledged as valid, pure, and divinely ordained for a specified period, as the doctrine of supersessionism holds, then there is no question of the Mohammedan community differing with them or a need of information regarding the differences. Third, the text asks that the response to this diversity be to compete with each other in righteous deeds. Given that any kind of meaningful competition can only be engaged in by contemporaneous communities who share similar advantages or disadvantages, one can only assume that the partners of these Muslims were to be those others who lived alongside them.

In the light of the above, the text can best be understood as follows: Looking at the context, one observes that it comes toward the end of a fairly lengthy discourse on the significance of specific scriptures for specific communities. Q. 5:44-45 deals with the Torah, which has "guidance and light," "should not be sold for a trivial price," and those Jews who do not judge by its injunctions are denounced as "ingrates" and "wrongdoers/oppressors." This is followed by Q. 5:46-47, which describes the revelations to Jesus Christ in similar terms ("light and guidance and an admonition for those who keep their duty") and a denunciation of the followers of Christ who do not judge by its standards as "transgressors" (see also Q. 7:170). It is at the end of this chronological discourse on the significance and importance of adhering to revealed scripture that the text appears: "To each of you we have given a path and a way." Given this context of recognizing the authenticity of the scriptures of the other, it follows that the text refers to the paths of the other in a similar vein.

As for its meaning, the essence of this text is located in the words *shir'a* and *minhaj*, both of which relate to "a path." While paths must be clear, comfortable, and scenic, and even at times a part of one's goal, they are never synonymous with it. The word *shari'a* and its variants appear only three times in the Qur'an; the word *Allah* appears approximately three thousand times. The text "There is no deity except Allah" thus means that God has determined a path for all people, both as individuals and as religious communities, and that one should be true to the path determined for him or her. Furthermore, should the path be so covered by cobwebs that it is no longer possible for one to move along it, then a person is free to choose another of the paths determined by Allah. The purpose is to vie with one another in righteousness toward Allah.

The text cited and discussed above (Q. 5:48) is one of two such verses that specifically employ the metaphor of competition. Both appear in a Medinan context of the Prophet engaging the People of the Book. The second one reads as follows:

> And each one has a goal toward which he strives [direction to which he turns] [*li kulli wijhah huwa muwalliha*]; so compete with one another in righteous deeds. Wherever you are, Allah will bring you all together. Surely Allah is able to do all things (Q. 2:148).

COMPETING IN RIGHTEOUSNESS

The metaphor of competition in righteousness is not regarded seriously in Qur'anic exegesis. The challenge to competition is immediately preceded by a statement on the diversity of religious paths: "And if God had pleased He would have made you a single *umma*. However, He desires to try you in what He gave you. So vie with one another in righteous deeds." Given that this competing in righteousness is between diverse communities, several implications follow: First, righteous deeds that are recognized and rewarded are not the monopoly of any single competitor. As the Qur'an says: "O humankind, We have created you from one male and female. We have made of you tribes and nations so that you may know one another. In the eyes of God, the noblest among you is the one who is most virtuous" (Q. 49:13). Second, the judge, God, has to be above the narrow interests of the participants. Third, claims of familiarity with the judge or mere identification with any particular team will not avail the participants. Fourth, the results of any just competition are never foregone conclusions.

The Qur'an makes several references to the theological difficulties of religious pluralism and of *kufr*. If God is One and if religion (*din*) originates with Him, why is it that humankind is not truly united in belief? Why do some people persist in rejection when "the truth is clearly distinguished from falsehood" (Q. 2:256; 23:90)? Why does God not will faith for everyone? These were some of the questions that appear to have vexed Mohammed and the early Muslims. In response to them, several texts urge an attitude of patience and humility; these questions are to be left to God, who will inform humankind about them on the Day of Requital. Other than the text under discussion (Q. 5:48), which addresses the people who have a *shir'a* and *minhaj*, saying "unto God you will return, so that he will inform you of that wherein you differed," the following text also conveys the call to patience and humility:

> God is your Lord and our Lord: Unto us our works and unto you your works; let there be no dispute between you and us. God will bring us together and to Him we shall return (Q. 42:15; 2:139).

As for those who persist in *kufr*, the Qur'an says:

> If your Lord had willed, all those on earth would have believed together. Would you then compel people to become believers? (Q. 10:99).

If God had so wanted, He could have made them a single people. But He admits whom He wills to His grace and, for the wrongdoers there will be no protector nor helper (Q. 42:8).

Revile not those unto whom they pray besides God, lest they wrongfully revile God through ignorance. Thus, unto every *umma* have we made their deeds seem fair. Then unto their Lord is their return, and he will tell them what they used to do (Q. 6:108).

Prophetic Responsibility in the Face of Religious Pluralism

If, as I have argued above, the Qur'an acknowledges the fact of religious diversity as the will of God, then a significant question which arises is that of Mohammed's responsibility to the adherents of other faiths. Rahman has correctly described the Qur'anic position regarding this relationship as "somewhat ambiguous."[18] From the Qur'an it would appear as if the fundamental prophetic responsibility was twofold. First, with regard to those who viewed themselves as communities adhering to a divine scripture, it was to challenge them regarding their commitment to their tradition and to engage them regarding their deviation from it. Second, with regard to all of humankind, to present the Qur'an's own guidance for consideration and acceptance. There are two ways of approaching this ambiguity: (1) to relate the first responsibility to the second one, for they are not entirely divorced from each other; and (2) to understand the context of different responsibilities and their applicability to specific components of the other at specific junctures in the relationship with the other.

The Qur'anic challenge to the exclusivist claims of the People of the Book has already been dealt with above. At other times various groups and individuals, among the People of the Book in particular, were challenged by Mohammed regarding their rejection of the signs of God (Q. 3:70-71; 3:98), their discouraging of others to walk the path of God (Q. 3:98-99), and their knowingly covering the truth with falsehood (Q. 3:70; 3:98-99). As for their scriptures, Mohammed, as indicated earlier, was expected to challenge them regarding their commitment to their own scriptures (Q. 5:68), their deviation from them, and their distortions thereof.

Muslim scholarship has largely argued that, given the distortion of non-Muslim scriptures, nothing in them has remained valid. In dealing with the Qur'anic references to the truth contained in these scriptures and exhortations to the People of the Book to uphold it, they have limited this obedience to the scripture to those texts that putatively predict Mohammed's prophethood. Notwithstanding this recognition of the legitimacy of the other revealed scriptures, Mohammed is still asked to proclaim: "O humankind! I am a Messenger of God unto all of you" (Q. 7:158). Mohammed thus had a task of proclaiming and calling in addition to that of challenging (Q. 16:125; 22:67).

On the face of it, these seem to be a set of contradictory responsibilities, for, if a text is distorted, how can one ask for adherence to it? In the second responsibility, that of inviting, the question arises regarding the purpose of inviting to one's own path if that of the other is also authentic. First, the problem of the authenticity of texts as against their being distorted, and thus invalid, only arises if one thinks in terms of a singularly homogeneous and unchanging entity called the People of the Book and if one divests all Qur'anic references to such an entity of their contextuality. It has been shown above that this is not the case. The Qur'an itself is silent about the extent and nature of this distortion and castigates "a section of the People of the Book." As indicated earlier, the uniformity of praise or blame for a particular religious group is contrary to the pattern of the Qur'an. It is thus possible that the references to the authenticity of their scriptures refer to those held by the rest. Indeed, even the Qur'anic denunciation of particular doctrinal "errors" is not uniform in tone. This indicates either a particular moment in the Muslim encounter with the other or different components of the other with specific nuances in reference to those "errors."

Mohammed's basic responsibility in inviting was to call to God. For some components of the other, the response to this call was best fulfilled by a commitment to Islam; thus they were also invited to become Muslims. For others, the call was limited to Islam. The invitation to the delegation from Najran is one such example. After they declined to enter into Islam, they were invited to "come to a word equal between us and you that we worship none but God, nor will we take from our ranks anyone as deities" (Q. 3:64). Thus the Qur'an is explicit only about inviting to God and to the "path of God." In the following text, for example, the instruction to invite people to God comes after an affirmation of the diversity of religious paths. Here again one sees the imperative of inviting to God, who is above the diverse paths that emanate from Him.

CONCLUSION: THE PREEMINENCE OF PLURALISM

The basis for the recognition of the other was clearly not the acceptance of a reified Islam and Mohammed's prophethood with all its implications, nor was it the absence of any principles. The fact that it was Mohammed and the Muslims who defined the basis of coexistence and who determined which form of submission was appropriate for which community clearly implies a Qur'anic insistence on an ideological leadership role for itself. This was explicit in the Qur'anic approach to relationships with other religious groups. This is a significant departure from the liberal position that equates coexistence and freedom with absolute equality for all. A fundamental question arises here: How is this Qur'anic position compatible with pluralism and justice?

The preeminence of the righteous does not mean a position of a permanently fixed socioreligious superiority for the Muslim community. It was not as if the Muslims as a social entity were superior to the other, for such a position would have placed them and their parochial God in the same category as others who were denounced in the Qur'an for the crimes of arrogance and desiring to appropriate God for a narrow community. There is no reason to suppose that the Qur'anic reprimand to other communities—that they cannot base their claims to superiority on the achievements of their forebearers—should not be applied to the post-Mohammedan Muslim community: "That is a community that is bygone; to them belongs what they earned and to you belongs what you earn, and you will not be asked about what they had done" (Q. 2:134).

Furthermore, the Qur'an does not regard all people and their ideas as equal but proceeds from the premise that the idea of inclusiveness is superior to that of exclusiveness. In this sense the advocates of pluralism have to be "above" those who insist that the religious expressions of others counts for nothing and that they are the only ones to attain salvation in the same way. The relationship between the inclusivist form of religion and the exclusivist form can be compared to that of a democratic state and fascist political parties, as Hassan Askari has cogently argued. If a group or party does not agree to the democratic rule and works to overthrow the government of the day by violent means in order to create a fascist social order wherein there is no room for democratic expression and exercise of opinion and power, that group cannot lay claim to those rights enjoined by a democracy. Inclusivity is not merely a willingness to let every idea and practice exist. Instead, it is directed toward specific objectives such as freeing humankind from injustice and servitude to other human beings so that they may be free to worship God. According to the Qur'an, the beliefs of non-accountability to God and *shirk* are intrinsically connected to the socioeconomic practices of the Arabs. In order to ensure justice for all, it was important for Mohammed and his community to work actively against those beliefs and not accord them a position of equality.

The responsibility of *da'wa*, "calling humankind" to God and to the path of God, thus remains. The task of the present-day Muslim is to discern what this means in every age and every society. Who are to be invited? Who are to be taken as allies in this calling? How does one define the path of God? These are particularly pertinent questions in a society in which definitions of self and other are determined by justice and injustice, oppression and liberation, and where the test of one's integrity as a human being dignified by God is the extent of one's commitment to defend that dignity.

Part Three

MAINLINE CHRISTIANITY

◆

7

PROSELYTISM AND WITNESS IN EARLIEST CHRISTIANITY

An Essay on Origins

———◆———

Luke Timothy Johnson

INTRODUCTION

Contemporary proselytism undoubtedly draws its linguistic and conceptual antecedents from the Jewish and Christian tradition. That it can appeal to those traditions for its moral warrant is far less certain. This chapter is an exercise in sorting out that distinction and begins with some general framing comments.

The basic linguistic point is the most obvious and easiest to make. The term *proselytos* ("one who has approached") appears for the first time in the Greek translation of the Hebrew Bible (the Septuagint) to render the term *ger*,[1] which referred primarily to those who were sojourners and aliens in the land of Israel,[2] and came to be applied to those—like Rahab and Ruth—who then attached themselves to the people and adopted Jewish identity through circumcision and the observance of the commandments of Torah.[3]

The basic conceptual point is more difficult. To what ancient or contemporary reality or practice does the term *proselytize* refer? The term can refer to five distinct postures taken by a group toward outsiders: (1) The group (and individuals within it) is open to new members and welcomes "those who approach." (2) The group and its representatives proclaim the group's message and seek to convince others of its worth so that they might join the group and share in its benefits. (3) The group and its emissaries seek to turn others away from their present allegiance out of the conviction that they are in error. (4) The group and its scouts seek to rescue others from imminent danger out of the conviction that they are under evil and destructive influences. (5) The group and its agents seek to coerce membership in the group as part of a strategy of religious or cultural hegemony.

The first and last of these options seem morally clear: the first is fully benign, and the last is totally wrong.[4] Moral ambiguity enters into the middle three options: The second seems to be not only morally defensible but also sociologically and psychologically inevitable, the natural overflow of sincere commitment and high levels of enthusiasm. The third and fourth options are increasingly problematic not so much for the methods they employ (which might be various) but for the judgment concerning outsiders on which they are based and the degree of coerciveness that might be implicit in the methods of recruitment. In the fourth option, even if one grants the validity of the "mortal danger" premise, there is still the questionable character of seeking to "rescue" those who may not in the least agree with the diagnosis.

In the first-century Mediterranean world within which Christianity arose, dramatically expanded its membership, and composed its canonical writings, the first three options are widely attested and regarded as morally unremarkable. The fourth option is unattested before Christianity and even within Christianity is hard to detect before the time of Constantine. After Constantine's establishment of Christianity as the imperial religion, even the fifth option makes an appearance. Augustine's interpretation of the phrase "compel them to come in" (*compelle intrare*) in Luke 14:23 as support for the forcible conversion of Donatists is perhaps the most infamous early example,[5] although the entire sequence of book-burnings, property seizures, controlling laws, and inquisitions offers an impressive catalogue of techniques by which Christendom sought a religiously uniform society.[6] It is the argument of the present chapter, however, that the normative New Testament writings offer no real support for such morally reprehensible actions, and, when properly assessed, provide compelling arguments against any form of proselytism that involves elements of coercion, including psychological pressure.

THE ANCIENT CONTEXT

In order to evaluate early Christian practice and ideology accurately, it is important to place the first Christian writings in their symbolic world.[7] Placing the texts in their original context does not by itself determine their meaning, but is the premise for any serious and disciplined engagement with them for the purpose of moral discernment.[8] Without knowing something of this context, neither contemporary approbation nor contemporary rejection of them is likely to be adequately based. The task here is to establish the basic options concerning persuasion and conversion for intentional communities within the Greco-Roman world. I consider in turn: Greco-Roman religion, Hellenistic philosophy, Judaism as a philosophy, and Christianity as a philosophy.

GRECO-ROMAN RELIGION

Proselytism in any form is virtually nonexistent in Greco-Roman religion. The reasons are not difficult to find. Religiosity was less private than public, less a matter of individual conviction than of social observance. It had more to do with a sharing in divine benefits than it did with attaining a future life. The polytheistic system that underlay all ancient Mediterranean cultures except the Jewish was, moreover, markedly inclusive and noncompetitive in its view of the divine power.[9]

If the divine realm is conceived as an extended family, and if the membrane separating mortals and immortals is permeable, then it is possible not only for the gods to metamorphose into humans but also for humans of outstanding virtue or valor to find a place among the gods.[10] The Hellenistic project of religious syncretism merely made this religious capaciousness more explicit by acknowledging that by whatever names the same divine power-field was engaged by all.[11] In the Hellenistic period we certainly find—for example, among some Stoics—ways of speaking about the divine that approach a monotheistic piety, as in Cleanthes' famous prayer to Zeus.[12] Implicit in such speech is a recognition of the unity of the divine energy. But we find no sign of a monotheism that excludes the divine character of the other gods. Zeus, if you will, is the personification of the entire divine family, rather than the only divine member among demonic pretenders.[13]

We have evidence of propaganda for various cults in the Hellenistic period, especially in connection with the new mystery cults from the East.[14] Certainly, Apuleius's novel *Metamorphoses* can be regarded as a recommendation of the Isis cult,[15] and Aelius Aristides' *Sacred Tales* as propaganda for the healing god Aesculapius.[16] These advertisements for the benefits to be gained by devotion to a particular god or goddess, however, never imply that such devotion should be exclusive.[17] Initiation into multiple mysteries was by no means uncommon and was regarded as a mark of exceptional piety rather than of unstable conviction.[18] A devotee of Serapis would not try to persuade a Jew to abandon YHWH in order to join his cult; devotion to Serapis, as to any god, was seen as an enrichment of other loyalties rather than a replacement of them.

GRECO-ROMAN PHILOSOPHY

The situation is strikingly different in the case of Greco-Roman philosophy as it develops in the early empire.[19] Philosophy took a turn from theory to therapy; its subjects were no longer the ideal city-state and the nature of knowledge, but the ways of being a good person in an alienating social environment.[20] Philosophy was regarded less as a set of ideas than as a way of life to which adherents committed themselves. In its patterns of organization—the formation of schools, memorization of teachings of founders, sharing of possessions, testing of recruits—philosophy revealed itself as a form of intentional community that was profoundly religious in character.[21]

Three aspects of philosophy's self-understanding as a vocation are of greatest importance for our subject. The first is the governing metaphor of medicine: vice is sickness, virtue is health, the philosophical school is a hospital, the philosophical teacher is the doctor of the soul.[22] If vice is spiritual sickness, then a person who is ignorant and immoral is not merely unfortunate but in grave danger. Turning to philosophy is a way of saving one's life. This leads to the second characteristic, which is the understanding of the turn to philosophy as a conversion demanding total dedication and a lifelong dedication.[23] Health is not won all at once but must be nourished within the framework of the proper treatment and teaching.[24] This sense of exclusive commitment to a teaching points in turn to the third characteristic, which is the competitive nature of philosophy in the early empire.[25] Though there was broad agreement on the basic goals of philosophy, schools differed sharply in the means to accomplish those goals. They competed for adherents and developed polemic intended to demean and diminish the teachings of other schools.[26] In contrast to the inclusive character of Greco-Roman religion, which saw multiple ways of gaining access to the divine power, Greco-Roman philosophy constructed exclusive and competing approaches to that form of salvation which was the virtuous life.

JUDAISM AS PHILOSOPHY

The most immediate context for earliest Christianity was a Judaism that had, under the influence of an aggressive Hellenistic culture, come to resemble Greco-Roman philosophy in more than superficial fashion. Judaism was still, of course, a "national cult" that more properly might be called a family religion. Its ancestral law was the *ethos* of this ancient *ethnos*.[27] Those who entered the land were welcomed into the people when they chose to live according to its norms, but there is no indication that ancient Israel sought "converts."[28] Intrinsic to its ethos, however, was the conviction that there was only one personification of the divine power. The observance of the Sabbath, the keeping of dietary and purity regulations, the practice of circumcision, the living of life according to the commandments, all these were in service of this one God, and a sign to the world that as this God was "Holy"—that is, different from the world—so would the people God had chosen be "Holy"—that is, different within the world (Lv 19:2). If YHWH was God, then all the gods of the nations are but idols—or, as in the Septuagint rendering, "demons."[29] Already in the exilic prophets this monotheistic conviction had come into conflict with the idolatry of the captor nations, generating a tradition of polemic against the gods of the Gentiles.[30]

The Jewish "way of life" (*halakha*), especially in the diaspora but also in Palestine, would naturally be perceived by Gentile observers as a form of philosophy: it had a coherent teaching, forms of fellowship, strict code of ethics, an altogether admirable form of wisdom. Nor is it surprising to find Josephus describe the "sects" of Judaism in Palestine as philosophical "schools," comparable to the Stoics, Pythagoreans, and Epicureans.[31] And writers such as Philo Judaeus not only think of life according to Torah as a philosophy but describe Moses as a philosopher from whom the Greeks learned their wisdom.[32] In the diaspora, separated from those "national" social and political institutions that could be found only in Palestine (the land, the Temple, the kingship), Judaism would appear even more like an intentional community, a philosophical school in competition with other forms of philosophy of the Greco-Roman world.

Given this profile, we are not surprised that Judaism in the Hellenistic period should have developed two new features pertinent to our subject. The first is the use of polemic against other traditions such as we find attested in Greco-Roman philosophical schools. Not only is such polemic found as an expression of the rivalry between the various Jewish sects, but it appears also against Greco-Roman religious traditions.[33] The ancient prophetic critique of idolatry now takes on a new urgency, as the practice of idolatry is not simply dismissed as foolish but is connected to every form of vice and societal malfeasance.[34] The corollary of such systematic deprecation of the Gentile world is that its inhabitants are in need of "saving"; they are not only in error, they are in danger. The competitive edge found in the philosophical schools is now connected to the unique claims of monotheism: only by belonging to the School of Moses can one fully live out the way of virtue.[35]

The second development—with the link to the first being obvious—is the practice of proselytism as an active interest in gaining converts to Judaism. The evidence is not extensive but is suggestive.[36] The synagogue functioned as a magnet for Gentiles, some of whom converted in the full sense by receiving circumcision and observing the laws, and some of whom were drawn into the circle of "God-Fearers" and perhaps observed some minimal obligations that enabled Jews to have table-fellowship with them.[37] Josephus reports one case in which circumcision was forcibly imposed.[38] What is most under dispute is the degree to which the evidence points to an active program of proselytizing.[39]

The New Testament itself provides the earliest and best evidence for missionary efforts by Jews, but its evidence is obviously colored by the perspective of a rival party. In Matthew 23:15 Jesus is made to address the "scribes and Pharisees," who, after the fall of the Temple in 70 C.E., became the other claimants to the heritage of Israel; his statement may be taken, however, as reflecting the historical situation of Matthew's church.[40] Matthew's gospel was written precisely in the context of conflict with this developing form of Judaism: "Woe to you, scribes and Pharisees, hypocrites, because you travel around the sea and the desert in order to make one proselyte, and when [he] becomes one, you make [him] twice the son of hell that you are!" The passage contains the conventional language of polemic,[41] but it suggests that there was real competition for conversions between these rival versions of Judaism around 85 C.E.[42] Far harder to evaluate is the evidence concerning the "Judaizers" in Pauline churches and their (possibly) Jewish sponsors.[43] Was the desire of some Gentile Christians to be circumcised and adopt the observance of Torah generated from within, or did it result from a sustained missionary activity by Jews among Gentiles in direct competition with Paul, using techniques of religious propaganda?[44]

EARLY CHRISTIAN PRACTICE

Christianity's first rapid expansion across the Mediterranean world must be assessed within the context just described.[45] Christianity was from the start an "intentional community" rather than a national cult, since it began as a sect of Judaism.[46] Within a generation, furthermore, it had not only established communities from Palestine to Rome but had extended membership to Gentiles, among whom the movement had significantly more success than among Jews.[47] It is obvious, therefore, that *some* form of proselytism was practiced by the first Christians, for its growth is otherwise incomprehensible.[48] More difficult to determine is the exact form of proselytism and the ideology underlying it.

It is only an apparent paradox to characterize the first expansion of Christianity as haphazard but purposeful. Despite the rapidity of the movement's expansion, the sources do not suggest a particularly high level of organization.[49] The evidence of persecution and harassment from both fellow-Jews and Gentiles from the beginning points to geographical expansion occurring at least in part as a result of necessity: being expelled from one location, Christians moved on to another.[50] Although there is evidence for some degree of consultation and cooperation among leaders,[51] this does not imply a centralized control of the mission.[52] And because the outward expansion began virtually at once, without a long period of time for stabilizing traditions, the many transitions demanded of the first adherents had to be negotiated by agents on the spot rather than according to the prescriptions of a master plan.[53]

The purposefulness of the expansion is well expressed by the compositions that speak of a sense of "mission" or of a "call" to announce the good news of what God had done through a crucified and raised Messiah.[54] The ending of each of the canonical Gospels contains an explicit statement of mission. The longer ending of Mark has Jesus tell his followers, "Go into all the world and preach the gospel to the whole creation. He who believes and is baptized will be saved, but he who does not believe will be condemned" (Mk 16:16).[55] At the end of Matthew, the resurrected Jesus tells his disciples: "All authority in heaven and earth has been given to me. Go therefore and make disciples of all nations, baptizing them in the name of the father and of the son and of the holy spirit, teaching them to observe all that I have commanded you" (Mt 28:19-20).[56] Luke-Acts contains a double commissioning. In Luke 24:46-48 Jesus tells his followers: "Thus it is written that the Christ should suffer and on the third day rise from the dead, and that repentance and forgiveness of sins should be preached in his name to all nations, beginning from Jerusalem. You are witnesses of these things." In Acts 1:8, "You shall receive power when the Holy Spirit comes upon you; and you shall be my witnesses in Jerusalem and in all Judea and Samaria and to the end of the earth."[57] In John's gospel the commission is more muted: "As the Father has sent me, even so I send you . . . receive the Holy Spirit. If you forgive the sins of any, they are forgiven; and if you retain the sins of any, they are retained" (Jn 20:21-22).[58] These texts, composed when the movement had been in existence already some forty to fifty years, clearly connect a sense of worldwide mission to the powerful presence and authorization of the risen Christ.

In the correspondence of the man who was, if not the key figure, at the very least a participant in the expansion of Christianity beyond its location as a Jewish sect into the Gentile world, we find the same sense of a divine commission from the resurrected Jesus (see Rom 1:1-5; 15:17; Gal 1:16; 2:8; Col 1:25-27; Eph 3:7). Paul considers himself to have been "called" to be an apostle (1 Cor 1:1), and to have been "entrusted" with the task of preaching it (1 Tm 1:11). He is "controlled by" the love of Christ (2 Cor 5:14) and under the necessity of preaching (1 Cor 9:16). The sense of urgency that enables Paul to undergo persecution, hardships, and rejection (1 Cor 4:9-13; 2 Cor 11:23-29) in order to fulfill his calling is also connected to a conviction that history is moving toward its climactic end and that his work is in service of God's plan.[59] The resurrection of Jesus is proleptic of a still greater and more definitive victory of God (1 Thes 1:9-10; 4:13–5:11; 1 Cor 15:51-58).

Earliest Christianity thus takes over from Judaism the outlook and behavior of a philosophical school but invests them with an even more specific focus. The call to monotheism is now articulated as faith in Jesus as Messiah (see 1 Thes 1:9-10; 1 Cor 8:8-10) with a definite eschatological edge. The resurrection is viewed as the beginning of God's cosmic victory (1 Thes 4:14; 5:9-10), but the in-between time (of whatever duration) is one in which the opponents of the church can easily be portrayed as instruments of the cosmic forces opposing God's victory.[60] The anti-idolatry polemic of Judaism therefore takes on an even sharper tone: the practices of the pagan world are not merely foolish or futile, they are sponsored by demons (1 Cor 10:20-21).[61] It does not take too great a leap to connect a spiritual triumph over such forces with a more palpable conquest of pagan practices.[62] Efforts to convert others also are affected by a sense of eschatological urgency. If God's final triumph is an expression of "wrath," in which God's enemies will be "destroyed by the breath of his mouth" (2 Thes 2:8),[63] then the desire to rescue or "save" as many people as possible from this future cataclysm is the more understandable; as it is put in the mouth of Peter at Pentecost, "save yourselves from this crooked generation" (Acts 2:40).[64]

Actual proselytizing practices in earliest Christianity are not entirely accessible. Certainly open-air proclamation or preaching, which is associated already with the ministry of Jesus,[65] and which is attested also among Cynic philosophers,[66] played some role. Acts shows Peter proclaiming the gospel at Pentecost to the crowd of pilgrims (Acts 2:14-40; 3:12-26); Paul debating with passers-by in the marketplace of Athens, which led to an opportunity to proclaim in the Areopagus (17:17-31); and Apollos debating Jews in public (Acts 18:28). The local synagogue also became the site of preaching and debate over the scriptures concerning the claims of the messianists (Acts 9:20; 13:5, 14-41; 14:1-2; 17:1, 17; 18:4, 19; 19:8).[67] Disturbances created in these contexts sometimes led to hearings before authorities, which provided further opportunities for proclaiming the message in the guise of defense speeches (Acts 4:8-12; 5:29-32; 7:2-53; 22:3-21; 24:1-10; 26:2-23) or to impressed jailers (Acts 16:25-34). The disturbance caused by Paul's preaching in the synagogue in Ephesus led to his having to use the lecture hall of a certain Tyrannus, which he then used for some two years as his base of operations (Acts 19:9-10). The proclamation of Jesus led to imprisonment for some (Acts 5:18; 8:3; 12:3-5; 16:23-24; 22:24-30; 23:35; 24:27; 28:16) and death for others (Acts 7:58-60; 12:2).

Acts also shows people opening their homes to missionaries, as Peter was welcomed by the friends of Tabitha (Acts 9:36-43), which led to a sojourn in the house of Simon (Acts 9:43), and into the house of Cornelius, where the entire Gentile household received the Holy Spirit when Peter proclaimed the good news (Acts 10:24-48). Likewise, Paul was invited to the house of Lydia (Acts 16:14-15). Paul also made use of contacts with the local gentry when they were of a religious bent: his confrontation with a magician before the proconsul Sergius Paulus on Cyprus (Acts 13:6-12), his friendship with the Asiarchs in Ephesus (Acts 19:31), and his visit to the leading citizen of Malta, Publius (Acts 18:7-10). Philip likewise takes advantage of a "chance" encounter with the treasurer of the queen of Ethiopia to preach Jesus (Acts 8:26-39). Thaumaturgy plays a definite role in drawing attention to the message delivered by the Christian missionaries and providing the opportunity for conversion (Acts 3:1–4:4; 8:4-8; 9:32-35; 13:11-12; 14:8-18; 16:25-34; 19:11-20; 28:1-10).[68]

Evidence from the letters of Paul for the actual process of proselytizing is sparse. They are addressed to communities already in existence and provide no account of a church's founding. His letters do, however, confirm the account of Acts in significant ways. Some sort of public proclamation or preaching, for example, is associated, at least ideally, with the community's formation (Rom 15:19-20; 1 Cor 2:1-5; 9:16; 2 Cor 2:12; Gal 3:1-5; 1 Thes 1:5-6; see also Heb 2:3; 1 Pt 1:25). The location of communities in households is also supported by Paul (1 Cor 1:16; 16:15-19; Phlm 1; Col 4:15), as is the significance of converting people of some visibility (1 Cor 1:16; 16:15-18; Rom 16:1-3, 23; Phlm 1; Phil 4:22).[69]

Paul by no means downplays the role of wonderworking in the foundation of a community; in fact, he emphasizes it (1 Thes 1:5; Gal 3:5; 2 Cor 12:12; 1 Cor 2:2; 4:20; Rom 15:18-19).[70] Finally, Paul confirms that his activities led to a variety of sanctions, including imprisonment, testifying to their socially disruptive character (2 Cor 11:24-29).[71]

The apocryphal acts of the apostles contain important evidence concerning the spread of Christianity. Even if much of their account is legendary in character, it has value as expressing perceptions of the mission from the perspective of the second and third century.[72] Once more, we find the apostles preaching in public as well as in domestic spaces.[73] Households that receive the wandering apostles are important locations for further conversions.[74] There is almost an obsession with making converts out of high-status persons like prefects and senators and kings.[75] Wonderworking emerges even more emphatically as an instrument for getting attention and persuading, in some cases leading directly to conversion.[76] These accounts also show the apostles suffering imprisonment and death for the ways in which they had disrupted the social order.[77]

The most notable disagreement in our earliest sources concerns a subject which is at the heart of the present-day concern about proselytism, namely, the degree to which witnessing to a religious conviction becomes intrusive or coercive. It is impossible to avoid the impression in the apocryphal acts that the portrayal of the various apostles steps over the line between enthusiastic sharing and psychological manipulation. This is most obvious in the cases of women whose devotion to the gospel—or to the apostle!—persuades them to abandon their intended or longtime spouse for the sake of a celibate existence as a Christian, with some of them explicitly told that this is the path they must follow.[78] Paul is accused by the outraged men in Iconium of being a sorcerer who has "corrupted all our wives."[79]

In the canonical letters of Paul to his delegates Timothy and Titus, in contrast, such tactics are ascribed to those teachers who have set themselves up in opposition to Paul's mission. On Crete, those from the circumcision party "are upsetting entire households" with their teaching on the necessity of keeping purity regulations (Ti 1:10-16). Even more strikingly, the false teachers in 2 Timothy are said to "make their way into households and capture weak women, burdened with sins and swayed by various impulses, who will listen to anybody and can never arrive at a knowledge of the truth" (2 Tm 3:6-7).[80] Whether or not these letters are regarded as Paul's own or as deriving from someone writing in Paul's name,[81] they demonstrate an awareness within the Pauline tradition that the sort of intrusiveness and manipulation suggested by the apocryphal acts is not an acceptable form of witness. The presence of these warnings within the canonical texts provides an important basis for a critical reflection on the practice and ideology of proselytism within Christianity.

ASSESSING THE CANONICAL SOURCES

In order to engage the discussion of the legitimacy or limits of proselytism in today's world, Christians must particularly engage the canonical writings of the New Testament that form the normative framework for debates over Christian identity and practice.[82] The apocryphal writings may be of great value in reconstructing the past, but precisely because they are not part of the church's canon, they do not enter into discussions concerning decisions for the present. Engagement with the canonical writings, furthermore, involves weighing them in a number of ways. Placing them in their historical context in order to understand both the range of and the reasons for their statements is fundamental. But assessing the diversity and divergence among the witnesses is equally important when trying to reach some sense of the witness of these writings. And all of this is still preliminary to the more difficult question of the role of that witness in decisions about present practice; exegesis is the basis rather than the essence of hermeneutics.[83]

It is important to assert in the flattest terms, however, that the New Testament offers no support for any sort of evangelization or proselytism that would seek conversions in order to strengthen the social or political agenda of Christian churches, nor any program of activity that would employ or accept the help of the state as an agent of proselytism. Any appeal to the New Testament in support of such efforts is a distortion of its witness.

Despite the amount of evidence concerning evangelism as carried out by leaders of the first generation, the New Testament is remarkably reticent concerning the place of such evangelization either as the mandate of the church as such or as an element in the life of the ordinary believer. Efforts to persuade others to believe are not ascribed or recommended to Christians apart from those with a commission, either from the risen Lord or by the community, to carry out such a task. In the sense of verbal proclamation with the intention of converting others, evangelism is nowhere stated as an essential dimension of Christian identity.[84] Although Peter exhorts his readers to be prepared to "make a defense (*apologia*) to anyone who calls you to account for the hope that is in you," he wants this to be done "with gentleness and reverence." He puts greatest emphasis on living in a way that will persuade more effectively than by words: "and keep your conscience clear, so that, when you are abused, those who revile your good name in Christ may be put to shame" (1 Pt 3:15).

The focus of the New Testament compositions is inward rather than outward. None of the compositions was written for the purposes of evangelization.[85] All were composed in order to persuade and transform those already part of the Christian community, in order to shape a certain character that can be expressed as "walking worthily of God" (1 Thes 2:12).[86] Such communal witness is to serve as a sign to the world of God's work and (we assume) is to attract others to join the community by the beauty and persuasiveness of its form of life.[87]

The emphasis is placed, however, not on witness as proclamation to others, but on witness as living true to God.[88] This sort of witness can draw people to the community, but it can also generate the exact opposite response, as the Johannine literature attests: a prophetic community that testifies to the truth of God and resists the seduction of the world's idolatry can find itself marginalized, rejected, and persecuted.[89] The measure of the church's success is not in any case the number of its members but the character of its life.[90] If its manner of life testifies to the reality of God's reconciling work in the world, then it has fulfilled its mission. This understanding of the church's mission is everywhere implicit in Paul's letters, and it is made explicit in Ephesians, which pictures the church as a *sacramentum mundi*, the effective sign of what the world might become, a place of reconciliation between those who are at enmity.[91]

Most of all, the moral teaching of the New Testament—the kind of behavior it inculcates among believers—moves in the exact opposite direction from any sort of proselytizing activity that involves psychological, much less physical, coercion or pressure.[92] There is to be mutual correction and exhortation in the community, yes, for how could there be a communal moral effort without such cooperation?[93] But it is always to tend toward the building up of the community. And the harsh manner of the Cynic philosophers attacking the morals of others is explicitly eschewed.[94] Paul adopts the gentle manner of the nurse with his communities[95] and recommends the same gentle manner to his delegates.[96] Judgment of others, in the sense of a moral condemnation of them, is explicitly forbidden.[97] Correction even of the most grievous faults is to be undertaken delicately, and with an eye toward healing and reconciliation. The words of Paul in Galatians 6:1-5 are typical:

> Brethren, if anyone is overtaken in any trespass, you who are spiritual should restore him in a spirit of gentleness. Look to yourself, lest you too be tempted. Bear one another's burdens, and so fulfill the law of Christ. For if anyone thinks he is something, when he is nothing, he deceives himself. But let each one test his own work, and then his reason to boast will be in himself alone and not in his neighbor. For each person will have to bear one's own load.

Even this pattern of mutual correction and edification is subject to limits. Paul's discussion of diversity in practice concerning diet and the observance of feasts in 1 Corinthians 8-10 and Romans 14 shows how seriously he takes the primacy of the individual conscience as determinant of behavior.[98] Far from allowing behavior that would impose on others standards that they are not yet ready to accept internally, Paul advocates the most delicate respect for the moral sensibilities of "the brother or sister for whom Christ died."[99]

CONCLUSIONS

Especially in the light of the way in which that strand within the New Testament that calls for a witness to all nations has been interpreted as an effort to make conversions, if necessary by means of coercion, Christians are today required to engage the texts of their tradition with particular rigor and honesty. They can neither deny the commission of their Lord to bear witness nor relinquish the teaching of that same Lord to live in a manner worthy of God. It seems appropriate therefore to reinterpret the mandate to mission in light of the moral imperative to respect the freedom of other humans.

In particular, it is necessary to reconsider the various practices revealed in these ancient texts in the light of changing circumstances, to see whether activities that may have been understandable and even laudable in another cultural context—as in a situation where Christianity was the tiniest and least powerful of minority movements—might be morally questionable in another cultural context, in which Christianity is a culturally and politically powerful agent. The ways in which Christian evangelism has been connected to programs of political and cultural hegemony in particular require the sharpest possible inquiry into the appropriateness of missionary activities. In this light the position taken by Paul's letters to Timothy and Titus are of particular value in pointing out that practices disruptive of households are off limits to Christian evangelists.

The bases for the concerted missionary effort in earliest Christianity also need to be reconsidered. The mission was driven, I have suggested, by the eschatological conviction that the end of time was approaching when those who were not among God's people would be punished. In this understanding, the gathering of people into the fold by virtually any means could possibly be justified as an act of mercy. This sense of eschatological urgency built on the prior perception of Judaism that Gentiles lived in a world of moral squalor and destruction, from which only the explicit worship of the one God of Israel could save them. Salvation, therefore, meant making that commitment to "the living and true God," now in terms of the raised Messiah Jesus, before the end of the ages (1 Thes 1:9-10).[100]

The experiences of Christians over the past two millennia have shown what disastrous results—for the church as well as for others—have come about by missionary practice based on such premises. The growth in understanding directed by the Holy Spirit has also fundamentally revised our very understanding of those premises. It is not necessary to understand eschatology as the imminent expectation of the end-time, not necessary to view non-Christians as in immediate peril of perdition, not necessary to view salvation as dependent on an explicit confession that Jesus is Lord.[101] A change in understanding does not mean the loss of a sense of witness or mission, but it does mean a modification of them.

It is possible to understand eschatology in terms of the church's witness to the contingency of all created things and the refusal to submit to any idolatrous claim made by creatures for themselves, a witness spelled out in a loyalty to God and a life in the world of "eschatological detachment." It is possible to view those outside the church as themselves gifted by God and responding to God in ways as yet unknown to us in lives that are not necessarily destructive but rather creative. It is possible to view salvation not as dependent on an explicit acknowledgment of Jesus' lordship but dependent rather on a faithful response to the truth as it is available in one's own circumstances. And within such an understanding, it is possible to understand the church's mission "to make disciples of all nations" in terms of making explicit for the world what God is already doing implicitly, and as inviting the world to join in a fellowship of explicit praise to God for a gift in which the world already to some degree shares.

If the church's presence in the world is to have moral probity in the context of global pluralism, then it must make the turn from a commitment to proselytism understood as the seeking of members to a commitment to witness understood as the task of providing a "light to the nations" by which they can actually see God.

8.

THE GREAT COMMISSION
AND THE CANON LAW

The Catholic Law of Mission

———◆———

James Muldoon

Christ's injunction to his apostles, "Go ye therefore, and teach all nations, baptizing them in the name of the Father, and of the Son, and of the Holy Ghost" (Mt 28:19; Mk 16:15, KJV) is the fundamental statement of the obligation of Christians to disperse throughout the world, spreading the good news of the gospel. For the first millennium of the Christian era this injunction was usually heeded by individuals, sometimes supported by secular rulers, who felt inspired to preach to one or another of the pagan peoples who lived along the borders of Christian Europe.[1] Patrick, Boniface, and scores of other missionaries whose names fill the histories of the Christian missionary endeavor acted not as agents of a church but as individuals who were impelled to heed Christ's injunction personally. Even the one example of papally directed missionary activity, the mission of Augustine of Canterbury to England in 597, was popularly believed to have been Pope Gregory I's (590-604) personal response to the sight of a group of Anglo-Saxon slaves in Rome, not to a formal papal policy of missionary work.[2]

MEDIEVAL FORMULATIONS

Only with the centralization of the church during the investiture controversy of the eleventh and twelfth centuries did missionary efforts become permanently associated with an organized institutional effort led by the papacy and, eventually, become incorporated within the law of the church. With the creation of the ecclesiastical structure that even now undergirds Catholic Christianity and with the formation of the canon law that articulated the principles of that ecclesiastical structure, missionary effort became part of the church's official policy.[3] Missionaries (like clerics everywhere) and their work became subject to direct papal supervision and the subject of legal discussion and analysis.

The two basic volumes of the canon law, Gratian's *Decretum* (c. 1140) and the *Decretales* (1234), did not devote any space to the specific issue of missionary endeavor. Furthermore, there was no legal treatise devoted to the status of the missionary and his task.[4] Curiously, much of the discussion of missionary effort came in connection with the Crusades. As Benjamin Kedar has pointed out, discussions of the morality of the crusading movement inevitably raised the issue of how best to deal with the Muslims. In the twelfth century, as he phrased it, "sword and word are first presented as two distinct approaches to the Saracens. . . . "[5] In a larger sense, the sword and the word can also be joined, as when the Crusader legitimately protects the missionary as he goes about his salvific preaching.

What might be termed the official position on the mission and the missionary appears in two related thirteenth-century documents, the papal bull *Cum hora undecima*, first issued by Pope Gregory IX (1227-41) in 1235, and a commentary on a chapter of the *Decretales* written by the most important canon lawyer of the thirteenth century, Sinibaldo Fieschi, better known as Pope Innocent IV (1243-54).[6] Innocent IV's commentary dealing with the issue of missionary activities is especially important because in his capacity as pope he began the so-called Mongol Mission, sending Franciscans to meet with the Mongol Khan in an attempt to ease tensions between the Christian world and the Mongols. In other words, he was both a theorist and a sponsor of missionary efforts. As part of his practical involvement in missionary efforts, Innocent IV also reissued *Cum hora undecima*.

The bull *Cum hora undecima* reflected the apocalyptic strain in thirteenth-century Christianity, a strain that was especially strong among the members of the newly formed Franciscan order.[7] The opening words of the bull, "Now that the eleventh hour has come in the day given to mankind," reflected the apocalyptic belief that the end of the world was near. That being the case, "it is necessary that spiritual men [possessing] purity of life and the gift of intelligence should go forth with John [the Baptist] again to all men and all peoples of every tongue and in every kingdom to prophesy. . . . "[8] Only then will Christ's injunction to his followers be fulfilled and the task for which the church was established be completed.

The first version of *Cum hora undecima* licensed, so to speak, missionaries who were expected to preach to a wide range of peoples. In addition to a general charge to preach to Saracens and pagans, the bull listed eighteen specific peoples to whom the missionaries should preach. These latter included a variety of schismatic and heretical Christian communities in the East, groups such as the Greeks, Armenians, and Nestorians.[9] When Innocent IV reissued the bull in 1245, he retained the basic structure and themes of the letter, adding more specific details about such matters as marriage law and other sacramental issues so that schismatics and heretics could be more easily reconciled with the Church of Rome. This version of the letter was the one that was periodically reissued as late as the early fifteenth century.[10]

Underlying *Cum hora undecima* was an assumption that schismatic, heretical, and non-Christian societies would (or should) accept Christian missionaries and allow them to preach in peace. In 1245, Innocent IV acted on this assumption when he sent the Franciscan John of Plano Carpini and a companion on a mission to the Mongol Khan. The friar carried with him two letters from the pope to the Khan outlining some of the principles of the Christian faith, but, more strikingly, emphasizing the common rationality of all mankind. By sending a pair of unarmed friars into the heart of the Mongol Empire, Innocent was demonstrating his adherence to the premise of Christ's missionary mandate: "Behold, I send you forth as sheep into the midst of wolves" (Mt 10:16).

Innocent IV's first letter to the Khan contained a brief outline of God's relationship to mankind, identifying the incarnation of Christ as the divine response to man's need for redemption from sin. Innocent pointed out that "human nature, being endowed with reason, was meet to be nourished on eternal truth as its choicest food," but, because of the chains of sin, could not have tasted of the divine nourishment without Christ's life and death. Innocent then turned to his own role in the work of preaching the message of Christ. As the head of Christ's church, he was responsible for ensuring the preaching of the message throughout the world. He then requested that the Khan "receive these Friars kindly and to treat them in considerate fashion" because they were his representatives. Furthermore, the pope requested the Khan to "furnish them with a safe-conduct and other necessities" so that they could return home safely.[11]

Innocent IV's other letter to the Mongol Khan dealt with the military threat that the Mongols presented to the Christians of eastern Europe. He opened this letter with a description of a naturally peaceful world order: "not only men but even irrational animals, nay, the very elements which go to make up the world machine, are united by a certain innate law after the manner of the celestial spirits, all of which God the Creator has divided into choirs in the enduring stability of peaceful order. . . . "[12]

By their attacks on eastern Europe, especially against the Christians who lived there, the Mongols were upsetting the natural order of the world. The pope had sent the friars to point out to the Khan the error of his ways, to ascertain his plans for the future, and to lead him and his people into the path of peace.

It is clear that the goals of the Mongol Mission were both religious and diplomatic. Although neither aspect of the mission proved successful, the letters of Innocent IV to the Khan contain some suggestions about how a thirteenth-century pope thought missionary work should proceed. In the first place, following a long tradition that stretched back to the late Roman Empire, Innocent IV addressed the leader of the Mongols and appears to have hoped that if the Mongol Khan became a Christian, his people would follow him to the baptismal font, as, for example, the Franks had followed Clovis in the fifth century and other medieval societies followed their rulers. As Christopher Dawson has pointed out, the medieval approach to missionary effort was "collective or communal," unlike modern approaches that are based "on the principle of individual conversion."[13] In taking this position, Innocent reflected the view that rulers had a responsibility for the spiritual well-being of their subjects, a view articulated in royal coronation oaths.[14] He also assumed that the Khan would respect the persons of the missionaries, even if he did not accept their message, because they came unarmed and in peace. Furthermore, the pope also appears to have believed that a rational presentation of the Christian worldview would be sufficient to win over the Khan to the Christian faith.[15]

The Mongol Mission provided a striking example of how the leadership of the medieval church attempted to fulfill Christ's injunction to preach his message to all mankind. If that experience was all that we had on which to base our understanding of medieval mission theory, it would be enough to enable us to draw some conclusions about the Christian theory of proselytization. As it happens, however, Innocent IV, in his commentary on the Decretal *Quod super* (X. 3.34.8), provided a fuller outline of such a theory, one that became the basis for all subsequent canonistic and papal thinking on the Christian mission effort as a legal issue. In effect, his commentary transformed Christ's spiritual injunction into a matter of law, because he placed the Christian missionary imperative within the larger context of Christian relations with non-Christian societies, developing an early theory of international law and relations.

Innocent IV's discussion of the legal status of missions and missionaries began with his commentary on the Decretal *Quod super his*, a decision of his predecessor, Pope Innocent III (1198-1216), in a case involving a vow to go on Crusade. The case dealt with a not uncommon problem, a man who took a vow to go on a Crusade and then failed to fulfill it. What could he do in place of actually going on Crusade? Unlike most other commentators on the Decretals, Innocent IV did not generally restate the opinions of other canonists on the *Decretales*, choosing instead to focus on what he believed to be the most significant point or points that the Decretal raised and deal with them, often in highly original ways.[16] In this case he focused not on the issue of the vow but on a line in the Decretal that referred to those "who vowed to go on pilgrimage for the defense of the Holy Land," thus moving away from the narrow question of fulfilling a vow and raising the larger question of the right of the pope to authorize Christians to wage war against the Muslims at all.[17] Innocent IV thus placed the discussion of missionary endeavor within the debate about the nature of the just war, an issue that the canonists had discussed at great length.[18]

Unlike some canonists, Innocent IV did not believe that Christians had a general right to invade and conquer any and all non-Christian societies.[19] He defended the crusader goal of regaining possession of the Holy Land because in his view the Muslims had taken it from Christians in an unjust war. That meant that their possession of that territory, their *dominium*, was illegitimate. On the other hand, Christians could not seize the lands that Muslims had acquired by legitimate means because Muslims, like all mankind, Christian and non-Christian alike, had the right to own property and to govern themselves.[20]

Having asserted the right of non-Christians to property and government, a right derived from the natural law that might be construed to mean that a non-Christian society could refuse admittance to missionaries, Innocent IV went on to explain why even non-Christian rulers were obligated to admit Christian missionaries. In his opinion the pope was responsible for the souls of all men, the baptized and the unbaptized. Quoting Christ's injunction to Peter, "Feed my sheep," Innocent IV asserted that Christ's command encompassed Christians and non-Christians because all were included in the "sheep of Christ by virtue of creation although they are not both of the flock of the Church."[21] Innocent did recognize, however, that the jurisdiction he claimed over non-Christians was de jure and not de facto.

Innocent IV transformed Christ's injunction to "feed my sheep" into a legal mandate, authorizing the pope to be the supreme judge of mankind, judging Christians according to canon law, Jews according to the law of Moses, and all others by the natural law, the universal law accessible to all by the use of reason. This tripartite division of papal responsibility would enable the pope to fulfill the responsibilities that Christ's injunction mandated. In addition, this statement of legal responsibilities provided the basis for a coherent position on the right of Catholics to proselytize in non-Christian society while limiting or preventing missionaries of foreign religions from entering Christian societies. The right to preach and the right to forbid preaching were two sides of the same responsibility.

According to Innocent IV, papal responsibility for the spiritual welfare of infidels would authorize him to punish infidels for violations of the natural law, although he was somewhat vague as to what would constitute such violations. He did suggest that sexual perversion and idol worship were two kinds of actions that would authorize such intervention. The latter was a violation of the natural law because, in his opinion, a monotheistic conception of god was ascertainable by natural reason.

In addition to claiming the right to intervene in infidel societies that were violating the natural law, Innocent IV also asserted the right of Christian missionaries to enter non-Christian countries in order to preach peacefully. Should a non-Christian ruler forbid Christian missionaries to enter, or if he was unable to ensure their safety, the pope would be justified in calling upon

Christian rulers to send troops to protect the missionaries. Furthermore, if a ruler persecuted those of his subjects who did choose to become Christians, then the pope had the right to call upon Christian rulers to come to the aid of their co-religionists. This did not imply any right to impose baptism on nonbelievers, only a right to present the gospel to the infidels safely. Finally, the pope was also careful to warn that Christian converts should not use their new religion as a reason for rebelling against their non-Christian rulers. Instead, they should be patient with their rulers in order to demonstrate that they were not subversive of the political order.[22]

Having justified the sending of troops to protect Christian missionaries, Innocent IV then asked if the right to send missionaries extended to other faiths, such as Islam, thus raising the possibility of a Muslim missionary preaching in Rome itself. The pope's answer was strongly negative "because they are in error, and we are on the righteous path."[23] Here we have a clear statement of the paradoxical position of the medieval canonists on missionary endeavor: on the basis of natural law, Catholics have the right to preach in non-Christian countries, but on the basis of ecclesiastical law, non-Christians cannot preach in Catholic countries

The obligation of the church to prevent the preaching of doctrines deemed schismatic or heretical within Christian society was deeply rooted within the canon law tradition. The *Decretum* dealt with the punishment of heretics and schismatics, while the *Decretales* dealt with Jews, Saracens, heretics, schismatics, and apostates.[24] The theme of these canonistic materials was that there was no right to preach doctrines that contradicted church doctrine. Furthermore, those who attempted to leave the church in order to become heretics, schismatics, or apostates had no right to do so. Once baptized, an individual remained subject to ecclesiastical discipline until death. In effect, these canons denied any possibility of successfully preaching new religious doctrines within a Christian society.[25]

The second area in which the canon law dealt with the issue of the right to proselytize concerned the Jews. Because it was a principle of canon law and of theology that conversion to Christianity had to be voluntary, there remained some Jewish communities in Christian Europe.[26] Ecclesiastical policy toward the Jews varied over time, but in the thirteenth century it reached its fullest development. Papal policy toward the Jews had two main thrusts. The first was to protect Christians from the allure of conversion to Judaism by restricting relations between Christians and Jews. The *Decretales* contained restrictions on Christian servants working in Jewish households and on the construction of new synagogues.[27] The goal of these restrictions was to prevent Christians from converting to Judaism. Throughout the Middle Ages, the church appears to have feared that Christians would be attracted to false doctrines unless prevented from doing so. In particular, Jewish converts to Christianity were seen as requiring such protection lest their former brethren entice them to return to the synagogue.[28]

Furthermore, several thirteenth-century popes took upon themselves responsibility for ensuring what they perceived as the purity of Jewish teaching by burning copies of the Talmud. Here again, Innocent IV played an important role. Following the example of Pope Gregory IX (1227-41), he asserted that the Jews were rejecting the ancient beliefs of their forefathers and that they were adopting beliefs that were insulting to Christianity. As a result, in 1244 he issued the bull *Impia iudaeorum* that outlined the errors of the Jews and ordered King Louis IX of France to seek out and burn copies of the Talmud, the text that contained these erroneous beliefs.[29]

The writings of Innocent IV provided the fullest discussion of the right to proselytize in the canonistic literature. For the remainder of the Middle Ages, when lawyers and popes discussed this issue, they did so in the terms that he had set out. His commentary on *Quod super his* received wide circulation because Joannes Andreae (1270-1348) included it in his own vast commentary on the *Decretales*.[30] Later canonists who cited Innocent's opinion often did so indirectly, through Joannes Andreae's volumes, and not from Innocent's own work.[31]

The collapse of the Mongol Empire in the fourteenth and fifteenth centuries and the expansion of Islam in the East gradually ended the Latin Christian presence in Asia.[32] To the extent that the Asian mission generated scholarly interest in the right of Christians to preach in non-Christian societies, the end of the mission meant the end of such discussion.[33] Innocent IV's views on the rights of non-Christian peoples, on the right of Christian missionaries to preach everywhere, and on the right of the pope to request Christian rulers to protect peaceful missionaries in the face of persecution remained the standard opinion among the canonists.

EARLY MODERN FORMULATIONS

Toward the end of the Middle Ages, Innocent IV's arguments reemerged in connection with Portuguese and Castilian expansion along the west coast of Africa. Between 1420 and 1500 this expansion generated more than 100 papal bulls that dealt with the Iberian rulers' acquisition of the islands in the Atlantic off of Africa.[34] It also led to the writing of legal treatises that justified Christian occupation of the newly discovered lands.[35] The bulls and the treatises continued to echo the opinions of Innocent IV. For example, Portuguese efforts to occupy the Canary Islands led Pope Eugenius IV (1431-47) to request of two canonists opinions on the legitimacy of the Portuguese occupation of these islands. These canonists agreed that the pope's responsibility for the salvation of all men could justify the occupation of these islands.[36] Eugenius subsequently issued a bull authorizing Portuguese occupation of these islands on the basis of his responsibility for the salvation of all men.[37] Neither the legal treatises nor the papal bulls reflected any new, more extensive analysis of the right to preach than existed in Innocent IV's writings. In effect, they simply applied Innocent's principles to the Portuguese situation in the Atlantic.

Eugenius's successor, Nicholas V (1447-55), subsequently issued a bull that stated the papal position on missionary efforts clearly and also indicated the temporal advantages that might accrue to a Christian ruler who chose to support missionary efforts. This letter reiterated the views of Innocent IV, blending crusading language with a call for missionary activity under the aegis of the pope's responsibility for all mankind.[38] Nicholas V authorized the Portuguese to defend Christendom against Saracens and other enemies of the faith, and, to support that effort, the Portuguese could conquer and possess their lands. Furthermore, the Portuguese ruler had, at his own cost, undertaken "to preach and cause to be preached to them the unknown but most sacred name of Christ. . . . "[39] As a reward for these crusading and missionary efforts and as an inducement for continuing those efforts, the pope granted the Portuguese a monopoly of trade with the newly discovered islands in the Atlantic and the mainland of West Africa. It was this tradition of rewarding those who defended and expanded Christendom that caused Alexander VI (1492-1503) to issue *Inter caetera* in 1493 so that the Portuguese and Castilian crowns would each possess a monopoly of trade with half of the newly discovered lands.[40]

The discovery of the Americas in 1492 and the subsequent European discovery of a variety of new worlds generated a great deal of interest in the right of Europeans to enter these lands in order to preach the gospel, because the encounter with the various newly encountered worlds provided the Christian church with an opportunity for missionary work on a scale unparalleled since the conversion of the barbarian invaders of the Roman world a millennium earlier.

At the same time, however, along with opportunities, the great age of discoveries also presented the papacy with several troublesome issues affecting missionary work. First, church leaders had to face the fact that the explorers had encountered not a single kind of non-European society but a wide range of human societies, from the most primitive to the most sophisticated. This meant that the missionaries might be required to bring the people they wished to convert to European standards of cultural behavior as part of the conversion process. Second, while in some mission territories such as the Americas, missionaries could count upon the support, military and economic, of Christian rulers, in others, such as China, they could not. Third, while the religious beliefs of many primitive societies faded before the coming of missionaries protected by Spanish arms, Confucianism and Hinduism presented much stronger opposition. The missionaries in China and India were able to function only because of the toleration granted by specific rulers, and they faced the arduous task of converting the members of ancient, well-entrenched religions that were deeply rooted in the social and cultural structure of their societies.[41] Finally, the work of converting the newly encountered peoples was complicated because of tension between the papacy and Catholic secular rulers. From the papal perspective, the secular rulers were expected to manage, so to speak, the missionary endeavor under license from the papacy. The *patronato*, "a combination of the rights and duties" exercised by the kings of Portugal and Castile in mission lands, included responsibility for building chapels and churches, maintaining a religious hierarchy, and sending missionaries to convert the heathen. ..." In return for carrying out these duties, the monarchs acquired the right of "presenting bishops to vacant sees, collecting tithes, and administering taxation."[42] Such arrangements had existed for several centuries in Europe and were not created specifically to meet the exigencies of the age of overseas exploration.

In theory, this *patronato* arrangement would seem to be a reasonable division of labor. The papacy would ensure the physical safety and the material maintenance of the missionaries in return for granting to a secular ruler the right of appointment to ecclesiastical office, a valuable form of patronage, and the right to appropriate various kinds of ecclesiastical income. Furthermore, as provided in *Inter caetera*, the ruler also received a monopoly of trade with the area specified in the letter of appointment. In the chancelleries where these documents were drawn up, such a division of land and responsibility no doubt appeared to be a neat solution to a potentially bloody conflict between Christian kingdoms.[43]

In practice, however, matters were more complicated, because the popes and the rulers of the Iberian kingdoms often had different and conflicting interests. Furthermore, some Catholic rulers, such as Francis I of France (1515-47), refused to accept Alexander's bull as the final word on expansion into the non-Christian world.[44] Moreover, once the Protestant Reformation broke over Europe there was a group of rulers for whom wresting control of access to the various newly encountered worlds from Catholic rulers was a religious as well as an economic goal.

Thus the encounter with the new world provided the Catholic church with great opportunities to fulfill Christ's injunction to preach to the entire world and great practical difficulties of implementing that charge. Within the broad spectrum of problems facing the church, three problems stood out. The first was the relationship between the rulers of Portugal and Castile and the churches established within the *patronato* that each enjoyed. The second was the degree of accommodation to local cultural practices that the missionaries would allow converts to retain. The third problem, and the one that was destined to have the greatest impact in the development of international law, especially as it affected missionaries, concerned the right of Christians to enter and to occupy the lands of non-Christians.

The first issue, the relationship between the papacy and secular monarchs who possessed a *patronato*, was most apparent in the Spanish Empire. Various Spanish writers wrote treatises that emphasized the monarchy's role in the direction of the church in the Americas and that limited the papacy's role to, at most, the power to license the king of Castile to administer the church there. Probably the most extreme royal claim to control of the church in the Americas was the attempt of Philip II (1556-98) to have Pope Pius II (1566-72) create "an 'Indian Patriarchate' which was to exist and be considered as a more or less autonomous church parallel to the Roman church. The patriarch was to be appointed by the King and reside in Madrid."[45] Pius V rejected this proposal for the obvious reason that it would have created for all practical purposes a church over which he had virtually no control, while Philip II would hold about the same position in it as Henry VIII did in the Church of England. The result was that, although Philip was unable to obtain the patriarchate he desired, until the end of the Spanish Empire in the Americas, the Spanish monarchs dominated the church there through the rights attached to the *patronato*.

The second problem that the papacy faced with regard to missionary work in the newly encountered worlds was the degree of cultural accommodation that missionaries could allow their converts. Although this issue arose virtually everywhere missionaries traveled, it reached its fullest expression in the Chinese Rites controversy. Two factors rendered the situation even more complex than it might have been otherwise. In the first place, Catholic missionaries in China and, for the most part, elsewhere in Asia could not rely on European Catholic rulers for protection. As a result, they could not afford to antagonize local officials who could prevent them from entering, who could oust them from the country, or who could even have them executed. The missionaries had to rely almost entirely on their ability to preach and teach without antagonizing those whom they sought to convert. Furthermore, as matters developed, it was also necessary for the missionaries to consider the situation of the potential converts. Did conversion require such a radical transformation of their way of life that the converts would be seen by their countrymen as subversive of the social order or even as potential agents of European conquest?

The issue of cultural accommodation arose most famously in the case of the Jesuit missionaries who learned the Chinese language, adopted the dress of Confucian intellectuals in place of traditional religious garb, and tolerated some traditional cultural practices, especially veneration of ancestors, by their converts. Members of other religious orders, most notably Franciscans and Dominicans, argued that the Jesuits had given away too much in order to accommodate the Chinese. Furthermore, the Jesuit approach to conversion stressed reaching the intellectual and political leadership in order to bring the great mass of society into the fold, a style of missionary effort that characterized the conversion of the barbarian invaders of Europe centuries earlier.[46]

The battle over Chinese Rites might not have gone the way it did if it had not been for the Protestant Reformation. In defending Catholic Christianity from Protestant attacks, the papacy placed special emphasis on the external signs of unity with Rome, a policy that stretched back to the days of the inves-

titure controversy in the late eleventh century. The Jesuit willingness to accommodate some Chinese cultural practices was seen by some as subversive of the
church in a time of great crisis, because deviation in external matters of ritual
and practice could be interpreted as a reflection of internal rejection of doctrine.

In the course of these conflicts a series of popes began to assert a greater
papal role in the work of missionaries. In 1622, Pope Gregory XV (1621-23)
established the Congregation of the Propagation of the Faith to direct missionary efforts and to resolve conflicts arising from the work. The actual power of
the seventeenth-century popes in missionary work remained limited, however,
by the rights that previous popes had granted to secular rulers. Furthermore,
the conflicts between religious orders about the proper methods of converting
infidels to Christianity came to be a major problem. Beginning shortly after
the establishment of the Congregation of the Propagation of the Faith, various
popes issued bulls designed to settle the issues that the critics of the Jesuits had
raised. Finally, with the bull *Ex quo singulari* (1742), Pope Benedict XIV (1740-
58) settled the issue for the next two centuries by forbidding the accommodations to Chinese cultural practices that the Jesuits had made.[47]

Conflicts between the papacy and the monarchs who possessed the
patronato; the conflict within the church between the Jesuits and their opponents regarding the degree to which cultural practices of the converts could be
accommodated; and the crisis of the Reformation and Counter-Reformation—
these were three conflicts that led to what one scholar politely described as
"[t]he manifest diminution of the missionary spirit in the seventeenth and eighteenth century. . . . "[48] The great religious enthusiasm that accompanied the
initial encounter with the new worlds, previously unknown to Europeans, faded
for the most part. As modern nation-states began to emerge and claim sovereignty, the papacy withdrew from leadership of, even involvement with, the
larger world. Not until well into the nineteenth century did popes reemerge
from this period of withdrawal. When they did, missionary activity again became a major interest of the papacy.[49]

One might conclude at this point that the Catholic church's encounter with
the new worlds opened to it as a result of Columbus's voyages resulted in
spiritual failure. That would be unfair. The faith was preached, converts were
made, new churches were established, and Christians could be found throughout the world. What did not happen, as apparently some enthusiasts had expected, was a new Pentecost resulting in the conversion of the great mass of
mankind. As C. R. Boxer pointed out, the reports of missionaries gave the
impression "that the conversion of uncounted thousands would be a relatively
simple matter, if only there were more missionaries in the field to help reap the
potentially rich harvest."[50] Indeed, the twelve Franciscans who were sent to
convert the people of Mexico were informed by the superior who sent them
that their mission was "the beginning of the last preaching of the gospel in the
eve of the end of the world."[51] In other words, the Great Commission was
about to be fulfilled.

In addition to the European exploration and conquest of much of the increasingly large known world and in addition to the efforts to bring Christ's message to the infidel inhabitants of the newly encountered worlds, there also emerged for the first time an extensive discussion of the legitimacy of conquest. Within that debate, which roiled (especially but not exclusively) the Spanish intellectual world, there emerged a discussion of the rights and responsibilities of missionaries with regard to infidel societies. The numerous treatises on the legitimacy of the conquest raised several points central to the missionary effort: Were the inhabitants of the Americas human beings and therefore legitimate objects of missionary preaching? Were infidel rulers obliged to admit peaceful missionaries? Did Christian rulers have the right to enter and occupy infidel societies in order to protect missionaries from harassment?

One of the most extensive discussions of these issues appeared in the lectures of the Dominican theologian Francis Vitoria (1480-1546), whose lectures on this topic were published as the *De Indis*.[52] Vitoria presented the entire range of positions on the legitimacy of the Spanish conquest and occupation of the Americas, citing a number of arguments for and against the legitimacy of Spanish possession of the Americas.

Vitoria discussed the sending of missionaries to the Americas in connection with both the legitimate and the illegitimate arguments for Spanish possession of the Americas. Among the arguments that he deemed illegitimate bases for the conquest of the Americas, Vitoria included the argument that the Indians' refusal to accept Christianity justified their conquest. He argued, however, that as "some of the requisite conditions for a legitimate choice were lacking, on the whole this title to occupying and conquering these countries is neither relevant nor legitimate."[53] The fundamental reason for taking this position was that nonbelievers cannot be forced to accept baptism. If, having admitted missionaries to their society and heard their message, the Indians, or anyone else, did not wish to receive baptism, they had done what could be legitimately required of them. At the same time, by having preached, the Christians had done what Christ had enjoined them to do.

If a non-Christian society refused to admit missionaries or harassed them, however, then, according to Vitoria, there could be a legitimate basis for occupying their lands. When he turned to the discussion of societies that refused to admit Christian missionaries, Vitoria did not assert Christ's injunction to preach the gospel to all mankind. Instead, he began by discussing the "natural partnership and communication" that link all mankind.[54] His position was that all mankind forms a single community with the result that the "Spaniards have the right to travel and dwell in those countries, so long as they do no harm to the barbarians and cannot be prevented by them for doing so." This right he traced to "the law of nations (*ius gentium*), which either is or derives from natural law. . . . "[55]

The right to travel freely in peace throughout the world that Vitoria asserted led to several statements about legitimate bases for the conquest of the

Americas. "The Spaniards may lawfully trade among the barbarians, so long as they do no harm to their homeland . . . and their [the Indians'] princes cannot prevent their subjects from trading with the Spaniards, etc. . . . "[56] Furthermore, Vitoria wrote, "if all other measures to secure safety from the barbarians besides conquering their communities and subjecting them have been exhausted, the Spaniards may even take this measure."[57]

Only after an extensive analysis of the right to travel for trade and other secular purposes did Vitoria come to a consideration of the right to preach the gospel in foreign lands. He raised the question of whether "Christians have the right to preach and announce the gospel in the lands of the barbarians" and cited Christ's injunction to preach the gospel to all men in support of this right, thus placing the Christian obligation within the context of the right of all men to travel freely. Nonbelievers must allow missionaries to enter because "if they [the Spaniards] have the right to travel and trade among them [the Indians], then they must be able to teach them the truth if they are willing to listen. . . . "[58] If the Indians or their rulers refused to admit Christian missionaries, it would then be legitimate for the pope to authorize a Christian ruler to occupy their lands in order to ensure that Christ's injunction was carried out under the terms of the law of nations. The pope's responsibility for the salvation of all mankind was the basis for his doing this.

Vitoria's discussion of the right to preach the gospel everywhere, even if it became necessary to occupy the lands of nonbelievers, was the most important discussion of this issue within the Catholic tradition. His reflections were widely read, studied, and cited by Spanish theologians, philosophers, lawyers, and bureaucrats. Subsequent generations of Spanish intellectuals continued to refer back to the *De Indis* throughout the sixteenth and seventeenth centuries.[59]

This sketch of what the medieval canon lawyers and their sixteenth-century successors had to say about the right to proselytize might seem at first not relevant to twentieth-century discussions of this issue. After all, Innocent IV, representing the fullest development of medieval thought on the issue, argued that while non-Christian societies must admit Christian missionaries, Christian societies were not obligated to admit representatives of other religions and to allow them to preach. Indeed, the canon law clearly mandated the punishment of Christians who defected to heretical sects or who converted to Judaism or Islam. Even if the right to preach in a Christian society was extended to a non-Christian missionary, no Christian could join the new faith because to do so was to bring down the church's punishment upon him. One might argue that Christian rulers such as the kings of Spain, who had not only Christian but Jewish and Muslim subjects, might allow missionaries of other religions to preach among these people because they were not subject to the church courts. Innocent IV's assertion of jurisdiction over all men according to the laws proper to them would of course explain why this was not possible. Christian rulers were expected to assist in the transformation of their non-Christian subjects into Christians, not into members of other religions.

At the same time, however, Innocent IV hinted at a way around this ban on non-Christian preaching in Christian societies. By recognizing the existence of natural rights possessed by all mankind, the pope raised the possibility that there might be a way to allow non-Christians to seek converts within Christian society. When Francis Vitoria developed his arguments about the legitimacy of the conquest of the Americas two and a half centuries later, he postulated the right of all men to travel in peace throughout the world. While he recognized that the spiritual mission of the church could override the natural right of a people to live and govern themselves if they refused to admit peaceful missionaries, he appears to have been hesitant to encourage military action. Furthermore, when he accepted the possibility of military action, he did not do so in terms of preaching the gospel. Instead, he emphasized that the failure of the Indians to adhere to the terms of the *ius gentium* could allow the Spanish to occupy their lands in order to allow the missionaries to exercise their right of free travel throughout the world.

Having focused attention on the natural right to travel, Vitoria made it possible to consider some other perspectives on the right to proselytize. For example, the church's condemnation of heretics, apostates, and schismatics, behavior that merited spiritual punishment, was supported by a series of secular laws mandating death by burning for those convicted of such ecclesiastical crimes. As Marsilius of Padua, admittedly a heretic, pointed out, ecclesiastical punishment could be separated from secular so that heresy could be punished as an ecclesiastical crime but not a civil one.[60] In such circumstances, non-Christian preachers could be admitted by a Christian ruler and Christians could accept the new faith, subject to ecclesiastical condemnation but not civil. By taking such a position, Christians could insist that other societies admit Christian missionaries because Christian societies admitted non-Christian missionaries.

The obvious drawback to this argument is that medieval and modern thinkers have very different conceptions of secular government. Innocent IV and Vitoria took for granted that the secular power would support the church's spiritual mission domestically and, when necessary, abroad. Furthermore, medieval and early modern rulers, Catholic and Protestant alike, generally assumed that religious uniformity was an essential part of a well-run society. The various Acts of Uniformity that the Tudor monarchs of England issued in the sixteenth century, for example, reflected the usual view on the need for religious conformity within the kingdom.[61] The individual who did not accept the officially supported religion was not only a heretic but a traitor as well. Likewise, the seventeenth-century colonial charters that the Stuart monarchs issued restated traditional Catholic teaching about the importance of converting the infidels to Christianity, thus assuming the right of Christians to enter other societies for "the Conversion and Reduction of the People in those Parts unto the true Worship of God and Christian Religion. . . . "[62] In effect, the English monarchs were restating the traditional canon law position on proselytization.[63]

MODERN REFLECTIONS

While the medieval and early modern worlds were quite different from the twentieth century in many ways, the canon law position on missionary efforts has some echoes in the position of some contemporary states around the world with regard to Christian missionaries. A number of states today forbid or severely restrict the activity of Christian missionaries for either religious or political reasons. In some cases a government may assume the truth of its religious position as some Islamic states do and see foreign missionaries as a threat to religious truth rather as the medieval canonists did. In other cases, foreign missionaries are seen as the agents of those who would overthrow the government, a fear that the medieval canonists recognized when they warned potential converts not to use conversion as an excuse for rebellion. Finally, modern states may see foreign religions as a threat to a national cultural heritage, rather as the leaders of the Russian Orthodox Church do.

Without extending the parallels excessively, it is possible to see the leaders of many modern states as facing the same dilemma that Innocent IV and Vitoria faced. In contemporary terms, the fundamental question has become: Is it possible to construct a modern state on a base of cultural and moral (or religious) diversity? Medieval and early modern writers would generally agree with the leaders of many modern states, especially emerging ones, that the state requires uniformity not diversity. From another perspective, the fundamental question has become: Does a society have the right to protect itself from what its people and its leaders see as a threat to dearly held beliefs? Innocent IV argued that the leaders of Christian societies had the right, indeed the obligation, to protect their subjects from the allure of heresy, Judaism, and Islam. Many contemporary political and religious officials around the world feel the same way about Christianity. Their people must be protected from it. Like medieval thinkers, these leaders see religion not simply as a personal commitment but as a matter of communal identity as well. Furthermore, they recognize more fully than their medieval predecessors who became Christian that conversion to Christianity will have a significant impact on the society's way of life. At the same time, leaders of those states that refuse to admit Christian missionaries, that persecute or harass converts, or that limit the practice of Christianity also know that their behavior has become an important issue in American politics. Like the medieval canonists, American congressmen are demanding the end to religious persecution and the opening of all societies to peaceful Christian missionaries. Failure to accede to these demands will lead to various kinds of sanctions, although not invasion, occupation, and conquest.

In a way, modern Americans find themselves facing the same problem as medieval Christians did when facing very different cultures. To what degree are cultural differences to be tolerated, to what degree should we strive to eliminate practices we define as wrong or immoral? One answer that at least some of the medieval canonists suggested is to distinguish between spiritual obligations and natural rights. Innocent IV, Vitoria, and other neglected Christian thinkers may have provided a key to resolving this issue in our day.

9.

MISSIONARY CHALLENGES
TO THE THEOLOGY OF SALVATION

A Roman Catholic Perspective

———————◆———————

Jozef Tomko

Salvation, redemption, liberation—these are various terms, perhaps with a different coloring, for a single reality that constitutes a central problem for humanity in search of the meaning of its own existence. This is a problem, often submerged by the course of life, but one that emerges with pressing urgency at crucial moments. It presents two fundamental aspects. One is negative: salvation or liberation *from* whom or *from* what? The other is positive: salvation or liberation *for* what or *in view* of what?

Salvation is a vital question for humanity and can bring doubt if not crisis to the woman or man who aspires to clarity, to certainty, indeed to security both on the level of physical existence and on the spiritual and religious levels.

This chapter combines edited excerpts from two chapters, "Missionary Challenges to the Theology of Salvation" and "Christian Mission Today," in *Christian Mission and Interreligious Dialogue*, ed. Paul Mojzes and Leonard Swidler (Lewiston/Queensland/Lampeter, 1990). The material is used herein with the kind permission of the editors and publisher. The two chapters were written respectively in 1988 and 1989. At least two subsequent official documents are important for the Roman Catholic perspective: (1) John Paul II's encyclical letter *Redemptori missio* (December 7, 1990); and (2) Pontifical Council of Interreligious Dialogue and Congregation for the Evangelization of Peoples, *Dialogue and Proclamation* (May 19, 1991), with presentations by Cardinal J. Tomko and Cardinal F. Arinze—EDS.

Salvation involves the fundamental vision of humanity: Who are humans? Do they need salvation? And which salvation?

The answers vary. There are those who speak of a purely *human* salvation: Humanity finds sufficiency and redemption in itself. The aspiration to salvation, so deeply rooted in the human heart, can have a satisfactory psychological and sociological explanation. There is no shortage of ideologies or systems that promise a secularized salvation. Other answers are *religious* in nature: In one form or another, salvation is considered a central theme in all the great religions of the world. For the Christian, salvation is one of the fundamental pillars of faith in God "who wishes to save every human being" (1 Tm 2:3), and in Jesus Christ, "who for us and for our salvation descended from heaven" (Nicene Creed). To bring and mediate salvation is also the mission of the church and so her reason for existence.

So we are at the heart of Christian missiology and of the very missionary activity of the church. Today, more than ever, it is necessary to make a thorough study of the problems of salvation; to present the reply the Christian faith gives to the problem of salvation; to clarify the Christian specific remedy in relation to the context of today's world, the great religions and cultures, and also the world of secularity. There are several precise reasons for urgency.

First, we need to clarify the missionary motivation of the church and of the missionaries themselves, who dedicate their lives and at least some years of their existence to evangelization. In the past, missionaries felt the pressing need to bring salvation to non-Christians with an almost dramatic anxiety. If their reading of the sacred texts was perhaps too fundamentalist, it is still vitally important to establish what is still valid in this motive.

Second, salvation is a complex reality. Perhaps also for this reason in the last two decades it has become an ambiguous concept that needs to be explained in light of the faith.

Third, the Second Vatican Council (1962-65) assumed a positive, respectful attitude toward the great non-Christian religions and so encouraged new reflection on the theology of religions and on the salvation of non-Christians. In view of the dialogue with these religions, Christians must have a clear awareness of their own identity and of the role of the Christian faith in the divine plan of salvation. There are many new ideas in this field, but they need a close examination and a serious critical maturation.

In this chapter I want to present some questions and some challenges that missionary life itself poses to missionaries. These questions come from direct experience, gathered in various mission lands, behind which are ideas that circulate in the various books and articles on the subject. These experiences above all invite theologians to have the greatest precision in formulating their own theses—a precision that is measured in the light of faith but also in the light of the practical disruptive consequences that these theses produce in the field of missions.

SALVATION AND NON-CHRISTIAN RELIGIONS

Today everyone admits the universal saving will of God, who "wishes to save every human being" (1 Tm 2:4)—though many stop at this point in the reading of the Pauline text and neglect or consider as less important what follows: "and to come to the knowledge of the truth" (1 Tm 2:4). However it may be, many questions remain open as to how God realized and realizes this universal plan in history: with what means, through which people and instruments.

One's attention immediately moves to three other points of interest: Jesus Christ, the church, and non-Christian religions. St. Peter, before the Sanhedrin, asserted that there is salvation only in the name of Jesus Christ, "and in no one else" (Acts 4:12). This affirmation gives theologians the difficult task of explaining whether and how people were saved before Christ and how, even after Christ, those who do not know or do not accept Jesus Christ are saved. The question of the necessity of the church for salvation comes as a consequence and in connection with the person and the work of Christ. And so the focus of the problem is reduced to two poles: Christ and non-Christian religions.

Paul Knitter had the merit of reducing all theological reflection on religions to four schemes or patterns of the relationship between Christ and non-Christian religions—and proposing a fifth way.[1]

The first pattern, which dominated nearly all the history of Christianity, was that of hostility toward "pagan" religions—*Christ against religions*. This hostile attitude was influenced by a rigid interpretation of the affirmation by the church fathers Origen and Cyprian, "Extra ecclesiam nulla salus," which limited divine grace to the church. The discoveries of other continents led later theologians, such as Robert Bellarmine and Francisco Suarez, to correct this narrow perspective—which Knitter calls "exclusive"—to a rather "inclusive" one: from no salvation "outside the church," they went to no salvation "without the church." This perspective has persisted until our own century in the form of various theories concerning invisible or potential membership in the church.

Some have objected that this schematization is not sufficiently objective.[2] It is true that the fathers of the church assumed a hostile attitude toward cults, rites, and myths considered to be idolatry and aberrations; yet it remains to be seen whether they were so in reality! However, among the church fathers and later writers there was also positive appreciation of the valid aspects of other religions. St. Justice spoke of "seeds of the Word" (*logos spermatikos*). St. Clement spoke of the "illumination of the Logos." St. Irenaeus spoke of the "divine teaching." Pope Gregory the Great gave wonderful missionary directives for the evangelization of England. Raymond of Penafort and Raymond Lulle supported dialogue with Islam. St. Thomas Aquinas spoke of "natural religion," which is a "preparation for the gospel" (*praeparatio evangelica*). Then there is the attitude of love and respect toward everything that is not an error in many missionaries, like St. Francis of Assisi, in Ricci and De Nobili, and in the famous 1659 "Instruction of the Congregation for the Propagation of the Faith." And what can be said of the theologians of at least four centuries who maintained that God's grace operated also outside the visible confines of the church but was always mediated by Christ and by the church, until the thesis that excluded non-members of the church from salvation was officially condemned in the Holy Office's letter to the archbishop of Boston in the case of Fr. Feeney (August 8, 1949).

The Second Vatican Council (1962-65) and its Declaration *Nostra aetate* opened a decidedly new perspective, which Knitter characterizes with the dual concept *Christ within religions*. The positive statements on the possibility of salvation also for non-Christians were "made clear," according to Knitter,[3] by Karl Rahner.[4] Rahner maintained that other religions are and can be ways of salvation positively included in God's plan of salvation; it is always the grace of Christ that operates in the non-Christian, offered through the respective non-Christian religion. The person thus touched by Christ is unconsciously directed to Christ and to Christ's church; he is an "anonymous Christian," who must, however, be transformed into an explicit, fully ecclesial Christian. Rahner's theory—especially as developed by Robert Schlette and Anita Röper,[5] and accepted by Edward Schillebeeckx—does not satisfy Knitter, because it would end up "only in a partial and provisional approval of them."[6]

Since the 1970s some theologians have been searching for a new perspective, which Knitter describes as *Christ above religions*. Not satisfied with Rahner's theory, these theologians maintain that other religions have an *independent* validity: even if Christ is not, in their opinion, the exclusive cause of saving grace, yet he remains *above* all religions and all peoples. To preserve the fact of faith in the uniqueness and finality of the normativity of Christ, they give various explanations. Christ is the only "critical catalyst" also for other religions, in the face of our modern world, claims Hans Küng.[7] Claude Geffré uses the universality of the *right* that Christ has over all peoples, in that he is the Word of God made flesh, whereas this would not be due to Christianity as a historical religion.[8]

To put Christ above religions does not seem very ethical if an honest dialogue is to be held. This, at least, is what the theologians think who propose a model that sees *Christ together with other religions* and with other religious figures. According to them, after the abandonment of "ecclesiocentrism," it is necessary to eliminate "Christocentrism" as well and put God at the heart of religion in a theocentric vision. Knitter himself upholds the theory of "unitive pluralism" or of "the coincidence of opposites," according to which "each religion (or religious figure) is unique and decisive for its followers; but it is also of universal importance." Christ and the Christian religion are neither exclusive (*against*) nor inclusive (*within* or *above*) other religions. But they are "essentially *related* to other religions," so that "perhaps . . . other revealers and saviors are as important as Jesus of Nazareth."[9]

Raimundo Panikkar reaches the same conclusions from the distinction between the Christ-Logos and the historical Jesus. There is more in the Christ-
Logos than there is in the historical Jesus, so that the Logos can appear in
different but real ways in other religions and historical figures, outside of Jesus
of Nazareth.[10] The faithfulness of this theology to Christ is assured because it
still maintains that God really spoke through Jesus, but it is fully open to
God's possible message in other religions.

Finally, Knitter also crosses this Rubicon in order to "liberate" the theology
of religions and missions. Using the methodological criteria of the theology of
liberation (with its themes of option for the poor and orthopraxis), Knitter
resolves to "go beyond theocentrism, toward *soteriocentrism*," so that the
primary concern of a theology of religions should not be "rightful belief" in
the uniqueness of Christ, but "rightful practice" with other religions, of the
"promotion of the Kingdom and of its soteria." "This means that the basis
and principal interest of every theological evaluation of other religions is not
their relationship with the church (ecclesiocentrism) or with Christ
(Christocentrism), or even with God (theocentrism), but rather the degree in
which they are able to promote *salvation*: the *well-being of humanity*."[11]

This well-being in which the kingdom, the reign of God, consists is the
reign of justice and of love to be reached in collaboration or dialogue with all.
Exalting interreligious dialogue, Knitter reduces faith in Christ to the level of
an ambiguous earthly "well-being." Here at last is a reassuring conclusion for
missionaries who are perhaps perturbed: "The missionary goal is reached if
the announcing of the Gospel to all peoples makes the Christian a better Christian and the Buddhist a better Buddhist," since "the primary mission of the
Church is not salvation business (to make people Christians so that they can
be saved), but the task of serving and promoting the kingdoms of justice and
of love."[12]

This reduction of evangelization has also occurred in other countries and
continents. It is justified in various ways, but it always starts from at least two
presuppositions: first, every religion is a way of salvation; second, it is necessary to seek dialogue with other religions, which must be reevaluated. This
reduction of evangelization also presents a common tendency to eclipse or
reduce the role of Christ, of the church, and of proclamation, and to concentrate all of the activity and finality of evangelization on the building up of the
reign of God, sometimes undefined and at other times identified with social
well-being, justice, peace, and love.

THE *MISSIO DEI* IN MODERN THEORIES OF MISSION

The most explicit theological motivation of this tendency is found in the most
radical derivations of the theory of the *missio Dei*.[13] The real protagonist of
mission is God. God's sovereignty or absolute lordship must in the end overcome the "Christomonism" in which the Christian missiology, both Protestant

and Catholic, was enclosed.[14] The "extra" promised by Jesus is realized in the building up of the reign of God. "The real end of the *missio Dei* is the King-dom of God, not the *ecclesia viatorum*," G. H. Anderson decrees.[15] God saves as God wants and when God wants; God's action is not bound to the church. Mission today is the action that tries to discover God in the world and serve God and not "to bring Christ" to the world. So also the church, like Christ, must practice *kenosis*, self-emptying, in this service.

Even more radically opposed to the church's role in mission is the tendency of "out-churchism." The Dutch Reformed theologian and missionary J. C. Hoekendijk asserts that the mission is realized with the proclamation of the "shalom" in hope. Mission is "pro-mission" in the service of the world, build-ing up peace, "shalom," that leads to intercommunion and participation. With this service to the world, people are brought together, rendering the church an event and not a structure.[16] Similarly, Catholic writer L. Rütti rejects the theol-ogy of the Second Vatican Council's decree on mission as being too ecclesiocentric and not very realistic when it refers to trinitarian missions and the mandate of the Lord. For Rütti, mission is the responsibility of Christians to hope for the transformation of the world, for the creation of a new world.[17] "The commitment of Christians (n.b., not of the Church!), bestowed with a new promise for the world, is not to maintain or spread a church, but it con-sists in efficacious responsibility for the present hope in the new world."[18]

THE CENTRALITY OF GOD'S REIGN

The centrality of the reign of God appears more and more frequently in these theories. And the reign of God, in the full ambiguity of interpretation, is also the cornerstone of the more recent reflections of some Asian theologians who were influenced by their experiences of direct contact with the great ancient religions and cultures of the East.

M. Amaladoss, for example, sees "a Copernican revolution of the theology of evangelization" in the fact that "the center of the approach moves from the Church to the Kingdom."[19] Amaladoss first analyses and then relativizes the role of the church for salvation. He then reports the opinion of some who "called the Church an extraordinary way in opposition to the other ordinary ways" of salvation represented by religions.[20] After Vatican II, Amaladoss writes, the relationship between the church and religions could not be presented in terms of the presence/absence of salvation, nor of light/darkness, and not even with the divine/human or supernatural/natural dichotomy. Today, the bino-mial explicit/implicit, or full/partial, is more common. Since "the Church, as she is, is a historically and culturally limited realization of the Good News," Amaladoss abandons ecclesiocentrism.[21]

> The Church does not offer an easier or a fuller salvation. Because of God's universal saving will and the socio-historical nature of the hu-man person, God's saving encounter with man occurs also through other

religions and their symbolic structures: writings, codes of conduct and rituals. . . . The Church is called not only to witness, to proclaim, but also to collaborate in humility and respect for the divine mystery that operates in the world.[22]

Indeed, "being a member of the Church is not an easier or surer way of salvation."[23] Amaladoss recognizes the saving role of Jesus Christ and refuses to set Christocentrism against theocentrism. But here too, with Panikkar, he distinguishes between the cosmic Christ and the historical Christ. The saving mediation of non-Christian religions is linked to the cosmic Christ, whereas the church's role is linked to the historical Christ and to his Paschal mystery. Today, he writes, we must not take advantage of the "communication idiomatum," attributing certain qualifications such as "final, last, unique, universal" to the historical Christ, because they belong not to Jesus, but to the Word. But in the end, how is the divine universal plan of salvation accomplished? Through evangelization that knows three patterns: the first ecclesiocentric, the second centered on the world, and the third on the reign of God. The author aims at an evangelization in the global sense, in which "the new focal point" is the reign of God, that is, the building up of a new humanity that will unite all people in a community of love, justice, and peace.[24] This is the mission in which the church must collaborate—with dialogue, with inculturation, and with liberation. Strangely, but significantly, proclamation is omitted from Amaladoss's definition. The explanation is found, perhaps, in his extremely radical doubt: "In this context of religious pluralism does it still make sense to proclaim Christ as the only Name in which all people find salvation and call them to be disciples through baptism and to enter the Church?"[25]

Another Indian theologian, J. Kavunkal, concludes similarly that

> the church's mission is not so much to bring salvation as to bring the manifestation, not to obtain the conversion to the church as the necessary means of salvation, but to help in the realization of the broader Kingdom of God as it develops in history. This includes the effort to help followers of other religions to follow those religions in a better manner.[26]

Such theories are now widespread and are beginning to bear fruit in the practical field. One pastoral magazine presented the following program of a missionary institute: "We go out on the missions not so much to plant the Church or to bring the faith, but rather to discover a faith and a goodness that already exist there."[27]

Some missionaries who work among the Indios in Latin America pose the same problem for themselves from a different angle. They were faced with the difficulty of changing the customs with which the Indios live happily and with an easy conscience. Why should they disturb their good faith with the severe demands of Christian morality, which is too hard for them and leads them to continuous spiritual distress? If the Indios follow their consciences, they are saved just the same, so why change them? Some of these missionaries then asked themselves whether it was not perhaps better to try to raise the level of social life and concern themselves more with the physical health of the Indios than with their salvation.

So the need for a clear answer to the problem is felt in many continents. It is even vaster with regard to the relationship between salvation and the human promotion in any form (economical, social, political, development, liberation, justice, and peace).

SALVATION AND HUMAN PROMOTION

Several recent theological opinions on non-Christian religions have weakened one of the motives that urged missionaries to sacrifice themselves for the salvation of non-Christians: announcing Jesus Christ and the Christian faith to them. These theories exalt the role of other religions and common commitments for the renewal of the world and for human promotion. Some reduce evangelization to this purpose. Others include this renewal in the very concept of salvation. Still others give human promotion priority ("First make men, then Christians," or, "First feed the hungry, then speak of God").

The radical position that reduces the church's mission to human promotion is expressed by G. Davies in one concise sentence: "The purpose of mission is not to make Christians, but to help people to become men."[28] Similarly, for some liberation theologians mission is a historical practice in the revolutionary process; without this participation mission becomes omission, whereas, "participation in the process of man's liberation is already, in a certain sense, the work of salvation."[29] Without adopting Karl Barth's diametrically opposed Puritan opinion, which maintains that the purpose of mission is exclusively eschatological salvation, it is necessary to confirm and deepen the balanced position reached by the church in the last two decades but only imperfectly passed into missionary practice and into certain theological theories.

CHALLENGES AND QUESTIONS TO THEOLOGIANS

After this wide-ranging but necessarily incomplete presentation of various opinions about salvation, it is necessary to explain at least some anxieties, challenges, and questions that the missionary world addresses to experts on mission.

The first series of questions concerns the *contents of salvation*; that is, with which salvation are we dealing? Salvation/liberation from what—or for what?

1. Is it an *essentially religious salvation*? And if this is so, does it concern only the next world, in the *exclusively eschatological sense*, as Karl Barth wished, assigning to the mission the task of bringing this salvation and of being a "crisis" of all human, cultural, and religious values?

2. According to divine revelation, can it be said that the salvation to which evangelization tends is of an economic, political, social, or cultural nature? Or is it limited to serve the "world," or for the "well-being" of the world? What are the *bonds between the human dimension of salvation* (liberation, progress, development, justice, and peace) and the *divine or spiritual dimension of salvation* (liberation from sin and from evil, which are its fruit and consequences)? Does salvation not entail the rebirth of God's children to the new life and final participation in the happiness and glory of God in life everlasting?

3. In evaluating the elements of salvation of non-Christian religions, should one not take into account the difference—maintained, for example, by Hans Urs von Balthasar—between the religions of revelations that profess a personal God (Judaism, Christianity, and Islam) and those that believe in an impersonal divinity and thus see the contents of salvation differently?[30]

A second series of fundamental questions, putting oneself on the level of the Christian faith, concerns *the divine plan of salvation* in its three pillars: *God, Christ,* and *church.*

1. "God desires to save all human beings" (1 Tm 2:4)—this is clear and is generally accepted in all theologies. It becomes more problematic if what is also revealed and follows immediately in the Pauline text is likewise respected: " . . . and to come to the knowledge of the truth" (1 Tm 2:4). What does this addition mean? Is the solemn *mandate* to preach the gospel to all peoples and to baptize those who believe not perhaps the interpretation that Jesus himself gives to God's saving will? How can one explain the solemn and decisive tone of this command? (cf. Mt 28:19; Mk 16:15). Obviously, what divine revelation understands as the *salvation* desired by God for all must be established.

2. Jesus Christ is humanity's only savior and the only mediator between God and humans, according to revelation. The Bible states this repeatedly: "And there is salvation in no one else, for there is no other name under heaven given among men by which we must be saved" (Acts 4:12). "For there is one God, and there is one mediator between God and humans, the man Christ Jesus, who gave himself as a ransom for all" (1 Tm 2:5). "No one comes to the Father, but by me" (Jn 14:6). With his death and resurrection Jesus became for all humans "the source of eternal salvation" (Heb 5:9) and "Leader and Savior" (Acts 5:31). Can the *only definitive* role Jesus Christ has in the work of salvation perhaps be disputed without neglecting these facts of the Christian faith? Or is it sufficient, following Knitter, to consider them as later Christologies of the New Testament and as emphatic statements on a level with those of the enamored husband who thinks his own wife is the most beautiful and most lovable woman in the world?

3. Does the fact that Jesus Christ is the Son of God made man, the incarnate Word, have some impact on the quality of his message and of the Christian faith? Can the "revelation" brought by him be put on the same level as the "revelations or divine inspirations" contained in other religions?

4. Can Christ be put "next to" or "together with" other founders of religion? Is he not a savior also for them?

5. Does God save those who do not believe in Christ, without Christ? Does Christ's grace constitute salvation? How does Christ reach those who do not believe in him?

6. What should one think of the difference between the cosmic Christ and the historical Christ?

7. The necessity of receiving baptism and of being part of the church is also contained in the divine plan of salvation: "He who believes and is baptized will be saved" (Mk 16:16). In fact, one cannot enter the reign of God unless "one is born of water and the Spirit" (Jn 3:5); through baptism one enters the church, which is by the will of Christ "the universal sacrament of salvation" (*Lumen gentium,* no. 48), and it is only through it "that the fullness of the means of salvation can be obtained" (*Unitatis redintegratio,* no. 3).

8. So is it necessary to believe with the Second Vatican Council and in the council itself when, "basing itself upon sacred Scripture and Tradition, it teaches that the Church, now sojourning on earth as an exile, *is necessary* for salvation" (*Lumen gentium,* no. 14)? We are well aware that the obligation to follow the church belongs only to those who know this necessity (ibid.) and that "those also can attain to everlasting salvation who through no fault of their own do not know the gospel of Christ or his Church, yet sincerely seek God and, moved by grace, strive by their deeds to do His will as it is known to them through the dictates of conscience" (ibid., no. 16).

9. So in what sense is the church the "universal sacrament of salvation"? Since non-Christians who lead a good life are excluded from formal and explicit membership of the church, can it still be said that the church is necessary for salvation and, if so, in what sense?

10. Is complete aversion to so-called ecclesiocentrism theologically justified? Must mission work forego planting the church as one of its goals? (cf. Eph 3:17; 2:19; *Ad gentes,* nos. 6, 9; *Evangelii nuntiandi,* no. 62)?

11. Have any other religions a "sacramental" function for salvation in the same way as the church, which is "the universal sacrament of salvation," or are they only "occasions" of salvation?[31]

A third series of fundamental questions seeks to clarify the *specific Christian purpose of mission.* The questions have already been partially asked in the first series of questions concerning the contents of salvation. But some theories expounded need a thorough critical examination, above all so far as concerns the reign of God and dialogue in relation to mission.

1. Can it be said that the reign of God is the center of Jesus Christ's mission (and of that of the church), separating it from or setting it against the great mandate that obliges us to "teach" and "make disciples of all nations, baptizing them," "teaching them to observe all that [he has] commanded you" (Mt 28:20); to "preach the gospel" (Mk 16:15), to preach "repentance and forgiveness of sins" (Lk 24:47); to announce and "testify that he is the one ordained by

God to be judge of the living and the dead" (Acts 10:42)? What meaning does the "reign" have on the lips of Jesus Christ?

2. Following the text and context of the gospel, does the reign of God precisely mean earthly social well-being? Are "the values of the reign" reduced to justice, fraternity, and peace?

3. Is the reign of God not at the same time the reign of Christ?

4. Has the reign of God no relationship to the church?

5. If "the proclamation of the Reign of God is evangelization,"[32] according to *Evangelii nuntiandi* (nos. 8-10), is it not also true that evangelization is a complex and rich reality? And that among other things it includes the "plantatio ecclesiae" (*Ad gentes*, no. 6; CIC c. 786; *Evangelii nuntiandi*, nos. 59, 62)? And yet is it not equally true that "evangelization will also *always* contain—as the *foundation, center* and at the same time *summit* of its dynamism—a clear proclamation that in Jesus Christ, the Son of God made human, who died and rose from the dead, salvation is offered to all humans, . . . and not an immanent salvation, . . . but a transcendent salvation" (*Evangelii nuntiandi*, no. 27)?

6. Does the fact that God operates with grace also on non-Christians release the church from *the obligation of announcing the gospel*?

7. Does dialogue replace the announcement-proclamation? Does the announcement eliminate dialogue? Or do both belong to the "complex and rich reality" of evangelization?

Such challenges and questions are not exhaustive, but they do show how important the theme of mission can be at the present moment. Today, the words of Paul VI's apostolic exhortation *Evangelii nuntiandi* are extremely true:

> The presentation of the gospel message is not an optional contribution for the Church. It is the duty incumbent on her by the command of the Lord Jesus, so that people can believe and be saved. This message is indeed necessary. It is unique. It cannot be replaced. It does not permit either indifference, syncretism or accommodation. It is a question of people's salvation. It is the beauty of the Revelation that it represents. It brings with it a wisdom that is not of this world. It is able to stir up by itself faith—faith that rests on the power of God (cf. 1 Cor. 2:5). It is truth. It merits having the apostle consecrate to it all his time and all his energies, and to sacrifice for it, if necessary, his own life (*Evangelii nuntiandi*, no. 5).

THE CHURCH'S MISSION TODAY

While the foregoing questions and challenges are not exhaustive, they do provide an entry into a larger discussion of the church's mission today. My aim in the remainder of this chapter is to address these questions and challenges from the position of the Roman Catholic Church. I do this as the head of the church's Congregation for the Evangelization of Peoples, with a sense of responsibility to the church, to the peoples of the world, and in fidelity to the gospel entrusted by Jesus Christ to his disciples.

The Contemporary Situation of the World Religions and the Church

We are living in a world that is becoming more and more interdependent economically, culturally, and even religiously. Animosities, hostilities, and suspicions that kept people and nations divided are gradually crumbling. Many ideological divisions of the past decades and centuries are also being leveled by new perceptions of interdependence and complementary roles. This is true also of the world religions—classical, primal, and animistic. There is today a growing appreciation of the riches, cultural and spiritual, of various religions. This is also a phenomenon that marks the contemporary church in its attitudes to the world and the world religions. Though not all antagonism based on religion, culture, ideology, and race is disappearing—for the new winds of fundamentalism are blowing—there is no doubt that new currents of tolerance, mutual acceptance, coexistence, exchange, sharing, and mutual enrichment are becoming stronger in the world of today.

It is in this context we must view the efforts of many theologians and missionaries to rethink the foundation of Christian mission theology and praxis, discover new insights, formulate a new mission theology, create new missionary attitudes, find new mission methods, set new mission goals, and observe new standards of measuring missionary work and its efficacy. Hence the efforts made by theologians to reinterpret the meaning of Christian mission today and the shape of Christian missions for the future are very laudable and indispensable to the church.

In such a situation, there is no doubt, the concerns of the church and the magisterium to preserve and transmit the original content of revelation-faith and proclaim them to the world of today will also be appreciated. The concerns of the church and the magisterium are not to be seen as obscurantist, retrograde action, but rather as an act of fidelity to God's mission to the world in God's Son, Jesus Christ, and the Holy Spirit.

The Central Issue in Mission Debate Today: Jesus Christ

With the Second Vatican Council's decree *Ad gentes* and with Paul VI's exhortation *Evangelii nuntiandi*, the Catholic church, theologians, and missionaries have to have a better perception of the complex aspects and dimensions of Christian mission. Although the new aspects were not totally absent or foreign to the prior concept of mission and evangelization, their inner interrelationship and connection with the central aspect of the proclamation of Jesus Christ are now better perceived and appreciated. Thus evangelization is understood to be witnessing to the life of Jesus Christ. It is promotion of the reign of God and of the values of justice, peace, and love. It is helping people of today to have a true God-experience, an experience that makes them aware of being children of the same God and Father of all. It is human promotion, a kind of social humanism that promotes the true well-being of humans everywhere. It is liberative action that removes unjust, sinful, exploitative, social, cultural, political, and economic structures that keep people in slavery of one kind or another. It is a kind of spiritual humanism that implies the promotion of previous human and spiritual values found in all religions.

All the above call for genuine dialogue with all religions and ideologies and authentic inculturation in order to promote human wholeness and the development of human potentialities. This human wholeness and well-being would seem to be the common platform where all religions and ideologies of the contemporary world can meet, stand, and speak a commonly intelligible religious and human language.

The implications of the above points would be that any opposing discourse, dogmatic or theological, is culture bound, historically dated, and tribalistic in its interpretation of religious truths. Religions and ideologies should, it is argued by some, shed such dogmatic, traditional pretensions and move on to the all-important question and problem of human salvation, wholeness, and well-being. To be saddled with the theological hangovers of colonial mission theologies and methods would be obstructing the onward march of Christian mission in theory and practice. Obviously, the above missiological position is not representative of all theologians and not everyone subscribes to all the new positions. But they are widespread, valuable, and influential enough to be taken seriously by all Christians and call for a response.

In the ultimate analysis, it is not the new aspects and dimensions of mission theology and evangelization methods that pose the problem. It is the central question of God's revelation in Jesus Christ for the salvation of humankind and its relationship to world religions as identical or independent ways of human salvation in the sense understood by each religion. It is argued by some that the mystery of God is not exhausted in the revelation in Jesus Christ, which is definitive, absolute, and unique, and constitutive of salvation only for Christians. Rather, the mystery of God is greater than Jesus, and God has revealed Self in other ways through other religions that are equally constitutive of salvation for their followers.

The central issue, therefore, in today's missiological debate is the person of Jesus Christ and the implications of this truth for human salvation. The proponents of some mission theologies demand that the missiological preoccupations of the past centuries and the accompanying missionary goals and methods be jettisoned in favor of more tolerant, respectful, mutually acceptable, noncontroversial, mutually enriching, and salvific missiologies, goals, and methods.

Thus, it is proposed by some that the unfounded ecclesiocentrism of mission theology and methods should be abandoned. Mission exists not to perpetuate and expand the church. As a kind of idolatry the church should be demolished. The church exists only to bring about the "reign of God," which is a reign of justice, peace, and love.

Christocentrism, likewise, has plagued and vitiated mission theology, goals, and methods of evangelization for centuries. Jesus' mission was not to promote his own "reign," but his whole life was at the service of ushering in God's reign. Christian mission has misunderstood and distorted Jesus' mission by making it an instrument of Jesus' reign and not of the "reign of God."

Again, some would say that theocentrism need not be the basis for mission today since considerable sections of the religious world have no reference to a personal God. The same is true of ideologies that have no transcendent reference, allegiance, and worship patterns. These, too, need and are in search of salvation. Hence ultimate meaning and salvation need to be found in God.

The common foundation for all missions, Christian and other, could then be reduced to soteriocentrism, understood as human well-being, wholeness, which in turn is salvation. Here all can concur, celebrate, strive for, collaborate, and speak the same religious language. This will obviate the religious conflicts and miseries of the past, serve the true meaning and goals of mission, and aid the formulation and adoption of acceptable and effective methods of evangelization.

In light of such radical theologies of mission, we have to ask: How can we reconcile these theologies of mission with Christian revelation and the traditional understanding of Jesus Christ as the Son of God and the fullness of God's salvific revelation; what is their significance for humankind's salvation, their relationship to other religions; what are their implications for Christian mission, missionary goals, and methods? Thus the missiological problem today is ultimately a christological and soteriological problem.

AN UNCLARIFIED PRESUPPOSITION IN TODAY'S CHRISTOLOGICAL-MISSIOLOGICAL DEBATE

A positive perception of all religions, their spiritual values and riches, their prayer experience, and their salvific significance has led some Christian theologians to think of Jesus Christ as one of the many revelations of the mystery of God and hence one of the many ways of human access to God and salvation. But behind this position there lies an uncritical assumption that the universal salvific will of God, which is clear from the record of Christian revelation, and the specific salvific will and historical revelation of God in Jesus Christ and its universal and absolute significance for human salvation, are irreconcilable.

Since the majority of humankind belongs to the general history of revelation and salvation of God, some theologians argue, it must be affirmed that world religions are independent ways to salvation. Hence all religions are the results of God's revelation and God's way of salvation for humankind. God's revelation in Jesus Christ can then be affirmed as absolute and universal only for Christians as a subjective truth, a mythos valid only for them.

This is a very questionable assumption. In reality, the God of creation and the Lord of the general history of salvation is also the God of historical revelation in Jesus Christ and salvation through faith in him. The unity of God, the unity of creation and salvation, and the unity of humankind lead us to believe that the two ways of revelation and salvation are intimately and essentially related. While there is distinction, there is also continuity and fulfillment. There is nothing inconsistent if the God who creates all things and wills the salvation of all peoples subsumes his universal salvific revelation and will into a specific revelation and will in his son Jesus Christ, which in turn constitutes an absolute, universal, and definitive way of salvation for all, even to those who live according to the former. Not only is there nothing inconsistent, incompatible, divisive, and intolerant in such a revelation and way of salvation; it is also eminently consistent, unifying, and gracious on the part of God to call all humans to the same revelatory knowledge and salvation. Besides, God could create the universe and all human beings in view of God's self-revelation and self-communication in the son Jesus Christ. We are dealing with the unfathomable mystery of God and the manifold wisdom of God in God's communication in creation and human salvation to be climaxed in God's self-communication in historical revelation in Jesus Christ and the salvation offered through faith in him.

If God has spoken to humankind in Jesus Christ, as the entire Christian tradition has been witnessing to in life, worship, and script, it is perfectly legitimate and even obligatory to believe that Jesus Christ has universal revelatory-salvific significance for all. There is no doubt that such truth is of the very essence of Christian revelation, faith, life, worship, and theology. Tampering with it, whatever the difficulties and however well-intentioned the motives for doing so, will only mean tampering with the content of God's revelation and offer of salvation. Humans are free to accept or reject this content but not to distort or vitiate it. Those who are unable to accept it, whether due to sociological or religious reasons, or due to philosophical difficulties, or due to the absence of credibility of the Christians to mediate it will certainly find their own ways to salvation, provided there is no resistance to God's general offer of salvation. In any case, truth is greater than the human mind; revelatory-salvific truth especially is not to be trimmed to fit the narrow frame of the human intellect.

Even our inability to define, articulate, and formulate satisfactorily the relationship between God's revelation and offer of salvation in the general history of salvation and God's historical and personalistic revelation and offer of salvation in Jesus Christ is no reason to undervalue or wish away one or the other. It is part of the existential tensions of the mystery of God's revelation and offer of salvation so that no human person may glory in one's own salvific efforts and search and sink into a challengeless salvific security.

The Centrality, Uniqueness, and Universal Significance of Jesus for Human Salvation

Humans look for meaning and wholeness, however they may be understood and expressed in cultural molds peculiar to particular peoples. Such search for meaning and wholeness of life leads them to the ultimate, transcendent reality most people call God or similar names. The ultimate meaning and wholeness is Transcendence itself. God, the transcendent Reality, may also reveal Self historically and thus encounter humans in their search for ultimate meaning and wholeness. Such a revelatory-salvific encounter in history in no way denies human search and freedom since the transcendent Reality does not force itself upon humans and their freedom. It is always a gracious offer. God's graciousness and goodness are infinite, so God can wait and encounter humans who continue their search for meaning and wholeness till the end of their salvific journey and they realize for themselves that the God of creation, and the God of revelation and salvation in Jesus Christ, is the one and the same God who offers meaning and wholeness to life.

Jesus Christ presented himself to humans as their ultimate meaning, Logos, and life, from God.

> Before the world was created, the Word already existed; he was with God, and he was the same as God. From the very beginning the Word was with God. Through him God made all things. The Word was the source of life, and this life brought light to humankind (Jn 1:1-4).

This is how his disciples perceived and understood him gradually and after his death-resurrection-Spirit event, as all the New Testament writers attest, though under varied imageries and languages. "I did come from the Father, and I came into the world; and now I am leaving the world and going back to the Father" (Jn 16:28). "You are the Messiah, the Son of the living God" (Mt 16:16). "We know that you know everything; you do not need someone to ask you questions. This makes us believe that you are from God" (Jn 16:30).

This revelation and offer of God to humankind in Jesus Christ has been authenticated by his life, teachings, death-resurrection, and the giving of the Spirit to his disciples. This is part of the very essence of Christian faith. Such faith is no myth but founded on the life, teachings, works, and especially the death-resurrection of Jesus and the giving of the Holy Spirit to all who accept him as God's offer of meaning and life. The Christian dogma of Jesus Christ as God and as human is to be understood as the formulation of the perception of Jesus by his disciples as God's definitive, unique, universal, and historical offer of salvation for all.

In many and various ways God spoke of old to our fathers by the prophets; but in these last days he has spoken to us by a Son, whom he appointed the heir of all things, through whom all he created the world. He reflects the glory of God and bears the very stamp of his nature, upholding the universe by his Word of power (Heb 1:1-3).

The Christian faith in Jesus Christ founded on historical facts does not negate or nullify the human search for meaning and wholeness, the salvific riches and insights into the mystery of God and human existence, or the truth and grace that God has revealed and offered in the course of humankind's age-old search for him. The Christian faith does not belittle or reject alternate expressions in faith, prayer, worship, conduct of life, and culture. Many of them even and often do enrich believers in Jesus Christ in their faith-worship expression. Believers in Jesus Christ can also be led to see the marvelous and mysterious wisdom and infinite graciousness of God to all. They can see the intimate connection between God's general revelation and offer of salvation and their historical expression in Jesus Christ. They can praise the one Father of all and the unity of all humankind as God's family, heirs to the same gracious salvation and wholeness as the early Christian witnesses tell us: "It is clear that God gave those Gentiles the same gift that he gave us when we believed in the Lord Jesus Christ. . . . When they heard this they stopped their criticism and praised God, saying, 'Then God has given to the Gentiles also the opportunity to repent and live'" (Acts 11:17-18). On the other hand, this conviction did in no way prevent Peter from baptizing the family of Cornelius.

While God's revelation and offer of salvation in Jesus Christ do not negate other searches and offers of salvation, God intended it as absolute, total, and final for all humankind. This is clear from the life and death-resurrection of Jesus. Jesus presented himself as God's final and definitive salvific covenant with humankind. "Then he took a cup, gave thanks to God, and gave it to them. Drink it, all of you, he said; this is my blood, which seals God's covenant, my blood poured out for many for the forgiveness of sins" (Mt 26:27-28). Jesus Christ, therefore, has constitutive salvific significance for all. By his absolute obedience to God's will and total solidarity with and self-giving to all, Jesus Christ became the absolute and unique norm for all ultimate meaning and wholeness of life, whatever may be the expressions of such meaning and salvation in creeds, worships, community structures, and philosophical, mystical, or spiritual interpretations and formulations.

The ultimate meaning and purpose of all religions are openness to God and one's neighbor, or at least to one's neighbor. Jesus Christ is the supreme expression of that core of all religiosity. He has, therefore, universal salvific significance, without, though, infringing upon human freedom. This is also the teaching of Vatican II:

All this holds true not for Christians only but also for all humans of good will in whose hearts grace is active invisibly. For since Christ died for all, and since all humans are in fact called to one and the same destiny, which is divine, we must hold that the Holy Spirit offers to all the possibility of being made partners, in a way known to God, in the paschal mystery (*Gaudium et spes*, no. 22).

It has been the constant conviction and belief of the church that Jesus Christ has universal salvific significance for all humankind. Through his incarnation, Jesus Christ has united himself with every human person and through his death and resurrection he has united all humans to his Paschal mystery in ways known to God. Again Vatican II confirms this view (ibid).

Jesus Christ is a twofold Logos, namely Word and Meaning. He is the ultimate meaning of God. He is God's ultimate meaning and revelation to humankind. He is also the ultimate meaning of human beings. He is the total openness to God and to humans and their total openness to God and to one another. Thus Vatican II says:

"It pleased God in his goodness and wisdom, to reveal himself and to make known the mystery of his will" (cf. Eph. 1:9). God's will was that humans should have access to the Father, through Christ, the Word made flesh, in the Holy Spirit and thus become sharers in the divine nature (cf. Eph 2:18; 2 Pet 1:4) (*Dei verbum*, no. 2).

THE ABSOLUTENESS AND UNIVERSAL SIGNIFICANCE OF THE CHRISTIAN MESSAGE FOR SALVATION

There was a time when some theologians claimed the Christian faith to be absolute for various sociohistorical reasons in a triumphalistic sense, along with a generally negative appraisal of other religions and religionists. The absoluteness of the Christian message for human salvation may have had little to do with sociohistorical reasons. It comes, rather, from God's absolute and definitive offer of salvation in Jesus Christ. It is God's offer of salvation in Jesus Christ. It is God's offer of Self as truth and life: "The Word became a human being and, full of grace and truth, lived among us" (Jn 1:14).

This self-revelation of God has been accepted uniquely and absolutely by humans in Jesus Christ, who is truly human, in his incarnation and through his death and resurrection, whose real significance is the human total surrender to God's will and self-giving to one's neighbor. Such surrender and self-giving constitute also the absoluteness and uniqueness of the Christian faith and message. They also constitute human meaning and wholeness, which we call salvation. The heart of the Christian message of salvation is sharing the absolute surrender and self-giving of Jesus. As such it has universal and absolute significance for all, even those who strive to do so through the working of the Spirit of God in their hearts. Somehow they are also in Christ, baptized into the real significance of his death and resurrection, though without the resultant creed and sacramental symbols but rather in their lives.

For Christian faith, Jesus is God's definitive and personal invitation to similar surrender and self-giving, overcoming the inborn resistance to God's will and deep-rooted selfishness whose power over humans cannot be underestimated. It is also a message to humans that such surrender and self-giving cannot be accomplished by human search and efforts; they are a gracious gift achieved through the power of Jesus's death-resurrection and the Spirit released through it.

Jesus Christ is the personal and historical witness of human surrender to God's will and self-giving to others. He is not only a model for all humans to do the same, but he also gives the power to do this by the gift of his Holy Spirit. Jesus is the pattern for self-surrender and self-giving, and he communicates the power of grace to do the same.

Such witness and communication of salvific power and grace are unique in human history. But that does not take away or deny the grace and power of other efforts for salvation, or other ways in which the Spirit communicated to humans the same saving grace. They are, however, not a different grace and salvific power but the same saving grace of Jesus Christ. As he himself has said: "No one comes to the Father except through me."

We may ask, then, why this unique way, when other ways are there and equally religious? To begin with, all other ways of salvation offered by God are part of God's unique plan of salvation. They are also the expressions of God's irreversible self-offer, authenticated, and personalistic, and expressive of total human salvation, overcoming sin and finally death itself, and symbol of human's final communion with God, as in the incarnate and risen Lord Jesus Christ. All other ways are subsumed into this one, unique, and universally applicable way of salvation. It is this that gives meaning and substance to all other ways of salvation and all other mediations of salvation. Such unique and universally applicable testimony of God's irreversible revelation-salvation is not seen anywhere else in the horizon of human history.

The uniqueness, absoluteness, and universal significance of the revelation-salvation in Jesus Christ gives no real ground for human pride, arrogance, superiority, boasting, or intolerance, for it is a call to total *kenosis*, self-emptying, letting God's rule take hold of the human heart and mind. It is to share in the "humiliation," even to the cross (Phil 2:5-11) and to become alive to God with a new life that looks to God (Rom 6:8).

The uniqueness and absoluteness of Christianity ought to give no real ground for exclusion or rejection of other religions, though in the course of history this has happened. All religions, in their original form, also existed for the same end, though they too became instruments of power in the course of history. Christianity is and ought to be more and more a call to authentic religion as human's surrender to God and self-giving to others. All have the same divine vocation (*Gaudium et spes*, no. 22), and Christianity offers its example and symbols to all in their attempt to fulfill the one divine-human vocation.

Far from generating an attitude of superiority, Christians are called to make the unique self-surrender of Jesus to God and his self-giving to others their own as individuals and as church, and thus become a sacrament of true religion to all others.

Jesus Christ gives concreteness and substance to what all religions are striving to achieve. As Lesslie Newbigin has put it:

> The central question is not "How shall I be saved?" but "How shall I glorify God by understanding, loving and doing God's will here and now in this earthly life?" To answer that question I must insistently ask: "How and where is God's purpose for the whole of creation and the human family made visible and credible?" That is the question about the truth—objective truth—which is true whether or not it coincides with my "values." And I know of no place in the public history of the world where the dark mystery of human life is illuminated, and the dark power of all that denies human well-being is met and measured and mastered, except in those events that have their focus in what happened under Pontius Pilate.[33]

THE PASCHAL MYSTERY OF JESUS CHRIST AND THE CHURCH

Conversion to God and salvation are not once-and-for-all events. They are a process by which humans are transformed into the image of God. The image of God has now been revealed in God's Son, Jesus Christ. Thus to be transformed into the image of Jesus Christ is also wholeness and salvation. The same God calls humans "to become like his Son so that the Son would be first among the many brethren" (Rom 8:29). Conversion and salvation are the process by which humans are assimilated into the image and likeness of Jesus Christ; thereby we let God transform us inwardly by a complete change of our minds (cf. Rom 12:2).

The church is nothing else but the community of believers who have accepted God's revelation and offer of salvation-life-wholeness in Jesus Christ, God's Son, and who strive to assimilate the Paschal mystery of Jesus Christ into their personal and community lives and thus be transformed into the likeness of God as Jesus Christ himself. Thus Paul exhorts his Christians: "Your minds and hearts must be made completely new, and you must put on the new self which is created in God's likeness and reveals itself in the true life that is upright and holy" (Eph 4:23-24).

The church is a communion in the Holy Spirit, taken into the mystery of the life of the Holy Trinity. It is a fellowship because of the indwelling of the Spirit: "Surely you know that you are God's temple and that God's Spirit lives in you" (1 Cor 3:16). This is exactly what Jesus promised before his death and resurrection: "When that day comes, you will know that I am in my Father and that you are in me, just as I am in you" (Jn 14:20).

The church is the result of the incarnation of the Word and the Paschal mystery of Jesus Christ. It is much more than a historical and sociological phenomenon; it exists only to proclaim God's offer of salvation in Jesus Christ to all humans and to transform individuals and society into God's children, in the image of God's Son. Conversion and salvation are a slow movement toward the wholeness of life; the church exists as its visible sign and instrument in proclamation, sacramental signs, worship, and a life modeled on Jesus Christ. The church, therefore, is not something optional. It is born of the Paschal mystery of Jesus: "For it was from the side of Christ as He slept the sleep of death upon the cross that there came forth the wondrous sacrament which is the whole Church" (*Sacrosanctum concilium*, no. 5).

Jesus gathered a community of disciples and taught them to live as he lived. He gave them the Holy Spirit to bring about the transformation into his image as God's children: "For the Spirit that God has given you does not make you slaves and cause you to be afraid; instead the Spirit makes you God's children and by the Spirit's power we cry to God, Abba, Father" (Rom 8:15).

Jesus commanded his disciples to be witnesses of his life, death, and resurrection to the ends of the earth, namely, to all humankind, and to teach all to live according to his precepts, Jews and Gentiles alike, without exception. The entire early church in its oral, liturgical, and scriptural tradition bears witness to this fact. Thus the apostles and the apostolic church, as well as the church of the fathers and the church of the subsequent centuries, confirm this understanding of Jesus Christ and of the church's mission to the world. The early fathers of the church faced openly the problem of other religions and ways of salvation. Their views were surprisingly open and go beyond the single phrase *extra ecclesiam nulla salus*—and even that was interpreted narrowly during later centuries.

The mission of the church is not based upon some isolated texts of scripture but on the incarnation, life, death, and resurrection of Jesus Christ and the giving of the Spirit to his disciples to go into the whole world, to bear witness to him and his life, to proclaim his message, and to do what he did in his memory, namely, his submission to the Father and self-giving to his disciples through the sacramental symbols of baptism and of bread and wine. All four gospels end with a solemn commission to go into the whole world and proclaim the good news of God's offer of forgiveness of sins and fullness of life by word, deed, and witness of life. Luke concludes his gospel as follows:

> Then he opened their minds to understand the Scriptures, and said to them, "This is what is written: the Messiah must suffer and must rise again from death three days later, and in his name the message about repentance and forgiveness of sins must be preached to all nations, beginning in Jerusalem. You are witness of these things" (Lk 24:45-48).

John, in different language, says the same thing:

> Jesus said to them again, "Peace be with you. As the Father has sent me, so I send you." Then he breathed on them and said: "Receive the Holy Spirit. If you forgive people's sins, they are forgiven" (Jn 20:21-23).

Before his ascension, Jesus promised his disciples the power of the Spirit to be his witnesses to the ends of the earth (Acts 1:7-9). The bestowal of the Spirit on Pentecost was also the solemn beginning of the mission of the church.

As the church springs from the incarnation and Paschal mystery of Jesus Christ, her mission and missionary motivation spring from the same sources. The fundamental methodology of doing mission today, as always, is provided by the same Paschal mystery of Jesus, though the concrete forms and shapes it takes and the methods used vary according to times and historical circumstances. The Paschal mystery of Jesus reveals also the need and urgency of Christian missions, even today in a climate of religious pluralism, as well as a positive evaluation of other religions. Indeed, the need and urgency of Christian mission are even greater today as we come to understand the close and essential connection between God's universal and cosmic plan of salvation and God's special plan of salvation. Indeed, the church's experience of redemption in Jesus Christ gives it a profound insight into God's plan of salvation of all. It has nothing to fear from any authentic religion. It has much to contribute to other religions, while it also learns from them about God's mysterious ways with them. In fact, Paul tells us in his letter to the Ephesians that God has made known to the church "the mystery of his will according to his purpose which is set forth in Christ as a plan for the fullness of time, to unite all things in him, things in heaven and things on earth" (Eph 1:9-10).

There is no real contradiction, therefore, between God's universal salvific will and the specific, historical, salvific revelation in Jesus Christ. As Paul put it: "His intent was that now, through the Church, the manifold wisdom of God should be made known to the rulers and authorities in the heavenly places" (Eph 1:11).

THE REIGN OF GOD, THE CHURCH, AND CHRISTIAN MISSION

The Church and the Reign of God

First, there is a tendency today among some theologians and missiologists to speak of the building up of the reign of God as the goal of all Christian missions. This is no new discovery. It is exactly what thousands of missionaries, men and women, have been doing in the remote villages, jungles, mountains, and valleys of Asia, Africa, Latin America, and Oceania—sharing the life of the poor, giving them the benefits of literacy, health care, and development, and thus making their lives more worthy of humans. Exceptions do not erase the overwhelming testimony of the majority. We need only to ask the Harijans, the Tribals, and the Campesinos, and they will bear witness to who is building up the reign of God in their midst. It is the missionaries who are really engaged in the work of building up God's reign among God's people.

Second, in today's missiological debate the mission of the church often is reduced to building up God's reign and promoting the values of God's reign, but both understood in a temporal sense. In general they reduce the reign of God and the values of God's reign to the earthly well-being of humans. "They would reduce her aims to a human-centered goal; the salvation of which she is a messenger would be reduced to material well-being" (*Evangelii nuntiandi*, no. 32).

But the biblical meaning of the reign is wider than mere material well-being. It is God's rule and presence in the heart of people. It is not an abstract concept but concretely revealed in Jesus Christ. It is established primarily in the death-resurrection of Jesus, when he became irreversibly God's reign. The proclamation of Jesus Christ is at the same time the proclamation of God's reign and of its values. He teaches all to let God's will rule over their hearts and become God's reign. God's reign must first be born in the hearts of individuals, and only then can human society become God's reign and live by the values of God's reign. The reign of God is primarily a spiritual reality in the New Testament; hence the role of Christian mission also is the reign of God understood in its biblical sense.

Third, the preaching of Jesus cannot be reduced to the imagery of God's reign. God's reign is not the only key concept in the New Testament. Discipleship and the body of Christ are also important concepts in the New Testament. Jesus spoke of his relationship with his disciples as that of the vine and the branches: "I am the vine, and you are the branches" (Jn 15:5). Paul expresses the same idea with the imagery of the body: "In the same way, all of us, whether Jews or Gentiles, whether slaves or free, have been baptized into the one body by the same Spirit, and we have all been given the one Spirit to drink" (1 Cor 12:13).

True, the reign of God is not exhausted by the church. Nor are the values of God's reign found only in the church. But the church and the reign of God are inseparably linked. The church, even if it fails to be fully God's reign, is the concrete expression of the reign of God. It is the community of those who accept God's rule in their hearts and seek to live as Jesus Christ did. The church strives to be the reign of God and to promote its values. It proclaims the reign of God and is its instrument in bringing it about in the world. As Vatican II says: "It becomes on earth the initial budding forth of that Reign. While it slowly grows, the church strains toward the consummation of the Reign and, with all her strength, hopes and desires to be united in glory with her King" (*Lumen gentium*, no. 5).

As Jesus is the revelation and the instrument of the reign of God, the church in a subordinate way is the revelation and instrument of the reign of God. It exists only for the reign of God: "Without doubt the Church has the Reign as her supreme goal, of which she on earth is its seed and beginning, and is therefore totally consecrated to the glorification of the Father" (*Christifideles laici*, no. 36).

The reign of God, on the other hand, is not a purely spiritual and eschatological reality. It is equally an earthly reality. The reign of God finds its expression in the values of justice, peace, freedom, and human dignity for all. The promotion of the reign of God and its values here on earth is an essential part of the mission of the church. Without it, the church's proclamation would lose its credibility and sacramental symbolic expression. Such values are not only symbols but the beginnings of the reign of God itself. Human promotion in all its wide variety and extension is vital to the mission of the church in its service to the reign of God.

The reign of God, therefore, has spiritual, eschatological, and temporal dimensions. These are interdependent and essential elements of the reign of God, and Christian mission cannot be reduced to any one of these without at the same time falsifying and distorting Christian mission and eventually making it ineffective and meaningless.

The Church and Religious Pluralism

The fact of religious pluralism is nothing new. Human existence has been pluralistic from its very beginning. There never was a time when humankind was not pluralistic in its social structures, economic, and political organizations; in its cultural expressions; and in its religious creeds, worship, and goals.

It was into this pluralistic world—dominated mostly by the Hebrew, Roman, and Greek cultures—that God sent the Son in the fullness of time that God might offer salvation to all. While Jesus showed the greatest respect to every person, he was not ashamed to bear witness to his Father in word, deed, and in gathering together a community of disciples.

Today's world is no different in its pluralistic situation. But the fact of religious pluralism and our new awareness of it cannot be an excuse for not proclaiming salvation in Jesus Christ. Our growing awareness of religious pluralism should help us to be tolerant, respectful, appreciative of other religions and cultures, but not to relativize the message of salvation we have received from God in Jesus Christ or to cease to proclaim and offer it as a way of salvation to all. We need to do mission in Jesus' way. The gospel is the power of salvation for all peoples, and we have an obligation to all, the civilized and the uncivilized, the educated and the ignorant, as Paul put it (Rom 1:15).

The Church, Dialogue and Mission

Dialogue is an essential part of Christian mission. Recent insights into the meaning of dialogue have helped the church to see its mission in a new light and context. But there are different meanings and levels of dialogue.

God sending the Son into the world is an act of salvific dialogue with humankind. Jesus' mission to the world was carried out in dialogue with the men and women of his time. But it was no neutral dialogue; it was a dialogue that offered God's salvation and demanded an obedience of faith. Christian mission, too, cannot be reduced to neutral dialogue.

Religious dialogue is not a meeting and sharing between two persons but a meeting and sharing in order to listen to God and accept what God has to offer to us; dialogue cannot be a substitute for proclamation. The Christian way of dialogue is to do it in Jesus's way—receiving, sharing, respecting, but also giving the message of salvation in Jesus Christ.

No doubt, there are different kinds or levels of dialogue. We can enter into dialogue with other religionists in order to clarify our own religious positions, to enrich our religious experience with their religious experience, to enter into mutual collaboration in the promotion of human and spiritual values, and to experience a conversion to our neighbor. We can also enter into dialogue with others as a means to evangelize, as Jesus entered into dialogue with others in order to reveal the Father and himself and thus offer fullness of life and salvation. There is nothing intellectually or morally unbecoming in it if it is done in respect and love for the other. It is part of the dialogue of salvation initiated even by God.

"For God loved the world so much that he gave his only Son, so that everyone who believes in him may not die but have eternal life" (Jn 3:16). Jesus entered into dialogue with his contemporaries because he loved the world. We also enter into dialogue because we love God and our neighbors and want to share with them the joy of salvation we have found in Jesus Christ.

The Church, Mission, Conversion, and Baptism

Conversion is a much abused word today. But its real meaning, "a change of heart," is always valid. This can have different levels. There is the conversion of the human person to God. We may speak of conversion to Jesus Christ. In fact, there are many who believe in and follow the teachings of Jesus without becoming Christians. But they have turned to Jesus Christ for the inspiration and the criterion of their lives. There is conversion to Jesus Christ in the Christian community with its sacraments and worship. There is also, finally, conversion to one's neighbor, even though one may have no religious or ecclesial affiliations.

Ultimately, all conversion is to God; all other conversions are meant to lead to conversion to God. The church is, in fact, the community of those who turn to God and want to continue being converted to God. In this sense, the church needs constant conversion. But the church also preaches conversion as Jesus gathered a community of disciples. Whenever it can, the church also wants to promote conversion at every level. The mission of Jesus involved a conversion of the heart and making people his disciples. Christian mission today implies also, among other things, a similar conversion and gathering together of the believing community through faith and baptism. Thus we see the apostles and disciples of Jesus proclaiming Jesus Christ in the power of the Spirit and gathering together communities of believers through repentance and baptism from the day of Pentecost onward. Peter tells the people gathered in Jerusalem:

> God raised this very Jesus from death, and we are all witnesses to this fact. . . . And when the people asked: "What shall we do brothers?" Peter answered, "Each one of you must turn away from his sins and be baptized in the name of Jesus Christ, so that your sins will be forgiven, and you will receive God's gift, the Holy Spirit" (Acts 2:32, 37-38).

Christian mission has many dimensions, such as dialogue, human promotion, promotion of the values of the reign of God, and promotion of spiritual values found in all religions and ideologies. But there are two primary and essential elements: (1) the proclamation of Jesus Christ; and (2) the gathering together of the believers in Jesus Christ, the church. Without these primary elements, all other elements of Christian mission will lose their validity and cohesion. As Paul VI stated in *Evangelii nuntiandi*, there can be no true evangelization without the proclamation of the life, death, and resurrection of Jesus Christ and the gathering together of the believing community through baptism.

CONCLUSION

Christian mission is based on God's plan to send the Son into the world and the saving Spirit to all who freely accept him. The salvation offered to humans in Jesus Christ is primarily a salvation from sin in all its individual and social manifestations and finally death itself. Such salvation has a religious, moral, and spiritual content in the first place. It is not to be reduced to a purely economical, political, or cultural liberation.

Human liberation and promotion of human dignity are essentially related to the spiritual salvation offered by God. They are the temporal expression of the eschatological salvation, the first fruits of the spiritual salvation, the necessary concomitants of the religious salvation. Without them, religious salvation would lack credibility and substance. Nonetheless, eschatological salvation offered by Jesus Christ through his death-resurrection cannot be arbitrarily reduced to its temporal expressions.

In God's offer of salvation of humankind, Jesus Christ is central; Jesus' mediation of salvation is unique and universal. The same God who creates all and gives revelation and salvation in ways known only to God can and does subsume God's universal salvific will in the Son Jesus Christ, according to Christian faith. This is our faith and conviction, based on the life and testimony of Jesus Christ, especially his death and resurrection. We hold this humbly yet firmly, respectfully yet unequivocally. We have the freedom to accept or reject it, but we do not have the right to relativize or syncretize it with other notions of ours against the cumulative witness of the early church, the scriptures, and a Christian tradition of twenty centuries.

The same God who wills the salvation of all wills also that all may come to the truth of Jesus Christ as the unique Savior of all (Jn 17:1-3; 1 Tm 2:3-4), even though we are not able to define satisfactorily how the grace of Jesus Christ is mediated to all.

The church is the community of the believers in Jesus Christ, where he is accepted in faith, celebrated in worship, and proclaimed in mission so that others may enter through conversion and baptism and find salvation, since it is willed by God for the salvation of all and hence necessary (*Lumen gentium*, no. 14). The fact that God saves those who do not know Jesus Christ (ibid., 16) does not in any way take away the necessity or urgency of proclaiming Jesus Christ for the church as the universal sacrament of salvation (ibid., no. 48). It is only in the believing, worshiping, and proclaiming community—the church—that the people of every age and place can encounter Jesus Christ, his salvific revelation. Without the church, the Christ-Spirit event, God's supreme revelation and salvific gift of life and wholeness to humankind cannot be mediated to the world.

The reign of God, Jesus Christ, and the church are not mutually exclusive realities but essentially related and interdependent and at the service of one another and the concrete expression and continuation of one another.

Our respect, love, and esteem for and sharing and collaboration with other religions and religionists need not lead us to dilute or distort our faith in the salvific revelation of God in Jesus Christ and his unique and universal significance. Doing so ultimately will be an act of disservice to the world and infidelity to God's will and gracious offer of salvation and impoverishment of the riches of God's salvific revelation.

What is required then in the contemporary world is not a relativized theology of mission and Christology, but that the church strive to become truly a church, namely, God's reign, as a clear sign, a forceful instrument, and a convincing invitation to all to share in the unsearchable riches of God's salvific revelation in Jesus Christ.

10.

DECIDING FOR GOD

The Right to Convert in Protestant Perspectives

———————◆———————

Max L. Stackhouse
Deirdre King Hainsworth

CONVERSION AS FREEDOM AND BONDING

The idea of conversion is, in some ways, a central Christian one, and it is one of several key ideas that led to the development of human rights—although the path is often indirect and has many non-Christian parallels and influences. The Greek terms *epistrepho* (to turn back, to return to the source and norm of life, meaning, and morality) and *metanoia* (to change mentality) are embedded in the Christian scriptures. Both were translated into the Latin *conversio* (to turn over). Of course, the idea is not exclusively Christian, even if it became centrally Christian. The prophets of ancient Israel used the Hebrew *shubh* to convey much the same thing, and Judaism long had a place for proselytism. Moreover, Hellenistic philosophers and devotees of various mystery cults sent teachers and preachers throughout the Middle East well before Christ, seeking converts to a "higher way," as had Hindu sages in South Asia before that. Indeed, the Buddha protested and reformed that tradition when he left his palace to seek enlightenment—a turn as dramatic for the East as that of Paul's was for the West, one that also inspired missionaries to go to the far reaches of civilization. Later, Islam also spread rapidly by conquest and conversion. The point of all conversion is that we are not simply what we are but are related to a greater reality than most of ordinary life discloses and have a duty, and thus the right, to turn to it intellectually, morally, and relationally.

Still, aspects of the idea remain centrally associated with Christianity,[1] especially those involving the freedom of religion and the right to change one's community membership. One is called into a new relationship with God and

201

has a renewed conviction that reorients both the inner life of the soul and the outer life of relationship. This becomes visible through the felt need to tell others of this connection and to form or join a community different from, even if related to, the "natural" institutions of society—what have variously been called the "estates," the "orders," or the "spheres"—the family, the regime, the economy, and the arts and sciences. In brief, a decision for the God whom Christians know through Jesus demands a turn to articulate conviction and an organized church. And this requires a freedom of conscience, a freedom of speech, and a freedom of association, and a right to attempt to convert others, even if converts hold that they were compelled to their decision by the grace of God, not by their free choice.[2]

For all who have known conversion, it is both the chief freedom and a primary bonding. No longer is one merely the product of one's biological, political, economic, cultural environment, or even of one's religious socialization. For all the influence of these forces, and all the profound insights of the sciences studying these phenomena, it is doubtful that they can explain all that is entailed in conversion.[3] Any who have known conversion may honor these realities but will also deny the ultimate significance of them, live in tension with them, seek to leave them behind, or try to reaffirm or reconstitute them on the basis of the newly acknowledged reality that transcends them.[4]

This feature of Christianity, and of many religions and philosophies, is also the reason that the prospect of fanaticism, dogmatism, and cultic jingoism haunts them all. But these possibilities, as the twentieth century seems to have demonstrated all too well, attend also those who deny the viability of Christianity, or of other universalist religions or philosophies, in favor of animistic, materialist, or merely humanist theories. National Socialism tried to resurrect paganism and convert the world to it. Marxist-Leninism sought to revolutionize the world on the basis of class-based secularism. And lesser efforts to make idols of societal or cultural images are on all sides. They have flooded our century with genocide, dogmatism, cultic fanaticism, and death more devastating than any Christian heresy hunt, crusade, inquisition, or witch trial. For all their complicity with evil, which Christians must confess, some strands of Christianity may be decisive for generating the convictions and institutions that sustain human rights and restrain these evils.[5]

This is not a matter of religious triumphalism or sectarian chauvinism. There is little doubt about the fact that Protestantism could not have developed the doctrine of human rights without the ethical universalism of the Hebraic traditions before it. And, in spite of the fact that Roman Catholicism has only come lately to embrace fully the ideas of religious human rights,[6] Protestants could not have developed the concept had it not been for theological, jurisprudential, and ecclesiological contributions of the Roman tradition, which they both internalized and altered. And it is likely that aspects of human rights thought and religious freedom remain unfinished and too much confined to distinctively Western conceptualities, and must, in the future, engage cultures and philosophies and religions beyond the West. Nevertheless, to insist on the contributions of Protestantism to this area is a demand for intellectual honesty. Moreover, if we do not preserve some of the ideas and institutions that Protestantism contributed to the generation of human rights, we may be again plunged into the intolerance, conflict, terror, and barbarism that attended the world without them.[7]

EARLY PROTESTANTISM AND RELIGIOUS FREEDOM

Protestant contributions to religious freedom have their roots in the biblical record to which the Reformation returned with such intensity, and which many felt had been subverted by the inflated claims of the authority of the pope.[8] The Bible is, among other things, a witness to a just God, one who has given to all peoples a universal moral law and whose image is conferred on every human being—a dignity not always evident in human behavior. However, the Creator, the law-giving God, is also a merciful, forgiving God. When that is recognized, converts discover a true freedom from sin and distortion that restores the relationship to God and neighbor and the capacity to reason rightly. Still, ideas of liberties and rights certainly were not advocated in contemporary terms by the earliest reformers, and would have been unpalatable to some of them.

Indeed, conscience was well bounded—by the idea of "right" conscience. An individual's conscience was not absolute, nor were a person's feelings or self-perceived rightness a sufficient test.[9] Instead, a "right" conscience was one in general conformity with right reason, the right use of scripture, right intent, and, thus, right doctrine. This emphasis on right conscience is indicative of the nature of religious liberty in the early Reformation; conscience was seen as moral "co-science," a common knowledge of standards before which life and thought were held accountable. Toleration in the early stages of the Reformation was a claim largely made against Rome. As the church had previously established the relative independence of the church from political control through long and too often forgotten battles between *imperium* and *sacerdotum*, and, within the church, between orders of various kinds (all of which claimed valid theologies), so now reformers claimed the right to form doctrines and practices on the basis of deeply held convictions and carefully debated arguments about sin and grace. The seeds of religious liberty were thus planted.

Martin Luther's celebrated break with the Roman hierarchy began over the issue of selling indulgences. Luther was an Augustinian monk in a chapter that had a long history of dealing with dissent under canon law, the only substantive international law of the time.[10] His local predecessors were famous for arguing the case of the Czech Jan Hus, who followed English dissident John

Wycliff in arguing for reform a century earlier. Like them, Luther's primary intent was to introduce necessary reforms within the church so that people in good conscience could become the more converted to the faith, and remain Catholic. In many respects he was in full continuity with a series of councils on this matter. From the early fifteenth-century Council of Constance to the Fifth Lateran Council in 1517, many had attempted to bring about a reform of church polity, piety, and practice. Scholars as diverse as William of Ockham and Erasmus of Rotterdam had returned to the scriptures with the insights of Renaissance learning, trying to uncover the sources and roots of a more authentic faith. Yet the intensity of the reaction against Luther's criticisms, the political climate, and the efforts to force his recantation pushed the issue of reform to a new level. Luther directly challenged the authority of the church hierarchy to dictate belief, arguing that conscientious Christians with scriptural support for their views had greater authority than the pope's edicts, if such edicts contradicted scripture and right reason. During his public questioning Luther refused to recant, arguing that "my conscience is a prisoner of God's Word."[11]

For Luther, the Word of God was revealed through Jesus Christ as known in scripture. In Christ, God restored the relationship broken by sin. This gospel (the good news of gracious forgiveness) surpassed the law (seeking to establish one's righteousness by the legal fulfillment of moral duties), although the law was not voided. Indeed, the law was necessary even if it was inadequate; it could restrain evil even if it could not generate good. When persons recognized this inadequacy and accepted, through God's grace, their need for salvation, the law ceased to be the controlling force in their lives. Instead, the converted heart was freed to act and work for God and neighbor without fear of punishment, and without assuming that their salvation was dependent upon doing everything perfectly.[12] This rejection of law as the ultimate clue to human salvation included a rejection of church laws or practices that linked salvation to prescribed behaviors, including tradition that prevented trust in Christ alone for one's salvation.[13]

Luther argued that the two kingdoms of law and gospel persisted into the present age, and that Christian believers had dealings with both of them. In each kingdom the ultimate duty of all persons was to God.[14] What this meant in practice changed significantly over time in Luther's writings. In *The Freedom of a Christian* (1520) Luther asserted that "a Christian is a perfectly free lord of all, subject to none" and "a Christian is a perfectly dutiful servant of all, subject to all."[15] Again, this is the freedom to serve without fear of the law. The public limits of that freedom are further described in Luther's tract *On Temporal Authority: To What Extend It Should Be Obeyed* (1523). There he argues that there would be no need for temporal law if everyone were truly faithful; but since not everyone is, the law must restrain evil.[16] Luther does limit temporal authority, arguing that civil authority only affects "life and property and external affairs on earth, for God cannot and will not permit anyone but himself to rule over the soul,"[17] and that the bishops are to deal with false doctrine, rather than the civil magistrates, for "heresy can never be restrained by force."[18]

These early teachings were to prompt many drives for religious freedom, but Luther inspired more radical changes than he intended. As forces loyal to Rome attacked him, his necessary reliance on the German princes who defended him also brought a change in his view of political authority. Nowhere was this more clear than in the Peasants' Revolts of 1524-25. German peasants appealed to local rulers for changes in working and living conditions with a set of demands accompanied by scriptural support. Luther first called for calm and pointed out the faults on both sides of the dispute, agreeing with the peasants' position that the preaching of the Word should be permitted. However, he went on to tell them that if the gospel was suppressed in their city, "you can leave these cities or places and follow the gospel to some other place . . . let the ruler have his city; you follow the gospel."[19] Luther viewed any thought of rebellion or violence, such as those of another reformer, Thomas Müntzer, as antithetical to Christian belief.[20] When the rulers refused to accede to the demands of the peasants, and armed conflict began, Luther urged the civil authorities to use all means to crush the revolt.

Luther's reaction was rooted in a concern for "right" doctrine and belief within the faith. Indeed, he argued for toleration for those outside the faith, although he advocated praying for their conversion and some of his later judgments about Jews became a part of the folklore of Germany that supported antisemitism.[21] No such toleration could be offered for perceived heresy within the Christian community; rather than an object for rebellion, the Protestant princes became its ally under God, to be respected and obeyed. Indeed, the authority of the state in Germany was strengthened by the 1555 Peace of Augsburg, which brought peace between Catholics and Lutherans with the establishment of *cuius regio eius religio* (the religion of the ruler is the religion of the state)—a principle that supported nationalism, the rise of the modern European nation-state, and sentiments behind the later (Hegelian) Declaration of Rights of 1848, which called for "the Rights of the German People." Under the 1555 Peace of Augsburg, religious freedom for individual subjects thus extended only to the right to emigrate to a region where their particular religion was protected, although the historic significance of this ought not be overlooked. When peasants were bound to the land and servants were bound to their lords, the right of migration for reasons of faith fundamentally altered the structure of authority and loyalty. It is doubtful that Luther imagined the implications of what he argued. But since slavery, bonded servanthood, and serfdom were accepted and practiced in most cultures at the time, approved by every major religion and social philosophy, this subordination of political duty and economic status to the dictates of the converted heart had consequences that were to echo for centuries. People had a right to exodus from the rule of earthly lords for the sake of faith. They may not have had the right to rebel against an established authority, but a new meaning flowed from Luther's earlier admonition to the peasants to "follow the gospel."

THE CALVINIST DIFFERENCE

In the generation after Luther it was the work of John Calvin that shaped the Reformation tradition. Trained as a lawyer, Calvin's early publications were about Stoic theories of justice.[22] Calvin became involved in the Protestant reform of the church in France. His efforts won him exile to Switzerland in 1535. The Reformation in Switzerland had begun in the 1520s, when pastor Ulrich Zwingli and the Zurich civil authorities rejected Catholic worship and theology. Zwingli's attempts to form a reforming alliance with Luther had failed, but in 1536 he helped draw Calvin from his studies to reform the Genevan church.

The scope and force of Calvin's work quickly made him a leader in the Reformation. The relationship of civil authority to church authority was everywhere in debate during this period, and Calvin's insistence on the right of church leaders, instead of civil authorities, to define who may take communion resulted in his expulsion from Geneva in 1538. By 1541, however, he was called back to assist again in the city's reform. His demand for the relative independence of church council and city council gave new shape to earlier Roman distinctions between *sacerdotum et imperium* and Luther's view of bishop and prince, and helped generate modern distinctions between church and state.

Minorities seek tolerance; majorities have to figure out how their principles shape the whole; great minds seek to grasp the larger picture. Calvin's early formulations were similar to Lutheran two-kingdoms theology, but with a stronger separation of church and state and a closer tie between spiritual and political liberty.[23] He sought to reform government so that it would support the church, led by a mixture of laity and clergy, in upholding the moral law and expanding the church's role in society. He extended the conciliar movement toward a representative polity in both church and state and saw both as agents for a "holy community" under principles of a moral law.[24] It was, in brief, a constitutional government with a balance of powers.[25]

Both his famous summary of Christian theology, *Institutes of the Christian Religion* (1536), and his *Ecclesiastical Ordinances* (1541) show a historic struggle to preserve both religious freedom and public order that would mark Reformed faith long after Calvin's death. His understanding of the scope of religious freedom was shaped by a firm insistence on the individual's discernment of scripture's truth: Each person stood in relationship with God and was wholly dependent upon God for salvation. Yet, the conversion of each person's heart, mind, and soul depended upon the Word rightly read and preached. As in Luther, so in Calvin, Christian doctrine and scriptural interpretation were bounded by standards of right and wrong, and one's responses to such interpretations were always subject to principles of order and the purposes of peace for the Christian community.[26] Thus the concern for civil law and the common good, enjoined to make God's moral law and salvific purposes effective in the world, limited expressions of conscience. Nevertheless, in the earliest versions of the *Institutes* Calvin advocated toleration for those of differing beliefs. Turks, Jews, and excommunicated persons were to be treated with kindness, prayer, and exhortation, in the hopes of bringing them to conversion.[27] Belief and conscience were not to be forced; many matters in the church were to be left as "adiaphora," judgments of prudence and preference; and while the state was to prevent idolatry, it was not otherwise to establish or interfere with religion.[28]

In later writings Calvin's emphasis fell on the protection of the broader community through regulation, as the subversive effects of heresy became clear. These writings demonstrate Calvin's conviction that while belief and conscience may not be enforced by law, conformity to degrees of virtuous behavior was within law's reach.[29] Thus Calvin urged civil magistrates to enforce the Decalogue as civil law. It would serve to teach basic morality to all, as well as to weed out those radically opposed to the first principles of morality in church and state.[30]

When the Reformation was under pressure, however, Calvin did not seek to prevent the civil magistrates from also controlling heresy by law. The most cited example of this was the 1553 trial and execution of Michael Servetus, a pioneering physician and lay theologian who had been driven out of Spain and taken refuge in Geneva. He objected to the fact that the doctrine of the Trinity used non-biblical, philosophical terms and had been developed in a council called by the Emperor Constantine. At stake was the issue of whether philosophy and political power had a place in the development of theology at all, and whether theology had a place in them. Servetus challenged, in brief, the legitimacy of the classic, catholic tradition precisely where the authority of Rome was negated. Calvin did not order the death of Servetus, but he provided evidence at his trial and attended his execution. This inspired a former disciple of Calvin's who had become a dedicated humanist, Sebastien Castellio, to write one of the earliest tracts against religious intolerance, *Concerning Heretics, Whether They Are to Be Punished.*[31]

Calvin's fear of heresy was twofold. First, he agreed with just about every other leader of the day that religion was the necessary glue of civilization. Like Luther (and the Catholics), he was aware of the possibility that heresy could easily become sedition. He was suspicious of the idea that theology and politics must be held apart, a view held by Castellio on humanist grounds; by those Lutherans who demanded a radical break between the inner and personal meanings of the gospel and the outer and social implications of the law on other grounds; and in still a third way by the Anabaptists, who thought that church was an enclave of "resident aliens" called out of a corrupt, irredeemable world that was inevitably unbelieving and immoral.

For Calvin, and most of the Reformed tradition after him, theology was necessary not only to clarify the beliefs of the church and to guide the formation and inevitably necessary repeated reformation of society, but to protect God's honor. God, of course, did not need human defense; but the honor of

God had to do with the place of religion in the common life. He believed, long before Dostoyevsky wrote, that "without God, everything is permissible." In a commentary on Deuteronomy he even argued that the ancient stoning of false prophets was justified—an injunction that accounts for some of the intensity of theological disputes in Protestant history.[32]

PROTESTANT CONFLICT; PROTESTANT TOLERANCE

During the latter half of the sixteenth century, both Lutheranism and Reformed Protestantism worked to define themselves in contrast to Anabaptists, Catholics, each other, and internal dissenters. Lutheranism sought to resolve its internal tensions with the 1577 Formula of Concord. Thereafter, Lutheran scholars developed an extensive dogmatic theology that gave one stream of Protestant theology, usually called evangelical, its distinctive stamp: theology was thought to be a matter of official doctrine on matters of faith and morals, organized into a "confession" to be honored by all in the church, or a territory where that church was strong. Of such trends the noted historian Steven Ozment wrote: "in Lutheran lands, Christian freedom in the end meant the right to dissent from Rome and to agree with Wittenberg."[33]

An attempt in 1606 forcibly to convert German Protestants to Catholicism broke the relative calm of European political and religious life. The Thirty Years War gripped Germany and involved most of the European political powers in battles between Catholic and Protestant alliances. This war ended with the Peace of Westphalia in 1648, which extended the earlier Peace of Augsburg and established the right of all persons to follow their religion, but it allowed a dominant religion (Catholic, Lutheran, or Reformed) to be established in each territory. This settlement did not, however, end religious persecution. In Catholic France, for example, Protestants protected under the 1598 Edict of Nantes found such toleration eroded over the seventeenth century, and finally, in 1685, the Edict of Fontainbleau made Protestantism illegal—a fact that strengthened the concern of Reformed believers for a legal order with freedom of religion.

The Reformed tradition, after Calvin's death, also had internal struggles over orthodox teaching during the period of the discovery and early settlement of America. These controversies came to a head over the teachings of Dutch theologian Jacob Arminius, who had a different view of the relation of divine will to human will than did Calvin. Was conversion and salvation a matter of God's choice, or did human choice play a major role in choosing God? If both played a role, how?[34] The Synod of Dordt (1618-19) sought to end the controversy but largely sided with the strict Calvinist position—although the Arminian position was later to become a hallmark of Methodists and others who disagreed with Calvinism, even though they shared a number of ethical convictions about religion and the common life.[35] The several sides of Calvinistic thought—a strong view of individual responsibility and proto-democratic order within the church polity linked to a strong view of the need for the civil regulation of individual behavior in public life, and an insistence on relative independence of not only church, but family, intellectual, and economic life from direct state control—allowed Calvin's heirs to claim very different legacies from his work.[36] They all, however, saw theology as necessary to justice and universal in implication—much as Ancient Israel and the traditions from Augustine and Thomas Aquinas also claimed.

All strands of Calvinism share at least a formal commitment to the separation of church and state, and the ordering of all spheres of life under the universal will of God. All share a commitment to some form of public participation by all members within the church polity, rooted in a recognition of the individual status and conscience of each believer before God since all are equally made in the image of God, equally sinners before God, and equally capable of being redeemed by God. However, several strands of Calvinism viewed the implications of such conscience differently outside the church context. One strand became quite "imperial," not far removed from earlier Catholic views. A second strand became "evangelical" in character and remained closer to Lutheran views. A third included sectarian motifs and is the most "Puritan."

INTERACTIONS WITH THE "RADICAL REFORMATION"

The Puritans of England and America, with some parallels in Holland, took the Calvinist separation of church and state in a new direction. They emphasized the freedom of individual believers to join in voluntary associations under God, covenanting to form a properly ordered faith community.[37] This strand shares the passion for public order found in other strains of Calvinism but preserves the freedom of believers by inviting them to use that freedom to serve and glorify God, first in the church and, later, by recognizing as a central task the formation of a just civil society and to the protection of even nonbiblical traditions. These "free-church" Calvinists took Calvin's view of the civil law as an expression of God's moral law quite seriously and sought to hold the political and civil authorities to such standards. Moreover, the demand that believers be allowed freely to gather and to covenant for religious purposes had social implications for the rights of the laity within the church (for instance, to be the trustees of its property and to elect or dismiss clergy) and eventually led to the expectation of rights beyond church polity and the formation of other associations. They actively engaged in the formation of schools, parties, federations, corporations, and improvement associations of all kinds according to the moral law and just ends revealed in scripture and as tested by right reason.[38] Thus, not only the church but also a host of associations around it constitute civil society and are seen as prior to and independent of the state. The "public," shaped by sound preaching, open debate, good education, freedom of the press, and a right to assemble and organize, was viewed as prior to the "republic," and the latter was accountable to the former.

Free-church Calvinism shares some features with the radical and Anabaptist reformation, whose leaders insisted on the separation of church and state and the duty of believers to form their own communities according to scriptural belief.[39] However, differences between free-church Calvinism and the Anabaptist reformers are also evident. The core religious belief of Anabaptist groups was more radically focused on Jesus and less engaged with society. It stressed the necessity of making a conscious decision before joining the believing community, one which separated believers clearly from nonbelievers.[40] Thus, only adult baptism or rebaptism was recognized; the traditional infant baptism that signaled the presence of God's grace even to those who were not and could not be conscious of it was rejected. The Swiss reformers Blaurock and Grebel, impatient with Zwingli's slower efforts, baptized each other in 1525 and began the Anabaptist movement in Zurich. While both free-church Calvinists and Anabaptists held to strong notions of freedom of conscience and conscious response to scripture, the Anabaptists often tried to form all business, marriage, and social arrangements entirely within the church. Although there was a militant branch of Anabaptism, one willing to use violence to purge church and society of all evil and compromise,[41] most advocated a pacifist stance. Many refused to accept political office, since politics always involves the use, or the threatened use, of coercion. These accents were largely absent from free-church Calvinism. Calvinists did not condemn society and culture or advocate total separation or withdrawal from them. They saw that as antithetical to the tasks of vocation, glorifying God in the world and protecting the neighbor through forming a just society—which sometimes required the just use of legitimate force.

Indeed, the very beliefs of the Anabaptists were often seen as seditious through their lack of engagement with society as a locus of God's providential care and their reliance on direct experience over theological analysis as a test of truth. Most Lutherans, Zwinglians, and Calvinists joined with Catholics in holding that even peaceful Anabaptists could be prosecuted, for, whether denying that the common life was of theological importance or insisting that God's purposes demanded a violent revolution, they undercut the complex view that public matters were both rational and theological in character.

It is of considerable importance in this regard, especially in view of several twentieth-century Reformed developments, to remember that a number of Calvinists had patterns of thought with affinities to Francisco Suarez, the Spanish Jesuit who is sometimes called the father of modern international law, and to some Lutherans, such as Samuel Pufendorf, who had strong humanist accents. They saw an intimate link between grace and reason: humans made in the image of God had a capacity, and a duty, to use their reason in the various "secular" areas of life, over which God also ruled. They viewed theology as a beacon to illuminate all areas of life, each of which had, in a limited sense, its own distinct mode of rationality. Thus they drew freely from philosophy and science, as necessary and God-given allies of theology, to deal with public matters. Later sixteenth- and seventeenth-century German covenant theologians of the Rhineland as well as Dutch legal theorists Johannes Althusius and Hugo Grotius, for example, retrieved the idea of humans being made in the image of God and thus being given the dignity of reason and the gravity of moral insight, even without full knowledge of the distinctive revelation of Jesus Christ—even as they held that reason and morality are only fulfilled in Christ and best understood through knowledge of Christ. These Calvinists saw moral order and right reason as gifts of "common grace," the true basis of natural law, a view that made it possible for all to see in each field of endeavor outside the church some traces of God's will, for believers to state their views in ways that nonbelievers could understand them without mystical leaps, and for believers and nonbelievers to interact responsibly in society.[42] Those who knew the "special grace" of Christ were called to the responsibilities of the church, but all of society was under God. This view later informed the work of John Milton, John Locke, and many later writers who shaped the American Constitution and Bill of Rights.

Reformed Protestantism took a different track in England and Scotland than on the Continent. Since Henry VIII's break with Rome, the Anglican church had became the established religion of England. Although Mary Tudor restored Roman Catholicism, Anglicanism was reestablished by Elizabeth I (1558-1603) and attempts at religious compromise were made. Still, upon Elizabeth's death, the English Calvinists, known as Puritans, saw the opportunity for more complete reform. The decisive issues had to do with how theology could and should both inform the common life and guarantee the freedom of religion. Extended political and military clashes dominated the early seventeenth-century struggle between the king and the Puritan-led Parliament over this issue. The Independent Puritan party, while not agreeing with the Parliament's advocacy of a strict Calvinist system, saw its advantages over episcopacy and joined the fight against the king.

Together they formed an uneasy alliance, but in spite of its military success, the alliance could not hold. The army, led by Oliver Cromwell, organized itself on covenantal-democratic lines. In 1646 Charles I was beheaded. Oliver Cromwell assumed control of England as Lord Protector[43] and sought to establish toleration to all who believed in God, consistent with the Independent Puritan party's beliefs. Cromwell is remembered with high ambiguity—both as an advocate of government under a written constitution with guarantees of religious liberty and human rights, and as a bloody suppressor of the Catholics in Ireland who resisted both British rule and toleration. During his time of leadership the right of freedom of the press was first claimed, the right to resist unjust authority exemplified, the demand for equal rights for women set forth, and the right of citizens in a civil society to form, dismantle, or reform an established, tyrannical government was actualized—a century and a half before the American and French Revolutions—all on the basis of the right to convert and to organize religious communities on that basis without interference from state authority.

In some ways, obviously, this revolution failed; but it established the first successful revolutionary model in the West—the second being the militantly secular French Revolution model, adopted later by the Marxists. Neither model could preserve either religious freedom or stable democracy.[44] Even in England, episcopacy was reestablished with the restoration of Charles II as monarch, and religious persecution spread once more. But the vision was partly kept alive in Scotland, where the efforts of English leaders to control politics and religion had been staved off, and the reform movements started by the Covenanters and carried through by Calvinist John Knox flourished through the seventeenth century. With the reign of William and Mary after the Glorious Revolution of 1689, powers were regained by Parliament, and religious toleration was again granted in England to those not deemed seditious or treasonous.

THE IMPACT ON AMERICA

While immigrants from many groups came to America, Puritanism most of all shaped church-state relations and religious freedom. The earliest settlement, at Jamestown in Virginia, was much influenced by Puritanism, although it became Episcopalian with the assertion of direct political control by James I of England in 1624. Northern settlements, notably Plymouth and the later Massachusetts Bay Colony, were strongly Puritan. Plymouth was founded in 1620 by Separatist Puritans who had first sought refuge in Holland. They asserted their right to form a government, as persons in a civil society under God, through the Mayflower Compact, a covenantal act that acknowledged the rights of both church members and nonmembers.[45]

The Massachusetts Bay Colony was founded in 1630 by another wing of the English Puritans. As Puritans were generally actively persecuted in England during this era, emigration to these colonies was often an attractive option, and colonies spread inland and down to Connecticut, often exhibiting all the ambiguities of the European background. In their insistence on the involvement of the laity, the right of self-governance of a community ultimately ruled only by God, and the concomitant recognition of the civil order's being subject to God's law and purposes, these Puritans broke down some of the hierarchical structures that bound European church and state. However, efforts to create a "holy commonwealth" involved very high levels of intervention in people's lives. This eventually proved unsustainable. The land was too open and the impulses for independence too strong; the desire for land and opportunity drew as many immigrants as did the desire for purity in faith and life. Dissenters who were driven out began alternative experiments.

Roger Williams was expelled from Massachusetts on religious grounds in 1635, and in 1636 began a new settlement at Providence.[46] He later wrote a protest against his treatment, *The Bloudy Tenent of Persecution* (1644), which pointed to a significant doctrinal contradiction in regard to a cornerstone of Calvinist theology. Unsure of their predestined status, knowing that they did not live up to God's standards, the Calvinists anxiously sought signs for determining one's election.[47] Confession of faith, disciplined activity in an effort to glorify God, and partaking of sacraments had been proposed by Calvin as sufficient to allay the fears of believers. Those who exhibited these signs were to assume their election. This meant that both the acknowledgment of sin and the demand for responsible action were encompassed in this theology; it also meant that both an ultimate modesty and a proximate confidence became marks of the Puritans. But these issues were complicated by the fact that New England Puritans added personal religious experience to the signs of "creed, deed, and sacrament."[48] "Conversion" became essential for membership in the established church—and for societal leadership.[49] Theology not only was to be related to the intellectual life of right reason and the interpretation of scripture, or to the formation of the common life in church and society, but to personal life and the affections. However, as it became clear that some who claimed personal transformation could not reasonably state their faith, did not glorify God in their dealings, or manifest transformation, the acceptance of these "elect" as leaders of the society and the use of civil law to enforce their authority met with resistance and dissent.

Roger Williams further argued that predestination rendered irrational the civil enforcement of the moral law in an effort to force parties to convert. If God controlled the decision of election, then human coercion of others could, at most, only lead to hypocrisy, feigned religious experience, a lie in the heart of conversion, and thus a radical violation of conscience.[50] Williams's colony at Providence resolutely demanded tolerance and attracted increasing numbers of dissenters. They flourished in Rhode Island, becoming some of the most eloquent advocates of religious liberty in the colonies, and sometimes allied with secular deists who, for other reasons, wanted religion disestablished.[51] Isaac Backus, for example, a Baptist dissenter in eighteenth century New England, wrote many influential tracts on the liberty of conscience and the right of civil disobedience.[52]

Other colonies offered toleration as well. The Maryland Colony, founded by Lord Baltimore in 1648, was initially Catholic and was the first to establish religious toleration by law. The regime was short-lived, however, for it became Anglican after Puritan revolts in 1655 and 1689 induced the English Crown to reclaim the colony and to establish the Anglican way.[53] The Quaker leader William Penn established a more enduring "Holy Experiment" in toleration in Pennsylvania. His *Frame of Government* of 1682 granted toleration to all professing belief in God.[54]

As noted above, New England Puritanism had expanded the role of the experience of regenerating grace as a test of election. Thus, even within the strictest churches, personal religious experience was recognized, and revival was possible. The first Great Awakening began in Jonathan Edwards's Congregational Church in Northampton, Massachusetts, in 1734. Like other eventual leaders and preachers of this revival, Edwards was a traditional, orthodox Calvinist.[55] Yet personal conversions and religious fervor swept his congregation and others in New England, and eventually down the entire Eastern seaboard in a dramatic movement that lasted for three years. At Edwards's invitation, British Methodist George Whitefield revived the movement in 1740. The American "evangelistic" tradition was born.

THE ISSUE OF MISSIONS

The "revival" of the Great Awakening highlighted another issue for Puritan theology: the possibility of preparation for conversion. Some interpreters of predestination held that humans are passive before God's decision on election and that the process of human decision cannot be helped at all. The preparationist belief, propounded by Edwards's grandfather Solomon Stoddard, held that while regeneration may not be forced, preparation through preaching and education is possible and assists in regeneration of the elect.[56] This brought a new emphasis on preaching and teaching to those beyond the church.

The issues of mission and proselytism, bound so closely to questions of conversion, had been present from the earliest days of American settlement, and, indeed, of the Reformation. To the extent to which church and state had been separated in the European context, individuals acted upon their religious convictions to join and to form different religious groups. The ability to preach publicly and to gather adherents to new religious movements was sharply limited, but already the first charter of the Massachusetts Bay Colony in 1629 had included the goal of turning Native Americans to the Christian faith. Missions to local tribes by Thomas Mayhew and John Eliot inspired the establishment of the Society for the Propagation of the Gospel in New England in 1649.[57]

The Great Awakening extended the mission field beyond Native Americans to other colonial and frontier communities. Such efforts at religious renewal or revival were not new to Protestantism. In Europe, Pietism, begun by Dutch Calvinists, had deeply influenced Lutheranism. P. J. Spener wrote his *Pia desideria* in 1675 and insisted on the relevance of one's living faith and the priesthood of all believers as vital to Lutheranism. His followers, including A. H. Francke, turned the renewal impulse to works of charity and international missions. This emphasis on missions and personal confrontation with the gospel also marked Count N. L. von Zinzendorf's Moravian movement, whose missions efforts deeply impressed the young Anglican John Wesley. Wesley, too, was personally affected by a religious experience and after his return from the American mission field worked with preacher George Whitefield to bring revival to the Church of England. By the 1780s his "Methodist" organization had publicly acknowledged its status as a separate religious organization from the Church of England in Great Britain and during the eighteenth century made significant gains in America as well.[58] Wesley argued for missions and liberty of conscience from his understanding of the Bible; of the "glory of rational beings," endowed by God with reason and perception; and of his own experience of conversion after years of ministry. Conscience required the freedom to hear and to heed the Spirit, to study scripture, and to be taught by the Spirit.[59]

The religious revival became one of many formative influences that aided toleration and religious liberty in eighteenth-century America. The emphasis on freedom of speech to prepare the heart for the grace of decision, freedom of assembly so that persons may be called to new associations, and freedom of the individual to find a personal response to grace and to the talents and callings given by God was evident not only in the revival movements but spilled over into an expanded view of the freedom of conscience and the place of the person in public affairs. Ideas of liberal democracy and economic freedom grew in this soil. John Locke, whose father had fought with Oliver Cromwell, and who had studied both at Westminster and in Holland, had developed an epistemology and view of natural rights grounded in the "common grace" of experience, in opposition to the Hobbesian view of interest-bound conflict requiring centralized sovereign authority. Protestants knew of the Hobbesian reality—it was the world of the Fall, of Sin. But they also believed that it was framed by a deeper and wider reality of self-evident truths and moral laws that made it possible, as Locke said, for people to govern themselves. Locke's views were warmly received in America, especially insofar as he placed great emphasis on the need for religious toleration as the best means of allowing each person to use his or her God-given reason to reach religious truth, echoing in a practical way Castellio's earlier arguments for toleration.[60]

Locke's fear that religious coercion could only cause hypocrisy, and thus hinder religious growth, was very similar to Williams's arguments.[61] Neither Locke nor Williams argued for toleration because they thought religion was irrelevant to public life. Although persons were to be allowed to come to their own reasoned convictions about religious belief, there was an overarching assumption that there was a right answer and that it was God-centered.[62] For Locke, Christianity was the religious system most evidently true through the use of human reason. Thus, Locke did not extend full toleration to atheists, for, in failing to acknowledge God at all, they perverted reason by rejecting its ground as well as the ground of faith. It was not that everyone had to become philosophical theologians or Christians, or that everything could be settled with absolute certainty. What the learned and wise could discern by reason, the uneducated and simple could essentially grasp by faith,[63] although many things remain uncertain, and people must be free to form opinions, and to form groups committed to their opinions, so long as they do not violate "self-evident" truths or their neighbor's rights.

Locke, Williams, and other advocates of religious liberty were reclaiming a strand of Christian tradition that could be traced back to early Reformation understandings of the freedom of conscience, rooted in both a Christology that advocated no use of force in conversion and a general theological expectation that truth—including the Truth of God—could fight its own battles in open debate. This is the tradition embraced by Erasmus, by Luther and Calvin in their early writings, and by a number of the covenantal and federal theologians. These motifs were never wholly lost from the Protestant churches, although they were sometimes obscured by confessional narrowness; coercive attempts to establish a holy community, which became confused with national identity; or the dictates of obedience to the civil order.

The constitutions adopted by the several states and the foundational documents of the new nation reveal the stamp of these influences.[64] An often neglected but decisive figure in this development was John Adams. As John Witte Jr. has shown,[65] Adams took a position quite distinct from that of either Roger Williams or the Lockean Thomas Jefferson, in whose correspondence we find the famous phrase about a "wall of separation" between church and state—defended on grounds of piety in Williams's case and on grounds of an Enlightenment-shaped philosophy of the state in Jefferson's. In consultation with a series of clergy, this heir of the Puritan tradition drafted the rights provisions of the Massachusetts Constitution (1780), the oldest constitution still in use. Adams supported the Jeffersonian formulas of the national Bill of Rights, but for reasons that recent court decisions and much historical scholarship seem to have obscured. For Adams, church and state were institutionally distinct, but the line between them was less a wall than a semipermeable membrane through which the nutrients of moral influence must be allowed to flow. The state was thus not only to protect the right of all faiths to exist and to propagate their views, but the state was also to protect a biblically based and rationally argued religion—by a favorable tax policy, for instance—since the state could and should recognize that the ethical principles and virtues that flowed from this classical heritage were indispensable to the well-being of civil society and to the protection of even nonbiblical traditions. Although how these tax policies are shaped has been altered over the years, Adams is perhaps more representative of what a large number of believers, conservative or liberal, continue to hold than either Williams or Jefferson. This view anticipates the current situation that permits the use of tax-collected funds for various chaplaincies and certain faith-based educational, social service, and welfare activities.

All the authors of the early documents agreed, however, that serious belief would be "reasonable," but that not all issues were settled. Thus the open communication of religious views and the right to organize around opinions or convictions were necessary to a viable society. Further, the emphasis on individual religious experience shifted the focus from those views of natural law that entailed a necessary, common teleology to a natural rights view that each has a duty to pursue the divergent ends, talents, and callings given by

God, and must be allowed to do so. Even more, the participatory, voluntary polity of many churches in America had schooled generations in the exercise of their rights and reason, and this shaped the fabric of the whole civil society. The state was to be the servant, not the master, of the common life; a creature, not the creator, of society. The 1776 Declaration of Independence and the 1791 Bill of Rights, especially the First Amendment, codified protections against many of the practices that had thwarted such notions previously. The establishment of any religion on the national level was prohibited. No national church after the Catholic, Lutheran, Anglican, or even Scottish Calvinist pattern would be permitted. Religious membership was separated from citizenship, voting rights, and office holding. This did not, however, infringe on the rights of religious groups to advocate ethical principles or policies in public discourse; it was presumed that they would and should.

CHRIST AND OTHER CULTURES

Although much ink and blood were spilled in establishing the new United States of America and its theologically driven view of constitutional democracy with human rights and religious freedom, it was not long before the French Revolution established civil rights on humanist, intentionally secular grounds and sought freedom from religion by overthrowing the influence of the Roman Catholic Church—which opposed democracy, human rights, and freedom at that time. Both the French Revolution and the American Revolution had a high place for reason in public discourse, and both established forms of governance that contrasted with traditional regimes elsewhere—though the implications of the two revolutions were to prove, over the next two centuries, to be quite different. At the time, however, the desire for land among the rising peasantry of Europe, the quest for profits among the rising bourgeois, and new sailing technologies brought both Christian and secular democrats, who looked quite similar to those from other cultures, into increased contact with those who had not been shaped by the Judeo-Christian heritage, modern science and technology, or constitutional democracy.[66] Protestant thought turned to missions among the new settlers and overseas, with both religious and cultural implications. Such issues were not entirely new, to be sure; in the early missions to the American Indians, John Eliot had argued that it was necessary to "carry on civility with religion."[67] He developed vernacular scriptures for the tribes, established towns for the "Praying Indians," conducted both religious and civil training, and sought to protect converts from unscrupulous white traders and traditionalist Indian influences.[68]

The relationships between missions, acculturation, and the purposes of the new nation were complex. While some thought that conversion of all peoples was decisive for the return of Christ, the matter was much disputed. More pressing was the question of who should be the primary target of missionary efforts. Baptist and Methodist groups, whose theology centered on the neces-sity of personal religious experience and response, were especially active in revival efforts on the American frontier among populations nominally Chris-tian. Jonathan Edwards, in whose Congregational Church the Great Awaken-ing began, had argued that the church was called by God to participate in bringing about the completion of God's plan for the world through conver-sion and sanctification of all. The church's obedience was necessary for the fulfillment of God's intentions in establishing the kingdom of God. Indeed, he held that the revivals in America marked the beginning of God's renewal of the world as a whole.[69] He saw that the diary of David Brainerd's account of revival and "heart religion" among some Native Americans was published, to the inspiration of many.

The publication of *Enquiry into the Obligations of Christians to Use Means for the Conversion of the Heathen* (1792) by William Carey, the English preacher and later missionary to India, offered arguments for working specifi-cally in missions abroad. Carey asserted that while conversions were necessary at home, those in other lands had "no Bible, no written language, no minis-ters, no civil government," and needed even more help.[70] Carey's plea spurred overseas missions by English Protestants in the 1790s. Pietist revivals, as al-ready mentioned, had inspired similar activity in Europe.[71] Overseas missions by American Protestants began when a small group of students at Williams College, inspired by revivalist preaching, pledged to become missionaries. While preparing for that at Andover Seminary, they also provided impetus for the establishment of the interdenominational American Board of Commissioners for Foreign Missions (ABCFM) in 1810. Numerous other associations were organized for support as well.[72] However, denominational splits were grow-ing, and national divisions along North-South lines were increasing. Some Southern churches focused on missions to slaves, to try to stabilize and bring Christian values to the master-slave relationship by linking theology to a hier-archical version of natural law theory, while Northern churches and missions increasingly worked to promote abolition, linking theology to human rights. By 1865 fifteen denominational missions boards had been established, each with its own area and style of missions, and each with its own sense of how church and society ought to be organized.[73]

Denominations sought to support their own missionaries not only because of personal ties but because missions also provided a way for local churches to participate in God's plan for the world. For many, this activity was rooted in a new understanding of the church itself as a missionary society. The church became less a holy community than an association of people of conviction with a task given by God. Denominational agencies became the Protestant version of the orders of Catholic monastic movements, each with its own dis-tinctive style and niche, with particular patterns for oversight of what mission-aries were transmitting overseas in terms of doctrine, church order, and cul-tural values.[74] Abroad, missionaries in the field were often quite ecumenical in outlook. While most recognized that conversion had to take on institutional embodiment if it was to endure in a society, and knew that church order would have many implications, often the question of how to preach in another culture or start a church at all was more decisive. In many societies the very idea that another worldview and way of organizing life were possible was shocking. To address these issues, missionaries needed to learn the language and develop some system for translating biblical and theological ideas into it, and this involved learning from the masters of the language—the indigenous leadership.[75] This mitigated, in some ways, the temptations to cultural imperialism and denominational chauvinism. While some disputes over mission territories arose, coordination among missions increased between denominations in several regions.[76]

One of the main controversies that affected Protestant missions in the nineteenth and twentieth centuries was the question of what constituted the proper scope for missions activity. The churches most involved in missions had all become advocates of the separation of church and state, at home and abroad. And they had very little influence with foreign governments where they were engaged in missions. But the question of the relationship of the gospel they preached to the culture was open. Were missionaries to evangelize through preaching the "pure" gospel? Or were they to engage in social reform and institution-building as preparation for and consequence of the spreading of the message? As the earliest domestic missions to Native American tribes had strongly emphasized the need to "civilize" as an adjunct and preparation for preaching, early foreign missions, too, found themselves increasingly drawn into the development of social institutions—schools, hospitals, agricultural centers, women's groups, orphanages, business training, labor organization, and legal aid associations. Often, missionary teams would include not only preachers but farmers or skilled tradesmen who would try to teach skills as practiced in the West, all in the name of furthering the gospel.[77] Was this "Westernization" simply colonialism?

One of the most impassioned opponents of "civilizing" missions efforts was Rufus Anderson, secretary of the ABCFM from 1826 to 1866. He argued that missions should involve preaching alone, rather than the extensive array of social services that nineteenth-century missions often involved. Anderson did not argue against social services out of hand; he recognized the need for linguistic work, translation, and the education of indigenous leaders.[78] Instead, he argued that those who developed social institutions tended to stay for extended periods of time, often developing dependency situations. They ended up transmitting a Western Christianity, in which particular cultural practices were added to the gospel. Thus an expression of Christianity appropriate to the culture, or the development of social institutions within the culture's particular framework, was blocked. Anderson asked missionaries to go into the mission field, plant seeds in the form of a native ministry that was, in his terms, "self-supporting, self-propagating, and self-governing," and go home.

Under his leadership some missions teams eliminated builders and farmers as missionaries to the field, and reduced support for auxiliary missions to women and for educational and health services.[79] Those in the field often resisted, protesting the closing of schools, hospitals, and other institutions.

In fact, missionaries altered the communities they reached simply by being there. Reading and writing (and thus new systems of communication and learning), schools (and thus new patterns of assembly and authority), and medical care (and thus new science and technology) were introduced alongside Christ and the church. Most missionaries came to admire many aspects of the cultures in which they worked, but they also found some cultural practices to be against human rights, and they openly opposed them. New converts often welcomed change. William Carey, the British Baptist, worked in India to stop suttee—widows' deaths on their husbands' funeral pyres. In Ceylon, missionaries and members of the native church signed a pledge to renounce "all caste and other distinctions, which tend to foster pride, impair the affections, and hinder the kindly offices of Christian love."[80] In Hawaii, Samoa, Tonga, and the East Indies, laws were changed to regulate sexual behavior that exploited women. Also in Hawaii, leaders invited missionaries to help write a new constitution based on biblical laws.[81] In Africa, missionaries confronted problems of indigenous slavery and polygamy.[82] In many mission contexts the practice of educating "lower status" people affected their social positions, and insistence on Sabbath laws changed how they were viewed as laborers. In Turkey, Congregationalists founded havens for racial minorities.[83] Throughout, the emphasis on equality, freedom, the dignity of the individual before God, and the right to convert and learn invited the reexamination of traditions.[84] Cultures, in this view, are not holy in and of themselves; they are necessary for human flourishing, but they can be questioned and judged.

Inevitably, the popular charge that missionaries brought Western culture with the gospel bore some truth. Some missionaries found it difficult to reinterpret Christianity outside of their home language and worship styles, and instead tried to import their own traditions directly.[85] In some areas the mission station served as the basis for a new community, along the lines of John Eliot's "praying towns" for Native American tribes. Converts were encouraged to break their ties with their past. Some did so with more energy than the missionaries advised; many resisted. These strategies were gradually abandoned, for they did not help prepare leaders who could spread the gospel in their native culture. However, missions leaders generally believed that part of what they had to offer included scientific learning, democracy, and human rights, in part because they held that these had been largely generated by the faith and were constitutionally related to it. To fail to transmit these would perpetuate restricted views of truth and justice and keep these cultures marginal to the future.

These issues of "civilizing" and structural change were far less debated on the American home front, as missions to immigrants in American cities also took on a new shape in the late nineteenth century. Huge waves of immigration from Europe, particularly Ireland and Germany, were met with a backlash of nativist hostility in the 1830s and 1840s. Immigrant missions were largely conducted by Catholic and Lutheran groups in this era in an effort to help newcomers assimilate while ensuring that they did not convert. After the Civil War, however, the population explosion in the cities spurred urban missions among Protestant denominations, often with efforts to convert, through education and social services, the children of immigrant Catholics. African-American churches also worked to provide education and services to African-Americans during Reconstruction, both in the South and in urban settings throughout the country.[86]

The Young Men's Christian Association (YMCA) was established in England in 1844 and in the United States in 1851. As in foreign missions, interdenominational voluntary organizations provided religious and social services to particular populations, thickening the fabric of civil society. Such urban organizations were significant not only for the recipients of this care, but also for the women who worked in them. Although the Women's Union Missionary Society had sent its first female missionary to Burma in 1860, most women's missions work was in home and urban organizations. Whether abroad or at home, women missionaries were able to extend missions into homes, and thus into women's lives, in ways men often could not.[87]

The early urban relief organizations were avowedly religious in orientation.[88] After 1880 increasing conflict between labor and industry, as well as the economic conditions of many in the cities, drew some Protestants to focus on the religious and moral aspects of business and to criticize the conduct of industry toward workers. The Social Gospel movement, famously articulated by Walter Rauschenbusch, attracted many to activism focusing on social and labor reform. Shailer Mathews—scholar, head of the new Federal Council of Churches, and a proponent of the Social Gospel—argued that "the Social Gospel proposed the teaching of Jesus as a call and a way to give salvation on earth," rather than the conservative, orthodox emphasis on salvation in heaven.[89] Other Protestants tried to establish urban missions churches that could bring the rich and poor together in worship and friendship.[90] Through the early twentieth century, city churches were established as large institutions, conducting worship but also a vast array of social services as "people's churches." Reading rooms, men's and women's clubs, and educational programs were offered both in these churches and in "settlement houses" for immigrants, as the scope of urban mission moved beyond the purely religious. Key features of both social work and sociology in America were generated by these developments.[91]

When the United States defeated Catholic Spain in the Spanish-American War (1898), some American Protestants became quite triumphalistic. Not only did political voices speak of "manifest destiny," but the home missions director, Josiah Strong, argued that the Anglo-Saxon as the bearer of the ideas of civil liberty and spiritual Christianity "sustains particular relations to the world's future, (and) is divinely commissioned to be, in a peculiar sense, his brother's keeper."[92] Strong's comments were made within a larger appeal for Christian responsibility regarding the need for social justice, and the need for strong home missions to preserve democratic values. But the white, Anglo-Saxon bias of some of his, and many others', sentiments was laden with racist arrogance. While this bias clearly existed, the other motifs were equally, often more, powerful.

EVANGELIZING THE WORLD

Various developments at home and abroad encouraged American Protestant optimism and the understanding of the church's calling. These took two forms: one was "the evangelization of the world in this generation." This was the "watchword" of the Student Volunteer Movement for Foreign Missions, established as a department of the YMCA in 1886; its impetus, like that of the ABCFM seventy-five years before, came from a group of newly converted students. The Student Volunteer Movement's leaders, John R. Mott and Robert H. Speer, argued that the preaching ministry was the central task of missions. The movement recruited the best and most articulate students it could find at the best colleges to enlist volunteers for the mission field. Student chapters spread overseas to Europe and Asia as well, and the organization sponsored international conferences to bring members together. Mott served as an apologist for the "watchword" but in later years was careful to limit the claims of the movement. Its goal was not to "Christianize" the world, nor was it to proclaim a new era.[93] Yet he and others argued that the goal of exposing every person in the world to the gospel message was within Protestantism's grasp; trade and communication routes were open to the world, and the church had the resources necessary to do the job. It was a basic principle of the faith that people ought to be free to preach and teach everywhere, and missionary efforts were necessary to counteract other, negative aspects of Western influence. The new world situation, he argued, both opened the door to the worldwide mission and made it more difficult.[94]

The second form of optimism sought the righting of human ills, and, within the Social Gospel movement, often identified such ills with the actions of industrialists and their national and international cartels or monopolies. However, the emphasis of the Social Gospel movement had its broader expression in liberal Christianity, with its ethical emphasis on human participation in establishing the kingdom of God, which fueled the growth of foreign missions activities focused on social reform and institution-building. Indeed, the Student Volunteer Movement's focus on preaching as its center was, in part, a response to the liberal, ethical Christianity in the various institutions and programs in the foreign fields; the idea of the missionary as preacher and "planter" gave way to the missionary as reformer and change agent. Conversion became defined as social transformation, emphasizing "applied Christianity" and social justice rather than personal experience or acceptance of creed.[95]

This emphasis on social reform and, more generally, the urgency with which American missionary groups approached missions caused rifts between American missionary groups and both European and indigenous ones.[96] Still, the 1910 World Missionary Conference began an era of international ecumenical understanding in Protestantism. At about the same time, however, Protestantism was racked by increasing controversies prompted by the rise of fundamentalism. Views of the Bible in relation to science, of the relationship of personal conviction to social context, of the relation of reason to experience were all at stake. These differences came to a head after World War I, particularly over the work of the Laymen's Foreign Missions Inquiry. This interdenominational committee for the study of foreign missions, headed by Harvard philosophy professor William Hocking, issued a report in 1932 which argued that while Christian missions should not be abandoned, their broader goal should be "world understanding on the spiritual level." This went beyond the call to recognize indigenous churches as full partners, although this, too, was urged. Rather, "it is clearly not the duty of the Christian missionary to attack the non-Christian systems of religion," the report argued.[97] Instead, missionaries were advised to focus on sharing the spirit of Christianity as an ethical and social expression of the teachings of Jesus, and to learn, in turn, from the truths of other faiths.[98] The committee also recommended that the number of missionaries in the field be reduced and those sent to the field be more rigorously trained in the issues pertinent to the host country. It further argued vigorously for social ministry to the "secular needs of man in the spirit of Christ," unsullied by preaching.[99] Missions boards received this "liberal," "social gospel" report with mixed reactions; even those who sought a broad appreciation of other cultures wanted also to stress the particularity and uniqueness of Christ.[100] Fundamentalist Protestants viewed the report as indicative of all that was wrong with mainline Christianity. By the 1930s, unity in missions became impossible; fundamentalists formed their own groups.[101]

The ecumenical strand of missions had begun in the missionary conferences of the early twentieth century and, more functionally, in the relations between missionaries in the field. They were driven by the need to coordinate efforts for witness, reform, and service. The Federal Council of Churches, founded in 1908, urged federation on the local level as well as support for its national efforts, and advocated *The Social Creed of the Churches* (1912) and *The Church and Social Reconstruction* after World War I, both of which stressed human rights, freedom of religion, and the duty of the church "to exert its vast educational influence and use its institutional organization for human happiness, social justice, and the democratic organization of society."[102] Social statements of individual denominations also displayed this focus on the church as social reformer. For example, the Methodist Social Creed focused on the areas of working conditions, job training, social security, and the regulation of the "profit motive," as well as the futility of nationalism and war, from the 1920s up until World War II.[103] These emphases were evident as major themes in domestic and foreign missions conferences through the 1920s, as missions groups and churches worldwide began to explore ecumenical partnership in social reform.[104]

Perhaps none of these conferences, however, was quite so important for our questions as the Madras Conference of the International Missionary Council in 1938. The previous year major themes on human rights had been articulated on a worldwide basis by the Universal Christian Council of Life and Work at its meeting in Oxford with the International Missionary Conference. In 1938, however, the conference met outside the West and, for the first time, included delegates in large numbers from around the world. The conference had a substantial representation from the younger churches of Asia, Africa, the Pacific Islands, and Latin America, and identified areas that needed concerted attention—including human rights and religious freedom. While colonialism was largely intact, while Hitler was purging Germany of Jews under the infamous Nuremberg laws and plotting the attack on Austria and Czechoslovakia, while Stalin was collectivizing the countryside and consolidating power by assassinating all opposition, while Mao was turning his army from flight to attack against the occupying Japanese after the Long March, while Gandhi was trying to extricate himself from the infighting of the Congress Party and move the masses to resistance against the British Raj, and while Roosevelt was organizing the "lend-lease" plan to aid the democratic countries of Europe in defense of freedom[105]—while all this was transpiring around the world, this worldwide Protestant gathering in Madras marked a new consensus about Protestantism's commitment to freedom and human rights in the inevitably global common life, in spite of obvious conflict.[106]

In the context of the vocation of Protestant missions to convert the hearts and minds of persons to God and to turn civilizations toward the relative freedom, justice, and peace possible in history, it is difficult to overestimate the intensity of the interaction of Protestantism and the social and political struggles of the nineteenth and twentieth centuries. Much of ecumenical Protestantism became convinced that the just ordering of the common life, shaped by faith, was decisive for individuals and groups, that a distorted ordering of society disrupted faith, dehumanized individuals, and destroyed community, and that it was among the duties of belief to monitor, shape, and guide, by persuasion and example, the fabric of institutional morality. In quite different terms than Luther, Calvin, Wesley, and Edwards had known, but in substantial continuity with them, church leadership became deeply involved in several struggles— against slavery and racism, for the rights of labor, against the evils of colonialism, for the recognition of a single humanity in a shrinking world, against the paganism of the Nazis and the militant secularism of the communists, and for the increased global embrace of constitutional democracy in politics, equality for women in home and society, and responsible development in economics. The churches were at the forefront of all of these developments, in spite of their residual nationalism, patriarchy, and class bias.

During World War II all these influences were present, intensified by the conflict. As the momentum toward the formation of the United Nations and a Declaration on Human Rights increased, Protestants felt, with some justification, that they had laid the groundwork for them, and that the subversion of the medieval conciliar ideals they had fought to preserve and make actual in church and society was finally being overcome. It was a step in the direction of that for which they had long preached, taught, and prayed. They welcomed the turn of the Roman Catholics, through the leadership of Jacques Maritain and John Courtney Murray, and later Popes John XXIII and John Paul II, who embraced human rights and made it a central teaching of that communion. They also applauded Evangelicals who, increasingly differentiated from both the fundamentalists and the liberals, took up issues of justice and human rights as a matter of faith.[107]

The Commission on a Just and Durable Peace (CJDP) was formed by the churches of the United States and Canada in 1941. It joined with the British Commission on Christian Social Responsibility in forming the International Round Table at Princeton, New Jersey, in 1943, with some sixty Christian leaders from around the world. The Round Table intentionally took as its task the attempt to shape the world order that would emerge after World War II. It evoked the formation of the Commission of the Churches on International Affairs (CCIA), endorsed by the (still emerging) World Council of Churches and the International Missionary Council.[108] The National Council of Churches of Christ in the USA also established a Committee on Religious Liberty, with overlapping membership. These groups became directly involved in formulating the United Nations Charter (1945) and the Universal Declaration on Human Rights (1948). Looking back on these events, Charles Malik, rapporteur of the U.N. Commission on Human Rights and later president of the General Assembly, wrote of the importance of the influence of Eleanor Roosevelt's leadership, of the cooperation of Jewish, Catholic, and Islamic delegates—and especially of the indefatigable leadership of Dr. O. Frederick Nolde, the Protestant representative of these groups and their convictions.[109]

Nolde's own account indicates that while these groups wanted to ensure a statement on the scope and source of human rights consonant with Christian teaching, it was without an expectation or desire that the statement would be explicitly Christian. This required advancing an understanding of human rights as a moral reality beyond human conferral. Nolde wrote: "[T]he CCIA unflaggingly . . . emphasized the principle that governments could not grant human rights, but only recognize the human rights which man, by virtue of his being and destiny, already possessed."[110] Human rights are not civil rights, which can be granted or revoked by governments. This view, to which others agreed, some reluctantly, resulted in the Preamble's final form: the basis of rights is "endowed."

A second, more difficult battle was waged over Article 18 of the Declaration. Nolde and other Protestant leaders worked tirelessly for the inclusion of the right to change one's religion or belief as central to the "freedom of religion," rather than simply "freedom of worship." The freedom to change one's belief, of course, is essential to ideas of conversion and the freedom of belief. In the development of both the Declaration and the U.N. Covenants resulting from it, however, other representatives resisted the freedom to change one's belief as opening the door to possible intervention in a society or culture by people or religions from other nations, and the possible formation of groups not loyal to the host country.[111] The distinction between "freedom of religion" with this understanding and "freedom of worship" was that the former necessitated the associated rights of assembly, speech, and property-holding as necessary to the free conduct of religion. Freedom of worship could have entailed, simply, the right to worship according to the tradition in which one is born, with all other religious behavior regulated by the state—a position practiced by the defeated fascist governments and advocated by the victorious communist ones. This matter was intensely debated by Hindu, Jewish, and Confucian believers also, for it involves a challenge to sometimes intricate relationship of ethnicity, nationality, religious culture, and political power. But the key issue, it was eventually recognized, is the difference between religion as an open quest and publicly debatable claim about the true basis of meaning and morality, and religion as an expression of a privileged group tradition or particular condition.[112]

After the Universal Declaration of Human Rights was passed in 1948, a CCIA statement argued what most Protestants have come to believe: while the Christian understandings of human dignity and responsibility had their source in "acts of creation and salvation," the Declaration, in its recognition of inherent human worth through endowment, was the fullest expression that could be assented to by a broad spectrum of faiths.[113] What some believed to be universally valid had to be stated in a way that others could embrace, and the wider acceptance tends to confirm it. The CCIA strategy had been to advocate an internationally recognized standard for religious liberty and human rights and to ask the churches worldwide to advocate domestic compliance with the standard through the endorsement and enforcement of the "covenants" of implementation.[114]

Nearly every Protestant denomination marked the Universal Declaration with a resolution or some other statement, although these varied. The Presbyterian Church in the United States of America stated that the Declaration "holds immense promise for the welfare of all mankind," and urged its ratification through "the passage of such legislation in this country as will be in keeping with our American traditions of freedom and justice to all men."[115] The 1953 General Synod of the Evangelical and Reformed Churches recognized the Declaration, urged the church to fight attempts to discredit or limit the covenants, and called for a recommitment to "the dignity and worth of the human person . . . human solidarity . . . national responsibility . . . [and] heightened personal commitment to an effective Christian witness in all of life."[116] The Protestant Episcopal Church endorsed the Declaration as a "statement of principles to be sought through which people of all religions and all faiths can give expression to their highest aspirations."[117] The Disciples of Christ in 1950 cited the "seeds of peace and hope" sown by the Declaration; in 1953 they began a series of resolutions of concern over the United States' failure to ratify human rights covenants. Such resolutions continued through the 1970s, as the United States had not ratified all the covenants made under the Universal Declaration.[118]

Still other denominations addressed the Universal Declaration as linked with, or secondary to, specific religious or evangelistic concerns. In 1950 the Congregational Christian Churches affirmed the Declaration, specifically regarding religious liberty, and urged both the support of the Declaration's broader freedoms and, at the same time, a renewed proclamation of the gospel, that it might be accepted by those who enjoyed such freedoms.[119] Ecumenically open Baptist denominations recognized the Declaration and recommended its ratification, but this was secondary to repeated resolutions concerning religious liberty and evangelism.[120] From 1950 onward such religious liberty resolutions first stated Baptist belief in "religious liberty for all people everywhere"; then the associated freedoms of freedom of conscience, press, speech, and assembly; and then offered support of the Declaration "in fulfilling our own principles." This defense of religious freedom has been consistently accompanied in Baptist statements by the advocacy of the absolute separation of church and state.[121] Broader ecumenical work on these concerns was expressed by the National Council of Churches, which called in 1952 for a "united expression of Christian opinion" regarding the U.N. human rights covenants and separately defended religious freedom for all while defining evangelism as the church's primary task.[122] A decade later the National Council passed a *Pronouncement on Human Rights*, which restated the international freedoms under an explicit theological preamble, saying that, under God, "religious liberty and indeed religious faith are basic both historically and philosophically to all our liberties. These religious and civil liberties are interdependent and indivisible."[123]

RECENT DEVELOPMENTS

Since the 1960s mainline Protestant churches and ecumenical bodies have addressed human rights as part of their understanding of world ministry and social mission, and often call believers to engage in broader social advocacy and action.[124] They have made major efforts to apply human rights ideas to minority, female, and oppressed groups, and many gains have been made in these areas. However, a good deal of focus has been placed on the conditions that inhibit the capacity of persons to claim or actualize their rights, rather than on the relative validity or basic nature of human rights and religious freedom directly. Some of the social analysis used in this way has become detached from explicit theological and missions discussions. At present, the relationship among missions, evangelism, and social reform is assumed by, but not well articulated in, the mainline churches,[125] and their connection to the root understandings of human rights and liberty, which extend back to the best of Protestant thinking, is only rarely being explored or claimed by them.[126] The Human Rights Office of the National Council of Churches has been closed; none of the major denominations has a full-time person working on human rights issues and religious liberty.

Other threats to Protestant thought on this matter are now at hand. The relationship of Christianity to non-Christian religions is one such pressing issue. The conversionist orientation of Protestant thought has left a legacy of condescension toward other religions in some circles and a suspicion of cultural neocolonialism in others. This can be seen, for instance, in the statements by Southern Baptists about Jews and Mormons and their recent renewal of efforts to convert them. Though they may not compromise the principles of religious liberty for which Baptists have been so famous vis-à-vis the state or in a way that involves coercion, these various statements and actions are sometimes socially abrasive and intimidating in ways that are both uncharitable and counterproductive in gaining converts.

But the deeper issue is whether Protestantism, in regard to religious liberty and human rights, did discern something that is, in fact, universally valid. If it did, and if others can discover aspects of their own heritage that support human rights and religious freedom once it is identified and actualized, it would mean that Protestantism would have to be more respectful of other traditions than it sometimes has been. At the same time it invites the question as to whether the universally valid ideas of religious liberty and human rights can be sustained without enduring support from the presuppositions that discovered them and made them central to modern life. If patterns of thought and social organization are present in many traditions but have been perennially subordinated to other dimensions of faith, morality, or polity, what would prevent the resubordination of rights and freedom to other concerns or priorities if the theological presuppositions are not acknowledged as critical also?

It must be admitted that mainline Protestants will remain suspicious of Roman Catholics and conservative Evangelicals, with whom there is much agreement on many points of Christian belief, if they speak of human rights but do not allow women to take a full role in the inner life of the churches and their leadership. They may also seek ways to cooperate with Islam, but will again remain critical of its views of women, Islam's restrictions on conversions that do not support its view of supersession, and its tendency to collapse religious, political, and social authority into a single regime. Similarly, Protestants may admire much in the Asian religious traditions, but will undoubtedly resist the tendencies of Hinduism to preserve caste, of Buddhism to deny the presence of an image of God at the core of the human self, and of Confucianism to place primary loyalty in the identities of family, clan, and nation. Protestants will also remain active in converting those adherents of tribal religions who worship local deities and construct life around particular communal memories of a specific ethnic group. We also expect that Protestants will increase their public witness against the persecution of Christians by other traditions and regimes around the world.[127]

However, it must also be admitted that current Protestant thought has undergone several shifts of accent that are ambiguous in their relationship to these themes. For one thing, the impact of "crisis theology"—particularly its rejection of liberal, natural law, and natural rights schools of thought, and often all jurisprudential accents in theology and ethics—has persuaded many that the human capacity to speak with non-Christians about a universal moral law is mistaken. Such antinomian tendencies are reinforced by sharp postmodern criticisms of any claim to the knowledge of universal or general principles. Further, many sectarian and ethnic groups who flooded to America to find religious freedom have developed intense moral sensibilities about personal and church ethics but seldom think theologically about how the whole is to be ordered, on what principles, for what reasons. And where the influential liberationist wing of contemporary Christian thought holds that ethics and theology are inescapably contextual, clearly rooted in the specific social and historical conditions of a specific time and place, it can downplay or deny the importance of claims of a general or universal moral or theological nature.[128] Those who view Protestantism as these several, disparate developments may easily dismiss the importance of Protestantism for human rights, except as another interest group.

Further, it is clear that much of Protestantism is no clearer about the relationship of the individual to the group than the rest of society. Human rights obviously pertain to persons, and religious freedom obviously pertains to groups; but how these two relate to each other, in what proportion, is quite unsettled in the culture. Protestants are today divided between (1) various forms of hyper-individualism, as in some theories of economic life and personal identity that have a diminished sense of responsibility to tradition, society, and institutions; and (2) various forms of communitarianism, which assume that the solutions to all personal and social difficulties are found by the right socialization of persons into their primary group—familial, religious, ethnic, and communal. In both of these, we would suggest, a crucial part of Protestant belief is lost; while conversion always involves a personal transformation, it is always properly viewed as authentic when it draws persons into new communities of discipline and responsibility.

Still, contemporary Protestantism accents advocacy for exploited workers, for women and minorities everywhere, for the freedom to change religion and share information of all kinds, and for the right to organize religious communities and unions, parties, protest groups, service organizations, and corporations. This is deep in the Protestant soul, and it will resist international bodies, foreign governments, or domestic policies that restrict these freedoms, even if its current modes of reflection do not adequately articulate its own deeper convictions. Indeed, it is likely that the more enduring side of the Protestant drive to convert will outlive current antinomian, sectarian, and ideological tendencies and extend the constant and ever-necessary reformation of persons, faith, church, and the world. The task facing mainline Protestantism is to reclaim the insights that gave it birth; to cooperate with Orthodox and Catholic churches who have adopted the commitment to religious freedom and human rights; to work with evangelical, pentecostal, and other Christians who have not fully claimed these roots; and to join them anew to a universal understanding of the freedom under God to convert, organize, and bring transformation to human hearts, civil society, and the new social conditions that are today generating a global civilization.

11.

EVANGELISM AND MISSION IN THE ORTHODOX TRADITION

◆

Vigen Guroian

In August 1992 the heads of the two most venerated episcopal sees in Armenian Christianity issued a joint encyclical entitled "Fatherly Advice." The late Catholicos Vazken I (1908-94) of the Mother See of Holy Etchmiadzin in Armenia and Catholicos Karekin II (1932-99) of the Great House of Cilicia in Antelias, Lebanon, condemned the proselytizing activities of religious groups who were arriving in Armenia after the collapse of the Soviet regime. The two patriarchs accused these foreign groups of unfairly "taking advantage of the principle of religious freedom," lately enshrined in the new Armenian law on religious conscience.[1] They explained that the Armenian Church was in a weakened condition and needed time to regain its strength after seventy years of Soviet rule. The patriarchs took umbrage at the notion that Armenia was a field ripe for proselytism. "Armenia is not a mission-field for Christian evangelization," they insisted. It is not "a heathen [non-Christian] world and therefore a field for mission work in the generally accepted meaning of this word."[2]

Vazken I and Karekin II described the activities of the Jehovah's Witnesses, Pentecostals, Nazarenes, Mormons, and others as self-serving and ignorant of Armenian faith and culture. They spoke of proselytism as "soul stealing," the illicit conversion of Christians from one confession to another within an already Christianized nation.[3] Their "purpose is not to provide spiritual care for already existing members or followers (factually non-existent); their clear aim consists in 'winning' adherents," in gaining "converts." The patriarchs regarded this activity as contradictory to the fundamental criterion and goal of legitimate Christian evangelism: This activity is "a threat to Christian unity . . . and to national unity."[4]

The sort of religious proselytism to which the Armenian Orthodox patriarchs objected is, of course, not limited to Armenia. It is being carried out by

231

Western Protestant churches and para-church organizations throughout the former Soviet Union and Eastern Europe. It has earned similar objections and denunciations from various Orthodox Church authorities in almost every instance.

More often than not, Western observers take notice of these events only insofar as they are interested in the protection and advancement of religious freedom and tolerance. Thus much attention has been given to new laws on freedom of conscience and religious organization that have recently been promulgated in the countries of the former Soviet Union. Virtually all of these new laws have set up a two-tier system that grants special privileges to a historic national Orthodox church while strictly limiting the activity and expression of all other religious organizations. Understandably, these laws have been viewed by many as mocking the religious freedom and tolerance they claim to embody.

One burden of this chapter is to admonish these critics to examine more closely the actual day-to-day situations of churches and religious groups in these historic Orthodox lands. For these situations and contexts are far more complicated than positive law often reveals and certainly very different from the denominational configurations of North America. Critics need to be more open to a recalibration of the formal concepts of religious liberty and human rights with which they judge the circumstances and behavior of distant others. And they need to take into account the distinctive theology and ecclesiology of the Orthodox churches. Most of all, Western observers need to keep in mind that they are witnessing only the beginning of a process in which ancient Christian churches are adjusting to conditions radically different from any they have known for more than a millennium.

Permit me just one example of how analysis of law alone does not adequately account for the actual behavior and relations of religious groups in these lands. Both Hare Krishnas and Protestant Armenian Evangelicals are categorized identically in the Armenian Law on Conscience and Religious Organization. I have seen a number of reports and video footage of Hare Krishnas being divested of their religious literature and sometimes violently abused by local villagers and Armenian priests—a lamentable plight by any and all humane standards of conduct. By contrast, the Protestant Armenian Evangelical Church, though in the same legal class, is afforded much greater freedom and latitude than the new Armenian Law on Conscience and Religious Organization prescribes. Many new Evangelical congregations have emerged throughout the country; members of this Protestant communion, who are overwhelmingly Baptist, have been invited to help teach in Armenian Orthodox parishes. Arrangements are even being discussed in some cities and towns for Armenian Orthodox and Armenian Protestants to share properties for the purposes of worship and religious instruction. And Protestants have founded a fully operational seminary. These new Protestant institutions are not without limitations and inhibitions, but their circumstance is far better than the stipulations of the Law on Conscience and Religious Freedom might lead one to believe.

Indeed, in 1996, on the occasion of the 150th anniversary of the establishment of the Armenian Evangelical Church, the newly elected Catholicos Karekin I (formally Karekin II of the Cilician See) gave an address in the capital city of Yerevan in which he openly welcomed the activities of the Armenian Evangelical Church. Karekin I reiterated the thesis regarding what constitutes legitimate evangelism as opposed to proselytism. However, His Holiness also distinguished Armenian Evangelicals and Armenian Catholics (Uniates) from the other religious groups in Armenia. He observed that both these churches had long histories in Armenia and had contributed to national unity.[5]

The Armenian Catholicos's greeting was noteworthy for both its inclusiveness as well as its implied exclusion of others. Nevertheless, on balance, it gives reason to hope for positive possibilities for religious freedom and tolerance in the future. The patriarch began his speech with these carefully chosen words:

> Dear believing and faithful brothers and sisters in Christ, children of both the Apostolic [i.e., Orthodox] and Evangelical Churches, all children of the Church of God and the Holy Gospel.[6]

Herein, Karekin I acknowledged an important equality of status between these churches. He asserted that in some real sense they are one church and all faithful followers of the gospel. What cannot be assumed from this greeting, however, is that the Armenian Catholicos was withdrawing in any strong sense from a claim for the ecclesiastical preeminence of the Armenian Church within Armenia.

This claim of supremacy should not come as a surprise, nor ought it to be viewed necessarily as in conflict with the principle of religious toleration. After all, the historic meaning of tolerance in Western religious history does not presume equality in doctrine or teaching but rather suggests forbearance and hospitality by the dominant party toward those who dissent from the established orthodoxy. Nor does tolerance necessarily include all groups. Even in America the beginnings of religious tolerance were rocky and spotty, to say the least.

But this analogy with America does not go very far. America embraced a plurality of churches and religious sects virtually from the beginning of European colonization; in Armenia, by contrast, the Orthodox Church has been the sole or dominant presence for seventeen hundred years. In Armenia, all other churches are late-comers; most did not arrive until the nineteenth and twentieth centuries. Even as Karekin I spoke in conciliatory terms, he was no doubt setting the stage for the commemoration of the 1700th anniversary of the official proclamation of Christianity as the state religion of Armenia. (The traditional date that is accepted by the Armenian Church is 301, although modern scholarship argues that a more accurate dating is 314.) The Armenian Church was the first state-established church in Christian history, a pride and memory easily as strong as that of other Orthodox churches that lay similar claims to an ancient presence and formative influence upon the nations whose names they carry.

The Armenian Orthodox Church did come in regular contact with the Roman Catholic Church during the Crusades, and it has carried on official relations with the papacy throughout much of its history. Few Armenian Orthodox, however, converted to Catholicism until the mid-nineteenth century, when changes in the Ottoman policy toward Christian minorities permitted the establishment of an official Armenian Rite Catholic *millet* (a millet is an ethnoreligious administrative unit). At the same time, Protestant missionary activity led to an Armenian Protestant community that was legally established in 1846. The Armenian Orthodox leadership had long vigorously opposed the grant of official status to these two religious communities. It is against this background that the Armenian Church's accusations of proselytism as well as Catholicos Karekin I's conciliatory gestures toward Armenian Catholics and Evangelical Protestants must be considered.

In his closing remarks, Karekin I not only delineated intelligible criteria for the acceptance or rejection of religious bodies in Armenia but also exposed the underlying ecclesiology and concept of mission that moved him to these positions. His Holiness stated:

> We welcome the impartial involvement of all those of our people in the movement of spiritual renewal, including our Armenian Catholic brothers and sisters. . . . But we . . . [do] not say the same thing to those who came individually, each one seeking his own profit, persons of foreign faiths, movements, and personal ambitions. They opened the Holy Bible and said what they wanted.
>
> Each person has an obligation to read the Bible; but the determination of biblical doctrine belongs to the Church, because it is the Church which said: "This is the Holy Bible, not that." We must keep the Church strong and steadfast in that, so that winds do not blow it about; as it is said even in our dear Bible [that] at the time of Christ and his apostles, many false prophets have come and gone. . . .
>
> Myriad cult-followers have come upon the rock of the Armenian Church and passed away, but the Church has remained strong, because our dear Armenian Catholic brothers and sisters and Evangelical brothers and sisters have stood firm with us, for the sake of the Church and for its rejuvenation. May you live long, and live in such a way that in this new era of freedom and independence in Armenia, the Armenian Church brings spiritual and moral health to our whole people. . . .
>
> Today our Armenian Church, together with her Catholic and Evangelical brethren, will continue that historic mission. . . . [7]

The Patriarch of Moscow has not offered this kind of approval to Russian Protestants or Catholics; and the tensions between the Russian and Ukrainian Orthodox churches and Catholic Uniates are well known. In this larger Orthodox context, therefore, Karekin I's speech was truly exceptional. The patriarch was forgiving a great deal with respect to Armenian Protestants and Uniate Catholics, but he was also defending and preserving an ancient theology of mission and a catholic ecclesiology that stresses unity of the church above all else.

MISSIONARY WORK IN THE HISTORY
OF ORTHODOX CHRISTIANITY

In a classic little volume published in 1963, Ernst Benz summarized and evaluated succinctly the history and theology of mission within the Orthodox Church. Benz began wisely by noting that "the Orthodox Church has often been charged with failure in its missionary work"[8] and that it is commonly thought that in character Orthodox Christianity is not oriented to missions. Nothing, of course, could be farther from the truth, Benz explained, even though Orthodox churches have not shown much evidence of mission in modern history. The seeming discordance between this Orthodox theology and practice of mission can be understood only by reference to the Islamic conquest of the Byzantine Empire in the fifteenth century and the rise of a powerful and far-reaching Ottoman Empire that prevailed until the beginning of the twentieth century.

Most of Orthodox Christianity—whether Syrian or Serbian, Russian or Rumanian, Greek or Bulgarian—was reduced during the long Ottoman captivity to a survival, rather than a missionary, mode of existence. The Ottomans divided the Orthodox peoples into millets. Under this administrative system ancient missionary churches were cast into national churches and began increasingly to identify themselves with distinct ethnic peoples and, later, with modern nation-states. Survivalism commingled with ethnocentrism and, later, with full-blown nationalist ideologies to narrow further the catholic vision of the Orthodox churches. Today, at the turn of the second millennium, we are able to see how this proclivity to ethnic particularism and secular nationalism within Orthodox churches colors their attitude toward other churches and gives rise to sometimes shrill protests of foreign intrusion and proselytism.

The late eighteenth and nineteenth centuries also featured growing modernization and secularization within the Orthodox churches. Faced with devastating wars of national liberation, the beleaguered Patriarchate of Constantinople granted Orthodox churches of Greece, Romania, Bulgaria, and Serbia autocephalous status. The last remnants of the old Orthodox *oekumene* were shattered, and the modern notion of a national Orthodox church was born. While this development did not generally bode well for Orthodox missions, the Russian Orthodox Church in particular engaged in important missionary activity in the century preceding the triumph of Bolshevism, spreading the Orthodox faith to Japan, Korea, China, and North America and the far reaches of Siberia and Alaska. The movement grew in part from a revival of monasticism within Orthodoxy. Monasticism in Russia, as elsewhere in the Orthodox East, had sometimes meant retreat. But it had also generated from within itself renewed religious fervor and the inspiration to go out and convert. Dostoyevsky explores these competing impulses through the character of Alyosha Karamazov and his relationship with the monk Zossima. Indeed, he modeled this Russian elder (*staretz*) after real and popular holy men of his own time. Zossima instructs his young disciple to leave the monastery and spread his new faith into the world.

The monastic spirit of mission within the Orthodox Church had combined with the colonizing activities of the Russian state as far back as the late Middle Ages, when Russian monks sometimes followed and sometimes preceded the Russian colonizers. In the fourteenth century St. Stefan of Perm took the gospel to the Zyrian (or Komi) people west of the Urals. Seventeenth-century bishop Filofey Lenchinsky is called the "beacon of light to the Siberian peoples." The most venerated of nineteenth-century monastic missionaries was undoubtedly Innokenty (St. Innocent) Venyaminov (1797-1879). He spread the Orthodox faith from Siberia to Alaska and the Aleutian Islands.

Three hallmarks of the Orthodox missionary vision and success ironically may also have contributed to the eventual fragmentation of Orthodox Christianity into national entities that today are finding it difficult to reengage in evangelistic activities and to compete with other churches.[9] First, Orthodox missiology stressed the use of the vernacular Bible and liturgy. Thus, for example, the Greek Septuagint version of the Bible was translated into Armenian in the fifth century, and the Byzantine liturgy was translated into Slavonic by the tenth century. St. Innocent translated St. Matthew's gospel, the Divine Liturgy, and a catechism into Aleutian. Second, Orthodox missiology stressed the training of an indigenous clergy. This was employed very effectively in Byzantium's mission to the Slavs, and was encouraged from the beginning by Saints Cyril and Methodius, who converted the Slavs. Third, Orthodox ecclesiology historically emphasized a conciliar conception of the church and of ecclesiastical authority. Within medieval Orthodox Christendom not even the See of Constantinople gained the kind of supremacy that was achieved by the Roman papacy. Whereas only one of the five historic patriarchal sees that claimed apostolic founding was located in the Latin West, four remained in the East: Constantinople, Alexandria, Antioch, and Jerusalem. Orthodox "canon law permits the establishment of local-churches, and to this end the noblest missionary efforts aspired."[10] Accordingly, autocephalous churches arose, beginning in Russia, which, in the fifteenth century, added another great independent patriarchal see alongside Constantinople, the Patriarchate of Moscow. Initially, these three hallmarks of Orthodox missiology—the use of the vernacular, the cultivation of indigenous clergy, and the tradition of conciliarity or decentralized organization—led to vigorous and highly successful missionary activity and the great expansion of the Orthodox faith. More recently, however, these same three hallmarks have been transformed into the corrupted elements of a secularized ideology and ossified vision of national churches.

Twenty years ago Alexander Schmemann noted two developments in modern history that dramatically challenged and permanently changed the face of Orthodox Christianity. "The first development is the tragically spectacular collapse, one after another, of the old 'Orthodox worlds' which appeared as the self-evident, natural and permanent 'home' and environment of the Orthodox Church—and not merely their collapse but also their transformation into the stage for a violent attack launched by an extreme and totalitarian secularism against religion." The second "event," Schmemann said, is "the rapid growth in the West of the Orthodox diaspora."[11]

The first development is the more germane for this discussion. The wounds that Communism inflicted upon churches and nations in the course of the twentieth century help us to understand the defensiveness with which Orthodox churches have reacted to religious pluralism and proselytism in recent years. The habits of survivalism and privatism that were deepened under Communism also help to account for the hesitancy and confusion with which these churches have mounted efforts since the fall of the Soviet empire to reevangelize their own peoples and to counter the intrusions, particularly of Western religious groups. The presence of large Orthodox diaspora communities in Western Europe and North America may not be as significant a factor in this analysis. But I surmise that by bringing Orthodox Christianity to the attention of Westerners, these diaspora communities inadvertently contributed to the identification of the old Orthodox worlds as potential mission fields for new adherents once the Soviet empire collapsed.

A third development, which Schmemann could not possibly have anticipated twenty years ago, is the rapid demise of the atheistic and totalitarian regimes in whose bowels most of the Orthodox churches lived for the greater part of this century. These recent developments have inaugurated a new and unprecedented era in the history of Orthodox Christianity that is not yet wholly comprehended even by the Orthodox churches themselves. These conditions bring to the fore an important dimension of the Orthodox vision of mission alluded to above. This is the relationship of mission and unity of the church. An understanding of the meaning of the vehement objections raised by Orthodox religious leaders against proselytism is not possible without taking into account this belief that mission must serve the goal of unity.

UNITY AND MISSION

The late John Meyendorff carefully presented the biblical and theological basis of the Orthodox theology of mission and unity of the church.

The Christian claim that Jesus is indeed the "Word of God," the Logos "through whom all things were made," is a universal claim which involves not only all men but also the entire cosmos. The Johannine identification between Christ and the Logos implies that Jesus is not just the "Savior of our souls." He is not only the carrier of a message limited to a peculiar field called "religion"; but in Him is the ultimate truth about the origin, the development, and the final destiny of *all things*. Hence His Church is necessarily the catholic Church . . . referring to the whole.[12]

The Orthodox understanding of mission is inseparable from Christology and ecclesiology, so that *mission is unity enacted*. When Vazken I and Karekin II protested that Armenia is not a mission field, at least not in the historical sense of evangelizing heathens, they lent voice to this principle. They were expressing their belief that proselytizing by "outside" groups only deepens the divisions among Christians. The spirit of denominationalism, leave aside sectarianism, is not welcome in Orthodox theology. Where denominationalism is a sociological given, Orthodox insist that Christians must work to unite a fragmented church. Where denominationalism is hardly present, as in Armenia, no good reason is found for encouraging it to increase.

Orthodox theology defines mission as an action to redeem a sinful and divided humankind and to reunite the race within the mystical body of Christ. Orthodox anthropology and soteriology contrast with the ontological individualism and modern human rights doctrines that predominate in the West.[13] In Orthodox theology, normative human nature is defined in strict relation to the divine acts of creation and Incarnation. The humanity assumed by the Creator Word is forever united with his divinity and is taken by him eternally to the Father in the Spirit. Humanity is itself created in the image and likeness of the triune God, as the Divinity itself is a perfect community of three divine Persons in a single Godhead. This trinitarian understanding of God and humanity answers doubts about whether in Orthodoxy the good and telos of the human being is autonomy or theonomy, individualism or communality. In modern liberalism and human rights theory, the good is autonomy. In Orthodoxy, the good is theonomy: the fulfillment of humankind is participation in and communion with the divine Life itself (2 Pt 1:4). No temporal human good exists apart from a movement either toward or away from holiness in the company of the saints.

By extension, therefore, Orthodox mission is premised on a strongly communal theological anthropology. Mission is a means of glorifying God by offering back to God the human community in communion as the one, holy, catholic, and apostolic church. The church is mission, and it constitutes itself as mission at each celebration of the eucharist. For in the eucharist Christ is present and the church is revealed as Christ's mystical body. Joined in all of its parts, this body is sent into the world to draw into itself all of humankind.

Pentecost is the crucial event in the history of the church that defines mission. In Pentecost the division of humankind at the Tower of Babel is reversed. "Pentecost saw the birth of the Church, the *koinonia*, which will gradually acquire structures and will presuppose continuity and authority and unity. Communion with God cannot, as such, be 'divided.' It can only be incomplete and deficient on the personal human level of man's lack of receptivity to the divine gift" of full communion in the Holy Spirit.[14] Any so-called mission activity that divides Christians further is condemned on the basis of this pentecostal theology of mission.

No doubt, the modality of mission changes when Christianity has literally spread to every corner of the globe. In a post-Reformation, post-Enlightenment world, the mission of the church must be conceived as an "inreach" every bit as much as an "outreach." Christianity has become global. But at the same time, Christendom has also disintegrated from within. While the gospel has spread to every corner of the earth, Christians have become pilgrims and sojourners in a "foreign land," much as they were in the first centuries of the church. The church is a "minority" even where once it was the heart of Christendom. As Aram I Armenian Catholicos of the Great See of Cilicia has stated: While "taking the Gospel to the ends of the earth is the unequivocal mission of the church," the "direction and modality of mission has changed. [Now] [m]ission is primarily inreach of the church, not simply an 'overseas' or 'foreign' enterprise."[15] With Christian churches in a new minority status almost everywhere, there are compelling practical reasons that they cooperate rather than compete. In an increasingly global and secularized human community, this practical necessity becomes painfully evident and pressing.

There has always been an even more compelling theological and—indeed ultimately christological—reason for this strategy and modality of mission. In Orthodox theology the only true mission is a mission that serves unity. This is a truth that is eternally validated in the person of Christ, that is, through the incarnation of the Word and his unity with the Father in the triune Godhead. The speech of Jesus in the Gospel of John about unity in him, and through him union with the Father, is the corollary to the Great Commission: "Go, therefore, and make disciples of all nations, baptizing them in the name of the Father and the Son and the Holy Spirit" (Mt 28:19, *NKJV*). In the gospel Jesus prays to the Father: "May they all be one, just as, Father, you are in me and I am in you, so that they also may be in us, that the world may believe that you sent me" (Jn 17:21, *NJB*). In our day this prayer for unity assumes great significance for the Christian churches and their mission in the world.

ECUMENISM AND THE MISSION OF THE CHURCHES

Both the Armenian encyclical "Fatherly Advice" and the address of Catholicos Karekin I that we have reviewed lay down serious theological and ecclesiological concerns. Theologically, the Orthodox churches maintain standards of dogma and practice that are interpreted not individualistically or voluntaristically but corporately and in relation to Armenian or Russian peoplehood. The American notion of a wall of separation between church and state has no place in Orthodox theology. For that implies not only legal separation but cultural separation and disembodiment of the faith.

The Orthodox Christianity of Armenia and Russia, or of Rumania and Georgia, is what Ernst Troeltsch called a "churchly form" of Christianity. The church is identified with a people and a land, with an ecology and a history. The sectarian or denominational understanding of church that is quite "natural" for Americans under the doctrine of a separation of church and state is quite "unnatural" for the Orthodox. For the Orthodox, the unity of the church is not merely a disembodied ideal; it is a process being worked out through long histories of conversion and triumph as well as conflict and defeat.

The Orthodox churches have held to this catholic vision of the faith and ecclesiology. Unity, based in trinitarian and christological dogma, is the compelling theological necessity. This necessity may have an eschatological horizon, but the principle seeks embodiment in this world just as the Word became flesh. So the local church—the particular Orthodox churches of the Russians, Serbians, or Armenians—transforms the culture and makes it its own body as Jesus took the flesh of his mother, Mary.

Thus at the heart of the modern struggle over proselytism is a conflict in beliefs, West against East, over the very nature of the church and its mission and over faith and culture. The Western individualistic and voluntaristic convictions and assumptions of many religious groups who arrive in old Orthodox lands are clashing with the corporate and organic concepts of church and peoplehood embraced by Orthodox theology. From the Orthodox point of view, proselytizing is mission mistakenly conceived by a church wrongly constituted.

In his 1996 address Catholicos Karekin I alluded to this individualism and voluntarism when he spoke of the differences in how scripture is read and received in Western and Eastern churches. Especially Western Protestants regard individual interpretation of the scripture as authoritative; Eastern Orthodox regard interpretation as an exercise of the whole body of believers gathered together liturgically around the apostolic episcopacy. Elsewhere in this same address Karekin I states: "We do not need to hear the truth of Christianity from others. Our Fathers have given us the truth; and taking it from Christ, taking it from their lives, and mixing it with their blood [the blood of martyrs], they have given it to us."[16] Contrary to Western individualistic and voluntaristic understandings of the church and its mission, Orthodox Christianity holds up concepts of history and tradition that are supported by stories of national conversion. Faith unifies a people historically. Evangelization is about conversion, but not just the conversion of individuals. The Slavs were converted by Saints Cyril and Methodius, not just individuals but a whole people converted. The Armenians were converted by St. Gregory the Illuminator, led by the Armenian King Tiridates III.

It is easy for transient Americans of recent immigrant origins to forget that these events of mission and conversion occurred in historically identifiable places, often stained with the blood of the martyrs and immortalized by monuments to their sacrifice. This is perhaps less inscrutable to Americans of the Old South, where religion, land, and sacrifice are still part of a common memory and regional identity. Factors such as these make the struggles between Orthodox Serbs and Muslim Bosnians, and between Armenians and Azeris in the dispute over Nagorno-Karabagh, virtually intractable. Not only are political boundaries arbitrarily drawn across the land, but the very earth and soil that are divided evoke collective memories of national identity that are linked with the veneration of saints and martyrs and marked by ancient churches and shrines of pilgrimage.

Once this corporate and communal principle in Orthodoxy is understood, then it is not difficult to grasp what proselytism really stands for in the contemporary rhetoric of Orthodox leaders. It is a term of opprobrium contrasted with true mission in continuity with the history of a people and the unity of church and nation. Proselytism is not only being carried on by persons and groups whose beliefs and religious practices are suspect or erroneous. Proselytism also threatens the unity of the church and so, practically speaking, the unity of the nation. It is particularly opprobrious and undesirable at this moment in history when long-frustrated national aspirations are at last within reach, and when the national church has been set free to teach once again the faith openly and to reevangelize the large numbers of unchurched persons.

These are some of the elements of Orthodox theology and ecclesiology that drive current Orthodox denunciations of proselytism. As the encyclical "Fatherly Advice" puts it:

> [Proselytizers] distort the Christian faith and cause new divisions within the Christian Church. . . . If they have the slightest consciousness and understanding of mission as taught by the Gospel, they should go to such countries and peoples which have not heard the name of Christ or accepted His faith. This is the proper way of mission as indicated and opened by our Lord Jesus Christ [in] Matthew 28:19-20.[17]

CONCLUSION: A CRITICAL LOOK AT THE ORTHODOX RESPONSE TO PROSELYTISM

Armenian Catholicos Aram I rightly contends that mission must now be a form of "inreach"—a reaching back into the concrete settings where the Christian faith was once planted but is now weakened by the secularization and atheism of modern life. This analysis of mission challenges the aggressive foreign proselytism being carried out in Orthodox lands.

This position, however, does not excuse the failures of the Orthodox churches themselves—particularly the embrace of uncritical nationalism. Virtually all Orthodox churches in formerly Soviet and Communist countries think of themselves as national churches and claim, by virtue of this title, a kind of ownership over the cultures and societies whose very names—Serbian, Bulgarian, Armenian, Ukrainian, and so forth—they have affixed as adjectives to the church. And the leaders of these churches often insist that their nations are Christian nations. For example, Karekin I states: "Armenia is a Christianized world . . . molded by the Christian principles of the Gospel, and with an existing culture permeated by the Christian faith. . . . Christianity for the Armenian nation remains the 'color of the skin,' yesterday, today, and forever."[18] Such a claim is subject to serious question.[19] Indeed, I believe it must be rejected if a serious remissionizing of Armenia is to proceed with full vigor and with real and lasting effect.

Today, Orthodox Christianity is not so much the "color of the skin" of a nation as it is the faded garment that the nation has grown out of or traded in for new secular clothing. To be sure, centuries of Ottoman captivity and decades of Communist rule have severely weakened and divided Orthodox Christianity, and these experiences give Orthodox churches current claims to special status and protection a measure of authenticity. But we must not underestimate the force of delusion and denial among Orthodox leaders, their unwillingness to admit that these societies are now post-Christian. Orthodox churches disadvantage themselves severely by persisting in their assertion that they are national churches with a special claim to privileges that outsiders must respect. This attitude contradicts the Orthodox principles of catholicity and unity. This contradiction is exacerbated by the globalization of the modern human community. In a world of increasingly globalized communications, technology, transportation, and economy, the notion of a "national Orthodox church" starts to look increasingly like claims of denominationalism that Orthodox principles of catholicity and unity have always firmly rejected.

With the fall of Communism in the East, the urgent question has become: How is it possible for the Orthodox Church, which is itself divided ecclesiastically into national churches, to present a unified witness on the world scale? The question is urgent and painful, because national Orthodox churches have not yet figured out how to act consistently with their theological vision of catholicity and unity. Their missionary spirit is still inhibited by the lie and cover of de facto separation and contentment with merely being present in a place and ceremonially representing a people.

Orthodox churches must admit that the evolution of local churches into national churches came at the price of allying with forces of secularism and nationalism that have ultimately eroded the Christian faith and compromised the church. Nationalist and secularist ideologies have supplanted the Orthodox theology of Christian mission. Vast parts of national populations that are claimed to be Orthodox are at best only nominally Christian. If such truth-telling were to prevail, the call made by Aram I for mission as inreach might bear real fruit: these churches might conscientiously retrain and reequip themselves for mission without illusion. In turn, this action would lend new perspective and positive insight into the issue of proselytism.

I cannot speak for all Orthodox churches. Each case is different. For example, religious pluralism in Russia far exceeds what obtains presently in Armenia. Indeed, Armenia might be one of the easiest Orthodox cases, since it is the most ethnically and religiously homogeneous of all the former republics of the Soviet Union. In Armenia, a reinvigorated Armenian Orthodox Church that truly viewed itself as "sent" would probably overwhelm most of the budding new sects and denominational forms of Christianity in Armenia. This alone would not answer the issue of religious freedom. A free and democratic Armenia will thrive only if it is open to the rest of the world. If Armenians invite others into their midst to do business, some of those who enter inevitably will also bring other faiths with them. Competition cannot be eliminated completely, and some religious pluralism, at least, cannot be avoided without destroying religious freedom.

This is why the rediscovery by the modern ecumenical movement of the relationship of mission and unity of the church is so important. In modern times, the Orthodox churches have stood foursquare in support of this principle. No doubt, their allegiance to it has been motivated in part by the protection it affords them. It makes it respectable to say to others, "Your activity on our territory jeopardizes the unity of the church." The trouble is that most of the religious groups that are now rushing into the old Orthodox lands have not been players in the modern ecumenical movement or the World Council of Churches, and have rather little sympathy with the theme of mission and unity in the church.

These foreign missionizing groups, however, have weaknesses that the Orthodox churches either have not recognized or have not fully exploited. Many of these foreign mission groups have little understanding of the peoples and their histories. And whatever their advantage in financial resources, they are greatly outnumbered by Orthodox. If Orthodox churches would recognize these simple facts and act upon them in a concerted way, they could mount "counteroffensives," not with bitter accusations and legal restrictions but in a true spirit of catholicity. They could teach these new religious groups a lesson or two in what constitutes the true marks of the church. This "counteroffensive" would be less a reaction to what others are doing than a free act of inner transformation, transformation once more into the ecumenical church. The Orthodox churches might use their rich tradition and ecclesiology and what they have learned from the ecumenical movement to press all of the Christian groups in their lands toward the goal of unity by the force of their own example. Implicit in this suggestion is a redefinition of religious freedom and toleration that is not entirely consistent with liberalism. But liberalism is not in all ways consistent with Orthodox theology and ecclesiology.

I have lent scant attention to the concerns of rights and legal processes that are of such paramount importance to many Western analysts. I only suggest that if Orthodox churches act consistently with their theology and tradition, these legal and procedural principles will have a rather different norm and form than now prevails in America and elsewhere. The Orthodox Church in all places is bound to act upon the knowledge and assurance of its theology that real peace and tolerance come, not from law and procedures, but only from a penitent spirit committed to the communion and unity of all who call on the name of Jesus as Lord.

Part Four

MODERN MISSION MOVEMENTS

◆

12.

The Missionary Work
of the Church of Jesus Christ
# of Latter-day Saints

————◆————

Dallin H. Oaks
Lance B. Wickman

We are pleased to be included in this global study of evangelism, proselytism, and human rights. We write as leaders and participants in the missionary work[1] of The Church of Jesus Christ of Latter-day Saints.[2] We seek to provide an inside perspective of an effort that includes approximately sixty thousand full-time missionaries in more than 125 nations and territories. Hopefully, the experience gained in that missionary effort will complement the other chapters in this important volume.

As we portray the missionary experience and philosophy of the people who are called Mormons or Latter-day Saints (LDS), we must explain the why and the how of their missionary work. This will necessarily include a description of doctrinal foundations, historical experience, and current missionary practices. We hope this will help explain why The Church of Jesus Christ of Latter-day Saints (hereafter "the church") deems it vital for religious liberty norms to protect and facilitate appropriate missionary work.

The driving force behind the missionary work of Christians is the spiritual duty to witness of Jesus Christ and his gospel. There are counterweights to that duty, but they are different in different religious traditions. In some there is a sense that the toleration for others mandated by the Golden Rule requires restraint in missionary efforts. In contrast, Mormons have such appreciation for the gospel message and the Great Commission to take it to all the world that the Golden Rule is not an obligation to refrain from witnessing to sincere adherents to other faiths but the central motivation of the duty to share.

The primary restraint on a Mormon's duty to witness is his or her profound respect for moral agency—the right of every soul to choose what he or she will believe and practice. A second restraint is the law, whose observance is a fundamental tenet of a Mormon's faith. Hence, missionary work is restrained by legal requirements or prohibitions. Over the years, this has given LDS missionaries and their leaders extensive experience with various tensions between legal regulation and spiritual witness.

The fundamental LDS attitude toward those of other faiths is respect and love and a desire to share with them a most precious possession. Latter-day Saints[3] do not seek to pull others away from the truth they have but to add to their knowledge, their happiness, and their peace. The church proclaims that it is neither Orthodox, Catholic, nor Protestant, but the *restored* church of Jesus Christ, bearing a message that was first given to God's spirit children in a pre-earth existence, which explains the purposes of mortal life, and which reveals important truths about the eternities to come. So far as they can do so without violating the law or infringing the moral agency of individuals, Latter-day Saints feel conscientiously impelled to share their gospel message with everyone in the world.

THE DOCTRINAL FOUNDATION

THE COMMAND TO WITNESS

As he neared the end of his earthly ministry, the Lord Jesus Christ commanded his disciples, "Go ye therefore, and teach all nations" (Mt 28:19). The Gospel of Mark reports this as a command to go "into all the world, and preach the Gospel to every creature," and promises that "[h]e that believeth and is baptized shall be saved; but he that believeth not shall be damned" (Mk 16:15-16). During one of his appearances to his apostles following his resurrection, Jesus reaffirmed that they should be "witnesses unto me both in Jerusalem, and in all Judaea, and in Samaria, and unto the uttermost part of the earth" (Acts 1:8).

To Latter-day Saints, this Great Commission is obligatory on all Christians. It imposes a sacred duty to witness "among all nations, kindreds, tongues, and people" (Doctrine and Covenants 112:1),[4] for, as the apostle Peter declared, "God is no respecter of persons" (Acts 10:34).

What was the gospel they were to preach? When Peter and the other apostles were arrested and brought before the authorities because they had violated the direction not to teach in the name of Jesus, they answered that they "ought to obey God rather than men." They explained God's command:

> The God of our fathers raised up Jesus, whom ye slew and hanged on a tree. Him hath God exalted with his right hand to be a Prince and a Saviour, for to give repentance to Israel, and forgiveness of sins. And we

are his witnesses of these things; and so is also the Holy Ghost, whom God hath given to them that obey him (Acts 5:29-32).

For Latter-day Saints, the command to be witnesses of Jesus Christ and to preach his gospel has been renewed in other works of scripture. The restored church of Jesus Christ began with the calling of a prophet, Joseph Smith,[5] whose first work was to translate an ancient book of prophecies and teachings given to Israelite refugees who had fled to the Americas. A purpose of this Book of Mormon,[6] as stated on its title page, was "to the convincing of the Jew and Gentile that JESUS is the CHRIST, the ETERNAL GOD, manifesting himself unto all nations." One of its teachings is that those who are desirous to come into the fold of God have the duty "to stand as witnesses of God at all times, and in all things, and in all places that ye may be in, even until death" (Book of Mormon, Mosiah 18:9).

Like the Bible (especially the New Testament), the Book of Mormon contains the witness and doctrine of Jesus Christ that is to be preached. Speaking to an audience in the New World, as recorded in the Book of Mormon, the Risen Lord declared:

> Behold I have given unto you my gospel, and this is the gospel which I have given unto you—that I came into the world to do the will of my Father, because my Father sent me.
>
> And my Father sent me that I might be lifted up upon the cross; and after that I had been lifted up upon the cross, that I might draw all men unto me, that as I have been lifted up by men even so should men be lifted up by the Father, to stand before me, to be judged of their works, whether they be good or whether they be evil. . . .
>
> Now this is the commandment: Repent, all ye ends of the earth, and come unto me and be baptized in my name, that ye may be sanctified by the reception of the Holy Ghost, that ye may stand spotless before me at the last day.
>
> Verily, verily, I say unto you, this is my gospel; and ye know the things that ye must do in my church; for the works which ye have seen me do that shall ye also do; for that which ye have seen me do even that shall ye do (Book of Mormon, 3 Nephi 27:13-14, 20-21).

In still another book of modern revelation, the Lord declared to early elders in the restored church: "Go ye into all the world, preach the gospel to every creature, acting in the authority which I have given you, baptizing in the name of the Father, and of the Son, and of the Holy Ghost" (Doctrine and Covenants 68:8).

In their attempts to fulfill this God-given responsibility, Latter-day Saints do not preach and teach merely to bring people into the church. They do not preach and teach merely to persuade people to live better lives. These are important, but the restored church offers something more.

The purpose of witnessing and missionary work by representatives of The Church of Jesus Christ of Latter-day Saints is to offer all of the children of God the opportunity to learn the fullness of the gospel of Jesus Christ as restored in these latter days and to give all the children of God the privilege of receiving the ordinances of salvation. By this means the door is opened for all the living and the dead to receive "eternal life, which gift is the greatest of all the gifts of God" (Doctrine and Covenants 14:7).

For Latter-day Saints, who believe that God has restored vital additional knowledge and power to bless the lives of all his children and who believe that they have a duty to share these treasures with all humankind, the command to witness is fundamental to all their belief and practice. It is a vital part of what it means to be a Latter-day Saint. To all who hold these convictions, the duty to witness and to share is a fundamental matter of conscience.

As we shall see, this duty and conviction has characterized Latter-day Saints from the beginning. It dictated the behavior of the earliest leaders and converts. It directed missionaries to scores of nations. It invited their converts to immigrate to join and strengthen the body of the new church on the frontier of the United States. And it shaped the growth of a nation as the Mormon pioneers colonized a substantial portion of the western part of the United States.

As we shall also see, this duty to witness and this conviction of its God-given importance are still vital to the self-image, faith, and practice of Latter-day Saints. They are people of faith and people of action. For them, lifelong participation in missionary work, including serving missions as young people and as retired couples, and striving to be worthy witnesses through precept and example throughout their lives, are the natural fruits of loving faith in action. Latter-day Saints believe and practice the word of the Lord given to early members of the church, "that the thing which will be of the most worth unto you will be to declare repentance unto this people, that you may bring souls unto me, that you may rest with them in the kingdom of my Father" (Doctrine and Covenants 15:6).

Moral Agency

Of course, each Christian denomination has its own interpretations of the gospel of Jesus Christ and its own points of emphasis. For Latter-day Saints, a point of emphasis that is critical to the way they conduct their missionary work is the importance of moral agency.

Among the profound questions pondered by all thoughtful people are these: Where did I come from? Why am I here? Where am I going when I die? Left unanswered, these questions gnaw at the edges of consciousness because they are fundamental to the nature and purpose of life.

In all ages God has provided answers to life's questions through his prophets. Central to the message of The Church of Jesus Christ of Latter-day Saints is the proclamation that God has called prophets in our time, as God did anciently, and that through these prophets God has revealed answers to these great questions to guide his children safely across the treacherous shoals of mortality.

Latter-day revelation teaches that all mankind dwelt with God the Eternal Father in the pre-mortal world as his spirit sons and daughters.[7] Every man, woman, and child is, therefore, a literal child of God, who loves each one with the perfect love of a divine Father. In that pre-mortal realm we knew him and his beloved Son, Jesus Christ, who was to be the Only Begotten in the flesh. Prior to the creation of the earth, God and all of his spirit offspring met in a Grand Council. The Father's plan pertaining to the Creation and divine purpose of the earth was presented by Jesus Christ:

> And there stood one among them [the hosts of Heaven] that was like unto God, and he [Jesus Christ] said unto those who were with him: We will go down, for there is space there, and we will take of these materials, and we will make an earth whereon these may dwell;
>
> And we will prove them herewith, to see if they will do all things whatsoever the Lord their God shall command them;
>
> And they who keep their first [pre-mortal] estate shall be added upon; and they who keep not their first estate shall not have glory in the same kingdom with those who keep their first estate; and they who keep their second [mortal] estate shall have glory added upon their heads for ever and ever (Pearl of Great Price, Abraham 3:24-26).

Earth was created as a proving ground for the spiritual children of God, to give them an opportunity to demonstrate by individual choice their faithfulness to God's commandments. Those who do so (that is, who "keep" their "second estate") will have "glory added upon their heads for ever and ever." Redemption for earthly sins and mistakes is made by Jesus Christ for those choosing to follow him. The rewards for righteous choices in mortality are eternal life and continual growth toward perfection in the presence of the Father and the Son.[8]

But this was not the only plan proposed in that heavenly council. Satan (or Lucifer, as he was then known) was also present, and he offered an alternative plan: "Behold, here am I, send me, I will be thy son, and I will redeem all mankind, that one soul shall not be lost, and surely I will do it; wherefore, give me thine honor" (Pearl of Great Price, Moses 4:1).

Satan offered to redeem all mankind—"that one soul shall not be lost." But there was an important qualification: In the redemption proposed by Satan, there would be no choice, no proving ground, and he insisted on receiving the Father's honor and glory as the perfidious price for his type of redemption. Earth as a proving ground, an avenue to eternal life for the sons and daughters of God, would be obviated. The privilege of individual choice or moral agency—central to Christ's plan—was eliminated from Satan's.

Satan's plan was rejected, and he was cast out of heaven down to earth where he continues his opposition to the divine principle of moral agency.[9]

The existence of opposition is a corollary of moral agency. Opposition is necessary, for the children of God cannot grow without exercising their agency by choosing between alternatives. It was so from the foundation of creation, it was so in the Garden of Eden, and it is so today: Good stands in opposition to evil, and it is given to men and women to choose between them. According to Latter-day revelation, "the Lord God gave unto man that he should act for himself," which he could not do "save it should be that he was enticed by the one or the other" (Book of Mormon, 2 Nephi 2:16). Thus, the Lord's great plan of happiness is grounded upon this exercise of moral agency in the face of opposition.

Latter-day Saints believe that Jesus Christ redeemed the children of men from the effects of Adam's choice in the Garden, the so-called fall of Adam. Thus redeemed from the effects of Adam's "original sin," all men are assured of resurrection and immortality[10] and are kept from ultimately returning to the presence of God only by their own sinful choices.[11] The Messiah's atonement for individual sin is conditioned upon individual repentance, meaning the exercise of moral agency in obedience to God's commandments. The Book of Mormon teaches that the righteous exercise of agency brings joy, which is the very purpose of man's existence.[12]

The underlying foundation is the grace and atonement of Jesus Christ,[13] and the operative principle is moral agency—the right to choose in a world where there is opposition and where alternative choices are available, and then to be accountable for one's choices. This right of choice is the key to happiness, and it is essential to salvation. Every person has a God-given right to hear and a right to choose. Because of the central importance of these rights to the very purpose of life, no man or government is justified in interfering with them.

A BRIEF HISTORY OF LDS MISSIONARY WORK

BEGINNINGS AND MESSAGE

Missionary work began during the translation of the Book of Mormon in 1829 and intensified after the church was formally organized in April 1830. Samuel H. Smith, a brother of the Prophet Joseph Smith, traveled through towns in upstate New York to acquaint people with the newly published Book of Mormon. In the fall of 1830 four men were called to go on a mission to the western frontier. They preached in what is now New York, Ohio, Indiana, Illinois, Missouri, and Kansas. In the next few years, missionaries were sent to other American states and to parts of Canada.

The primary message of these missionaries was millennialist Christianity, deeply rooted in the Bible but generously flavored with the novelty of the new witness of the Book of Mormon, and strongly moved by the urgency inherent in the calling of a new prophet and the restoration of long-lost doctrines and authority.[14]

Within a decade missionary outreach had extended across the Atlantic. The calling of missionaries to England is representative of the boldness with which this missionary work was undertaken and the spirit of sacrifice with which it was carried out. This first overseas initiative came in June 1837, at a time when the still newly organized church consisted of only about fourteen thousand members struggling for economic survival on the frontiers of western America, in Ohio and Missouri. During a Sunday meeting, the Prophet Joseph Smith whispered to Heber C. Kimball, one of the twelve apostles, that the Spirit of the Lord had spoken that Heber should "go to England and proclaim my Gospel, and open the door of salvation to that nation."[15] Heber recorded his reaction:

> O, Lord, I am a man of stammering tongue, and altogether unfit for such a work; how can I go to preach in that land, which is so famed throughout Christendom for learning, knowledge and piety; the nursery of religion; and to a people whose intelligence is proverbial![16]

The idea of such a mission was almost more than Heber could bear, but his faith and obedience prevailed:

> However, all these considerations did not deter me from the path of duty; the moment I understood the will of my Heavenly Father, I felt a determination to go at all hazards, believing that He would support me by His almighty power, and endow me with every qualification that I needed; and although my family was dear to me, and I should have to leave them almost destitute, I felt that the cause of truth, the Gospel of Christ, outweighed every other consideration.[17]

In less than two months Kimball and several associates were preaching to congregations in England. Eight months later hundreds of converts had joined the church and many branches had been organized.

METHODS/PROCEDURES

The organization and procedures for the pursuit of missionary work by the new Church of Jesus Christ of Latter-day Saints were dictated by scripture and by early prophetic direction that continues to the present day. The missionaries were more than volunteers. They were called to service by a prophet, and the place and duration of their labors were given to them by that same authority. They did not go forth alone. They were commanded to go "two by two"

(Doctrine and Covenants 42:6). They were not compensated for their labors. Like the early disciples, they were even commanded to go without purse or scrip.[18] As with the early disciples, that command was later relaxed,[19] but LDS missionaries remain uncompensated.

The method of their preaching was consistent with Bible teachings, amplified and reaffirmed by modern revelation. The early apostles taught that Christians should "follow after the things which make for peace" (Rom 14:19). They should avoid contention, debate, strife, and wrath, and they should communicate with others in gentleness and meekness.[20] In revelations given specifically to the restored church by its prophet and applied faithfully by its missionaries, the Lord reaffirmed these directions: "And let your preaching be the warning voice, every man to his neighbor, in mildness and in meekness" (Doctrine and Covenants 38:41). There should be no contention. The gospel was not to be preached "in wrath nor with strife" (60:14). In publishing their glad tidings, the elders should "do it with all humility, trusting in me, reviling not against revilers" (19:30).

The Prophet Joseph Smith gave instructions that imposed limits on missionaries' teaching children without the consent of the head of the household, an apparent effort to preserve family harmony and honor the government of the home.

> And first, it becomes an Elder . . . instead of commencing with children, or those who look up to parents or guardians to influence their minds, thereby drawing them from their duties, which they rightfully owe these legal guardians, they should commence their labors with parents, or guardians; and their teachings should be such as are calculated to turn the hearts of the fathers to the children, and the hearts of children to the fathers; and no influence should be used with children, contrary to the consent of their parents or guardians. . . . [T]herefore, first teach the parents, and then, with their consent, persuade the children to embrace the Gospel also.[21]

In its content the message of the Mormon missionaries was confident but not confrontational, firm but not negative. Its essence is expressed in parts of two sermons by Brigham Young, one of the church's earliest and most successful missionaries, later the second president of the church.

> When I first came into the Church it was a subject of considerable thought to me why people whom I knew to be as good and moral as they could be, should have to repent. But I could see afterwards that if they had nothing else to repent of they could and ought to repent of their false religions, of their narrow, contracted creeds in which they were bound, of the ordinances of men, and get something better. . . . "Well," say the ministers, "we have lived according to the light we have received." We say, are you willing to receive more? If so, here is more for you. So far as

your faith in Christ goes, and your morality, we say, Amen. But here is something more.[22]

If this is the work of God, let us understand its beauty and glory. I do not say that all are like myself; but from the day I commenced preaching the gospel to this present moment, I never had a feeling in my heart to occupy much time in preaching hell to the people, or in telling them much about being damned. There are the kingdoms and worlds which God has prepared, and which are waiting for the just. There are more beauty, glory, excellency, knowledge, power, and heavenly things than I have time to talk about, without spending my time in talking about the hells prepared for the damned. I have not time to talk much about them.[23]

PERSISTENCE

Despite the severe persecution and extreme poverty of the leaders and members of the church in its first twenty-five years (including the murder of Joseph Smith, the expulsion of Mormons from the states of Missouri and Illinois, and the epic migration of Mormon pioneers across the great plains of America from 1846 through 1869), the early Mormons continued to carry out their commission to send missionaries to every nation.

In late 1839 seven of the twelve apostles left to fulfill their call to the British Isles. Two more apostles joined them there. They preached as missionaries in England for over a year.[24] These missionaries departed on their assignments in that stressful period when the Mormons, driven out of Missouri, were just beginning to settle in a swampy, sickly area along the Mississippi River in western Illinois. Some of these men were sick when they departed; all of them left families in stressful circumstances. The nobility of the Mormon wives who supported their husbands in this undertaking is no less than their husbands'. A recent history gives this description:

Many members of the Twelve were struck with the ague as they prepared to depart for England. Wilford Woodruff, who was very ill, left his wife, Phoebe, almost without food and the necessities of life. George A. Smith, the youngest Apostle, was so sick that he had to be carried to the wagon, and a man who saw him asked the driver if they had been robbing the graveyard. Only Parley P. Pratt, who took his wife and children with him, his brother Orson Pratt, and John Taylor were free from disease as they left Nauvoo, although Elder Taylor later became terribly ill and almost died as they traveled to New York City.

Brigham Young was so ill that he was unable to walk even a short distance without assistance, and his companion, Heber C. Kimball, was no better. Their wives and families, too, lay suffering. When the Apostles reached the crest of a hill a short distance from their homes, both lying in a wagon, they felt as though they could not endure leaving their families in so pitiful a condition. At Heber's suggestion, they struggled to their feet, waved their hats over their heads, and shouted three times, "Hurrah, Hurrah, for Israel." Their wives, Mary Ann and Vilate, gained strength enough to stand and, leaning against the door frame, they cried out, "Good-bye, God bless you." The two men returned to their wagon beds with a spirit of joy and satisfaction at seeing their wives standing instead of lying sick in bed.[25]

Their preaching was notably successful. After one year, in the spring of 1841, there were 5,864 members in the British Isles, with a steady stream of new members flowing across the Atlantic to gather with the Saints in Illinois and strengthen the new church.[26] This flow of emigrants from Europe (first from England and later from Scandinavia and the continent) to gather with the Saints in what they called Zion would continue for almost a century.

In the midst of all of the adversities suffered by the Mormon people and the difficulties of transportation and communication in the mid-nineteenth century, the missionaries of this restored faith were comforted and strengthened by the promise God had given them:

> And the voice of warning shall be unto all people, by the mouths of my disciples, whom I have chosen in these last days.
>
> And they shall go forth and none shall stay them, for I the Lord have commanded them (Doctrine and Covenants 1:4-5).

One of the greatest examples of the seriousness with which the early Mormons took their missionary responsibilities is their continuing to send missionaries even during the demands and disruptions of their western migration. Only two years after the initial band of pioneers arrived in the valley of the Great Salt Lake, at a time when the pioneers' grip on survival in that hostile area was still tenuous and when most Mormons were still on the trail westward or struggling to get resources to make the trip, the church sent out a new wave of missionaries. At the general conference in the city of the Great Salt Lake on October 6, 1849, the church called missionaries to go to Scandinavia, France, Germany, Italy, and the South Pacific.[27] Similarly, at a special conference in August 1852, ninety-eight men were assigned to missions. One of the church leaders remarked: "The missions we will call for during this conference, are generally, not to be very long ones; probably from 3 to 7 years will be as long as any man will be absent from his family."[28]

The group of missionaries who were called from the pioneer settlements in that first decade preached the gospel in various countries of Europe, in South America, South Africa, China, India, Australia, Hawaii, New Zealand, and other islands in the South Pacific. As these missionaries rode or walked eastward along the pioneer trail, they passed other Saints headed for the gathering place in the Rocky Mountains.

Missionary Impact on LDS Growth and Personal Goals

The missionary work of the first half-century of the church (1830-80) gave a mighty impetus to the ranks of its members. It also provided an indelible impression on the thinking and commitment of its members. It does not over-state the point to say that missionary zeal, including potential, preparation, and performance, is fundamental to the identity of Latter-day Saints. It sets them apart.

Since its organization in 1830 the membership of The Church of Jesus Christ of Latter-day Saints has increased at a rate a non-LDS sociologist, Rodney Stark, has described as "the Mormon 'miracle' of rapid growth."[29] From six members in April 1830, the church grew to 16,865 at the conclusion of 1840. At the end of 1850, after a decade of persecution and forced exodus to the West, the total was 51,839. Membership totals at the end of the succeeding decades through 1900 were 61,082; 90,130; 133,628; 188,263; and 283,765. A half-century later, at the end of 1950, the total membership was 1,111,314. By the end of 1990 it was 7,761,179.[30]

Observers have noted that the church growth rate since 1860 has never been less than about 30 percent per decade. In some decades it has exceeded 40 percent, and since 1950 the growth rate has accelerated to more than 50 percent in each decade.[31] In 1984, Stark's "high estimate" of LDS total mem-bership was 10.4 million in the year 2000 and 23.5 million in the year 2020.[32] So far, the church is well ahead of these predictions, having noted its 10 mil-lionth member early in 1997.

The enormous continuing impact of missionary work on the thinking, con-scientious beliefs, and behavior of Latter-day Saints is attributable in impor-tant measure to two unusual LDS doctrines or practices involving individual and family histories.

First, obedient to one of the earliest revelations given through their prophet,[33] Latter-day Saints have been faithful history-writers and journal-keepers. As a result, the sacrifices and accomplishments of Mormon missionaries from the earliest days are well recorded and proudly disseminated within the families of their posterity.

Second, in furtherance of their unique belief in the eternal duration of fam-ily relations, Latter-day Saints have been avid genealogists, assembling the world's greatest collection of family records and pioneering techniques for searching out and disseminating family connections and histories. As a result, Mormons are unusually conscious of their ancestry, including where and how their forebears came into the church.

All of this gives Latter-day Saints an unusual sensitivity and sophistication about the general effects of missionary work upon the growth and accomplish-ments of their church and an unusual appreciation of the effects of missionary work upon them personally. Pride in missionary forebearers and appreciation for the missionary work that converted their own ancestors provide Latter-day Saints with a strong foundation for personal commitments and sacrifices to continue that missionary tradition.

THE NATURE OF MISSIONARY WORK IN THE CHURCH OF JESUS CHRIST OF LATTER-DAY SAINTS TODAY

PROSELYTING: AN INVITATION

The Savior's gentle summons to "come and see" (Jn 1:39) provides the lode-star of formal missionary work in the church. What do you know about the Mormons? Would you like to know more? Known as the Golden Questions, these two questions give substance to the slogan first coined some four decades ago by church president David O. McKay: "Every member a missionary."

In their simplicity and widespread application, the Golden Questions give expression to a member's duty to "share the gospel" with everyone—neighbors, coworkers, and even strangers casually encountered in the common-place affairs of life. Their tenor and openness reveal much about the Mormons' low-key approach to missionary work. In the Latter-day Saint lexicon, the word *proselyting* means missionary work, which is simply an invitation. Mormons eschew any tactic that smacks of coercion, high pressure salesman-ship, argumentation, or economic incentive.

The Golden Questions offer every invitee an opportunity to exercise personal choice to "know more" or to decline the invitation with a graceful exit from the encounter. They are universally appealing. Neither intimidating nor confrontational, these questions softly beckon, "come and see."

The church's "come and see" philosophy is manifest in the conservatively dressed young men and women who make up the body of the church's full-time missionary force and who are a familiar presence in many communities across the earth. A later section will describe the missionary culture from which these young people come and the policies and practices that govern their missionary labors.

The church's "come and see" philosophy is also apparent in numerous "visitors' centers" at church points of interest, usually temples or historic sites. These visitors' centers, such as the world-famous Temple Square in Salt Lake City, Utah, are often "mini-museums" of church history related to the site and virtually always have displays illustrating essential beliefs of the church. They are staffed by full-time missionaries, usually retired couples and sister mission-aries serving from six to eighteen months, who provide guided tours and an-swer questions in a spirit of warmth and friendliness. Members in the vicinity of a visitors' center are encouraged to invite their nonmember friends and acquain-tances to visit the center with them. Those who are interested are encouraged to learn more about the church by inviting missionaries to their homes. But there is no pressure; the approach is always the same: "Come and see."

The church uses many opportunities to present itself and the gospel in an accurate and positive light through the public media. The renowned Mormon Tabernacle Choir, whose weekly nondenominational worship services are the oldest continuous network radio program in the United States, may be the best known example. Other media efforts take the form of brief paid announcements on radio and television, such as the church's award-winning "Home Front" series, which highlights various aspects of positive family life. Whether directly or indirectly, such media efforts are intended to bring together the gospel and those who are seeking for answers to life's questions.

The mild summons to "come and see" that is the substance of formal missionary work and public relations also guides most of the other activities of the church. Some of these carry a direct outreach because they are made available to all. Examples include efforts to translate and disseminate modern scriptures and other church publications and the church's pioneering work in microfilming and preserving family history records—the largest such data base in the world—and in encouraging their use.

The church's activity program is broad spectrum, almost literally from cradle to grave. Children's activities are conducted by the Primary. Young Men and Young Women organizations sponsor a multifaceted program of social, educational, athletic, and spiritual activities for adolescent youth. Priesthood quorums provide religious instruction and social activities for men. Relief Society, the oldest women's organization in the United States, provides opportunities for compassionate service and personal enrichment for women. Associated Priesthood and Relief Society activities serve the special interests of single adults. In all of these, rank and file Latter-day Saints beckon their nonmember friends to come, see, and participate.

But it is the lives of church members themselves that are the most compelling manifestation of the "come and see" philosophy. Just as the Savior taught that "ye shall know them by their fruits" (Mt 7:16), so the "fruits" of the doctrines of the restored gospel are woven into the fabric of the lives of Latter-day Saint men and women, youth, and children. The Latter-day Saints are a gracious, family-oriented, Christian people. They gently urge all to "come and see."

Thus, for Latter-day Saints, proselyting is a diffuse notion that permeates every facet of the church. But in its essence it is simply an invitation to learn more. Full-time missionaries, with their conservative apparel and distinctive name tags, are merely the most visible aspect of this invitation.

PREPARATION FOR FULL-TIME MISSIONARY SERVICE

> I hope they call me on a mission,
> When I have grown a foot or two.
> I hope by then I will be ready
> To teach and preach and work as missionaries do.[34]

Such are the words of a song learned by every Latter-day Saint child in Primary, the organization for children ages three through eleven. It expresses the hope of every Mormon boy, and many Mormon girls, to have the opportunity of serving as a full-time missionary.

This children's song is but one manifestation of the "witnessing culture" in which Latter-day Saint children are raised. The church's hymnal[35] is filled with missionary-oriented hymns, some of them dating to the earliest days of the church and many others familiar to all Christians. No fewer than thirty-six hymns relate to missionary work. Some are directly related to those called to full-time service, such as "Go, Ye Messengers of Glory":

> Go, Ye messengers of glory;
> Run ye legates of the skies.
> Go and tell the pleasing story
> That a glorious angel flies,
> Great and mighty,
> Great and mighty,
> With a message from the skies.[36]

Others, such as "I'll Go Where You Want Me to Go," have more general application:

> It may not be on the mountain height or over the stormy sea,
> It may not be at the battle front my Lord will have need of me.
> But if, by a still, small voice he calls to paths that I do not
>   know,
> I'll answer, dear Lord, with my hand in thine:
> I'll go where you want me to go.
> I'll go where you want me to go, dear Lord,
> Over mountain, or plain or sea;
> I'll say what you want me to say, dear Lord,
> I'll be what you want me to be.[37]

In every case, these inspiring hymns, sung from childhood, reinforce a spiritual call of conscience for every faithful Latter-day Saint. Their words inspire Mormons of all ages to carry the gospel message far and near: "Because I have been given much, I too must give." "Come, all ye sons of God, who have received the priesthood." "Called to serve him, heavenly King of glory." "The time is far spent, there is little remaining." "We are sowing, daily sowing, countless seeds of good and ill." These first lines are but a sampler from the rich treasury of missionary hymns loved by church members everywhere.

A mission is an experience that most LDS young men and their families prepare for, literally from the moment of birth. While young women are eligible for missionary service and are very effective as part of the missionary force if they choose to serve, missionary service is the special province of young men as a priesthood obligation. It also provides full-time preparation for a life of part-time service in the church's lay priesthood.

In family settings, such as the weekly Family Home Evening, parents teach their sons of the great opportunity and duty that awaits them when they reach age nineteen. Fathers and mothers who have served as missionaries share treasured missionary experiences, emphasizing not only their love for the lands, peoples, and languages where they served, but also the rich spiritual experiences they received in teaching the gospel of Jesus Christ.

From the time they are old enough to receive an allowance or a gift of a few coins from relatives or friends, children are taught to pay 10 percent of their financial increase as tithing for the Lord and to set aside an additional amount toward the cost of their missions. Since missionaries are not compensated by the church, the cost of their service is borne by them, their families, and for those with insufficient means, by other church members in their local units. So that no willing young person will be denied the opportunity of serving a mission, a general missionary fund is maintained from member contributions for missionaries whose families or local units are too poor to sustain them.

Church organizations further the young people's preparation for missionary service. Besides singing missionary-oriented songs and hymns, Primary children are taught to prepare themselves to receive a missionary call from the prophet. Stories and experiences of great missionaries are shared. Present and former full-time missionaries are invited periodically to share their testimonies of missionary work.

Preparation for missionary service is a prime focus of the Aaronic (lesser) Priesthood, which is held by young men aged twelve and older. Sunday lessons extol the virtues of missionary service and teach practical skills necessary for such service. Through corollary youth activities, such as Boy Scouts in the United States and Canada, youth are taught self-reliance and the development of virtue and character that will make them exemplary missionaries, as well as exemplary citizens and church members all their lives.

Another resource for preparing future missionaries is the LDS "seminary," which provides scriptural and theological instruction for young men and women of high school age. It is available in some locations during the school day as "released time" from secular education, but for most Mormon youth the world over it is an early morning program conducted daily before school. Seminary students arise early in order to attend their seminary class of approximately forty-five minutes and then hurry to their high schools for the normal school day. Seminary requires a significant measure of self-discipline by LDS students, who must also satisfy academic demands and often participate in extracurricular activities or part-time employment. A young man or woman who graduates from the four-year seminary program has developed a solid grounding in the scriptures and has received excellent preparation for missionary service.

Through all of this, young men and women are encouraged to maintain high moral standards that they may be worthy to accept a call to missionary service. This includes complete obedience to the law of chastity (abstinence from sexual relations of any kind outside the bonds of marriage) and adherence to the "Word of Wisdom" (abstinence from tobacco, tea, coffee, alcohol, and drugs). Leaders of local congregations (usually bishops and their counselors) meet individually with every young man and woman twice a year in an interview to encourage them to maintain standards of righteousness and to assist them in meeting the challenges of adolescence. The bishop, who presides over the ward, understands that his first duty is to help these young people prepare for life, and in the case of young men, to help them prepare for missionary service.

When a young man nears his nineteenth birthday, the bishop interviews him as to his worthiness, helps him complete the necessary forms, and recommends him to the president of the church for a call as a missionary. Then begins an anxious period of waiting for the prospective missionary and his family. The arrival of the long-awaited letter of call for missionary service in an assigned geographical area is an event that, in many cases, the missionary has looked forward to literally all his life. Now he will lay aside education and other plans in order to serve the Lord.

Mature couples who have reached retirement and who are healthy and financially able are also encouraged to make themselves available for missionary service for periods ranging from six to eighteen months. Besides sharing the gospel with nonmembers, such couples often render valuable service in strengthening the church, especially where it is relatively new and the local leaders are still inexperienced. For them, the sacrifice is somewhat different from the young missionaries. Retired couples leave behind the comforts of home and the joy of association with their children and grandchildren. Yet they do so gladly because missionary service is such a part of being a Latter-day Saint. Many serve two or more missions.

A missionary call is an experience in which the entire congregation participates. On a Sunday before departure, a "missionary farewell" is held in the weekly sacrament service. The missionary and members of his or her family are invited to participate, praying and delivering brief sermons on appropriate gospel subjects. And when a missionary returns, he or she again speaks in the sacrament meeting, giving a report of service and sharing spiritual experiences. These farewells and homecomings do much to foster the missionary culture that pervades the church in every ward and branch.

Bidding goodbye to family and loved ones, who will not be seen again for two years, the newly called missionary reports to a Missionary Training Center (MTC). Here, he or she will receive instruction in the scriptures, a standard missionary lesson plan, and the rules of conduct expected of missionaries. Missionaries assigned to missions where they will speak their native tongue normally spend three weeks in the MTC. A missionary called to learn a new language spends nine weeks in the MTC, beginning the difficult task of mastering a new tongue—one that he will come to love as dearly as his own.

It is in the MTC that the new missionary joins his voice with dozens, even hundreds, of other missionaries in singing that spirited anthem of many Christians:

Called to serve Him, heavenly King of glory;
Chosen e'er to witness for his name,
Far and wide we tell the Father's story,
Far and wide his love proclaim.

Onward, ever onward, as we glory in his name,
Forward, pressing forward, as a triumph song we sing.
God our strength will be; press forward ever
Called to serve our King.[38]

Missionary Work in the Field

Missionaries come from many lands and cultures. Some are assigned to serve in their own land; others serve far from home. An American may be assigned, as it were, in Peoria, Perth, or Paris; a Canadian in Montreal or Montevideo; a Russian in St. Petersburg (Russia) or St. Petersburg (Florida). The young men are all unmarried, between the ages of nineteen and twenty-five, and are called to serve for a period of two years. Young women, also unmarried, are eligible to serve at age twenty-one and serve for eighteen months. All have received their call from the president of the church. All devote their full-time efforts to missionary service.

They are young, but as Paul wrote to Timothy, "Let no man despise thy youth" (1 Tm 4:12). Commenting on that verse to young men and women called as missionaries, Church President Gordon B. Hinckley has said:

> What he [Paul] is saying is that if you reflect in your lives the elements of the gospel, people will look beyond your youth as in the faces of men and women who are believers in word, in their conversations, in their acts of love and charity, in spirit, their attitude, in faith, in purity.[39]

Missionaries of the church serve in approximately 125 nations across the earth. In every land their standards of behavior are the same. They are expected to live according to a strict code of conduct. Among other things, missionaries are expected (1) to keep their thoughts, words, and actions in harmony with the message of the gospel; (2) to dress neatly, bathe frequently, polish shoes, and keep clothes clean, mended, and wrinkle-free; (3) never to be alone with anyone of the opposite sex or to participate in dating or flirtation; (4) to obey mission rules, civil regulations, visa requirements, and laws of the land where they serve; (5) never to become involved in political or commercial activities; and (6) to respect the customs and culture of those among whom they serve, including their religious beliefs, practices, and sacred sites.

Going forth two-by-two in their labors, Mormon missionaries reside in the midst of the people and become fluent in their language and knowledgeable of their culture. They grow to love the land and people where they serve, often to the point that their feelings run almost as deeply as for their native lands. These feelings are carried home at the conclusion of their missionary service.

Although functioning independently in their assigned pairs, missionaries are carefully supervised by the mission president, the presiding officer in the mission. A mission has specific geographic limits, and each missionary is assigned to a specific local area within it. Each is expected to remain with a missionary companion within that area at all times. Periodically, on the basis of inspiration, the mission president will transfer a missionary to a new locale and assign a new companion. Periodic transfers benefit the missionary and the work. The freedom to transfer missionaries throughout the mission is vital to mission operations.

The mission president is a mature church leader and man of experience and sound judgment. He is very carefully selected by the First Presidency and the Quorum of the twelve apostles. Usually he is already proficient in the predominant language of the mission. Accompanied by his family, he relocates to the area of his mission, where he normally presides for a period of three years.

From within his missionary force, the mission president calls other leaders to assist him in looking after the missionaries. These missionary leaders live and serve in the same locale as the missionaries they supervise. Their greatest influence is through their own exemplary service, but they also spend considerable time meeting and working with those missionaries under their supervision. Leadership opportunities are rotated among qualified missionaries in order to provide experience to as many as possible.

TEACHING THE GOSPEL

The principal responsibilities of missionaries are to teach the restored gospel of Jesus Christ to those wishing to hear it, to baptize those desiring baptism, and to help local church members strengthen new converts in their recently adopted faith. All of these responsibilities depend in the first instance on finding people to teach. Missionaries locate "investigators" in a number of ways. Local members introduce them to family members, friends, and acquaintances. Where church messages are broadcast on television or radio, potential investigators often seek out the missionaries directly. Where permitted by local law and custom, missionaries "tract" by going door to door; where tracting is not permitted, the missionaries merely extend an invitation to learn more to those persons whom they encounter in the normal course of daily life.

When someone expresses interest in learning more, the missionaries meet with him or her in a series of discussions organized according to a standard lesson plan. Based upon foundational scriptures, this lesson plan presents basic doctrinal principles in an organized manner designed to assist the sincere investigator to a fuller understanding of the gospel of Jesus Christ. As President Hinckley recently said, "[We are] not argumentative. We do not debate. We, in effect, simply say to others, 'Bring all the good that you have and let us see if we can add to it.'"[40]

Missionaries explain gospel principles, but each investigator must ascertain the truthfulness of such principles by personal study and prayer.[41] Each additional step is predicated on the investigator's interest. The missionaries invite investigators to attend church meetings and to make key commitments, such as to pray, to read the Book of Mormon and other scriptures, and, eventually, to be baptized once the Spirit witnesses that the teachings of the missionaries are true.[42] Agreement to such commitments leads naturally to baptism; unwillingness to make such commitments gracefully terminates the discussions with the missionaries. Because of the profound importance of each person's moral agency, the desires of the investigators are always paramount and determinative. They will be invited—even urged—but not pressured or coerced.

Missionary work is not a numbers game or a recruiting exercise. The goal of the church's missionary program is baptism and eternal life for those who accept the increased understanding and ordinances offered by the missionaries. That understanding teaches that baptism and eternal life are the greatest of all the gifts of God and are available to all God's children.

Baptism and the acceptance of membership in the church are a significant, life-changing commitment. By modern revelation, the Lord has set forth the following requirements to be baptized into the church:

> All those who humble themselves before God, and desire to be baptized, and come forth with broken hearts and contrite spirits, and witness before the Church that they have truly repented of all their sins, and are willing to take upon them the name of Jesus Christ, having a determination to serve him to the end, and truly manifest by their works that they have received of the Spirit of Christ unto the remission of their sins, shall be received by baptism into his Church (Doctrine and Covenants 20:37).

Since baptism is for the remission of sins, it must be preceded by genuine repentance. Among other things, this means that a person applying for baptism commits (1) to live a good and Christian life; (2) to adhere to principles of strict virtue and chastity; (3) to keep the Lord's law of health (the Word of Wisdom); (4) to attend church meetings regularly; (5) to serve actively in the church; and (6) to contribute one-tenth of his or her income annually to the Lord as tithing, as well as other offerings.

Why are people willing to make such commitments? The answer is found in the testimony of individual converts that they are joining the church of Jesus Christ restored to the earth in these latter days and that the authority by which they are being baptized is in very deed the priesthood of God, efficacious in this world and in the world to come. The message of The Church of Jesus Christ of Latter-day Saints is that it has that priesthood and the fullness of the gospel of Jesus Christ. It extends an invitation to every man, woman, and child upon the earth to "come and see."

CHURCH ACTIVITIES WITH INCIDENTAL MISSIONARY EFFECTS

While the spirit of missionary work is woven into the very fabric of the church, not every church activity is intended to produce converts. Some have an effect on missionary work only incidentally and unintentionally. The same spirit of concern for all people that motivates formal missionary work inspires other church activities, such as those focusing on temporal welfare and humanitarian services.

Welfare Program

The church is concerned with the temporal and physical welfare of its members as well as their spiritual well-being. Less than a year after the church was organized in 1830, the Lord revealed to the church through the Prophet Joseph Smith that "[T]hou wilt remember the poor, and consecrate of thy properties for their support that which thou hast to impart unto them, with a covenant and a deed which cannot be broken" (Doctrine and Covenants 42:30). The bishop and his counselors were appointed by the Lord to the particular stewardship of husbanding the "substance" set aside for the benefit of the poor. This concern for the poor and needy of the church has developed into an extensive commodity system of "bishop's storehouses" and includes monthly cash "fast offerings" contributed by church members, both used to assist the poor.

Every member has ready access to these welfare resources. Bishops authorize distribution of commodities from the storehouses and dispense fast-offering funds when commodities will not meet a particular need. Members must look first for help from their extended families before turning to the church. Those receiving church assistance are expected to work for what they receive. Since assistance is intended to be for limited duration, bishops and other church leaders help those assisted to regain the capability to provide for themselves. Thus, want is alleviated while preserving the dignity of the individual.

Just as welfare is not administered as a dole for members, neither is it used as an incentive to bring people into the church. Pre-baptismal interviews determine the willingness of a baptismal candidate to accept the obligations of membership and filter out any who might be seeking membership for ulterior reasons. Rather than being a "meal ticket," church membership is an opportunity for service to others. As stated in Latter-day Saint scripture:

[N]ow, as ye [baptismal candidates] are desirous to come into the fold of God, and to be called his people, and are willing to bear one another's burdens, that they may be light;

Yea, and are willing to mourn with those that mourn; yea, and comfort those that stand in need of comfort. . . .

Now I say unto you, if this be the desire of your hearts, what have you against being baptized in the name of the Lord? (Book of Mormon, Mosiah 18:8-10).[43]

Humanitarian Services

The same concern for people that sparks LDS missionary work and the welfare program for church members also motivates humanitarian assistance to the poor and needy of the world without regard to their religious affiliation. Indeed, church humanitarian aid is intended primarily for those who are not Mormons. To avoid any risk that such aid might be misunderstood as a subtle inducement to seek membership, this humanitarian aid is not distributed by missionaries or through the church's missionary organization. Rather, the church acts through a satellite organization, Latter-day Saint Charities, in distributing vast quantities of food, clothing, and material, as well as financial assistance.

This humanitarian work extends across the earth in dozens of countries where assistance with health, sanitation, and personal hygiene are desperately needed. In the immediate wake of earthquakes, hurricanes, typhoons, floods, famines, wars, and other disasters, the church has distributed cash contributions and large quantities of needed commodities and supplies.

While humanitarian and charitable aid have been given throughout the history of the church, such aid has significantly increased in recent years. Since 1985 the church has been involved in more than 2,340 humanitarian projects in 137 countries (including Mexico, Bangladesh, China, the Philippines, Bosnia, Croatia, Serbia, North Korea, and Ethiopia, to name only a few), contributing over $170 million worth of aid. In addition, the church supports and promotes a wide array of humanitarian initiatives around the world, such as village banking in Guatemala, micro-enterprise projects in Armenia, surgical initiatives in the Philippines, and vocational skill training in India. In 1996 alone the church distributed more than 1 million pounds of medical and educational equipment and supplies in seventy countries and sufficient clothing for an estimated 8.7 million people in fifty-eight countries. In North Korea, where the church has no members, assistance has amounted to $3.1 million and has included 2,150 tons of corn, powdered milk, flour, and medical supplies, 400 tons of fertilizer, pesticides, and seeds, and more than 500 seedling apple trees. In 1999 the church sent over 2.5 million pounds of food, clothing, blankets, and soap, and over $500,000 in cash contributions to help refugees from Kosovo.[44] Where possible, humanitarian projects are designed to help strengthen individual self-reliance and local autonomy, instead of merely providing a handout. Thus, the church donated twenty-five tractors to help the cleanup and farming efforts of returning Kosovar refugees.

One moving example of such assistance came in the aftermath of World War II. In 1946 and 1947 Dutch members of the church sent some 160 tons of potatoes to Germany, even though they themselves were still on meager rations. In 1985 members of the church were asked to participate in two "fast Sundays" (that is, to donate the value of two meals not eaten on those days) to assist the hungry in Ethiopia. The proceeds of this endeavor ultimately totaled $9.6 million distributed in food and other necessary goods to starving

Ethiopians, virtually entirely through non-LDS channels such as the International Red Cross and Red Crescent and Catholic Relief Services.[45]

All such humanitarian aid is distributed without strings. The church does not seek "rice Christians." Rather, such assistance is given in love to help those in need without regard to their religious affiliation or interest in Mormonism.

RELATIONS WITH GOVERNMENTS

In a letter dated March 1, 1842, the Prophet Joseph Smith responded to a request from Mr. John Wentworth, the editor and proprietor of the *Chicago Democrat*, for a written "sketch of the rise, progress, persecution, and faith of the Latter-day Saints."[46] After giving the requested historical information, the Prophet's response, the "Wentworth Letter," concludes with thirteen short declarative statements summarizing the central doctrines of the church. These have since been extracted and canonized in a doctrinal statement known as the Articles of Faith. Two of these Articles of Faith are directly pertinent in describing the church's attitude toward governments and their rightful place in the religious affairs of men.

A COMMITMENT TO OBEY, HONOR, AND SUSTAIN THE LAW

The Twelfth Article of Faith states: "We believe in being subject to kings, presidents, rulers and magistrates, in obeying, honoring, and sustaining the law" (Articles of Faith, Pearl of Great Price). Events occurring shortly after this declaration illustrate the seriousness of the Latter-day Saints' commitment to this principle.

The early history of the church was marred by intense persecution. Some of this was in response to Joseph Smith's claim that he had seen and conversed with God the Father, his son Jesus Christ, and other heavenly beings. Some of it was spawned by economic and political jealousies in the developing communities along the remote western frontier where the church had its origins. Whatever its causes, the effect of the persecution was to force the Mormons to move repeatedly. Initially organized in upstate New York, the main body of the church moved to Kirtland, Ohio, and then in succession to Jackson County, Missouri; Daviess and Caldwell Counties, Missouri; Nauvoo, Illinois; and ultimately to the Great Basin. In each frontier community, law enforcement was either impotent or in league with those conspiring against the Mormons. Repeated appeals to state officials in Ohio, Missouri, Illinois, and even to the United States government elicited no protection.

Then, in June 1844, Joseph Smith and his brother, Hyrum, were assassinated by a mob while incarcerated in Carthage, Illinois.[47] By February 1846 mob persecution around Nauvoo, Illinois, where most church members were then congregated, became so intense that the Mormon people were forced to commence their withdrawal from Illinois. Though it was the dead of winter, many Mormons, under the leadership of Brigham Young, loaded what belongings they could into wagons and, abandoning their comfortable homes, crossed the frozen Mississippi River and headed west across Iowa. Within eight months virtually all had left Nauvoo—the last group at gunpoint! The privation and suffering of the Saints as they struggled across Iowa, destitute and mired in a seemingly endless sea of mud, was heart-rending. They were homeless, with only the great wilderness before them. With the Rocky Mountains their destination, they were leaving the United States.

Into that desperate situation, in late June 1846, Captain James Allen of the 1st U.S. Dragoons rode with an urgent appeal to the Mormons from the United States government. The United States had declared war on Mexico, and President James K. Polk asked the Mormons to raise a battalion of five hundred men to march to Santa Fe as part of General Stephen Kearny's Army of the West. To rank-and-file Mormons, this appeal was stupefying. Not only would their indigent families be left without able-bodied men, but this appeal was coming from the very government that had stood by disinterestedly time and again while mobs forced their depredations upon the Mormons, sometimes under color of state law. In the minds of some, they had every right to ignore the appeal and to turn their backs on the United States.

President Brigham Young, their leader, saw it differently. For one thing, the Saints could use the soldiers' wages to buy needed equipment and supplies for the trek west to the Great Basin. More fundamentally, their country was in need, and their government had called. President Young decided: the Saints would respond to the call. At his personal appeal, the Mormon Battalion was organized, literally overnight. Its 497 men marched away leaving wives and mothers, sisters and daughters to provide and care for their needy families. Their country had called, and the Mormons responded.

Suffering tremendous hardships, the Mormon Battalion ultimately pioneered a road across the Great American Desert to San Diego on the shores of the Pacific Ocean, a road that would later be followed by many thousands seeking their fortunes in California. The Mormon Battalion's march of more than two thousand miles was to be the longest foot march of infantry in the nation's history. Their courage and fortitude is a storied chapter in the history of the United States. It stands as a monument to church members' deep commitment to their Twelfth Article of Faith.

Latter-day Saints are law-abiding and loyal citizens. They obey the law, participate in the affairs of government at all levels, vote in elections, and serve in the armed forces of their respective nations. No government need ever view with suspicion the Latter-day Saint congregations within its borders. To the contrary, it can take comfort in the assurance that none of its citizens is more committed to "obeying, honoring, and sustaining the law" than its Mormon citizens.

In a revelation given to Joseph Smith in 1831, the Lord said: "Let no man break the laws of the land, for he that keepeth the laws of God hath no need to break the laws of the land" (Doctrine and Covenants 58:21). Accordingly,

Latter-day Saints take seriously the Savior's admonition: "Render therefore unto Caesar the things which are Caesar's; and unto God the things which are God's" (Mt 22:21). This philosophy is manifest in the church's missionary program.

Most nations have specific legal requirements governing religion and religious representatives. While there are many similarities, each country has its own different requirements. Most require churches to register with the national government; many also require registration at the regional and/or local level as a condition of holding meetings, acquiring real property, opening bank accounts, and engaging in missionary activity. In some countries foreign religious representatives may need visas.

The church strives to identify and to comply with all legal requirements. It approaches every nation through the "front door" (that is, by complying with legal requirements). It expects its missionaries to abide by the law of the jurisdiction where they are serving and to respect local customs and culture.

GOVERNMENT'S DUTY TO GUARANTEE THE RIGHT TO WORSHIP

Latter-day Saints, who believe in "rendering unto Caesar" that which is properly Caesar's, also believe that governments have a responsibility to distinguish between "the things which are Caesar's" and "the things which are God's" and to guarantee religious freedom for the latter.

The church's Eleventh Article of Faith states: "We claim the privilege of worshiping Almighty God according to the dictates of our own conscience, and allow all men the same privilege, let them worship how, where, or what they may" (Articles of Faith, Pearl of Great Price).

In furtherance of the God-given right of moral agency, including the right to hear and to choose among competing philosophies, doctrines, and religions, Latter-day Saints believe that governments have a solemn duty to protect and preserve that agency to every person within the reach of their jurisdictions. The church's declaration of belief states:

> We believe that no government can exist in peace, except such laws are framed and held inviolate as will secure to each individual the free exercise of conscience, the right and control of property, and the protection of life (Doctrine and Covenants 134:2).

No government can long endure that does not secure these basic freedoms to its citizens. The scrap heap of history is strewn with the tattered remnants of regimes that behaved otherwise.

The Book of Mormon account of an ancient people in the Americas records what modern history teaches with tragic eloquence, namely, that the fire of freedom burns naturally in the human breast:

> And now the design of the Nephites was to support their lands and their houses, and their wives, and their children, that they might preserve them

from the hands of their enemies; and also that they might preserve their rights and their privileges, yea and also their liberty, that they might worship God according to their desires (Book of Mormon, Alma 43:9).

Nevertheless, the Nephites were inspired by a better cause [than their enemies], for they were not fighting for monarchy nor power but they were fighting for their homes and their liberties, their wives and their children, and their all, yea, for their rites of worship and their church (Book of Mormon, Alma 43:45).

The chronicles of God, as with the chronicles of history, teach that every man recognizes in his heart the God-given gift of freedom, or agency. Truly, "no government *can* exist in peace" that does not guarantee this to its citizens.

In no aspect of life are these fundamental freedoms more important than as they relate to every man's freedom of worship—his moral agency. Mormons believe that "[i]t is [not] just to mingle religious influence with civil government" (Doctrine and Covenants 134:9). This means that "religious societ[ies] [do not have] authority to try men on the right of property or life . . . " (ibid., 10).[48] But government also has a duty to preserve moral agency. The Latter-day Saint declaration of belief states:

We believe that religion is instituted of God; and that men are amenable to him, and to him only, for the exercise of it unless their religious opinions prompt them to infringe upon the rights and liberties of others; but we do not believe that human law has a right to interfere in prescribing rules of worship to bind the consciences of men, nor dictate forms for public or private devotions; that the civil magistrate should restrain crime, but never control conscience; should punish guilt, but never suppress the freedom of the soul (Doctrine and Covenants 134:4).

Within broad limits relating to legitimate concerns for health and safety, government has no place in directly or indirectly regulating matters of conscience, including religious opinion, expression, and exercise. Every person should be free in choosing who, where, and how he worships and his "forms for public or private devotions." The church believes that it is beyond the legitimate powers of government to compel membership or participation in one church while preventing or restricting them in another. Once again, as a voice from the dust, come these divine principles defining the rightful roles of government and individual conscience as they existed in an ancient American civilization:

And it came to pass that king Mosiah sent a proclamation throughout the land round about that there should not any unbeliever persecute any of those who belonged to the church of God. And there was a strict command throughout all the churches that there should be no persecutions among them, *that there should be an equality among all men* (Book of Mormon, Mosiah 27:2-3, emphasis added).

Mormons believe deeply that one of government's most fundamental duties is to preserve "an equality among all men" when it comes to matters of religion and conscience. Every person is entitled to the right to speak his or her mind on such matters, and everyone else has the right to listen, or not. Every person is entitled to exercise the right to worship where, how, and as he or she pleases.

And every citizen, while exercising his or her own rights, has the duty to respect those same rights in others. Government has no stake in any point of view. Its only legitimate role between its citizens on such matters is to maintain their individual rights:

> We believe that . . . governments have a right, and are bound to enact laws for the protection of all citizens in the free exercise of their religious belief; but we do not believe that they have a right in justice to deprive citizens of this privilege, or proscribe them in their opinions, so long as a regard and reverence are shown to the laws and such religious opinions do not justify sedition nor conspiracy (Doctrine and Covenants 134:7).

Hence, while some may assert that there is an inherent conflict between a religionist's exercise of his religion, including his need to express his convictions, and the right of others not to suffer the imposition of his exercise, for Latter-day Saints there is no tension between the Great Commission and the Golden Rule. Latter-day Saints desire the opportunity to proclaim the gospel of Jesus Christ as they understand it to any and all who wish to listen, they accord every other man that same right, and they acknowledge that all have the right not to listen. They pledge to honor such principles and ask only that government guarantee them that right and protect them in its exercise.

What does the church expect from government in practical terms? Simply put, the church asks for room to perform its divine mission to preach the gospel to all men and women, who have a right to *hear it* and *choose* for themselves whether to embrace it. As a minimum, this means the following:

1. *The right to worship.* Church members should have the right to practice their religion without interference by the agencies of government.
2. *The right to meet together.* Church members should have the right to meet together in public and in private in adequate facilities and without government scrutiny. The right of assembly is basic to religious freedom.
3. *The right to self-governance.* The church claims the right to non-interference by government in its internal affairs. Church doctrines and practices should be free from government regulation. The church has the right to determine who will serve as its officers, how long they will serve, and how the affairs of the church will be conducted.

4. *The right to communicate with church members.* Church members should have the right to regular communication with church leaders and other members, whether in person, in writing, or electronically. Such communications should not be prohibited, impeded, monitored, or otherwise interfered with.

5. *The right to legal entity status and action.* While the church respects the right of government to establish reasonable requirements for churches to become recognized as a legal entity, it asserts that it has a right to legal recognition upon reasonable conditions. Thus recognized, the church should be able to acquire, hold, and dispose of property, to open bank accounts, and to transact business necessary to church operations.

6. *The right to declare beliefs publicly.* Church missionaries should have the right to proclaim the gospel individually or before assemblies of people. This should include the right to print and distribute literature explaining the teachings and doctrines of the church, the right to display videos, tape recordings, and other electronic or graphic presentations concerning the church and its beliefs, and the right of reasonable access to the public press, radio, and television to disseminate messages and information concerning the church and its teachings.

7. *The right to travel freely.* Church members should have the right to travel freely to attend church meetings and activities and to visit with other members. Similarly, full-time missionaries and other church representatives, even if citizens of another nation, should have the right, consistent with reasonable government regulations, to enter the government's jurisdiction and to proclaim the gospel and participate in church meetings and activities.

On its part, the church reaffirms its commitment to obey the law and to respect the rights of all persons. As previously mentioned, high-pressure salesmanship, coercion, and inducement are not part of the church's program or approach. Consistent with the "come and see" principle, missionaries and other church representatives fulfill their callings by inviting those whom they meet to learn more. Courtesy and good will are the hallmarks of the approach of church representatives and members to nonmembers. They see their duty to "witness" in the first instance as extending an invitation and subsequently to explain gospel principles to those who wish to learn them.

RELATIONS WITH OTHER CHURCHES

What pertains between individuals should also pertain between organizations. The principle of moral agency, central to the very purpose of morality, must be as sacrosanct in relationships with religious organizations as in relationships with individuals. Each church deserves to be respected in its legitimate individual operations. In addition, there is a pressing need for cooperative action in today's world. In a time of wrenching poverty, increasing intolerance, and cascading evil and immorality in many communities, religious organizations sharing common principles have ample opportunities for shared action to improve the overall welfare of the community.

Because of the nature of its divine mandate, the church is not free to engage in ecumenical discourse aimed at amalgamating its doctrines with other denominations. At the levels of doctrine and ecclesiastical polity, the church understands itself as a restored church charged with maintaining its integrity and independence from all other religious organizations. For this reason, the church does not engage in ecumenical dialogue aimed at homogenizing or compromising doctrine.

However, the church regards interfaith efforts differently than ecumenism in the foregoing sense. Churches can cooperate on an interfaith basis on common principles without compromising their own doctrines and teachings. Thus, the church welcomes interfaith opportunities for joint venturing of worthwhile projects in areas of common concern. Such projects may include alleviating the effects of poverty and homelessness, fostering standards of community decency (especially for children and youth), strengthening families, and championing laws buttressing morality, to name only a few. Such projects do not require an amalgamation of beliefs and doctrines, only mutual respect and a common purpose.

Despite its independence and the singularity of its beliefs, the church regards other churches and religions with good will. Although Utah is predominantly Mormon, the church has over the years assisted its Jewish, Roman Catholic, and Protestant friends in a variety of ways, from making contributions to the remodeling or refurbishing of a church, cathedral, or synagogue to the sharing of facilities with other congregations temporarily dislocated from their usual places of worship.[49] When representatives of other denominations come to Utah, the church's attitude is as expressed recently by President Gordon B. Hinckley, "We are going to welcome them. We are going to do everything we can to make them feel at home."[50]

CONCLUSION

A genuine courtesy for others and respect for their beliefs is a hallmark of Latter-day Saints' relationship with others. Rather than attempting to challenge others' beliefs, they merely proffer the additional truths of the restored gospel to augment truths already possessed. Hence, Mormons manifest a sincere good will for other churches and for those with differing beliefs. This neighborliness and respect are an application of Mormon doctrine.

As a matter of principle, the Mormons are law-abiding and good citizens, and they conscientiously seek the good will of governments. But they also expect that governments and their representatives will reciprocate that same respect, good will, and cooperation. The right to worship, to hold meetings without governmental interference, to enjoy unfettered self-governance, to receive legal recognition, and to communicate among themselves as well as with others are among the rights they believe governments should guarantee to them and to all churches.

Mormon missionaries go about their work in accordance with these commitments and expectations. Serving for two years in the midst of the people, they master their language and embrace their culture. Traveling in pairs and observing a strict code of moral rectitude and comely appearance, these young men and women strive to reflect in their lives the precepts of the gospel truths they are teaching.

The driving force behind the work of missionaries and members of the church is their strongly felt spiritual duty to witness of Jesus Christ and his restored gospel to every nation and people. Their history has abundant evidence of the sincerity of their missionary efforts and their willingness to sacrifice for them. Their record of rapid growth for over 150 years, culminating in a present worldwide membership of over 10 million, shows that their message is meaningful to many.

In carrying out their duty to witness, Mormons have two external restraints. Since the observance of law is strictly required, they must comply with all legal requirements in seeking admission to nations and in delivering their message. And since moral agency—the right of every soul to choose what he or she will believe and practice—is a fundamental tenet of the faith, Mormons cannot seek converts by coercion or consideration but only by invitation and persuasion. The proofs of their message are found in the lives of the members and in the witness of the Spirit. Their invitation to all the world is, "Come and see."

13.

HUMAN RIGHTS, EVANGELISM, AND PROSELYTISM

A Perspective of Jehovah's Witnesses

———————◆———————

W. Glen How
Philip Brumley

Most people in the Western world, indeed in most parts of the world, have encountered Jehovah's Witnesses at one time or another. Prominent scholars have described Jehovah's Witnesses as the most rapidly growing religious movement in the Western world.[1] Neither public indifference, nor abuse, nor outright persecution seems to discourage them in their persistent evangelism. What is the point this group is trying to make? What do they achieve by their constant community visitation—Bible in hand, offering copies of *The Watchtower* and *Awake!*, seeking to engage people in biblical discussions?

Reverence for Jehovah God and the Holy Scriptures has impelled Jehovah's Witnesses to engage in a campaign of Bible education. It is one of their fundamental beliefs that each person should have his or her own copy of the Bible and that it should be read daily. The Watch Tower Society, the legal entity used by Jehovah's Witnesses to organize and accomplish this Bible distribution and educational work, has not only translated the Bible into an easy-to-read modern version, *The New World Translation of the Holy Scriptures,* but it has also printed numerous other translations, such as the *American Standard Version,* Byington's translation, and the Holy Scriptures in Russian, a recently discovered translation by Makarios, an Orthodox priest of the nineteenth century. To date, *The New World Translation of the Holy Scriptures* has been translated into thirty-one languages with a total printing of 101 million copies.

The *1999 Yearbook of Jehovah's Witnesses* lists branch offices in 106 locations worldwide to oversee the evangelizing work in 87,644 congregations

276

spread across 233 lands. In 1998 it reported a total of 5,888,650 evangelizers. Some outstanding figures for the increase in evangelizers are noted in the Ukraine, which reported a 15 percent increase over the previous year, Mozambique a 17 percent increase, Lithuania an 18 percent increase, Russia a 17 percent increase, and Albania a 30 percent increase. In 1998 a total of 1,186,666,708 hours of activity were spent in all forms of their evangelizing service, including conducting, on an average, 4,302,852 home Bible studies around the world. This does not include many additional hours spent on internal shepherding ministry, such as caring for the sick and for those needing assistance inside and outside the congregation, along with international relief work and other activities.[2]

ALL CHRISTIANS ARE COMMANDED
TO SPREAD THE GOSPEL

At the heart of the Jehovah's Witness belief is that all Christians are commanded to spread the gospel. The ministry of Jesus Christ was characterized by active preaching in local synagogues and public marketplaces throughout Judea and Palestine. Jesus traveled through towns and villages, preaching the good news about the kingdom of God. The twelve disciples went with him (Lk 8:1, *GNB*; Mt 5:1, 9, 10, 28, 35). Jesus did not wait for people to come to him. Rather, he encouraged his disciples actively to preach, instructing them: "Into whatever city or village you enter, search out who in it is deserving" (Mt 10:7, 11-14).[3] This searching out required personal contact with people at their homes. This is confirmed in the Gospel of Luke, where Jesus directed his followers: "But wherever you enter into a home, stay there and leave from there" (Lk 9:1-6).

In addition to the twelve apostles, Jesus trained seventy others whom he sent forth in pairs to publicize the kingdom message. That the work of these seventy disciples was done in the homes of individuals is obvious from Jesus' words: "Wherever you enter into a house say first, 'May this house have peace.' And if a friend of peace is there, your peace will rest upon him. But if there is not, it will turn back to you. So stay in that house eating and drinking the things they provide, for the worker is worthy of his wages" (Lk 10:5-7).

Jehovah's Witnesses are evangelizers who follow these scriptural injunctions. They accept the command of Christ Jesus, which spans nearly twenty centuries of human history from his time to ours: "Go therefore and make disciples of people of all the nations, baptizing them in the name of the Father and of the Son and of the Holy Spirit" (Mt 28:19). This mandate guides the activity of Jehovah's Witnesses. For a person to be one of Jehovah's Witnesses, he or she must be an evangelizer. Many millions of people study the Bible with Jehovah's Witnesses and associate with them at their Kingdom Halls but are not included in the list of evangelizers.

Jehovah's Witnesses have the same basic attitude toward all people everywhere, whether these may be perceived as non-Christian, nonreligious, or part of the pluralistic religious world of Christendom. Their form of evangelizing is basically one on one, talking to people in their homes or in the streets, marketplaces, and other convenient public locations. Witnesses are prepared to accept reasonable local regulations by police and other authorities to allow them to do their work in a place and manner that does not unduly interfere with traffic or the movement of other people. However, they do not accept that authorities, whether secular or religious, have any right to prohibit their evangelizing work or to require them to apply for official permission to preach. The individual citizen has a right to hear and make a personal choice as to the beliefs he or she will adopt.

WHAT IT MEANS TO BE A WITNESS (EVANGELIZER)

The original-language words translated as "witness" provide insight into what it means to be a Witness for Jehovah. In the Hebrew scriptures the noun rendered witness (*'edh*) is derived from a verb (*'udh*) meaning "return or repeat, do again." "A witness [*'edh*] is one, who by reiteration, emphatically affirms his testimony. The word is at home in the language of the court."[4] The original meaning of the verb *'udh* was probably "he said repeatedly and forcefully."[5]

In the Christian scriptures the Greek words rendered witness (*mar'tys*) and bear witness (*mar'ty're'o*) also had a legal connotation, although in time they took on a broader meaning. "[T]he concept of witness [is used] both in the sense of witness to ascertainable facts and also in that of witness to truths, i.e., the making known and confessing of convictions."[6] So witnesses relate facts from direct personal knowledge or proclaim views or truths of which they are convinced.

The faithful course of first-century Christians carried the meaning of witness a step further. Many of those early Christians witnessed under persecution and in the face of death (Acts 22:20; Rv 2:13). As a result, by the second century C.E., the Greek word for witness (*mar'tys*, from which is also derived the word *martyr*) acquired the meaning that applied to persons who were willing to seal the seriousness of their witness or confession by death.[7] They were not called witnesses because they died; they died because they were loyal witnesses.

When on trial before Roman governor Pontius Pilate, Jesus stated: "For this I have been born, and for this I have come into the world, that I should bear witness to the truth" (Jn 18:37). As the Faithful Witness, Jesus was outstandingly a proclaimer of God's kingdom. He emphatically said: "I must declare the good news of the kingdom of God, because for this I was sent forth" (Lk 4:43). He proclaimed that kingdom throughout Judea and Palestine. He preached wherever there were people who would listen: lake shores, hillsides, cities and villages, synagogues and the Temple, marketplaces, and peoples' homes. He set a precedent followed by Jehovah's Witnesses to this day.

THE RISE OF JEHOVAH'S WITNESSES

While there were prototype evangelists throughout church history, Jehovah's Witnesses were organized as an evangelical group in the 1870s in the United States. They first used the name International Bible Students Association. The best known figure in the early years was Charles Taze Russell, better known as Pastor Russell, born in 1852. While still in his early twenties and fired with the zeal for evangelism, he left a profitable business career to dedicate his whole time and effort to evangelism. The small group organized by Russell quickly came to understand that evangelism is an essential part of Christianity.

To accomplish this ministry, Russell and his associates founded Zion's Watch Tower and Tract Society (now, The Watch Tower Bible and Tract Society) with original headquarters in Pittsburgh, Pennsylvania. The Society began publishing and distributing tracts, originally entitled Bible Students Tracts, in 1880. In the following year the magazine *Zion's Watch Tower* (now *The Watchtower*) carried an article entitled "Wanted 1000 Preachers," which requested men and women to "go forth into large or small cities, according to your ability, as Colporteurs or Evangelists, seek to find in every place the earnest Christians."[8] Even though few in number, they undertook to spread the message of the gospel wherever and whenever they could. This tiny group was quick to utilize a variety of methods to reach people.[9] In addition to books and pamphlets on doctrinal questions, Russell showed a lot of imagination in preparing in 1914 an early pictorial presentation, partly moving pictures, with recorded explanation; it was entitled, *The Photo Drama of Creation* and was shown throughout America and Europe.

C. T. Russell and his associates saw newspapers as an effective way of reaching large numbers of people. The December 1, 1904, issue of *Zion's Watch Tower*, the official journal of Jehovah's Witnesses, announced that sermons by C. T. Russell were appearing in three newspapers. The next issue of *Zion's Watch Tower*, under the heading "Newspaper Gospelling," reported: "Millions of sermons have thus been scattered far and near; and some at least have done good. If the Lord wills we shall be glad to see this door keep open, or even open still wider." The door of "newspaper gospelling" opened still wider. In fact, by 1913 it was estimated that through two thousand newspapers Russell's sermons were reaching 15 million readers![10]

As a further means of expanding the evangelizing work, the Witnesses in the 1920s began to use radio stations, a number of which they built and owned. Less than two years after regular commercial radio broadcasting began, radio was being used to transmit the Kingdom message. On February 24, 1924, the Watch Tower Society's own radio station, WBBR, began broadcasting from Staten Island, New York. Eventually, the Society organized worldwide networks to broadcast Bible programs and lectures. By 1933, there were 408 stations carrying the kingdom message to six continents![11]

In January 1942 the Watch Tower Bible and Tract Society appointed Nathan Homer Knorr as its president. Although World War II was raging, Knorr quickly recognized that missionary work needed to be organized, and the Watch Tower Society set up a missionary school called Gilead at South Lansing, New York. By 1943 a course in theocratic ministry was established in each congregation of Jehovah's Witnesses around the world for the training of individual Witnesses.[12] These courses continue operating in every congregation of Jehovah's Witnesses to this day.

N. H. Knorr soon realized that a tremendous organization would be needed to do the evangelizing work that Jehovah's Witnesses foresaw as being required around the world. In 1942, when he became president, there were 25 branch offices of the Society in other countries. By 1946, despite the bans and carnage of World War II, there were branches in 57 lands. Over the next thirty years, down to 1976, the number of branches increased to 97. While some have been consolidated and reorganized, the Witnesses report a total of 106 branches operating in 1999, directing the work of evangelism in more than 230 lands.[13]

Since 1942 the Witnesses have widely recognized the need to be teachers or evangelists, and a major thrust of the worldwide organization has been directed to training, educating, and preparing people to share in the evangelizing work. Many families have left their homes and gone to other countries where there was a recognized need for evangelizers, and thus the evangelizing continues.

THE RIGHT TO WITNESS

Jehovah's Witnesses do not only engage in evangelizing, but concern themselves in many other fields closely related to the evangelizing work, most notably litigation in support of religious freedom. In the first century C.E. the apostles and other disciples often met with strong opposition. The apostle Paul spoke to Christians in Philippi, in what is now Greece, about defending and legally establishing the good news (Phil 1:7). Following that precedent, the Witnesses established in 1936 a legal department at their world headquarters. It is now located at the Watchtower Educational Center in Patterson, New York, and assisted by lawyers in a number of other countries. The legal department continues to aid in a modern-day, worldwide struggle for religious freedom.

The decades of the 1940s and 1950s were difficult for Jehovah's Witnesses even in the most liberal parts of the Western world. The United States and Canada stood at the forefront of the international litigation arena, where Jehovah's Witnesses fought for the right to evangelize. Hayden C. Covington, a dynamic Texas lawyer and one-time vice-president of the Watch Tower Bible and Tract Society, carried the legal defense of the Witnesses' right to evangelize through many state courts, and ultimately he appeared a number of times before the Supreme Court of the United States. There he planted his feet firmly on the Constitution of the United States and insisted on the Witnesses' right to evangelize under the First Amendment. In Canada, W. Glen How, Q.C., was closely associated with Covington and was equally vocal before the lower courts and the Supreme Court of Canada in maintaining evangelism as a right of free religious expression.

In the landmark case of *Murdock v. Pennsylvania*, Justice Douglas, speaking for the United States Supreme Court, said concerning Jehovah's Witnesses:

> The hand distribution of religious tracts is an age-old form of missionary evangelism, as old as the history of printing presses. It has been a potent force in various religious movements down through the years. This form of evangelism is utilized today on a large scale by various religious sects whose colporteurs carry the Gospel to thousands upon thousands of homes and seek through personal visitations to win adherents to their faith. It is more than preaching; it is more than distribution of religious literature. It is a combination of both. Its purpose is as evangelical as the revival meeting. This form of religious activity occupies the same high estate under the First Amendment as do worship in the churches and preaching from the pulpits. It has the same claim to protection as the more orthodox and conventional exercises of religion. It also has the same claim as the others to the guarantees of freedom of speech and freedom of the press.[14]

In *Saumur v. City of Quebec*, Justice Rand of Canada's Supreme Court discussed the right to communicate with citizens on the public streets:

> That public ways, in some circumstances the only practical means available for any appeal to the community generally, have from the most ancient times been the avenues for such communications, is demonstrated by the Bible itself: in the 6th verse of ch. xi of Jeremiah these words appear: "Proclaim all these words in the cities of Judah, and in the streets of Jerusalem"; and a more objectionable interference, short of complete suppression, with that dissemination which is the "breath of life" of the political institutions of this country than that made possible by the by-law can scarcely be imagined.[15]

Freedom of speech and free interchange of thoughts, whether written or oral, are part of the freedom of expression that distinguishes a free country from a dictatorship. Justice Cannon of the Supreme Court of Canada described freedom of information as the right of the people to be informed through sources independent of the government.[16] Justice Rand of the same court has said that free speech demands the condition of a virtually unobstructed access to and diffusion of ideas.[17]

William Kaplan, professor of law at the University of Ottawa, has commented on the valuable contribution Jehovah's Witnesses have made to the law of Canada:

> The Jehovah's Witnesses taught the state, and the Canadian people, what the practical content of legal protection for dissenting groups should be. Moreover, the events of the Second World War ban were but a dress rehearsal for post-war persecution of Jehovah's Witnesses in the province of Quebec. That persecution led to a series of cases that, in the 1940s and 1950s, made their way to the Supreme Court of Canada. They too made an important contribution to Canadian attitudes about civil rights, and they constitute the bedrock of civil-liberties jurisprudence in Canada today.[18]

One of the long-standing practices regarding dissemination of ideas is to visit the homes of citizens. This has been a practice of religious, political, charitable, and other associations. Homeowners who wish to listen are entitled to do so. Those not interested need only say so. This is a matter of decision left to the individual, not to local government. The citizen can decide what ideas he or she wishes to accept or reject. The value of this practice from the standpoint of freedom of information has been discussed by the United States Supreme Court in *Martin v. Struthers*, one of the cases involving Jehovah's Witnesses:

> For centuries it has been a common practice in this and other countries for persons not specifically invited to go from home to home and knock on doors or ring doorbells to communicate ideas to the occupants or to invite them to political, religious, or other kinds of public meetings. Whether such visiting shall be permitted has in general been deemed to depend upon the will of the individual master of each household, and not upon the determination of the community. . . .
>
> Of course, as every person acquainted with political life knows, door to door campaigning is one of the most accepted techniques of seeking popular support, while the circulation of nominating papers would be greatly handicapped if they could not be taken to the citizens in their homes. Door to door distribution of circulars is essential to the poorly financed causes of little people.[19]

Fifty years ago, the United States Supreme Court took an enlightened step forward in *Hague v. C.I.O.*:

> Wherever the title of streets and parks may rest, they have immemorially been held in trust for the use of the public and, time out of mind, have been used for purposes of assembly, communicating thoughts between citizens, and discussing public questions. Such use of the streets and public places has, from ancient times, been a part of the privileges, immunities,

rights, and liberties of citizens. The privilege of a citizen of the United States to use the streets and parks for communication of views on national questions may be regulated in the interest of all; it is not absolute, but relative, and must be exercised in subordination to the general comfort and convenience, and in consonance with peace and good order; but it must not, in the guise of regulation, be abridged or denied.[20]

After decades of litigation, Jehovah's Witnesses have largely secured the unabridged right to evangelize in the United States and Canada, but this is not the case for Witnesses worldwide. While Jehovah's Witnesses maintain organized evangelical work in over 230 nations of the world, they have, over the years, experienced and survived tremendous religious and political oppression. In many countries their evangelizing work has been totally banned; in others it is partially suppressed. In some places Witnesses of Jehovah have experienced intense persecution, at times even forfeiting their lives because of doing the evangelizing work they have considered so important.

What are the practical problems when one begins a whole new territory of, say, 50 million people? Where to start? What to say? What does one do if local people do not appreciate the intrusion of strangers? How long does one put up with serious official opposition, both religious and political? How long does it take to move from outsider status to accepted? What cooperation does one extend to local government? How does one deal with the chilling hatred still prevalent in some places?

We believe these and many other questions can be understood and answered only as one sees what really happens firsthand. Also, it quickly becomes apparent that one can only understand the attitude of Jehovah's Witnesses on this subject by studying what they do. A pattern emerges. Small beginnings, dynamic evangelism, church and political persecution, and finally a measure of acceptance, during all of which the Witnesses have persevered and grown. Sometimes, this requires more than a lifetime. The evangelizing never stops. Herewith are a few case studies, drawn from each continent, illustrating what Jehovah's Witnesses have done in the 233 nations of the world where they operate.

BRAZIL

Brazil offers a fairly typical illustration of the Witnesses' activities in Central and Latin America. In 1920 a group of eight young Brazilian sailors, on leave from their ship *São Paulo* docked in New York, read a window display in Brooklyn under the heading, "The Chart of the Ages." This was at the meeting place (closed at the time) of a group of International Bible Students, the name by which Jehovah's Witnesses were then known. Discerning that the chart was based on the Bible, the group returned on another occasion and enjoyed some Bible discussions. They also obtained a Bible in Portuguese and some copies of *The Watchtower* and the book *Divine Plan of the Ages*, in Spanish, which they could understand reasonably well. They studied the Bible using these publications and, when their ship returned to Brazil, they began to talk to others about what they were learning. That was the beginning of the Witnesses' evangelizing work in Brazil.

Other means were used to get the kingdom message to Brazil's honest-hearted people, especially in the city of São Paulo. A commercial radio station began to be used as early as 1937 carrying five-minute Bible lectures by the Watch Tower Society's president, Judge Rutherford, three times a week in Spanish, English, and German. After four months, however, the radio station succumbed to religious pressure and refused to carry any more programs.

Another powerful instrument used to proclaim the kingdom message in São Paulo was the sound car, a 1936 Chevrolet with an amplifier mounted on its roof. For eight months Bible talks were given weekly in seven different languages in São Paulo's public parks near the city center. However, religious pressure was again brought to bear on the city authorities so that they ordered that Jehovah's Witnesses obtain a license from the city to operate the sound car. When their efforts to obtain a license proved futile, another means to sound out the message was initiated, the use of individual phonographs. In 1938 about twenty of these were being used, playing records in eight different languages. Pressure continued against the work until May 31, 1940, when a ban was decreed by the Ministry of Justice, a Kingdom Hall (as the meeting places of Jehovah's Witnesses are called) was closed, and the Witnesses were obliged to meet in private homes.

In October 1945 a petition was drawn up and addressed to the president of Brazil, requesting that the Watch Tower Society be registered and that its educational activity be renewed. The petition was signed by 44,411 persons and presented to President Eurico Gaspar Dutra in April 1946. Finally, after eleven years, in April 1957 the new president, Dr. Juscelino Kubitschek, granted the petition and the Watch Tower Society began to function freely again.[21]

As time passed it was noticed that many persons associated with the congregations had a minimum of education, some even having difficulty in reading. For this reason, the Watch Tower Society produced its own reading aid entitled *Learn to Read and Write* in Portuguese and, at the same time, appointed qualified Jehovah's Witnesses in the congregations, where needed, to serve as instructors in classes of reading and writing. The results have been very encouraging.

"Speech is like a bee: It has honey and also a sting." With these words Chief of Police Leo Machado in Ferrors, MG, Brazil, began his letter of August 2, 1991, to the Watch Tower Society in Brazil, in which he highly commended the work of three young female Witnesses of Jehovah. He went on to explain: "I could not let the matter pass without saying something. Like a fine rain that falls silently but which causes rivers to overflow, these Witnesses have done much, both in a spiritual and material way, in the sense of reintegrating into society those under sentence collaborating with this Chief of Police in teaching the prisoners how to read and write." The above illustrates another phase of the evangelizing activity.

Through the years there has been a constant increase in the number of Witnesses and congregations in Brazil. The report for 1998 indicates that there are now 7,386 congregations throughout the country, with 487,661 evangelizers of the good news. In 1998 the attendance at the Memorial commemorating the death of Jesus Christ was 1,216,268.

BRITAIN

Why do Jehovah's Witnesses feel the need to evangelize in countries that are already traditionally Christian? Is their work carried out in stable, democratic lands without interference or impediments? The history of Jehovah's Witnesses in Britain answers these questions.

Two close associates of C. T. Russell arrived in Britain from the United States in 1881 to engage in evangelizing work.[22] Tom Hart, a railroad shunter working at night in London, enjoyed reading when he returned home early in the morning. A lad in the street gave Tom a copy of *Food for Thinking Christians*. Impelled by what he read, Tom Hart enthusiastically shared his new knowledge with his wife and friends. Many of these left the chapel they attended because they were convinced that what they heard there was not truly scriptural. This little group began distributing tracts to passersby in their neighborhood. Thus began the evangelizing work of Jehovah's Witnesses in Britain.

Unfortunately the public preaching activity of Jehovah's Witnesses in Britain has not been accomplished without opposition. The fever of both the First and Second World Wars brought Jehovah's Witnesses before the courts. Many legal problems focused on the determination of who is a minister of religion. Soon more than forty Bible Students were imprisoned because of their conscientious objection to military service. The Bible Students circulated a petition to protest these sentences. This was eventually signed by some five thousand persons and presented to the prime minister, the Right Honourable H. H. Asquith, M.P.[23]

Opposition to Jehovah's Witnesses in Britain was not, however, limited to questions about their status as ministers. At the beginning of World War II, supplies of the magazines *The Watchtower* and *Consolation* were imported under special permit.[24] But on December 31, 1940, notice was given that no further import licenses would be issued, all payments to the United States for these publications would be stopped, and all Watch Tower publications placed under censorship. Watch Tower literature was put on the prohibited list.[25] When printers refused to print Watch Tower Society publications without censoring them, a Witness, Harry Briggs, bought a printing firm and operated it as though it was the Society's, printing everything as requested.[26] Then, in 1945, the London branch office of Jehovah's Witnesses organized a campaign for congregations to acquaint the members of Parliament with the facts of the ban and request that it be lifted. Two hundred and fifty members were interviewed, and repeated questions were asked in the House of Commons.[27] Eventually on February 28, 1945, the ban was lifted.[28]

Jehovah's Witnesses are now free to go about their public ministry without hindrance in Britain. There are no current proceedings that affect their evangelizing work in that country. The Witnesses never attempted to export American culture and impose it on British society. The Witnesses did not enter Britain as a well-organized and well-financed institution, but rather on a one-on-one basis. In 1998 the number of Witnesses who associate with the 1,452 congregations throughout Britain reached 131,981.[29] Their public preaching, has made Jehovah's Witnesses well-known throughout the whole country. Their journals *The Watchtower* and *Awake!* now enjoy an annual distribution of over 20 million in Britain.[30]

How do the English view Jehovah's Witnesses? Among the favorable comments are the following: "Witnesses, in disputing the beliefs of other religions, are doing no more than maintaining an attitude that has been common to the major churches of the Christian tradition," observes Oxford University reader *emeritus* in sociology Bryan R. Wilson. "In practice," he continues, "they constitute . . . a responsible, diligent, respectable, and respectful community whose operation is ultimately very much for the public good and the creation of a more caring and orderly society."[31] Lord Avebury, chairman of the British Parliamentary Human Rights Group, argues: "It is manifestly absurd to contend that [Jehovah's Witnesses] pose any threat to the security of the state, and the fact that they operate in a great many other countries without impediment proves that they are not regarded as such a threat in those countries."[32]

GERMANY

The history of the Jehovah's Witnesses in Germany is a grimmer tale. In 1893 German emigrants who had become Bible Students (Jehovah's Witnesses) returned from the United States to their German homeland. The organized activity of the Watch Tower Society began in 1897, when a literature depot was opened in Berlin. In 1902 an office of the Watch Tower Society was opened in Elberfeld, and scattered classes were organized that later became the foundation for local congregations.

These Witnesses soon faced increasingly vicious persecution. In 1931 Bavarian officials falsely applied the Emergency Decree of April 28, 1931, which properly was to be reserved for political riots. On November 14, 1931, officials confiscated the Witnesses' publications in Munich and banned all literature of the Bible Students. By the end of 1932 pending court cases involving Witnesses totaled 2,335. By the middle of 1933 the work of Jehovah's Witnesses was banned in most German states. On June 28, 1933, their headquarters building in Magdeburg was occupied by thirty SS men, their factory closed down, and the swastika hoisted over the building. An official police decree prohibited all Bible study and prayer on the Society's property. On June 29 this action was reported to the entire German nation by radio. Some sixty-seven tons of books, Bibles, and pictures were taken from the Society's printery in August 1933, brought to the edge of Magdeburg, and publicly burned. This was only a foretaste to the persecution by the Third Reich, which is more generally known. Many Bible Students were sent to concentration camps. The intense persecution of Jehovah's Witnesses under the Third Reich has been carefully documented in the Holocaust Museum located in Washington, D.C.

Despite this repression and the strictest surveillance, even in the concentration camps Witness publications were available, and a certain amount of evangelizing was carried out. The historian Kirsten John describes this:

> Along with secret letters the women placed issues of the *Watchtower* under gravestones on the Wewelsburg cemetery or in other dead mailboxes in the neighborhood of the labor groups. The prisoners were able to smuggle the messages and publications from there into camp without making a stir.[33]

Prisoners in the Wewelsburg concentration camp even found ways to mimeograph publications. Kirsten John writes:

> In the rubble of a building destroyed by fire Jehovah's Witnesses found a typewriter which they used to write stencils for the *Wachtturm [The Watchtower]*. A simple mimeograph machine was produced. The women Bible Students, who were already doing courier work, provided the necessary material and paper. The issues of the *Wachtturm* produced on the simple mimeograph machine came out of the camp in the same manner. The sisters took over the further distribution of the publications. A large part of Westphalia and Northern Germany could be provided with issues of the *Wachtturm* in this manner. The Jehovah's Witness, Georg Klohe, who took part in the illegal mimeographing remembers: "We never saw the sisters, but they were dear to us and we were appreciative that they waited in the night under many dangers in order to give us the opportunity of service. It was very hair-raising, but a wonderful time. This courier service, directly under the eyes of the SS, was continued until the concentration camp was liberated in 1945."[34]

In other concentration camps, Jehovah's Witnesses were busy speaking to others about their faith. Detlef Garbe explains:

> Within the concentration camp Jehovah's Witnesses put forth every effort to win new members for their faith. Numerous fellow prisoners became—often to their regret—objects of proselytism. In connection with a missionary campaign at the beginning of 1943 in the concentration camp Neuengamme, the camp was divided into territories, which were

to be "worked" by special "assault detachments." In order to reach the largest possible number of fellow prisoners, small groups of Jehovah's Witnesses went from block to block and witnessed to their faith. For this purpose they had prepared witnessing cards in several languages. These contained a short biblical passage and an offer to have a discussion about the Kingdom hope. Even talks were given which were translated for the Russian and Polish inmates.

Baptisms were performed several times in the Neuengamme camp. Baptismal candidates—it is reported about a Russian and a young Polish prisoner—were infiltrated into the labor groups who were doing weeding and had to dig ditches to drain water. There they slipped as though being clumsy. With words such as "if you are already in anyway, then at least go under properly," the Bible Student grabbed the head of the one willing to be baptized, and to the cheers of the SS guards who thought it was for general amusement, thrust him under water, whereas the Jehovah's Witnesses devoutly followed the action with their silent prayers.[35]

The Nazi period offers more insight into religions mixing in politics. Many thinking people have wondered, How did Catholic and Evangelical Lutheran clergymen deal with Hitler and his brutal Nazis? Paul Johnson describes the norm: "Both churches, in the main, gave massive support to the regime. . . . Of 17,000 Evangelical pastors, there were never more than fifty serving long terms [for not supporting the Nazi regime] at any one time. Of the Catholics, one bishop was expelled from his diocese, and another got a short term for currency offences." Johnson continues: "The bravest were the Jehovah's Witnesses, who proclaimed their outright doctrinal opposition from the beginning and suffered accordingly. They refused any cooperation with the Nazi State."[36]

After a thorough study of Jehovah's Witnesses and their determination to evangelize in Nazi Germany, Professor Christine E. King, vice-chancellor of Staffordshire University, England, concludes:

> Their concerns, in my experience, are with their relationship with their God, Jehovah, and with ways in which they can serve Him best. These ways in my view are non-political, they are concerned with spreading the Word of God as they see it and in living lives which demonstrate their faith.[37]

The integrity of Jehovah's Witnesses in Germany during the Nazi regime continues to be a testimony to their love for God and for peace even now, more than fifty years later. A booklet published by the United States Holocaust Memorial Museum in Washington, D.C., states: "Jehovah's Witnesses endured intense persecution under the Nazi regime. . . . The courage the vast majority displayed in refusing [to renounce their religion], in the face of torture, maltreatment in concentration camps, and sometimes execution, won them the respect of many contemporaries." Then it adds: "During the liberation of the camps, Jehovah's Witnesses continued their work, moving among the survivors, making converts."[38]

The possibility to exercise one's faith, which also includes evangelizing, is guaranteed today in the constitution of the Federal Republic of Germany. Freedom of creed, conscience, and freedom to profess a religion has come about through various developments and trends in church-state laws and intellectual history.

Jehovah's Witnesses have engaged in missionary work in Germany for more than a century, sometimes under brutal persecution. Today, Jehovah's Witnesses have become a recognized religious association in Germany; in 1998 there were 171,704 evangelizers, associated with 2,083 local congregations. In the last twenty-five years more than 150,000 persons have indicated that they are Jehovah's Witnesses by undergoing water baptism. Moreover, there are thousands of others who attend the religious services of Jehovah's Witnesses or who are in contact with them. For example, Jehovah's Witnesses in Germany are conducting over fifty-nine thousand free Bible study courses at the present. These are held in the homes of families and individuals. On April 11, 1998, over 270,000 attended the celebration of the Memorial of Christ's death in the Kingdom Halls of Jehovah's Witnesses.[39]

GREECE

Jehovah's Witnesses began their evangelical activity in Greece around the turn of the century. By 1912 there were twelve Bible Students (Jehovah's Witnesses) at work in Greece. They made extensive use of the printed page, distributing books and tracts that served as Bible study aids.

One of the most difficult periods began in 1936, when the Metaxas dictatorship was established. The oppressive laws against proselytism that were enacted during his administration have been used against Jehovah's Witnesses ever since. Many Witnesses were thrown into prison, while others were exiled to the arid islands of the Aegean. The darkest time of all came during the German occupation and immediately afterward. Because of the politically neutral stand Jehovah's Witnesses maintained, some received prison sentences of from seven to twenty years; others were sentenced to life in prison.

During the 1950s and 1960s the plight of the Jehovah's Witnesses in Greece improved. Although persecution continued, it often took subtler forms. Then, in 1967, the seven-year rule of the military junta began, and articles of the Constitution protecting freedom of assembly and of the press were suspended. As in the past, the Witnesses simply continued their evangelizing work underground. Their numbers continued to grow, from 10,940 in 1967 to 17,073 in 1974. In 1998 the Witnesses numbered over 27,000 active preachers in Greece, and over 43,000 persons attended the Witnesses' most important religious gathering, the Memorial of Jesus' death.[40]

Throughout this period, however, Greek authorities have continued their harassment and repression. From 1938 to 1992 Witnesses were victims of 1,059 cases of physical abuse by the police, 252 cases of physical abuse by priests, and 708 cases of physical abuse by others. From 1983 to 1992 Greek authorities carried out some 2,000 arrests and 400 convictions of Witnesses for proselytism, a criminal offense in Greece. These statistics include only severe physical maltreatment, most of which goes beyond the boundaries of cruel and inhumane treatment and torture. In the past four decades thousands of other Witnesses of Jehovah in Greece have been subjected to all kinds of degrading treatment; have faced mob violence, jeering, and slapping; have had their clothing torn and their literature destroyed; have faced threats, obscene behavior, and grievous insults; and have been subjected to psychological pressure and serious discrimination on the basis of their religion.

The legal case that proved to be a turning point in the treatment of Jehovah's Witnesses in Greece was *Kokkinakis v. Greece*, which was ultimately decided before the European Court of Human Rights in Strasbourg.[41] On March 2, 1986, Minos Kokkinakis, then a retired seventy-seven-year-old businessman, and his wife called at the home of Mrs. Georgia Kyriakaki in Sitia, Crete. Mrs. Kyriakaki's husband, who was the cantor at a local Orthodox church, informed the police. The police arrested Mr. and Mrs. Kokkinakis, who were then taken to the local police station. There they were forced to spend the night in prison, charged with the criminal offense of proselytizing. The Criminal Court at Lasithi, Crete, heard the case on March 20, 1986, and found Mr. and Mrs. Kokkinakis guilty of proselytism. Both were sentenced to four months in prison. The court declared that "the defendants had intruded on the religious beliefs of Orthodox Christians . . . by taking advantage of their inexperience, their low intellect and their naïvety. The defendants were further charged with encouraging [Mrs. Kyriakaki] by means of their judicious, skillful explanations . . . to change her Orthodox Christian beliefs."[42]

The decision was appealed to the Crete Court of Appeal. On March 17, 1987, this court acquitted Mrs. Kokkinakis. It upheld her husband's conviction, although it reduced his prison sentence to three months. In a dissenting opinion, one of the appeal judges wrote that Mr. Kokkinakis "should also have been acquitted, as none of the evidence shows that Georgia Kyriakaki . . . was particularly inexperienced in Orthodox Christian doctrine, being married to a cantor, or of particularly low intellect or particularly naive, such that the defendant was able to take advantage and . . . [thus] induce her to become a member of the Jehovah's Witnesses sect."[43] Mr. Kokkinakis appealed the case to the Greek Court of Cessation, the Supreme Court of Greece. But that court dismissed the appeal on April 22, 1988.

On August 22, 1988, Mr. Kokkinakis applied to the European Commission of Human Rights. His petition was eventually accepted on February 21, 1992, and was admitted to the European Court of Human Rights. In a six-to-three vote decision issued on May 25, 1993, the Court held that the Greek government had violated the religious freedom of Minos Kokkinakis, now eighty-four years old. In addition to vindicating his life course of public ministry, it awarded him $14,400 in damages.

Jehovah's Witnesses understand that not everyone agrees with their explanation or application of the scriptures. Since we live in a pluralistic society, tolerance of differences in lifestyles, ethnic backgrounds, and religious beliefs is an essential ingredient in harmonious living. Many Greek journalists, judges, and others have commented on the fine spirit and positive contributions that Jehovah's Witnesses have made to the communities in which they live. For example, journalist Zeta Karagiannis noted in the weekly magazine *Ena*: "Jehovah's Witnesses do not smoke, and they have been organized into 338 churches all over Greece, which, as they maintain, function according to the pattern of the early Christian Church."[44] A year later, the same magazine noted concerning an assembly of Witnesses: "As we saw them praying, we were impressed by their peaceable attitude. The presence of the police was limited to only a few men. You see, there was not such a need. . . . These are people with strong family ties, they are taught to love and to live by their conscience so as not to harm others. . . . Among them one can find educated men and people of the arts."[45] Emphasizing the international unity among Witnesses, as well as the neutral stand they always take, journalist George Alexandrou wrote the following after visiting the war-torn former Yugoslavia, where the Witnesses carried out extensive relief work: "Jehovah's Witnesses from Greece were able to cross all the borders carrying humanitarian aid, with the following inscription in Greek, Serbian, and English: Jehovah's Witnesses, and nobody harmed them."[46] Vasilis Vasilikos, a well-known Greek intellectual and writer, stated on the same subject:

> Jehovah's Witnesses try to bring back to their lives Christianity, in its early virgin stage, before it became armed and imperialistic. . . . Edward Gibbon wrote of early Christians in his book *History of Christianity*: "They refused to take any active part in the civil administration or the military defence of the empire. . . . [I]t was impossible that the Christians, without renouncing a more sacred duty, could assume the character of soldiers, of magistrates, or of princes." In our days, however, the role of the arch-martyr for solely ideological reasons has been shouldered by Jehovah's Witnesses.[47]

In another article the same writer made this appeal: "Jehovah's Witnesses are pure gold. . . . You have to help them. And rescue them. If you are Christians, and, above that, if you are humans."[48]

ITALY

What can possibly be accomplished by evangelizing in the country that is the seat of Catholicism? What good can come from time spent preaching in a land that hosts Vatican City? A brief analysis of the history of Jehovah's Witnesses in Italy may shed some light on those questions.

In 1891 Charles Taze Russell visited Italy and had contacts with Professor Daniele Rivoir, a Waldense and language teacher in Torre Pellice. Professor Rivoir never became a Bible Student (one of Jehovah's Witnesses) but was greatly interested in circulating in Italian the biblical explanations printed by Russell and his associates. In 1903 Rivoir translated into Italian Russell's book *The Divine Plan of the Ages*, which was published the following year. He also began to translate *The Watchtower*. Meanwhile, in 1903, at S. Germano Chisone, Pinerolo, a group of Bible Students held its first meetings in the home of a Waldense, Fanny Lugli. She had begun to study the Bible with the aid of Watch Tower Society publications. The Bible Students held their first assembly in Italy in Pinerolo in 1925. In order to avoid obstacles from the Fascist authorities, the seventy or so who attended that convention disguised it as a wedding celebration.

In 1915, during World War I, Remigio Cuminetti, a Bible Student, objected to military service based on his Bible-trained conscience. He endured five court cases as the first conscientious objector in contemporary Italian history.[49]

Between 1929 and 1940 five circulars emanated from the Ministry of the Interior. These led to the conclusion that Jehovah's Witnesses were one of the principal objectives of Fascist religious discrimination. Circular No. 442/41732, dated September 21, 1929, for example, invited prefects to furnish information on subscribers to *The Watchtower* magazine and on their international association. It was specified that punishment for those who were arrested was to be exemplary.[50]

Although the Italian Constitution was officially promulgated in 1948, it was not until 1956, with the institution of the Constitutional Court, that the laws against freedom of worship and proselytism gradually began to be abolished, often prompted by actions and cases brought by the Jehovah's Witnesses. During the 1950s Jehovah's Witnesses attempted to obtain legal recognition of the organization that directed their activities in Italy. The requests were routinely rejected.[51] In June 1957 police interrupted a peaceful assembly of Witnesses that was to take place in Milan —"an unheard act of tyranny," according to the newspaper *Avanti!*[52] The Rome periodical *Il Mondo* wrote of the same episode of intolerance: "Evidently there is no loyalty, legality, or civil spirit that can prevail against the malice of a State functionary who wants to interpret the Fascist laws of public security [still] in force, in such a way as to satisfy an archbishop"—referring to the archbishop of Milan, Giovan Battista Montini, the future Pope Paul VI.[53]

The social climate of the postwar years "turned out, on the whole, to be rather denominational," recognizes Catholic historian Andrea Riccardi.[54] "Molestations (not to use the all-too-grave term persecution) of the harmless attempts at proselytism by Jehovah's Witnesses and Pentecostals, were encouraged by the tendency toward Catholic fundamentalism," observes Arturo

Carlo Jemolo.[55] The climate of intolerance, however, did not stop the Witnesses from arriving at the figures of 1,000 active evangelists toward the end of the 1940s, 10,000 halfway through the 1960s, and 100,000 at the beginning of the 1980s.

In 1976 the organization of Jehovah's Witnesses obtained their first governmental recognition on the basis of the so-called Pact of Friendship between Italy and the United States (ratified in 1949).[56] In 1976 the state granted permission for the ministers of Jehovah's Witness to perform marriages. During the late 1970s and early 1980s a number of ministerial decrees granted religious ministers of Jehovah's Witnesses the opportunity to be included in health insurance and pension plans available to religious ministers of other denominations. Another decree authorized a certain number of Witnesses to provide spiritual assistance to persons in prison who requested it.[57] By means of a Decree of the President of the Republic, dated October 31, 1986, following a favorable opinion expressed by the Council of State, juridical recognition of the Congregazione cristiana dei testimoni di Geova (Christian Congregation of Jehovah's Witnesses) as an association representing Jehovah's Witnesses was granted.[58]

Jehovah's Witnesses continue peacefully carrying out their preaching activity in Italy. A Catholic periodical reported: "It has to be said that Jehovah's Witnesses are the first to live the faith they propagandize. They do not get mad, they do not smoke, they do not accumulate money, they abstain from political arguments, . . . they pay their taxes, live a virtuous and honest life, they are cheerful and helpful toward their neighbors. All of this wins them many friends."[59]

At present the evangelizing work by Jehovah's Witnesses is not subject to any restrictions in Italy. Many are progressively becoming aware of the social utility of the work carried out by Jehovah's Witnesses. A survey among the congregations of Jehovah's Witnesses in Italy in 1997 (based on the responses of 96.7 percent of the congregations) indicated that among the more than 200,000 preachers of the good news, at least 41,722 persons had been helped to free themselves of the vice of smoking, 2,424 had overcome alcohol abuse, and 2,089 had conquered drug abuse. Some 1,626 who once had problems with the law have been helped to put their lives in order.

As of January 1999 the peak of Witnesses taking part in the preaching work was 232,145. This represents a ratio of one Witness to every 248 people in the population. At the last Memorial celebration of the death of Jesus Christ, the attendance was 385,387.[60] It may be said that Jehovah's Witnesses are the second largest religion practiced by the local population in Italy.

RUSSIA

Jehovah's Witnesses began their work in Russia more than a hundred years ago. *The Watchtower* magazine of February 1887 published a letter from a reader to Charles Taze Russell: "I shall also mail copies of the Watch Tower to different places, even Russia."[61]

It was about the same time that Cimeon Kozlicki, a graduate of a Russian theological seminary, returned to Russia from the United States with the teachings of the Bible Students (Jehovah's Witnesses). He zealously sought to bring the good news to those who were searching for it. Even in western Siberia, where he later lived, preaching God's Word remained the most important thing in his life.

In 1911, when the Herkendells, a young German couple, got married, the bride requested a dowry of her father—money for an unusual honeymoon. She and her husband had in mind making a strenuous trip into Russia to reach German-speaking people there with the Bible's message.

After the revolution in Russia in 1917, the Watch Tower Bible and Tract Society received an unexpected letter from a teacher in Siberia who was earnestly seeking Bible knowledge. He wrote: "Here [in Russia] publications that enlighten are very much needed." As a result of those early beginnings, small Bible study groups and congregations of Bible Students were formed in various parts of Russia and other territories of the Soviet Union.

Many Russian citizens, along with millions of people of other nationalities, suffered greatly in concentration camps under Germany's cruel totalitarian dictatorship. But these difficult experiences led to some unexpected blessings. Many Russian prisoners met Jehovah's Witnesses in concentration camps and then became Witnesses themselves. In the Ravensbruck camp, for example, about thirty Russian women became Jehovah's Witnesses. Madame Genevieva de Gaulle, niece of the former president of France, Charles de Gaulle, who was in the Ravensbruck concentration camp, said with reference to Jehovah's Witnesses:

> They were among the first deportees in the camp. . . . We recognized them by their distinctive badge. . . . It was absolutely forbidden for them to talk about their beliefs or to have any religious books, and especially the Bible, which was considered the supreme book of sedition. . . . What I admired about a lot of them was they could have left at any time just by signing a renunciation of their faith. Jehovah's Witnesses had their strength, and it was their willpower that no one could beat.[62]

Russians who had become Jehovah's Witnesses while in German concentration camps returned to their homeland and took with them the good news of God's kingdom. By 1946 there were 4,797 Witnesses active in the Soviet Union. Many of these were moved from place to place by the government over the years. Some were consigned to prison camps. Wherever they went they witnessed. Their numbers grew. Even before the government granted them legal recognition, groups of them were active all the way from Lviv to Vladivostok.[63]

After 1951, Jehovah's Witnesses began to flourish not only in Moldova, Ukraine, Belarus, the Baltic States, and all of western Russia, but also beyond the Urals, in Kazakstan, Siberia, the Far East, Sakhalin Island, and the Kamchatka Peninsula. A report on Russia written in Poland, November 4, 1955, provides the following compelling story:

> [T]he days of April 1, 7 and 8, 1951, will forever remain in the memory of Jehovah's Witnesses in Russia. During these three days there were arrests in Western Ukraine, White Russia, Bessarabia, Moldova, Latvia, Lithuania, and Estonia involving more than 7,000 persons. The arrests were carried out during the cover of night. Those arrested were not allowed to take any clothes or food with them. Whole families were loaded on carts and carried to the railroad station. The Witnesses were transported to . . . Irkutsk on the picturesque Lake of Baykal where for thousands of miles there is a virgin forest. What the persons found there was only trees, snow, and cold up to minus 72 degrees celsius. Individual families or small groups of persons were distant from each other by 80 to 120 kilometers and without any means of communication. When they arrived, their food consisted of roots and nuts. The task assigned to them by the authorities was formulated as follows: "Clear the forests, build the houses and remain here forever, work and live."[64]

What was the outcome? Walter Kolarz, in *Religion in the Soviet Union*, writes: "This was not the end of the Witnesses in Russia, but only the beginning of a new chapter in their proselytizing activities. . . . [T]he Soviet Government could have done nothing better for the dissemination of their faith."[65]

Anany Grogul's story of the work of the Jehovah's Witnesses in the Ukraine is of interest:

> My parents became Jehovah's Witnesses during World War II, in 1942, when I was 13 years old. Shortly thereafter, my father was arrested, put in jail and later transferred to the Soviet camps in the Ural Mountains. When I was 15, in 1944, the military authorities called me to service in preparation for the armed forces. As I already had a firm hold on the faith, I refused to learn war. For this reason, at the tender age of 15, I was sentenced to five years in prison. . . . 1950 was a very difficult year for me; I was again arrested and was sentenced to 25 years of incarceration because of my preaching activity. I was 21 years old. I served seven years and four months in the labor camps. I saw many people die, bloated by hunger and worn-out by hard labor. . . . After the death of Stalin in 1953, conditions began to change, and in 1957 the authorities released me from the prison. Once again I stepped into freedom, but not for long. This time they banished me to Siberia for ten years. . . . In prison I was reunited with my fleshly sister, who had already become an invalid. . . .

Her investigation was carried on in an absolutely atrocious manner. They locked her up in solitary confinement and then let rats loose in her cell. They gnawed at her feet and ran all over her body. Finally, her tormentors made her stand in cold water up to her chest and watched her agony. She was sentenced to 25 years imprisonment because of her preaching activity. Both her legs became paralyzed. For five years they kept her in the camp hospital until they finally wrote her off as dead. Then they sent her back to our parents, who had also been sent into exile in Siberia in 1951. Even in Siberia we kept up our preaching work. Every night my brother Jacob and I were busy in the basement, duplicating *The Watchtower*. We had two typewriters and a homemade duplicating machine. . . . My exile came to an end. I moved on to the Ukraine, but persecution followed me. Several times a month, members of the State Security came to my workplace and tried to persuade me to compromise my faith. They arrested me and took me to the State Security offices in Kiev. They tried to confuse me with atheistic propaganda. Then the chief of police came to see me and asked me whether I was really convinced of what I was defending. . . . I declared my readiness to die for the truth. His answer was: "If I were convinced that this is the truth, I would be ready not only to stay in prison for 3 or 5 years but to stand on one leg in prison for 60 years!" After a brief pause, he said: "Go home!"[66]

Thousands of Jehovah's Witnesses endured similar horrors in Russia due to their faith. The Witnesses' fine record is now well-known to all those who have researched the history of twentieth-century religion in Russia. On July 28, 1997, while speaking to a Washington, D.C., audience at a briefing sponsored by the Commission on Security and Cooperation in Europe, Lawrence A. Uzzell of the Keston Institute, Oxford, England, stated the following about Jehovah's Witnesses: "Thanks to Stalin, there is an unusually large concentration of Jehovah's Witnesses in eastern Siberia. . . . If Stalin could not destroy Jehovah's Witnesses and other religious minorities, no government that is likely to come to power in Russia is going to be able to."[67]

By the end of the 1980s a new period began for Jehovah's Witnesses in the territory of the Soviet Union—an era of freedom of worship. In 1989 and 1990, when the government authorities stopped viewing them as enemies, thousands of Witnesses were given the opportunity to receive Bible education at a convention held in Poland. Millions of their fellow believers around the world watched with keen interest and anticipation and wondered: When will Jehovah's Witnesses be legally recognized in the Soviet Union? On March 27, 1991, the Administrative Center of the Religious Organization of Jehovah's Witnesses in the USSR was registered.[68] Following this legal registration, a series of conventions was held in different cities throughout Russia. Freedom of worship made the Witnesses' hearts sing with joy and gave them greater zeal for Bible truth.

As of December 1996, on the territory of the former USSR, excluding the Baltic states, Moldova, and Ukraine, there are 754 congregations, 103,573 evangelizers, 111,825 Bible studies, and at the annual celebration of the Memorial of Jesus Christ's death, 275,806 persons attended. A government official of St. Petersburg, Russia, explained:

> Jehovah's Witnesses were presented to us as some kind of underground sect, sitting in the darkness and slaughtering children and killing themselves. Now I see normal, smiling people, even better than many people I know. They are peaceful and calm, and they love one another very much. I really do not understand why people tell such lies about them.[69]

Alexander Stamm wrote:

> They call each other sisters and brothers regardless of age and status in the community. . . . Children who are raised in families who are Jehovah's Witnesses are kind, decent, and neat. It is practically impossible that from these children will come alcoholics, drug addicts, scoundrels, and debauched persons. . . . Jehovah's Witnesses do not push their teaching upon anyone. They may start a conversation with you, but if you are not interested, they will not insist. Additionally, the main criterion for entering the organization is a voluntary and willing desire to prove their love for God through actions. . . . The history of the organization is old and deeply rooted in the first century of our Common Era, the time of the foundation of the first Christian communities.[70]

Those who herald freedom of religion and freedom of worship as rights rather than privileges are concerned with the implementation of the law on the freedom of conscience and on religious associations signed by President Yeltsin and officially published on October 1, 1997. On April 29, 1999, the Russian Ministry of Justice reregistered the centralized religious organization under the 1997 religion law as the "Administrative Center for Jehovah's Witnesses in Russia." Still, the struggle for freedom of religion is not over as Jehovah's Witnesses recently have had to defend themselves in unfounded civil trials and have already filed cases challenging the constitutionality of the new federal and provincial anti-proselytism laws.

MALAWI (FORMERLY NYASALAND)

The plight of the Jehovah's Witnesses in the small country of Malawi is rather typical of their plight in the continent of Africa. The evangelizing work of Jehovah's Witnesses began in Nyasaland in 1907. By 1963 the number of evangelists had increased to a peak of more than fifteen thousand in 394 congregations, and their work had begun to prosper.

In 1963 Dr. Hastings Kamuzu Banda returned to Malawi from his many years of study and medical practice abroad and was installed as an internal prime minister in the colony. He stirred up the people to fight for their independence. It was agreed with Britain that full self-rule would be granted in mid-1964 after a general election. To this end the government arranged for voluntary registration of voters to take place from December 30, 1963, to January 19, 1964.

It was at this time that Jehovah's Witnesses first found themselves thrust into what the *San Francisco Examiner* described as "a religious war . . . a very one-sided war, pitting force against faith. This meant Jehovah's Witnesses Bible-based stand of Christian neutrality versus the allegiance and loyalty demanded by Dr. Banda and his party."[71]

The Witnesses exercised their right not to register, but strong persecution broke out as efforts were made to force them to change their mind and buy party membership cards, costing the equivalent of 25 cents (U.S.). Officials were incensed at the "disrespect" shown by Jehovah's Witnesses' refusal to purchase party cards, claiming that buying one was the "one way in which we, the people of this country, can show appreciation to our Life Leader, the Ngwazi [Dr. Banda], for developing this country of Malawi."[72] For thirty years this would be cited as the crime of which the Witnesses were guilty.

In the meantime, the Watch Tower Society worked diligently to persuade the authorities to put a stop to the unwarranted persecution. To this end an interview was eventually granted with Dr. Banda on January 30, 1964. Jack Johansson, a missionary of Jehovah's Witnesses, was able to explain clearly the neutral stand of Jehovah's Witnesses. Dr. Banda seemed quite pleased with what had been said, and when Johansson left, he was thanked very much.

Four days later, on February 3, an attack was made on a group of Witnesses in the Mulanje region. Elaton Mwachande was murdered, and an elderly woman, Mona Mwiwaula, seriously wounded and left for dead. When news of this incident reached the branch office, a telegram was immediately sent to the prime minister, leading to another meeting with Dr. Banda on February 11, 1964. This time the mood was different. Dr. Banda claimed that the Witnesses were deliberately provoking their attackers and that they were not supportive of community projects. The meeting ended on a negative note: Dr. Banda alleged that Jehovah's Witnesses were the cause of the confused situation in Nyasaland and threatened that he could ban the work any time he wished.

In 1967 the situation came to a head. More and more pressure was put on the Witnesses to buy party membership cards, although doing so was supposedly voluntary. Dr. Banda, in various addresses broadcast on radio, falsely accused the Witnesses of not paying taxes and trying to prevent others from doing so. He also condemned them for not buying party cards. On October 13, 1967, Dr. Banda personally signed an order declaring Jehovah's Witnesses to be an unlawful society dangerous to the good government of Malawi. This banning order was published in a *Malawi Gazette Supplement* on October 20,

1967.[73] The banning order was taken as carte blanche by the feared Malawi Young Pioneers and Youth League, described as a kind of Hitler Youth, to unleash a wave of vicious and brutal atrocities against Jehovah's Witnesses. The police and courts, although sometimes sympathetic, were powerless to stop the violence, as the Witnesses were now outlawed in the land.

Articles describing the atrocities committed appeared in the February 1968 issues of *The Watchtower* and *Awake!*, which aroused a public outcry throughout the world. Thousands of protest letters began pouring in; additional postal workers had to be employed to work extra shifts in order to cope with the influx of mail. As a result of this public outcry, Dr. Banda issued a decree prohibiting the persecution against Jehovah's Witnesses. On October 6, 1969, he even went on record stating publicly that no one in the country should be forced to buy a political card.

The 1972 resolutions adopted at the Annual Convention of the Malawi Congress Party led to a third wave of brutal persecution, the most widespread and intense to date. These resolutions, in effect, called for Jehovah's Witnesses to be cast out of human society. A purge began. The Malawi Young Pioneers and Youth League took the lead in a virtual holy war. In the area of Blantyre, Malawi's major city, Richadi Nyasulu, Greyson Kapininga, and other Jehovah's Witnesses were taken to the headquarters of the Southern Region of the Malawi Congress Party. They were asked why they had not bought political membership cards. Upon replying that they were completely nonpolitical because of their Bible beliefs, the Witnesses were turned over to some sixteen Young Pioneers and members of the Youth League. These took turns beating each Witness. When they still refused to buy political cards, the youths rubbed a mixture of salt and red pepper into their eyes. Some were beaten on their back and buttocks with a plank of wood with nails in it. When any showed signs of pain, their attackers beat harder, saying, "Let your God come and save you." In addition, they broke a bottle and used the broken edge to shave some Witness men. Jasteni Mukhuna of the Blantyre area was beaten until his arm was broken. At Cape Maclear, at the southern end of Lake Malawi, Witness Zelphat Mbaiko was covered with bundles of grass, which were tied around him. Petrol was poured on the grass, and it was set afire. He died as a result of the burns. Southeast of Blantyre, at Kavunje Village, all the Witnesses, men and women, were badly beaten and forced to walk naked on the road. One of their children died from the beating. In the northern region of Malawi, at Nkhotakota, a Witness woman, pregnant, was stripped of her clothing and badly beaten. The local leader told small children to kick her in the stomach, his purpose being to try to cause a miscarriage. At Kamphinga Village, Matilina Chitsulo of Gwizi Village was raped by party branch chairman Kachigongo. At Mkombe Village, on October 2, 1972, Velenika Hositeni was kept in a room of the office of the M.C.P. for an entire night by the local party chairman and the party secretary, and both raped her. Seven men raped another Witness named Nezelia at the same office.

Amnesty International's 1973 report on torture confirmed these reports, stating:

> Well-substantiated reports indicate that both in 1967 and in 1972 the Young Pioneers and their supporters inflicted torture on the Jehovah's Witnesses in the form of rape, beatings, shaving with broken bottles, and burning. In the autumn of 1972 these persecutions caused a number of deaths and the migration of some 21,000 Jehovah's Witnesses to Zambia, where several hundred died in an inadequate refugee camp.[74]

Following this the Witnesses fled to Mozambique, then under Portuguese control, where eventually thirty-four thousand men, women, and children settled in twelve refugee camps. By the third week of December 1975, over three thousand male Witnesses had been confined in the infamous Dzaleka Detention Camp near Dowa, north of Lilongwe, in Malawi. All had been charged, convicted, and imprisoned for two years. Women members of the Witnesses were put into similar camps. By January 1976 more than five thousand Christian men and women were imprisoned in Malawi. The heads of these detention camps employed the Witnesses as slave laborers. Officers are quoted as telling them: "As the government has arranged, we shall make you our tractors." One of the imprisoned Witnesses wrote: "Prisoners being so many, there are only four hundred plates. So, some have hot *nsima* [a customary Malawian food] put on one hand and relish on the other. Brothers often must put the hot *nsima* on the ground and eat it from there."

Finally, on August 12, 1993, the twenty-six-year ban on the Witnesses' evangelizing work was lifted. This was announced in a *Malawi Gazette Supplement* on September 10, 1993.[75]

Interestingly, it was just a few weeks after the registration of the Society that the headquarters of the Malawi Young Pioneers, who had so brutally persecuted and harassed the Witnesses, was destroyed by the army, much to the delight of all in the country. All of their offices were closed and many of them were hunted down and killed by the army. Others fled for their lives into Mozambique, where they now live in exile.

When reports were collated properly for the first time in many years, over thirty thousand evangelizers were active in the country! A general election in 1994 saw the M.C.P. lose its thirty-year stranglehold on power. The new government has been very favorable to the Witnesses and authorities have been helpful in many ways. Since the lifting of the ban, the work has progressed. In 1998 a new peak of 42,770 evangelizers was reached. In 1998 the Memorial of Jesus Christ's death was attended by over 120,412[76] and the 1996 series of district conventions was attended by over 117,000.

The integrity of Jehovah's Witnesses has been remarkable in this small Central African state. Despite the years of persecution, described as one of the most brutal, inhuman persecutions of Christians in the twentieth century, the Witnesses have come through with their strong faith intact.

NIGERIA

Nigeria is more than twice the size of California and has three times its population—about 107 million. It is the most populous country in Africa and has the largest population of Witness preachers in that continent. Almost a quarter of all Witnesses in Africa live in Nigeria.

The outbreak of World War II brought severe trials to Jehovah's Witnesses in Nigeria, as in other lands. On May 10, 1940, an Order in Council prohibited the importation of Watch Tower Society publications into Nigeria, claiming that they contained seditious and undesirable matter.

When the war had ended, Jehovah's Witnesses in Nigeria were delighted to see the increase in their numbers. They had weathered six hard years and yet had grown from 636 in 1939 to 3,542 in 1946. The time now seemed right to attempt to have the ban on the Society's literature lifted. The Witnesses requested the general public to sign a petition and then provided it to the Legislative Council on March 18, 1946. The 1947 Yearbook of Jehovah's Witnesses reported:

> We had barely a fortnight to get matters through, but the brethren worked hard and were privileged to secure over 10,000 signatures of the educated class. . . . The authorities were astonished to see the names of almost all the leading citizens. . . . [Two months later] the ban was rescinded, to the joy of the brethren and the general public, who cheered us wherever we went. The news was gazetted by the government on May 18, 1946, and on the following morning the local press blazed it out in bold headlines.[77]

Jehovah's Witnesses also had severe problems during the Nigerian civil war (1966-70), but the war years did not slow the growth of the evangelizing work. In 1965 there were 37,392 Witnesses preaching in Nigeria. After the war ended on January 15, 1970, there were 62,641 Witnesses. During those five years, 24,486 new ones had been baptized, compared with 12,230 for the previous five years. By 1971 the number of evangelizers had grown to 75,372. In 1976 an average of 107,924 shared in the preaching. In 1998 a new peak in evangelizers of 222,306 was reached.

In order to make the evangelizing work more effective, Jehovah's Witnesses in Nigeria provide a literacy program. The first classes started in October 1949 in each congregation, using manuals that were prepared locally by the Watch Tower Society. This literacy program continues to this day and has produced good results. Between 1970 and 1996 Jehovah's Witnesses taught over twenty-two thousand persons in Nigeria to read and write.

Today, Jehovah's Witnesses in Nigeria are generally well respected. Dr. Nnamdi Azikiwe, the governor-general of Nigeria in 1960, told his Council of Ministers: "If all the religious denominations were like Jehovah's Witnesses, we would have no murders, burglaries, delinquencies, prisoners, and atomic bombs. Doors would not be locked day in and day out."[78] An editorial in the *Daily Sketch* said: "Jehovah's Witnesses are good citizens. They pay their taxes regularly and promptly. They do not give wrong information that would lead to their being under-assessed [by tax officials]. They are consistent and hard workers indeed, ideal citizens."[79]

CONCLUSION: EVANGELISM AT THE CLOSE OF THE TWENTIETH CENTURY

These stories of evangelism of Jehovah's Witnesses can be duplicated for many other countries around the world. Many other countries feature a similar narrative: the first visits and work of Charles Russell or other early Witnesses; the faithful distribution of Bible literature; the courageous stands on conscientious objection to the military in World War II or during revolutionary wars; the struggle for registration of their churches and publication societies; the insistence of Witnesses on abiding by the teaching of the Bible, sometimes at the cost of severe persecution and torture; and the insistence of all to be Witnesses for Jehovah.

Jehovah's Witnesses, of course, are not alone in recognizing the need for evangelism. Britain's churches, for example, have united in 1990 behind the slogan "A Decade of Evangelism." But the consistent position of Jehovah's Witnesses (who avoid political entanglements) is attractive to thinking people glad to have a biblical position that is clear and straightforward. The rapid growth among Jehovah's Witnesses is understandable.

Jehovah's Witnesses, who carefully abstain from politics, still have a positive contribution to make through their evangelism. Let us quote the following from Professor Eke-Henner W. Kluge, University of Victoria, Canada, in a letter written specifically to the government of Latvia:

> As the former Director of the Department of Ethics and Legal Affairs of the Canadian Medical Association and as a member of the Advisory Committee on Ethical Issues in Health Care to the British Columbia Ministry of Health, I have had some considerable experience with members of said faith. I have found that the preceding allegations to the contrary, Jehovah's Witnesses constitute a law-abiding, fair-minded and industrious community that cherishes family values and ties. While their beliefs may differ from those of others, this cannot be construed as undermining the value of religious freedom that should be the hall-mark of a democratic society.
>
> Rather than constituting a threat to the peace and order of society, their actions have been entirely in keeping with the fundamental values of the society in which I live, which is to say, with the values of personal integrity, religious freedom, and obedience to the duly constituted laws of our society.[80]

Similar thoughts are expressed by Eugene Meehan:

The history of Jehovah's Witnesses as a recognized religion in Canada dates back more than 100 years. They are highly respected for their courage and their contribution to Canadian freedoms, especially during the dark days of World War II and the decades following, and in particular leading to the Canadian Charter of Rights and Freedoms. On ten occasions, Jehovah's Witnesses have appeared before the Supreme Court of Canada to advocate issues essential to the peace, good order and tolerance of a free society. Their landmark decisions in the Supreme Court are studied in Canadian universities and elsewhere as models in the legal process of democratic nation-building. The importance of these decisions is such that by necessity, before they graduate from university, all lawyers in Canada study the legal contribution of Jehovah's Witnesses to national law and freedoms. . . . [81]

Also note the comments of Bernard Dickens:

My first and major observation is that the community of Jehovah's Witnesses is a peaceable community devoted to living in harmony with neighbours. As a group of people deeply committed to their religious convictions, they naturally assert their beliefs in the face of oppression, and find it right to seek converts to a faith they find convincing and beneficent within the limits of tolerance in societies committed to religious freedom and pluralism. When their convictions are reasonably accommodated in civil societies, none of their practices is objectionable, and many are praiseworthy. They are a self-disciplined community, taking proper pride in the extent to which they give witness to their faith.[82]

Finally, we conclude our discussion of evangelism of Jehovah's Witnesses by referring again to the early Christian Church and the honorable position of those who paved the way:

With that they called them and charged them, nowhere to make any utterance or to teach upon the basis of the name of Jesus. But in reply Peter and John said to them: "Whether it is righteous in the sight of God to listen to you rather than to God, judge for yourselves. But as for us, we cannot stop speaking about the things we have seen and heard" (Acts 4:18-20).

"We positively ordered you not to keep teaching upon the basis of this name, and yet, look! You have filled Jerusalem with your teaching, and you are determined to bring the blood of this man upon us." In answer Peter and the [other] apostles said: "We must obey God as ruler rather than men" (Acts 5:28-29).

When the apostle Paul knew that his martyrdom was approaching, he sent to Timothy this instruction that rings out to Christians over the centuries: "I solemnly charge you before God and Christ Jesus, who is destined to judge the living and the dead, . . . preach the word, be at it urgently in favorable season, in troublesome season, . . . keep your senses in all things, suffer evil, do [the] work of an evangelizer, fully accomplish your ministry" (2 Tm 4:1,2,5). This divinely inspired directive is as alive and as necessary today as on the day it was written. Jehovah's Witnesses are happy to follow it.

14.

Proselytism and Religious Freedom
in the
Seventh-day Adventist Church

Norman K. Miles

Religious movements often develop a self-identity based on their concept of mission. This self-identity includes the group's reason for existence and may determine its position on a host of social, political, and ethical issues. Sects that developed as reform groups often followed the logical course of their reforms into areas such as dress, diet, social arrangements, economic theory, and political stance. This was especially true of groups that developed in the United States during the Second Great Awakening (ca. 1800-60). Of the groups formed during this period, the Seventh-day Adventist Church has emerged as the most diverse in scope and international in membership. It operates schools, churches, hospitals, clinics, and other institutions in almost every country, and its active evangelistic posture has made it one of the fastest-growing churches in the world.

This chapter discusses the Seventh-day Adventist positions on proselytization and religious freedom—two issues that in Adventist thinking are intertwined. The key ideals of the Seventh-day Adventist Church in these areas were well-developed by 1865, as an outgrowth of its understanding of self-identity, mission, and biblical eschatology. In subsequent decades these concepts were analyzed and refined in the light of further theological understanding, but they have remained essentially unchanged. Since 1975 there has been significant movement within the church to reemphasize the importance and veracity of these traditional Adventist ideals. In order to develop a clear understanding of the church's stance on these two issues, and how they relate to one another, it is necessary to understand the roots of Adventism, its self-identity and concept of mission.

ADVENTIST ROOTS

The Seventh-day Adventist Church has its roots in the Millerite movement of the 1830s and 1840s, which was one of the most vital religious movements of the Second Great Awakening.[1] William Miller, a New York farmer and Baptist preacher, was the catalyst of the movement, which was to dominate much of the religious debate during the early years of the Second Great Awakening. In his early years Miller expressed little religious fervor, and as a young man was a self-declared Deist. As a captain in the United States Army during the War of 1812, Miller saw combat action during the battles around Lake Champlain. He became convinced that his life had been miraculously spared. When he returned home after the war he became a Baptist minister and set out systematically to study the Bible. Armed with a *Cruden's Concordance* as his only study aid, Miller became a relentless student of the prophecies of the Bible, especially the time prophecies of the books of Daniel and the Revelation. Using generally accepted principles of biblical interpretation of the day, and calculating the time prophecies, Miller came to the conclusion that the second advent of Christ would take place sometime between 1838 and 1845. He developed a number of charts to support his conclusions and began to preach his message in the various churches around upstate New York. His message of the imminent return of Christ might have only been an interesting historical footnote had it not been for Joshua V. Himes.

Joshua V. Himes was the pastor of a large Congregationalist Church in Boston. In 1840 he heard Miller preach and was impressed with his message. He was surprised that Miller preached his message only in the small communities around his home. Convinced of the truth of Miller's message, Himes took it upon himself to spread the message further. His first step was to invite Miller to conduct a series of meetings at his church in Boston. A first-class publicist, Himes succeeded in assembling a large audience to hear Miller preach. The meetings made such an impact that soon Miller received invitations to speak in large cities throughout the Northeast. Himes was also instrumental in the development of an Adventist journal, *The Signs of the Times*, which was widely distributed. Before long thousands of adherents of William Miller's teachings scattered throughout various churches across the country, especially in New England and upstate New York. In 1842 Himes founded an additional Adventist paper, *The Midnight Cry*. Other followers of Miller developed pamphlets and newsletters to help spread the news of the imminent second coming of Christ. Joseph Bates, a retired seaman living in Maine, began to publish various pamphlets. He was aided by a group of young men, the most notable being one James White, who rapidly became a leader of the New England Millerites.

Before 1844 Miller was constantly pressured to refine his message and more closely determine the day of the Lord's appearing. After several calculations and recalculations, Miller finally announced that he expected the Lord to return on October 22, 1844. A firm date for the return of the Lord galvanized the Millerite communities across the country. Pamphlets were printed and distributed at a breakneck pace. People sold property so they could make greater financial contributions to the work of warning the world, and the number of Millerite believers began to swell. The reaction of the established churches was swift and strong. Most opposed Millerite teachings as heresy and were put off by the extreme denunciations by some Millerites against church leaders who opposed their message. It is estimated that by the summer of 1844 over sixty thousand people who claimed to believe the advent message were expelled from their various churches. Some felt that their rejection by the mainline churches was the last great sign of the correctness of their position and accepted their place in the long line of those who suffered persecution for righteousness sake. They had only to wait for the Master's return.

The Millerite movement faced harsh opposition for reasons besides its predictions of the coming of Christ. Many religious movements of the period made predictions about the coming of Christ and the new millennium. But most groups were *post*millennialists, who believed that revival preaching and societal reform would bring about a thousand years of Eden-like peace, and then Jesus would come and set up his kingdom. The Millerites were *pre*millennialists, who believed that Jesus would come first and that the millennium would follow his second advent. What turned out to be most troubling about the Millerites was their belief that the second coming would be accompanied by catastrophic disaster and a fiery destruction of the world before Jesus set up his kingdom. This concept of the advent set them apart from almost all Christian groups of the time. Their success in publishing their views gave them a visibility other groups did not have, thus making them a target for abuse and ridicule—particularly when Jesus failed to return on the appointed day.

The folklore surrounding the Great Disappointment is rich, and much of it is fictional. Stories of people making ascension robes or standing on the rooftops so that they would be closer to Jesus and the angels were certainly untrue. There is little evidence that there was widespread destitution among the advent believers following the disappointment, but there were some people who failed to dig their potatoes and conduct other business in the belief that it would soon be unnecessary. What is abundantly clear is that October 22, 1844, was more than the day Jesus failed to return. It was the watershed event in the history of American Adventism. The disappointment and depression of the Millerite believers on the night of October 22, 1844, was almost overwhelming. They had put their trust and fondest hopes in the belief that Jesus would return on this date. Some had been expelled from their churches and ridiculed by their families, while others suffered financial loss. What went wrong? Was there an answer to this dilemma, or were they just the victims of a cruel religious hoax?

Almost immediately, advent believers came up with a variety of answers. Some came to the conclusion that the whole teaching about the advent was just a hoax. Some of them gave up on religion completely. Most humbly made their way back to their former spiritual communities, acknowledged that they were victims of a deception, and tried to forget their Millerite enthusiasm. But others came to the conclusion that there had been a miscalculation, and they immediately pressed Miller to predict another date. Those who accepted this position continued to predict dates, which came and went uneventfully. After the Lord failed to appear in 1850, this group faded out of existence.

Perhaps the smallest Millerite segment continued to believe that Miller's calculations were correct and that something did happen on October 22, 1844. Initially, some believed that the 1844 date marked the time of the end, and that they were in the tarrying time. They noted that in the parable of the Ten Virgins there was a period of time when the virgins slumbered while waiting for the bridegroom. Believing that the church was in the tarrying time, these believers embraced what came to be known as the "Shut Door Theory." This theory held that all who were going to be saved had been marked in the books of heaven and that the door was shut on further converts. Further attempts to evangelize were unnecessary; they had only to wait a little while longer through this "testing" period. During the first few days after the Great Disappointment, *The Midnight Cry* speculated that the testing time would not be long and that the believers needed only to remain faithful. Within a few weeks *The Midnight Cry* abandoned the Shut Door Theory and embraced a new position postulated by Hiram Edson of New York.

Edson and a number of upstate New York Millerites were convinced that their biblical computations were correct. They came to believe that they were mistaken not about their calculations of time but about the nature of the event predicted in the Bible. Their Bible study led them to reexamine the ante-typical day of judgment enacted in the sanctuary system. They concluded that on October 22, 1844, Jesus's priestly ministry on behalf of the human family moved from the holy place to the most holy place, signaling the beginning of the judgment of the human race ("the investigative judgment"). They determined that the biblical phrase "cleansing of the sanctuary" referred not to the second advent of Christ but to the beginning of the final phase of judgment. This theory was shared among those who remained within the circle of Millerite communications, and within a short time New England Adventists such as Joseph Bates and James and Ellen White, came to agree with Hiram Edson and his New York co-religionists. This position energized those advent believers who accepted it. There was a reasonable explanation for the Great Disappointment that did not destroy the original basis of their beliefs. There was a new imperative to work toward evangelizing the general population, and a strong emphasis on continual reform of the group and society. It was in the areas of evangelism and societal reform that the infant group would become the founders of the Seventh-day Adventist Church.

Between 1850 and 1860 the advent believers were hard at work studying the Bible, shaping doctrinal positions, and sharing those positions with others. Itinerant evangelists encouraged advent believers and shared with them the emerging body of doctrinal beliefs. This was not a period of true proselytization, because there was no religious organization to which people could be brought. Indeed, many of the advent believers strongly resisted the development of a formal church structure, fearing that formal organization would hinder believers from following the lead of the Holy Spirit and would enslave the movement with adherence to formal creeds. Much of the work of people like Ellen and James White, Hiram Edson, Joseph Bates, John Byington, and other emerging leaders was to keep the believers united and to manage the rapid changes within the movement. *The Sabbath Review and Advent Herald*, a paper printed and published by James White, was a vital instrument during this period, providing important communication, doctrinal and devotional articles, and news of work in various Adventist communities. Between 1850 and 1860 the advent believers accepted and wove into their system of beliefs a whole series of doctrines—sabbatarianism, trinitarianism, justification, sanctification, bodily resurrection of the dead, freedom of the will, and the beginning of health reform. *The Review and Herald* was probably the single most important vehicle for convincing believers of the veracity of these new beliefs and for uniting them with a sense of common belief and destiny. Within the pages of the *Review* the advent movement was increasingly identified as the "remnant church" of Bible prophecy, which kept the commandments of God and had the testimony of Jesus. As early as 1855 the pages of the *Review* contained articles stressing the importance of sharing these gospel understandings with the entire world.

As the movement grew in scope and complexity, it became essential that some sort of organization be formed to consolidate the gains made, give the group a sense of identity, and provide direction for the future. By 1860 a core group of Adventist leaders met in Battle Creek, Michigan, and organized a new church organization. They named this new organization the Seventh-day Adventist Church to emphasize their cherished hope in the imminent return of Jesus and their concern that the entire Christian world should keep all of the Ten Commandments, especially the Fourth Commandment concerning observance of the Sabbath. The new Seventh-day Adventist Church saw itself responsible to warn the world about the reality of living within the judgment hour and to call Christian communities to a higher standard of living in the light of the reality of the judgment hour.

For Adventists, this could be accomplished only by vigorous evangelism and absolute religious freedom. Like other religious groups shaped during the Second Great Awakening, religious freedom was an absolute prerequisite to any meaningful conversion. True conversion could occur only if there was freedom to refuse the entreaties of the Lord. Thus from the very beginning the Seventh-day Adventist Church endorsed vigorous proselytization while championing absolute religious freedom for all. During the next 130 years this position became central to the beliefs and operational philosophy of Seventh-day Adventists.

THE PROSELYTIZATION IMPULSE

The word *proselytization* is seldom found in Seventh-day Adventist vocabulary. The more common expressions referring to proselytization are *evangelism* and *soul winning*. Seventh-day Adventists believe that evangelism, the proclamation of the gospel, is fundamental to the mission of the church. Aggressive evangelism has played a major role in the growth of the church. In the early years of the church's development there were no settled pastors. Evangelism was carried on by a few itinerant evangelists assisted by local elders. The first generation of Adventist evangelists emphasized the necessity of local members assisting in the work of reaching people for Christ. Members were encouraged to assist the evangelists in giving Bible studies and sharing the gospel with their friends. Although times have changed, evangelism, especially of the personal nature, is still considered fundamental to the Seventh-day Adventist faith and lifestyle. Each member is encouraged to share the good news of the gospel with others in the hope that they might accept the teachings Adventists hold so dear. This concept is summed up in commitment seven in the baptismal vows of the Seventh-day Adventist Church:

> Do you look forward to the soon coming of Jesus and the blessed home when "this mortal shall . . . put on immortality"? As you prepare to meet the Lord, will you witness to His loving salvation by using your talents in personal soul-winning endeavor to help others to be ready for His glorious appearing?[2]

The Seventh-day Adventist Church takes very seriously the Great Commission (Mt 28:10-20). In accordance with the injunction to preach the gospel to every person in every nation, the church at a very early time in its history embarked on an aggressive program of world evangelism. This work was considered all the more imperative since the church holds that society is living in the last days before the second advent of Christ. Advent urgency and the belief in complete obedience to the commandments of God are their unique contribution to the world. For Adventists, this is more than an ideal; it represents what is considered the duty of each individual member of the church. "Every church member is under a sacred command from Jesus to use his talents in personal soul-winning work in helping to give the gospel to all the world," reads the *Seventh-day Adventist Church Manual*. "When this work is finished Jesus will come (Matt. 25:14-29)."[3]

In 1900 Ellen G. White, the prophetic voice of the Seventh-day Adventist Church, wrote:

> We should now feel the responsibility of laboring with intense earnestness to impart to others the truths that God has given for this time. We cannot be too much in earnest. . . . Now is the time for the last warning

to be given. There is a special power in the presentation of the truth at the present time; but how long will it continue? Only a little while. If there was ever a crisis it is now. All are now deciding their eternal destiny. Men need to be aroused to realize the solemnity of the time, the nearness of the day when human probation shall be ended. Decided efforts should be made to bring the message for this time prominently before the people. The Third angel is to go forth with great power.[4]

While Adventists are encouraged to share their faith with their immediate neighbors, the church has always urged its members to adopt a worldwide perspective regarding the mission of the church. Between 1880 and 1900 the church initiated a strong missionary outreach throughout the world beginning in Western Europe, the southern parts of the United States, the major cities throughout the United States, and Australia. The plan was to develop a strong missionary apparatus, including schools, churches, health institutions, and publishing facilities, in the developed nations. These were to be the places where workers would be trained to perform medical, educational, and evangelistic work in the areas of the world considered undeveloped and uncivilized. As Ellen White put it:

> At this time there should be representatives of present truth in every city, and in the remote parts of the earth. The whole earth is to be illuminated with the glory of God's truth. The light is to shine to all lands and all peoples. And it is from those who have received the light that it is to shine forth. . . .
>
> Certain countries have advantages that mark them as centers of education and influence. In the English speaking nations and the Protestant nations of Europe it is comparatively easy to find access to the people, and there are many advantages for establishing institutions and carrying forward our work. . . . America has many institutions to give character to the work. Similar facilities should be furnished for England, Australia, Germany, and Scandinavia, and other continental countries as the work advances. In these countries the Lord has able workmen, laborers of experience. These can lead out in the establishment of institutions, the training of workers, and the carrying forward of the work in its different lines. God designs that they shall be furnished with means and facilities. The institutions established would give character to the work in other countries, and would give opportunity for the training of workers for the darker heathen nations. In this way the efficiency of our experienced workers would be multiplied a hundredfold.[5]

This pattern of world missionary enterprise was carried forward for decades, with the United States, Europe, and Australia producing thousands of missionaries who went to all points of the globe to win souls. So successful was the missionary enterprise of the Adventist church that by 1965—100 years after the organization of the church—schools, churches, hospitals, and publishing houses were operated by Seventh-day Adventists in almost every country of the world. Today the fastest-growing areas of the church are in Africa and Latin America. About 85 percent of the membership of the Seventh-day Adventist Church today is in areas outside North America. International broadcasts such as the Voice of Prophecy, Faith for Today, It Is Written, Breath of Life, and Adventist World Radio are among the many modern methods of reaching large numbers of people around the world with the gospel.

PROSELYTIZING AMONG OTHER FAITHS

Because Seventh-day Adventists believe that theirs is a holistic message for all people near the end of time, Adventist evangelists have always welcomed people who come to the Adventist church from other denominations. All of the original Adventist pioneers, of course, came from other Christian faiths, and a large number of those who join the church today are converts from other denominations. As the Adventist evangelistic work developed during the last quarter of the nineteenth century, some evangelists denounced ministers of other faiths, particularly Catholics, in their public presentations. Some evangelists and writers also shared too readily in the general anti-Catholic bias of the time as they preached Adventist doctrine. Ellen White was very forthright in condemning such practices and constantly advised against evangelizing in a way that would stir up ill will.

> Let not those who write for our papers make unkind thrusts and allusions that will certainly do harm, and that will hedge up the way and hinder us from doing the work that we should do in order to reach all classes, the Catholics included. It is our work to speak the truth in love, and not to mix in with the truth the unsanctified elements of the natural heart, and speak things that savor of the same spirit possessed by our enemies. All sharp thrusts will come back upon us in double measure when the power is in the hands of those who can exercise it for our injury. Over and over the message has been given to me that we are not to say one word, not to publish one sentence, especially by way of personalities, unless positively essential in vindicating the truth, that will stir up our enemies against us, and arouse their passions to a white heat. . . .
>
> It is true that we are commanded to "cry aloud, spare not, lift up thy voice like a trumpet, and show My people their transgression, and the house of Jacob their sins" Isa. 58:1. This message must be given, but while it must be given, we should be careful not to thrust and crowd and condemn those who have not the light that we have. We should not go out of our way to make hard thrusts at the Catholics. Among the Catholics there are many who are most conscientious Christians, and who

walk in the light that shines upon them, and God will work in their behalf. Those who have failed to improve their physical, mental, and moral powers, but who have lived to please themselves, and have refused to bear their responsibility, are in greater danger and in greater condemnation before God than those who are in error upon doctrinal points, yet who seek to live to do good to others. Do not censure others; do not condemn them.[6]

Ellen White also recommended that definite work be initiated to seek to convert Jews:

There is a mighty work to be done in our world. The Lord has declared that the Gentiles shall be gathered in, and not the Gentiles only, but the Jews. There are among the Jews many who will be converted and through whom we shall see the salvation of God go forth as a lamp that burneth. There are Jews everywhere, and to them the light of present truth is to be brought. There are among them many who will come to the light, and with wonderful power. The Lord God will work, He will do wonderful things in righteousness.[7]

For Seventh-day Adventists, the whole world is their responsibility, and people who choose to convert to Adventism from other faith communities are welcomed. Winning converts from other faiths is not regarded as a negative outcome by Seventh-day Adventists. Most people who convert to Adventism come from other faith groups rather than from the unchurched. This has led to accusations of Adventists as "sheep stealers," but the church and many who join the church see Adventism as a progression in the Christian journey. For many of them, joining the Seventh-day Adventist Church is a logical step in their desire to follow biblical teachings and to grow spiritually.

Seventh-day Adventists sometimes refer to themselves as the "remnant church," a term which was embraced by early Adventists who were scattered and unorganized but who were faithful to the advent hope. The term appears numerous times in the Bible, often referring to a small group of people who are faithful to God in the midst of a largely unfaithful society. In Revelation 12:7 the term "remnant" is derived from the Old Testament usage, which describes a succession of Israelites who remained faithful to God despite overwhelming cultural apostasy. These were the chosen people of their generations who were usually misunderstood and sometimes persecuted for their faithfulness to divine instruction. The faithful groups from Old Testament times to the Protestant Reformation were considered the remnant people of their day who preached a special and often unpopular message and sought to purify the spiritual community. Early Adventists saw themselves as another group in a long line of remnant groups who sought to serve the Lord in purity and obedience. Adventists believed that the Protestant churches constituted the remnant churches of their time, but that they became satisfied with their progress and were unwilling to journey theologically beyond their founders. Because of this theological impasse, God raised up another group to preach the last message to the world with power and to call nominal Christians to a higher standard of piety and obedience. Since Adventists believed that the messages of the three angels in Revelation 14:6-12 were God's last great appeal to sinners, they identified themselves with the remnant of the seed of the woman (the church) of Revelation 12:17.

The first known use of the term *remnant church* by Adventists appeared in the first Seventh-Day Adventist pamphlet, Ellen G. White's *A Word to the Little Flock* (1847), one of whose chapters was entitled, "To the Remnant Scattered Abroad." Successive publications would emphasize the development of a remnant theology, which identified the Seventh-day Adventist Church as having a special role in the great controversy between God and Satan throughout history. Early Seventh-day Adventist writers such as Uriah Smith and James White linked the term *remnant* directly with the Adventist movement on the basis that:

1. Seventh-day Adventists are the only ones who meet the conditions specified in Revelation 12:17 which describe the remnant in that they keep the faith of Jesus and keep all of the commandments of God.

2. Satan's war on the remnant is the last series of prophetic events, and comes after the 1260 days of Revelation 12:6 (after 1844).

3. The figurative word, remnant, must represent the latest members of the church of Jesus Christ living in the time just prior to the second advent.[8]

Today, Seventh-day Adventists emphasize the biblical usage of the term but see themselves as the continuation of the Reformation with a special message of reform and revival for the last days in earth's history. As part of the message of the end, Adventists believe that Revelation 13:15-17 indicates that one of the methods used by Satan in the last deception is to compel people to compromise their consciences in matters of religion. They therefore see freedom of religion as critical for the salvation of humanity.

FREE TO BELIEVE

From the earliest days of the organization of the Seventh-day Adventist Church the leadership upheld concepts of religious liberty and separation of church and state. In part, this was a reflection of the strong support of religious liberty that prevailed in America during the church's formative years. As a church born in the northern portions of the United States during the middle of the nineteenth century, the church readily incorporated the republican ideals of liberty into its understanding of how its members should relate to society. More important, however, the church believed that freedom of conscience was an unqualified gift from God that Satan's last great deception would be combined with an attempt to force people to act against their consciences in matters of religion.

Adventists believe that liberty of conscience in matters of religion is a basic human right and that any type of compulsion in matters of religious conscience is wrong. The church defines religious liberty as:

> freedom from coercion in religious matters, by way of either compulsion or interference, in respect to one's choice, profession, or practice of any religion (or no religion); a freedom limited only at the point of infringement on the rights of others.[9]

Because the church views religious liberty as a fundamental human right, it stands against mere toleration alone. For Adventists, religious toleration implies sufferance granted to nonconformists. Such a concept is unacceptable, for it contemplates that the freedoms granted to religious nonconformists may also be withdrawn. Since God has given humanity freedom of choice it is unacceptable for human powers to compel anyone in matters of conscience and religion.

Adventists predicated their position on religious liberty on basic biblical principles: (1) the kingdom of Christ is not a political entity (John 18:36); (2) Christians have an obligation to obey civil authority (Mt 22:16-21; Rom 13:1-8); and (3) Christians are to obey God if there is a conflict between divine and human requirements (Acts 5:29, Dn 3:6). Basic to the Adventist concept of religious freedom is the belief that people can best fulfill their obligations to God and the nation under a government which holds the separation of church and state as a basic tenet.

The Seventh-day Adventist position on religious liberty began to take shape as early as the 1850s, under the leadership of several Adventist writers. J. N. Andrews and Hiram Edson, for example, identified the two horns of the lamb-like beast of Revelation 13:11 as representing civil and religious liberty.[10] R. F. Cottrell sought to clarify the Adventist position in an 1865 article entitled "Should Christians Fight?," which dealt with issues of separation of church and state and the Christian's responsibility to the state. By the end of the Civil War in 1865 the Adventist position on these issues was fairly well-formed. Adventists considered it their duty to be good citizens and to obey the laws of the land. They also held that the church as a spiritual body should be apolitical in nature and considered any union of church and state to be dangerous to the spiritual integrity of the church and the political integrity of the state.

In the nineteenth century many of the religious laws on the books, especially Sunday laws, had become dead letters. In 1863, however, the National Reform Association was created to institute a moral revival in the United States. One of its specific goals was to unite the mainstream Christian churches in their promotion of the sacredness of Sunday and to have Sunday legally established as the day of public worship in the United States. By the 1880s this movement had achieved measurable success. Sunday laws were revived, and Seventh-day Adventists suffered greatly as a result. In some places Adventists were imprisoned or subject to heavy fines for violation of the Sunday laws.

Adventists saw these developments as dangerous to religious freedom, not just of themselves but of all people. They responded in two ways.

First, in 1883 the General Conference of Seventh-day Adventists agreed to launch a massive public information and education campaign passing the following resolutions:

> 26. Whereas, we as students of prophecy, have for years anticipated the present Sunday movement, and understand that there is a conflict before us, the magnitude of which can scarcely be appreciated: and
>
> Whereas, thousands of earnest Christians are laboring sincerely for the enforcement of the Sunday laws, who would not do so if the claims of the true Sabbath were placed before them: therefore
>
> Resolved, that we remind our people of their duty to place the great light which God has given them upon the Sabbath question before others; and we urge that this be done before the leaders of this Sunday movement have opportunity to represent the issues of this question in a false light.
>
> 27. Resolved, that we need tracts, both large and small, upon the present issues of the Sunday movement.
>
> 28. Whereas, the ever-shifting front of this Sunday question calls constantly for new arguments, and the stealth of their movements calls for constant vigilance; therefore
>
> Resolved, that we recommend the publication of a four-page paper the size of the *Review*, monthly, whose mission shall be to oppose this Sunday law enforcement, this paper to be conducted by a committee of five, appointed by this Conference.[11]

Accordingly, in 1884 the proposed journal, the *Sabbath Sentinel*, was established. Its purpose was to sound the alarm on the true nature and implications of uniting church and state and agitating for religious legislation.[12]

Second, in 1889 the National Religious Liberty Association was organized in Battle Creek, Michigan—the first of several organizations formed by the Seventh-day Adventist Church to promote religious freedom. In its Declaration of Principles the following four resolutions dealing directly with religious liberty were set forth:

> We believe in supporting the civil government, and submitting to its authority.

We deny the right of any civil government to legislate on religious questions.

We believe it is the right, and should be the privilege, of every man to worship according to the dictates of his own conscience.

We also believe it to be our duty to use every lawful and honorable means to prevent religious legislation by the civil government; that we and our fellow citizens may enjoy the inestimable blessings of both civil and religious liberty.[13]

In 1887 the General Conference recommended that the various state conferences form committees to assist in the defense of those members who faced prosecution for the violation of Sunday laws. So successful was their work that religious persecution and the move to enact further Sunday legislation began to wane appreciably by 1890. Efforts to educate the public in the area of religious liberty became sporadic, and some even questioned the necessity of the religious liberty department and the publication of the *Sabbath Sentinel*. A revival of interest in Sunday legislation between 1913 and 1917 and a renewed prosecution of Seventh-day Adventists, however, spurred the religious liberty arm of the church back into action. It has remained continuously active under various names until today.

In many countries the religious liberty department acts in an advisory capacity. In the United States the department, officially known as the Public Affairs and Religious Liberty Department of the General Conference of Seventh-day Adventists, has been very active in combating every type of religious discrimination—involving cases of Sunday legislation, freedom to distribute religious literature, employment discrimination, and the right to receive unemployment compensation benefits. The department has also allied with other groups in submitting briefs as friends of the court (*amici curiae*) in various religious liberty cases. Although the Seventh-day Adventist Church has adopted an apolitical stance with regard to partisan politics, it is very involved in the struggle to preserve the right to worship according to one's conscience around the world. Each Seventh-day Adventist church is considered an informal religious liberty association and is expected to choose a leader who will work with the local pastor to support efforts to ensure the maintenance of freedom of religion.[14]

Seventh-day Adventists are very sensitive to religious liberty issues, and during a great part of the church's history its members have faced discrimination, particularly with regard to their pacifism and Sabbath observance. The experience of being a religious minority that has suffered persecution has deeply affected the psyche of the church. Seventh-day Adventists understand the nature of religious persecution and know that sincere people with the best motives can act repressively and inhumanely. Adventists realize that religious persecution and intolerance are most often the results of forced conformity in a misguided attempt to bring about social stability and spiritual development. They understand that true spirituality can flourish best when people are given the opportunity to worship and believe as they are persuaded by their own conscience.

This understanding is eloquently expressed in the fundamental principles of religious liberty, which are a part of the official policy statement of the church.

1. In a changing world it is essential to retain in clear focus the unchanging principles that govern the relationships between God the creator and humanity, between church and government, and to make clear the application of those principles to specific situations as they develop. Seventh-day Adventists believe these fundamental principles to be:

a. That God as Creator of all things has established the relationships that should prevail between Himself and humanity, and between church and government.

b. That God endowed humanity with intelligence, with the means for obtaining a knowledge of the Creator's purpose and will for the individual, with moral perception and conscience, with the power of free choice to determine one's own destiny, and with responsibility to the Creator for the use one makes of these faculties: and that the first and supreme duty is to know and to cooperate with the Creator's revealed will.

c. That an individual's relationship to other human beings rests on the basic principle of unselfish love as illustrated in the words, "Whatsoever ye would that men should do to you, do ye even so to them" (Matthew 7:12), and that application of this principle involves recognition of the equal rights of others under God and a direct responsibility to God for our treatment of one another.

d. That the Church is a divinely ordained institution, the role of which is to preserve and to proclaim God's message to humanity, to assist individuals in making His design effective in their hearts and lives, and to unite its members in fellowship, worship and service.

e. That civil government is ordained by God: that its divinely-appointed function is to protect individuals in the legitimate exercise of their rights, to provide a suitable environment in which they can pursue the objectives set for them by their Creator.

f. That in view of its divinely-ordained role, civil government is entitled to humanity's respectful and willing obedience in temporal matters to the extent that civil requirements do not conflict with those of God; in other words, humanity is bound to "render therefore unto Caesar the things that are Caesar's" but to reserve for "God the things that are God's" (Matthew 22:21), to exercise an active, personal interest and concern in matters affecting the public welfare and to be an exemplary citizen.

g. That humanity's two-fold duty to God and to government implies that God has delegated authority over strictly temporal matters to government, while reserving to Himself authority over strictly spiritual matters; that in matters where secular and religious interests overlap, government, in the best interests of both church and government, must observe strict neutrality in religious matters, neither promoting nor restricting individuals or the Church in the legitimate exercise of their rights.

h. That religious freedom consists of the inalienable right to believe and to worship God according to conscience, without coercion, restraint or civil disability, and to practice or to change one's religion and to promulgate it without interference of penalty.

i. That the right to religious freedom includes the obligation to grant the same right to others.

j. That each community of faith has the right to organize and operate in harmony with its own religious beliefs.[15]

CONCLUSIONS

Unlike other religious groups that have had to struggle with issues of evangelism and religious liberty, the Seventh-day Adventist Church has had a consistent philosophy almost from the beginning of its existence. First, Seventh-day Adventists understand that churches grow as a result of vigorous efforts to win whoever will accept the gospel message. For them, evangelism is what the church exists for, and they embrace people from every nation, class, race, and former belief. Second, Seventh-day Adventists believe in the freedom of the will and reject any compulsion with regard to religious belief. Third, Seventh-day Adventists believe that the nonreligious state is the best guarantee for full religious freedom for all. Unlike some faiths, they are not uncomfortable with the secular state but embrace it as the protector of the faith or lack of faith of all people. Fourth, Seventh-day Adventists believe that they are a people of destiny with a global ministry and mission, but their weapons are not those of political influence or state support, but rather those of preaching, education, and healing.

On the cusp of the twenty-first century the Seventh-day Adventist Church continues in its tradition of seeking to reach people from every circumstance of life while standing firmly for the rights of all people to live according to their conscience. This modern ideal may help keep people of strong faith and belief from reverting to an intolerant past and destroying each other in the name of God. The Seventh-day Adventist Church may be able to provide leadership in faith communities, which must constantly balance personal faith and piety with public freedom and liberty. In the end only those who are free to say no to the gospel are really free to say yes.

15.

A Bahá'í Perspective on Tolerance, Human Rights, and Missions

———————◆———————

Firuz Kazemzadeh

Like Christianity and Islam, the Bahá'í Faith is a universal religion. Its message is directed to all humanity and crosses the barriers of race, ethnicity, nationality, and culture. In the century and a half since its inception the Bahá'í Faith, first perceived as a sect of Islam, has been widely acknowledged as an independent religion. It has spread to every continent and virtually every country in the world. Its followers are found among the Indians of Bolivia; the aborigines of Australia; South Africans, both black and white; the English; the Maoris; the Japanese; the Finns; the Russians; the Portuguese; the Pacific islanders; the Turks; and the Iranians. In the United States, Bahá'ís reside in some seven thousand cities and towns in every state of the Union. In 1998 there were approximately 5.5 million Bahá'ís worldwide.

The rapid expansion of a faith that originated in the nineteenth century in Shi'ite Muslim Iran to become a world religion in the twentieth was neither accidental nor automatic but the result of deliberate propagation. From its earliest day the Bahá'í Faith, as well as its immediate and inseparable precursor, the Bábí religion, enjoined its adherents to proclaim and teach their belief.

After sunset on May 22, 1844, in the southern city of Shiraz, a young merchant, Sayyid Ali Muhammad, proclaimed himself the return of the twelfth Imam, the long-awaited messiah of Shi'ite Islam. His interlocutor, Mullá Husayn Bushrúí, a learned divine, accepted the claim and became the first disciple of the man who would become known to history as the Báb (Arabic for "gate"). Filled with enthusiasm at finding the Promised One, Mullá Husayn was ready to carry the glad tidings to others who, like himself, were expecting the advent.

320

However, the Báb declared that the next seventeen to believe in him must come to him unbidden. Over the months after the Báb's declaration of his mission, sixteen men and one woman from various regions of the country found the Báb and accepted his mission without having been taught. To them and to Mullá Husayn, as the first and most prominent disciples, the Báb gave the title of Letters of the Living.

The further spread of the faith, however, would not proceed in the same fashion. The Báb now instructed the Letters of the Living actively to propagate his cause throughout Iran and beyond. In an eloquent address to this small band of self-recruited believers, the Báb reminded them of the words of Christ to his apostles as he sent them forth to spread his teachings. The eighteen disciples of the Báb were entrusted with a similar mission.

> You are the lowly [the Báb declared], of whom God hath thus spoken in His Book: "And We desire to show favour to those who were brought low in the land, and to make them spiritual leaders among men, and to make them Our heirs." You have been called to this station; you will attain to it only if you arise to trample beneath your feet every earthly desire, and endeavour to become those honoured servants of His who speak not till He has spoken, and who do His bidding.[1]

The new faith immediately ran into fierce opposition from both the Muslim religious establishment and the government. The Báb, who had addressed messages to the shah and his ministers, acquainting them with his claim and his teachings, was himself arrested and after years of imprisonment executed by a firing squad in 1850 in Tabriz. In spite of severe persecution the faith attracted ever larger numbers of people dissatisfied with the arid preachment of the mullahs and hopeful of a spiritual renewal. The Báb's following was diverse, including government officials, clergymen, merchants, artisans, and peasants. Many of them, including most of the Letters of the Living, lost their lives spreading the new religion. Among the martyrs was Táhirih, an outstanding poetess and advocate of the emancipation of women.[2] Between 1850 and 1854 some twenty thousand Bábís were killed and the rest driven under ground.

The religion lived on largely because its surviving adherents firmly believed in the Báb's prophecy of the advent of another messenger, one greater than himself, who would usher in a new religious cycle and a new age in the history of humanity. Thus the apparent defeats that the faith had suffered would be transmuted into victories with the coming of "him whom God shall make manifest." In 1863 one of the leaders of the Bábís, Mírzá Husayn Alí Núrí, known as Bahá'u'lláh, living in exile in Baghdad, proclaimed himself to be the one whose appearance the Báb had foretold. Bahá'u'lláh's emissaries carried the word to the scattered remnant of the Bábí community in Iran. Over the next decade most Bábís accepted Bahá'u'lláh's claim and became known as Bahá'ís.[3]

Oneness of humanity—the paramount principle of the religion founded by Bahá'u'lláh—demanded that his faith be proclaimed to the entire world. Its principles and spirit must be shared with all. Thus teaching the faith and its propagation were from the beginning important concerns of the community of his followers. Bahá'u'lláh wrote:

> Teach ye the Cause of God, O people of Bahá, for God hath prescribed unto every one the duty of proclaiming His Message, and regardeth it as the most meritorious of all deeds. Such a deed is acceptable only when he that teaches the Cause is already a firm believer in God, the Supreme Protector, the Gracious, the Almighty. He hath, moreover, ordained that His Cause be taught through the power of men's utterance, and not through resort to violence.[4]

> The Pen of the Most High hath decreed and imposed upon everyone the obligation to teach this Cause. . . . God will, no doubt, inspire whosoever detaches himself from all else but Him, and will cause the pure waters of wisdom and utterance to gush out and flow copiously from his heart.[5]

Teachers of his religion, Bahá'u'lláh wrote, must themselves exemplify the principles they strive to propagate, and while "God hath prescribed unto every one the duty of teaching His Cause," this duty must be carried out under certain conditions. "Whoever arises to discharge this duty, must needs, ere he proclaimeth His Message, adorn himself with the ornament of an upright and praiseworthy character, so that his words may attract the hearts of such as are receptive to his call. Without it, he can never hope to influence his hearers."[6]

In presenting their faith to adherents of other religions, Bahá'ís had the great advantage of never having to use a negative approach, never having to belittle any religion or to attack its founder. Accepting the validity not only of Judaism, Christianity, and Islam but also of Hinduism, Zoroastrianism, Buddhism, and other faiths, believing that no human society had ever been deprived of divine guidance, Bahá'ís offered their faith as a fulfillment of universal messianic expectations. They did not invite believers in other religions to repudiate the truths or the founders of such religions but rather offered a more inclusive way of seeing the progressive revelation of divine will in history.

Bahá'u'lláh set down rules Bahá'í teachers must strictly follow. Teachers must show respect for the religions of those whom they teach, if for no other reason than their own belief in the truth contained in such religions. They must be considerate of the feelings of their hearers and not insist that their hearers agree with them. "Proclaim the Cause of thy Lord," Bahá'u'lláh wrote, "unto all who are in the heavens and on the earth. Should any man respond to thy call, lay before him the pearls of the wisdom of the Lord, thy God. . . . And should anyone reject thy offer, turn thou away from him, and put thy trust and confidence in the Lord of all worlds."[7] And again:

Consort with all men, O people of Bahá'í, in a spirit of friendliness and fellowship. If ye be aware of a certain truth, if ye possess a jewel of which others are deprived, share it with them in a language of utmost kindness and goodwill. If it be accepted, if it fulfill its purpose, your object is attained. If anyone should refuse it, leave him to himself and beseech God to guide him. Beware lest you deal unkindly with him. A kindly tongue is the lodestone of the hearts of men. It is the bread of the spirit, it clotheth the words with meaning, it is the fountain of the light of wisdom and understanding.[8]

Bahá'u'lláh's prohibition on imposing one's beliefs on others, engaging in any form of intimidation, offering material inducements to conversion, or taking unfair advantage of one's hearers explains the frequent assertions by Bahá'ís that the Bahá'í Faith prohibits proselytism. Such assertions obviously refer to the negative sense the term has acquired in common parlance, not to its traditional meaning of an activity aimed at causing someone "to come over or turn from one opinion, belief, creed, or party to another; *esp.* to convert from one religious faith to another."[9] Since Bahá'u'lláh states that the purpose of spreading his cause is "that fire may turn into light, and hatred may give way to fellowship and love," Bahá'í teachers must be on guard not to compromise the principles they strive to propagate.[10] They must "be careful not to teach in a fanatical way."[11] To establish a balance between vigor in proclaiming the message and care not to force it upon the unwilling has always been a concern both of individual Bahá'ís and of Bahá'í institutions.

Addressing the Bahá'í community in 1957, Shoghi Effendi, Head of the Faith from 1921 to 1957, wrote that Bahá'í teachers

in their contact with the members of divers creeds, races and nations . . . must neither antagonize them nor compromise with their own essential principles. They must be neither provocative nor supine, neither fanatical nor excessively liberal, in their exposition of the fundamental and distinguishing features of their Faith. They must be either wary or bold, they must act swiftly or mark time, they must use the direct or indirect method [of teaching], they must be challenging or conciliatory, in strict accordance with the spiritual receptivity of the soul with whom they come in contact, whether he be a nobleman or a commoner, a northerner or a southerner, a layman or a priest, a capitalist or a socialist, a statesman or a prince, an artisan or a beggar. In their presentation of the Message of Bahá'u'lláh they must neither hesitate nor falter. They must be neither contemptuous of the poor nor timid before the great. In their exposition of its verities they must neither overstress nor whittle down the truth which they champion, whether their hearer belong to royalty, or be a prince of the church, or a politician, or a tradesman, or a man of the street.[12]

Before he passed away in 1892, Bahá'u'lláh appointed as his successor and authorized interpreter of his teachings his eldest son, 'Abdu'l-Bahá', who for forty years had shared his father's exile. 'Abdu'l-Bahá's systematic efforts to spread the faith throughout the world opened a new phase in its history. While in Bahá'u'lláh's time it had been taken from Iran and the Ottoman Empire to India, Burma, Transcaspia, the Caucasus, and Egypt, where most of its converts were recruited from Islam and some from Zoroastrianism and Judaism, under 'Abdu'l-Bahá's guidance Bahá'í teachers began to penetrate the Christian West. In 1894 a Syrian, Ibráhím Khayrulláh, who had been converted in Egypt, arrived in the United States and established the first American Bahá'í community in Chicago. Khayrulláh held classes that offered students a peculiar mix of Bahá'í teachings with the then-popular notions of healing and mysticism.[13]

From 1910 to 1913 'Abdu'l-Bahá' himself made extensive journeys to Egypt, several European countries, the United States, and Canada.[14] His visits had been prepared for by local Bahá'ís who arranged his itineraries; secured halls for public lectures; and contacted the press, religious leaders, and many individuals prominent in government, education, business, and the arts. In churches and synagogues, at universities and in private homes, before large gatherings and small, 'Abdu'l-Bahá' expounded the fundamental principles of the Bahá'í Faith:

> The independent search after truth, unfettered by superstition or tradition; the oneness of the entire human race, the pivotal principle and fundamental doctrine of the Faith; the basic unity of all religions; the condemnation of all forms of prejudice, whether religious, racial, class or national; the harmony which must exist between religion and science; the equality between men and women, the two wings on which the bird of humankind is able to soar; the introduction of compulsory education; the adoption of a universal auxiliary language; the abolition of the extremes of wealth and poverty; the institution of a world tribunal for the adjudication of disputes between nations; the exaltation of work, performed in the spirit of service, to the rank of worship; the glorification of justice as the ruling principle in human society, and of religion as the bulwark for the protection of all peoples and nations; the establishment of a permanent and universal peace as the supreme goal of all mankind. . . .[15]

'Abdu'l-Bahá's example and his continuous emphasis on the obligation to teach the faith had a profound effect on Bahá'ís, particularly in the nascent Bahá'í communities of North America. Linking the teaching of the faith to other moral and spiritual obligations, 'Abdu'l-Bahá' wrote to the followers of the faith:

> Soon will your swiftly passing days be over, and the fame and riches, the comforts, the joys provided by this rubbish-heap, the world, will be gone

without a trace, summon ye then the people of God, and invite humanity to follow the example of the Company on high. Be ye loving fathers to the orphan, and a refuge to the helpless, and a treasury for the poor, and a cure for the ailing. Be ye the helpers of every victim of oppression, the patrons of the disadvantaged. Think ye at all times of rendering some service to every member of the human race. Pay ye no heed to aversion and rejection, to disdain, hostility, injustice: act ye in the opposite way.[16]

Thus, in conformity with the commandments of Bahá'u'lláh, teaching became an organic part of every believer's striving for spiritual growth and the attainment of virtue. A mere verbal conveyance of principles was not enough: "Know thou," 'Abdu'l-Bahá' wrote, "that delivering the Message can be accomplished only through goodly deeds and spiritual attributes, an utterance that is crystal clear and the happiness reflected from the face of that one who is expounding the Teachings. It is essential that the deeds of the teacher should attest the truth of his words."[17]

During World War I, while cut off from contact with his North American followers, 'Abdu'l-Bahá, between March 26, 1916, and March 8, 1917, penned fourteen messages to the Bahá'ís of the United States and Canada. Collectively these epistles, known as the *Tablets of the Divine Plan*, constituted a charter that has guided Bahá'í efforts for the worldwide expansion of the faith. In addition to general exhortations to perfect their character and cultivate their spiritual life, 'Abdu'l-Bahá provided the Bahá'ís of the United States and Canada with specific instructions as to the countries to which they must take the faith. In the message dated April 8, 1916, he mentions Alaska, Mexico, Guatemala, Honduras, Salvador, Nicaragua, Costa Rica, Panama, and Belize. He then enumerates the countries of the West Indies and of South America. In his message of April 11, 1916, 'Abdu'l-Bahá lists the Pacific islands, including Japan, as well as Australia, Tasmania, and New Zealand.[18] Turning to the Atlantic, 'Abdu'l-Bahá lists its islands and then the continents of Europe and Africa, thus closing the circle around the world.[19]

In response to 'Abdu'l-Bahá's appeal, there arose a number of intrepid Americans who left their country for distant lands where, at great sacrifice, they engaged in teaching the faith to whomever they found willing to hear their message. They traveled as far as Tahiti, Japan, and Australia, some settling there and laying the foundations of Bahá'í communities in those countries. Among the early pioneers, women played a predominant role. Several became internationally revered Bahá'í heroines. American Bahá'í women were among the first to help the Iranian Bahá'í community to foster the education of women and organize schools for girls, and to acquaint Iranian women with the principles and methods of Bahá'í administration. It is noteworthy that the first woman elected to the National Spiritual Assembly of the Bahá'ís of Iran, the national governing body of the Bahá'í community, was an American teacher who had been the principal of the Bahá'í school for girls in Tehran.

Yet 'Abdu'l-Bahá's plan could not be carried very far by individual Bahá'ís thinly spread over a small number of countries. To accomplish the expansion of the faith, strong, well-organized communities had to be created. After the passing of 'Abdu'l-Bahá in 1921, under the leadership of his successor, Shoghi Effendi, the Bahá'ís raised an administrative order, which grew to be a well-functioning organization that could execute the plan in a regular and methodical way. The next phase of the expansion of the Bahá'í Faith, therefore, was the work of individuals acting within the framework of regularly elected institutions that have continued to implement 'Abdu'l-Bahá's original design.

In 1925 the Bahá'ís of the United States and Canada elected a National Spiritual Assembly, the governing body for the two Bahá'í communities. Their example was soon followed by the Bahá'ís in Germany, Great Britain, Iran, India, and in other countries as soon as Bahá'í communities were established. The national assemblies invariably appointed national and regional teaching committees that encouraged Bahá'ís to teach the faith wherever they resided and also to travel for the purpose of spreading the faith. Local spiritual assemblies in many communities followed the pattern and appointed local teaching committees. Bahá'ís who were the first to settle in a given locality were called pioneers, the term missionary being eschewed because of its association with professional clergy, which does not exist in the Bahá'í Faith. A large majority of Bahá'í pioneers were unpaid volunteers who made a living at whatever occupation was open to them in foreign countries where they settled. A minority that could not find work or lacked private means was supported through a system of deputization established by Bahá'u'lláh. Under that system those who wished to leave their homes to teach the faith but were for some reason unable to do so were encouraged to provide for someone who needed support.

Since 1937 the Bahá'ís have been carrying out specific propagation plans whose time spans have ranged from three to ten years. The first one of these, the Seven Year Plan, was initiated by the National Spiritual Assembly of the United States and Canada in 1937 and completed in 1944.[20] It established local assemblies in every state of the United States, every province of Canada, and every country of Latin America, creating a network of Bahá'í communities and institutions that stretched from Alaska to the southern tip of Chile. The Second Seven Year Plan, which greatly enlarged the scope of teaching activity, resulted in a considerable expansion of the Bahá'í community, particularly in Africa, preparing the ground for the first global teaching enterprise, the Ten Year Plan. Bahá'í communities of Central and South America, Australia, New Zealand, India, Pakistan, Burma, the United Kingdom, Germany, Austria, Iran, Iraq, and Egypt devised and carried out plans of their own.

Launched in 1953 by Shoghi Effendi, the Ten Year Plan, frequently referred to as the Ten Year World Crusade, took the faith to every continent and every country and dependency where there were no legal restrictions against proselytism. In a decade the number of countries where Bahá'ís resided doubled. The number of national spiritual assemblies, national governing bodies of Bahá'í communities, increased from twelve to fifty-six, twenty-one of them in Latin America. Three temples were erected on three continents: one in Kampala, Uganda; one near Sidney, Australia; and one in Langenhein, near Frankfurt, Germany. In the Pacific, in India, and in Africa the Bahá'í Faith began to attract tens of thousands of new adherents who represented both rural and urban populations and all strata of society. In recognition of the sacrifices made by Bahá'í pioneers who opened new territories to the faith, Shoghi Effendi named them Knights of Bahá'u'lláh. Their names were inscribed on a roll of honor, which was ceremonially placed at Bahá'u'lláh's resting place in 1992, during the commemoration of the hundredth anniversary of his passing.

In the expansion and consolidation of the Bahá'í community a most important part was played by the Hands of the Cause of God, men and women of singular accomplishment appointed by the Head of the Faith to work directly under his guidance in propagating and protecting the faith. This institution, originally established by Bahá'u'lláh, was continued by 'Abdu'l-Bahá, and given its final form by Shoghi Effendi. Since after his passing in 1957 no new Hands could be appointed, the Universal House of Justice, the supreme governing body of the Bahá'í Faith, made provisions in 1968 designed to carry on their functions of protection and propagation of the faith. This new institution, the Continental Boards of Counselors, whose members are appointed from among the most distinguished persons in the Bahá'í community, actively participates in stimulating teaching activity, continuously provides advice and counsel to the elected national spiritual assemblies, and directs the work of its own auxiliary boards, which interact with local spiritual assemblies and work at the grass roots.[21] Continental counselors and the members of their auxiliary boards, unencumbered with administrative duties, concentrate on the propagation of the faith, are involved in every aspect of the teaching work of the Bahá'í community, and actively participate in the training of teachers in specialized institutes.

It must be noted that in their teaching activities Bahá'ís were concerned not only with the geographical and numerical expansion of the community. They were vitally concerned with its quality and character as well. Commitment to the principle of unity demanded that Bahá'í communities everywhere include members of all races, religious and ethnic backgrounds, cultures, and levels of education. This necessitated paying special attention to teaching minority groups. As a result, the Bahá'í community of Iran had, relative to the country's general population, a disproportionately large number of members of Jewish and Zoroastrian backgrounds. In India the same held for the untouchables, in Egypt for the Copts, in the United States for African-Americans, in Canada for the Indians. The integration of these and other groups into one global community on the basis of equality and mutual acceptance has been one of the outstanding achievements of the Bahá'í Faith.

While Bahá'ís were commanded to teach the faith to all humankind, they were simultaneously enjoined, first, to obey the law and the governments under which they lived and to abstain from partisan politics, and from all dissension and strife. Second, they were forbidden the Shi'ite practice of *taqíya* (dissimulation); and they were never to deny their faith, even if threatened with death. These two commandments could not be reconciled under despotic regimes. When faced with the choice, Bahá'ís bowed to the law, even if they found it unjust. They disbanded their institutions in Germany under the Nazis and in the Soviet Union under the Communists. In countries where they were persecuted without the government enacting laws that prohibited their activities, they maintained their community institutions and taught the faith. Nevertheless, the growth of the faith often provoked opposition from entrenched religious establishments as well as from some governments, opposition that in some cases took tragically violent forms.

In 1955, in Iran, during the month of Muslim fasting, the Ramadan, a prominent Shi'ite cleric, Shaykh Muhammad Taqí Falsafí, daily preached incendiary sermons in a mosque in Tehran, attacking the Bahá'ís, accusing them of being enemies of Islam, and calling upon his listeners to rise against that "false religion." His hate sermons were broadcast throughout the country by government radio, providing Falsafí with a vast and highly impressionable audience. On May 7 the Iranian army took over the Bahá'í National Center in Tehran. Symbolizing the close cooperation of religion and state, high army officers joined the mullahs in demolishing the dome over the large meeting hall of the Center.

> This was followed by an orgy of senseless murder, rape, pillage, and destruction the like of which has not been recorded in modern times . . . shops and farms were plundered; crops burned; livestock destroyed; bodies of Bahá'ís disinterred in the cemeteries and mutilated; private homes broken into, damaged and looted; adults executed and beaten; young women abducted and forced to marry Muslims; children mocked, reviled, beaten and expelled from schools; boycott by butchers and bakers was imposed on hapless villagers; young girls were raped; families murdered; Government employees dismissed and all manner of pressure brought upon the believers to recant their faith.
>
> Yet, despite a thousand provocations and acts of medieval barbarism, the Bahá'ís held firm, and by their firmness opened the way for remarkable progress in teaching the Cause and opening the doors of public knowledge of the Faith.[22]

Antagonism toward the Bahá'ís was actively promoted by religious extremists and some nationalists in other countries as well. In 1960 all Bahá'í activities were prohibited by a decree of President Nasser of Egypt. This led to the dissolution of the National Spiritual Assembly of the Bahá'ís of Egypt; the confiscation of community properties, including cemeteries and libraries; and other severe restrictions. The Egyptian Bahá'í community, established almost a century earlier, now found itself silenced and deprived of all rights, its membership dwindling due to the emigration of the younger people. The harassment of the Bahá'ís continues to this day. Similar treatment befell the Bahá'ís of Indonesia at the hands of President Sukarno. In Morocco in 1962 fourteen Bahá'ís were arrested and, after six months of detention, remanded for trial before the local criminal court in the town of Nador "on the charges of (1) rebellion and disorder, (2) attacks on public security, (3) constitution of an association of criminals, (4) constitution of an association, and (5) attacks on religious faith."[23] In spite of absence of any proof, nine of the defendants were found guilty—three were sentenced to death, five to imprisonment for life, and one to imprisonment for fifteen years.[24] Bahá'ís rapidly organized a worldwide campaign to save their Moroccan co-religionists from execution and imprisonment. The pressure of international public opinion and the intervention of foreign governments induced Moroccan authorities to spare the lives of the three who had been condemned to death and vacate the sentences.[25] While such attacks did prevent the spread of the faith in the countries where they occurred, elsewhere the Bahá'ís were achieving and even surpassing the goals of the Ten Year Plan.

The global expansion of the Bahá'í community in the preceding decade made it possible for the first time in 1963 to elect the Universal House of Justice. The year after its election the Universal House of Justice launched the Nine Year International Teaching Plan, which envisaged the formation of forty-six more national spiritual assemblies, twenty-six of them in Africa, four in the Americas, eight in Asia, six in Australia, and two in Europe. Seventy new territories were to be opened to the faith, Bahá'í literature was to be translated into 133 additional languages, two temples were to be erected, and sites for sixty-two additional temples were to be acquired. The plan included an array of other goals that would strain the energy and the resources of the Bahá'í community for the next nine years but would result in the further expansion of the faith and the consolidation of Bahá'í communities on every continent.[26] In the closing years of this plan many Bahá'í communities began to experience rapid growth in the number of believers. In the United States the 1970s witnessed an influx into the Bahá'í community of thousands of men and women of college age and of minorities, particularly of African-Americans in the South. By the end of that decade South Carolina had more Bahá'ís than any state except California. In India the faith expanded at a rate surpassing its expansion rates anywhere else, the number of believers soon exceeding a million.

The successful completion of the Nine Year Plan was followed by the launching, in 1974, of a Five Year Plan, in 1979 a Seven Year Plan, in 1986 a Six Year Plan, in 1993 a Three Year Plan, and in 1996 a Four Year Plan.[27] The latest plans have included the countries of the former Soviet Union and the Eastern Bloc, where Bahá'í communities had been repressed for many decades. The Bahá'í Faith had first been brought to the Russian Empire by Iranian Bahá'ís in the late nineteenth century. A large and prosperous community had sprung up in Ashkhabad, Turkmenistan (then the province of Transcaspia), where the Bahá'ís erected their very first temple, established schools for boys and girls, published literature, and founded extensive charitable institutions. Bahá'í communities sprang up in other cities of Central Asia as well as in the Caucasus. All were banned by the Soviet government during the terror in the 1930s. Many Bahá'ís perished in concentration camps or were exiled. However, a few hundred survived, who quietly transmitted their faith to their children. A small community reemerged during the *perestroika* and began to grow in every part of the former Soviet Union.

The expansion of the faith did not proceed without reverses, the most serious of which was the major assault on the Bahá'í community in Iran by the Islamic regime. In 1979, as a result of the revolution, the Shi'ite clergy took full control of the Iranian state. The most extreme among the fundamentalist mullahs, old antagonists of the Bahá'í Faith, advocated the complete destruction of the Bahá'í community. In the next several years at least 214 Bahá'ís, most of them community leaders, were put to death. Of the twenty-seven members of the three consecutively elected national spiritual assemblies, twenty-three were killed, and three were imprisoned and tortured. Only one succeeded in leaving the country. Bahá'í institutions were banned, and membership in them was regarded as a punishable crime. Bahá'ís were unprotected infidels, virtual outlaws denied the most fundamental human rights. They were discharged from government employment and ordered to pay back the salaries they had received during their years of service. Retired Bahá'ís had their hard-earned pensions canceled. Bahá'í students and faculty were dismissed from universities. Bahá'í holy places were destroyed or desecrated. All Bahá'í community properties were confiscated, including cemeteries. Frequently, private homes were invaded and in many cases taken over without compensating the owners. Thousands were arrested and kept in jails for varying periods of time. Well over thirty thousand fled the country, seeking refuge abroad. While the initial fervor of the persecution has abated, the war against the Bahá'ís has not ceased.[28] Yet in spite of all pressure the Iranian Bahá'í community survives, and the faith is better known in the country of its birth to the general population than ever before.

While the Iranian Bahá'ís struggled for existence and Bahá'ís in a number of other countries were deprived of the right to practice their religion freely, elsewhere the expansion of the Bahá'í community went on at a fast pace. Teachers continued to travel to new territories, pioneers continued to settle in areas where none had settled before. This global endeavor took the Bahá'í Faith to most countries and dependencies in the world, establishing viable communities in tens of thousands of localities on every continent, and resulting in the election of more than 170 national spiritual assemblies, and of more than 17,000 local spiritual assemblies. In 1997 the worldwide membership in the faith was estimated at 5.5 million, which included representatives of every race, virtually every nationality, ethnic group, and tribe. Bahá'í temples have been raised on every continent; Bahá'í literature has been translated into hundreds of languages and dialects; Bahá'í schools have been functioning in urban and rural settings; and Bahá'í individuals and institutions have been active in the promotion of human rights, equality of races, equality of sexes, social and economic development, and moral education. The Bahá'í International Community (BIC), an organization that represents all national spiritual assemblies at the United Nations and in the international arena in general, has acquired consultative status with the U.N. Economic and Social Council and participated in many of the activities of various U.N. agencies.

The Bahá'í position on human rights, including religious freedom and tolerance, was made explicit on many occasions since the 1947 publication of *A Bahá'í Declaration of Human Obligations and Rights*. A year later the Bahá'ís welcomed the Universal Declaration of Human Rights and fully endorsed Article 18, which expresses their own conviction that every person must be free to have and practice a religion, to change religions, or not to have one. In 1985 the Bahá'í International Community welcomed the "report of the seminar [organized by the United Nations] on the encouragement of understanding, tolerance and respect in matters relating to freedom of religion or belief," and expressed the hope that the conclusions adopted by the seminar "will provide the inspiration for action by individuals, non-governmental organizations, governments and international organizations to implement the religious rights enshrined in the 1981 Declaration on the Elimination of All Forms of Intolerance and Discrimination Based on Religion or Belief."[29] The Bahá'í International Community, through its U.N. office in New York, published the statements *Elimination of Intolerance* (1987), *Religious Intolerance* (1988), *Promoting Religious Tolerance* (1989), and *Elimination of Intolerance* (1990). All these statements expressed the fundamental Bahá'í teaching that every individual must be free to engage in independent investigation of truth; that blind imitation destroys the essence of religion; that peace, love, and fellowship must not be sacrificed to doctrine; and that coercion must never be used in matters of faith.

In its statement to the U.N. Sub-Commission on the Prevention of Discrimination and Protection of Minorities, the Bahá'í International Community deplored the feeling experienced by many religious believers that they had "discovered the one and only truth" and the temptation "to relegate the remaining masses of humanity, adhering to other beliefs, to the status of apostates or unbelievers, spiritually doomed, deserving pity at best, or outright ridicule and persecution at worst."[30]

The Bahá'í International Community wrote to the United Nations Commission on Human Rights at its fifty-first session in Geneva in January 1995 that freedom of religion, one of the most cherished of human rights, in the exercise of which people have been willing to lay down their lives, has been frequently and openly violated. The BIC pointed out the paradox that "the violators are most often those who consider themselves faithful followers of a religion," and recommended that in addition to legislation to suppress acts of religious persecution education be used as a tool for the cultivation of positive attitudes. Such education would include the study of history and culture, which, if based on the premise of the oneness of humanity, should lead to a growing appreciation of the divers religious traditions. This appreciation will be strengthened by interaction with people of different faiths if the purpose is to promote unity.[31]

The Bahá'í views on religious tolerance stem from the deeply held conviction that the source of all religions is one and "that religion must be the cause of unity, harmony and agreement among mankind. If it be the cause of discord and hostility, if it leads to separation and creates conflict, the absence of religion would be preferable in the world."[32] Belief that the source of all religion is one and that revelation is progressive precludes exclusivity and makes it mandatory for Bahá'ís to accept the validity of religions other than their own.[33]

> That the diverse communions of the earth and the manifold systems of religious belief should never be allowed to foster the feelings of animosity among men is, in this Day, of the essence of the Faith of God and His Religion. These principles and laws, these firmly-established and mighty systems, have proceeded from one Source, and the rays of one Light. That they differ one from another is to be attributed to the varying requirements of the ages in which they were promulgated. . . . Religious fanaticism and hatred are a world-devouring fire, whose violence none can quench. The Hand of Divine power can, alone, deliver mankind from this desolating affliction. . . .
>
> The utterance of God is a lamp whose light are these words: Ye are the fruits of one tree and the leaves of one branch. Deal ye one with another with the utmost love and harmony, with friendliness and fellowship. He Who is the Day-Star of Truth beareth Me witness! So powerful is the light of unity that it can illumine the whole earth.[34]

Thus Bahá'ís are explicitly prohibited from maltreating members of other religions or those who profess no religion at all and must consider all humanity their friends. Adherence to a religion must be an act of free will, and no person should be compelled to remain a member of a religion once he or she has lost faith in it. Therefore, the issue of apostasy does not arise for Bahá'ís. Anyone who loses his or her faith is free to leave the Bahá'í community. Children of Bahá'í parents are considered members of the Bahá'í community, but when they reach the age of fifteen they are free to leave the faith if they so choose.

Over the years the Bahá'ís developed many methods of both individual and institutionalized teaching. The process itself may be divided into three consecutive but distinct stages: proclamation, designed to attract general interest to the faith; teaching proper, conveying information about Bahá'u'lláh and the religion he founded; and consolidation, the deepening of a convert's knowledge and his or her integration in the community.

The first stage of proclamation activities is carried out by placing announcements of Bahá'í meetings or quotations from Bahá'í writings in newspapers, discussing the faith on radio and television, conducting public meetings on subjects of broad interest approached from a Bahá'í point of view, mailing pamphlets, donating books to libraries, setting up booths with displays of literature at exhibitions and fairs, and even entering Bahá'í floats in parades. Proclamation methods, of course, vary from country to country and, within a country, from region to region, depending on the customs and sensitivities of the local population.

The second stage, teaching proper, which leads to the acceptance of the faith and the expansion of the community, may begin at small meetings in private homes, gatherings that Bahá'ís call firesides (irrespective of the presence or the absence of a fire). In a quiet, relaxed, and intimate atmosphere, an experienced Bahá'í teacher writes: "Our minds are clearer, keener, and more receptive to new ideas. Our hearts are less agitated."[35] Domestic firesides have been for many years the most successful method of teaching, at least in North America, parts of Europe, and parts of the Middle East. Teaching takes other forms as well. Regular study classes may be conducted at the local center, if there is one. Bahá'í college clubs may conduct meetings at which the faith is studied in detail. In rural areas Bahá'í teachers may go from house to house and engage the inhabitants in conversation, always being careful not to impose and not to force their message on the unwilling.

The third stage of the process, consolidation, involves continuing the education of the convert in Bahá'í writings and his or her participation in the regular activities of the community—electing or being elected to the local spiritual assembly, serving on its various committees, and becoming a teacher of the faith. Consolidation is carried out by many means—at summer schools, in "deepening" sessions and discussion groups, through national and local Bahá'í publications, and, perhaps most important of all, through constant encouragement for new and old Bahá'ís to study the scriptures on their own.

Literature has always played a most important role in teaching the Bahá'í Faith, whose very first believer was converted by the cogency, the persuasive argumentation, and the spiritual power of a written commentary on a sura of the Qur'an. Bahá'í scriptures, as well as books about the faith, have been ever since an indispensable instrument of teaching. Bahá'u'lláh's and 'Abdu'l-Bahá's voluminous writings in Arabic and Persian, as well as those of Shoghi Effendi in Arabic, Persian, and English constitute Bahá'í authoritative texts, some of which have been translated into many languages. Bahá'ís believe the writings of Bahá'u'lláh to be endowed with special spiritual potency that influences the sincere seeker after truth. Therefore these writings, "the creative word," are extensively used in teaching the faith.

In addition, there is a body of writings of early Iranian Bahá'í scholars who had mastered traditional Islamic learning and applied their knowledge to investigations of and reflections on topics of particular interest to Muslims. The most outstanding among them, Mírzá Abu'l Fadl Gulpáygání, a scholar who had taught in religious schools in Iran and at the famed Al-Azhar University in Cairo, spent some time in the United States and produced several works specifically aimed at Western readers.[36] In France, the orientalist Hyppolite Dreyfus wrote a long introductory essay, in effect a book, that was also translated into

English.[37] In England, John E. Esselmont wrote a comprehensive introduction to the Bahá'í Faith that has been translated into dozens of languages and probably has been the most widely used work of that genre.[38] As the Bahá'í community expanded, the production of books and pamphlets, many of which were intended as teaching tools, increased from year to year, as did the publication of works on biography, history, theology, and other aspects of the faith. A complete bibliography of the Bahá'í Faith would run to hundreds of pages and include thousands of entries for published documentary sources, autobiographies, memoirs, secondary accounts, pamphlets, articles in scholarly and popular journals and magazines, and newspaper stories.

Bahá'í journals and magazines are yet another tool in teaching the faith. Among them should be mentioned *One Country*, a news magazine published by the Bahá'í International Community in English, French, Spanish, and Russian; *Bahá'í Studies* (Ottawa, Canada); *Opinioni Bahá'í* (Rome, Italy); *La Pensee Bahá'í* (Bern, Switzerland); *Pensamienta Bahá'í* (Murcia, Spain); *Herald of the South* (Canberra, Australia); and *World Order* (Wilmette, Illinois, USA). These publications address themselves to the general reader, both Bahá'í and non-Bahá'í.

Such, then, are the beliefs and practices of the Bahá'ís concerning the propagation of their faith. For over a century and a half they have been carrying on this activity, first in relative obscurity, later in full view of the world. They have offered the principles and the spirit of their faith to anyone who wished to accept them, without offering material inducements, without forcing their views on the unwilling, without denigrating the convictions of others. They hold that every human being has the right to the independent investigation of truth, that religious freedom must be guaranteed to all, and that religion itself must never be the cause of enmity, conflict, and strife.

16.

EVANGELISM *SANS* PROSELYTISM

A Possibility?

———————◆———————

M. Thomas Thangaraj

Is it possible to envision and speak of evangelism without proselytism? Is it possible to think of and articulate the idea of evangelism without any reference or linkage to a significant effort to persuade people to join the Christian religion or Christian church? If one considers this to be a possibility, is it desirable after all? Will such a view of evangelism end up as a denial of all that evangelism stands for? If one concludes that it is desirable to conceive of evangelism in this way, how does one go about constructing such a view of evangelism? These are the questions that I address in this chapter. These questions demand that we first offer some tentative and working definitions of both *evangelism* and *proselytism*.

EVANGELISM

A definition of evangelism can be very elusive. This is seen in the variety of definitions of *evangelism* one encounters. These vary from "evangelism is social action,"[1] to evangelism is "announcing the gospel to non-Christians with a view to faith and conversion and their eventual incorporation into the Church by baptism."[2] There is actually a broad spectrum of definitions. Some highlight the task of proclaiming; others give prominence to the acting out of the gospel in and through acts of mercy. One can detect how the various elements that are highlighted in these differing definitions are woven into a comprehensive definition or a set of guidelines. To cite a few examples, George Morris defines evangelism as "spreading the gospel of the kingdom of God by word and deed and then waiting in respectful humility and working with expectant hope."[3] David Bosch lists a set of eighteen propositions to get to a constructive

335

understanding of evangelism today, including propositions such as "I perceive mission to be wider than evangelism," "Evangelism is always an invitation," and "Evangelism is not the same as church extension."[4] We encounter a variety of opinions and a host of ambiguities with regard to defining evangelism. Therefore, it is helpful to look at how this word has evolved in our recent history.

The word *evangelism* comes from the Greek words *euaggelion* (good news), and *euaggelizomai* (to preach the good news), as they are used in the New Testament. Jesus begins his ministry by announcing, "The time is fulfilled, and the kingdom of God has come near; repent, and believe in the good news" (Mk 1:15).[5] The Greek word for good news here is *euaggelion*—made up of two words *eu* (good) and *aggelion* (message). The verb form of this word, *euaggelizomai*, is translated "preaching or announcing the good news." Based on these two words, *evangelism* can be defined, in most cases, as "the act of preaching or proclaiming the good news of Jesus the Christ."

In the New Testament two major ideas emerge with regard to the meaning of these terms. First, the good news is primarily the good news of the reign of God, though in a few places the good news is associated with Christ or simply God. It is good news about the coming or the already-come reign of God. Second, the verb form *euaggelizomai* need not always be translated as "preaching" the good news. A literal translation would be "goodnewsing." In other words *euaggelizomai* can easily be translated as "living the good news" or "being the good news."

Both the terms *evangelism* and *evangelization* are used today. For most, these two terms are synonyms. Yet, broadly speaking, one may say that Roman Catholics and some Evangelicals prefer the term *evangelization*, whereas ecumenically minded Protestants tend to prefer the term *evangelism*. These two groups may not mean the same thing by these two terms. But it is clear that these terms are late arrivals in the history of mission. As Kenneth Cracknell notes:

> The terms "evangelism" and "evangelization" are comparative late-comers in Christian vocabulary. Rare indeed are the sightings of either term before the mid-nineteenth century. An evangelist was one of the writers of the four Gospels or a title of an office in the early church, and that virtually was it![6]

Given all the ambiguities surrounding the definition of the word *evangelism*, I want to propose a working definition so that we can examine evangelism in relation to proselytism. I define evangelism as the task of sharing the good news of Jesus the Christ, inviting people to a personal commitment to Christ, and consequently to join the church.

Such a definition immediately raises some important issues for the question of human rights, especially religious human rights. If Christians are to perform the task of "sharing" the good news, they need a setting in which they are free to share. They need a societal structure that offers them the possibility to invite people to a commitment to Christ. So the question is: Is evangelism—as an act of sharing and inviting—one of the fundamental rights of humans? If a recipient of such a sharing and invitation decides consequently to join a church, should it be backed by the fundamental human right of a person to choose a religious tradition of his or her liking? Thus one can see that the very definition of evangelism calls for a discussion of human rights.

PROSELYTISM

In defining the term *proselytism*, I find the five categories offered by Luke Johnson helpful. Johnson sees proselytism as "postures taken by a group toward outsiders."[7] He discovers five distinct postures: (1) openness to people who want to join the group; (2) inviting and convincing others to join the group; (3) seeking to turn others from their present allegiance because of the error of their position; (4) reaching out to save others from the danger and evil that surrounds their present membership; and (5) coercing others to accept membership in the group.

If we look at these five postures in the light of our definition of evangelism, it is clear that most Christians will see evangelism as "openness," "inviting," and "convincing." Some may include the fourth posture of "seeking to turn others from their present allegiance" and "reaching out to save." But most Christians would hesitate to include the fifth posture as being a part of their understanding of evangelism. The distinctions that are made between evangelism and proselytism are quite subtle and nuanced here. In this sense *evangelism* and *proselytism* do not mean the same thing. Do all Christians make the kind of distinctions that I have made here? Do people who do not belong to the Christian tradition see evangelism as being different from proselytism? Is it not the case that many do not see a distinction between evangelism and proselytism?

Such a blurring of boundaries between these two terms has led to a reduction of proselytism to the latter part of Johnson's definition, namely, the view of others as being in total error and thus deeming it necessary to coerce them to join one's own religion. Once proselytism is seen in such narrow and most often pejorative sense, it raises significant issues with regard to human rights and religious human rights. Coercing another to join one's religious group will be a violation of the other's fundamental right to follow his or her own religious tradition. Similarly, reducing evangelism to a "membership drive" leads to a view of evangelism that is also not very different from proselytism. Such an evangelism does raise issues regarding the fundamental human right of a person to practice his or her own religious tradition. As we can see, a reductionist understanding of both these terms has led to viewing evangelism and proselytism as synonyms. How did this happen?

Some historical incidents have contributed to this conflation of *evangelism* and *proselytism*. First, viewing the mission of the church as *expansion* of the

Christian religion began mostly during the period following the conversion of Emperor Constantine in the fourth century c.e. At this time the large-scale persecutions of Christians had ended, and it became realistic to envision the task of the church as expanding its boundaries. The Edict of Milan (313 c.e.) and subsequent imperial laws changed the situation of persecutions to a setting in which Christianity was ultimately bestowed with royal favor. Once Christianity secured for itself a place of both comfort and honor, the view of evangelism was altered. It did not simply signify bearing witness in the midst of suffering and martyrdom; increasingly, it signified expanding the boundaries of the powerful new religion of the emperors. This led to a vision of mission as expansion. This expansionist program had highly recognizable political overtones and moves.

For example, St. Augustine of Canterbury was sent by Pope Gregory the Great to England in 596 c.e. and was received by the king of Kent. From the very beginning the mission to England was backed by royal favor and support. Such royal favor was a great boon to the growth and expansion of the church in other parts of Europe as well. While this is true of the early centuries, it is also something that is associated with the modern missionary movement of the last five centuries. The Roman Catholic missionaries to the Americas had the blessings of Spanish and Portuguese rulers.[8] Bartholomew Ziegenbalg, the first Protestant missionary to India, was sent by the king of Denmark in 1706 to land in the Danish colony in South India.[9] One can narrate several more examples of this kind of political patronage of missionary work.

Of course this was not true of all the missionary movements during the colonial days. There were moments when the missionary movement and colonial expansion could not go hand in hand. But most often the missionary and the colonizer helped each other. Discussing this "unholy" alliance, David Bosch points out that while the Western missionary enterprise was compromised with colonial powers, there was also a "persistent minority" who "withstood the political imposition of the West on the rest of the world."[10]

This expansionist view of mission often also promoted a *militant* view of mission. The birth and rapid spread of Islam into Europe was the setting in which this militancy first developed. Islam and its rapid spread was seen as a threat to Christianity. By 715 c.e. Spain, Syria, Palestine, and Persia had come under the rule of Muslims. In 846 c.e. Rome was attacked and plundered by Muslim forces. By 902 c.e. Sicily had been conquered by the followers of Islam. In such circumstances, mission came to be understood increasingly in militant terms. Tragic and dark pages of Christian history were opened. Western Christians saw their mission as military invasion against the Muslims of their day. The late eleventh to thirteenth centuries witnessed the Crusades (the wars of the Cross). These wars were understood as efforts to recover the Holy Land from the hands of the Muslims and block the further expansion of Islam into Europe. There were eight such Crusades, and they had disastrous effects on the mission of the Church: The Crusades permanently injured the relations between Eastern Orthodox Christians and Western Christians. They sowed seeds of bitterness between Christians and Muslims, the harvest of which we reap even today. And they lowered the "moral temperature" of Christianity.[11] Of course, the Crusades were not meant to be missionary enterprises. Yet they brought a significant element of militancy into the life and mission of the Christian church.

Even before the Crusades the militant character of expansionist mission could be seen in the way in which European kings saw their wars with neighboring kingdoms as part of their Christian mission. For example, the ninth-century Frankish Emperor Charlemagne's campaign against the Saxons was his way of expressing the extension of the Christian religion. Saxons who refused to become Christians and accept baptism were by law condemned to death by sword.[12] Conversion to Christianity was woven into many peace treaties and into royal marriages as well.

Whatever one thinks of its merits, the militaristic imagery and language born of such early experiences have remained part of modern mission vocabulary. Hymns, writings, and speeches use militaristic imagery that promotes the idea of mission as coercion and expansion in subtle and hidden ways. Moreover, the host of books published in recent years with regard to increasing membership in the churches all over the world has given way to a reductionist view of evangelism as membership drive. For example, the writings of mission thinkers such as Donald McGavarn have made church growth the measuring rod for the effectiveness of the evangelistic task of the church. Most parishes in the United States today see the word *evangelism* as directly related, and sometimes only related, to membership drive. This, too, has vague overtones of militarism, conquest, and expansion.

A second factor, besides "expansion," that has contributed to the conflation of *evangelism* and *proselytism* is the perception that the primary task of the church is to work toward the *conversion of heathens*. The dictionary lists two meanings for the term *heathen*: "an unconverted member of a people or nation that does not acknowledge the God of the Bible" and "a person whose culture or enlightenment is of an inferior grade."[13] The Christian church, throughout its history, has sometimes labeled as heathens those who were outside the church. But this perception has become a much more dominant model during the modern missionary movement of the last three centuries. William Carey's historic *An Enquiry into the Obligations of Christians to Use Means for the Conversion of the Heathens* (1792) is sustained by such a view of outsiders.[14] Carey wrote this booklet mainly to motivate Christians in the West, especially in England, to sponsor generously overseas missionary work. He described inhabitants of the world without a written language or literary tradition as the "poor, barbarous, and destitute of civilization." Though Carey was writing in the eighteenth century, his attitude toward non-Western peoples has persisted within the church. Even today there are Christians who view people of other cultures and other religious traditions as "heathens."

The social, political, and economic situation in the world of the eighteenth and nineteenth centuries made such a condescending view of others both possible and sustainable. The success of the colonial expansion of the West appeared to confirm the supremacy of its culture and Christian religion. The missionaries, including Carey, were shaped by the prevailing culture of that day, even though, as persons they were totally dedicated to their missionary task and to a sympathetic and appreciative understanding of other peoples. Of course, not all missionaries from the West operated with such a view of others, even when they used the word *heathen* to refer to the non-Western peoples. For example, the first Protestant missionary to India, Ziegenbalg, recognized the worth of the so-called heathens when he wrote: "I do not reject everything they teach, rather rejoice that for the heathen long ago a small light of the Gospel began to shine. . . . One will find here and there such teachings and passages in their writings which are not only according to human reason but also according to God's word."[15] Such views, however, were exceptions to the dominant view that non-Western peoples were inferior and thus needed to be converted to Christianity.

Viewing the missionary task as the conversion of heathens also led to a highly negative view of religions other than Christianity. Other religions were often pictured as enemies of God that ought to be annihilated and abolished. Of course, not all missionaries thought and acted this way. There were those who viewed other religions with respect, understanding, and appreciation. Kenneth Cracknell, writing about theologians and missionaries in the period from 1846 to 1914, mentions and discusses eight missionaries and five theologians from this period who viewed other religious traditions with understanding and thus practiced "justice, courtesy, and love."[16] While some practiced courtesy, the overall picture of the other religions and its members has been very negative.

These two factors—the expansionist program of the Christian church and the perception of non-Christians as heathens—have ultimately led to an easy equation of evangelism to proselytism in its pejorative sense.

A MOVE TOWARD RECONSTRUCTION

I have argued thus far that in the history of the Christian church the two words *evangelism* and *proselytism* have not been carefully nuanced and differentiated, and that these two words have been seen as synonyms due to some particular historical developments. How does one reconstruct a view of evangelism that is not easily reducible to proselytism?

I suggest that we make two specific moves. The first move is to locate the discussion and exposition of the idea of evangelism within the framework of a wider concept, such as mission. The second move is to articulate a theology of mission that takes seriously into account both the fact of religious pluralism and the history of interreligious dialogue and cooperation that we have had, alongside the efforts to invite people to change their religion and join the Christian church.

LOCATING EVANGELISM WITHIN MISSION

Let me begin with the first move—to locate evangelism within the framework of a wider concept such as mission. One can easily notice that the words *mission* and *evangelism* have come to have widely varied meanings—from synonyms to antonyms—in the history of the church, especially in this century. For example, when the leaders of the World Missionary Conference at Edinburgh in 1910 used the slogan, "Evangelization of the world in our generation," they were not specific about the difference between the terms *mission* and *evangelism*. But since Edinburgh in 1910, these two terms have begun to change their meanings.

When the ecumenical movement progressed under the Life and Work movement and the Faith and Order movement, it appeared that the peculiar thrust of Christian mission for the proclamation of the Christian message was being lost in the ecumenical discussion. While the Faith and Order movement was concerned with seeking unity at the level of doctrine, the Life and Work movement focused on unity through participation in acts, programs, and events of service to the community at both local and global levels. These two movements appeared to have lost sight of the proclamatory character of mission. In response, the International Missionary Council (IMC) was formed in 1921. Though the IMC emphasized the role of *evangelism* in the life of the churches, it was more concerned about unity in mission. But the terms *mission* and *evangelism* had still not been sufficiently refined.

With the rise of the Evangelical movement in the United States and Europe (1921-61), however, *mission* and *evangelism* were more sharply distinguished.[17] These two words came to be assigned three sets of meanings. First, while *mission* meant the outreach activity of the church in service, *evangelism* was seen as the proclaiming of the Lordship of Christ and inviting people to join the church. In other words, mission emphasized the *activities* of love, justice, and peace, while evangelism highlighted the verbal *announcing* of the good news of Jesus Christ. One could engage in mission without mentioning the name of Christ. But evangelism required one to name the name of Christ and to invite people to accept Christ as their Savior and Lord. Second, while *mission* came more and more to be associated with "overseas" missionary efforts, *evangelism* came to mark the efforts of the local church to preach the gospel to its immediate neighbors and invite them to join the church. This distinction is clearly seen in many churches in the United States that have two separate committees or boards— one for missions (overseas) and one for evangelism (local membership drives). Third, some defined *mission* as a broader term that included both acts of charity and the ministry of announcing the good news. This meant that the word *evangelism* was more and more limited to the verbal proclamation of the good news of Jesus Christ.

Such a sharp distinction between *mission* and *evangelism* was further strengthened by the Lausanne Committee on World Evangelization, which called Evangelicals all over the world to be united under the banner of "evangelization." The word *evangelization* came to be seen as more inclusive than the word *mission*.[18] This was, in part, a reaction to the reduction of the word *evangelism* to mean simply the verbal proclamation within ecumenical circles. It was also a way of regaining the fuller meaning of the word *evangelization* as both announcing and living the good news.

For our task here, we need to locate evangelism as a part of the larger vision of mission. This is very clear in the way in which David Bosch proposes eighteen guidelines for the understanding of evangelism. He makes it clear that any definition of evangelism should be done in the context of mission. The eighteen guidelines actually begin, "I perceive mission to be wider than evangelism."[19] Then he proceeds to offer a set of highly dialectical propositions to get at a nuanced understanding. For example, he writes, "Evangelism is not the same as church extension," and immediately follows that by saying, "To distinguish between evangelism and membership recruitment is not to suggest, though, that they are disconnected."[20]

One of the advantages of locating evangelism within mission is that the activities of love and care that are an integral part of the mission of the church are no longer seen simply as the ways of luring people into the Christian religion. Quite often people who see evangelism as coercive proselytism operate with an instrumental idea of all the service programs of the church. The idea of coercion that is linked to proselytism cannot be maintained if evangelism is envisioned as within a broader concept of mission.

A NEW THEOLOGY OF MISSION

The second move is to construct a theology of mission that is not merely guided by proselytizing concerns, but that is significantly shaped by our new and fresh awareness of modern religious pluralism and that incorporates the history of interreligious dialogue and cooperation. Such a theology of mission cannot be constructed following traditional methodologies. For example, such a theology of mission will have to be constructed by taking interreligious conversation as the locus of theological reflection. If such a conversation is taken as the locus, one cannot simply begin to construct a theology of mission with either the Bible or the mission of God (*missio Dei*).

I have argued in detail elsewhere how one might employ a discussion of the mission of humanity (*missio humanitatis*) as the starting point and then move on to an explication of a Christian theology of mission.[21] Let me simply summarize my arguments here. A discussion of the mission of humanity is one in which all humans can join, irrespective of their religious loyalties and views. One may object that such a discussion is impossible when our understandings of what it means to be human are so varied. I argue that the fact that humans are self-conscious and "biohistorical" beings helps us to see how we have come up with multiple understandings of what it means to be human and also prods us to a conversation on issues facing humanity. One can thus engage in a conversation on the mission of humanity, taking into consideration a wider circle of discussion.

As a Christian theologian I thus offer a paradigm to discuss the mission of humanity: The mission of humanity may be defined as *"an act of responsibility, in a mode of solidarity, shot through with a spirit of mutuality."*[22] Humans have a mission to one another in terms of taking responsibility for one another and for the environment. This responsibility cannot be exercised as something solely "for" others but rather as something "with" others. It is a responsibility that is exercised in a mode of solidarity. Responsibility without solidarity can lead to disastrous consequences, as we have seen in the politics of dictators and in the human exploitation of the ecological order of the universe. This sense of solidarity needs further strengthening by a spirit of mutuality, which rescues solidarity from an attitude of condescension. Humans in taking responsibility for one another and with one another need to learn from one another, especially in our modern world of intense religious pluralism.

Once the mission of humanity is expounded in these formal categories of *responsibility*, *solidarity*, and *mutuality*, one can move to a specifically Christian theology of mission. This is done by bringing the mission of God in Christ and the mission of the early disciples to bear on the discussion of the mission of humanity. When such a theological move is taken, one comes to define the mission of the church as *"the working out of its commitment to cruciform responsibility, liberative solidarity, and eschatological mutuality."*[23] Let me explain each of these phrases briefly.

By *cruciform responsibility* I mean our willingness to see ourselves as partners with God, always acknowledging that ultimate responsibility for this universe rests in God. Such a stance relativizes human responsibility and rescues it from its oppressive and demonic distortions. It also transforms the act of responsibility into a form of service that is carried out in vulnerability and humility. *Liberative solidarity* invokes the idea of incarnating oneself in the setting of the other and working for the liberation of all by opting for the poor and the oppressed. Such a sense of solidarity sees the liberation of all from the sociopolitical, economic, cultural, and spiritual bondage of our time as the final goal and marches toward that total liberation in and through concrete acts of expressing a "preferential option for the poor." *Eschatological mutuality* points to the work of the Holy Spirit in luring us toward fullness and consummation, and thus invites us to exercise mutuality in our relation with our neighbors in light of the *eschaton*. Thus the formal categories—responsibility, solidarity, and mutuality—are now given Christian theological and material content by linking them to the cross of Christ, the liberative stance of the Bible, and the eschatological vision in Christian theology.

EVANGELISM *SANS* PROSELYTISM

Having made these two moves—locating evangelism within the larger concept of mission, and explicating Christian mission in terms of cruciform responsibility, liberative solidarity, and eschatological mutuality—we are now in a position to reconstruct the idea of evangelism.

The theology of mission we have worked out does maintain that Christians who have been formed and transformed by the good news of Jesus the Christ have the responsibility of sharing that good news with their neighbors. Mission is an act of responsibility. To be responsible is to share. If one thinks that the story of Jesus is transformative and worth sharing, then it is exercising one's sense of responsibility to retell that story to one's neighbors. Evangelism is a legitimate activity of a Christian community. But it has to be a *cruciform* activity. The sharing of the good news ought to be done in a spirit of vulnerability and humility. Cruciform responsibility points to the Christian act of responsibility that is chastened by the vision of the cross as God's expressing of God's responsibility in vulnerability and suffering. Those who equate evangelism with proselytism, and thus reject it as unnecessary and even "unchristian," should note that evangelism done in a cruciform spirit is not conquest minded or militant. David Bosch draws from the writings of Ronald Allen and D. T. Niles the following:

> Allen, who was comparing Paul's missionary methods with ours, was actually suggesting the model of the "victim" missionary. So was D. T. Niles, one of the most remarkable Third World Christians of our time, who was wont to depict mission or evangelism as one beggar telling other beggars where to find bread. The point is that we are as dependent on the bread as those are to whom we go. And it is only as we share it with them that we experience its true taste and nutritious value.[24]

When evangelism is shaped by the idea of cruciform responsibility, one understands the issue of church growth very differently. We are called to invite people to join the Christian community, yet it cannot be done in any other way than the way of vulnerability and humility. Evangelism cannot simply be reduced to a membership drive. It should remain as an invitation and invitation only. Once we focus strongly on the *invitation*, we will see that increase in membership of the church is one possible consequence of evangelism and not the only result. It cannot function as the norm or measuring rod for the effectiveness of evangelism. The notion of Donald McGavarn that church growth is the sign of faithfulness to the task of evangelization is highly misleading. McGavarn defines "today's supreme task" as "effective multiplication of churches in the receptive societies of earth."[25] Such a view, however, makes church growth a goal and measuring rod of evangelism, rather than a byproduct. Such a view is contrary to the portrayal of the early church in the Acts of the Apostles. In the early church the disciples shared the good news of Jesus Christ more as an invitation than as a program. They did so in ordinary, unplanned, and spontaneous settings, and they continued to maintain that it was God who was bringing people into the fellowship of the church. They were quite aware that their task was not a membership drive. Acts 2:46-47 reads: "Day by day, as they spent much time together in the temple, they broke bread at home . . . praising God and having the goodwill of all the people. And day by day the Lord added to their number those who were being saved."

The history of the missionary movement clearly shows that not all those who heard the good news of Jesus the Christ felt the need to join the church. There have always been individuals and groups who accepted the Lordship of Christ in their lives, lived a life of discipleship, and never joined the fellowship of the church. Mahatma Gandhi is a grand example of this kind of discipleship. He followed the teachings of Jesus with a great sense of commitment and determination but never saw the need to join a church. I know a group of Christians in the town of Sivakasi, South India, who have been called secret Christians for decades. The women in the business community of Sivakasi who secretly admire and follow Christ have refrained from accepting baptism and publicly joining the local church for personal and family reasons. One may not agree with the way in which they have responded to the evangelistic invitation. But they have responded to the invitation in a way they deem appropriate. Another illustration is the life and work of Simone Weil. In describing her life Diogenes Allen has this to say: "Weil is . . . an outsider to institutional Christianity. . . . [S]he was critical of superficial understanding of Christianity which can be found both inside and outside the Church. . . . [S]he was born a Jew and was never baptized."[26] Weil did claim herself to be a Christian and agreed with many of the Christian beliefs, though she did not accept baptism and did not officially join any church. These illustrations show that evangelism is not always followed by church membership or church growth in the institutional sense.

Liberative solidarity has significant implications for the task of evangelism. First, it brings under severe criticism the kind of "hit-and-run evangelism" practiced in several churches. Let me illustrate what I mean by "hit-and-run evangelism" with the following autobiographical notes. As a lay person, and later as a minister in the Church of South India, I participated in evangelistic programs in which a group of Christians would choose a village or town several miles away from their congregations to engage in evangelistic work. They would visit that village, preach in the various spots within that village, distribute tracts and booklets, and return home after a few hours. In such an enterprise there is no sustained relationship between the evangelist and the hearers of the good news, and thus the evangelist fails to express any form of solidarity with the hearers. Judging from the theology of mission that I have proposed, such acts of evangelism exhibit a total lack of solidarity. Moreover, they fail to recognize and practice the incarnational dimension of the Christian faith.

There is another issue that confronts us. We defined mission as *liberative* solidarity. In mission we are called to express our solidarity with the poor and work with them toward their, and eventually everyone's, liberation. "Hit-and-run" evangelism aims more at inviting people to join the church than at offering them good news about their liberation from all those things that oppress and marginalize them. Such an evangelistic effort is unaware of the kinds of economic and social conditions in which people live. It fails to recognize that the good news that one shares has serious implications for human liberation and not simply for increasing the membership of the Christian community. Biblically, evangelism includes sharing the good news in word *and* deed. While evangelism offers an invitation to join the church, it is the reign of God, which is a community of justice and peace, that is the ultimate goal of evangelism.

Eschatological mutuality has its own implications for the understanding of evangelism. The eschatological vision offered by the Christian faith invites one to be open to the movement of the Spirit in the world and thus to exercise mutuality in one's relation with others. We ought to listen to one another, learn from one another, and correct and challenge one another in our common "missionary" enterprise. Therefore, evangelism is always a two-way street. In evangelism we witness to one another. While we bear witness to the love of God manifested in the life, death, and resurrection of Jesus the Christ, our neighbors of other religious traditions and ideologies should be allowed to share their witness with us. In such a setting evangelism becomes an exercise in mutuality.

One may argue that the Christian church has always listened to those outside of its membership. Have not the missionaries listened to the native peoples in various countries? If they had not listened to them, they could not have translated the Bible into the language of the various peoples, one may maintain. Most often, however, Christians have listened to people of other traditions only to gather their questions to which we may present Christ as the answer. The kind of mutual witnessing I would propose here is that which allows the partners to witness to each other. While Christians share the good news of Jesus Christ, Hindus, for example, may share the way they have come to witness God's dealing with them in their faith community. Such a willingness to allow the other to witness to us is founded on a vision of the *eschaton*, in which all are brought into a community of peace, justice, and love.

On the basis of what I have said so far, we begin to see that evangelism in light of this proposed theology of mission can only be done in a mode of vulnerability and humility, can only be aimed at the holistic liberation of peoples, and can only be exercised in a setting of mutual witness. Such a form of evangelism may or may not lead people to join the church. The discussion so far forces us to redefine evangelism in dialogical terms and in a spirit of mutuality. Kenneth Cracknell rightly ends his book on evangelism thus:

> For most people the good news has to be told for the first time. Perhaps they are people who live within one of the great world religions. . . . For all such people that Christian message needs to be made known in a way in which they can understand it, question it, bring their own insights to bear upon it, and make their own response to it. This requires "discernment, seriousness, respect and competence." The way in which this will happen is more likely to be dialogue than proclamation. And the process

itself, by the grace of God, will lead us to a place where neither they nor we have ever been before.[27]

Any discussion of evangelism in light of our theology of mission will invariably lead us to examine the idea of dialogue.

Before we examine the interrelationship between evangelism and dialogue, we need to note that evangelism *sans* proselytism will be seen purely as being nice to one another, not really offering a challenge to those who are outside the Christian church, if we do not face the question of conversion. When evangelism is seen as synonymous with proselytism, the primary goal of evangelism is to convert people from one religion to another. The concept of church growth and membership recruitment are closely connected to the idea of conversion. One could argue that the history of the missionary movement in the last three centuries and the perception of Christian mission by those outside the Christian tradition have turned the word *conversion* into a dirty word. Therefore, many recommend that we leave people to remain in the religious traditions that they are born into. Mahatma Gandhi, for example, was opposed to the traditional Christian view of conversion. Gandhi said, "I am against conversion, whether it is known as *shuddhi* by Hindus, *tabligh* by Mussalmans or proselytizing by Christians."[28] Such criticisms of conversion have altered the view of Christian mission in such a way that it is equated with "change of religion" in its best sense and "proselytism" in its most pejorative sense. We need to examine the word *conversion* with care.

My first real encounter with the word as such was in the year 1961 when I first read a book on conversion by E. Stanley Jones, a famous Methodist missionary in India.[29] This book had a profound influence on me. Jones quotes William James's definition of *conversion:*

> To be converted, to be regenerated, to receive grace, to experience religion, to gain assurance, are so many phrases which denote the process, gradual or sudden, by which a self, hitherto divided, and consciously wrong, inferior and unhappy, becomes unified and consciously right, superior and happy, in consequence of its firmer hold upon religious realities.[30]

Jones considers James's definition as "sound and penetrating in its psychological phases." Yet he criticizes it as theologically insufficient because the commitment to a Person (like the person of Jesus the Christ) is not taken seriously in the process of conversion. According to James, conversion is a very positive and welcome experience, which one may wish for all.

The theology of mission that I have outlined here would affirm and celebrate the idea of regeneration and receiving of grace among all peoples of the world. Conversion, in this sense, is strongly recommended for all. Evangelism can and should lead to conversion in this sense. But the important thing is that the people who announce the good news and the people who hear it come to experience a conversion. Both come to a "firmer hold upon religious realities." Such conversion can take forms other than leaving one's religion and joining another. It may take the form of one's revision and reformulation of one's own religious tradition. Many of the Hindu reformers in India—Raja Ram Mohan Roy, Keshub Chunder Sen, Vivekananda, Mahatma Gandhi, and Radhakrishnan—reformulated the Hindu faith in light of their exposure to Christianity. Of course, in some other cases evangelism can and may lead to leaving one's native tradition, community, and beliefs behind and joining a totally new community and tradition. Others in India, M. M. Thomas points out, were "converted" to taking Jesus's teachings and his self-sacrifice on the cross as their leading religious symbols while continuing to be Hindus or secularists:

> In India, the crucifixion of Jesus as the symbol of God as Suffering Love identifying himself with the agony of the oppressed humanity has been a most potent spiritual vision, inspiring many Indians irrespective of religious or secular labels to identify themselves with the poor and the downtroddens.[31]

All these are cases of conversion. But they are not all the same. Our view of mission as responsibility, solidarity, and mutuality offers us a wide variety of possibilities in conversion. Conversion is not limited to change of religion alone.

It is becoming clear that the task of evangelism is not simply to proclaim verbally the good news in Jesus the Christ. Nor is it merely to recruit members for the Christian church. Then what exactly is the purpose of evangelism? Does not our evangelism aim for some transformation in the hearers or recipients? Does not one anticipate a transformation of the world due to the work of evangelism?

While evangelism is not limited to recruiting members for the church, it does aim at transformation. I would describe the transformation that is aimed at in three dimensions. The first is what I call a *personal transformation*. This dimension is often referred to by terms, such as *salvation, conversion, regeneration,* or *being born again.* It is one of the major elements in the transformation that is aimed at by evangelism. One is invited to move from a self-centered or uncentered life to a life that is centered in God. People are invited to transform themselves into centered and holistic humans. The gospel of Jesus the Christ is offered as a way to achieve such centeredness and wholeness. The idea of cruciform responsibility supports the idea of taking responsibility for others by offering them the personal transformation that is available in the gospel of Christ. Yet this is done in humility, recognizing that those who offer this are not fully transformed and perfect. They do so only in a mode of humility and hope. Moreover, the ideas of solidarity and mutuality require that the personal transformative elements in traditions other than our own will have to be acknowledged and celebrated. For example, if my Muslim or Hindu friends share with me their experience of personal transformation through their traditions, I need to recognize them as valid and true experiences of transformation and see such instances as those that enhance my own journey toward becoming a fully centered human being.

The second dimension is *societal transformation*. By *societal*, I mean the social, political, and economic dimensions of human life. The history of missions amply illustrates the way the church has always been concerned not simply with individuals but also with societies, nations, and indeed with the globe itself. The dramatic social changes that were brought about by Christian mission throughout the world bear witness to this. The idea of cruciform responsibility that we have outlined sees the cross as a symbol of protest against political and economic forces in our society.

Several considerations attract our attention when we understand mission as leading to societal transformation. The foremost consideration is that we need to be self-conscious about the political character of mission and the political implications of mission. A lack of awareness of the political side leads us to fall prey to the dominant political ideology of the given moment and thus does not ultimately contribute to societal transformation; rather, it only strengthens the status quo and by its silence fails to transform reality.

Moreover, the kind of liberative solidarity that we have put forward demands that one pays attention to the question of sociopolitical and economic structures of society. It is not enough to organize instruments of charity (charity understood as almsgiving); rather, one should set in motion a movement that attempts to alter the prevailing unjust structures of society that perpetuate poverty, inequality, and oppression. Latin American liberation theologians have been foremost in conscientizing the theological community with regard to the primacy of structures in dealing with societal problems. Thus, legal, organizational, and constitutional changes are all very much a part of the program of mission that aims at societal transformation.

Furthermore, our idea of eschatological mutuality demands that our engagement in societal transformation cannot and should not be achieved in isolation from other communities of faith and commitment. Our partners in other religious and secular traditions are our companions in our journey toward a just and peaceful community all over the world. To use the words of George Rupp, we are called to establish "communities of collaboration" that celebrate our "shared commitments and common tasks."[32]

The third dimension is *ecological transformation*. We today have a heightened awareness about the ecological problems of the world. Several international conferences and congresses have met during the last two decades to increase this awareness. The Earth Summit at Rio de Janeiro especially has "elevated the awareness of people and their leaders to the crisis our civilization faces as a result of the damage we are inflicting on our earth's environment and development goals. Rio altered the environment and development dialogue fundamentally, linking poverty, equity and social justice with the achievement of sustainable development."[33] Thus, today, we are keenly aware that the personal and societal dimensions of human life are closely interwoven with the ecological dimension. Therefore, mission should promote and work for ecological transformation.

The ideas of responsibility, solidarity, and mutuality that we have examined provide a strong foundation and impetus for engaging in healthy and sustainable ecological transformation. They also warn us against an irresponsible and excessive exploitation of nature and the environment to satisfy the greed of humans and their societies. We need to express our responsibility with a deep sense of solidarity and mutuality with all living beings and nonliving things in the universe. One can see how the personal and the societal dimensions of transformation come together in the task of ecological transformation. As Constantin Voicu writes, "A better environment will never exist without a more just social order."[34] Similarly, a better environment will not be available to humans if there is not a personal transformation in humans that leads to a loving and sharing attitude to the earth and a lifestyle that promotes simplicity and love.

One more issue demands our attention. I suggested earlier that the new understanding of evangelism that we have developed here involves a strong and lively connection between evangelism/mission and dialogue. Dialogue has been acknowledged more and more in recent years as a form of witness, especially through the work of the World Council of Churches (WCC) and the writings of the theologians from Asia and Africa. Since the subunit of the WCC on Dialogue with Living Faiths and Ideologies began its operation in 1971, dialogue—specifically, interreligious dialogue—has become a household term in the ecumenical ecclesial communities. One of the significant milestones in the life of this subunit was the production of *Guidelines on Dialogue with People of Living Faiths and Ideologies* (1979).[35] Many churches, seminaries, and other Christian groups have taken the task of interreligious dialogue seriously and have been engaged in such dialogues for several years now.

Though evangelical theologians have traditionally been suspicious and skeptical of dialogue as a form of witness, today more and more of them affirm the need for dialogue to be recognized as a form of witness and mission. Though the Lausanne Covenant—the historic document of Evangelicals on world evangelization—mentions dialogue only in passing and only in reference to understanding the hearer of the word, an increasing number of evangelical theologians see dialogue as genuine form of witness.[36]

As for Roman Catholics, the Second Vatican Council (1962-65) gave a boost to the engagement in and the promotion of interreligious dialogue. Pope Paul VI established a separate Secretariat for Non-Christians, now called the Pontifical Council for Interreligious Dialogue. Since Vatican II, the church has issued several encyclicals and documents encouraging Catholics to engage in dialogue as a form of witness. The document *Dialogue and Proclamation,* published by the council in 1991, has been important for the Roman Catholic Church. Currently the Pontifical Council for Interreligious Dialogue and the Office of Interreligious Relations of the World Council of Churches hold consultations together and thus promote the cause of interreligious dialogue.

The Roman Catholic document *Dialogue and Proclamation* lists four types of dialogue: (1) *dialogue of life*, in which people strive to live in an open and neighborly spirit, sharing their joys and sorrows, their human problems and preoccupations; (2) *dialogue of action*, in which Christians and others collaborate for the integral development and liberation of people; (3) *dialogue of theological exchange*, in which specialists seek to deepen their understanding of their respective religious heritages and to appreciate each other's spiritual values; (4) *dialogue of religious experience*, in which persons rooted in their own religious traditions share their spiritual riches, for instance, with regard to prayer and contemplation, and faith and ways of searching for God or the Absolute.[37]

All four of these forms of dialogue are capable of being avenues for the kind of mission and evangelism that we have constructed. Dialogue becomes an expression of our cruciform responsibility, liberative solidarity, and eschatological mutuality. To recognize dialogue in these terms, the following remarks are germane.

First, dialogue is not merely a way of being nice to one another. People who criticize dialogue quite often see it merely as mutual affirmation, appreciation, and admiration. Dialogue does involve a great deal of mutual admiration and appreciation. But dialogue in the context of mission and evangelism means much more than that. It is a form of *engagement* with the other, not simply pleasant *talk*. Genuine dialogue involves challenging, correcting, and criticizing one another and truly learning from one another.

Second, dialogue is a form of witness even when there is no explicit proselytism agenda. In dialogue one lives out the good news that God accepts all as God's own children and engages in a dialogue with God's own creation. In expressing our responsibility, solidarity, and mutuality with others in the various types of dialogue that we have outlined earlier, we are, in fact, making the good news present in the midst of our dialogue. It is a witness that simply expresses itself through "being there" with others in conversation, exchange, and action. In this sense one is engaged in evangelism when one is in dialogue with the other.

Third, dialogue does not preclude inviting people to hear good news in Jesus the Christ. The kind of dialogue I am referring to here is a conversation between people who are committed to their respective religious traditions. Wesley Ariarajah expresses this well:

We must begin with the affirmation that dialogue does not exclude witness. In fact, where people have no convictions to share, there can be no real dialogue. In a multilateral dialogue meeting in Colombo, one of the Hindu participants rejected any idea of "levelling down" religious convictions, and said that he had no interest in entering into dialogue with Christians who had no convictions about their faith. In any genuine dialogue authentic witness must take place, for partners will bear testimony to why they have this or that conviction.[38]

Authentic witness can and should happen in a dialogical situation. The only difference is that such a witness can be done only in the form of *mutual* witnessing. It cannot be a one-way invitation.

CONCLUSIONS

What I have offered is a view of evangelism that locates it firmly within a broader concept of mission and focuses more on the invitational side of evangelism than on the recruitment side of it. Such an evangelism cannot be reduced to or equated with a condescending and coercive form of proselytism. It can only be seen as an act of sharing that is carried out in a mode of solidarity and mutuality and is open to a variety of forms of response to the good news.

Now we can return to the questions with which we began. Is evangelism *sans* proselytism possible? Yes, it is. It is possible to envision evangelism within a broader understanding of mission, especially when mission is seen as an act of cruciform responsibility, done in a mode of liberative solidarity, and shot through with a spirit of eschatological mutuality. Is evangelism *sans* proselytism desirable? Yes, it is. It is desirable because such a view of evangelism conforms more to the spirit, the life, and the teachings of Jesus the Christ, and the central teachings of the Bible. It is desirable as well because it is a form of evangelism that respects and values the religious human rights of both the evangelist and the evangelized.

NOTES

PREFACE

1. The phrase is from Irwin Cotler, "Jewish NGOs and Religious Human Rights: A Case Study," in *Human Rights in Judaism: Cultural, Religious, and Political Perspectives*, ed. Michael J. Broyde and John Witte Jr. (Northvale, N.J./Jerusalem, 1998), 165.

2. See sources and discussion in John Witte Jr. and Michael Bourdeaux, eds., *Proselytism and Orthodoxy in Russia: The New War for Souls* (Maryknoll, N.Y., 1999).

3. See sources and discussion in Abdullahi Ahmed An-Na'im, ed., *Proselytization and Self-Determination in Africa* (Maryknoll, N.Y., 1999).

4. Paul E. Sigmund, ed., *Religious Freedom and Evangelization in Latin America: The Challenge of Religious Pluralism* (Maryknoll, N.Y., 1999).

5. For a good sampling, see Tad Stahnke and J. Paul Martin, eds., *Religion and Human Rights: Basic Documents* (New York, 1998). For analysis, see Kevin Boyle and Juliet Sheen, *Freedom of Religion and Belief: A World Report* (London and New York, 1997); Malcolm D. Evans, *Religious Liberty and International Law in Europe* (Cambridge, 1997); John Witte Jr. and Johan D. van der Vyver, eds., *Religious Human Rights in Global Perspective*, 2 vols. (The Hague/Boston/London, 1996).

6. See esp. Wolfgang Huber and Hans-Richard Reuter, *Friedensethik* (Stuttgart/Berlin/Köln, 1990), esp. 209-352; Donald W. Shriver, "Religion and Violence Prevention," in *Cases and Strategies for Prevention Action*, ed. Barnett R. Rubin (New York, 1998), 169-97.

7. *New York Trust Co. v. Eisner*, 256 U.S. 345, 349 (1921).

INTRODUCTION

1. Quoted in Ernest Gellner, *Legitimation of Belief* (Cambridge, 1974), 147.

2. W. H. Auden, *Collected Poems* (New York, 1976), 179.

3. These are not Auden's words but condensations of poems by Joseph Warren Beach, *Obsessive Images: Symbolism in Poetry of the 1930's and 1940's* (Minneapolis, 1960), 109-10.

4. The Auden quotations and the comments by Beach are in ibid., 113, 121-22.

5. George Santayana, *Reason in Religion*, quoted by Clifford Geertz, *The Interpretation of Cultures: Selected Essays by Clifford Geertz* (New York, 1973), chap. 4 epigraph.

1. PROSELYTISM IN JUDAISM

1. The term is Kant's (*Critique of Pure Reason*, B311), but I use it as did Wittgenstein when he wrote: "So we cannot say in logic, 'The world has this in it, and

353

this, but not that' . . . since it would require that logic should go beyond the limits of the world; for only in that way could it view those limits from the other side as well" (*Tractatus Logico-Philosophicus*, 5.61, trans. D. F. Pears and B. F. McGuiness [London and New York, 1961], 115). In the case of conversion, one side is Judaism and the other the non-Jewish world. The border, though, has been drawn at different points at different times in the history of Judaism.

2. Parts of the following sections are adapted from David Novak, "The Legal Question of the Investigation of Converts," *Jewish Law Association Studies* 3 (Atlanta, 1987), 153, and idem, *The Image of the Non-Jew in Judaism* (New York and Toronto, 1983), chap. 1.

3. See T. J. Meek, "The Translation of *Ger* in the Hexateuch," *Journal of Biblical Literature* 49 (1930): 177.

4. All translations, unless otherwise noted, are by the author.

5. See, also, Genesis 15:13, 23:4; Exodus 2:22, 18:3, 22:20; Leviticus 19:34, 25:35 and 47; Deuteronomy 10:19, 16:11 and 14, 23:8.

6. See Novak, *The Image of the Non-Jew in Judaism*, 93ff.

7. See *Palestinian Talmud* (Talmud Yerushalmi, hereafter Y.): Kiddushin 3.14/ 64d re Numbers 1:18.

8. Numbers 18:1-24.

9. Leviticus 25:13-18.

10. *Sifre*: Bemidbar, no. 78. See *Sifre*: Devarim, no. 352. Thus the full integration of *gerim* into the patrimony of the land of Israel had to be a messianic innovation (see Ezekial 47:22-23).

11. See R. de Vaux, *Ancient Israel*, trans. J. McHugh (New York, 1965), 1:74.

12. See *Sifre*: Behar, ed. Weiss 110a re Leviticus 25:47; *Babylonian Talmud* (Talmud Bavli, hereafter B.): Kiddushin 20a.

13. See J. Pedersen, *Israel* (Copenhagen, 1926), 1:40ff.

14. Deuteronomy 23:4-9. Cf. *Mishnah* (hereafter M.): Yadayim 4.4; Y. Yevamot 8.3/9.3.

15. See Joshua 16:10, 17:13; Judges 1:28ff.; 2 Samuel 11:3.

16. *Sifre*: Devarim, no. 200; Y. Sheviit 6.1/36c.

17. In rabbinic sources, however, formal conversion had to take place before any such marriage could be valid. See Y. Yevamot 2.6/4a; B. Kiddushin 68b re Deuteronomy 7:4. Cf. B. Kiddushin 22a re Deuteronomy 21:11 and Rashi, s.v. "leequhin."

18. Deuteronomy 7:3-2. Cf. B. Avodah Zarah 36b.

19. See Deuteronomy 25:5-10.

20. B. Baba Kama 118a.

21. B. Yevamot 47b; *Ruth Rabbah* 2.17ff.

22. Ruth 4:22.

23. In Ezekial 20:32, when the people of Israel assume that because of their exile from the land of Israel "we shall become like the nations (*ka-goyyim*), like the families of the other lands, serving wood and stone," the prophet emphasizes to them that God rules over his people wherever they happen to be (ibid., 33ff.). Recalling the wilderness experience in the days of Moses (v. 35) seems to mean that Israel in her exile had returned to the wilderness, as it were. Thus, although King David equates exile from the land of Israel with "worship of other gods" (1 Samuel 26:19), the Rabbis have to qualify the statement by concluding that for "one who lives outside the land of Israel, it is *as if* (*k'ilu*) he were an idolater" (*Tosefta* [hereafter T.]: Avodah Zarah 4.5; B. Ketubot 110b). That is, living in the land of Israel enhances a Jew's

relationship with God and living outside it diminishes it, but the basic covenantal relationship obtains wherever.

24. See Arakhin 29a.

25. *Antiquities*, 20.38.

26. Ibid., 20.41.

27. Ibid.

28. See ibid., 20.139; also, LXX on Esther 8:17 and Judith 14:10.

29. *Antiquities*, 13.257. Cf. Jubilees 15:26-27.

30. See ibid., 15.1ff.

31. Cf. B. Yevamot 24b for rabbinic suspicion of converts who converted because of political subservience to Jewish rule.

32. See ibid., 46a and Rashi, s.v. "le-toqfo be-mayyim."

33. Ibid. Cf. Y. Kiddushin 3.13/64d.

34. This was the position of Paul, which more than anything else led to the schism between Judaism and Christianity (see Acts 15:1ff.; B. J. Bamberger, *Proselytism in the Talmudic Period*, rev. ed. [New York, 1968], 48ff).

35. See Josephus, *Antiquities*, 14.110; *Contra Apionem*, 2.123, 210, 279-83; *Bellum Judaicum*, 2.463; Juvenal, *Satires*, 14.96; Tacitus, *History*, 5.5.

36. See Martin Goodman, *Mission and Conversion* (Oxford, 1994), 129ff.

37. *De Vita Mosis*, 2.43-44, trans. F. H. Colson (Cambridge, Mass., 1935), 468-71.

38. See B. Berakhot 22b re Jeremiah 23:29. Cf. M. Kelim 1.8.

39. *Beresheet Rabbah* 43.7.

40. Ibid. See Y. Berakhot 4.4/8a; B. Yevamot 79a re 1 Kings 5:29.

41. *Mekhilta*: Yitro, ed. Horovitz-Rabin, 194-95.

42. Ibid., 199-200 re Exodus 18:27.

43. B. Gittin 57b.

44. B. Shabbat 31a. For a variety of modern Jewish interpretations of this story, which draw legal implications from it, see the chapter by Michael J. Broyde herein.

45. See, e.g., Aristotle, *Nicomachean Ethics*, 1132b21 and 1166a1; *Politics*, 1253a15.

46. See B. Yevamot 24b and Tosafot (hereafter Tos.), s.v. "lo" re Menahot 44a.

47. See B. Yevamot 22a.

48. M. Avot 1.12.

49. Matthew 23:15.

50. See Salo W. Baron, *A Social and Religious History of the Jews*, rev. ed. (New York, 1952), 1:375, n.15.

51. Acts 10:2, 13:16, 18:4.

52. See Novak, *The Image of the Non-Jew in Judaism*, 28ff.

53. Cf. Hullin 13a and parallels.

54. T. Demai 2.4-5; Bekhorot 30b; B. Yevamot 47a.

55. B. Sanhedrin 58b-59a.

56. T. Sanhedrin 13.2 and B. Sanhedrin 105a re Psalms 9:18.

57. *Mishneh Torah* (hereafter MT): Melakhim, 10.9.

58. Keritut 9a. See J. Neusner, *A Life of Yohanan ben Zakkai* (Leiden, 1962), 162ff.

59. See M. Yoma 3.6; Y. Yoma 3.3/40b; B. Yoma 30a; M. Pesahim 8.8.

60. Keritut 9a. See Y. Demai 2.1/22c.

61. Keritut 9a.

62. See B. Sanhedrin 2b-3a.

63. B. Yevamot 46b re Numbers 15:16.

64. Ibid., Tos., s.v. "mishpat."

65. See B. Gittin 88b and Tos., s.v. "be-milta."

66. See T. Rosh Hashanah 1.18; B. Rosh Hashanah 25a-b.

67. See *Yalqut Shimoni*: Ruth, no. 596.

68. For the ramifications of just what such acceptance entails, see the chapter of Michael J. Broyde herein.

69. B. Yevamot 47a-b.

70. R. Joseph Karo, *Shulhan Arukh*, Yoreh Deah 263.3.

71. See B. Sanhedrin 44a re Joshua 7:11; also, D. Novak, *The Election of Israel* (Cambridge, 1995), 189ff.

72. B. Yevamot 46b-47a.

73. Ibid., 47a, Tos., s.v. "be-muhzaq."

74. B. Pesahim 3b, Tos., s.v. "ana"; Maimonides, MT: Isurei Biah, 13.10.

75. B. Yevamot 47a.

76. B. Ketubot 11a re M. Eruvin 7.11.

77. See B. Yevamot 22a and 62a; Maimonides, MT: Ishut, 15.6.

78. B. Ketubot 44a, Tos., s.v. "ha-giyoret."

79. *Sifre*: Behar, 109d; B. Yevamot 46a. See B. Kiddushin 22a.

80. MT: Avadim, 8.20. See MT: Isurei Biah, 13.7 and Melakhim, 10.3.

81. B. Ketubot 11a, Tosfot Rid.

82. Ran on *Alfasi*: Ketubot, ed. Vilna, 4a.

83. See Y. Yevamot 8.1/8d re M. Makhshirin 2.7.

84. B. Yevamot 22a and parallels. See B. Shabbat 68a and R. Menahem ha-Meiri, *Bet ha-Behirah*: Shabbat 68a, ed. Lange, 256.

85. R. Solomon Luria, *Yam shel Shlomoh*: Ketubot 11a.

86. B. Ketubot 11a, Rashi, s.v. "ger qatan"; R. Yom Tov ben Abraham Ishbili, *Hiddushei ha-Ritva* thereon.

87. R. Menahem ha-Meiri, *Bet ha-Behirah*: Ketubot 11a, ed. Sofer, 51.

88. See Tacitus, *History*, 5.5.

89. See M. Nedarim 3.11; Herodotus, *Persian War*, 2.36; Philo, *De Specialus Legibus*, 1.210; *Epistle of Barnabas*, 9.6.

90. T. Shabbat 15.9.

91. B. Eruvin 13b.

92. B. Shabbat 135a.

93. See Maimonides, MT: Isurei Biah, 14.5.

94. See B. M. Lewin, *Otsar ha-Geonim*: Shabbat 135a (Jerusalem, 1930), 127, no. 391.

95. *Hiddushei ha-Ramban*: B. Shabbat 135a; also, R. Solomon ibn Adret, *Teshuvot ha-Rashba* 1, no. 329. Cf. Karo, *Shulhan Arukh*, Yoreh Deah 268.1.

96. B. Yevamot 47b.

97. Cf. Hullin 31a.

98. B. Yevamot 45b.

99. MT: Isurei Biah, 13.9.

100. *Hiddushei ha-Ramban*: B. Yevamot 45b.

101. Y. Kiddushin 3.13/64d.

102. B. Yevamot 47a.

103. B. Kiddushin 71a. See M. Eduyot 8.6; B. Kiddushin 72a.

104. M. Hagigah 1.7 re Ecclesiastes 1:15. See D. Novak, *Halakhah in a Theological Dimension* (Chico, Calif., 1985), chap. 2.

105. M. Baba Metsia 4.10.

106. B. Baba Metsia 58b.

107. See B. Sanhedrin 94a.

108. See B. Yoma 71b.

109. Y. Bikkurim 1.4/64a.

110. For the question of whether permission to accept converts requires the approval of the non-Jewish authorities under whose jurisdiction Jews are living, see the chapter by Michael J. Broyde herein.

111. See Josephus, *Contra Apionem*, 2.168; Philo, *De Specialus Legibus*, 4.61.

112. See B. Sanhedrin 74a; Y. Sanhedrin 3.6/21b; Maimonides, MT: Yesodei ha-Torah, 5.1ff.; R. Abraham Gumbiner, *Magen Avraham* on Karo, *Shulhan Arukh*: Orah Hayyim, 128.37.

113. *Kuzari*, 1, intro.

114. Ibid., 1.1.

115. See *Nicomachean Ethics*, 1177a25-30.

116. See Leo Strauss, *Persecution and the Art of Writing* (Glencoe, Ill., 1952), 103; Novak, *The Election of Israel*, 210ff.

117. *Kuzari*, 1.2. See Plato, *Republic*, 473D.

118. *Kuzari*, 1.4.

119. Ibid., 1.9.

120. Ibid., 1.11ff.

121. See ibid., 2.48.

122. Ibid., 2.1.

123. MT: Melakhim, 10.9 re B. Sanhedrin 59a. Much of this section is based on the author's Samuel Goldenson Memorial Lecture, "Maimonides on Judaism and Other Religions," delivered in February 1997 at the Hebrew Union College-Jewish Institute of Religion in Cincinnati, Ohio.

124. Ibid., 9.1. See T. Avodah Zarah 8.4; B. Sanhedrin 56b.

125. *Sefer ha-Mitsvot*, pos. no. 9. See D. Novak, *Jewish-Christian Dialogue* (New York, 1989), chap. 3.

126. *Teshuvot ha-Rambam* 1, ed. J. Blau (Jerusalem, 1960), no. 149, pp. 284f.

127. B. Yevamot 47a.

128. MT: Melakhim, 12.1, 4.

129. Ibid., chap. 11, ed. M. D. Rabinowitz (Jerusalem, 1962), 416.

130. See Maimonides, *Guide of the Perplexed*, 2.40; 3.27.

131. It should be noted that the first heresy rejected by the Church was that of Marcion, who advocated a total break from the God of Israel and the Torah of Israel. See H. Chadwick, *The Early Church* (New York, 1967), 38ff.

132. See *Teshuvot ha-Rambam* 2, no. 293.

133. Ibid., 1, no. 149, p. 285.

134. See Maimonides, *Guide of the Perplexed*, 1.50.

135. See Thomas Aquinas, *Summa Theologiae* 2/1, q. 103, a. 3.

136. See ibid., q. 100, a. 1 and a. 3.

137. For his earlier view, see *Commentary on the Mishnah*: Avodah Zarah 1.3-4.

138. *Teshuvot ha-Rambam* 1, no. 149, p. 285.

139. Thus the most influential nineteenth-century Protestant theologian, Friedrich Schleiermacher, subtitled his 1799 book *On Religion*, "Speeches to Its Cultured Despisers."

140. See Hermann Cohen, *Reason and Hope*, ed. and trans. E. Jospe (New York, 1971), 186.

141. See Leo Baeck, *Judaism and Christianity*, ed. and trans. W. Kaufmann (Philadelphia, 1958), 274ff.

142. See Novak, *The Election of Israel*, 216ff.

143. See D. Novak, *Jewish Social Ethics* (New York, 1992), 228ff.

144. Cf. Ignaz Maybaum, *The Face of God after Auschwitz* (Amsterdam, 1965); also, L. J. Epstein, *The Theory and Practice of Welcoming Converts to Judaism* (Lewiston, N.Y., 1992).

145. See Novak, *The Election of Israel*, 152ff.

2. PROSELYTISM AND JEWISH LAW

1. Jewish law (*halakha*) is used herein to denote the entire subject matter of the Jewish legal system, including public, private, and ritual law. For discussion of its sources and evolution, see sources and discussion in Michael J. Broyde, "Forming Religious Communities and Respecting Dissenters' Rights," in *Human Rights in Judaism: Cultural, Religious, and Political Perspectives*, ed. Michael J. Broyde and John Witte Jr. (Livingston, N.J., 1998), 35-76, esp. 36-37.

2. Although there was a time when the Jewish tradition was more amenable to various forms of proselytizing, this era appears to be considerably more than twenty-five hundred years past. Undoubtedly, this is related to the Talmud's repeated need to address the difficulty caused by the neo-Jewish nation referred to as *kutim*, perhaps Samaritans, who repeatedly troubled the Jewish community in a variety of different manners for more than five hundred years in the rabbinic era. For an excellent survey of many different facets of conversion, see Menachem Finkelstein, *Hagiyur, Halacha Uma'aseh* (Bar Ilan, 1994).

3. For example, the Talmud recounts that a Gentile who observes the Sabbath is liable for divine punishment (see Sanhedrin 58b and Maimonides, Kings 10:9).

4. See *Tosafot*, Megillah 9a, s.v. "elokim echad."

5. See generally, Maimonides, *Law of Kings*, chaps. 9 and 10. See the chapter by David Novak herein, and idem, *The Image of the Non-Jew in Judaism* (New York, 1983).

6. Maimonides, *Laws of Kings*, 12:1.

7. Yevamot 24b.

8. Sanhedrin 56a.

9. According to Samuel ben Hofni, thirty specific commandments are included; see generally, appendix to Shlomo Yosef Zevin, ed., *Encyclopedia Talmudit* (Jerusalem, 1976), 3:394-96.

10. See Aaron Lichtenstein, *The Seven Laws of Noah* (New York, 1986), 90-91.

11. Ibid.

12. See further Michael J. Broyde, "Public Policy and Religious Law: Assisting in a Deliberate Violation of Noahide Law that is Permitted by Secular Law," *Jewish Law Association Studies VIII: The Jerusalem 1994 Conference Volume* (Atlanta, 1996), 11-20, and idem, "Jewish Law and the Obligation to Enforce Secular Law,"

in *The Orthodox Forum Proceedings VI: Jewish Responsibilities to Society*, ed. D. Shatz and C. Waxman (Livingston, N.J., 1997), 103-43.

13. Judah Loewe of Prague (*Maharal Me-Prague*), *Ber Hagolah* (Jerusalem, 5731), 38-39; see further, Michael J. Broyde, "Cloning People," *Connecticut Law Review* 30 (1998): 503-35.

14. One such duty, for example, is to return lost objects to one another, but not to Gentiles (see Michael J. Broyde and Michael Hecht, "The Return of Lost Property according to Jewish and Common Law: A Comparison," *Journal of Law and Religion* 13 [1996]: 225-54).

15. This point is not trivial. Even when the Jewish tradition acknowledges that others may engage in this conduct as it is "good" to do, it insists that others are not legally obligated to engage in such conduct. The absence of the "yoke of heaven" compelling obligation *reduces*, rather than increases, the reward given to a person (see Kidushin 28a). In Jewish law, the reward is greater for one who is obligated to observe the law and does so than for one who is not obligated in the law, and does so, as the second person has no "yoke of heaven" compelling the activity.

16. This is of no small theological significance, as the Jewish tradition is comfortable stating that conversion to Judaism is bad for a person if he or she subsequently decides not to observe Jewish law. This is explicitly noted in Joseph Karo, *Shulhan Arukh* (Vilna, 1896), Yoreh Deah 268:2. Rabbi Moses Feinstein, in *Responsa Iggrot Moshe Yoreh Deah* (New York, 1959), Even Haezer 4:26(3), notes a contrary sentiment is possible when one is involved in the conversion of minors (and perhaps adults too), when one can aver that the violations of Jewish law by those individuals is unintentional, rather than purposeful. This is itself questionable.

17. Exodus 19:6.

18. See, for example, Maimonides, *Law of Kings*, 9:1-11.

19. *Shulhan Arukh*, Yoreh Deah 268:2, and 13.

20. Ibid., 268:2.

21. The simple language of the *Shulhan Arukh* (ibid.) makes this clear. There is no duty to seek converts, and no reasons, other than practical ones, to undertake such conduct. But see Yerucham Perlow, *Sefer Hamitzvot LeRav Sadia Gaon*, Positive Commandment 19, who adopts the view that it is an ethically positive act of kindness to convert a worthy convert.

22. There remains the fascinating theoretical discussion among the early and late decisors of Jewish law as to whether a person who actually does convert to another faith loses his or her status as a Jew, and if so, whether that loss of status is full, absolute, and irrevocable. Most Jewish law authorities rule that one who converts out of Judaism develops the status of a Gentile only for a small number of technical prohibitions, such as the ability to lead prayer, but does not generally have that status for most matters—for example, the marriage of such a person to another Jewish apostate would be governed by Jewish law, and the children would be Jewish. Other authorities rule that this person develops the status of a Gentile for many areas of Jewish law, and it is only in the area of core status issues and procreation that this person remains Jewish. Yet a third group (a very small minority) contemplates that such a person is required to reconvert to Judaism, and until such time as he or she reconverts, is not Jewish. While the first and second approach have some support in normative Jewish law, the third does not. For a thoughtful discussion of this topic, see *Iggrot Moshe*, Even Haezer 4:83, and *Maharashdam*, Even Haezer 1:10. This last response is one of the very few that accepts this third position as normative, and the

author of *Iggrot Moshe* notes that its approach is "in error and writing about it [as normative Jewish law] a waste of ink." For a review of the sources in English, see Aaron Lichtenstein, "Brother Daniel and the Jewish Fraternity," *Judaism* 12 (1963): 260-80.

23. See Dov Katz, *Tenuat HaMussar*, 5th ed. (Jersualem, 1987), 1:22-25.

24. This parenthetical is a significant one in the area of outreach, as there are a significant number of decisors of Jewish law who permit one to entice a person to sin in a manner that leads to fuller observance in the long run. While this dispute touches on a number of obscure areas of Jewish law, its modern-day variation is simple: In order to introduce people to the Jewish tradition, many Jewish organizations will run events on the Sabbath that entice violations of the Sabbath laws by people who are going to these events. These specific violations would not happen but for these events, although the purpose of these events is to convince people, in the long run, to cease engaging in these violations. Many modern decisors of Jewish law insist that such events are permissible or even proper, while others insist that they are not (see Michael Broyde and David Hertzberg, "Enabling a Jew to Sin: The Parameters," *Journal of Halacha and Contemporary Society* 19 [1990]: 5-33).

25. See Menachem Elon, *Jewish Law: History, Sources and Principles* (Philadelphia, 1994), 1575-1618.

26. Indeed, the exact parameters of who is to enforce these norms, and why, are subject to a considerable debate (see Compare Nahum Rakover, "Jewish Law and the Noahide Obligation to Preserve Social Order," *Cardozo Law Review* 12 [1991]: 1073-1136; Arnold Enker, "Aspects of Interaction between the Torah Law, the King's Law, and the Noahide Law in Jewish Criminal Law," *Cardozo Law Review* 12 [1991]: 1137-56; J. David Bleich, "Jewish Law and the State's Authority to Punish Crime," *Cardozo Law Review* 12 [1991]: 829-57, esp. 856).

27. *Shulhan Arukh*, Hoshen Mishpat 163:3. These rules are found, not surprisingly, in the rules relating to the financial obligations imposed on all citizens, and not in the discussion of ritual law.

28. See Broyde, "Forming Religious Communities and Respecting Dissenters' Rights."

29. Maimonides, *Book of Commandments*, Commandment 1.

30. See Yom Tov Ashbeilli, Ritva, Ketubot 86a, and Betzalel Ashkenazi, Shita Mekubetzet, Kebubot 86a.

31. Abraham Isaiah Karletz, Chazon Ish, Hoshen Mishpat 10:6. For more on what exactly precipitated this exchange, see Shabtai ben Meir Hacohen, Shach, Hoshen Mishpat 87(80) and Ketzot Hachoshen commenting on ibid. This argument can be parsed even further, by distinguishing between a person who will properly engage in the prescribed ritual worship when compelled to do so, and one who will not. It is apparent that coercion cannot be effective as a matter of technical Jewish law in the later case, as intent, in some form, is needed to fulfill *mitzvot*. The rationale for nonenforcement is that compelled worship is of no value, and a fruitless exercise. Jewish law insists that worship requires a positive intent actually to revere the Divine in one's heart, and that can never be compelled.

32. This concept requires some elaboration, and explanation, in order to understand why this case is different from love of God or Sabbath prayers. Simply put, worship through coercion is valueless in the Jewish tradition, as most positive commandments require specific intent to fulfill the *mitzvah*. Thus, one who prays with no intent to pray has fulfilled no good deed. On the other hand, one who refrains from

eating prohibited food lest he be punished, just as one who chooses not to rob banks because of the guards, has, in the end, conducted himself in accordance with the law and avoided criminal liability. (A technical digression into the details of Jewish law is needed here. Even those authorities who insist that the fulfillment of *mitzvot* requires no actual intent—a dispute in the Talmud—agree that one who has absolutely no idea why he is doing this action, or an affirmative subconscious desire not to fulfill the obligation, has not fulfilled any *mitzvah*. Thus, one who prays under threat of harm from another, if he does not pray, has not prayed, as the Jewish tradition would view such prayers as without any intent.) So, too, one has to note that even when the Jewish tradition allows for no formal punishment of a violation, that approach does not logically compel one to observe that one cannot force another to cease ongoing violations.

33. None of the classical commandments designed to deter sinning by Jews (except the biblical prohibition of facilitating sin [*lifnei ivver*]) is generally thought applicable to Gentiles. Thus, there is no obligation to admonish (*tokhahah*) a Gentile who sins (see generally, Sanhedrin 75a and *Rashi ad locum*). So, too, there is no notion of cooperative activity (*arevut*) that compels collective responsibility (see generally, Aaron Kirschenbaum, "'Covenant' with Noahides Compared with Covenant at Sinai," *Dinei Israel* 6 [1977]: 31).

34. This is stated quite unambiguously by Rabbi Yehiel Mikhel Epstein, who writes: "You should know that the obligation to admonish is only applicable to a Jew who is generally committed to Jewish law but who has been overtaken by desire to commit [this sin]. In such a case, admonition applies; concerning those who completely deny the words of the Sages, the obligation of admonition does not apply" (Arukh ha-Shulhan, Orah Hayyim 608:7). Similar sentiments are expressed by *Mishnah Berurah* 608, Be'ur Halakhah s.v. "*aval*" (see Eliezer Waldenberg, *Tzitz Eliezer* 17:37).

35. See, e.g., Joseph Babad, *Minhat Hinuch*, Commandment 339, who notes that the obligation to assist Jews in their religious search is, at the minimum, subsumed under the obligation of a person to return the lost object of another.

36. See Norman Lamm, "Loving and Hating Jews as Halakhic Categories," *Tradition* 24, no. 2 (1989): 98-122.

37. See David ha-Levi, *Turei Zahav, (Taz),* Yoreh Deah 334:1, and remarks of Shakh as found in *Nekudat ha-Kesef* commenting on it.

38. *Pesahim* 22b.

39. *Moed Katan* 17a and *Kiddushin* 29b.

40. See Exodus 21:15, which lists striking one's parents as a capital offense.

41. See Exodus 22:24 and Leviticus 25:36-37.

42. Bava Metzia 75b.

43. Genesis 39:14.

44. Mechilta commenting on Exodus 22:20.

45. Yevamot 109b.

46. Niddah 13b.

47. Finkelstein, *Hagiyur, Halacha Uma'aseh*, 98-107.

48. Thus, for example, *Shulhan Arukh*, Yoreh Deah 268:2, requires that one tell the convert that the Jewish people are subject to religious persecution, which the convert will now be subject to, also.

49. *Shulhan Arukh*, Yoreh Deah 268:3, which explicitly notes that absent a Jewish law court witnessing the acceptance of the commandments and the desire to enter the Jewish people, the conversion is void. Although the matter is in some dispute,

Jewish law now recognizes that neither immersion nor conversion absolutely needs a Jewish court to witness it, although in both cases the presence of a court is preferred.

50. Finkelstein, *Hagiyur, Halacha Uma'aseh*, 283-305.

51. At least three theories explain this. One theory states that the presence of a foreskin is a sign of spiritual impurity such that immersion in the *mikva* or *ma'ayan* cannot be valid, and thus circumcision is needed only to validate immersion. Others aver that circumcision is required to mimic the conversion of Abraham. Yet others aver that a male, upon conversion, would be in violation of Jewish law the second he converts (which would be improper, as explained in the next section), and thus circumcision is needed to prevent this Jew from starting his life as a Jew in sin.

Significant differences in terms of normative Jewish law arise among these doctrines. Consider the problem of one who immerses in the *mikva* and then is circumcised. Has that man undergone a proper conversion? One school of thought avers that immersion by a man who is uncircumcised is a void immersion; the other school of thought maintains that sequence is not important, and so long as one both immerses and circumcises, the conversion is valid. Consider also a pregnant woman who converts and subsequently gives birth to a boy, whether that child needs circumcision as a part of his conversion, as he was not fully converted yet, or whether his circumcision is as a born Jew. Finally, consider the question of the requirement of circumcision for a man who already was circumcised as a Gentile and now seeks to convert to Judaism. While all agree that such a person needs a nominal circumcision (*hatafat dam brit*), some authorities aver that such is not needed as part of the circumcision but for a different reason (see Finkelstein, *Hagiyur, Halacha Uma'aseh*, 165-76).

52. See Mishnah, Mikvaot, 1:1-6.

53. *Mikva* is the term used for a pool of approximately 100 gallons of rainwater, or water in contact with or derived from rainwater, suitable for an average person to immerse in.

54. *Ma'ayan* denotes a flowing body of water, of no fixed amount, suitable for a person to immerse in.

55. See *Shulhan Arukh*, Yoreh Deah 268:12.

56. See Finkelstein, *Hagiyur, Halacha Uma'aseh*, 218-20.

57. One other condition for conversion is sometimes mentioned: permission from the secular government. In a wide variety of Jewish law works spanning a number of centuries, the caveat is often recited that permission for a Jewish court to receive converts requires consent of the local government (see, for example, *Shulhan Arukh*, Yoreh Deah 268:1). I am inclined to believe that such permission is not genuinely required according to Jewish law, and these comments were placed in these works as a form of self-censorship to indicate that the Jewish community understood that proselytizing was deemed improper by the pre-emancipation governments of Europe; out of respect for the wishes of the local government, such conversions were very rare. More generally, a Jewish law court is under no duty to accept a convert when the convert's conversion will lead to other difficulties for the community. Conversion is not a commandment (*mitzvah*) in the Jewish faith, and thus a bet din can opt not to convert one for a variety of social, economic, or other reasons.

58. Paul Johnson, *A History of the Jews* (New York, 1987), 147 notes that the requirement of conversion was the point that deterred many pagans from converting to Judaism and drove many pagans to become Christians rather than Jewish, as paganism

disappeared as a faith. This view is unsupported in the Jewish sources dealing with this topic. Those areas of interaction with converts in talmudic times that seemed most stressful to the talmudic rabbis related to the lack of commitment to observance of Jewish law—even in talmudic times—by prospective proselytes or partial converts. Thus, the conduct of the Samaritans (converts to Judaism whose observance of Jewish law was incomplete) was the problem most frequently addressed in the Talmud. So, too, when the potential converts approach Hillel and Shamai about the possibility of conversion with conditions, all of the conditions proposed relate to Jewish law observance, and not to the procedural requirements of Jewish law. There is no discussion of potential converts who wish to convert "except for circumcision." If Johnson were correct, there would be a noticeably larger number of female, rather than male, converts. The *responsa* literature indicates the exact opposite to be true; there are more male converts to Judaism than female converts discussed in every single volume of medieval *responsa* that this writer has examined.

59. Yevamot 47a-b; *Shulhan Arukh*, Yoreh Deah 268:2.

60. *Shabbat* 68a and *Tosafot* on ibid., s.v. *"ger."*

61. *Keretut* 30b.

62. Consider Maimonides' formulation for a resident alien, which explicitly notes that a resident alien who obeys all the laws, without agreement that God directed to Moses that they be obeyed, has not properly become a resident alien (see Maimonides, Kings 8:10 and Issurai Biah 14:7; *Shulhan Arukh*, Yoreh Deah 124:2). It is worth noting that this formulation is itself changed slightly in one of Maimonides' *responsa* (see *Responsa of Maimonides* 1:146 Blua edition). See further discussion in the chapter by David Novak herein.

63. *Shabbat* 31a.

64. In practical terms, sometimes it is difficult to distinguish between individuals in this third category and individuals who fully commit to Jewish law without any information about how to observe it. Again, consider the case of one who completely, and with no reservations, violates the Sabbath. Is such a person in category 3, or merely one who was properly converted and never informed about the Sabbath? Mere observation of this person's behavior cannot answer this question in a meaningful way, as in both cases the behavior is identical.

65. This is a bit of a simplification, in that a claim can be made that a person who is immersed (and, if a man, circumcised) has left the status of Gentile and simply not yet become Jewish. This claim, first formulated by Maimonides in reference to a person who has been circumcised and not yet immersed, could just as well be applied to one who is immersed and circumcised but has not yet accepted the commandments (for more on this, see Howard Jachter, *Beinyan Kedushat Yisrael Lichazayin* [New York, 5752], Beit Yitzchak 24:425-27).

66. The vast majority of converts seek conversion for social and not theological reason; typically that social reason is that they have met a person whom they wish to marry, who is Jewish, and who will only marry a Jew. Simply put, since the vast majority of Jews in both the United States and Israel are themselves not observant of Jewish law and fall into either category 2 or 3, it would seem likely that the individuals undergoing conversion to Judaism for the sake of a potential Jewish spouse would be unlikely to be interested in a level of observance markedly higher than that of their potential spouse. Even if they were to express such interest, it is unlikely that their spouse would approve of such, as they themselves do not desire to live a life of fidelity to Jewish law and would discourage their spouses from so doing.

67. See *Iggrot Moshe*, Yoreh Deah 3:108, about the woman who set out to violate festival law, and knew she would, for economic need.

68. Another approach sometimes mentioned argues that Hillel did not convert the Gentile until after he had convinced him to accept all of Jewish law (see Responsa of Rabbi Akiva Eiger 41). As noted by Rabbi Isaac Herzog (*Hachal Yitzchak*, Even Haezer 1:19:7), this approach is very difficult to understand on a variety of levels: first, because it seems inconsistent with the words of the Talmud; and second, because it makes the story insignificant, which the Talmud itself indicates that it is not.

69. Rashi commenting on Shabbat 31a.

70. See Ovadia Yosef, "Questions of Conversion in our Era," *Torah She'bal Pe* 13 (5731): 26-27, which clearly notes that a person who has not affirmatively rejected a specific commandment, but merely does not trust the rabbi's interpretation, has not rejected a commandment. This approach is explicitly rejected by *Iggrot Moshe*, Yoreh Deah 3:106.

71. *Iggrot Moshe*, Yoreh Deah 3:106.

72. Isaac Herzog, *Hechal Yitzchak Even Haezer* 119(9).

73. *Beit Yitzchak,* Yoreh Deah 2:100(10). See also, Abraham Isaac Kook, *Dat Kohein* 152 and Abrahm Shapiro, *Dvar Avraham* 3:28. Rabbi Moshe Feinstein, who elsewhere insists that this approach is wrong, acknowledges its correctness in *Iggrot Moshe*, Yoreh Deah 3:106: "but, post fact, if one accepts a convert [who accepts all except for one thing] such a person is a convert, and obligated in all the commandments, including the one that they chose not to accept." This seems to be in conflict with Rabbi Feinstein's general approach to this topic, which will be discussed infra. For a clue as to how Rabbi Feinstein perhaps could reach this result, consistent with his principles, see his *Dibbrot Moshe*, Yevamot, 507.

74. See also Yoab Weingarten, *Helkat Yoab* 1:13.

75. See, for example, Isser Yehuda Unterman, "The Laws of Conversion and Their Practical Application," *Torah Shebal Pe* 13 (1971): 1-20. (Rabbi Unterman was one of the chief rabbis of Israel.) For a survey of some of these issues, see Shmuel Shilo, "Halakhic Leniency in Modern *Responsa* regarding Conversion," *Israel Law Review* (1988): 353-64.

76. It is in this matter that Jewish theological belief that Gentiles are proper in their rejection of Jewish law for themselves, and are under no duty to accept it, plays a significant role. In order for a Gentile to join the Jewish people, he must voluntarily accept the parallel version of the covenant at Sinai. However, voluntary acceptance does not preclude the possibility that a person might voluntarily accept *and subsequently violate*.

77. *Responsa Acheizer* 3:26(4).

78. Ibid. See the long and thoughtful discussion of this in Ovadia Yosef, "Questions of Conversion in Our Era," who endorses the broad approach of Rabbi Grodzinski.

79. Finkelstein, *Hagiyur, Halacha Uma'aseh*, 357; the quotation is from *Iggrot Moshe*, Yoreh Deah 1:157.

80. The forcefulness of Rabbi Feinstein's view is reflected in one of the *responsa* in which he considers the validity of a conversion done when the convert intended to observe Jewish law fully but had committed to going to work on the last days of Passover immediately after her conversion. The convert herself, after twelve years of observance, questioned her status; Rabbi Feinstein maintained that she was Jewish. Although his reasoning combines a number of diverse factors, he limits the ability of

converts to continue to violate Jewish law after their conversion to cases where their violation was due to duress (economic or physical) and of a temporary nature. When both of those factors are not present, the conversion would appear to be void (see *Iggrot Moshe*, Yoreh Deah 3:108).

81. Although one might assume that there is a general theological undertone to this dispute also, such, I think, is not correct. Some have argued that the underlying dispute reflects a disagreement within the Jewish tradition as to whether one is better off being a Gentile or a Jew without Jewish observance. One could claim, with considerable basis in Jewish law, that Jewish law and theology treat a Gentile observant of Noahide law with greater reverence than a Jew who does not observe Jewish law at all, or a heretic. Indeed, the standard Jewish law code notes without any reservation that "heretics [or perhaps, apostates] are worse than Gentiles" (*Shulhan Arukh*, Hoshen Mishpat 334:22). While this issue is of considerable interest and relevance in our times, there is little correlation between those authorities who view being Jewish as always better than being a Gentile, or the reverse, with their view on conversion of those who reject Jewish law. Consider the case of Rabbi Moses Feinstein, the intellectual leader of the school within Jewish law that insists that conversions are only valid when accompanied by full observance. Yet it is he—the same Moses Feinstein—who insists that it is better to be an unobservant Jew than a Gentile (see *Iggrot Moshe*, Yoreh Deah 4:26[3]).

3. ANTISEMITISM AND PROSELYTISM

1. The term *antisemitism* was coined in German in 1879 by Wilhelm Marr, a professed antisemite. In English, the word is often written with a hyphen, which is an absurd construction in that there is no such thing as "semitism" to which it might be opposed. In German and Hebrew the term has no hyphen, and it is therefore more accurate to write the English word without a hyphen (see Y. Bauer, "In Search of a Definition of Antisemitism," in *Approaches to Antisemitism*, ed. M. Brown (Jerusalem, 1994), 10.

2. R. Wistrich, "The Anti-Zionist Masquerade," *Midstream* (August/September 1983): 8-18.

3. R. L. Rubenstein, *After Auschwitz* (Indianapolis, 1966), 19.

4. Y. Bauer, *The Jewish Emergence from Powerlessness* (Toronto, 1979), 41.

5. See, e.g., Emil Fackenheim, *The Jewish Return into History Reflections in the Age of Auschwitz and a New Jerusalem* (New York, 1978).

6. D. Berger, ed., *History and Hate: The Dimensions of Anti-Semitism* (Philadelphia, 1986), 5.

7. Rosemary Radford Ruether, "Anti-Semitism and Christian Theology," in *Auschwitz: Beginning of a New Era*, ed. E. Fleischner (New York, 1977), 81.

8. When Herzl met Pope Pius X in 1904, he was received with theological hostility, because the Holy See found it difficult to conceive of the return of the Jews to Palestine or to accept that, if such an event were to take place, it would be carried out by secular Jews (see D. V. Segre, "Is Anti-Zionism a New Form of Antisemitism?" in *Antisemitism in the Contemporary World*, ed. M. Curtis (Boulder, Colo., 1986), 153n.

9. G. Steiner, "Jewish Values in the Post-Holocaust Future," *Judaism* 16, no. 3 (Summer 1967): 276-81.

10. F. H. Littel, *The Crucifixion of the Jews* (New York, 1975), 2.

11. Rubenstein, *After Auschwitz*, 56.

12. *The Condition of Jewish Belief: A Symposium Compiled by the Editors of Commentary Magazine* (New York, 1966), 90.

13. Rubenstein, *After Auschwitz*, 186.

14. There is, for example, a haunting scene in Claude Lanzmann's film of the Holocaust, "Shoah," in which a group of Poles claims to have witnessed a rabbi interpreting the Jewish fate during the Holocaust as a "deserved" punishment for the crime of deicide.

15. Cited by A. L. Eckhardt, "The Holocaust, the Church Struggle, and Some Christian Reflections," in *Faith and Freedom: A Tribute to Franklin H. Littel*, ed. R. Libowitz (New York, 1987), 33.

16. E. L. Fackenheim, "Philosophical Reflections on Claude Lanzmann's 'Shoah,'" in Libowitz, *Faith and Freedom*, 13.

17. H. Maccoby, "Theologian of the Holocaust," *Commentary* 74, no. 6 (December 1982).

18. C. Huchet-Bishop, "Response to John Pawlikowski," in Fleischner, *Auschwitz*, 183.

19. Ibid., 180.

20. Bernard Lewis, "Antisemitism in the Arab and Islamic World," in *Present-Day Antisemitism*, ed. Y. Bauer (Jerusalem, 1988), 57.

21. J. S. Gerber, "Anti-Semitism in the Muslim World," in Berger, *History and Hate*, 73-93.

22. Ibid., 80.

23. Ibid.

24. Lewis, "Antisemitism," 60.

25. Ibid., 61.

26. Awareness of the Dreyfus trial in France, for example, resulted in the first Arabic translations of specifically antisemitic books. These, however, had limited influence at the time.

27. Lewis, "Antisemitism," 62.

28. Ibid., 63.

29. Ibid., 65.

30. See R. Wistrich, *Hitler's Apocalypse: Jews and the Nazi Ideology* (London, 1985).

31. Lewis, "Antisemitism," 70.

32. Segre, "Anti-Zionism," 145-54.

33. Ibid.

34. N. Glazer, "Anti-Zionism—A Global Phenomenon," in Curtis, *Antisemitism*, 155-63.

35. I. Rabinovitch, "Antisemitism in the Muslim and Arab World," in Bauer, *Present-Day Antisemitism*, 265.

36. B. Rivlin and J. Fomerand, "Changing Third World Perspectives and Policies towards Israel," in *Israel and the Third World*, ed. M. Curtis and S. A. Gitelson (New Brunswick, N.J., 1976), 325-60.

37. Ibid.

38. Ibid., 328.

39. Ibid., 339.

40. Ibid., 342.

41. Ibid., 348.

42. Ibid., 346.

43. Ibid., 347.

44. Ibid.

45. Ibid.

46. Lewis, "Antisemitism," 65.

47. Ibid.

48. It should be noted that the Christian theology of the Jews as a reprobate people was also disturbed by this decisive historic event.

49. Osama bin Laden, the man alleged to have been behind the bombings of the American embassies in Kenya and Tanzania, is reported to have invited "all Muslims to join his jihad against the Americans and against the Jews" (*The Sunday Independent*, August 23, 1998, 4).

4. *JIHAD* FOR HEARTS AND MINDS

1. During the decade since the Ayatollah Khomeini issued his *fatwa* of death against Salman Rushdie, one of the novelist's translators has been killed and another seriously wounded, while other Muslim authors have been murdered in Egypt, Algeria, and Saudi Arabia (see *For Rushdie: Essays by Arab and Muslim Writers in Defense of Free Speech*, ed. Anouar Abdallah [New York, 1993]).

2. See Richard W. Bulliet, "Conversion Stories in Early Islam," in *Conversion and Continuity: Indigenous Christian Communities in Islamic Lands, Eighth to Eighteenth Centuries*, ed. Michael Gervers and Ramzi Jibran Bikhazi (Toronto, 1990), 123; Richard W. Bulliet, *Conversion to Islam in the Medieval Period: An Essay in Quantitative History* (Cambridge, Mass., 1979), 128; Larry Poston, *Islamic Da'wah in the West: Muslim Missionary Activity and the Dynamics of Conversion to Islam* (New York, 1992), 158.

3. U.N. Human Rights Committee, General Comment on Article 18, ICCPR, U.N. Doc. CCPR/C/48/CPR.2/Rev.1 (1993), para. 5. See Bahiyyih Tahzib, *Freedom of Religion or Belief: Ensuring Effective International Legal Protection* (The Hague, 1996), 325-27.

4. On the variety of streams of thought within Islam, see Donna E. Arzt, "The Treatment of Religious Dissidents under Classical and Contemporary Islamic law," in *Religious Human Rights in Global Perspective: Religious Perspectives*, ed. John Witte Jr. and Johan D. van der Vyver (The Hague/Boston/London, 1996), 408-10.

5. See C. G. Weeramantry, *Islamic Jurisprudence: An International Perspective* (New York, 1988).

6. Sura 10:65. Unless quoting the Qur'an from a secondary source or deliberately comparing different English translations, this chapter follows the English translation in Marmaduke Pickthall, *The Glorious Koran: A Bi-Lingual Edition with English* (London, 1976). Pickthall is both a Muslim and a native English speaker who consulted Egyptian experts in rendering his translation. According to Islamic law, the Qur'an should not be read in translation, because to do so is to alter Allah's revelation (ibid., vii). Thus, any translation is, at best, an interpretation. For a comparison of Pickthall with Yusufali and Shakir, two other English translators, see www.usc.edu/dept/MSA/quran.

7. Weeramantry, *Islamic Jurisprudence*, 39.

8. See generally, Hamilton A. R. Gibb, *Studies on the Civilization of Islam* (London, 1962).

9. See Abdulaziz A. Sachedina, "The Development of Jihad in Islamic Revelation and History," in *Cross, Crescent and Sword: The Justification and Limitation of War in Western and Islamic Tradition*, ed. James Turner Johnson and John Kelsay (New York, 1990), 40-41. On Islamic schools of jurisprudence as well as the Sunni and Shi'i divisions, see generally, N. J. Coulson, *A History of Islamic Law* (Edinburgh, 1964); Henry Corbin, *History of Islamic Philosophy* (London, 1993); and Weeramantry, *Islamic Jurisprudence*.

10. "He hath ordained for you that religion which He commended unto Noah, and that which We inspire thee (Mohammed), and that which We commended unto Abraham and Moses and Jesus, saying: 'Establish the religion, and be not divided therein'" (Q. 42:13). See T. W. Arnold, *The Preaching of Islam* (Lahore, 1914), 30-31.

11. The other four pillars are daily prayer at dawn, noon, mid-afternoon, evening, and night; fasting during the month of Ramadan; almsgiving (*zakat*); and the pilgrimage to Mecca (*hajj*) for all who are capable (Geddes MacGregor, *Dictionary of Religion and Philosophy* [New York, 1989], 251-52).

12. Arnold, *Preaching of Islam*, 418. See generally, Bulliet, *Conversion to Islam in the Medieval Period*.

13. This is the Yusuf Ali translation, with which Shakir closely concurs: "And it is naught but a reminder to the nations." By contrast, in the Pickthall translation, the universality is lost "When it is naught else than a Reminder to creation" (www.usc.edu/dept/MSA/quran).

14. See Mahmood Ahmad Ghazi, *The Hijrah: Its Philosophy and Message for the Modern Man* (Lahore, n.d.), 51-59.

15. See, e.g., Q. 13:38, 21:10, 31:33, and 68:52.

16. See Eugene P. Heideman, "Proselytism, Mission, and the Bible," *International Bulletin of Missionary Research* 20, no. 1 (January 1996): 10-12.

17. See Betty Beard, "Antioch Conversion Tactics Rile Muslims," *The Arizona Republic* (August 19, 1995). See generally, Edward W. Said, *Orientalism* (New York, 1978); idem, *Culture and Imperialism* (New York, 1983); idem, *Covering Islam: How the Media and the Experts Determine How We See the Rest of the World* (New York, 1981).

18. Sachedina, "The Development of Jihad in Islamic Revelation and History," 36-38.

19. Ibid., 36.

20. "Tell those who disbelieve that if they cease [from persecution of believers] that which is past will be forgiven them; but if they return [thereto] then the example of the men of old hath already gone [before them for a warning]. And fight them until persecution is no more, and religion is all for Allah. But if they cease, then lo! Allah is Seer of what they do" (Q. 8:38-39).

21. See later sections of this essay concerning the taxes imposed on non-Muslims. See further, Albert Hourani, *A History of the Arab Peoples* (New York, 1991), 35, and Daniel C. Dennett, *Conversion and the Poll Tax in Early Islam* (Cambridge, Mass., 1950).

22. Yusuf Ali translates this as "nor would We visit with Our Wrath until We had sent a messenger (to give warnings)" (www.usc.edu/dept/MSA/quran). See also Q. 22:67, which instructs to "summon thou unto thy Lord."

23. Poston, *Islamic Da'wah in the West*, 14, citing a *hadith* recorded by Bukhari.

24. Rudolph Peters, *Islam and Colonialism: The Doctrine of Jihad in Modern History* (New York, 1979), 18, cited in Poston, *Islamic Da'wah in the West*, 14.

25. This call for patience is reinforced by proximity. It appears immediately after the passage quoted earlier that requires a summons to the unbelievers and reasoning with them.

26. Majid Khadduri, *The Islamic Conception of Justice* (Baltimore, 1984), 163-64. *Imam* is the term used by Shi'i, and *khalifah* is the term used by Sunnis to refer to the community's leader. The Shi'i require their imam to be a descendent of 'Ali, Mohammed's son-in-law.

27. Ibid., 165-66. After the classical period, when Islamic power began to decline, some scholars construed *jihad* as only a defensive duty, dormant until actual danger loomed (ibid., 168-70). Sa'id Hawa, a member of the Muslim Brotherhood movement in Syria, derived five varieties of *jihad* from the Qur'an and Hadith: *jihad* through language; *jihad* through learning; *jihad* through body and mind; political *jihad*; and financial *jihad*. Ibrahim Malik, "*Jihad*—Its Development and Relevance," *Palestine-Israel Journal* 2 (Spring 1994): 32-33.

28. Bulliet quotes a hadith about Mohammed's stipulation that a group of people should surrender/convert (*aslamu*): "He sent them his emissaries and governors to familiarize them with the laws of Islam and his practices and to collect their alms and the poll tax on those of them who remained Christians, Jews or Zoroastrians." Bulliet then comments: "But the language does not allow the reader to disentangle the meanings 'surrender' and 'convert.' This raises the question as to whether these meanings were actually raised in the minds of the actors. After all, the notion of religious conversion as a moral or spiritual act that could be taken independently of other political or social action may not have been widespread in seventh-century Arabia" (Bulliet, "Conversion Stories in Early Islam," 124).

29. See Joan Fitzpatrick, "Protection against Abuse of the Concept of 'Emergency,'" in *Human Rights: An Agenda for the Next Century*, ed. Louis Henkin and John L. Hargrove (Washington, D.C., 1994), 203-28.

30. See John Esposito, *The Islamic Threat: Myth or Reality* (New York, 1992), 33; Abdulaziz A. Sachedina, "Freedom of Conscience and Religion in the Qur'an," in *Human Rights and the Conflict of Cultures: Western and Islamic Perspectives on Religious Liberty*, ed. David Little et al. (Columbia, S.C., 1988), 84; Majid Khadduri, *The Islamic Conception of Justice* (Baltimore, 1984), 164-70. Note that all three translators, Pickthal, Yusuf Ali, and Shakir, use the word "fight" in the verse beginning "Fight those who do not believe in Allah. . . . "(Q. 9:29) (www.usc.edu/dept/MSA/quran).

31. Most verses of the Qur'an that employ the derivative form of *hijra*, *hajaru* ("they migrated") are paired with *jahadu* ("they waged war"), thus implying a close relationship between *hijra* and *jihad*. Mohammed Khalid Masud, "The Obligation to Migrate: The Doctrine of *Hijra* in Islamic Law," in *Muslim Travelers: Pilgrimage, Migration and Religious Imagination*, ed. Dale F. Eickelman and James Piscatori (Berkeley, Calif., 1990), 32.

32. "Human Rights, Migration and Asylum: The 'Three Traditions' in Middle Eastern-Islamic Civilizations," unpublished and undated paper prepared by a group of unnamed Islamic scholars for the United Nations High Commissioner on Refugees, 4. See also Sami A. Aldeeb Abu-Sahlieh, "The Islamic Conception of Migration," *International Migration Review* 30, no. 1 (1996): 37.

33. Eickelman and Piscatori, *Muslim Travelers*, 37 and 259, citing Ismail R. Faruqi, *The Hijrah: The Necessity of Its Iqamat or Vergegungwärtigung* (Islamabad, 1985).

34. Hourani, *A History of the Arab Peoples*, 18, 22.

35. Hugh Goddard, *Christians and Muslims: From Double Standards to Mutual Understanding* (Surrey, England, 1995), 126-27. See generally, Philip Khuri Hitti, *History of the Arabs* (London, 1937); Khalid Yahya Blankinship, *The End of the Jihad State: The Reign of Hisham Ibn Abd al-Malik and the Collapse of the Umayyads* (Albany, N.Y., 1994).

36. Majid Khadduri and Herbert J. Liebesny, eds., *Law in the Middle East* (Washington, D.C., 1955), 367; Hourani, *A History of the Arab Peoples*, 19; Majid Khadduri, *War and Peace in the Law of Islam* (Baltimore, 1955), 202-22.

37. *The Islamic Law of Nations: Shaybani's Siyar*, trans. Majid Khadduri (Baltimore, 1966).

38. Abdullahi Ahmed An-Na'im, "Islamic Ambivalence to Political Violence: Islamic Law and International Terrorism," in *German Yearbook of International Law* 31 (Berlin, 1988): 323.

39. Goddard, *Christians and Muslims*, 140.

40. Sachedina, "Freedom of Conscience and Religion," 84. See also Khadduri, *The Islamic Conception of Justice*, 164-170.

41. Poston, *Islamic Da'wah in the West*, 14.

42. Hourani, *A History of the Arab Peoples*, 41-42. However, large communities of Christians and Jews remained.

43. Bulliet, *Conversion to Islam in the Medieval Period*, 2. Bulliet undertook a detailed study of the timetable of conversion in six major regions, based primarily on the adoption of distinctive Muslim names by converts. He then correlated these timetables with other known events. One of his observations was that non-Muslim revolts died out at about the middle point of the conversion process, as the population base to draw on steadily shrank (ibid., 44-45, 128). See further the chapter by Richard C. Martin herein.

44. These taxes were, according to Qur'anic instruction, an acknowledgement by the payers that they were in a state of subjugation to the Muslims. See Q. 9:29.

45. See Hourani, *A History of the Arab Peoples*, 27. Local civil control, however, including tax collection, was usually left to the non-Muslims (see M. Shaban, "Conversion to Early Islam," in *Conversion to Islam*, ed. Nehemia Levtzion [New York, 1979], 27-28).

46. Larry Poston, *Islamic Da'wah in the West*, 15, citing Marshall G. S. Hodgson, *The Venture of Islam* (Chicago, 1974), 1:209. Garrisons were used to house Muslim soldiers in Iraq and Northern Africa but not Syria (see Shaban, "Conversion to Early Islam," 28).

47. Poston, *Islamic Da'wah in the West*, 52.

48. Ibid., 14. The "osmosis method" is confirmed by Bulliet, who observes about a collection of conversion stories: "None give[s] any indication of a systematic conversion effort directed by the government or by any religious body. None refers to supernatural or spiritual experiences. None details any special charisma or spiritual gift possessed by the Muslims who called non-Muslims to Islam" (Bulliet, "Conversion Stories in Early Islam," 128).

49. This verse may technically refer to the *musta'min*, the unbelievers who were passing through Muslim territory under a temporary grant of safe-conduct (*aman*), merchants for instance. But it is analogous to the longer-term *dhimma* covenant for

People of the Book, which included an indefinite *aman* (Khadduri, *War and Peace in the Law of Islam*, 163-65, 177).

50. Bulliet, "Conversion Stories in Early Islam," 131. See also Dennett, *Conversion and the Poll Tax in Early Islam*.

51. The closest equivalent to missionaries might be the mystical Sufi orders. Sufism is believed to have been the principal agent in attracting non-Muslims to Islam after the tenth century (Levtzion, *Conversion to Islam*, 17).

52. Poston, *Islamic Da'wah in the West*, 16-17: "[I]n the case of the trader, his well-known and harmless avocation secures to him an immunity from any such feelings of suspicion [for professional missionaries], while his knowledge of men and manners, his commercial *savoir-faire*, gain for him a ready reception. . . . "

53. Bulliet, "Conversion Stories in Early Islam," 127-29.

54. Gibb, *Studies on the Civilization of Islam*, 5.

55. Bulliet, *Conversion to Islam in the Medieval Period*, 132.

56. Maan Z. Madina, "The Disruption and Decline of the Arab Empire," in *The Columbia History of the World*. ed. John A. Garraty and Peter Gay (New York, 1972), 271, 267-79; and Hourani, A *History of the Arab Peoples*, 30.

57. Conversely, for Muslims, submission to foreign domination is a religious crime; actual conversion to another religion was traditionally a capital offense (see Abdullahi A. An-Na'im, *Toward an Islamic Reformation: Civil Liberties, Human Rights and International Law* [Syracuse, N.Y., 1990], 88-91, 144-49; idem, "Civil Rights in the Islamic Constitutional Tradition: Shared Ideals and Divergent Regimes," *John Marshall Law Review* 25 [1992]: 289).

58. "Human Rights, Migration and Asylum," 5.

59. See Donna E. Arzt, "Heroes or Heretics: Religious Dissidents under Islamic Law," *Wisconsin International Law Journal* 14, no. 2 (1996): 349, 381-83; Bernard Lewis, *The Jews of Islam* (Princeton, N.J., 1984).

60. Weeramantry, *Islamic Jurisprudence*, 90-91; Raphael Patai, *The Seed of Abraham: Jews and Arabs in Contact and Conflict* (New York, 1986), 45-46; Bat Ye'or, *The Dhimmi: Jews and Christians under Islam* (London, 1985), 57-67. However, scholars disagree as to whether *dhimmis* were free to engage in practices that conflicted outright with Islam, such as the consumption, sale, and production of alcohol (see Arzt, "Heroes or Heretics," 382n).

61. Pickthall, Yusuf Ali, and Shakir all translate "God" in this verse as "Allah" (www.usc.edu/dept/MSA/quran). But the sense of the verse is that the People of the Book worship God, the same God as the Muslims, albeit of a different name (Pickthall, 103). The third *khalifah*, Umar, added the Zoroastrians of Persia to the People of the Book classification; Mandaeans and others were added later.

62. Weeramantry, *Islamic Jurisprudence*, 86. Another hadith reports that Mohammed lodged several members of the tribe of Thaqif, who were non-scriptural "unbelievers," in his own mosque (ibid.).

63. Ibid, 85-86, citing S. A. Ali, *The Spirit of Islam* (London, 1896).

64. Non-indigent, able-bodied *dhimmi* males paid the *jizya* poll tax in exchange for avoiding military conscription, in addition to property taxes (*kharaj*) (see *Law in the Middle East*, 363-64; Patai, *The Seed of Abraham*, 45-46; An-Na'im, *Toward an Islamic Reformation*, 88-91, 144-49). Hence, modern scholars such as An-Na'im consider the *dhimma* contract to constitute coerced submission rather than a charter of rights. *Dhimmis* were treated in a discriminatory manner, which sometimes rose to the level of outright persecution, such as when they were massacred or subjected to

forced conversions (see Ye'or, *The Dhimmi*, 60-61, citing examples in Armenia in 704-5 and 852-55 C.E., and numerous similar examples after the classical era).

65. Madina, "The Disruption and Decline of the Arab Empire," 271.

66. Amir Hasan Siddiqi, *Non-Muslims under Muslim Rule and Muslims under Non-Muslim Rule* (Karachi, 1969), 2. The author also notes that non-Muslims "got more than their due share in government service. In such lucrative occupations as banking, large commercial ventures, linen trade, land ownership, medical profession, etc., the Christians and Jews were well represented and firmly established" (ibid., 8-9).

67. Ye'or, *The Dhimmis*, 57-58.

68. Abdulaziz A. Sachedina, "Context for the Ayatollah's Decree: The Religious and Political in Islam," in *The Rushdie File*, ed. Lisa Appignanesi and Sara Maitland (Syracuse, N.Y., 1990), 223.

69. Abdullahi Ahmed An-Na'im, "The Islamic Law of Apostasy and Its Modern Applicability: A Case from the Sudan," *Religion* 16 (1986): 197, 213. Some scholars insisted that such rejection of *shari'a* must be based on the belief that non-Islamic rules are better and more just than Islamic rules (ibid.).

70. Kanan Makiya, *Cruelty and Silence: War, Tyranny, Uprising and the Arab World* (New York, 1993), 90.

71. Technically, Islam has no precise equivalent to the term *blasphemy*, which is derived from the Greek "to hurt" and "to speak" and used as the opposite of *euphemy*, the source of *euphemism* (see David Lawton, *Blasphemy* [London, 1993], 14; Arzt, "Heroes or Heretics," 374n).

72. See Aly Aly Mansour, "*Hudud* Crimes," in *The Islamic Criminal Justice System*, ed. M. Cherif Bassiouni (London, 1982), 195, 197; Taymour Kamel, "The Principle of Legality and Its Application in Islamic Criminal Justice," in ibid., 150, 163-66. Some jurists omit rebellion from the list of seven *hudud* offenses, while others also omit drinking wine and apostasy, as neither the Qur'an nor Sunna prescribed specific penalties for them (ibid., 227).

73. Majid Khadduri, *War and Peace in the Law of Islam*, 150. The Hanbali school put apostates to death immediately, while the other three Sunni schools of jurisprudence gave apostates three days to reconsider, after which, if they refused to retract their apostasy, they were executed. The Hanafis did not execute women apostates, presumably because women would not engage in war against Muslims (Mohammed Talbi, "Religious Liberty: A Muslim Perspective," in *Religious Liberty and Human Rights*, ed. Leonard Swidler [Philadelphia, 1986], 182-83).

74. See An-Na'im, "The Islamic Law of Apostasy," 211-12.

75. Some modern scholars, however, believe that Abu Bakr was committing a political act of counter-rebellion for which a *hudud* sanction was invoked collectively and which was not intended to be applied to "pure" cases of individual apostasy (Khadduri, *The Islamic Conception of Justice*, 238).

76. Talbi, "Religious Liberty: A Muslim Perspective," 183. Therefore, it should not even be cited as a case of apostasy, though it often is. Sachedina, "Freedom of Conscience and Religion in the Qur'an," 80-82; and Abdulaziz A. Sachedina, "Al-Bukhari's *Hadith* on Killing Those Who Refuse to Fulfill the Duties Enjoined by God and Considering Them Apostates," in Little et al. *Human Rights and the Conflict of Cultures*, 97.

77. Talbi, "Religious Liberty: A Muslim Perspective," 182.

78. An-Na'im, "The Islamic Law of Apostasy," 212. See also Ann Elizabeth Mayer, *Islam and Human Rights* (Boulder, 1991), 178, on the "civil death" of Bahá'ís in present-day Iran.

79. At least two Islam scholars, al-Tabari and al-Razi, concluded that non-coercion in the matter of religion was to be afforded only to the People of the Book—Jews, Christians, and Zoroastrians—implying that others could be coerced into converting to Islam. Others, such as al-Zamakhshari, believed that all human beings, not only the People of the Book, were entitled to exercise free volition regarding religion (see Sachedina, "Freedom of Conscience and Religion in the Qur'an," 67-68).

80. See Bulliet's linguistic commentary on the confusion between the meaning of *surrender* and *convert* (Bulliet, "Conversion Stories in Early Islam").

81. Ibid., 128.

82. Hourani, *A History of the Arab Peoples*, 23.

83. Of the Five Pillars of Islam, the latter four are behavioral, and even the first, the *shahada*, is a public recitation, though it was meant to be fully believed. (Fasting on Ramadan and the Hajj were added after the Qur'anic itemization.) Contrast the Judaic version of "Pillars," Maimonides' Thirteen Articles of Faith, each of which begins, "I believe with perfect faith" (Abraham Milgram, *Jewish Worship* [Philadelphia, 1971], 420-23).

5. CONVERSION TO ISLAM BY INVITATION

1. Toshihiko Izutsu, *God and Man in the Koran: Semantics of the Koranic Weltanschauung* (Tokyo, 1964), 147.

2. See Katherine P. Ewing, "The Dream of Spiritual Initiation and the Organization of Self-Representations among Pakistani Sufis," *American Ethnologist* 17, no. 1 (February 1990): 56-74.

3. See Richard J. McCarthy, *The Theology of al-Ash'ari* (Beirut, 1953), and the article on al-Ash'ari in the *Encyclopaedia of Islam* (second edition).

4. The connotation of the verb *aslama* ("he became Muslim") is "he converted to Islam." We shall discuss below the curious absence of a technical term for religious conversion in general.

5. For a nuanced discussion of the terms *Islamdom* and *Islamicate*, see Marshall G. S. Hodgson, *The Venture of Islam*, 3 vols. (Chicago, 1974), 1:57-60.

6. Michael Morony, in a point made at a faculty seminar on Islam and comparative studies in religion at Ohio State University, 1987.

7. Ibn Ishaq, *The Life of Mohammed: A Translation of Ibn Ishaq's Sirat Rasul Allah*, trans. and ed. Alfred Guillaume, repr. ed. (Oxford, 1980), 642-43 (Arabic text 4:435).

8. Ibn Ishaq, *Sirat Rasul Allah*, 645 (Arabic text 4:438).

9. Ibid. (Arabic text 4:438, lines 15, 20). Guillaume's English translation (645-46) renders this phrase the "institutions of Islam," in the sense, presumably, of John Calvin's *Institutes of the Christian Religion*.

10. Ibn Ishaq, 561-62 (Arabic, 4:324-25).

11. For this meaning of *saba'a*, see Lane, *An Arabic-English Lexicon*, 4:1640, entry for "saba'a'" (sad/ba'/hamza). See also M. Shaban, "Conversion to Early Islam," in *Conversion to Islam*, ed. Nehemia Levtzion (New York, 1979), 24ff.

12. Al-Tabari, *The History of al-Tabari,* trans. W. Montgomery Watt and M. V. McDonald (Albany, N.Y., 1987), 7:80.

13. On Christian proselytism among pagans in Iraq, see Michael G. Morony, *Iraq after the Muslim Conquest* (Princeton, 1984), 384-430, esp. 395.

14. Morony, *Iraq,* 394. The passage he refers to is translated in *The Life and Works of Jahiz: Translations of Selected Texts [by] Charles Pellat,* trans. D. M. Hawke (Berkeley and Los Angeles, 1969), 162-63.

15. The classic study of the political struggle between monotheism and paganism is Charles Norris Cochrane, *Christianity and Classical Culture: A Study of Thought and Actions from Augustus to Augustine* (London and New York, 1944). For a more recent study that includes Islam, see Garth Fowden, *Empire to Commonwealth: Consequences of Monotheism in Late Antiquity* (Princeton, 1993), esp. 158-65.

16. Marshall Hodgson has revised the earlier view of scholars that Islam was primarily a product of Arabian culture. His point is that the seventh-century *oikumene* from northeast Africa to the Steppes of Central Asia was the geographical and cultural context within which Islam became a world civilization. This he refers to as the "Nile to Oxus" region in comparative world history (see Hodgson, *The Venture of Islam,* 1:60-62).

17. T. W. Arnold, *The Preaching of Islam: A History of the Propagation of the Muslim Faith,* 2d ed. (Delhi, 1913 [1896]), 7.

18. Ibid., 46. In the second (1913) edition, Arnold took his data on the conquests and their interpretation from Leone Caetani, *Studi di Storia Orientale* (Rome, 1905), 1:365ff.

19. Arnold, *The Preaching of Islam,* 46.

20. See Fred McGraw Donner, *Early Muslim Conquests* (Princeton, 1981).

21. Horton summarizes his several writings about conversion in Robin Horton, *Patterns of Thought in Africa and the West: Essays on Magic, Religion, and Science* (Cambridge, 1993), 359-69, 374-75.

22. Horton, *Patterns of Thought,* 315, quoted by Richard M. Eaton, "Comparative History as World History: Religious Conversion in Modern India," *Journal of World History* 8, no. 2 (1997): 248.

23. For his more theoretical work on conversion to Islam, see Richard M. Eaton, *The Rise of Islam and the Bengal Frontier, 1204-1760* (Berkeley, 1993), chap. 5 ("Mass Conversion to Islam: Theories and Protagonists"). More recently he has tested Horton's theory on three communities in Nagaland that began converting from local traditional religions to Christianity in the late nineteenth century (in Richard M. Eaton, "Comparative History as World History," 243-71).

24. Richard W. Bulliet, *Conversion to Islam in the Medieval Period: An Essay in Quantitative History* (Cambridge, Mass., 1979). A shorter presentation of his methods and conclusions as they apply to Iran is presented in Richard W. Bulliet, "Conversion to Islam and the Emergence of a Muslim Society in Iran," in Levtzion, *Conversion to Islam,* 30-51.

25. Bulliet, *Conversion to Islam,* 10.

26. Bulliet, "Emergence of Muslim Society in Iran," 36.

27. Ibid., 37-41.

28. Ibid., 31.

29. While the great majority of the Shi'a, such as those living in Iran and Iraq, believe that eleven Imams descended from 'Ali, Mohammed's cousin and son-in-law, a dispute arose as to whether Isma'il or Musa al-Kazim was the true seventh Imam.

The Isma'ili broke away from the Ithna 'Ashari or Twelver Shi'a, becoming a minority within a minority, and soon produced a counter-da'wa aimed equally at other Shi'a and Abbasid civilizations as a whole. The most violent opposition came from the Isma'ilis at Alamut, known as the Assassins (Hashishiyun), for which see Bernard Lewis, *The Assassins: A Radical Sect in Islam* (London, 1967) and Marshall G. S. Hodgson, *The Order of the Assassins: the Struggle of the Early Nizari Isma'ilis against the Islamic World* (The Hague, 1955).

30. Hodgson, *The Order of Assassins*, 12.

31. Maya Shatzmiller, "Marriage, Family, and the Faith: Women's Conversion to Islam," *Journal of Family History* 21, no. 3 (1996): 236.

32. Ibid., 258.

33. The Mu'tazili theologian 'Abd al-Jabbar (d. 1024) gives the rationale for "Commanding the Good and Prohibiting Evil" in his theological compendium titled *Kitab al-usul al-khamsa* [*Book of the Five Fundamentals (of religion)*], which I have translated in Richard C. Martin and Mark R. Woodward, *Defenders of Reason in Islam: Mu'tazilism from Medieval School to Modern Symbol* (Oxford, 1997), 107-110; see also the commentary in ibid., 82-87.

34. Lane, *Arabic-English Lexicon*, 2:392, entry for root "j-d-l."

35. An excellent article on the cultural practices of *mujadala* in Islamicate culture is Josef van Ess, "Disputationspraxis in der islamischen Theologie: Eine vorläufige Skizze," *Revue des Études Islamiques* 44 (1976): 23-60. On the textual history of manuals written on the art of disputation, see Larry Benjamin Miller, "Islamic Disputation Theory: A Study of the Development of Dialectic in Islam from the Tenth through Fourteenth Centuries" (Ph.D. diss., Princeton University, 1984).

36. Cited in al-Humaydhi, *Kitab al-Jadhwa*, 101-2.

37. Michel Hayek, ed., *'Ammar al-Basri, Apologie et Controverses* (Beyrouth, 1977), 135-36, translated by Sidney H. Griffith, "Comparative Religion in the Apologetics of the First Christian Arab Theologians," *Proceedings of the Patristic, Medieval, and Renaissance Conference* (Villanova, 1979), 4:64.

38. For a discussion of Islamic modernism and its historical links with Mu'tazili theology, see Martin and Woodward, *Defenders of Reason in Islam*.

6. MUSLIMS ENGAGING THE OTHER AND THE *HUMANUM*

1. I tell this story in more detail in Farid Esack, *Qur'an, Liberation and Pluralism: An Islamic Perspective of Interreligious Solidarity against Oppression* (Oxford, 1997).

2. The Arabic phrase, meaning "rejection (of non-Muslim society) and withdrawal (from it)," has functioned as a label for Islamist groups that are pessimistic about the ability of the Islamic *da'wa* to reform and Islamize society—EDS.

3. The primary proponents of this view are Bruce Lawrence, *Defenders of God: The Fundamentalist Revolt against the Modern Age* (San Francisco, 1989), esp. 1-5; and Martin E. Marty and Scott Appleby, eds., *Fundamentalisms Observed* (Chicago and London, 1991), vii-xiii.

4. The phrase, as explained by Donna Arzt in her chapter herein, is an Islamic legal concept, which distinguishes land under Islamic rule from "the Abode of Conflict" (*dar al-harb*), or territory not under Islamic rule and hence theoretically subject to the Islamic *da'wa*—EDS.

5. Sa'ad Ghrab, "Islam and Christianity: From Opposition to Dialogue," *IslamoChristiana* 13 (1987): 107.

6. Mohammed Arkoun, "New Perspectives for a Jewish-Christian-Muslim Dialogue," in World Conference on Religion and Peace, *Weltkonferenz der Religionen für den Frieden, Rundbrief von W.C.R.P. Europa* 26 (June 1990): 20.

7. Leonard Binder, *Islamic Liberalism: A Critique of Development Ideologies* (Chicago, 1988), 5.

8. Juan Luis Segundo, *The Liberation of Theology* (Maryknoll, N.Y., 1976).

9. David Tracy, *Plurality and Ambiguity: Hermeneutics, Religion, Hope* (San Francisco, 1987), 90.

10. Martin Lings, *The Eleventh Hour* (Lahore, 1987), 34.

11. Ibid., 63-64.

12. Ibid.

13. H. A. R. Gibb and J. H. Kramers, eds., *Shorter Encyclopaedia of Islam* (Ithaca, N.Y., 1960), s.v. "shirk."

14. Fazlur Rahman, "Islam's Attitude toward Judaism," *Muslim World* 72, no. 1 (1982): 1.

15. Ibid.

16. Fakhr al-Din al-Razi, *Tafsir*, 32 vols. (Mecca, 1990), 3:112-13.

17. Abu Ja'far Mohammed b. Jarir al-Tabari, *Jami'al-bayan 'an ta'wil ay al-qur'an*, 30 vols., ed. M. M. Shakir (Cairo, 1954), 5:212-14.

18. Rahman, "Islam's Attitude toward Judaism," 5.

7. PROSELYTISM AND WITNESS IN EARLIEST CHRISTIANITY

1. See, e.g., LXX Ex 12:48; 20:10; 23:9; Lv 16:29; 17:3-15; 18:26; Nm 9:14; Dt 5:14; 24:14-21; Jos 9:1; 20:9.

2. The point is not infrequently made that Israel itself had also been a "sojourner" in Egypt before coming to its own land (see Ex. 22:21; 23:9; Lv 19:34; Dt 10:19).

3. For rabbinic traditions concerning Rahab as a proselyte and as a model of hospitality, see *b.Meg.* 14b-15a; *Mekilta* on Exod. par. Jith. Amal. 18:1; *Exodus Rabbah* 27:4; *Numbers Rabbah* 3:2; 8:9; *Deuteronomy Rabbah* 2:26-27; Josephus, *Antiquities of the Jews*, 5:5-30. For Ruth, see, e.g., *b.Shab.* 113b; *b.Yeb.* 47b; *b.San.* 39b; *b.BabKam.* 38a-b; *Ruth Rabbah* 2:22-23; 3:5.

4. The last option is unacceptable not only because of its motivation (religious or cultural hegemony) but also because of the means it employs; physical or psychological coercion is such a fundamental assault on the integrity of conscience that it must be regarded as morally wrong.

5. Augustine, *Letter* 185; for a review of the texts and a contextualization, see F. Van der Meer, *Augustine the Bishop* (London, 1961), 78-128.

6. See the literature cited in Luke Timothy Johnson, "Religious Rights and Christian Texts," in *Religious and Human Rights in Global Perspective: Religious Perspectives*, ed. John Witte Jr. and Johan D. van der Vyver (The Hague/Boston/London, 1996), 66-70.

7. For "symbolic world" as encompassing social structures and dynamics as well as the systems of language supporting such social arrangements, see Luke Timothy

Johnson, *The Writings of the New Testament: An Interpretation*, rev. ed. (Minneapolis, 1999), 1-19.

8. For two perspectives on the way in which moral discourse engages the texts of the New Testament, see R. B. Hays, *The Moral Vision of the New Testament* (San Francisco, 1996), and Luke Timothy Johnson, *Scripture and Discernment: Decision Making in the Church* (Nashville, Tenn., 1996).

9. For accessible sketches of Greek and Roman religious sensibilities, see M. P. Nilsson, *Greek Piety*, trans. H. J. Rose (New York, 1969); W. K. C. Guthrie, *The Greeks and Their Gods* (Boston, 1950), and R. M. Ogilvie, *The Romans and Their Gods in the Age of Augustus* (New York, 1969). Modern editions of the classic texts cited herein are available in the Loeb Classical Library.

10. Note the reaction of the Phrygians to Paul and Barnabas in Acts 14:1-18: from their display of divine *dynamis*, the townspeople infer the presence of Zeus and Hermes. The story echoes the account of Baucis and Philemon's encounter with Zeus and Hermes in Ovid's *Metamorphoses* 8:611-724.

11. For the complexity of the category "syncretism," see C. Colpe, "Syncretism," in *Encyclopedia of Religion*, ed. Mircea Eliade (New York, 1987), 14:218-27. The basic idea of syncretism is magnificently expressed by the self-identification of Isis in Apuleius's *Metamorphoses* 11:5. For an example of a pagan author equating the Jewish God with Dionysos, see Plutarch, *Table Talk* 4, 6, 2 (Mor. 671D-672C).

12. See Epictetus, *Encheiridion*, 53; *Discourses* II, 23, 42.

13. See the meditation on Zeus in Dio Chrysostom's "Olympic Discourse," *Oration* 12: 74-85.

14. See, e.g., Euripides' *Bacchae* for the cult of Dionyios, and the "Isis Aretalogy" from Cyme; the new cult established by Alexander of Abunoteichos was pilloried by Lucian in *Alexander the False Prophet*. See also D. Georgi, "Socioeconomic Reasons for the 'Divine Man' as a Propagandistic Pattern," in *Aspects of Religious Propaganda of Judaism in Early Christianity*, ed. Elisabeth Schüssler-Fiorenza (Notre Dame, Ind., 1976), 27-42.

15. The hero, Lucius, whose careless dabbling in magic has caused Fortune to change him into the form of an ass and to torture him with a series of escapades that lead him ever further into alienation, is finally granted salvation by the goddess Isis. Having been initiated into her cult, and then into that of her consort, Osiris, Lucius enjoys both the hope of immortality and worldly success (see *Metamorphoses*, 11).

16. The chronically ill (perhaps psychosomatically ill) rhetorician never wavered in his devotion to the god and endured many hardships of travel to spend time at the deity's shrine in Pergamum. Inscriptions from the fourth century B.C.E. testify to the cult of healing associated with Aesculapius at Epidaurus.

17. See M. Goodman, *Mission and Conversion: Proselytizing in the Religious History of the Roman Empire* (Oxford, 1994), 20-32.

18. Apuleius of Madura claims to have been multiply initiated into mysteries (much like his hero, Lucius), in *Apology*, 55. Libanius reports of Emperor Julian that he had engaged in countless rites (see A. D. Nock, *Conversion: The Old and New in Religion from Alexander the Great to Augustine of Hippo* [Oxford, 1933], 115).

19. In my view, Goodman, *Mission and Conversion*, 33-37, gives far too little attention to the extensive evidence on the phenomenon of philosophical proselytizing.

20. For a survey of the preoccupations of philosophy in this period, see A. J. Malherbe, "Hellenistic Moralists and the New Testament," in *Aufstieg und Niedergang*

der römischen Welt, ed. A. Haase and H. Temporini (New York, 1992), II, 26; 1:267-333; Martha Nussbaum, *The Therapy of Desire: Theory and Practice in Hellenistic Ethics* (Princeton, N.J., 1994).

21. The religious character of Hellenistic philosophy was recognized already by Samuel Dill, who speaks of "the philosophic theologian" in his classic, *Roman Society from Nero to Marcus Aurelius* (New York, 1956 [1904]), 384-440. For the organization of schools, see E. A. Judge, "The Early Christians as a Scholastic Community," *Journal of Religious History* 1 (1960): 4-15, 125-37; R. A. Culpepper, *The Johannine School: An Evaluation of the Johannine School Hypothesis Based on an Investigation of the Nature of Ancient Schools* (Missoula, Mont., 1975), 1-260.

22. A classic text is Epictetus, *Discourses* III, 23, 27-32; see also Nussbaum, *Therapy of Desire*, 13-47, and A. J. Malherbe, "Medical Imagery in the Pastorals," in *Texts and Testaments*, ed. W. E. March (San Antonio, Tex., 1980), 19-35.

23. See the discussion of philosophic conversion in Nock, *Conversion*, 156-86. The classic example is the account of conversion in Lucian of Samosata, *Nigrinus*.

24. See, e.g., Plutarch, *Progress in Virtue*, Mor. 75B-86A.

25. The rivalry between philosophical schools and the ways in which competition for recruits led to philosophers betraying their own ideals was a favorite target for Lucian (see, e.g., *Carousel, Icaromenippus, The Double Indictment, Philosophers for Sale,* and above all, *The Eunuch*).

26. For examples of such polemic, see R. J. Karris, "The Background and Significance of the Polemic of the Pastoral Epistles," *Journal of Biblical Literature* 92 (1973): 549-64, and Luke Timothy Johnson, "II Timothy and the Polemic against False Teachers—A Reexamination," *Journal of Religious Studies* 6/7 (1978-79): 1-26.

27. See S. G. Wilson, *Luke and the Law* (Cambridge, 1973).

28. See J. R. Rosenbloom, *Conversion to Judaism: From the Biblical Period to the Present* (Cincinnati, Ohio, 1978), 3-31; B. J. Bamberger, *Proselytism in the Talmudic Period* (New York, 1939), 13-16.

29. The LXX of Ps 95:5 translates the Hebrew "all the gods of the nations are idols" as "all the gods of the nations are demons (*daimonia*)"; for the pagan worship of demons, see also Dt 32:17; Bar 4:7, and Ps 105:37 (LXX).

30. Is 40:18-20; 41:7, 29; 44:9-20; Jer 10:1-16; Hos 4:11-19; 13:1-3; Mi 5:10-15; Hb 2:18-19.

31. Josephus, *Jewish War* II, 8, 2-14; *Antiquities* XVIII, 1, 4.

32. See Philo, *Life of Moses*; Josephus, *Against Apion* I, 165; II, 168; II, 281; *Letter of Aristeas* 187-293; Artapanus, *Fragment* 3.

33. For examples, see Luke Timothy Johnson, "The New Testament's Anti-Jewish Slander and the Conventions of Ancient Polemic," *Journal of Biblical Literature* 108 (1989): 419-41.

34. See, e.g., Philo, *The Contemplative Life* 1:8-9; *The Embassy to Gaius* 18:120; 19:131; 20:132; 25:162; *The Wisdom of Solomon* 13:1–14:28; *Sibylline Oracles* 3:545-49; 601-7. In *Mission and Conversion*, 55-59, Goodman again dramatically under-reports and under-reads the evidence.

35. See Philo, *Life of Moses* 2:36, and E. R. Goodenough, "Philo's Exposition of the Law and His *De Vita Mosis*," *Harvard Theological Review* 26 (1933): 109-24. See also, P. Borgen, "Aristobulus and Philo," in *Philo, John and Paul: New Perspectives on Judaism and Early Christianity* (Atlanta, 1987), 7-16.

36. Among the texts that must be taken into account for the period before 100 C.E., are *2 Baruch* 41:4; 42:5; *Sentences of Pseudo-Phocylides* 39; *Tobit* 1:8;

4QFlorilegium 1:4; *2 Maccabees* 9:17; Horace, *Satires* 1,4, 142-43; *Esther* 8:17; Epictetus, *Discourses* II, 9, 20; Josephus, *Jewish War* 2:559-61; 7:45; *Antiquities* 13:257-58; 13:319; 18:81-83; 20:17-96; 20:139; 20:145; *Against Apion* 2:123; 2:210; 2:261; 2:282.

37. The very existence, much less the technical nomenclature and relationship to proselytes of this group called "fearers of God," is much debated; important texts are Acts 10:2, 22, 35; 13:26, 43, 50; 16:14; 17:4, 17; 18:7; Josephus, *Antiquities* 14:116-117; *Against Apion* 2:39; 2:282-86; Juvenal, *Satires* 14:96-108. See M. Wilcox, "The 'God-Fearers' in Acts—A Reconsideration," *Journal for the Study of the New Testament* 13 (1981): 102-22; T. M. Finn, "The God-Fearers Reconsidered," *Catholic Biblical Quarterly* 47 (1985): 75-84.

38. Josephus, *Antiquities* 13:257-258; 319.

39. The standard position—that Judaism, especially in the diaspora, was actively proselytizing, is stated by J. R. Rosenbloom, *Conversion to Judaism*, 35-60, and Bamberger, *Proselytism in the Talmudic Period*, who states confidently, "during the period of the Second Temple, there was a vigorous missionary movement in Judaism, both in the Diaspora and in Palestine. Converts were eagerly sought, and they were obtained in large numbers" (ibid., 24). A revisionist reading is offered by Goodman, who reviews the evidence and concludes: "The missionary hero in search for converts to Judaism is a phenomenon first approved by Jews well after the start of the Christian mission, not before it. There is no good reason to suppose that any Jew would have seen value in seeking proselytes in the first century with an enthusiasm like that of the Christian apostles. The origins of the proselytizing impulse within the church should be sought elsewhere" (*Mission and Conversion*, 90). The tone of the last sentences suggests the reasons why Goodman, as I suggest above, under-reports and under-reads the evidence. If Bamberger overstates, then Goodman understates. The reality is probably somewhere in the middle.

40. See J. A. Overman, *Matthew's Gospel and Formative Judaism: The Social World of the Matthean Community* (Minneapolis, 1990), and A. J. Saldarini, "The Gospel of Matthew and Jewish-Christian Conflict," in D. Balch, *Social History of the Matthean Community: Cross-Disciplinary Approaches* (Minneapolis, 1991), 38-61.

41. Johnson, "The New Testament's Anti-Jewish Slander and the Conventions of Ancient Polemic," 433-34; see also S. Freyne, "Vilifying the Other and Defining the Self: Matthew's and John's Anti-Jewish Polemic in Focus," in *"To See Ourselves as Others See Us": Christians, Jews, "Others," in Late Antiquity*, ed. J. Neusner and E. S. Frerichs (Chico, Calif., 1985), 117-43.

42. D. E. Garland, *The Intention of Matthew 23* (Leiden, 1979). Once more, Goodman (*Mission and Conversion*, 69-72) takes a minimalist position, arguing—I think unconvincingly—that the passage envisages only a program by which Pharisees were recruiting other Pharisees.

43. The issue of Gentile Christians seeking circumcision under the influence of someone's persuasion occurs in Paul's letters to the Galatians, Colossians, and Titus. What is sometimes taken as a polemic against Judaizers in Philippians 3 is in reality a presentation of Paul as an example of one who has given up status in view of a better reality (see W. Kurz, "The Kenotic Imitation of Paul and Christ in Phil. 2 and 3," in *Discipleship in the New Testament*, ed. F. Segovia [Philadelphia, 1985], 103-26). For the identity of Paul's opponents in Galatia and Colossae, see R. Jewett, "The Agitators and the Galatian Community," *Novum Testamentum* 10 (1968): 241-54 and W. A. Meeks and F. O. Francis, *Conflict in Colossae*, rev. ed. (Missoula, Mont., 1975).

44. The fullest argument along these lines is made by D. Georgi, *The Opponents of Paul in 2 Corinthians: A Study of Religious Propaganda in Late Antiquity* (Philadelphia, 1985).

45. Although in need of revision on many points, these older studies remain valuable for their survey of the evidence: Adolf von Harnack, *Mission and Expansion of Christianity in the First Three Centuries*, 2 vols., trans. J. Moffatt (New York, 1908), and Kenneth S. Latourette, *A History of the Expansion of Christianity*, vol. 1, *The First Five Centuries* (Grand Rapids, Mich., 1937).

46. By "intentional community" I mean one that draws its adherents not through birth but through choice. Baptism as a ritual of initiation continues the principle of intentionality within Christianity, even though, after the first generation, it became, like Judaism, a tradition into which one could be born. For the intentional character of the earliest *ekklēsia*, see above all, W. A. Meeks, *The First Urban Christians: The Social World of the Apostle Paul* (New Haven, Conn., 1983), 74-110.

47. If we combine the (admittedly partial and biased) geographical framework provided by Luke's Acts of the Apostles with the evidence from first-generation epistolary literature (Paul, James, Peter, Hebrews), we can support both these assertions: (1) within twenty-five years there were Christian cells scattered in cities and towns through Palestine, Syria, Asia Minor, Macedonia, Achaia, Illyricum, and Italy, with possible foundations also in Cyprus and Crete; and (2) Gentiles began to join the community already in the 30s C.E. (see Acts 10–15) and probably before the year 70 C.E. occupied a majority position within the movement.

48. See Goodman, *Mission and Conversion*, 104-8.

49. The scene in the *Acts of Thomas* 1, which portrays all the apostles being sent to divers regions, is obviously idealized. In fact, the precise administrative role (if any) of "the Twelve," even within the Jerusalem church, is difficult to determine (see Acts 1:15-26). Three years after his call Paul traveled to Jerusalem to consult with Cephas (Peter) but declared he saw none of the other "apostles except James the brother of the Lord" (Gal 1:18-19); at a still later date the leadership of that church seems to consist in "three pillars," namely, Cephas, James, and John (Gal 2:9). In Acts 12:17 Peter is said to leave the Jerusalem church "for another place." He reappears as one of the discussants at the Jerusalem Council in 15:3-11 but is clearly subordinate to James, who speaks as leader of the community (Acts 15:13-21). James again appears at the head of a board of elders in the Jerusalem church at the time of Paul's final visit to the city (Acts 21:18).

50. In addition to the narrative account in Acts (8:1-3; 9:1, 23-25; 12:1-17; 14:5-6, 19-20; 16:19-24; 17:5-9, 13-14; 18:12; 19:8-10), there is the testimony of the earliest letters concerning harassment and persecution (1 Thes 1:6; 2:14-16; 2 Thes 1:5-12; 2 Cor 11:24-27; Heb 10:32-34; 1 Pt 1:6; 3:15; 4:12), and the fact that several of Paul's letters were written from captivity (Philemon, Philippians, Colossians, Ephesians, 2 Timothy).

51. See Rom 16:3-16; 1 Cor 3:5–4:6; 15:3-11; Gal 1:18; 2:9-10; Acts 15.

52. The Jerusalem church not only had what appears as an unstable leadership, but it was also impoverished, requiring gestures of support from other communities (see Acts 11:27-30; 12:25; Gal 2:10; 1 Cor 16:1-4; 2 Cor 8–9; Rom 15:25-32). Obviously, the mission lacked *textual* controls, since there was yet no "New Testament," and the use of Torah (in the form of scrolls) would have been difficult in some circumstances.

53. There was obviously a geographical transition as the movement spread beyond Palestine to the diaspora. There was also a sociological shift from the rural, itinerant ministry of Jesus to the urban churches we encounter in our earliest writings. Although Hellenism was well diffused in Palestine, the spread of the movement into the diaspora also implied a more profound cultural transition to a predominantly Greco-Roman world. A linguistic transition was required from the (presumably) Aramaic speech of Jesus to the Greek form in which his words appear in the Gospels. Finally, and most portentously, there was the demographical transition from a largely Jewish movement to an almost exclusively Gentile one.

54. This sense is given its most direct expression by Paul: "When he who had set me apart before I was born, and had called me through his grace, was pleased to reveal his son to me, in order that I might preach him among the Gentiles . . . " (Gal 1:15-16).

55. Although most scholars today think, on the basis of the best manuscript evidence, that Mark's gospel originally ended at 16:8, the so-called "longer ending" (16:9-20) was added very early and entered the main textual tradition. As such, it has been read as scripture down to the present day. As its popularity among Pentecostals and "snake-handling" Christians attests, its understanding of mission has had a not insignificant impact.

56. The passage is the subject of an enormous amount of literature. See, e.g., P. Perkins, "Christology and Mission: Matthew 28:16-20," *Listening* 24 (1989): 302-9; J. P. Meier, "Nations or Gentiles in Matthew 28:19?" *Catholic Biblical Quarterly* 39 (1977): 94-102; O. Michel, "The Conclusion of Matthew's Gospel: A Contribution to the History of the Easter Message," in *The Interpretation of Matthew*, ed. G. N. Stanton (Edinburgh, 1995), 30-41.

57. For Luke 24, see R. J. Dillon, *From Eye-Witnesses to Ministers of the Word: Tradition and Composition in Luke 24* (Rome, 1978), 157-225; for Acts 1:8, see Ph.-H. Menouds, "The Plan of the Acts of the Apostles," *Jesus Christ and the Faith*, trans. E. M. Paul (Pittsburgh, Penn., 1978), 121-32.

58. See R. E. Brown, *The Gospel according to John, XIII-XXI* (Garden City, N.Y., 1970), 1018-45.

59. See esp. J. Munck, *Paul and the Salvation of Mankind*, trans. F. Clarke (Richmond, Va., 1959), 36-68.

60. Note Paul's language about "Satan" (Rom 16:20; 1 Cor 5:5; 7:5; 2 Cor 2:11; 11:14; 12:7; 1 Thes 2:18; 2 Thes 2:9; 1 Tm 1:20; 5:15), about the "devil" (Eph 4:27; 6:11; 1 Tm 3:6-7; 2 Tm 2:16), about "demons" (1 Cor 10:20-21; 1 Tm 4:1), about "elements of the universe" (Gal 4:3, 9; Col 2:8, 20), and about "powers and principalities" (Rom 8:38; Eph 1:21; 3:10; 6:12; Col 1:16, 18; 2:10).

61. For the way in which this identification gets carried into the anti-Gentile polemics of patristic writers, see Johnson, "Religious Rights and Christian Texts," 79-80.

62. For the way in which this gets expressed narratively in Acts, see S. R. Garrett, *The Demise of the Devil: Magic and the Demonic in Luke's Writings* (Minneapolis, 1989), and Luke Timothy Johnson, *The Acts of the Apostles* (Collegeville, Minn., 1992).

63. The prophetic image of "God's wrath" (*orgē tou theou*) as the punishment of an unfaithful people in history (see LXX Is 5:25; 13:9; Jer 21:5; Ez 6:12; 21:31) gains an additional intensity in the New Testament writings (see Mt 3:7; Lk 3:7; 21:23;

Rom 1:18; 2:5; 9:22; 13:4-5; Eph 2:3; 5:6; Col 3:6; 1 Thes 2:16; 5:9; Rv 6:17; 11:18; 16:19; 19:15).

64. See also Paul's statements: "How you turned to God from idols, to serve a living and true God, and to wait for his son from heaven, whom he raised from the dead, Jesus, who delivers us from the wrath to come" (1 Thes 1:9-10); "Since, therefore, we are now justified by his blood, much more shall we be saved by him from the wrath of God" (Rom 5:9).

65. See, e.g., Mt 4:16-5:1; 11:1-30; 12:46; 13:1; Lk 5:1; 6:17-19; 8:1; 11:29; 12:54; 13:22; 20:9.

66. See Epictetus, *Discourses* III, 22, 26-49; Dio Chrysostom, *Oration* 13:9-23.

67. According to Acts 13:15, the first such occasion was by invitation of the rulers of the synagogue. Paul's proclamation of Jesus as Messiah after the reading of the Law and the Prophets at first met with some welcome (13:42) but then resistance (13:45). Given that the synagogue was also the *Beth ha Midrash*, where disputations over the meaning of Torah were a regular event, Paul's behavior might be regarded as provocative but not outside the protocols of that social setting. I do not think, therefore, that, even though ultimately disruptive, his preaching and disputation in the synagogue would be itself then considered as an inappropriate means of persuasion.

68. See Elisabeth Schüssler-Fiorenza, "Miracles, Mission, and Apologetics: An Introduction," in Schüssler-Fiorenza, *Aspects of Religious Propaganda*, 1-26.

69. Paul's letters provide no information concerning how he might have met such leading figures as Stephanus, Achaichus, Fortunatus and Erastus, in the Corinthian community (see 1 Cor 16:15-18; Rom 16:23). Was it through public proclamation, personal contacts, or even business dealings? For a fascinating glimpse at a more private part of Paul's teaching activity, see R. Hock, *The Social Context of Paul's Ministry: Tentmaking and Apostleship* (Philadelphia, 1980).

70. See also Mk 16:17; Heb 2:4, for the role of miracles in confirming the proclamation of the message.

71. See also 1 Pt 2:20-25; Heb 10:32-34.

72. For translations and introductions to the apocryphal acts, see E. Haennecke, *New Testament Apocrypha*, 2 vols., ed. W. Schneemelcher, trans. R. M. Wilson, (Philadelphia, 1964).

73. *Acts of Peter* 2, 7, 8, 20; *Acts of Paul* 3:4-6; *Acts of Thomas* 38, 37.

74. *Acts of Peter* 6, 19, 29; *Acts of Paul* 3:2, 7, 36.

75. *Acts of John* 19; *Acts of Peter* 3, 8, 28, 34; *Acts of Paul* 3:36; *Acts of Thomas* 4-8, 17, 62, 82.

76. *Acts of John* 23, 30-37, 47; *Acts of Peter* 9, 11, 12, 13, 25-27, 28-29; *Acts of Paul* 3:24; *Acts of Thomas* 33, 42-49, 52). See P. J. Achtemeier, "Jesus and the Disciples as Miracle Workers in the Apocryphal New Testament," in Schüssler-Fiorenza, *Aspects of Religious Propaganda*, 149-86.

77. *Acts of Peter* 36; *Acts of Paul* 3:17-18; 11:17; *Acts of Thomas* 105-7; 159-70.

78. See *Acts of Thomas* 15-16, 96-101; *Acts of Peter* 33-34; *Acts of Andrew* 4-13; *Acts of Paul* 3:7-13.

79. *Acts of Paul* 3:15.

80. For a discussion of these passages, see Luke Timothy Johnson, *Letters to Paul's Delegates: 1 Timothy, 2 Timothy, Titus* (Valley Forge, Penn., 1996).

81. For the view that the Pastoral Letters are written as a conservative response to a more radical, egalitarian mission being carried out in the name of Paul, see S. L. Davies, *The Revolt of the Widows: The Social World of the Apocryphal Acts*

(Carbondale, Ill., 1980); D. R. MacDonald, *The Legend and the Apostle: The Battle for Paul in Story and Legend* (Philadelphia, 1983); D. R. MacDonald, "Virgins, Widows, and Paul in Second Century Asia Minor," *1979 SBL Seminar Papers,* ed. P. J. Achtemeier (Missoula, Mont., 1979), 1:165-84; J. Bassler, "The Widow's Tale: A Fresh Look at 1 Tim. 5:3-16," *Journal of Biblical Literature* 103 (1982): 23-41.

82. See Johnson, *Scripture and Discernment.*

83. See the more extensive discussion of these points in Johnson, "Religious Rights and Christian Texts," 71-73, 80-88.

84. See Goodman, *Mission and Conversion,* 92-94.

85. The passage that at first seems most clearly to express an evangelistic intention, namely John 20:30-31, occurs in the gospel whose overall literary and thematic character argues most strongly for internal consumption (see W. A. Meeks, "The Man from Heaven in Johannine Sectarianism," *Journal of Biblical Literature* 91 [1972]: 44-72). For a discussion of the text that shows its inherent ambiguity, see Brown, *The Gospel according to John, XIII-XXI,*1055-61.

86. See W. A. Meeks, *The Origins of Christian Morality* (New Haven, Conn., 1993), esp. 150-73; and W. T. Wilson, *The Hope of Glory: Education and Exhortation in the Epistle to the Colossians* (Leiden, 1997).

87. This is what I take to be the distinctive outlook of 1 Peter among the canonical compositions. The contribution that 1 Peter might make to the topic of Christian witness has not yet adequately been exploited; for a sense of the composition's tone, see W. C. van Unnik, "The Teaching of Good Works in 1 Peter," *New Testament Studies* 1 (1954): 92-110; D. L. Balch, *Let Wives Be Submissive: The Domestic Code in 1 Peter* (Chico, Calif., 1981), and J. H. Elliott, "Backward and Forward in His Steps," in Segovia, *Discipleship in the New Testament,* 184-209.

88. The language of "witnessing" and being a "witness" does occur, especially in Acts, in connection with the proclamation of the message to others (for "witness," see Acts 1:8; 2:32; 3:15; 10:39; 13:31; 22:15; for "witnessing," see 13:22; 14:3; 23:11). But even in Acts, being a witness is more complex than simply "testifying" (see 1:22; 6:3; 15:8; 16:2; 22:20). For witnessing as involving more than verbal proclamation, see, e.g., Jn 2:25; 5:32-36; 8:18; 10:25; 18:37; Rom 10:2; 2 Cor 8:3; Gal 4:15; 1 Tm 6:13; Heb 10:15; 11:39; Rv 1:9; 19:10). Note also how, in 1 Corinthians 5:9-13, Paul rebukes the Corinthians for their preoccupation with judging those outside the community while refusing to tend to their own moral integrity.

89. This outcome is exemplified best by the book of Revelation, which understands the church to be a community of prophets, servants, and witnesses who carry on the witness of Jesus to the claims of God ("the spirit of prophecy is the witness of Jesus" [Rv 19:10]), and as a consequence experience persecution. See Elisabeth Schüssler-Fiorenza, *The Book of Revelation: Justice and Judgment* (Philadelphia, 1985); A. Yarbo Collins, "The Political Perspective of the Revelation to John," *Journal of Biblical Literature* 96 (1977): 241-56; A. Trites, "Martyrs and Martyrdom in the Apocalypse," *Novum Testamentum* 15 (1973): 72-80.

90. Elsewhere I put it this way: "Only if Christians and Christian communities illustrate lives transformed according to the pattern of faithful obedience and loving service found in Jesus does their claim to live by the Spirit of Jesus have any validity. The claims of the gospel cannot be demonstrated logically. They cannot be proved historically. They can be validated only existentially by the witness of authentic Christian discipleship" (Luke Timothy Johnson, *The Real Jesus: The Misguided Quest for*

the Historical Jesus and the Truth of the Traditional Gospels [San Francisco, 1996], 168).

91. See R. Schnackenburg, *The Church in the New Testament* (New York, 1965), 77-85; L. Cerfaux, "The Revelation of the Mystery of Christ," *Christ in the Theology of St. Paul* (New York, 1959), 402-38.

92. On this point, one should read R. B. Hays's chapter "Violence in Defense of Justice," in Hays, *The Moral Vision of the New Testament*, 317-46, for a moral roadmap.

93. For extensive reference to the practice of mutual correction in the Greco-Roman world, Judaism, and the New Testament, see Luke Timothy Johnson, *The Letter of James* (Garden City, N.Y., 1995), 27-79, esp. 337-46.

94. For the Cynic emphasis on severity in correction, see, e.g., Dio Chrysostom, *Oration* 32:11, 18; 77/78:37-45; Epictetus, *Discourses* III, 22, 26-30. For the abuses of such boldness in speech, see Julian, *Oration* 7:225; Epictetus, *Discourses* III, 22, 9; Lucian, *Timon* 7; *The Runaways* 13-16.

95. See A. J. Malherbe, "'Gentle as a Nurse': The Cynic Background to 1 Thessalonians 2," in *Paul and the Popular Philosophers* (Minneapolis, 1989), 35-48.

96. 2 Tm 2:20-3:9. For a discussion of this important passage in its cultural context, see Johnson, *Letters to Paul's Delegates*, 79-91.

97. Mt 7:1; Lk 6:37; Rom 14:3-22; Jas 4:11-12. For the moral logic of such hostile judging, see Johnson, *The Letter of James*, 291-309.

98. For the importance of Paul's argument in the development of Christian sensitivity to issues of religious pluralism, see Johnson, "Religious Rights and Christian Texts," 89-92.

99. Richard Hays has made a fundamental contribution to the understanding of the moral vision of the New Testament in his identification of the way in which the "story of Jesus"—understood as a character paradigm—undergirds Christian moral consciousness (see his *Moral Vision of the New Testament*, 27-32; see also Johnson, *The Real Jesus*, 141-66).

100. See Luke Timothy Johnson, "The Social Dimensions of *sōtēria* in Luke-Acts and Paul," in *1993 SBL Seminar Papers*, ed. E. H. Lovering Jr. (Atlanta, 1993), 520-36.

101. It is not necessary to belabor the point that precisely the refusal to renegotiate these premises is what most characterizes that segment of Christianity whose program of cultural and political hegemony in the name of salvation has been provided fresh fuel for frenzy by the approaching millennium.

8. THE GREAT COMMISSION AND THE CANON LAW

1. There is a convenient survey of medieval missionary efforts in Kenneth Scott Latourette, *A History of Christianity* (New York, 1953), 99-108, 342-52, 385-406. For a documentary survey of early Christian missionary efforts, see J. N. Hillgarth, ed., *Christianity and Paganism* (Philadelphia, 1986), 350-750; see also James Muldoon, ed., *Varieties of Religious Conversion in the Middle Ages* (Gainesville, Fla., 1997).

2. Recent scholarship has stressed that Pope Gregory I did have a policy of missionary work that did not depend on a personal experience. See R. A. Markus, "The Chronology of the Gregorian Mission to England: Bede's Narrative and Gregory's Correspondence," *Journal of Ecclesiastical History* 14 (1963): 16-30; idem, "Gregory

the Great and a Papal Missionary Strategy," in *Studies in Church History: The Mission of the Church and the Propagation of the Faith*, ed. G. J. Cuming (Cambridge, 1970), 6:29-38. Both of these articles are reprinted with their original pagination in R. A. Markus, *From Augustine to Gregory the Great* (London, 1983).

3. On the early development of the canon law, see James A. Brundage, *Medieval Canon Law* (London, 1995), 44-69.

4. It is somewhat curious that the status and responsibilities of missionaries were not the subject of a canonistic treatise, but, as James Brundage has pointed out, even the Crusades were not the subject of a treatise. Instead, the Crusades were seen as a particular form of pilgrimage (James A. Brundage, *Medieval Canon Law and the Crusader* [Madison, Wis., 1969], 189-90).

5. Benjamin Z. Kedar, *Crusade and Mission: European Approaches toward the Muslims* (Princeton, N.J., 1984), 99.

6. According to F. W. Maitland, Innocent IV was "the greatest lawyer that ever sat upon the chair of St. Peter." F. W. Maitland, "Moral Personality and Legal Personality," in *The Collected Papers of Frederic William Maitland*, 3 vols., ed. H. A. L. Fisher (Cambridge, 1911), 3:304-20 at 310.

7. E. Randolph Daniel, *The Franciscan Concept of Mission in the High Middle Ages* (Lexington, Ky., 1975), 76-98.

8. James Muldoon, *Popes, Lawyers, and Infidels: The Church and the Non-Christian World 1250-1550* (Philadelphia, 1979) 36-37.

9. Ibid., 37.

10. Ibid., 133.

11. "First Letter of Innocent IV to the Emperor of the Tartars," in Christopher Dawson, ed., *Mission to Asia*, repr. ed. [originally *The Mongol Mission*] (New York, 1966), 73-75, esp. 75. See also Muldoon, *Popes, Lawyers, and Infidels*, 42-43.

12. "Second Letter of Innocent IV," in Dawson, *Mission to Asia*, 75-76 at 75.

13. Christopher Dawson, *Christianity in East and West* (LaSalle, Ill., 1981), 99.

14. On the development of coronation ceremonies and their political implications, see Joseph Canning, *A History of Medieval Political Thought 300-1450* (London, 1996), 53-59.

15. A subsequent Franciscan missionary to the Mongols, William of Rubruck, who went to Mongolia in 1253, was asked to engage in a debate with Muslims and with representatives of another religion, perhaps Taoism (Dawson, *Mission to Asia*, 188-94).

16. There is no modern edition of his commentary. The edition used here is Innocent IV, *Commentaria doctissima in Quinque Libros Decretalium* (Turin, 1581).

17. Muldoon, *Popes, Lawyers, and Infidels*, 6.

18. The standard work on the theory of the just war is Frederick H. Russell, *The Just War in the Middle Ages* (Cambridge, 1975).

19. Muldoon, *Popes, Lawyers, and Infidels*, 15-16. There is a translation of part of this commentary in James Muldoon, *The Expansion of Europe: The First Phase* (Philadelphia, 1977), 191-92.

20. Muldoon, *Popes, Lawyers, and Infidels*, 89.

21. Ibid., 10.

22. Ibid., 11-12. This fear was justified in the late sixteenth century when, in Japan, Christian converts were among the leaders of a rebellion (see C. R. Boxer, *The Christian Century in Japan* [Berkeley, 1951]; Conrad Totman, *Early Modern Japan* [Berkeley, 1993], 46-47, 55-56).

23. Muldoon, *Popes, Lawyers, and Infidels*, 14.

24. Emil Friedberg, ed., *Corpus Iuris Canonici*, 2 vols., repr. ed. (Graz, 1959), vol. 1, *Decretum*; vol. 2, *Decretales*: see *Decretales*, C. 23, q. 7, cc. 1-4; C. 24, q. 1; *Decretales*, bk. 5, chs. 6-9.

25. Beginning in the thirteenth century, secular rulers enacted laws decreeing the death penalty for heretics. The first of these was a statute of Emperor Frederick II (1220-50) (see James M. Powell, ed., *The Liber Augustalis or Constitutions of Melfi* [Syracuse, 1971], 7-10; David Abulafia, *Frederick II: A Medieval Emperor* [London, 1988], 211-13). In England, Henry IV issued such a statute, "For the Burning of Heretics," in 1401 (see Carl Stephenson and F. G. Marcham, eds., *Sources of English Constitutional History* [New York, 1937], 274).

26. *Decretales*, bk. 5, ti. 6, ch. 9.

27. Ibid., bk. 5, ti. 6.

28. Edward Peters, "Jewish History and Gentile Memory: The Expulsion of 1492," *Jewish History* 9 (1995): 9-34 at 10.

29. Muldoon, *Popes, Lawyers, and Infidels*, 30-31.

30. Joannes Andreae, *In quinque decretalium libros novella commentaria* (Venice, 1581), repr. ed. (Turin, 1963).

31. Muldoon, *Popes, Lawyers, and Infidels*, 18.

32. The term *Latin Christian* is employed here because various Christian communities, such as the Nestorian, Jacobite, etc., did survive.

33. Before the collapse of the Mongol Mission, some of the missionaries were beginning to establish Christian communities that did not depend on the leadership of secular rulers but on the preaching of "personal salvation to the masses" (see James D. Ryan, "Conversion vs. Baptism? European Missionaries in Asia in the Thirteenth and Fourteenth Centuries," in Muldoon, *Varieties of Religious Conversion*, 146-67, esp. 147).

34. James Muldoon, "Papal Responsibility for the Infidel: Another Look at Alexander VI's *Inter Caetera*," *Catholic Historical Review* 64 (1978): 168-84, esp. 169, n.2.

35. Muldoon, *Popes, Lawyers, and Infidels*, 119ff.

36. Ibid., 128.

37. Ibid., 129.

38. The text of this bull, *Romanus Pontifex* (January 8, 1455) is in F. G. Davenport, ed., *European Treaties Bearing on the History of the United States and Its Dependencies to 1648* (Washington, D.C., 1917), repr. ed. (Gloucester, Mass., 1967), 13-26.

39. Ibid., 22.

40. Muldoon, *Popes, Lawyers, and Infidels*, 137-39.

41. Benjamin Z. Kedar's observation about the failure of missionaries to make any significant headway among Muslims applies to the situation in Asia: missionary "work among adherents of that self-confident high culture, Islam, was doomed to fail wherever the preaching was not backed by power" (*Crusade and Mission*, 202).

42. C. R. Boxer, *Four Centuries of Portuguese Expansion, 1415-1825: A Succinct Survey* (Johannesburg, 1961), repr. ed. (Berkeley, Calif., 1969), 64.

43. For an analysis of *Inter caetera*, see Muldoon, "Papal Responsibility for the Infidel," 168-84.

44. Francis I wanted to see "the clause in Adam's will which excluded me from my share when the world was being divided" (ibid.).

45. Hubert Jedin, *History of the Church*, trans. Gunther J. Holst, ed. Jay Dolan (New York, 1981), 6:232.

46. Other Jesuits developed a similar accommodation with Indian culture. They adopted the garb and caste status of the Brahmins and made other concessions to the local situation. Here again, Franciscans and Dominicans asserted that the Jesuits had compromised too much (see Latourette, *A History of Christianity*, vol. 3, *Three Centuries of Advance A.D. 1500-1800* [New York, 1939]).

47. George Minamiki, S.J., *The Chinese Rites Controversy from Its Beginning to Modern Times* (Chicago, 1985), 69-76.

48. Jedin, *History of the Church*, 6:232.

49. For a brief but very detailed survey of the missionary work during this period and the difficulties the missionaries faced in various parts of the world, see ibid., 6:232-325.

50. C. R. Boxer, *The Church Militant and Iberian Expansion 1440-1770* (Baltimore, 1978), 95.

51. John Leddy Phelan, *The Millennial Kingdom of the Franciscans in the New World*, 2d ed. (Berkeley, Calif., 1970), 23.

52. The most extensive selection of Vitoria's writings available in English is Francisco de Vitoria, *Political Writings*, ed. Anthony Pagden and Jeremy Lawrence (Cambridge, 1991). This edition contains not only the *De Indis* but several other texts as well.

53. Ibid., 276.

54. Ibid., 278. An earlier edition of the *De Indis* that contained both the Latin text and an English translation gave the Latin as "naturalis societatis et communicationis," and translated the phrase as "natural society and fellowship." This would seem to be a more felicitous way of expressing Vitoria's meaning (Francisco de Vitoria, *De Indis et de Iure Belli Relectiones*, ed. Ernest Nys, trans. John Pawley Bate [Washington, D.C., 1917], repr. ed. [New York, 1964], 151, 257).

55. Vitoria, *Political Writings*, 278.

56. Ibid., 279.

57. Ibid., 283.

58. Ibid., 284.

59. On Vitoria's importance, see Quentin Skinner, *The Foundations of Modern Political Thought*, 2 vols. (Cambridge, 1978), 2:135-38. In addition, Vitoria was an important figure in the formation of international law (see James Muldoon, "The Contribution of the Medieval Canon Lawyers to the Formation of International Law," *Traditio* 28 [1972]: 483-97).

60. Cary Nederman, "Tolerance and Community: A Medieval Communal Functionalist Argument for Religious Toleration," *The Journal of Politics* 56 (1994): 901-18.

61. Stephenson and Marcham, *Sources of English Constitutional History*, 325-27, 346-48.

62. "Second Charter of Virginia," in *Select Charters and Other Documents Illustrative of American History 1606-1775*, ed. William MacDonald (New York, 1899), 11-16, esp. 16. The charter also banned Catholic missionaries from Virginia.

63. James Muldoon, "Discovery, Grant, Charter, Conquest, or Purchase: John Adams on the Legal Basis for English Possession of North America" (forthcoming).

9. MISSIONARY CHALLENGES
TO THE THEOLOGY OF SALVATION

1. Paul Knitter, *No Other Name? A Critical Survey of Christian Attitudes toward World Religions* (Maryknoll, N.Y., 1985); idem, "La teologia cattolica delle religioni a un crocevia," *Concilium* 22, no. 1 (1986), 133-43. See also John Hick and Paul Knitter, *The Myth of Christian Uniqueness: Toward a Pluralistic Theology of Religions* (Maryknoll, N.Y., 1987).

2. See D. Colombo, "Missionari senza Cristo?" *Mondo e Missione* 10 (1988): 317.

3. Knitter, "La teologia cattolica," 135.

4. Karl Rahner, "Das Christentum und die nicht christlichen Religionen," in Karl Rahner, *Schriften zur Theologie* (Einsiedeln, 1962), vol. 5.

5. H. Robert Schlette, *Le religioni come tema della teologi* (Brescia, 1968; German ed. Freiburg, 1964); Anita Röper, *Die anonymen Christen* (Mainz, 1963).

6. Knitter, "La teologia cattolica," 136.

7. Hans Küng, *Cristianesimo e religioni universali* (Milan, 1986); Hans Küng, "Per una teologia ecumenica delle religioni," *Concilium*, 22 no. 1 (1986): 156-65.

8. Claude Geffré, "La Mission de l'Eglise a l'age de l'oecumenisme interreligieux," *Spiritus* (1987): 6.

9. Knitter, "La teologia cattolica," 139.

10. Raimundo Panikkar, *The Unknown Christ of Hinduism* (Maryknoll, N.Y., 1981).

11. Knitter, "La teologia cattolica," 141-42.

12. Knitter, *No Other Name*, 222.

13. See H. H. Rosin, *Missio Dei* (Leiden, 1972).

14. See, e.g., the work of A. Van Ruler and M.K. Miskotte.

15. Quoted by J. Lopez-Gay, "Missiologia contemporanea," in *Missiologia oggi* (Rome, 1985), 98.

16. J. C. Hoekendijk, *The Church Inside Out* (Philadelphia, 1964); Die Zukunft der Kirche und die Kirche der Zukunft (Stuttgart/Berlin, 1964).

17. L. Rutti, *Zur Theologie der Mission: Kritische Analysen und neue Orientierung* (Mainz/München, 1972).

18. Ibid., 345; see also Lopez-Gay, "Missiologia contemporanea," 105.

19. M. Amaladoss, S.J., "Faith Meets Faith," *Vidyajyoti* (1985): 109; M. Amaladoss, S.J., "Dialogue and Mission: Conflict or Convergence?" *Vidyajyoti* (1986): 63.

20. Amaladoss, "Dialogue and Mission," 65.

21. Ibid., 72.

22. Ibid., 78.

23. Ibid., 82.

24. M. Amaladoss, S.J., "Evangelization in Asia: A New Focus?" *Vidayajyoti* 51, no. 2 (1987): 7-28.

25. Amaladoss, "Faith Meets Faith," 110.

26. J. Kavunkal, "The 'Abba Experience' of Jesus: The Model and Motive for Mission Today," *FABC Papers* 43 (1986): 14; idem, *To Gather Them into One* (Nettetal, 1985).

27. "Maryknoll's Changing Concepts of Mission," *Tripod* (Spring 1988): 65.

28. G. Davies, *Dialogue with the World* (1968), chap. 4, quoted in Lopez-Gay, "Missiologia contemporanea," 114.

29. Gustavo Gutierrez, *Teologia della liberazione* (Brescia, 1972), 79, see also 94, 202, 272.

30. Hans Urs von Balthasar, *Das Christentum und die Weltreligionen* (1979), translated as *Il Cristianesimo e le religioni universali* (Piemme, 1987), 6.

31. See S. Maggiolini, "Le catholicisme et les religions non chretiennes," *Nouvelle Revue Theologique* 109 (1987): 509-20.

32. M. Amaladoss, S.J., "Reply to the Objections," *Vidyajyoti* 10 (1985): 478 (quoting *Evangelii nuntiandi*, no. 8).

33. Lesslie Newbigin, "Religious Pluralism and the Uniqueness of Jesus Christ," *International Bulletin of Missionary Research* 13 (1989): 54.

10. DECIDING FOR GOD

1. This is so because no one is born a Christian; no one is automatically a member. Baptism marks, in principle, a break between religious identity and community and the identity and community given by genetic or cultural roots. Further, baptism is open to all; this "initiation rite" is not defined by sex or caste, ethnicity or nation, status or citizenship to any. Among the world religions, Buddhism and Islam are closer to Christianity on this point than Judaism or Hinduism. Neither Buddhism nor Islam, however, generated enduring traditions of human rights regarding the universal right to convert, although they have advocated conversion in many contexts.

The debate on this matter is present also within Christianity. Recently the noted Roman Catholic scholar Bryan Hehir offered a definition of the social virtue of *solidarity*: "the conviction that we are born into a fabric of social relationships, that our humanity ties us to others, that the Gospel consecrates those ties, and that the prophets tell us that those ties are the test by which our very holiness will be judged" (see *Woodstock Report* #54 [June 1998], 1). In some understandings of this concept, the primary and natural matrix of social relationships into which one is born is seen to be of ultimate theological and moral significance. To break with it, to be converted from it to another set of relationships, would be wrong. But most Christians hold that while we are to respect the communities of origin that brought us into being ("Honor your father and your mother," etc.), solidarity implies a duty to protect the dignity and just claims of each person, including the right to leave a particular social matrix and join a new community on the basis of conversion (see The Ramsey Colloquium, "On Human Rights: The Universal Declaration of Human Rights Fifty Years Later," *First Things* 82 [April 1998]: 19).

2. The debates as to how much "free will" people exercise in the process of conversion, as compared to the predestined influence of God's grace, is one of the heatedly debated issues in theology that came to focus at the Synod of Dordt, as we will see. R. Seeborg traced much of this conflict in his *Dogmageschichte* (Erlangen, 1895). An artful contemporary sorting of the issues can be found in J. H. Whittaker, *Matters of Faith and Matters of Principle* (San Antonio, Tex., 1981), esp. chap. 3. He shows that, from the standpoint of human experience, a sense of freedom attends the decision, but that after the fact we become aware that we could not have made the choice on our own had it not been for a prior influence. In any case, the right to turn to God, or to be turned to God, is not something that can be controlled by any

earthly authority, and any authority that seeks to forbid it forfeits its legitimacy from the standpoint of every profound religion that understands conversion.

3. See Lewis R. Rambo, "Current Research on Religious Conversion," *Religious Studies Review* 8 (1982): 146-59; Max L. Stackhouse, "Missionary Activity," in *Encyclopedia of Religion*, ed. Mircea Eliade (New York, 1987), 9:563-570.

4. A typology of the various relationships between a theological-ethical view of transcendent reality and the social and cultural matrix of institutions in which people live is worked out for Christians in H. R. Niebuhr, *Christ and Culture* (New York, 1951).

5. That is the central conclusion of Max L. Stackhouse, *Creeds, Society and Human Rights* (Grand Rapids, Mich., 1984), repr. ed. (New York, 1994). It differs from the secularist views of Louis Henkin, who edited the volume in which K. J. Partsch pointed out convincingly that the right of religious freedom was the first and central right, established "long before the idea of systematic protections of civil and political rights was developed" (see Louis Henkin, ed., *The International Bill of Rights* [New York, 1981]). But, as Natan Lerner pointed out in "Religious Human Rights under the United Nations," in *Religious Human Rights in Global Perspective: Legal Perspectives*, ed. Johan D. van der Vyver and John Witte Jr. (The Hague/Boston/London, 1996), 81, Henkin fails to include a chapter on the issues in *Human Rights: An Agenda for the Next Century* (New York, 1994), co-edited with J. L. Hargrove, or to treat religion seriously as a source in other writings. Ironically, this view is paralleled in the widely read volume by Alasdair MacIntyre, *After Virtue* (Notre Dame, Ind., 1981), and even by Sumner Twiss and Bruce Grelle, who claim to initiate a new method for studying religious ethics by reducing all the main factors to cultural ones (see their "Human Rights and Comparative Religious Ethics," *The Annual of the American Society of Christian Ethics* [1995]: 21-48, esp. 23).

6. See John Courtney Murray, ed., *Religious Freedom* (New York, 1966); Walter J. Burghardt, *Religious Freedom* (New York, 1977); John T. Ford, *Religious Liberty* (Brescia, 1995).

7. The perils of denying human rights and religious freedom is clearly stated by the noted Roman Catholic writer George Weigel, "Religious Freedom: The First Human Right," *This World* (Spring 1988): 31-45.

8. See the classic study by J. N. Figgis, *Studies in Political Thought from Gerson to Grotius* (Cambridge, 1907). A contemporary view of the earlier period from a Roman Catholic scholar of considerable note on this issue is Brian Tierney, "Religious Rights: An Historical Perspective," in Witte and van der Vyver, *Religious Human Rights in Global Perspective*, 17-45, and further in Brian Tierney, *The Idea of Natural Rights: Studies on Natural Rights, Natural Law, and Church Law, 1150-1625* (Atlanta, 1997).

9. Randall C. Zachman, *The Assurance of Faith: Conscience in the Theology of Martin Luther and John Calvin* (Minneapolis, 1993), 39.

10. See Harold J. Berman, *Law and Revolution: The Formation of the Western Legal Tradition* (Cambridge, Mass., 1983), esp. 199-255.

11. Quoted in Zachman, *The Assurance of Faith*, 22.

12. Marilyn J. Harran, *Luther on Conversion* (Ithaca, N.Y., 1983), 56. Luther understood conversion in two ways, used interchangeably in his writings. First, conversion involved the initial movement from unbelief to faith—the beginning of the Christian life. Second, conversion could involve the repenting and returning of a Christian to God.

13. Ibid., 129.

14. F. Edward Cranz, *An Essay on the Development of Luther's Thought on Justice, Law and Society* (Cambridge, Mass., 1959), 162.

15. Martin Luther, "The Freedom of a Christian," in *Luther: Selected Political Writings*, ed. J. M. Porter (Philadelphia, 1974), 25.

16. Martin Luther, "Temporal Authority," in Porter, *Luther*, 56.

17. Ibid., 61.

18. Ibid., 63. See also William K. Anderson, "Luther and Calvin: A Contrast in Politics," *Religion in Life* 9, no. 2 (Spring 1940): 261.

19. Martin Luther, "Admonition to Peace, A Reply to the Twelve Articles of the Peasants in Swabia," in Porter, *Luther*, 80.

20. See Thomas Müntzer, "Sermon Before the Princes," in *Spiritual and Anabaptist Writers*, ed. George Huntston Williams (Philadelphia, 1957).

21. Martin Luther, "On War against the Turks," in Porter, *Luther*, 128. See also James Luther Adams, "No Authority But from God" (four documentary videotapes of the religious background of the rise of the Nazis in Germany) (James Luther Adams Foundation, Harvard Divinity School, 1936-38, edited with commentary, 1988-90).

22. Günther H. Haas, *The Concept of Equality in Calvin's Ethics* (Carlisle, 1995).

23. John Witte, Jr., "Moderate Religious Liberty in the Thought of John Calvin," in *Religious Liberty in Western Thought*, ed. Noel B. Reynolds and W. Cole Durham Jr. (Atlanta, 1996), 88.

24. A. V. Hiester, "Calvin and Civil Liberty," *Reformed Church Review* (1909): 133.

25. Sheldon Wolin, *Politics and Vision* (Boston, 1960).

26. Zachman, *Assurance of Faith*, 233.

27. Walter G. Hards, "A Critical Translation and Evaluation of the 1536 Edition of Calvin's *Institutes*" (Th.D. Diss., Princeton Theological Seminary, 1955), 198-200; see also Hiester, "Calvin and Civil Liberty," 140.

28. Witte, "Moderate Religious Liberty," 89.

29. Hans Höpfl, *The Christian Polity of John Calvin* (Cambridge, 1982), 189-90. See Calvin, "Draft Ecclesiastical Ordinances (1541), in John Dillenberger, ed., *John Calvin: Selections from His Writings* (Ann Arbor, Mich., 1975), 199-244.

30. Witte, "Moderate Religious Liberty," 106.

31. Roland H. Bainton, *The Travail of Religious Liberty* (Philadelphia, 1951), 108-9.

32. Ibid., 69.

33. Steven Ozment, "Martin Luther on Religious Liberty," in Reynolds and Durham, eds., *Religious Liberty in Western Thought*, 77.

34. Some of this dispute appears to rest on a logical error. If God is all-powerful, but then one attributes some power to humans, it seems to diminish God—if "all" is thought of as 100 percent; but if "all" is "infinite," then infinity minus some, or much, still equals infinity.

35. This point has often been made from a sociological point of view (see Max Weber's much-discussed *Protestant Ethic and the Spirit of Capitalism* [1904], trans. Talcott Parsons [New York, 1958] and Ernst Troeltsch, *The Social Teaching of the Christian Churches* [1911], trans. O. Wyon [New York, 1931]).

36. Stackhouse, *Creeds, Society, and Human Rights*, 55-60.

37. For documentary examples of this in the English context, see excerpts from Richard Mather, "An Apology for Church Covenant," and from "The Saints' Apology,"

in A. S. P. Woodhouse, *Puritanism and Liberty* (London, 1938), 299-300. For a current review of the significance of the concept of the covenant in civil society, see Max L. Stackhouse, *Covenant and Commitments* (Louisville, Ky., 1996).

38. See, e.g., Frederick S. Carney, "Associational Thought in Early Calvinism," in *Voluntary Associations: A Study of Groups in Free Societies*, ed. D. B. Robertson (Richmond, Va., 1966), 40-53.

39. The most exhaustive treatment of the cluster of movements here under discussion, with special attention to religious freedom, is George Huntston Williams, *The Radical Reformation*, 3d ed. (Philadelphia, 1992).

40. For a basic typology of the several forms of Anabaptist thought, see "Introduction," in Williams, *Spiritual and Anabaptist Writers*.

41. See Norman Cohn, *The Pursuit of the Millennium: Revolutionary Messianism in Medieval and Reformation Europe and Its Bearing on Modern Totalitarian Movements* (New York, 1961).

42. Johannes Althusius, *Politica Methodice Digesta* (Cambridge, Mass., 1932), with introduction by Carl J. Friedrich; Charles McCoy and J. W. Baker, *Fountainhead of Federalism: Heinrich Bullinger and the Covenantal Tradition* (Louisville, Ky., 1991). This tradition was to influence British and New England Puritans as well as the Scottish Enlightenment.

43. See Ivan Roots, ed., *Speeches of Oliver Cromwell* (London, 1989), 120-143.

44. See Woodhouse, *Puritanism and Liberty*, esp. primary sources at 179-302. See also Christopher Hill, *The Century of Revolution* (Edinburgh, 1961); Michael Walzer, *The Revolution of the Saints* (New York, 1968); David Little, *Religion, Law and Order* (New York, 1969).

45. Sydney E. Ahlstrom, *A Religious History of the American People* (New Haven, 1972), 136.

46. Williams's call for religious liberty and full separation from the Church of England inspired strong reactions. Nathaniel Ward of the Massachusetts Bay Colony replied that agitators for toleration such as Williams "shall have free liberty to keep away from us" (see Edwin S. Gaustad, *Liberty of Conscience: Roger Williams in America* [Grand Rapids, Mich., 1991], 43-44).

47. Bainton, *The Travail of Religious Liberty*, 67

48. Ibid.; Ahlstrom, *A Religious History of the American People*, 128.

49. See Charles Lloyd Cohen, *God's Caress: The Psychology of Puritan Religious Experience* (New York, 1986); Norman Pettit, *The Heart Prepared* (New Haven, Conn., 1966).

50. Bainton, *The Travail of Religious Liberty*, 21.

51. David Little, "Conscience, Theology and the First Amendment," *Soundings* 72 no. 2/3 (Summer/Fall 1988): 359-78.

52. Backus drew on the work of Roger Williams, disagreeing only with what he saw as a synthesis of natural and revealed religion in Williams's thought (see Stanley J. Grenz, "Isaac Backus and Religious Liberty," *Foundations* 22 [1979]: 352-60). Earlier Baptist arguments on religious liberty drew from the experiences of English Baptists to plead for toleration both on religious grounds (the relationship of conscience between God and humans should not be violated) and on social and political grounds (persecution slows immigration and only drives divisions underground) (see Barrie White, "Early Baptist Arguments for Religious Freedom: Their Overlooked Agenda," *Baptist History and Heritage* 24 [October 1989]: 3-10). For a general yet

thorough discussion of Baptists and religious liberty, see William G. McLoughlin, *Soul Liberty: The Baptists' Struggle in New England, 1630-1833* (Hanover, 1991).

53. Kenneth Lasson, "Free Exercise in the Free State: Maryland's Role in Religious Liberty and the First Amendment," *Journal of Church and State* 31 (1989): 419-49.

54. J. William Frost, *A Perfect Freedom: Religious Liberty in Pennsylvania* (Cambridge, 1990). A sociohistorical study that inquires as to the capability of Quaker theology to sustain a viable civil society, however, can be found in E. Digby Batzell, *Puritan Boston and Quaker Philadelphia* (New York, 1979).

55. For a summary of Edwards's theological and political views see Gerald R. McDermott, *One Holy and Happy Society: The Public Theology of Jonathan Edwards* (University Park, Penn., 1992), chaps. 3-5.

56. David Laurence, "Jonathan Edwards, Solomon Stoddard, and the Preparationist Model of Conversion," *Harvard Theological Review* 72 (1979): 267-83.

57. Ahlstrom, *A Religious History of the American People*, 156-57.

58. In the North American experience the early Wesleyans on the local level understood themselves to be "mission societies." That was their rationale for existence; the church was derived from mission (James C. Logan, "The Evangelical Imperative: A Wesleyan Perspective," in *Theology and Evangelism in the Wesleyan Heritage*, ed. James C. Logan [Nashville, Tenn., 1994], 16).

59. Leon O. Hynson, "John Wesley's Concept of Liberty of Conscience," *Wesleyan Theological Journal* 7 (1972): 36-46; John C. English, "John Wesley and the Rights of Conscience," *Journal of Church and State* 37 (1995): 349-63. For a discussion of similarities between Wesley's understanding of the role of religious experience and that of Jonathan Edwards, see Robert Doyle Smith, "John Wesley and Jonathan Edwards on Religious Experience: A Comparative Analysis," *Wesleyan Theological Journal* 25 (1990): 130-46.

60. For Locke, the ability of humans to use reason to see religious truth only came with Christ; before Christ, power was an appropriate tool for religious ends. Since Christ has opened the authority of reason to see Christ's light, humans may not block the use of reason in others (see Joshua Mitchell, "John Locke: A Theology of Religious Liberty," in Reynolds and Durham, *Religious Liberty in Western Thought*, 143-60).

61. The connection between Williams and Locke cannot be made with great accuracy (Gaustad, *Liberty of Conscience*, 196-99).

62. This shaped his proposed understanding of an "evangelical" toleration for Jews, rooted in his understanding of the difference Christ made to the use of reason (Nabil I. Matar, "John Locke and the Jews," *Journal of Ecclesiastical History* 44, no. 1 [1993]: 45-62).

63. Wioleta D. Polinska, "Faith and Reason in John Locke" (Ph.D. diss., Princeton Theological Seminary, 1996).

64. See Georg Jellinek, *The Declaration of the Rights of Man and of Citizens*, trans. Max Farrand (New York, 1901). It remains the classic study of this issue.

65. John Witte Jr., "'A Most Mild and Equitable Establishment of Religion': John Adams and the Massachusetts Experiment," *Journal of Church and State* 41 (1999): 213.

66. It is not possible to pause here to consider the rich and largely compelling hypothesis of Arendt van der Leeuwen, *Christianity in World History* (New York,

1962) that democracy and technology are among the worldly implications of Christianity, especially Protestantism, and that where they are accepted the deep presuppositions of Christianity are also de facto approved—with unintended implications for receiving cultures.

67. William R. Hutchison, *Errand to the World* (Chicago, 1987), 27.

68. Henry W. Bowden and James P. Ronda, eds., "Introduction," *John Eliot's Indian Dialogues* (Westport, Conn., 1980), 34-40.

69. Jonathan Edwards, *Thoughts on the Revival of Religion* (1740), in Carl J. C. Wolf, ed., *Jonathan Edwards on Evangelism* (Grand Rapids, Mich., 1958), 46.

70. William Carey, *An Enquiry into the Obligations of Christians to Use Means for the Conversion of the Heathens* (1792), repr. ed. (London, 1934), 13.

71. Andrew S. Burgess, *Lutheran Churches in the Third World* (Minneapolis, 1970), 10-12.

72. Andrew Walls argues that the organizations allowed greater lay participation and power in religious activity (see Andrew Walls, "Missionary Societies and the Fortunate Subversion of the Church," in *The Missionary Movement in Christian History: Studies in the Transmission of Faith* [Maryknoll, N.Y., 1996], 241-54). The importance of the role of these associations in the formation of women's organizations ought not be overlooked and is well documented.

73. William R. Estep, *Whole Gospel, Whole World: The Foreign Mission Board of the Southern Baptists Convention 1845-1995* (Nashville, Tenn., 1994), 34-37.

74. Clifford Merrill Drury, *Presbyterian Panorama: One Hundred and Fifty Years of National Missions History* (Philadelphia, 1952), 85-89.

75. Lamin Sanneh, *Translating the Message* (Maryknoll, N.Y., 1989).

76. See M. Searle Banks, "The Theology of American Missionaries in China, 1900-1950," in *The Missionary Enterprise in China and America*, ed. John King Fairbanks (Cambridge, 1974), 139-43; Kenneth Scott Latourette, *A History of the Expansion of Christianity*, Vol. 6: *The Great Century in Northern Africa and Asia, 1800-1914* (New York, 1944).

77. John A. Andrew, III, *Rebuilding the Christian Commonwealth: New England Congregationalists and Foreign Missions 1800-1830* (Lexington, Mass., 1976), 87.

78. Rufus Anderson, *The Theory of Missions to the Heathen: A Sermon at the Ordination of Mr. Edward Webb, as a Missionary to the Heathen* (Boston, 1845), 12-13. This idea of Anderson's is the ideological source of the Three-Self Church in the Republic of China.

79. Hutchison, *Errand to the World*, 98.

80. ABCFM, *Memorial Volume*, 296-97.

81. Kenneth Scott Latourette, *A History of the Expansion of Christianity*, Vol. 5: *The Great Century in the Americas, Australia, and Africa* (New York, 1943), 249-50.

82. For accounts of African-American churches and nineteenth-century missions, see Sandy D. Martin, *Black Baptists and African Missions* (Macon, Ga., 1989); Walter L. Williams, *Black Americans and the Evangelization of Africa 1877-1900* (Madison, Wis., 1982).

83. In an analysis of missions to Turkey and China, James Field writes that American missionaries' teachings "upheld the integrity of the empires against external pressures while undermining it by support of religious, linguistic or ethnic minorities" (James A. Field Jr., "Near East Notes and Far East Queries," in Fairbank, *The Missionary Enterprise in China and America*; see also Latourette, *A History of the Expansion of Christianity*, 6:51.

84. Torben Christensen, "Danish Missions in India," in Torben Christensen and William Hutchison, *Missionary Ideologies in the Imperialist Era, 1880-1920*, 2d ed. (Arhus, 1982), 122-25.

85. See the essays in Christensen and Hutchison, *Missionary Ideologies in the Imperialist Era, 1880-1920*, for the ways in which a variety of missions navigated between their home traditions and the missions context. Many of the missteps in communication seem to have been clumsiness rather than wholesale rejection of the native context.

86. Clara Merritt DeBoer, *His Truth Is Marching On* (New York, 1995).

87. See Dana L. Robert, *American Women in Mission: A Social History of Their Thought and Practice* (Macon, Ga., 1996).

88. Aaron Ignatius Abell, *The Urban Impact on American Protestantism, 1865-1900* (Cambridge, Mass., 1943), 37-46.

89. Shailer Mathews, *New Faith for Old* (New York, 1936), 126.

90. Abell, *The Urban Impact on American Protestantism, 1865-1900*, 85-86.

91. See A. J. Vidich and S. M. Lyman, *American Sociology* (New Haven, Conn., 1985).

92. Josiah Strong, *Our Country* (1883), Jürgen Herbst, ed. (Cambridge, Mass., 1963), 202.

93. John R. Mott, *The Evangelization of the World in This Generation* (New York, 1900), 9-14.

94. John R. Mott, *The Present World Situation* (New York, 1915), 97-127.

95. Hutchison, *Errand to the World*, 102-11.

96. At the Edinburgh Conference these viewpoints were each represented in a series of speeches entitled "The Problem of Cooperation between Foreign and Native Workers." Speaking on June 20, 1910, The Right Reverend Bishop Roots, a missions leader in China, advocated a paternalistic attitude, and The Reverend V. S. Azariah, who would become the first native Indian Anglican bishop in India, rejected the "master-servant" relationship he saw between some missionaries and native leaders in India (see World Missionary Conference, *The History and Records of the Conference, Together with Addresses Delivered at the Evening Meetings* [Edinburgh, 1910], 289-93, 306-14). On the issue of self-governance, see also Richard L. Deats, *Nationalism and Christianity in the Philippines* (Dallas, Tex., 1967).

97. Laymen's Foreign Missions Inquiry: Commission of Appraisal, *Re-Thinking Missions* (New York, 1932), 40.

98. Ibid., 45-47, 56.

99. Ibid., 68-70.

100. Robert E. Speer, *"Re-Thinking Missions" Examined* (New York, 1933). Speer asserted, "For us, Christ is still the Way, not a Way" (ibid., 31).

101. The Interdenominational Foreign Missions Association began in 1917 for missions agreeing to adhere to "the fundamental doctrines of the historic Christian church." During the 1920s, conservative, nondenominational "faith" missions, which had their initial success in the China Inland Mission, spread to Latin America, the West Indies, and India. These missions stressed evangelism through preaching, leaving broader institutional concerns to other missions groups.

102. "The Church's Distinctive Program," in Commission on the Church and Social Service, Federal Council of the Churches of Christ in America, *The Church and Social Reconstruction* (New York, 1919), 17.

103. See Methodist Episcopal Church, "Social Creed of the Churches," in *Doctrines and Discipline of the Methodist Episcopal Church* (New York, 1920-38), revised annually.

104. The International Missionary Council's 1928 Conference in Jerusalem, for example, established a "Department for Social and Economic Research and Counsel."

105. The famous speech in defense of the "Four Freedoms"—freedom of speech, freedom of religion, freedom from want, and freedom from fear—was not delivered until January 6, 1941, but the formation of the alliance that led to the Atlantic Charter, which officially included the first two of these, was underway.

106. See Max L. Stackhouse, *Apologia: Contextualization, Globalization and Mission in Theological Education* (Grand Rapids, Mich., 1988).

107. Non-Christian scholars of human rights have credited the ecumenical Protestant churches, especially, with having a major impact on the development of human rights theory before the formation of the United Nations (see, e.g., Natan Lerner, "Proselytism, Change of Religion, and International Human Rights," *Emory International Law Review* 12 [1998]: 477-562).

108. O. F. Nolde, "Ecumenical Action and International Affairs," in *The Ecumenical Advance*, ed. H. E. Fey (London, 1970), 2:262-64.

109. C. H. Malik, "On The Universal Declaration of Human Rights," in *Free and Equal*, ed. O. F. Nolde (Geneva, 1968), 7-13.

110. Ibid., 27-28.

111. Ibid., 39-40. See Malik, "On The Universal Declaration of Human Rights," 11: "The very essence of freedom is the right to become, not the right to be." For the debates over the inclusion of the right to change one's belief in the 1966 Covenant on Civil and Political Rights, see also Marc J. Bossuyt, *Guide to the "Travaux Preparatoires" of the International Covenant on Civil and Political Rights* (Dordrecht, 1987), 351-71; K. J. Partsch, in Henkin, *The International Bill of Rights*, 209-45.

112. For the debates over state interests in the control of religion in the drafting of Article 18, see Martin Scheinin, "Article 18," in Asbjorn Eide, *The Universal Declaration of Human Rights: A Commentary* (New York, 1992), 263-74. O. Frederick Nolde points out that even the comprehensive nature of Article 18 has not resolved all questions of the scope of religious expression, particularly in regard to conscientious objection in times of war.

113. See Nolde, *Free and Equal*, 49-50.

114. Ibid., 35-36. See also Lowell Livesey, "US Religious Organizations and the International Human Rights Movement," *Human Rights Quarterly*, 11, no. 1 (February 1989): 14-81. Livesey documents the ways in which the churches became advocates for the Universal Declaration and its provisions around the world after it was passed.

115. Presbyterian Church in the USA, *Minutes of the 161st General Assembly* (1949), 250.

116. Evangelical and Reformed Church, *Minutes of the Ninth General Synod of the Evangelical and Reformed Church* (1953), 277, 274.

117. Protestant Episcopal Church in the USA, *Journal of the General Convention of the Protestant Episcopal Church in the USA* (1949), 352-53. A 1964 Episcopal resolution urging the U.S. ratification of U.N. human rights covenants passed, while an expanded resolution on such ratification failed three years later (see Protestant

Episcopal Church in the USA, *Journal of the General Convention of the Protestant Episcopal Church in the USA* [1964], 307-8; [1967], 448-49).

118. Disciples of Christ, *Yearbook and Directory of the Disciples of Christ* (1950), 31-32; (1953), 82; (1974), 168-69; (1978), 213-14.

119. Congregational and Christian Churches, *Minutes of the 1950 General Council of the Congregational and Christian Churches of the United States* (New York, 1950), 43. In a separate statement on Protestant-Catholic relations the denomination urged the clarification of the American Protestant position on religious liberty and church and state: "We cannot compromise on essential principles, but we must know what these principles are" (ibid., 48).

120. Southern Baptists generally supported the United Nations and its efforts to promote religious liberty, but the denomination's mistrust of the ecumenical movement, particularly the Councils of Churches on the national and world level, kept them apart from the CCIA efforts on the UN Declaration (see George D. Kelsey, *Social Ethics among Southern Baptists 1917-1969* [Metuchen, N.J., 1972], 23-28, 123). *The Southern Baptist Handbook, 1949* (Nashville, Tenn., 1949), 35, mentioned the Universal Declaration insofar as it failed to mention God. The National Association of Evangelicals urged revision of the Universal Declaration on similar grounds, "not because we do not favor basic freedoms for all mankind," but because in its estimation, the Declaration presented such rights as "man's due reward for his goodness" rather than as gifts from God (see *Evangelicals Move Forward for Christ: A Report of the Eighth Annual Convention of the National Association of Evangelicals* [1950], 14-15). The group also rejected the Universal Declaration's inclusion of economic and social rights as a form of socialism (ibid., 23).

121. See National Baptist Convention, *Minutes of the General Assembly of the National Baptist Convention, 1949*, 146-47; idem, *Minutes of the General Assembly of the National Baptist Convention, 1950*, 193. For international Baptist statements regarding religious liberty, see "Mid-Century Call to Religious Freedom," *Minutes of the Eighth Baptist World Conference, 1950* (Philadelphia, 1950), 336-38; "Golden Jubilee Declaration on Religious Liberty," *Minutes of the Ninth Baptist World Conference, 1955* (London, 1955), 369-70; see also statements on religious liberty in *Official Report of the Tenth Baptist World Conference* (Nashville, Tenn., 1961), 297-300, and *Official Report of the Thirteenth Baptist World Conference* (Nashville, Tenn., 1976), 255-58.

122. National Council of Churches, "A Letter to the Christian People of America," *Minutes of the 1952 Biennial General Assembly of the National Councils of the Churches of Christ in the USA*, 187-91.

123. "Pronouncement on Human Rights," in National Council of Churches, "A Letter to the Christian People of America," 3. In the Methodist Social Creed, by World War II, the explicit commitment to "equal rights and complete justice" for all persons was included as well, although the scope of such rights was not fully enumerated, and the U.N. not specifically mentioned (see Methodist Church, *Doctrines and Discipline of the Methodist Church* [Nashville, Tenn., annual revisions]).

124. See Allen O. Miller, ed., *A Christian Declaration on Human Rights* (Grand Rapids, Mich., 1977), adopted by the World Alliance of Reformed Churches, with commentary by Jürgen Moltmann, et al., "Human Rights: Doing Justice in God's World"; adopted by the Ninth Biennial Convention, Lutheran Church in America, 1978, in Christa R. Klein and Christian D. Von Dehsen, *Politics and Policy*

(Minneapolis, 1989), 227-34; adopted by the United Church of Christ, "Pronouncement on Human Rights," Twelfth General Synod of the United Church of Christ, reprinted in Stackhouse, *Creeds, Society and Human Rights*; adopted by the United Methodist Church, "Human Rights" (1980) and "New Issues in Human Rights" (1988), in *Book of Resolutions, United Methodist Church, 1988* (Nashville, Tenn., 1988), 444-58.

125. See, e.g., Jean Stromberg, *Mission and Evangelism: An Ecumenical Affirmation* (Geneva, 1983).

126. See John Witte Jr., "Law, Religion, and Human Rights," *Columbia Human Rights Law Review* 28 (1996): 1.

127. The mainline churches have been relatively silent on the issue of persecutions of Christians, with most public advocacy being conducted by conservative and evangelical groups. However, recent detailed documentation of such persecution by Paul Marshall, Nina Shea, the human rights group Freedom House, and the U.S. State Department has brought the matter to a new level of public and church awareness (see Paul Marshall, *Their Blood Cries Out* [Dallas, Tex., 1997], as well as the July 22, 1997, report by the Bureau of Democracy, Human Rights and Labor Affairs, U.S. State Department, "United States Policies in Support of Religious Freedom: Focus on Christians").

128. Max L. Stackhouse has worked with a number of colleagues to identify and evaluate the presuppositions and implications of these developments and to suggest why they are problematic with regard to the issues of human rights (see, e.g., *Christian Social Ethics in a Global Era,* with Peter Berger, Dennis McCann, and Douglas Meeks [Nashville, Tenn., 1996]; "Religion and Human Rights: A Theological Apologetic," with Stephen Healey, in Witte and van der Vyver, *Religious Human Rights in Global Perspective*, 485-516; "Public Theology and Ethical Judgment," *Theology Today* 54, no. 2 [July 1997]: 165-79; "Human Rights and Public Theology," Columbia University Seminar on Religion and Human Rights [forthcoming from M. E. Sharpe]; "A Symposium on Human Rights," *Journal of Religious Ethics* 26, no. 2 [1988]: 225-330).

11. EVANGELISM AND MISSION
IN THE ORTHODOX TRADITION

1. "Fatherly Advice: Joint Statement of Catholicoi Regarding Religion in Armenia," *Window: View on the Armenian Church* 3, no. 1 (1992): 33. This encyclical has been translated subsequently as "A Fatherly Word."

2. Ibid., 3.

3. For other Orthodox statements that make similar distinctions between proselytism and evangelization, see Ion Bria, ed., *Go Forth in Peace: Orthodox Perspectives on Mission* (Geneva, 1986) and "Message of the Primates of the Most Holy Orthodox Churches," *Ecumenical Trends* 21 (April 1992): 57.

4. "Fatherly Advice," 3-4.

5. The Armenian Apostolic Orthodox Church is separated from the Byzantine family of Orthodox churches (Greek, Russian, Finnish, Rumanian, and others) and is in strict communion with other so-called Oriental Orthodox churches (Coptic, Ethiopian, Syrian, and others). This "Oriental" family of churches has dissented from the christological teaching of the Great Ecumenical Council of Chalcedon (451 c.e.). At

issue in particular has been the Council of Chalcedon's employment of the phrase "two natures" to describe Christ as fully human and fully divine. See further, note 13 below.

6. "Speech of His Holiness Karekin I Catholicos of All Armenian on the Occasion of the 150th Anniversary of the Armenian Evangelical Church," delivered on July 7, 1996, in Yerevan, Armenia. An unpublished transcript in English translation was provided to the author by the Armenian Missionary Association of America, Paramus, New Jersey.

7. Ibid.

8. Ernst Benz, *The Eastern Orthodox Church: Its Thought and Life* (Garden City, N.Y., 1963), 103.

9. See James J. Stamoolis, *Eastern Orthodox Mission Theology Today* (Maryknoll, N.Y., 1986), chap. 3.

10. Ibid., 22.

11. Alexander Schmemann, *Church, World, Mission* (Crestwood, N.Y., 1977), 8.

12. John Meyendorff, *Living Tradition* (Crestwood, N.Y., 1978), 92.

13. It is my persuasion that a strongly *dyophysitic* accent in mainstream Protestant and Roman Catholic Christology has contributed to what are now deeply embedded notions of human autonomy and rights in Western thought. These notions contradict Orthodox Christianity's insistence upon the theonomous nature of humanity revealed by the divine Word's incarnate existence. I do not discount that the deepest inspiration of the doctrine of human rights has roots in Christian convictions. God is person and so are human beings that are created in God's image and likeness. Every human hypostasis has needs and makes claim to certain advantages that assist it in flourishing.

Hypostasis is the Greek word that was adopted by the theologians of the Council of Nicaea (325 C.E.) to designate personal existence. It permitted the council to draw the distinction between human, angelic, and divine beings while also attributing personhood to all three. My own Armenian tradition—with its Cyrillian monophysitism, represented in the dogmatic statement "one nature, and that incarnate, of the divine Word"—understood from the outset of the great christological debates of the fifth and sixth centuries the hazards of speaking of natures or essences in the abstract, whether pertaining to the divinity or humanity of Jesus. The Council of Nicaea had employed the term *ousia* to connote concrete existence. God is one *ousia*, one being and nature. The Son is of the same being and nature of the Father. This is how the council interpreted Jesus' words: "Whosoever has seen me has seen the Father. . . . I am in the Father and the Father is in me" (Jn 14:9-10). The theologians of Nicaea employed *nature* with a sense analogous to what modern physics means by a solid. A solid, like a diamond or an ice cube, is a discrete substance that cannot be mixed into another solid in the way that one liquid or gas might be mixed with another. Thus, when at the Council of Chalcedon (451 C.E.) discussion shifted to a sharp distinction between *ousia* and *hypostasis* that entailed a language of "two natures" in reference to Christ, Armenians balked. This was reminiscent of Nestorianism, especially as the language of two natures appeared in Pope Leo's time. How could it be said, as Leo did, that "the Word performs what pertains to the Word, the flesh what pertains to the flesh," without dividing Christ in two? How could Christ be two "solids," two natures, Armenians asked, except he be two and not one? For Cyril of Alexandria, it was possible to say in the abstract that there is a oneness of two natures in Christ, but Leo's language suggested the impossible, namely, a unification of two natures in the concrete. Ultimately, the Armenian Church rejected this "two natures" doctrine because it wanted to honor and safeguard the ancient teaching of "One Lord, one faith, one baptism" (Eph 4:5).

What does this curious piece of the history of Christian doctrine have to do with how one stands on human rights? The answer: From the standpoint of Armenian Christianity the legacy of Western dyophysitism extends into the Enlightenment in two essentially Christian heresies: deism and the rights of man. In deism, God is removed from creation and the Incarnation is denied—implicitly if not explicitly. In the concept of the rights of man, humanity gains an autonomy that a consistently incarnational faith will not permit. Human freedom is not autonomy, that is, pure self-determination, it is *autexouisian*, a graced capacity to achieve full ethical personhood and mystical participation in divine life. There is always a synergy of nature and grace. For more, see Vigen Guroian, "Human Rights and the Modern Faith," *Journal of Religious Ethics* 26, no. 2 (Fall 1998): 241-47.

14. Meyendorff, *Living Tradition*, 152.

15. Aram I, "Report of the Moderator: The Incarnation of the Gospel in Culture: A Missionary Event," *The Ecumenical Review* 48, no. 1 (January 1995): 104.

16. "Speech of His Holiness Karekin I."

17. "Fatherly Advice," 34.

18. "Speech of His Holiness Karekin I on the 150th Anniversary of the Armenian Evangelical Church."

19. See Vigen Guroian, *Ethics after Christendom: Toward an Ecclesial Essay* (Grand Rapids, Mich., 1994), chap. 5 ("Church and Armenian Nationhood: A Bonhoefferian Reflection on the National Church"); idem, *Faith, Church, Mission: Essays for Renewal in the Armenian Church* (New York, 1995).

12. THE MISSIONARY WORK
OF THE CHURCH OF JESUS CHRIST
OF LATTER-DAY SAINTS

1. The term *missionary work* is preferred by Mormons, who rarely use the term *evangelism*. For them, *proselyting* is synonymous with missionary work, connoting religious persuasion in its most positive sense without any of the coercive connotations some infer from that term.

2. This is a personal expression and not an official statement of the church.

3. The term *Saints* is used in its biblical sense of members of the church who are striving for holiness (see, e.g., Acts 9:13, 32, 41; Rom 1:7).

4. The canonical texts or standard works of the church are the Bible, the Book of Mormon, the Doctrine and Covenants (a compilation of modern revelations), and the Pearl of Great Price (another compilation).

5. See, generally, Joseph Smith—History, in Pearl of Great Price; Richard L. Bushman, *Joseph Smith and the Beginnings of Mormonism* (Urbana, Ill., 1984).

6. See, generally, "Book of Mormon," in *Encyclopedia of Mormonism*, ed. Daniel H. Ludlow (New York, 1992), 1:139-216.

7. See, generally, Gerald N. Lund, "Plan of Salvation," in Ludlow, *Encyclopedia of Mormonism*, 3:1088-91; M. Russell Ballard, *Our Search for Happiness* (Salt Lake City, 1993).

8. See, generally, James E. Talmage, *Jesus the Christ* (Salt Lake City, 1984); Jeffrey R. Holland, "Atonement of Jesus Christ" and various authors' articles on "Jesus Christ," all in Ludlow, *Encyclopedia of Mormonism*, 1:82-86, 2:723-53.

9. See Rev. 12:7-9.

10. "For as in Adam all die, even so in Christ shall all be made alive" (1 Cor 15:22).

11. Latter-day Saints' understanding of original sin and of the Fall is illuminated by their understanding of individual moral accountability, as expressed in the church's Second Article of Faith: "We believe that men will be punished for their own sins, and not for Adam's transgression" (Pearl of Great Price).

12. "Adam fell that men might be; and men are, that they might have joy" (Book of Mormon, 2 Nephi 2:25).

13. "For we labor diligently to write, to persuade our children, and also our brethren, to believe in Christ, and to be reconciled to God; for we know that it is by grace that we are saved, after all we can do" (Book of Mormon, 2 Nephi 25:23).

14. See Jan Shipps and John W. Welch, eds., *The Journals of William E. McLellin* (Urbana and Chicago, 1994), 5-7, 14, 18, 382-84.

15. *History of The Church of Jesus Christ of Latter-day Saints*, 8 vols. (Salt Lake City, 1948), 2:490.

16. Orson F. Whitney, *The Life of Heber C. Kimball* (Salt Lake City, 1992), 104.

17. Ibid.

18. See Lk 10:4; Doctrine and Covenants 24:18, 84:78.

19. See Lk 22:35-36.

20. See 1 Cor 11:16; 2 Cor 12:20; 2 Tm 2:24-25; Ti 3:9; Jas 1:19-20.

21. *History of The Church of Jesus Christ of Latter-day Saints*, 2:262.

22. *Discourses of Brigham Young* (Salt Lake City, 1978), 157.

23. Ibid., 235.

24. See James B. Allen, Ronald K. Esplin, and David J. Whittaker, *Men with a Mission* (Salt Lake City, 1992); V. Ben Bloxham, James R. Moss, and Larry C. Porter, *Truth Will Prevail: The Rise of The Church of Jesus Christ of Latter-day Saints in the British Isles, 1837-1987* (Solihull, West Midlands, England, 1987), 104-62.

25. *Our Heritage* (Salt Lake City, 1996), 56-57.

26. See Allen, Esplin, and Whittaker, *Men with a Mission*, 301.

27. See "Minutes of the General Conference of 6 October 1849," General Church Minutes Collection, Historical Department, The Church of Jesus Christ of Latter-day Saints, Salt Lake City, Utah.

28. "Remarks of George A. Smith" (August 28, 1852), in "Minutes of Conference," *Deseret News* (September 18, 1852).

29. Rodney Stark, "The Rise of a New World Faith," *Review of Religious Research* 26 (1984): 18.

30. See *Deseret News, 1997-98 Church Almanac* (Salt Lake City, 1996), 529-31.

31. See Rodney Stark, "So Far, So Good: A Brief Assessment of Mormon Membership Projections," *Review of Religious Research* 38 (1996): 176; Kay H. Smith, "Conversion," in Ludlow, *Encyclopedia of Mormonism*, 1:323.

32. Stark, "The Rise of a New World Faith," 18.

33. See Doctrine and Covenants 69:2-8.

34. "I Hope They Call Me on a Mission," *Children's Songbook* (Salt Lake City, 1995), 169.

35. *Hymns of The Church of Jesus Christ of Latter-day Saints* (Salt Lake City, 1985).

36. "Go, Ye Messengers of Glory," in ibid., no. 262.

37. "I'll Go Where You Want Me to Go," in ibid., no. 270.

38. "Called to Serve," in ibid., no. 249.

39. *Teachings of Gordon B. Hinckley* (Salt Lake City, 1997), 258-59.

40. President Gordon B. Hinckley, "The BYU Experience," *Brigham Young University Speeches* (1997-98), 64.

41. See Book of Mormon, Moroni 10:4-5: "And when ye shall receive these things, I would exhort you that ye would ask God, the Eternal Father, in the name of Christ, if these things are not true; and if ye shall ask with a sincere heart, with real intent, having faith in Christ, he will manifest the truth of it unto you, by the power of the Holy Ghost. And by the power of the Holy Ghost ye may know the truth of all things."

42. President Gordon B. Hinckley has stated: "[Conversion] is the great process by which those with responsive hearts listen to the teachings and testimonies of missionaries and change their lives, leaving the past behind them, and moving forward into a new life. There is no miracle quite like it in all the world" (*Teachings of Gordon B. Hinckley*, 144).

43. Amulek, a famous missionary in the Book of Mormon, emphasized this same duty of service as a qualification for church membership even more bluntly: "And now behold, my beloved brethren [of the church], I say unto you . . . if ye turn away the needy, and the naked, and visit not the sick and afflicted, and impart of your substance, if ye have, to those who stand in need—I say unto you, if ye do not any of these things, behold, your prayer is vain, and availeth you nothing, and ye are as hypocrites who do deny the faith" (Book of Mormon, Alma 34:28).

44. Figures on North Korea are from President Thomas S. Monson, "Am I My Brother's Keeper?," *Church News* (November 29, 1997), 3, 6. Figures on Kosovo are from "Humanitarian Service," *Church News* (July 17, 1999); *Congressional Record*, August 5, 1999, 510366.

45. Monson, "Am I My Brother's Keeper?," 40.

46. *History of the Church*, 4:535.

47. See generally, Dallin H. Oaks and Marvin S. Hill, *Carthage Conspiracy: The Trial of the Accused Assassins of Joseph Smith* (Urbana and Chicago, 1975).

48. The full text of Doctrine and Covenants 134:9-10 is as follows:

We do not believe it just to mingle religious influence with civil government, whereby one religious society is fostered and another proscribed in its spiritual privileges, and the individual rights of its members, as citizens, denied. We believe that all religious societies have a right to deal with their members for disorderly conduct, according to the rules and regulations of such societies; provided that such dealings be for fellowship and good standing; but we do not believe that any religious society has authority to try men on the right of property or life, to take from them this world's goods, or to put them in jeopardy of either life or limb, or to inflict any physical punishment upon them. They can only excommunicate them from their society, and withdraw from them their fellowship."

49. See, e.g., Bernice Maher Mooney, "The Cathedral of the Madeleine," *Utah Historical Quarterly* (Spring 1981); "Soup Kitchen Equipped," *Church News* (January 17, 1987); "LDS Ward Building Given to Salvation Army," *Church News* (June

25, 1988); "Church Lends to Charitable Center," *Church News* (March 24, 1990); "President Monson Represents LDS Church at Ceremony in Catholic Cathedral," *Church News* (February 27, 1993); "Madeleine's Miracle," *Salt Lake City* (Winter 1993); "Jewish Congregations Note High Holy Days in LDS Meetinghouses," *Church News* (September 25, 1993); "Helping Rebuild Burned Chapels," *Church News* (November 9, 1996).

50. Hinckley, "The BYU Experience," 64.

13. HUMAN RIGHTS, EVANGELISM, AND PROSELYTISM

1. Rodney Stark and Laurence R. Iannaccone, "Why the Jehovah's Witnesses Grow So Rapidly: A Theoretical Application," *Journal of Contemporary Religion* 12, no. 2 (1997): 133.

2. *1999 Yearbook of Jehovah's Witnesses* (Watchtower Bible and Tract Society, 1999), 31-39.

3. Unless otherwise indicated, all biblical references in this article are from the New World Translation of the Holy Scriptures.

4. R. Laird Harris, ed., *Theological Wordbook of the Old Testament* (Chicago, 1980), s.v. "'*edh.*"

5. Ernest Klein, *A Comprehensive Etymological Dictionary of the Hebrew Language for Readers of English* (New York, 1987), s.v., "'*edh.*"

6. Gerhard Friedrich, ed., *Theological Dictionary of the New Testament*, trans. Geoffrey W. Bromiley (Grand Rapids, Mich., 1985), s.v., "witness."

7. *Jehovah's Witnesses—Proclaimers of God's Kingdom* (Watch Tower Bible and Tract Society, 1993), 12, 13.

8. *Zion's Watch Tower* (April 1881): 7.

9. *Jehovah's Witnesses—Proclaimers of God's Kingdom*, 42.

10. Ibid., 55.

11. Ibid., 80.

12. Ibid., 721.

13. *1999 Yearbook*, 33.

14. *Murdock v. Pennsylvania*, 319 U.S. 105, 108-9 (1943) (footnotes omitted).

15. *Saumur v. City of Quebec* [1953] 2 S.C.R. 299, 332.

16. *Re Alberta Statutes* [1938] S.C.R. 100, 145.

17. *Switzman v. Elbling* [1957] S.C.R. 285, 306.

18. W. Kaplan, *State and Salvation, The Jehovah's Witnesses and Their Fight for Civil Liberties* (Toronto, 1989), xii.

19. *Martin v. Struthers*, 319 U.S. 141, 146 (1943).

20. *Hague v. C.I.O.*, 307 U.S. 496, 515-16 (1939).

21. *1973 Yearbook*, 66, 69.

22. Ibid., 47, 48.

23. *The Watchtower* (July 15, 1916).

24. *Unabridged History of Britain Branch* [International Bible Students Association] (London, 1971), 283.

25. Ibid., 294.

26. *1973 Yearbook*, 127.

27. *Unabridged History*, 341.

28. Ibid., 342.

29. "1998 Service Year Report of Jehovah's Witnesses Worldwide," *The Watchtower* (January 1, 1999): 12.

30. "1996 Annual Field Service Report for Britain" (Britain Branch Files, unpublished).

31. "Letter from Bryan R. Wilson to CB & M Law Offices," Riga, Latvia, November 3, 1996 (unpublished) (on file with the authors).

32. "Letter from Lord Avebury, Chairman of the Parliamentary Human Rights Group," November 6, 1996 (unpublished) (on file with the authors).

33. Kirsten John, *"Mein Vater wird gesucht"*: *Häftlinge des Konzentrationslagers in Wewelsburg* (Essen, 1996), 128.

34. Ibid., 129, 130.

35. Detlef Garbe, "Der Lila Winkel," in *Dauchauer Hefte, Täter und Opfer* (Dachau, 1994), 26.

36. Paul Johnson, *History of Christianity* (Harmondworth, Middlesex, 1976), 488-89.

37. "Letter from Professor Christine E. King, Vice-Chancellor, Staffordshire University, Stafford, England, to Watch Tower Bible and Tract Society of Pennsylvania," January 9, 1997 (unpublished) (on file with the authors).

38. *Jehovah's Witnesses Victims of the Nazi Era 1933-1945* (Washington, D.C., n.d.), 1, 14.

39. "1998 Service Year Report," 13.

40. Ibid.

41. *Kokkinakis v. Greece* (1993) 17 E.H.R.R. 397.

42. *Kokkinakis v. Greece* (March 20, 1996) Lisithi Criminal Court.

43. *Kokkinakis v. Greece* (March 17, 1997) Crete Court of Appeal.

44. *Ena* (June 23, 1992): 44.

45. *Ena* (July 28, 1993): 114-16.

46. *Beta* (Athens, April 1993): 17.

47. *Ta Nea* (Athens, February 11, 1976): 3.

48. *Eleftherotypia* (Athens, September 26, 1975): 2.

49. Sentence No. 309 (August 18, 1916), is found in the Archives of the Turin Military Tribunal.

50. Associazione europa dei testimoni di Geova per la tutela della libertà religiosa, *Intolleranza religiosa alle soglie del Duomila* (Rome, 1990), 247-82.

51. Florenzo Dentamaro, *La politicia dei culti acattolici* (Florence, 1979), cols. 72-84.

52. *Avanti!* (Rome, June 28, 1957): 4.

53. *Il Mondo* (Rome, July 30, 1957): 2.

54. Andrea Riccardi, "La Chiesa cattolica in Italia nel secondo dopoguerra," in *Storia dell Italia religiosa*, Vol. 3, *Letà contemporanea*, ed. G. De Rosa, T. Gregory, and A. Vauchez (Rome, 1995), 348-49.

55. Arturo Carlo Jemolo, *Chiesa e Stato in Italia dalla unificazione ai giorni nostri* (Turin, 1981), 314.

56. Dentamaro, *La politica dei culti acattolici*, cols. 72-84.

57. *Intolleranza religiosa*, 283-92.

58. *Gazetta Ufficiale della Repubblica Italiana* 127(275) (November 26, 1986): 31-32.

59. "Le nuove fedi [New Faiths]," *Mondo erre*, Supplement 50 (March 1986): 6.

60. "1998 Service Year Report," 13.

61. *The Watch Tower* (February 1887): 7.

62. "The Evils of Nazism Exposed," *Awake!* (August 22, 1995): 10.

63. *Proclaimers of God's Kingdom*, 509.

64. "Branch Report on Russia from Poland" (November 4, 1955) (Berne, November 16, 1955): 3-4.

65. Walter Kolarz, *Religion in the Soviet Union* (New York, 1961), 340.

66. "Victorious in the Face of Death," *Awake!* (May 8, 1993): 7.

67. Lawrence A. Uzzell, "Address to Commission on Security and Cooperation in Europe, Washington, D.C." (July 28, 1997) (unpublished).

68. Recorded in *Jehovah's Witnesses in Russia* (Watchtower Bible and Tract Society of New York, 1996), 10.

69. Ibid., 13.

70. Reported in *Golos Azli (Alma-Ata)* (November 15, 1991).

71. "Malawi's Citizens Face a Vital Decision," *The Watchtower* (May 1, 1973): 264.

72. "The Worship of the Wild Beast: Why True Christians Refuse," *The Watchtower* (October 15, 1976), 635.

73. "Shocking Religious Persecution in Malawi," *The Watchtower* (February 1, 1968): 76.

74. *Amnesty International Report on Torture* (New York/London, 1973), 124.

75. *Malawi Gazette Supplement*, Government Notice No. 85, File sub D 7:01, No. 36A, p. 315.

76. "1998 Service Year Report," 14.

77. *1947 Yearbook of Jehovah's Witnesses* (Watchtower Bible and Tract Society, 1947), 247, 248.

78. "A Little One Became Thousands," *The Watchtower* (September 15, 1962): 568.

79. *Daily Sketch* (Ibadan, Nigeria, December 22, 1988): 2.

80. "Letter from Professor Eke-Henner W. Kluge, Ph.D., to Latvian Government," November 11, 1996 (unpublished) (on file with authors).

81. "Letter from Dr. Eugene Meehan, LL.D., to Latvian Government," November 12, 1996 (unpublished) (on file with authors).

82. "Letter from Bernard Dickens, Ph.D., LL.D., Professor of Medical Law, Faculty of Law, Faculty of Medicine, University of Toronto, Ontario, Canada, to Latvian Government," November 6, 1996 (unpublished) (on file with authors).

14. PROSELYTIZATION AND RELIGIOUS FREEDOM IN THE SEVENTH-DAY ADVENTIST CHURCH

1. Standard accounts of the early development of Adventism include Edwin S. Gaustad, ed., *The Rise of Adventism: Religion and Society in Mid-Nineteenth-Century America* (New York, 1974); Gary Land, ed., *Adventism in America: A History* (Grand Rapids, Mich., 1985); Francis D. Nichol, *The Midnight Cry: A Defense of William Miller and the Millerites* (Washington, D.C., 1944); M. Ellsworth Olsen, *History of the Origin and Progress of Seventh-day Adventists* (Washington, D.C., 1925); and Richard W. Schwarz, *Light Bearers to the Remnant* (Mountain View, Calif., 1979).

2. *Seventh-day Adventist Church Manual*, 15th ed. (Hagerstown, Md., 1995), 30-31.

3. Ibid., 192.

4. Ellen G. White, *Testimonies to the Church* (1900), 6:16.

5. Ibid., 6:24-26.

6. Ibid. (1909), 9:241-44.

7. Ellen G. White, *Manuscript 87* (1907).

8. *Review and Herald* (February 28, 1856) and (January 8, 1857).

9. Don F. Neufeld, ed., *Seventh-day Adventist Encyclopedia, Commentary Reference Series*, rev. ed. (Washington, D.C., 1976), 10:1197-98.

10. J. N. Andrews, "Thoughts on Revelation XIII and XIV," *Review and Herald* 1 (May 19, 1851): 83; Hiram Edson, "The Times of the Gentiles," *Review and Herald* 7 (January 24, 1856): 129.

11. *Seventh-day Adventist Yearbook* (1884), 42 (Resolutions 26-28).

12. *Review and Herald* 16 (January 1, 1884): 61.

13. "Declaration of the Principles of the International Religious Liberty Association," which appears on the masthead of *Liberty: A Magazine of Religious Freedom*.

14. *Seventh-day Adventist Church Manual*, 117.

15. *North American Division of the General Conference Working Policy* (Hagerstown, Md., 1996-97), 267-68.

15. A BAHÁ'Í PERSPECTIVE ON TOLERANCE, HUMAN RIGHTS, AND MISSIONS

1. Nabil Zarandi, *The Dawn-Breakers* (Wilmette, Ill., 1974), 93, quoting in part from the Qur'an.

2. Ibid., 626.

3. Shoghi Effendi, *God Passes By* (Wilmette, Ill., 1987), 127-63.

4. Bahá'u'lláh, *Gleanings from the Writings of Bahá'u'lláh* (Wilmette, Ill., 1982), 278.

5. Ibid., 314.

6. Ibid., 335.

7. Bahá'u'lláh, quoted by Shoghi Effendi, *The Advent of Divine Justice* (Wilmette, Ill., 1990), 61.

8. Ibid., 65.

9. The *Oxford English Dictionary* gives no negative connotations in its definitions of the terms *proselyte, proselytism, proselytize*. Some dictionaries list special inducement to conversion as a second meaning.

10. Bahá'u'lláh, *Tablets of Bahá'u'lláh* (Haifa, 1978), 44.

11. Letter to an individual written on behalf of Shoghi Effendi (October 20, 1956), in *The Individual and Teaching*, comp. Research Department of the Universal House of Justice (Wilmette, Ill., 1977), 38.

12. Shoghi Effendi, *Citadel of Faith* (Wilmette, Ill., 1965), 25-26.

13. For the origins of the Bahá'í communities in the United States and Canada, see Robert H. Stockman, *The Bahá'í Faith in America*, vol. 1 (Wilmette, Ill., 1985); vol. 2 (Oxford, 1995).

14. 'Abdu'l-Bahá's travels in Europe and America have been chronicled by Mírzá Muhmud Zarqání, *Kitáb-i-Badáyi'u'l-Athár*, 2 vols. (Bombay, 1914, 1921). Only

some segments of this chronicle have been translated into English. Hasan Balyuzi, *'Abdu'l-Bahá* (London, 1972) devotes almost half of his 495 pages to 'Abdu'l-Bahá's travels. Allan Ward, *239 Days* (Wilmette, Ill., 1979) examines 'Abdu'l-Bahá's inter-action with individuals and the press in North America.

15. Shoghi Effendi, *God Passes By*, 281-82.

16. *Selections from the Writings of 'Abdu'l-Bahá* (Haifa, 1979), 3.

17. Ibid., 175.

18. 'Abdu'l-Bahá, *Tablets of the Divine Plan* (Wilmette, Ill., 1993), 32-33.

19. Ibid., 40-43.

20. The United States and Canada were under the jurisdiction of a single assembly between 1925 and 1948.

21. For the formation of the Continental Boards of Counselors see *Messages from the Universal House of Justice: 1963-1986* (Wilmette, Ill., 1996), 130 and passim.

22. *The Bahá'í World: An International Record* (Haifa, 1970), 13:292.

23. Ibid., 289.

24. Ibid.

25. Ibid., 794.

26. For the full text of the plan and the statistics of the Bahá'í world community, see *The Bahá'í World* 14 (1974): 101-40.

27. Detailed information on these plans is found in the consecutive volumes of *The Bahá'í World*.

28. There exists a considerable literature on the persecution of Iranian Bahá'ís. The Bahá'í International Community (BIC) has published a number of papers detail-ing the relevant facts and reproducing Iranian government documents. The *Congres-sional Record* contains speeches made in both houses of Congress in defense of Ira-nian Bahá'ís and in condemnation of the human rights record of the Iranian government. The U.N. Commission on Human Rights and the General Assembly have passed numerous resolutions condemning Iran's treatment of religious minori-ties, specifically mentioning the Bahá'ís.

29. Bahá'í International Community, "On the Elimination of Religious Intoler-ance," written statement circulated as official U.N. document E/CN.4/1985/NGO/47 of 27 February 1985 (referring to document ST/HR/SER.A/16).

30. Bahá'í International Community, "Ending Religious Intolerance," statement to the U.N. Sub-Commission on the Prevention of Discrimination and Protection of Minorities, Geneva, Switzerland, August 1993; BIC Document #93-0803.

31. Bahá'í International Community, "Promoting Religious Tolerance," written statement submitted to the fifty-first session of the United Nations Commission on Human Rights, Geneva, Switzerland; BIC Document #95-0110.

32. 'Abdu'l-Bahá, *Bahá'í World Faith: Selected Writings of Bahá'u'lláh and 'Abdu'l-Bahá* (Wilmette, Ill., 1976), 247.

33. The concept of the unity of religion and the spiritual identity of all founders of great religion is presented by Bahá'u'lláh in *The Kitáb-i-Iqán* [The Book of Certi-tude] (New York, 1931), 99-103.

34. Bahá'u'lláh, *Epistle to the Son of the Wolf* (Wilmette, Ill., 1963), 13-14.

35. Nathan Rutstein, *Teaching the Bahá'í Faith* (Oxford, 1984), 124.

36. Mírzá Abu'l-Fadl's major work intended for American readers, *The Bahá'í Proofs* (Hujaja'l-Bahíyyih), was translated into English and published in 1902. The second edition appeared in 1914, the third in 1929, the fourth was brought out in 1983 by the Bahá'í Publishing Trust, Wilmette, Illinois.

37. Hyppolite Dreyfus, *The Universal Religion: Bahaism* (London, 1909).

38. John E. Esselmont, *Bahá'u'lláh and the New Era* (London, 1923).

16. EVANGELISM *SANS* PROSELYTISM

1. William J. Richardson, *Social Action vs. Evangelism: An Essay on the Contemporary Crisis* (South Pasadena, Calif., 1977), 26.

2. John Power, *Mission Theology Today* (Maryknoll, N.Y., 1971), 159.

3. H. Eddie Fox and George Morris, *Faith-Sharing: Dynamic Christian Witnessing by Invitation* (Nashville, Tenn., 1986), 44.

4. David Bosch, *Transforming Mission* (Maryknoll, N.Y., 1991), 411-20.

5. See also Acts 15:7; Rom 1:16; Mt 4:23.

6. Kenneth Cracknell, *Protestant Evangelism or Catholic Evangelization* (Keswick, 1992), 3.

7. See the chapter by Luke Timothy Johnson herein.

8. See the chapter by James Muldoon herein.

9. Robin Boyd, *An Introduction to Indian Christian Theology* (Madras, India, 1975), 15

10. Bosch, *Transforming Mission*, 310.

11. Stephen Neill, *A History of Christian Missions,* rev. ed. (London, 1969), 54, 97ff.

12. Ibid., 68.

13. *Webster's Third International Dictionary* (Chicago, 1976), 2:1046.

14. William Carey, *An Enquiry into the Obligations of Christians to Use Means for the Conversion of the Heathens* (1792), fasc. ed. (London, 1942).

15. Bartholomew Ziegenbalg, quoted in Boyd, *An Introduction to Indian Christian Theology*, 15.

16. Kenneth Cracknell, *Justice, Courtesy, and Love: Theologians and Missionaries Encountering World Religions, 1846-1914* (London, 1995).

17. Therefore, when the IMC finally joined the WCC to form the Commission on World Mission and Evangelism, these two words had to be coupled together in the naming of this Commission. It could not simply be named either "Commission on World Mission" or "Commission on World Evangelization." These two words had to be combined at all times.

18. Bosch, *Transforming Mission*, 411.

19. Ibid.

20. Ibid., 415.

21. See M. Thomas Thangaraj, "Toward a Dialogical Theology of Mission," in *Theology at the End of Modernity*, ed. Sheila G. Davaney (Philadelphia, 1991), 161-76; idem, *The Common Task: A Theology of Mission* (Nashville, Tenn., 1999).

22. Thangaraj, "Toward a Dialogical Theology of Mission," 170.

23. Ibid., 175.

24. David Bosch, "The Vulnerability of Mission," in *New Directions in Mission and Evangelism*, ed. James Scherer and Stephen Bevans (Maryknoll, N.Y., 1994), 1:83ff.

25. Donald A. McGavarn, *Understanding Church Growth* (Grand Rapids, Mich., 1970), 49; see also, "today's paramount task, opportunity, and imperative in missions is to multiply churches" (ibid., 63).

26. Diogenes Allen, *Three Outsiders* (New York, 1983), 97.

27. Cracknell, *Justice, Courtesy, and Love*, 19.

28. Gandhi, quoted in M. M. Thomas, *The Acknowledged Christ of the Indian Renaissance*, 2d ed. (Madras, India, 1976), 209.

29. William James, quoted in E. Stanley Jones, *Conversion* (Nashville, Tenn., 1959).

30. Ibid., 46ff.

31. M.M. Thomas, *Faith and Ideology in the Struggle for Justice* (Bombay, 1984), 4.

32. George Rupp, "Communities of Collaboration: Shared Commitments/Common Tasks," in Davaney, *Theology at the End of Modernity*, 201.

33. Wesley Granberg-Michaelson, *Redeeming the Creation: The Rio Earth Summit: Challenges to the Churches* (Geneva, 1992), vi.

34. Constantin Voicu, "Orthodox Theology and the Problems of the Environment," *The Greek Orthodox Theological Review* 38, nos. 1-4 (1993): 175.

35. World Council of Churches, *Guidelines on Dialogue with People of Living Faiths and Ideologies* (Geneva, 1979).

36. "The Lausanne Covenant," in Scherer and Bevans, *New Directions in Mission and Evangelization*, 1:255.

37. *Dialogue and Proclamation*, reprinted in Scherer and Bevans, *New Directions in Mission and Evangelization*, 187.

38. Wesley Ariarajah, *The Bible and People of Other Faiths* (Geneva, 1985), 39.

CONTRIBUTORS

Donna E. Arzt is Professor of Law and Director of the Center for Global Law and Practice, Syracuse University.

Michael J. Broyde is Associate Professor of Law and Academic Director of the Law and Religion Program, Emory University, Atlanta.

Philip Brumley is General Counsel for Jehovah's Witnesses, World Headquarters, Brooklyn, New York.

Farid Esack is Professor of Arabic and Islamic Studies, University of Western Cape, South Africa.

Vigen Guroian is Professor of Religion, Loyola College, Baltimore, Maryland.

Deirdre King Hainsworth is a Ph.D. Candidate at Princeton Theological Seminary, Princeton, New Jersey.

Jocelyn Hellig is Professor of Religious Studies, University of the Witwatersrand, Johannesburg, South Africa.

W. Glen How, Q.C., is General Counsel for Jehovah's Witnesses in Canada, Halton Hills (Georgetown), Ontario.

Luke Timothy Johnson is Robert W. Woodruff Professor of New Testament and Christian Origins, Emory University, Atlanta.

Firuz Kazemzadeh is Professor of History, *Emeritus*, Yale University, and Member of the National Spiritual Assembly of the Bahá'ís of the United States and Canada.

Richard C. Martin is Professor of Religion and Chair of the Department of Religion, Emory University, Atlanta.

Martin E. Marty is Fairfax M. Cone Distinguished Service Professor, *Emeritus*, The University of Chicago, and Director of the Public Religion Project, Chicago.

Norman K. Miles is President of the Lake Region Conference, Seventh-day Adventist Church.

James Muldoon is Professor of History, *Emeritus*, Rutgers University, Camden, New Jersey.

David Novak holds the J. Richard and Dorothy Shiff Chair of Jewish Studies, The University of Toronto.

Dallin H. Oaks is Member of the Quorum of the Twelve Apostles, The Church of Jesus Christ of Latter-day Saints, Salt Lake City, Utah, and former Professor of Law, The University of Chicago.

Max L. Stackhouse is Stephen Colwell Professor of Christian Ethics, Princeton Theological Seminary, Princeton, New Jersey.

411

M. Thomas Thangaraj is Brooks Professor of World Christianity, Emory University, Atlanta.

Jozef Tomko is Cardinal and Head of the Congregation for the Evangelization of Peoples, The Vatican.

Lance B. Wickman is Member of the Quorum of the Seventy and General Counsel of The Church of Jesus Christ of Latter-day Saints, Salt Lake City, Utah.

John Witte Jr. is Jonas Robitscher Professor of Law and Ethics, and Director of the Law and Religion Program, Emory University, Atlanta.

INDEX

413